MW01243322

Introduction to Social and Political Philosophy

Ann E. Cudd

University of Kansas

KENDALL/HUNT PUBLISHING COMPANY
4050 Westmark Drive   Dubuque, Iowa 52002

Cover images from the Library of Congress.

Copyright © 2007 by Kendall/Hunt Publishing Company

ISBN 978-0-7575-4579-5

Printed in the United States of America
10 9 8 7 6 5 4 3 2 1

Contents

⟋⟋⟋⟋

Part Two—Democracy

PART THREE—Rights

Part Four—Freedom and Oppression

Part One

---- ⤲⊙⤳ ----

Theories of Human Nature, Governmental Authority, and Political Legitimacy

Political Authority and Legitimacy

overnment can be defined as the *ruling authority* over a territory and its people. To be a ruling authority is to have the ability to make and enforce laws, to adjudicate disputes, and to claim a monopoly on the use of force or coercive measures to maintain peace. To do all these things, governments are financed by their people through some form of taxation. This ruling authority applies both internally, in ruling within the territory, and externally, by claiming the sole right to make treaties, conduct negotiations, transfer goods to other governments, make or accept loans, and conduct war on behalf of the people. So described, government is authoritative, and to ask whether a body constitutes a government is to ask a *descriptive question*, that is, a question of *fact*.

As we all know, governments can be good or bad, just or unjust with respect to their own people, and with respect to other governments they can be decent or rogue, peaceful or aggressive states. An important question that this book will concentrate on is the question of legitimacy: when is governmental authority legitimate? This is a *normative question*, the answer to which cannot be determined by a simple check of the facts. By *legitimate* we mean *justified* in its use of authority. *Normative*, to a philosopher, means how things *ought* to be, which is often not how things are, even some of the time. Thus, we cannot discover the answer to a normative question empirically, that is, by observing the world. This is not to say, though, that empirical fact has no bearing on the issue. Many philosophers hold to the dictum that "ought implies can", or in other words, normative claims should not prescribe conditions that are impossible for humans to meet. There are many different ways to look at the justification of governmental authority, (including that there are no justified governmental authorities), which forms the topic of this first section of the book.

Philosophers study justification in a variety of areas of human life, including knowledge claims (epistemology) and ethical claims (moral philosophy). Social and political philosophy studies the justification of claims about such matters as governmental authority, law, rights, freedom, and justice. Because we organize our political lives primarily by means of government, the most fundamental issue for political philosophy is the question of legitimacy. In the readings in this section we will be looking at the long tradition of political philosophy concerning the legitimacy of the governmental authority, beginning with what philosophers term the ancient classics from Greek and Chinese political thought, through some important readings from the modern and contemporary periods of political philosophy. Near the end of the section we turn to readings about three views about the relation of individual to the state: Liberalism, Socialism, and Communism. The section concludes with readings that question the legitimacy of some specific practices (colonial conquest and slavery) of governments and the duty of citizens to obey the law even when the law is immoral.

ANCIENT POLITICAL THOUGHT

Although governments existed long before then, political philosophy really began almost simultaneously in Greece and China in roughly the 5th century before the common era (BCE). In the city state of Athens, home of the first long-standing Democracy, Socrates and his pupil Plato thought and wrote about virtue, including the virtue of justice. Largely because they were citizens of a Democracy, in which they were given equal voice and equal responsibility for the state, they were concerned about the questions of how states can be harmonious within and secure from attack from outsiders, while at the same time that individuals can follow their own pursuits. Ancient Chinese political philosophers, on the other hand, were members of very hierarchical societies, in which each person had a predetermined role, and the roles were highly unequal. Their main concerns include harmony among unequals, and the nurturing of leaders and rulers to maintain balance and not succumb to the temptations of despotic power. There are four main schools of ancient Chinese political thought represented by the readings here: Confucianism, Mohism, Taoism, and Legalism, which take different stances is the best way to maintain harmony and avoid despotism.

HISTORY OF ANCIENT POLITICAL THOUGHT TIMELINE

Greek History

Athenian Democracy (roughly 507–320 BCE)
   Socrates (479–399 BCE)
   Plato (428–348, BCE)
   Aristotle (384–322 BCE)

Chinese History

Chou Dynasty (894–476 BCE)
Spring and Autumn Period, China (722–481 BCE)
   Confucius (551–479 BCE)
Warring States Period, China (403–221 BCE)
   Mo Tzu (470–391 BCE)
   Mencius (385–302 BCE)
   Chuang Tzu (369–286 BCE)
   Hsün Tzu (310–237 BCE)

Socrates and Plato
Ancient Greece

Plato (428–348, BCE) was the most important student of Socrates (479–399 BCE) and the teacher of Aristotle. Plato wrote many philosophical works in the form of dialogues, like the following selection. In each of them he explores a virtue, such as justice or courage, or a concept, such as knowledge, love, virtue itself, or truth. His early dialogues place Socrates in the role of protagonist, as this one, *The Republic*, does. Socrates and Plato founded the Academy, a famous school in Athens that was later taken over by Aristotle.

Socrates was the great philosopher famous for the saying, "the unexamined life is not worth living." He was a teacher who took no money for teaching and lived a simple, virtuous life. He did not write any philosophy, but taught it and lived it. In his lifetime, a famous oracle that said about him: none is wiser than Socrates. He believed that virtue was knowledge, and that to know the Good is to do the good. Socrates was tried and executed in 399 BCE for the crime of corrupting the youth. He was immortalized by the dialogues of Plato, especially the series of dialogues about his trial and death, one of which, *The Crito*, is included in this collection.

Athens was, of course, the first great democratic city-state, and its Democracy lasted for nearly 200 years. The Athenian Democracy was a pure or Direct Democracy: agendas for voting were decided by randomly selected persons who served on the council, then every decision on each issue on the agenda was made by majority rule by the citizens (and this did not include a majority of the people living there), including trials such as Socrates. During the time of Socrates execution it was falling into the hands of a few corrupt oligarchs.

The Republic is the Utopian vision of Plato that is supposed to illustrate justice, and its virtues for a state and for an individual. The selection here is Book One, in which the topic is only introduced. Socrates argues that justice is good, but not by looking at the nature of justice, but in effect by arguing that it is good by definition. The rest of the dialogue (ten books in all) is an attempt to illustrate the just state and relate it to the soul of the just person.

STUDY QUESTIONS:

1. What definitions of justice do the characters contemplate? How would you define justice?

2. What does Thrasymachus think about justice? Does he offer a competing definition?

3. Why does Socrates think that one ought to be just?

The Republic: Book 1

Translated by G.M.A. Grube

On his way back to Athens from the Piraeus Socrates is stopped by Polemarchus who persuades him to come to his house, where he is received by Polemarchus' old father Cephalus. They have a brief but interesting conversation on the burdens of old age, and Cephalus admits that these are lightened by his wealth, which enables one to speak the truth and to pay one's debts to men and gods. Here we slip almost unawares into an attempt to define justice (i.e. right conduct toward others). Cephalus retires from the argument and Polemarchus takes over. He quotes Simonides that justice consists in giving everyone what is owed them. This definition is queried by Socrates and proved to be unsatisfactory, and this refutation is a good example of the Socratic method. Although Polemarchus shifts his ground more than once, he has to admit that his definition will not do.

At this point the Sophist Thrasymachus intervenes somewhat vehemently. He sneers at the Socratic method and is with apparent reluctance persuaded to give his own definition, that justice is the advantage of the stronger (i.e. that might is right). He is a much more formidable opponent than Polemarchus, though Socrates soon makes him contradict himself, but he gets out of that difficulty rather subtly, and it takes Socrates

some time and difficulty to show the Sophist that he is wrong. Thrasymachus fights back by appealing to the facts against Socrates' theoretical view of justice. The interplay of characters has full play here. So has the Socratic irony and in the end Thrasymachus is, if not convinced, at least argued into submissiveness, but Socrates himself points out that this leaves us without a definition of what justice really is.

The first book might well be called the most dramatic and artfully contrived of the Socratic dialogues. It is extremely vivid throughout and forms an excellent introduction to the whole Republic.

I went down to the Piraeus yesterday with Glaucon, the son of Ariston. I intended to say a prayer to the goddess,[1] and I also wanted to see how they would manage the festival, since this was its first celebration. I thought our own procession was a fine one and that which the Thracians had sent was no less outstanding. After we had said our prayer and witnessed the procession we started back toward the city. Polemarchus saw us from a distance as we were setting off for home and he told his slave to run and bid us wait for him. So the slave caught hold of my cloak from behind: Polemarchus, he said, bids you wait for him. I turned around and asked where Polemarchus was. There he is, coming up behind you, he said, please wait for him. And Glaucon said: All right, we'll wait.

Just then Polemarchus caught up with us. Adeimantus, the brother of Glaucon,[2] was with him, and so were Niceratus, the son of Nicias, and some others, presumably on their way from the procession.

Then Polemarchus said: Socrates, it looks to me as if you had started on your way back to the city.

Quite right, said I.

Do you see how many we are? he said.

Of course I do.

Well, he said, you must either be stronger than we are, or you must stay here.

Is there not another alternative, said I, namely that we may persuade you to let us go?

Could you, said he, persuade men who do not listen?

Not possibly, said Glaucon.

Well, you can take it that we are certainly not going to listen.

Adeimantus intervened: Do you really not know that there is to be a torch race on horse-back this evening in honour of the goddess?

On horseback? said I, that is a novelty. Are they going to race on horseback and hand the torches on in relays, or how do you mean?

That's it, said Polemarchus, and there will be an all night festival besides, which will be worth seeing, and which we intend to watch after dinner. We shall be joined by many of our young men here and talk with them. So please do stay.

And Glaucon said: It seems that we'll have to stay.

If you think so, said I, then we must.

So we went to the home of Polemarchus, and there we found Lysias and Euthydemus, the brothers of Polemarchus, also Thrasyma-chus of Chalcedon, Charmantides of Paiania, and Cleitophon the son of Aristonymus. Pole-marchus' father Cephalus was also in the house. I thought he looked quite old, as I had not seen

him for some time. He was sitting on a seat with a cushion, a wreath on his head, for he had been offering a sacrifice in the courtyard. There was a circle of seats there, and we sat down by him.

As soon as he saw me Cephalus welcomed me and said: Socrates, you don't often come down to the Piraeus to see us. You should. If it were still easy for me to walk to the city you would not need to come here, we would come to you, but now you should come more often. You should realize that, to the extent that my physical pleasures get feebler, my desire for conversation, and the pleasure I take in it, increase. So be sure to come more often and talk to these youngsters, as you would to good friends and relations.

I replied: Indeed, Cephalus, I do enjoy conversing with men of advanced years. As from those who have travelled along a road which we too will probably have to follow, we should enquire from them what kind of a road it is, whether rough and difficult or smooth and easy, and I should gladly learn from you what you think about this, as you have reached the point in life which the poets call "the threshold of old age,"[3] whether it is a difficult part of life, or how your experience would describe it to us.

Yes by Zeus, Socrates, he said, I will tell you what I think of old age. A number of us who are more or less the same age often get together in accordance with the old adage.[4] When we meet, the majority of us bemoan their age: they miss the pleasures which were theirs in youth; they recall the pleasures of sex, drink, and feasts, and some other things that go with them, and they are angry as if they were deprived of important things, as if they then lived the good life and now were not living at all. Some others deplore the humili-ations which old age suffers in the house-hold, and because of this they repeat again and again that old age is the cause of many evils. However, Socrates, I do not think that they blame the real cause. For if old age were the cause, then I should have suffered in the same way, and so would all others who have reached my age. As it is, I have met other old men who do not feel like that, and indeed I was present at one time when someone asked the poet Sophocles: "How are you in regard to sex, Sophocles? Can you still make love to a woman?" "Hush man, the poet replied, I am very glad to have escaped from this, like a slave who has escaped from a mad and cruel master." I thought then that he was right, and I still think so, for a great peace and freedom from these things come with old age: after the tension of one's desires relaxes and ceases, then Sophocles' words certainly apply, it is an escape from many mad masters. As regards both sex and relations in the household there is one cause, Socrates, not old age but the manner of one's life: if it is moderate and contented, then old age too is but moderately burdensome; if it is not, then both old age and youth are hard to bear.

I wondered at his saying this and I wanted him to say more, so I urged him on by saying: Cephalus, when you say this, I don't think most people would agree with you; they think you endure old age easily not because of your manner of life but because you are wealthy, for the wealthy, they say, have many things to encourage them.

What you say is true, he said. They would not agree. And there is something in what they say, but not as much as they think. What Themistocles said is quite right: when a man from Seriphus[5] was insulting him by saying that his high reputation was due to his city and not to himself, he replied that, had he been a Seriphian, he would not be famous, but neither would the other had he been an Athenian. The same can be applied to those who are not rich and find old age hard to bear–namely that a good man would not very easily bear old age in poverty, nor would a bad man, even if wealthy, be at peace with himself.

Did you inherit most of your wealth, Cephalus, I asked, or did you acquire it?

How much did I acquire, Socrates? As a moneymaker I stand between my grandfather and my father. My grandfather and namesake inherited about the same amount of wealth which I possess but multiplied it many times. My father, Lysanias, however, diminished that amount to even less than I have now. As for me, I am satisfied to leave to my sons here no less but a little more than I inherited.

The reason I asked, said I, is that you did not seem to me to be overfond of money, and this is generally the case with those who have not made it themselves. Those who have acquired it by their own efforts are twice as fond of it as other men. Just as poets love their own poems and fathers love their children, so those who have made their money are attached to it as something they have made themselves, besides using it as other men do. This makes them poor company, for they are unwilling to give their approval to anything but money.

What you say is true, he said.

It surely is, said I. Now tell me this much more: What is the greatest benefit you have received from the enjoyment of wealth?

I would probably not convince many people in saying this, Socrates, he said, but you must realize that when a man approaches the time when he thinks he will die, he becomes fearful and concerned about things which he did not fear before. It is then that the stories we are told about the underworld, which he ridiculed before—that the man who has sinned here will pay the penalty there—torture his mind lest they be true. Whether because of the weakness of old age, or because he is now closer to what happens there and has a clearer view, the man himself is filled with suspicion and fear, and he now takes account and examines whether he has wronged anyone. If he finds many sins in his own life, he awakes from sleep in terror, as children do, and he lives with the expectation of evil. However, the man who knows he has not sinned has a sweet and good hope as his constant companion, a nurse to his old age, as Pindar too puts it. The poet has expressed this charmingly, Socrates, that whoever lives a just and pious life

Sweet is the hope that nurtures his heart,
companion and nurse to his old age,
a hope which governs the repidly changing
thoughts of mortals.

This is wonderfully well said. It is in this connection that I would say that wealth has its greatest value, not for everyone but for a good and well-balanced man. Not to have lied to or deceived anyone even unwillingly, not to depart yonder in fear, owing either sacrifices to a god or money to a man: to this wealth makes a great contribution. It has many other uses, but benefit for benefit I would say that its greatest usefulness lies in this for an intelligent man, Socrates.

Beautifully spoken, Cephalus, said I, but are we to say that justice or right[6] is simply to speak the truth and to pay back any debt one may have contracted? Or are these same actions sometimes right and sometimes wrong? I mean this sort of thing, for example: everyone would surely agree that if a friend has deposited weapons with you when he was sane, and he asks for them when he is out of his mind, you should not return them. The man who returns them is not doing right, nor is one who is willing to tell the whole truth to a man in such a state.

What you say is correct, he answered.

This then is not a definition of right or justice, namely to tell the truth and pay one's debts.

It certainly is, said Polemarchus interrupting, if we are to put any trust in Simonides.[7]

And now, said Cephalus, I leave the argument to you, for I must go back and look after the sacrifice.

Do I then inherit your role? asked Polemarchus.

You certainly do, said Cephalus laughing, and as he said it he went off to sacrifice.

Then do tell us, Polemarchus, said I, as the heir to the argument, what it is that Simonides stated about justice which you consider to be correct.

He stated, said he, that it is just to give to each what is owed to him, and think he was right to say so.

Well now, I said, it is hard not to believe Simonides, for he is a wise and inspired man, but what does he mean? Perhaps you understand him, but I do not. Clearly he does not mean what we were saying just now, that anything he has deposited must be returned to a man who is not in his right mind; yet anything he has deposited is owing to him. Is that not so?—Yes.

But it is not to be returned to him at all if he is out of his mind when he asks for it?—That's true.

Certainly Simonides meant something different from this when he says that to return what is owed is just.

He did indeed mean something different by Zeus, said he. He believes that one owes it to one's friends to do good to them, and not harm.

I understand, said I, that one does not give what is owed or due if one gives back gold to a depositor, when giving back and receiving are harmful, and the two are friends. Is that not what you say Simonides meant?—Quite.

Well then, should one give what is due to one's enemies?

By all means, said he, what is in fact due to them, and I believe that is what is properly due from an enemy to an enemy, namely something harmful.

It seems, I said, that Simonides was suggesting the nature of the just poetically and in riddles. For he thought this to be just, to give to each man what is proper to him, and he called this what is due.—Surely.

Then by Zeus, I said, if someone asked him: "Simonides, what does the craft[8] which we call medicine give that is due, and to whom?" What do you think his answer would be?

Clearly, it is the craft which prescribes medicines and food and drink for our bodies.

And what does the craft which we call cooking give that is due and fitting, and to whom?—It adds flavor to food.

Very well. What, and to whom, does that craft give which we would call justice?

It must follow from what was said before, Socrates, that it is that which benefits one's friends and harms one's enemies.

He means then that to benefit one's friends and harm one's enemies is justice?—I think so.

And who is most capable of benefiting his friends and harming his enemies in matters of health and disease?—A physician.

And who can do so best when they are sailing and heading into a storm?—A pilot.

What about the just man? In what activity and what task is he most able to benefit his friends and harm his enemies?—In waging war and in alliances, I think.

Very well. Now when people are not ill, my dear Polemarchus, the physician is no use to them?—True.

Nor is the pilot when they are not sailing?—That is so.

So to people who are not fighting a war the just man is useless?—I do not think so at all.

Justice then is useful also in peace time?—It is.

And so is farming, is it not?—Yes.

For the producing of a harvest?—Yes.

And the cobbler's craft too?—Yes.

I think you would say for getting shoes?—Certainly.

Well then, what is it which justice helps one to use or acquire in peace time?—Contracts, Socrates.

By contracts you mean dealings between people, or something else?—That is what I mean.

Is the just man a good and useful associate in a game of checkers, or is the checkers player?—The checkers player.

And for putting together bricks and stones, is the just man a better and more useful associate than the builder?—Not at all.

In what kind of dealings then is the just man a better associate than the builder or the musician, as the musician is better than the just man in matters of music?—In money matters, I think.

Except perhaps, Polemarchus, when money is to be used, for whenever one needs to buy or sell a horse together, I think the horse breeder is a more useful associate. Is that not so?—Apparently.

And when one needs to buy a boat, the shipbuilder or the captain of a ship?—So it seems.

In what joint use of silver and gold is the just man a more useful associate than the others?—Whenever one needs to deposit it and keep it safe.

You mean whenever there is no need to use it, but to keep it?—Quite so.

So it is whenever money is not being used that justice is useful?—I'm afraid so.

And whenever one needs to keep a pruning knife safe, but not to use it, justice is useful both in associations and in private. When you need to use it, however, it is the craft of vine dressing that is useful.—So it seems.

You will agree then that when one needs to keep a shield or a lyre safe and not use them, justice is a useful thing, but when you need to use them, it is the hoplite's or the musician's craft which is useful.—That necessarily follows.

So with all other things, justice is useless in their use, but useful when they are not in use.—I fear so.

In that case, my friend, justice is not a very important thing if it is only useful for things not in use. Let us, however, investigate the following point: is not the man most capable of landing a blow in a fight, be it boxing or any other kind, also the most capable of guarding against blows?—Certainly.

And the man most able to guard against disease is also the man most able to inflict it unnoticed?—So it seems.

Further, the same man is a good guardian of a camp who is also able to steal the plans of the enemy and be aware of their actions?—Quite so.

Whenever a man is a good guardian of anything, he is also a good thief of it.—Apparently.

If then the just man is good at guarding money, he is also good at stealing it.—So our argument shows.

The just man then has turned out to be a kind of thief. You may well have learned this from Homer, for he likes Odysseus' maternal grandfather Autolycus, and at the same time he says that he excelled all men in thieving and perjury. It follows that justice, according to you and Homer and Simonides, appears to be a craft of thieving, of course to the advantage of one's friends and to the harm of one's enemies. Is this not what you meant?

No, by Zeus, he said, I don't any longer know what I meant, but this I still believe to be true, that justice is to benefit one's friends and harm one's enemies.

When you say friends, do you mean those whom a man believes to be helpful to him, or those who are helpful even if they do not appear to be so, and so with enemies?

Probably, he said, one is fond of those whom one thinks to be good and helpful to one, and one hates those whom one considers bad and harmful.

Surely people make mistakes about this, and consider many to be helpful when they are not, and often make the opposite mistake about enemies?—They do.

Then good men are their enemies, and bad people their friends?—Quite so.

And so it is just and right for these mistaken people to benefit the bad and harm the good?—It seems so.

But the good are just and able to do no wrong?—True.

But according to your argument it is just to harm those who do no wrong.

Never, Socrates, he said. It is the argument that is wrong.

It is just to harm the wrongdoers and to benefit the just?

That statement, Socrates, seems much more attractive than the other.

Then, Polemarchus, for many who are mistaken in their judgment it follows that it is just to harm their friends, for these are bad, and to benefit their enemies, who are good, and so we come to a conclusion which is the opposite of what we said was the meaning of Simonides.

That certainly follows, he said, but let us change our assumption; we have probably not defined the friend and the enemy correctly.

Where were we mistaken, Polemarchus?

—When we said that a friend was one who was thought to be helpful.

How shall we change this now? I asked.

Let us state, he said, that a friend is one who is both thought to be helpful and also is;

one who is thought to be, but is not, helpful is thought to be a friend but is not. And so also with the enemy.

According to this argument then, the good man will be a friend, and the bad man an enemy.—Yes.

You want us to add to what we said before about the just, namely that it is just to benefit one's friend and harm one's enemy; to this you want us to make an addition and say that it is just to benefit the friend who is good and to harm the enemy who is bad?

Quite so, he said. This seems to me to be well said.

But, I said, *is it the part of the just man to harm anyone at all?*

Why certainly, he said, those who are bad and one's enemies.

Do horses become better or worse when they are harmed?—Worse.

Do they deteriorate in their excellence as dogs or as horses?—As horses.

And when dogs are harmed, they deteriorate in their excellence as dogs, not in that of horses?—Necessarily.

Shall we not say so about *men too, that when they are harmed they deteriorate in their human excellence?*—Quite so.

And is not justice a human excellence?—Of course.

Then men who are harmed, my friend, necessarily become more unjust.—So it appears.

Can musicians, by practising music, make men unmusical?—Not possibly.

Or can teachers of horsemanship, by the practice of their craft, make them into non-horsemen?—Impossible.

Well then, can the just, by the practice of justice, make men unjust? Or, in a word, can good men, by the practice of their virtue, make men bad?—They cannot.[9]

It is not the function of heat to cool things, but the opposite?—Yes.

Nor of dryness to make things wet but the opposite?—Quite so.

And it is not the function of the good to harm people, but the opposite?—It seems so.

And the just man is good?—Certainly.

It is not then the function of the just man, Polemarchus, to do harm to a friend or anyone else, but it is that of his opposite, the unjust man?—I think that you are entirely right, Socrates.

If, then, anyone tells us that it is just to give everyone his due, and he means by this that from the just man harm is due to his enemies and benefit due to his friends—the man who says that is not wise, for it is not true. *We have shown that it is never just to harm anyone.*—I agree.

You and I, I said, will therefore together fight anyone who tells us that Simonides said this, or Bias or Pittacus or any other of our wise and blessed men.—Yes, and I am quite willing to join that fight.

Do you know, I said, to whom I think this saying belongs, that it is just to benefit one's friends and harm one's enemies?—To whom?

I think Periander said that, or Perdiccas, or Xerxes, or Ismenias of Corinth, or some other wealthy man who believed himself to have great power.[10]—What you say is very true.

Very well, said I. Since neither justice nor the just appears to be that either, what else might one say it is?

While we were speaking Thrasymachus often started to interrupt, but he was restrained by those who were sitting by him, for they wanted to hear the argument to the end. But when we paused after these last words of mine he could no longer keep quiet. He gathered himself together like a wild beast about to spring, and he came at us as if to tear us to pieces.

Polemarchus and I were afraid and flustered as he roared into the middle of our company: What nonsense have you two been talking, Socrates? Why do you play the fool in thus giving way to each other? If you really want to know what justice is, don't only ask questions and then score off anyone who answers, and refute him. You know very well that it is much easier to ask questions than to answer them. Give an answer yourself and tell us what you say justice is. And don't tell me that it is the needful, or the advantageous, or the beneficial, or the gainful, or the useful, but tell me clearly and precisely what you mean, for I will not accept it if you utter such rubbish.

His words startled me, and glancing at him I was afraid. I think if I had not looked at him before he looked at me, I should have been speechless. As it was I had glanced at him first when our discussion began to exasperate him, so I was able to answer him and I said, trembling: do not be hard on us, Thrasymachus, if we have erred in our investigation, he and I; be sure that we err unwillingly. You surely do not believe that if we were searching for gold we would be unwilling to give way to each other and thus destroy our chance of finding it, but that when searching for justice, a thing more precious than much gold, we mindlessly give way to one another, and that we are not thoroughly in earnest about finding it. You must believe that, my friend, for I think we could not do it. So it is much more seemly that you clever people should pity us than that you should be angry with us.

When he heard that he gave a loud and bitter laugh and said: By Heracles, that is just Socrates' usual irony. I knew this, and I warned these men here before that you would not be willing to answer any questions but would pretend ignorance, and that you would do anything rather than give an answer, if anyone questioned you.

You are clever, Thrasymachus, I said, for you knew very well that if you asked anyone

how much is twelve, and as you asked him you warned him: "Do not, my man, say that twelve is twice six, or three times four, or six times two, or four times three, for I will not accept such nonsense," it would be quite clear to you that no one can answer a question asked in those terms. And if he said to you: "What do you mean, Thrasymachus? Am I not to give any of the answers you mention, not even, you strange man, if it happens to be one of those things, but am I to say something which is not the truth, or what do you mean?" What answer would you give him?

Well, he said, do you maintain that the two cases are alike?

They may well be, said I. Even if they are not, but the person you ask thinks they are, do you think him less likely to answer what he believes to be true, whether we forbid him or not?

And you will surely do the same, he said. Will you give one of the forbidden answers?

I shouldn't wonder, said I, if after investigation that was my opinion.

What, he said, if I show you a different answer about justice from all these and a better one? What penalty do you think you should pay then?

What else, said I, but what is proper for an ignorant man to pay? It is fitting for him to learn from one who knows. And that is what I believe I would deserve.

You amuse me, he said. You must not only learn but pay the fee.

Yes, when I have the money, I said.

We have the money, said Glaucon. If it is a matter of money, speak, Thrasymachus, for we shall all contribute for Socrates.

Quite so, said he, so that Socrates can carry on as usual: he gives no answer himself, and then, when someone else does give one, he takes up the argument and refutes it.

My dear man, I said, how could one answer, when in the first place he does not know and does not profess to know, and then, if he has an opinion, an eminent man forbids him to say what he believes? It is much more seemly for you to answer, since you say you know and have something to say. Please do so. Do me that favour, and do not begrudge your teaching to Glaucon and the others.

While I was saying this, Glaucon and the others begged him to speak. It was obvious that Thrasymachus was eager to do so and earn their admiration, and that he thought he had a beautiful answer, but he pretended that he wanted to win his point that I should be the one to answer. However, he agreed in the end, and then said: "There you have Socrates' wisdom; he himself is not willing to teach but he goes around learning from others, and then he is not even grateful."

When you say that I learn from others you are right, Thrasymachus, said I, but when you say that I am not grateful, that is not true. I show what gratitude I can, but I can only give praise. I have no money, but how enthusiastically I praise when someone seems to me to speak well is something you will realize quite soon after you have given your answer, for I think you will speak well.

Listen then, said he. I say that *the just is nothing else than the advantage of the stronger.* Well, why don't you praise me? But you will not want to.

I must first understand your meaning, said I, for I do not know it yet. You say that the advantage of the stronger is just. What do you mean, Thrasymachus? Surely you do not mean such a thing as this: Pouly damas, the pancratist athlete, is stronger than we are; it is to his advantage to eat beef to build up his physical strength. Do you mean that this food is also advantageous and just for us who are weaker than he is?

You disgust me, Socrates, he said. Your trick is always to take up the argument at the point where you can damage it most.

Not at all, my dear sir, I said, but tell us more clearly what you mean.

Do you not know, he said, that some cities are ruled by a despot, others by the people, and others again by the aristocracy?—Of course.

And this element has the power and rules in every city?—Certainly.

Yes, and *each government makes laws to its own advantage*: democracy makes democratic laws, a despotism makes despotic laws, and so with the others, and *when they have made these laws they declare this to be just for their subjects, that is, their own advantage*, and they punish him who transgresses the laws as lawless and unjust. This then, my good man, is what I say *justice is, the same in all cities, the advantage of the established government*, and correct reasoning will conclude that the just is the same everywhere, the advantage of the stronger.

Now I see what you mean, I said. Whether it is true or not I will try to find out. But you too, Thrasymachus, have given as an answer that the just is the advantageous whereas you forbade that answer to me. True, you have added the words "of the stronger."

Perhaps, he said, you consider that an insignificant addition!

It is not clear yet whether or not it is significant. Obviously, we must investigate whether what you say is true. I agree that the just is some kind of advantage, but you add that it is the advantage of the stronger. I do not know. We must look into this.—Go on looking, he said.

We will do so, said I. Tell me, do you also say that obedience to the rulers is just?—I do.

And are *the rulers in all cities infallible, or are they liable to error?*—No doubt they are *liable to error.*

When they undertake to make laws, therefore, they make some correctly and make others incorrectly?—I think so.

"Correctly" means that they make laws to their own advantage, and "incorrectly" not to their own advantage. Or how would you put it?—As you do.

And whatever laws they make must be obeyed by their subjects, and this is just?—Of course.

Then, according to your argument, it is just to do not only what is to the advantage of the stronger, but also the opposite, what is not to their advantage.

What is that you are saying? he asked.

The same as you, I think, but let us examine it more fully. Have we not agreed that, in giving orders to their subjects, the rulers are sometimes in error as to what is best for themselves, yet it is just for their subjects to do whatever their rulers order. Is that much agreed?—I think so.

Think then also, said I, that you have agreed that it is just to do what is to the disadvantage of the rulers and the stronger whenever they unintentionally give orders which are bad for themselves, and you say it is just for the others to obey their given orders. Does it not of necessity follow, my wise Thrasymachus, that it is just to do the opposite of what you said? The weaker are then ordered to do what is to the disadvantage of the stronger.

Yes by Zeus, Socrates, said Polemarchus, that is quite clear.

Yes, if you bear witness for him, interrupted Cleitophon.

What need of a witness? said Polemarchus. Thrasymachus himself agrees that the rulers sometimes give orders that are bad for themselves, and that it is just to obey them.

Thrasymachus maintained that it is just to obey the orders of the rulers, Polemarchus.

He also said that the just was the advantage of the stronger, Cleitophon. Having established

those two points he went on to agree that the stronger sometimes ordered the weaker, their subjects, to do what was disadvantageous to themselves. From these agreed premises it follows that what is of advantage to the stronger is no more just than what is not.

But, Cleitophon replied, he said that the advantage of the stronger is what the stronger believes to be of advantage to him. This the weaker must do, and that is what he defined the just to be.

That is not how he stated it, said Polemarchus.

It makes no difference, Polemarchus, I said. If Thrasymachus now wants to put it that way, let us accept it. Tell me, Thrasymachus, was this what you intended to say justice is, namely that which appears to the stronger to be to his advantage, whether it is so or not? Shall we say that this is what you mean?

Not in the least, said he. Do you think that I would call stronger a man who is in error at the time he errs?

I did think you meant that, said I, when you said that the rulers were not infallible but were liable to error.

You are being captious, Socrates, he said. Do you call a man a physician when he is in error in the treatment of patients, at the moment of, and in regard to this very error? Or would you call a man an accountant when he makes a miscalculation at the moment of, and with regard to this miscalculation? I think that we express ourselves in words which, taken literally, do say that the physician is in error, or the accountant, or the grammarian. *But each of these, in so far as he is what we call him, never errs, so that, if you use language with precision—and you want to be precise—no practitioner of a craft ever errs. It is when the knowledge of his craft leaves him that he errs, and at that time he is not a practitioner of it. No craftsman, wise man, or ruler is in error at the time that he is a ruler in the precise sense.*

However, everyone will say that the physician or the ruler is in error. Take it then that this is now my answer to you. To speak with precision, the ruler, in so far as he is a ruler, unerringly decrees what is best for himself and this the subject must do. The just then is, as I said from the first, to do what is advantageous to the stronger.

Very well, Thrasymachus, said I. You think I am captious?

You certainly are, he said.

And you think that it was deliberate trickery on my part to ask you the questions I did ask?

I know it very well, he said, but it will not do you any good, for I would be well aware of your trickery; nor would you have the ability to force my agreement in open debate.

I would not even try, my good sir, I said, but in order to avoid a repetition of this, do define clearly whether it is the ruler in the ordinary or the precise sense whose advantage is to be pursued as that of the stronger.

I mean, he said, the ruler in the most exact sense. Now practise your trickery and your captiousness on this if you can, for I will not let any statement of yours pass, and you certainly won't be able to.

Do you think, I said, that I am crazy enough to try to shave a lion or trick Thrasymachus?

You certainly tried just now, he said, though you are no good at it.

Enough of this sort of thing, I said. But tell me: is the physician in the strict sense, whom you mentioned just now, a moneymaker or one who treats the sick? Tell me about the real physician.—He is one who treats the sick, said he.

What about the ship's captain? Is he, to speak correctly, a ruler of sailors or a sailor?—A ruler of sailors.

We should not, I think, take into account the fact that he sails in a ship, and we should not call him a sailor, for it is not on account of his sailing that he is called a ship's captain, but because of his craft and his authority over sailors.—True.

And there is something which is advantageous to each of these, that is: patients and sailors?—Certainly.

And *is not the purpose of a craft's existence to seek and secure the advantageous in each case?*—That's right.

Now is there any other advantage to each craft, except that it be as perfect as possible?—What is the meaning of that question?

It is this, said I. If you asked me whether our body is sufficient unto itself, or has a further need I should answer: "It certainly has needs, and for this purpose the craft of medicine exists and has now been discovered, because the body is defective, not self-sufficient. So to provide it with things advantageous to it the craft of medicine has been developed." Do you think I am correct in saying this or not?—Correct.

Well then, is the craft of medicine itself defective, or is there any other craft which needs some further excellence—as the eyes are in need of sight, the ears of hearing, and, because of this need, they require some other craft to investigate and provide for this?—is there in the craft itself some defect, so that each craft requires another craft which will investigate what is beneficial to it, and then the investigating craft needs another such still, and so ad infinitum? Or does a craft investigate what is beneficial to it, or does it need neither itself nor any other to investigate what is required because of imperfections? There is in fact no defect or error of any kind in any craft, nor is it proper to any craft to seek what is to the advantage of anything but the object of its concern; it is itself pure and without fault, being itself correct, as long as it is wholly itself in the precise sense. Consider this with that preciseness of language which you mentioned. Is it so or otherwise?—It appears to be so.

The craft of medicine, I said, does not seek its own advantage but that of the body.—Yes.

Nor does horse-breeding seek its own advantage but that of horses. Nor does any other craft seek its own advantage—it has no further need—but that of its object.—That seems to be the case.

And surely, Thrasymachus, the crafts govern and have power over their object.

He agreed, but with great reluctance at this point.

No science of any kind seeks or orders its own advantage, but that of the weaker which is subject to it and governed by it.

He tried to fight this conclusion, but he agreed to this too in the end. And after he had, I said: Surely no physician either, in so far as he is a physician, seeks or orders what is advantageous to himself, but to his patient? For we agreed that the physician in the strict sense of the word is a ruler over bodies and not a moneymaker. Was this not agreed?

He said yes.

So the ship's captain in the strict sense is a ruler over sailors, and not a sailor?—That has been agreed.

Does it not follow that the ship's captain and ruler will not seek and order what is advantageous to himself, but to the sailor, his subject.

He agreed, but barely.

So then, Thrasymachus, I said, no other ruler in any kind of government, in so far as he is a ruler, seeks what is to his own advantage or orders it, but that which is to the advantage of his subject who is the concern of his craft; it is this he keeps in view; all his words and actions are directed to this end.

When we reached this point in our argument and it was clear to all that the definition of justice had turned into its opposite, Thrasymachus, instead of answering, said: Tell me, Socrates, do you have a nanny?

What's this? said I. Had you not better answer than ask such questions?

Because, he said, she is letting you go around with a snotty nose and does not wipe it when she needs to, if she leaves you without any knowledge of sheep or shepherds.

What is the particular point of that remark? I asked.

You think, he said, that shepherds and cowherds seek the good of their sheep or cattle, whereas their sole purpose in fattening them and looking after them is their own good and that of their master. Moreover, you believe that rulers in the cities, true rulers that is, have a different attitude towards their subjects than one has towards sheep, and that they think of anything else, night and day, than their own advantage. You are so far from understanding the nature of justice and the just, of injustice and the unjust, that you do not realize that the just is really another's good, the advantage of the stronger and the ruler, but for the inferior who obeys it is a personal injury. Injustice on the other hand exercises its power over those who are truly naive and just, and those over whom it rules do what is of advantage to the other, the stronger, and, by obeying him, they make him happy, but themselves not in the least.

You must look at it in this way, my naive Socrates: *the just is everywhere at a disadvantage compared with the unjust.* First, in their contracts with one another: wherever two such men are associated you will never find, when the partnership ends, the just man to have more than the unjust, but less. Then, in their relation to the city: when taxes are to be paid, from the same income the just man pays more, the other less; but, when benefits are to be received, the one gets nothing while the other profits much; whenever each of them holds a public office, the just man, even if he is not penalized in other ways, finds that his private affairs deteriorate through neglect while he gets nothing from the public purse because he is just; moreover, he is disliked by his household and his acquaintances whenever he refuses them an unjust favour. The opposite is true of the unjust man in every respect. I repeat what I said before: the man of great power gets the better deal. Consider him if you want to decide how much more it benefits him privately to be unjust rather than just. You will see this most easily if you turn your thoughts to the most complete form of injustice which brings the greatest happiness to the wrongdoer, while it makes those whom he wronged, and who are not willing to do wrong, most wretched. This most complete form is depotism; it does not appropriate other people's property little by little, whether secretly or by force, whether public or private, whether sacred objects or temple property, but appropriates it all at once.

When a wrongdoer is discovered in petty cases, he is punished and faces great opprobrium, for the perpetrators of these petty crimes are called temple robbers, kidnappers, housebreakers, robbers, and thieves, but when a man, besides appropriating the possessions of the citizens, manages to enslave the owners as well, then, instead of those ugly names he is called happy and blessed, not only by his fellow-citizens but by all others who learn that he has run through the whole gamut of injustice. Those who give injustice a bad name do so because they are afraid, not of practising but of suffering injustice.

And so, Socrates, injustice, if it is on a large enough scale, is a stronger, freer, and more powerful thing than justice and, as I said from the first, *the just is what is advantageous to the stronger, while the unjust is to one's own advantage and benefit.*

Having said this and poured this mass of close-packed words into our ears as a bathman might a flood of water, Thrasymachus intended to leave, but those present did not let him, and made him stay for a discussion of his views. I too begged him to stay and I said: My dear Thrasymachus, after throwing such a speech at us, you want to leave before adequately instructing us or finding out whether you are right or not? Or do you think it a small thing to decide on a whole way of living, which, if each of us adopted it, would make him live the most profitable life?

Do I think differently? said Thrasymachus.

You seem to, said I, or else you care nothing for us nor worry whether we'll live better or worse, in ignorance of what you say you know. Do, my good sir, show some keenness to teach us. It will not be without value to you to be the benefactor of so many of us. For my own part, I tell you that I do not believe that injustice is more profitable than justice, not even if one gives it full scope and does not put obstacles in its way. No, my friend. Let us assume the existence of an unjust man with every opportunity to do wrong, either because his misdeeds remain secret or because he has the power to battle things through; nevertheless he does not persuade me that injustice is more profitable than justice. Perhaps some other of us feels the same, and not only I. Come now, my good sir, really persuade us that we are wrong to esteem justice more highly than injustice in planning our life.

And how, said he, shall I persuade you, if you are not convinced by what I said just now? What more can I do? Am I to take my argument and pour it into your mind?

Zeus forbid! Don't you do that, but first stick to what you have said and, if you change your position, do so openly and do not deceive us. You see now, Thrasymachus—let us examine again what went before—that, while you first defined the true physician, you did not think it necessary later to observe the precise definition of the true shepherd, but you think that he fattens sheep, in so far as he is a shep-herd, not with what is best for the sheep in mind, but like a guest about to be entertained at a feast, with a banquet in view, or again a sale, like a moneymaker, not a shepherd. The shepherd's craft is concerned only to provide what is best for the object of its care; as for the craft itself, it is sufficiently provided with all it needs to be at its best, as long as it does not fall short of being the craft of the shep-herd. That is why I thought it necessary for us to agree just now that every kind of rule, as far as it truly rules, does not seek what is best for anything else than the subject of its rule and care, and this is true both of public and private kinds of rule. Do you think that those who rule over cities, the true rulers, rule willingly?—I don't think it, by Zeus, I know it, he said.

Well but, Thrasymachus, said I, do you not realize that in other kinds of rule no one is will-ing to rule, but they ask for pay, thinking that their rule will benefit not themselves but their subjects. Tell me, does not every craft differ from every other in that it has a different func-tion? Please do not give an answer contrary to what you believe, so that we can come to some conclusion.

Yes, that is what makes it different, he said.

And each craft benefits us in its own particular way, different from the others. For example, medicine gives us health, navigation safety while sailing, and so with the others.—Quite so.

And the craft of earning pay gives us wages, for that is its function. Or would you call medicine the same craft as navigation? Or, if you wish to define with precision as you proposed, if the ship's captain becomes healthy because sailing benefits his health, would you for that reason call his craft medicine?—Not at all, he said.

Nor would you call wage-earning medicine if someone is healthy while earning wages?—Certainly not.

Nor would you call medicine wage-earning if someone earns pay while healing?—No.

So we agree that *each craft brings its own benefit?*—Be it so.

Whatever benefit all craftsmen receive in common must then result clearly from some craft which they pursue in common, and so are benefited by it.—It seems so.

We say then that if the practitioners of these crafts are benefited by earning a wage, this results from their practising the wage earn-ing craft.

He reluctantly agreed.

So this benefit to each, the receiving of pay, does not result from the practice of their own craft, but if we are to examine this precisely, medicine provides health while the craft of earning provides pay; house building provides a house, and the craft of earning which accom-panies it provides a wage, and so with the other crafts; each fulfills its own function and bene-fits that with which it is concerned. *If pay is not added, is there any benefit which the practitioner gets from his craft?*—Apparently not.

Does he even provide a benefit when he works for nothing?—Yes, I think he does.

Is this not clear now, Thrasymachus, that *no craft or rule provides its own advantage, but, as we have been saying for some time, it procures and orders what is of advantage to its subject; it aims at his advantage, that of the weaker, not of the stronger.* That is why, my dear Thrasymachus, I said just now that no one willingly wants to rule, to handle and straighten out the affairs of others. They ask for pay because the man who intends to practise his craft well never does what is best for himself, nor, when he gives such orders, does he give them in accordance with his craft, but he pursues the advantage of his subject. *For that reason, then, it seems one must provide remuneration if they are to be willing to rule, whether money or honour, or a penalty if he does not rule.*

What do you mean, Socrates? said Glaucon. I understand the two kinds of remuneration, but I do not understand what kind of penalty you mean, which you mention under the heading of remuneration.

Then you do not understand the remuneration of the best men, I said, which makes them willing to rule. Do you not know that *the love of honour and money are made a reproach, and rightly so?*—I know that.

Therefore good men will not be willing to rule for the sake of either money or honour. They do not want to be called hirelings if they openly receive payment for ruling, nor, if they provide themselves with it secretly, to be called thieves. Nor will they do it for honour's sake, for they have no love for it. So, if they are to be willing to rule, some compulsion or punishment must be brought to bear on them. That is perhaps why to seek office willingly, before one must, is thought shameful. Now *the greatest punishment is to be ruled by a worse man than oneself if one is not willing to rule.* I think it is the fear of this which makes men of good character rule whenever they do. They approach office not as something good or something to be enjoyed, but as something necessary because they cannot entrust it to men better than, or even equal to, themselves. In a city of good men, if there were such, they would probably vie with each other in order not to rule, not, as now, in order to be rulers. There it would be quite clear that the nature of the true ruler is not to seek his own advantage but that of his subjects, and everyone, knowing this, would prefer to receive benefits rather than take the trouble to benefit others. In this matter I do not at all agree with Thrasymachus that the just is the advantage of the stronger, but we will look into this matter another time. What

seems to me of greater importance is what Thrasymachus is saying now, namely that *the life of the unjust man is to be preferred to that of the just.* Which will you choose, Glaucon, and which of our views do you consider the more truly spoken?

I certainly think that the life of the just is more profitable.

You have heard, said I, all the blessings of the unjust life which Thrasymachus enumerated just now?

I heard, said he, but I am not convinced.

Do you want us to persuade him, if we could find the means to do so, that what he says is not true?

Of course I want it, he said.

If we were to oppose him, I said, with a parallel set speech on the blessings of the just life, then another speech from him in turn, then another from us, we should have to count and measure the blessings mentioned on each side, and we should need some judges to decide the case. If, on the other hand, we investigate the question, as we were doing, by seeking agreement with each other, then we can ourselves be both the judges and the advocates.—Quite so.

Which method do you prefer? I asked.—The second.

Come then, Thrasymachus, I said, answer us from the beginning. You say that complete injustice is more profitable than complete justice?

I certainly do say that, he said, and I have told you why.

Well then, what about this: you call one of the two a virtue and the other a vice?—Of course.

That is, you call justice a virtue, and injustice a vice?

Is that likely, my good man, said he, since I say that injustice is profitable, and justice is not?

What then?—The opposite.

Do you call being just a vice?—No, but certainly high-minded foolishness.

And you call being unjust low-minded?—No, I call it good judgment.

You consider the unjust then, Thrasymachus, to be good and knowledgeable?

Yes, he said, those who are able to carry injustice through to the end, who can bring cities and communities of men under their power. Perhaps you think I mean purse-snatchers? Not that those actions too are not profitable, if they are not found out, but they are not worth mentioning in comparison with what I am talking about.

I am not unaware of what you mean, I said, but this point astonishes me: do you include injustice under virtue and wisdom, and justice among their opposites?—I certainly do.

That makes it harder, my friend, and it is not easy now to know what to say. If you had declared that injustice was more profitable, but agreed that it was a vice or shameful as some others do, we could have discussed it along the lines of general opinion. Now, obviously, you will say that it is fine and strong, and apply to it all the attributes which we used to apply to justice, since you have been so bold as to include it under virtue and wisdom.—Your guess, he said, is quite right.

We must not, however, shrink from pursuing our argument and looking into this, so long as I am sure that you mean what you say. For I do not think you are joking now, Thrasymachus, but are saying what you believe to be true.

What difference, said he, does it make to you whether I believe it or not? Is it not my argument you are refuting?

No difference, said I, but try to answer this further question: *do you think that the just man wants to get the better of the just?*

Never, said he, for he would not then be well mannered and simple, as he is now.

Does he want to overreach a just action?[11]

Not a just action either, he said.

Would he want to get the better of an unjust man, and would he deem that just or not?

He would want to, he said, and he would deem it right, but he would not be able to.

That was not my question, said I, but whether the just man wants and deems it right to outdo not a just man, but an unjust one?—That is so.

What about the unjust man? Would he deem it right to outdo the just man and the just action?

Of course he does, he said, since he deems it right to get the better of everybody.

So the unjust man will get the better of another unjust man or an unjust action and he will strive to get all he can from everyone?—That is so.

Let us put it this way, I said. *The just man does not try to get the better of one like him but of one unlike him, whereas the unjust man overreaches the like and the unlike?*—Very well put.

The unjust man, I said, is knowledgeable and good, and the just man is neither?—That is well said too.

It follows, I said, that the unjust man is like the knowledgeable and the good, while the just man is unlike them?

Of course that will be so, he said, being such a man he will be like such men, while the other is not like them.

Good. Each of them has the qualities of those he is like?—Why not? Very well, Thrasymachus. Now you speak of one man as musical, of another as unmusical?—I do indeed.

Which is knowledgeable and which is not?

Of course the musical man is knowledgeable, the unmusical is not.

What he has knowledge of he is good at,[12] and he who has no knowledge is bad?—Yes.

Is not the same true of the physician?—The same.

Do you think, my dear sir, that any musician, when tuning his lyre, desires, in the tightening and relaxing of the strings, to do better than another musician or deems it right to get the better of him?—I don't think so.

But he wants to do better than a non-musician?—Necessarily.

What of a physician? When prescribing food or drink, does he want to 350 do better than another medical man or action?—Certainly not.

But better than the non-medical?—Yes.

In matters involving any kind of knowledge or ignorance, do you think that any expert would wish to achieve more than any other expert would do or say, rather than, in respect to the same action, achieve the same as anyone like himself?—Well perhaps, it must be as you say.

What about the non-expert? Does he not want to outdo the expert and the non-expert equally?—Perhaps.

The man with knowledge is wise?—I agree.

And the wise is good?—I agree.

So *the good and wise does not wish to get the better of one like himself, but of the unlike and opposite*?—Apparently.

But the bad and ignorant would want to get the better of his like and his opposite?—So it appears.

Now Thrasymachus, I said, we found that the unjust man tries to get the better of both those like and those unlike him. Did you not say so?—I did.

Yes, and the just man will not get the better of his like, but of one unlike him?—Yes.

The just man then, I said, resembles the wise and good, while the unjust resembles the bad and ignorant?—It may be so.

Further, we agreed that each will be such as the man he resembles?—We did so agree.

So we find that the just man has turned out to be good and wise, and the unjust man ignorant and bad.

Thrasymachus agreed to all this, not easily as I am telling it, but reluctantly and after being pushed. It was summer and he was perspiring profusely. And then I saw something I had never seen before:

Thrasymachus blushing. After we had agreed that justice was virtue and wisdom, and injustice vice and ignorance, I said: Very well, let us consider this as established, but we also said that injustice was powerful, or don't you remember, Thrasymachus?

I remember, he said, but then I am not satisfied with what you are now saying. I could make a speech about it, but if I should speak I know that you would say I am delivering a public oration. So either allow me to speak or, if you want to ask questions, ask them, and I will say "very well," and nod yes and no, as one does to old wives' tales.

Don't ever do that, I said, against your own opinion.

Just to please you, he said, since you won't let me speak. What else do you want?

Nothing at all, said I. If you will do this, do it. I will ask my questions.—Ask them then.

I am asking what I asked before, so that we may proceed with our argument about the relation of justice and injustice in an orderly way. It was said that injustice is more powerful and stronger than justice. But now, I said, since justice is wisdom and virtue, it will easily be shown to be also stronger than injustice which is ignorance; nobody could still not know that. However, I do not want to state this thus simply, Thrasymachus, but to look into it in some such way as this: would you say that it is unjust for a city to undertake to enslave other cities unjustly and hold them in subjection, having enslaved many cities to its power?

Of course, he said, this is what the best city will do, the most completely unjust.

I understand that this was your argument, I said, but let me examine this point: will the city which has become stronger than another achieve this power without justice, or must it do so with the help of justice?

If what you said just now stands—that justice is wisdom—with the help of justice, but if things are as I stated them, with injustice.

I am delighted, Thrasymachus, that you do not merely nod yes or no, but that you answer in a very fine manner.

I am doing it to please you, he said.

You are doing well. Now please me also by answering this question: do you think that a city, an army, a band of robbers or thieves, or any other body of men which engages unjustly upon a common course, could achieve anything if they wrong one another?—No indeed.

What if they do not wrong one another? Would they not achieve more?—Certainly.

Yes, for injustice, Thrasymachus, causes factions and hatreds and fights with one another, while justice brings a sense of common purpose and friendship. Is that not so?—Be it so, to agree with you.

You are doing well my good friend. Tell me this: *if it is the result of injustice to bring hatred wherever it occurs, then its presence, whether among free men or slaves, will make them hate each other and quarrel, and be unable to achieve any common purpose?*—Quite so.

What if it occurs between two men? Will they not be at odds, hate each other, and be hostile to each other as well as to the just?— They will be.

Does injustice, my good sir, lose this capacity for dissension when it occurs within one individual, or will it preserve it intact?

Let it be preserved intact, he said.

It seems to follow that injustice, wherever it occurs, be it in a city, a family, an army, or anything else results in making it incapable of achieving anything as a unit because of the dissensions and differences it creates, and, *further, it makes that unit hostile to itself, to its every enemy, and to the just. Is that not so?—* Quite.

Even in one individual it has the same effect, which follows from its nature. First, it makes that individual incapable of achievement because he is at odds with himself and not of one mind. It makes him his own enemy, as well as the enemy of the just, does it not?—It does.

The gods too, my friend, are just.—Be it so.

So the unjust man is also an enemy of the gods, while the just man is their friend.

Bravely enjoy your feast of words, he said. I will not oppose you, to avoid unpopularity in this company.

Come then, said I, complete the feast for me by answering as you are now doing. The just are shown to be wiser and more able in action, while the unjust are not even able to act together, for surely, when we speak of a powerful achievement by unjust men acting in common, we are altogether far from the truth. They could not have kept their hands off each other if they had been completely bad, but clearly they had some justice which forbade them to wrong each other and their enemies at the same time. It was this which enabled them to do what they did. They started on their unjust course being half evil with injustice, for those who are completely evil and completely unjust are also completely incapable of achievement. I can see that this is so, and not as you at first assumed.

We must now examine whether the just also live a better life than the unjust and are happier, a point which we deferred for later investigation. I think it is clear even now that they are, yet we must look into this further, for *the argument concerns no casual topic, but one's whole manner of living.*—Look into it, then.

I am looking, said I. Do you think there is such a thing as the function of a horse?—I do.

And would you define the function of a horse, or of anything else, as to do that which can be done only, or be done best, by means of it?

I do not understand your question, he said.

Put it like this: is it possible to see by any other means than the eyes?—Certainly not.

Further, could you hear by any other means than the ears?—Not possibly.

Then we are right to say that these are the functions of eyes and ears?—Quite so.

Further, would you use a dagger or a carving knife to trim the branches of a vine, or many other instruments?—Of course.

But you would not do it as well with any other instrument as with a pruning knife which was made for the purpose?—That is true.

Then shall we put it that this is the function of a pruning knife?—We shall.

Now I think you will understand my recent question better, when I inquired whether the function of each thing is to do that which it alone can perform, or perform better than anything else could.—I understand, he said, and I think that is the function of each.

Very well, said I. *Does each thing to which a particular task is assigned* also have its excellence? Let us go over the same ground again. We say that the eyes have a particular task?—Yes.

They also have their own excellence?—They have.

The ears too have a function?—Yes.

So they have their excellence?—That too.

Is that not the case with all other things?—It is.

Moreover, could the eyes perform their function well if they did not possess their own excellence or virtue, but their own vice instead?

How could they? he said. You mean blindness instead of sight?

Whatever their virtue is, for I am not now asking that, but whether any agent performs its function well by means of its own excellence or virtue, or badly through its own badness or vice.—What you say is true.

So the ears, too, deprived of their own virtue, would perform their function badly.—Quite so.

And we could say the same about all other things?—I think so.

Come now, consider this point next: *There is a function of the soul which you could not fulfill by means of any other things, as for example: to take care of things, to rule, to deliberate, and other things of the kind*; could we entrust these things to any other agent than the soul and say that they belong to it?—To no other.

What of living? Is that not a function of the soul?—It most certainly is.

So there is also an excellence of the soul?—We say so.

And, Thrasymachus, will the soul ever fulfill its function well if it is deprived of its own particular excellence, or is this impossible?—Impossible.

It is therefore inevitable that *the bad soul rules and looks after things badly and that the good soul does all these things well.*—Inevitable.

Now we have agreed that justice is excellence of the soul, and that injustice is vice of soul?—We have so agreed.

The just soul and the just man, then, will live well, and the unjust man will live badly.—So it seems, according to your argument.

Surely the one who lives well is blessed and happy, and the one who does not is the opposite.—Of course.

So the just man is happy, and the unjust one is wretched.—So be it.

It profits no one to be wretched, but to be happy.—Of course.

And so, my good Thrasymachus, injustice is never more profitable than justice.

Let that be your banquet of words, he said, at the feast of Bendis, Socrates.

Given by you, Thrasymachus, I said, after you became gentle and ceased to be angry with me. Yet I have not had a good banquet, but that was my fault, not yours. I seem to have behaved as gluttons do, snatching at every dish that passes them and tasting it before they have reasonably enjoyed the one before. So I, before finding the answer to our first enquiry into the nature of justice, let that go and turned to investigate whether it was vice and ignorance or wisdom and virtue. Another argument came up after, that injustice was more profitable than justice, and I could not refrain from following this up and abandoning the previous one so that the result of our discussion for me is that I know nothing; for, when I do not know what justice is, I shall hardly know whether it is a kind of virtue or not, or whether the just man is unhappy or happy.

NOTES

1   "The goddess" in an Athenian writer, especially when the scene is laid in Athens, usually means Athena, and it may do so here. However, we know from the mention of the Thracians here, that the festival was that of Bendis, a Thracian goddess whose worship had recently been introduced in the Piraeus, and the reference may be to her.

2   Glaucon and Adeimantus are the brothers of Plato, who is not present. They carry the main burden of the conversation with Socrates from the beginning of the second book to the end of the work. The scene is the house of old Cephalus, father of Polemarchus, Lysias, and Euthydemus. Lysias is a well-known writer of speeches of the late fifth century, and a number of them are extant. He later became the model of the simple style. He takes no part.

We have a dialogue named after Euthydemus. Thrasymachus was a Sophist of the younger generation, known for his powerful emotional appeals. He is the main objector in the first book, but after that says very little. We have a short dialogue, the *Cleitophon* which criticizes Socrates for his lack of positive teaching. The first book, like many early or "Socratic" dialogues, discusses several definitions of "justice" but comes to no conclusion. The whole discussion is probably supposed to have taken place about 411 B.C.

3   The phrase occurs several times in Homer (e.g. *Iliad* 22, 60). It refers to old age as the threshold on leaving life.

4   The old saying that like consorts with like.

5   Seriphus was a small island of little importance.

6   It should be kept in mind through out the *Republic* that the Greek word *dikaios* and the noun *dikaiosyne* are often used, as here, in a much wider sense than our word "just" and "justice" by which we must usually translate them. They then mean "right" or "righteous," i.e. good conduct in relation to others, and the opposite *adikia* then has the general sense of wrongdoing.

7   Simonides was a well-known lyric and elegiac poet, and author of many epigrams. He died about 468 B.C., around the time of Socrates' birth.

8   By *technê*, here translated "craft," Socrates refers to any art or craft which requires special knowledge. The word "art" has been avoided in the translation because it implies for us other factors than knowledge, and it is knowledge alone which Socrates has in mind. He then proceeds to equate "justice" with such a *technê*, as implying the knowledge of how to behave, on the well-known Socratic belief that virtue is knowledge.

9 We should note that in arguing against the popular ethic that it is right to harm one's enemies, Socrates is rising to a higher ethic when he maintains that the good man will harm no one.

10 Bias of Priene in Ionia and Pittacus of Mytilene (both early sixth century) were counted among the seven wise men of Greece. Periander (650–570) was tyrant of Corinth. Perdiccas probably refers to the first king of Macedonia (eighth century) and Xerxes was the king of Persia who invaded Greece in the second Persian war. All three are mentioned here as typical despots.

11 *pleon echein or pleonexia*, literally to have more, comes to mean "to outdo, to over-reach, to do better than." Now there is one right note to strike in music and the musician has the necessary knowledge to do so. He will want to do this, but he will not want to do better than another musician with the same knowledge, which would be absurd. So the just man, if justice is a *technê*, a matter of knowledge (see note 8) will have the knowledge to do the right thing, and cannot want to do better than that, so he will not desire to outdo another just man with the same knowledge.

12 As before, the craftsman with sufficient knowledge is good at his craft, and his virtue or excellence as a craftsman depends on, in a sense is, that knowledge. Socrates assumes throughout that *dikaiosune* or justice in the sense it is here used (see 331c and note 6) is also a matter of knowledge, a *technê*. So the notion of "being good at one's craft" being a matter of knowledge is broadened to "being good is a matter of knowledge," i.e. the famous Socratic paradox that "virtue" (*aretê*) is knowledge.

Confucius and Mencius
Ancient China

Confucius (551–479 BCE) lived in a time of political and social change, known as Spring and Autumn Period, when the separate states of ancient China were moving from Feudal Aristocracy to Autocracy. It was a time of great creativity in philosophical and political thought, and like Socrates in the West, Confucius was the first of the great philosophers of ancient China.

Confucius was from the state of Lu, a small state of the North of China. His father died when he was very young, and he grew up in relatively poor circumstances. However, he was descended from a Duke of State of Sung and from a Great Officer of Lu, and these connections contributed to the fact that he was able to secure a good education, which means that he was able to have access to the official documents of several states, and the leisure to read and study them. These documents would have mainly consisted of descriptions of ritual and musical texts, poetry, and various court records.

Confucius's public life consisted of three elements: service in government, teaching, and compiling texts. He served only briefly in government, though he rose to the level of a Great Officer, as a Minister of Justice, and made a couple of significant contributions to his Duke's government. It seems that he began teaching at about the age of 30, and was a demanding but much esteemed teacher. It is mainly because of his teachings that we know him, because, like Socrates, he left no writings of his own. All of Confucius's words come from his students or their students. He was himself a great student of the texts of previous eras and ordered and organized the state archives while making his own interpretations of them. He established a body of thought and learning, based on older traditions, by means of which the scholar, the gentleman could advance in office and which he could use for making decisions in practical circumstances. Because of his lasting and even continuing influence on China, Confucius must be considered the single most important thinker in the history of China.

Mencius was a follower of the teachings of Confucius, though not a contemporary. He lived approximately (385–302 BCE), which was during a period of time in China known as the Warring States period. As its name suggests, this was a time of many wars and military campaigns, as the crumbling feudal structure gave rise to competition. Shortly after this time, China was united under a single emperor.

Most of the following selection comes from *The Analects of Confucius*, a collection of the teachings of Confucius, and are recorded by his students and passed down over the centuries. They provide an ethical orientation to the world, but not a direct political philosophy. For this we will have to appeal to the *Book of Mencius*, which applies Confucian thought in instructing rulers.

STUDY QUESTIONS:

1. What qualities must a gentleman possess, and how should he live to cultivate those qualities?

2. What is valuable about living a gentleman's life?

3. What are the most important qualities of a ruler, according to Mencius?

The Analects

Confucius
Translated by James Legge

BOOK I

Chapter I

The whole work and achievement of the learner, first perfecting his knowledge, then attracting by his fame like-minded individuals, and finally complete in himself.

1. The Master said, "Is it not pleasant to learn with a constant perseverance and application?

2. "Is it not delightful to have friends coming from distant quarters?

3. "Is he not a man of complete virtue, who feels no discomposure though men may take no note of him?"

BOOK II

Chapter IV

Confucius's own account of his gradual progress and attainments.

1. The Master said, "At fifteen, I had my mind bent on learning.

2. "At thirty, I stood firm.

3. "At forty, I had no doubts.

4. "At fifty, I knew the decrees of Heaven.

5. "At sixty, my ear was an obedient organ for the reception of truth.

6. "At seventy, I could follow what my heart desired, without transgressing what was right."

Chapter XI

To be able to teach others one must from his old stores be continually developing things new.

The Master said, "If a man keeps cherishing his old knowledge, so as continually to be acquiring new, he may be a teacher of others."

Chapter XII

The general aptitude of the Chün-tsze.

The Master said, "The accomplished scholar is not a utensil."

Chapter XX

Example in superiors is more powerful than force.

Chî K'ang asked how to cause the people to reverence their ruler, to be faithful to him,

---

From *The Analects of Confucius* translated by James Legge, Clarendon Press, 1893.

and to go on to nerve themselves to virtue. The Master said, "Let him preside over them with gravity; —then they will reverence him. Let him be final and kind to all; —then they will be faithful to him. Let him advance the good and teach the incompetent; —then they will eagerly seek to be virtuous."

BOOK III

Chapter III

Ceremonies and music vain without virtue.

The Master said, "If a man be without the virtues proper to humanity, what has he to do with the rites of propriety? If a man be without the virtues proper to humanity, what has he to do with music?"

Chapter V

The anarchy of Confucius's time.

The Master said, "The rude tribes of the east and north have their princes, and are not like the States of our great land which are without them."

Chapter VII

The superior man avoids all contentious striving.

The Master said, "The student of virtue has no contentions. If it be said he cannot avoid them, shall this be in archery? But he bows complaisantly to his competitors; thus he ascends the hall, descends, and exacts the forfeit of drinking. In his contention, he is still the Chün-tsze."

Chapter XI

The profound meaning of the great sacrifice.

Some one asked the meaning of the great sacrifice. The Master said, "I do not know. He who knew its meaning would find it as easy to govern the kingdom as to look on this"— pointing to his palm.

Chapter XIV

The completeness and elegance of the institutions of the Châu dynasty.

The Master said, "Châu had the advantage of viewing the two past dynasties. How complete and elegant are its regulations! I follow Châu."

Chapter XVII

How Confucius cleaved to ancient rites.

1. Tsze-kung wished to do away with the offering of a sheep connected with the inauguration of the first day of each month.

2. The Master said, "Ts'ze, you love the sheep; I love the ceremony."

Chapter XVIII

How the princes should be served: —against the spirit of the times.

The Master said, "The full observance of the rules of propriety in serving one's prince is accounted by people to be flattery."

Chapter XXVI

The disregard of what is essential vitiates all services.

The Master said, "High station filled without indulgent generosity; ceremonies performed without reverence; mourning conducted without sorrow; —wherewith should I contemplate such ways?"

BOOK IV

Chapter II

Only true virtue adapts a man for the varied conditions of life.

The Master said, "Those who are without virtue cannot abide long either in a condition of poverty and hardship, or in a condition of enjoyment. The virtuous rest in virtue; the wise desire virtue."

Chapter V

The devotion of the Chün-tsze to virtue.

1. The Master said, "Riches and honors are what men desire. If it cannot be obtained in the proper way, they should not be held. Poverty and meanness are what men dislike. If it cannot be avoided in the proper way, they should not be avoided.

2. "If a superior man abandon virtue, how can he fulfill the requirements of that name?

3. "The superior man does not, even for the space of a single meal, act contrary to virtue. In moments of haste, he cleaves to it. In seasons of danger, he cleaves to it."

Chapter VI

A lament because of the rarity of the love of virtue; and encouragement to practice virtue.

1. The Master said, "I have not seen a person who loved virtue, or one who hated what was not virtuous. He who loved virtue, would esteem nothing above it. He who hated what is not virtuous, would practice virtue in such a way that he would not allow anything that is not virtuous to approach his person.

2. "Is any one able for one day to apply his strength to virtue? I have not seen the case in which his strength would be insufficient.

3. "Should there possibly be any such case, I have not seen it."

Chapter XVIII

How a son may remonstrate with his parents on their faults.

The Master said, "In serving his parents, a son may remonstrate with them, but gently; when he sees that they do not incline to follow his advice, he shows an increased degree of reverence, but does not abandon his purpose; and should they punish him, he does not allow himself to murmur."

Chapter XIX

A son not ought to go to a distance where he will not be able to pay the due services to his parents.

The Master said, "While his parents are alive, the son may not go abroad to a distance. If he does go abroad, he must have a fixed place to which he goes."

Chapter XXIV

Rule of the Chün-tsze about his words and actions.

The Master said, "The superior man wishes to be slow in his speech and earnest in his conduct."

Chapter XXV

The virtuous are not left alone: —an encouragement to virtue.

The Master said, "Virtue is not left to stand alone. He who practices it will have neighbors."

BOOK VI

Chapter XXVIII

The true nature and art of virtue.

1. Tsze-kung said, "Suppose the case of a man extensively conferring benefits on the people, and able to assist all, what would you say of him? Might he be called perfectly virtuous?" The Master said, "Why speak only of virtue in connection with him? Must he not have the qualities of a sage? Even Yâo and Shun were still solicitous about this.

2. "Now the man of perfect virtue, wishing to be established himself, seeks also to establish others; wishing to be enlarged himself, he seeks also to enlarge others.

3. "To be able to judge of others by what is nigh in ourselves; —this may be called the art of virtue."

BOOK VII

Chapter XV

The joy of Confucius independent of outward circumstances.

The Master said, "With coarse rice to eat, with water to drink, and my bended arm for a pillow; —I have still joy in the midst of these things. Riches and honors acquired by unrighteousness, are to me as a floating cloud."

Chapter XVI

The value which Confucius set upon the study of the Yî.

The Master said, "If some years were added to my life, I would give fifty to the study of the Yî, and then I might come to be without great faults."

Chapter XXIV

The subjects of Confucius's teaching.
There were four things which the Master taught, —letters, ethics, devotion of soul, and truthfulness.

Chapter XXV

The paucity of true men in, and the pretentiousness of, Confucius's time.

1. The Master said, "A sage it is not mine to see; could I see a man of real talent and virtue, that would satisfy me."

2. The Master said, "A good man it is not mine to see; could I see a man possessed of constancy, that would satisfy me.

3. "Having not and yet affecting to have, empty and yet affecting to be full, straitened and yet affecting to be at ease: —it is difficult with such characteristics to have constancy."

Chapter XXVI

The humanity of Confucius.

The Master angled, —but did not use a net. He shot, —but not at birds perching.

BOOK VIII

Chapter XIII

The qualifications of an officer, who will always act right in accepting and declining office.

1. The Master said, "With sincere faith he unites the love of learning; holding firm to death, he is perfecting the excellence of his course.

2. "Such a one will not enter a tottering state, nor dwell in a disorganized one. When right principles of government prevail in the kingdom, he will show himself; when they are prostrated, he will keep concealed.

3. "When a country is well governed, poverty and a mean condition are things to be ashamed of. When a country is ill governed, riches and honor are things to be ashamed of."

Chapter XIV

Every man should mind his own business.

The Master said, "He who is not in any particular office has nothing to do with plans for the administration of its duties."

Book of Mencius

Translated by James Legge

MENCIUS

Chapter I

Benvolence and righteousness Mencius's only topics with the princes of his time; and the only principles which can make a country prosperous.

1. Mencius went to see king Hûi of Liang.

2. The king said, 'Venerable sir, since you have not counted it far to come here, a distance of a thousand lî, may I presume that you are provided with counsels to profit my kingdom?'

3. Mencius replied, 'Why must your Majesty use that word "profit?" What I am provided with, are counsels to benevolence and righteousness, and these are my only topics.

4. 'If your Majesty say, "What is to be done to profit my kingdom?" the great officers will say, "What is to be done to profit our families?" and the inferior officers and the common people will say, "What is to be done to profit our persons?" Superiors and inferiors will try to snatch this profit the one from the other, and the kingdom will be endangered. In the kingdom of ten thousand chariots, the murderer of his sovereign shall be the chief of a family of a thousand chariots. In the kingdom of a thousand chariots, the murderer of his prince shall be the chief of a family of a hundred chariots. To have a thousand in ten thousand, and a hundred in a thousand, cannot be said not to be a large allotment, but if righteousness be put last, and profit be put first, they will not be satisfied without snatching all.

5. 'There never has been a benevolent man who neglected his parents. There never has been a righteous man who made his sovereign an after consideration.

6. 'Let your Majesty also say, "Benevolence and righteousness, and let these be your only themes." Why must you use that word—"profit?".

Chapter II

Rulers must share their pleasures with the people. They can only be happy when they rule over happy subjects.

From *The Works of Mencius* translated by James Legge, Clarendon Press, 1895.

1. Mencius, another day, saw King Hûi of Liang. The king went and stood with him by a pond, and, looking round at the large geese and deer, said, 'Do wise and good princes also find pleasure in these things?'

2. Mencius replied, 'Being wise and good, they have pleasure in these things. If they are not wise and good, though they have these things, they do not find pleasure.

3. 'It is said in the Book of Poetry,

   He measured out and commenced his marvellous tower;
   He measured it out and planned it.
   The people addressed themselves to it,
   And in less than a day completed it.
   When he measured and began it, he said to them—
   Be not so earnest:
   But the multitudes came as if they had been his children.
   The king was in his marvellous park;
   The does reposed about,
   The does so sleek and fat:
   And the white birds came glistening.
   The king was by his marvellous pond;
   How full was it of fishes leaping about!"

   'King Wan used the strength of the people to make his tower and his pond, and yet the people rejoiced to do the work, calling the tower "the marvellous tower," calling the pond "the marvellous pond," and rejoicing that he had his large deer, his fishes, and turtles. The ancients caused the people to have pleasure as well as themselves, and therefore they could enjoy it.

4. 'In the Declaration of T'ang it is said, "O sun, when wilt thou expire? We will die together with thee." The people wished for Chieh's death, though they should die

with him. Although he had towers, ponds, birds, and animals, how could he have pleasure alone?'

Chapter III

Half measures are of little use. The great principles of royal government must be faithfully and in their spirit carried out.

1. King Hûi of Liang said, 'Small as my virtue is, in the government of my kingdom, I do indeed exert my mind to the utmost. If the year be bad on the inside of the river, I remove as many of the people as I can to the east of the river, and convey grain to the country in the inside. When the year is bad on the east of the river, I act on the same plan. On examining the government of the neighboring kingdoms, I do not find that there is any prince who exerts his mind as I do. And yet the people of the neighboring kingdoms do not decrease, nor do my people increase. How is this?'

2. Mencius replied, 'Your majesty is fond of war;—let me take an illustration from war.—The soldiers move forward to the sound of the drums; and after their weapons have been crossed, on one side they throw away their coats of mail, trail their arms behind them, and run. Some run a hundred paces and stop; some run fifty paces and stop. What would you think if those who run fifty paces were to laugh at those who run a hundred paces?' The kind said, 'They should not do so. Though they did not run a hundred paces, yet they also ran away.' 'Since your Majesty knows this,' replied Mencius, 'you need not hope that your people will become more numerous than those of the neighboring kingdoms.

3. 'If the seasons of husbandry be not inter-fered with, the grain will be more than can be eaten. If close nets are not allowed to enter the pools and ponds, the fishes and turtles will be more than can be consumed. If the axes and bills enter the hills and for-ests only at the proper time, the wood will more than can be used. When the grain and fish and turtles are more than can be eaten, and there is more wood than can be used, this enables the people to nour-ish their living and mourn for their dead, without any feeling against any. This con-dition, in which the people nourish their living and bury their dead without any feeling against any, is the first step of royal government.

4. 'Let mulberry trees be planted about the homesteads with their five mâu, and per-sons of fifty years may be clothed with silk. In keeping fowls, pigs, dogs, and swine, let not their times of breeding be neglected, and persons of seventy years may eat flesh. Let there not be taken away the time that is proper for the cultivation of the farm with its hundred mâ, and the family of several mouths that is supported by it shall not suffer from hunger. Let careful attention be paid to education in schools, inculcating in it especially the filial and fraternal duties, and grey-haired men will not be seen upon the roads, carrying bur-dens on their backs or on their heads. It never has been that the ruler of a State, where such results were seen,—persons of seventy wearing silk and eating flesh, and the black-haired people suffering neither from hunder nor cold,—did not attain to the royal dignity.

5. 'Your dogs and swine eat the food of men, and you do not make any restrictive arrangements. There are people dying from famine on the roads, and you do not issue the stores of your granaries for them. When people die, you say, "It is not owing to me; it is owing to the year." In what does this differ from stabbing a man and killing him, and then saying—"It was not I; it was the weapon?" Let your Majesty cease to lay the blame on the year, and instantly from all the nation the people will come to you.'

Chapter IV

A continuation of the former chapter, carry-ing on the appeal, in the last paragraph, on the character of king Hû's own government.

1. King Hûi of Liang said, 'I wish quietly to receive your instructions.'

2. Mencius replied, 'Is there any difference between killing a man with a stick and with a sword?' The king said, 'There is no difference!

3. 'Is there any difference between doing it with a sword and with the style of govern-ment? 'There is no difference,' was the reply.

4. Mencius then said, 'In your kitchen there is fat meat; in your stables there are fat horses. But your people have the look of hunger, and on the wilds there are those who have died of famine. This is leading on beasts to devour men.

5. 'Beasts devour one another, and men hate them for doing so. When a prince, being the parent of his people, administers his government so as to be chargeable with leading on beasts to devour men, where is his parental relation to the people?'

6. Chung-nî said, 'Was he not without pos-terity who first made wooden images to bury with the dead? So he said, because that man made the semblances of men,

and used them for that purpose:— what shall be thought of him who causes his people to die of hunger?'

Chapter VII

Loving and protecting the people is the characteristic of royal government, and the sure path to the royal dignity.

1. The king Hsüan of Ch'î asked, saying, 'May I be informed by you of the transactions of Hwan of Ch'î, and Wan of Tsin?'

2. Mencius replied, 'There were none of the disciples of Chuncg-nî who spoke about the affairs of Hwan and WAn, and therefore they have not been transmitted to these after-ages;—your servant has not heard them. If you will have me speak, let it be about royal government.'

3. The king said, 'What virtue must there be in order to attain to royal sway?' Mencius answered, 'The love and protection of the people; with this there is no power which can prevent a ruler from attaining to it.'

4. The king asked again, 'Is such an one as I competent to love and protect the people?' Mencius said, 'Yes.' 'How do you know that I am competent for that?' 'I heard the following incident from Hû Ho:—"The king," said he, "was sitting aloft in the hall, when a man appeared, leading an ox past the lower part of it. The king saw him, and asked, Where is the ox going? The man replied, We are going to consecrate a bell with its blood. The king said, Let it go. I cannot bear its frightened appearance, as if it were an innocent person going to the place of death. The man answered, Shall we than omit the consecration of the bell? The king said, How can that be omitted? Change it for a sheep." I do not know whether this incident really occurred.'

5. The king replied, 'It did,' and then Mencius said, 'The heart seen in this is sufficient to carry you to the royal sway. The people all supposed that your Majesty grudged the animal, but your servant knows surely, that it was your Majesty's not being able to bear the sight, which made you do as you did.'

6. The king said, 'You are right. And yet there really was an appearance of what the people condemned. But though Chî be a small and narrow State, how should I grudge one ox? Indeed it was because I could not bear its frightened appearance, as if it were an innocent person going to the place of death, that therefore I changed it for a sheep.'

7. Mencius pursued, 'Let not your Majesty deem it strange that the people should think you were grudging the animal. When you changed a large one for a small, how should they know the true reason? If you felt pained by its being led without guilt to the place of death, what was there to choose between an ox and a sheep? The king laughed and said, 'What really was my mind in the matter? I did not grudge the expense of it, and changed it for a sheep!—There was reason in the people's saying that I grudged it.'

8. 'There is no harm in their saying so,' said Mencius. 'Your conduct was an artifice of benevolence. You saw the ox, and had not seen the sheep. So is the superior man affected towards animals, that, having seen them alive, he cannot bear to see them die; having heard their dying cries, he cannot bear to eat their flesh. Therefore he keeps away from his slaughter-house and cook-room.'

9. The king was pleased, and said, 'It is said in the Book of Poetry, "The minds of others, I am able by reflection to measure;"—this is verified, my Master, in your discovery

of my motive. I indeed did the thing, but when I turned my thoughts inward, and examined into it, I could not discover my own mind. When you, Master, spoke those words, the movements of compassion began to work in my mind. How is it that this heart has in it what is equal to the royal sway?'

10. Mencius replied, 'Suppose a man were to make this statement to your Majesty:— "My strength is sufficient to lift three thousand catties, but it is not sufficient to lift one feather;—my eyesight is sharp enough to examine the point of an autumn hair, but I do not see a waggon-load of faggots;— "would your Majesty allow what he said?' 'No,' was the answer, on which Mencius proceeded, 'Now here is kindness sufficient to reach to animals, and no benefits are extended from it to the people.— How is this? Is an exception to be made here? The truth is, the feather is not lifted, because strength is not used; the waggon-load of firewood is not seen, because the eyesight is not used; and the people are not loved and protected, because kindness is not employed. Therefore your Majesty's not exercising the royal sway, is because you do not do it, not because you are not able to do it.'

11. The king asked, 'How may the difference between the not doing a thing, and the not being able to do it, be represented? Mencius replied,' In such a thing as taking the T'âi mountain under your arm, and leaping over the north sea with it, if you say to people—"I am not able to do it," that is a real case of not being able. In such a matter as breaking off a branch from a tree at the order of a superior, if you say to people-"I am not able to do it," that is a case of not doing it, it is not a case of not being

able to do it. Therefore your Majesty's not exercising the royal sway, is not such a case as that of taking the T'âi mountain under your arm, and leaping over the north sea with it. Your Majesty's not exercising the royal sway is a case like that of breaking off a branch from a tree.

12. 'Treat with the reverence due to age the elders in your own family, so that the elders in the families of others shall be similarly treated; treat with the kindness due to youth the young in your own family, so that the young in the families of others shall be similarly treated:—do this, and the kingdom may be made to go round in your palm. It is said in the Book of Poetry, "His example affected his wife. It reached to his brothers, and his family of the State was governed by it."—The language shows how king Wan simply took his kindly heart, and exercised it towards those parties. Therefore the carrying out his kindness of heart by a prince will suffice for the love and protection of all within the four seas, and if he do not carry it out, he will not be able to protect his wife and children. The way in which the ancients came greatly to surpass other men, was no other but this:—simply that they knew well how to carry out, so as to affect others, what they themselves did. Now your kindness is sufficient to reach to animals, and no benefits are extended from it to reach the people.—How is this? Is an exception to be made here?

13. 'By weighing, we know what things are light, and what heavy. By measuring, we know what things are long, and what short. The relations of all things may be thus determined, and it is of the greatest importance to estimate the motions of the mind. I beg your Majesty to measure it.

14. 'You collect your equipments of war, endanger your soldiers and officers, and excite the resentment of the other princes;—do these things cause you pleasnre in your mind?'

15. The king replied, 'No. How should I derive pleasure from these things? My object in them is to seek for what I greatly desire.'

16. Mencius said, 'May I hear from you what it is that you greatly desire?' The king laughed and did not speak. Mencius resumed, 'Are you led to desire it, because you have not enough of rich and sweet food for your mouth? Or because you have not enough of light and warm clothing for your body? Or because you have not enough of beautifully coloured objects to delight your eyes? Or because you have not voices and tones enough to please your ears? Or because you have not enough of attendants and favourites to stand before you and receive your orders? Your Majesty's various officers are sufficient to supply you with those things. How can your Majesty be led to entertain such a desire on account of them?' 'No,' said the king; 'my desire is not on account of them.' Mencius added, 'Then, what your Majesty greatly desires may be known. You wish to enlarge your territories, to have Ch'in and Ch'û wait at your court, to rule the Middle Kingdom, and to attract to you the barbarous tribes that surround it. But doing what you do to seek for what you desire is like climbing a tree to seek for fish.'

17. The king said, 'Is it so bad as that?' 'It is even worse,' was the reply. 'If you climb a tree to seek for fish, although you do not get the fish, you will not suffer any subsequent calamity. But doing what you do to seek for what you desire, doing it moreover with all your heart, you will assuredly afterwards meet with calamities.' The king asked, 'May I hear from you the proof of that?' Mencius said, 'If the people of Tsâu should fight with the people of Ch'û, which of them does your Majesty think would conquer?' 'The people of Ch'û would conquer.' 'Yes;—and so it is certain that a small country cannot contend with a great, that few cannot contend with many, that the weak cannot contend with the strong. The territory within the four seas embraces nine divisions, each of a thousand lî square. All Ch'î together is but one of them. If with one part you try to subdue the other eight, what is the difference between that and Tsâu's contending with Ch'û? For, with such a desire, you must turn back to the proper course for its attainment.

18. 'Now if your Majesty will institute a government whose action shall be benevolent, this will cause all the officers in the kingdom to wish to stand in your Majesty's court, and all the farmers to wish to plough in your Majesty's fields, and all the merchants, both travelling and stationary, to wish to store their goods in your Majesty's market-places, and all travelling strangers to wish to make their tours on your Majesty's roads, and all throughout the kingdom who feel aggrieved by their rulers to wish to come and complain to your Majesty. And when they are so bent, who will be able to keep them back?'

19. The king said, 'I am stupid, and not able to advance to this. I wish you, my Master, to assist my intentions. Teach me clearly; although I am deficient in intelligence and vigour, I will essay and try to carry your instructions into effect.'

20. Mencius replied, 'They are only men of education, who, without a certain

livelihood, are able to maintain a fixed heart. As to the people, if they have not a certain livelihood, it follows that they will not have a fixed heart. And if they have not a fixed heart, there is nothing which they will not do, in the way of self-abandonment, of moral deflection, of depravity, and of wild license. When they thus have been involved in crime, to follow them up and punish them;—this is to entrap the people. How can such a thing as entrapping the people be done under the rule of a benevolent man?

21. 'Therefore an intelligent ruler will regulate the livelihood of the people, so as to make sure that, for those above them, they shall have sufficient wherewith to serve their parents, and, for those below them, sufficient wherewith to support their wives and children; that in good years they shall always be abundantly satisfied, and that in bad years they shall escape the danger of perishing. After this he may urge them, and they will proceed to what is good, for in this case the people will follow after it with ease.

22. 'Now, the livelihood of the people is so regulated, that, above, they have not sufficient wherewith to serve their parents, and, below, they have not sufficient wherewith to support their wives and children. Notwithstanding good years, their lives are continually embittered, and, in bad years, they do not escape perishing. In such circumstances they only try to save themselves from death, and are afraid they will not succeed. What leisure have they to cultivate propriety and righteousness?'

23. 'If your Majesty wishes to effect this regulation of the livelihood of the people, why not turn to that which is the essential step to it?

24. 'Let mulberry-trees be planted about the homesteads with their five mâu, and persons of fifty years may be clothed with silk. In keeping fowls, pigs, dogs, and swine, let not their times of breeding be neglected, and persons of seventy years may eat flesh. Let there not be taken away the time that is proper for the cultivation of the farm with its hundred mâu, and the family of eight mouths that is supported by it shall not suffer from hunger. Let careful attention be paid to education in schools,—the inculcation in it especially of the filial and fraternal duties, and grey-haired men will not be seen upon the roads, carrying burdens on their backs or on their heads. It never has been that the ruler of a State where such results were seen,—the old wearing silk and eating flesh, and the black-haired people suffering neither from hunger nor cold,-did not attain to the royal dignity.'

Book of Mencius

Translated by James Legge

MENCIUS

Chapter VIII

Killing a sovereign is not necessarily rebellion or murder.

1. The king Hsüan of Ch'î asked, saying, 'Was it so, that T'ang banished Chieh, and that king Wû smote Châu?' Mencius replied, 'It is so in the records.'

2. The king said, 'May a minister then put his sovereign to death?'

3. Mencius said, 'He who outrages the benevolence proper to his nature, is called a robber; he who outrages righteousness, is called a ruffian. The robber and ruffian we call a mere fellow. I have heard of the cutting off of the fellow Châu, but I have not heard of the putting a sovereign to death, in his case.'

Chapter X

The disposal of kingdoms rests with the minds of the people.

Chapter XII

The affections of the people can only be secured through a benevolent government. As they are dealt with by their superiors, so will they deal by them.

1. There had been a brush between Tsâu and Lû, when the duke Mû asked Mencius, saying, 'Of my officers there were killed thirty-three men, and none of the people would die in their defence. Though I sentenced them to death for their conduct, it is impossible to put such a multitude to death. If I do not put them to death, then there is the crime unpunished of their looking angrily on at the death of their officers, and not saving them. How is the exigency of the case to be met?'

2. Mencius replied, 'In calamitous years and years of famine, the old and weak of your people, who have been found lying in the ditches and water-channels, and the able-bodied who have been scattered about to the four quarters, have amounted to several thousands. All the while, your granaries, 0 prince, have been stored with grain, and your treasuries and arsenals have been full, and not one of your officers has told you of the distress. Thus negligent have the superiors in your State been, and cruel to their inferiors. The philosopher Tsang

From *The Works of Mencius* translated by James Legge, Clarendon Press, 1895.

said, "Beware, beware. What proceeds from you, will return to you again." Now at length the people have paid back the conduct of their officers to them. Do not you, 0 prince, blame them.

3. 'If you will put in practice a benevolent government, this people will love you and all above them, and will die for their officers.'

CHAPTER V

How Mencius convinced a Mohist of his error, that all men were to be loved equally, without difference of degree.

1. The Mohist, Î Chih, sought, through Hsü Pî, to see Mencius. Mencius said, 'I indeed wish to see him, but at present I am still unwell. When I am better, I will myself go and see him. He need not come here again.'

2. Next day, Î Chih again sought to see Mencius. Mencius said, 'To-day I am able to see him. But if I do not correct his errors, the true principles will not be fully evident. Let me first correct him. I have heard that this Î is a Mohist. Now Mo considers that in the regulation of funeral matters a spare simplicity should be the rule. Î thinks with Mo's doctrines to change the customs of the kingdom;—how does he regard them as if they were wrong, and not honour them? Notwithstanding his views, Î buried his parents in a sumptuous manner, and so he served them in the way which his doctrines discountenance.'

3. The disciple Hsü informed Î of these remarks. Î said, 'Even according to the principles of the learned, we find that the ancients acted towards the people "as if

they were watching over an infant." What does this expression mean? To me it sounds that we are to love all without difference of degree; but the manifestation of love must begin with our parents.' Hsü reported this reply to Mencius, who said, 'Now, does Î really think that a man's affection for the child of his brother is merely like his affection for the infant of a neighbour? What is to be approved in that expression is simply this:—that if an infant crawling about is likely to fall into a well, it is no crime in the infant. Moreover, Heaven gives birth to creatures in such a way that they have one root, and Î makes them to have two roots. This is the cause of his error.

4. 'And, in the most ancient times, there were some who did not inter their parents. When their parents died, they took them up and threw them into some water-channel. Afterwards, when passing by them, they saw foxes and wildcats devouring them, and flies and gnats biting at them. The perspiration started out upon their foreheads, and they looked away, unable to bear the sight. It was not on account of other people that this perspiration flowed. The emotions of their hearts affected their faces and eyes, and instantly they went home, and came back with baskets and spades and covered the bodies. If the covering them thus was indeed right, you may see that the filial son and virtuous man, in interring in a handsome manner their parents, act according to a proper rule.'

5. The disciple Hsü informed Î of what Mencius had said. Î was thoughtful for a short time, and then said, 'He has instructed me.'

Mo Tzu

M o Tzu (470–391 BCE) lived during the Warring States period (403–221 BCE), which
was characterized by increasing prosperity, because of the increased use of iron in agriculture, but also by great social upheaval. The ancient city states and their primitive
democracies were coming to an end, kings were consolidating their rule over greater areas of
land, and the cities were growing. The result was a growing, impersonal, and bureaucratic style
of government.

Although Mo Tzu was said to be educated at a Confucian school, he rejected many of the
doctrines of Confucianism. His school of thought, called Mohism, was quite influential for several
hundred years, but then fell out of favor. It is now only studied as a part of the history of Chinese
political thought.

Mo Tzu's writings are in the form of a monologue, much more like the philosophical writing
of more modern times. But like the previous selections, it is presented as a series of vignettes of the
master, in this case Mo, speaking with various rulers.

Mo Tzu's philosophical orientation could be termed proto-utilitarian, in that he holds that
the right action is that which will bring about the satisfaction of the needs of the greatest number.
Utilitarianism is a 19th century British Ethical Theory (though there are still adherents today)
that holds that the right act is that act which will bring about the greatest happiness of the greatest number. (A reading from the work of John Stuart Mill, who was one of the proponents of
Utilitarianism, comes later in this anthology.) Mo Tzu was an opponent of Confucianism. The
most important difference with Confucianism is over whether morality must be impartial. While
Confucius held up family relationships, in particular father-son and elder brother-younger brother
relations, as ethically all important, Mohism holds that such partiality is wrong. Instead, we are
to love everyone universally. Another difference is that while Confucius thought that happiness
was necessarily a by-product state, to be achieved only by focusing on other things, Mo holds that
happiness and love are to be sought directly. The resulting differences in their political philosophies
are very great, (although this is not so apparent from the short passage included here):

- Confucianism offers no clear principle of legitimacy, but rather offers guidelines for rulers to
  maintain their authority. Mo Tzu argues that the state must be run for the greatest satisfaction
  of basic needs, which is his principle of legitimacy.

- Confucian rulers are benevolent and responsive to the desires of the people; Mohist rulers are authoritarian and run the state like a machine.
- Individuals matter for Confucians; individuals are only part of a greater state machine for Mohists.
- Confucius modeled government on the family; Mo Tzu views government as a machine.

STUDY QUESTIONS:

1. What is universal love? Is it an emotion? A rational attitude?

2. Would universal, mutual love be effective in securing peace and order if it were instituted?

3. Is it possible for universal mutual love to be effected?

Universal Love

Translated by James Legge

UNIVERSAL LOVE. PART I

It is the business of the sages to effect the good government of the world. They must know, therefore, whence disorder and confusion arise, for without this knowledge their object cannot be effected. We may compare them to a physician who undertakes to cure men's diseases:—he must ascertain whence a disease has arisen, and then he can assail it with effect, while, without such knowledge, his endeavours will be in vain. Why should we except the case of those who have to regulate disorder from this rule? They must know whence it has arisen, and then they can regulate it.

It is the business of the sages to effect the good government of the world. They must examine therefore into the cause of disorders; and when they do so they will find that it arises from the want of mutual love. When a minister and a son are not filial to their sovereign and their father, this is what is called disorder. A son loves himself, and does not love his father—he therefore wrongs his father, and seeks his own advantage: a younger brother loves himself, and does not love his elder brother—he therefore wrongs his elder brother, and seeks his own advantage: a minister loves himself, and does

not love his sovereign—he therefore wrongs his sovereign, and seeks his own advantage:—all these are cases of what is called disorder. Though it be the father who is not kind to his son, or the elder brother who is not kind to his younger brother, or the sovereign who is not gracious to his minister:—the case comes equally under the general name of disorder. The father loves himself, and does not love his son—he therefore wrongs his son, and seeks his own advantage: the elder brother loves himself, and does not love his younger brother—he therefore wrongs his younger brother, and seeks his own advantage: the sovereign loves himself, and does not love his minister—he therefore wrongs his minister, and seeks his own advantage. How do these things come to pass? They all arise from the want of mutual love. Take the case of any thief or robber:—it is just the same with him. The thief loves his own house, and does not love his neighbour's house—he therefore steals from his neighbour's house to benefit his own: the robber loves his own person, and does not love his neighbour—he therefore does violence to his neighbor to benefit himself. How is this? It all arises from the want of mutual love. Come to the case of great officers throwing each

From *The Chinese Classics*, VOLUME II, James Legge, translator, Oxford: The Clarendon Press, 1895.

other's Families into confusion, and of princes attacking one another's States:—it is just the same with them. The great officer loves his own Family, and does not love his neighbour's—he therefore throws his neighbour's Family into disorder to benefit his own: the prince loves his own State, and does not love his neighbour's—he therefore attacks his neighbour's State to benefit his own. All disorder in the kingdom has the same explanation. When we examine into the cause of it, it is found to be the want of mutual love.

Suppose that universal, mutual love prevailed throughout the kingdom—if men loved others as they love themselves, disliking to exhibit what was unfilial. . . . And moreover would there be those who were unkind? Looking on their sons, younger brothers, and ministers as themselves, and disliking to exhibit what was unkind. . . . the want of filial duty would disappear. And would there be thieves and robbers? When every man regarded his neighbour's house as his own, who would be found to steal? When every one regarded his neighbour's person as his own, who would be found to rob? Thieves and robbers would disappear. And would there be great officers throwing one another's Families into confusion, and princes attacking one another's States? When officers regarded the Families of others as their own, what one would make confusion? When princes regarded other States as their own, what one would begin an attack? Great officers throwing one another's Families into confusion, and princes attacking one another's States, would disappear.

If, indeed, universal, mutual love prevailed throughout the kingdom; one State not attacking another, and one Family not throwing another into confusion; thieves and robbers nowhere existing; rulers and ministers, fathers and sons, all being filial and kind:—in such a condition the nation would be well governed.

On this account, how may sages, whose business it is to effect the good government of the kingdom, do but prohibit hatred and advise to love? On this account it is affirmed that universal mutual love throughout the country will lead to its happy order, and that mutual hatred leads to confusion. This was what our master, the philosopher Mo, meant, when he said, "We must above all inculcate the love of others."

UNIVERSAL LOVE. PART II

Our Master, the philosopher Mo, said, "That which benevolent men consider to be incumbent on them as their business, is to stimulate and promote all that will be advantageous to the nation, and to take away all that is injurious to it. This is what they consider to be their business."

And what are the things advantageous to the nation, and the things injurious to it? Our Master said, "The mutual attacks of State on State; the mutual usurpations of Family on Family; the mutual robberies of man on man; the want of kindness on the part of the ruler and of loyalty on the part of the minister; the want of tenderness and filial duty between father and son and of harmony between brothers:—these, and such as these, are the things injurious to the kingdom."

And from what do we find, on examination, that these injurious things are produced? Is it not from the want of mutual love?

Our Master said, "Yes, they are produced by the want of mutual love. Here is a prince who only knows to love his own State, and does not love his neighbour's—he therefore does not shrink from raising all the power of his State to attack his neighbour. Here is the chief of a Family who only knows to love it, and does not love his neighbour's—he therefore does not shrink from raising all his powers to seize on that other Family. Here is a man who only knows to love his own person, and does not love his neighbour's—he therefore does not shrink from using all his resources to rob his neighbour. Thus it happens, that the princes, not loving one another, have their battle-fields; and the chiefs of Families, not loving one another, have their mutual usurpations; and men, not loving one another, have their mutual robberies; and rulers and ministers, not loving one another, become unkind and disloyal; and fathers and sons, not loving one another, lose their affection and filial duty; and brothers, not loving one another, contract irreconcilable enmities. Yea, men in general not loving one another, the strong make prey of the weak; the rich do despite to the poor; the noble are insolent to the mean; and the deceitful impose upon the stupid. All the miseries, usurpations, enmities, and hatreds in the world, when traced to their origin, will be found to arise from the want of mutual love. On this account, the benevolent condemn it."

They may condemn it; but how shall they change it?

Our Master said, "They may change it by the law of universal mutual love and by the interchange of mutual benefits."

How will this law of universal mutual love and the interchange of mutual benefits accomplish this?

Our Master said, "It would lead to the regarding another's kingdom as one's own: another's family as one's own: another's person as one's own. That being the case, the princes, loving one another, would have no battle-fields; the chiefs of families, loving one another, would attempt no usurpations; men, loving one another, would commit no robberies;

rulers and ministers, loving one another, would be gracious and loyal; fathers and sons, loving one another, would be kind and filial; brothers, loving one another, would be harmonious and easily reconciled. Yea, men in general loving one another, the strong would not make prey of the weak; the many would not plunder the few; the rich would not insult the poor; the noble would not be insolent to the mean; and the deceitful would not impose upon the simple. The way in which all the miseries, usurpations, enmities, and hatreds in the world, may be made not to arise, is universal mutual love. On this account, the benevolent value and praise it."

Yes; but the scholars of the kingdom and superior men say, "True; if there were this universal love, it would be good. It is, however, the most difficult thing in the world."

Our Master said, "This is because the scholars and superior men simply do not understand the advantageousness of the law, and to conduct their reasonings upon that. Take the case of assaulting a city, or of a battle-field, or of the sacrificing one's life for the sake of fame:—this is felt by the people everywhere to be a difficult thing. Yet, if the ruler be pleased with it, both officers and people are able to do it:—how much more might they attain to universal mutual love, and the interchange of mutual benefits, which is different from this! When a man loves others, they respond to and love him; when a man benefits others, they respond to and benefit him; when a man injures others, they respond to and injure him; when a man hates others, they respond to and hate him:—what difficulty is there in the matter? It is only that rulers will not carry on the government on this principle, and so officers do not carry it out in their practice."

Hsün Tzu

Hsün Tzu (310–237 BCE), now called Xun Zi, was a Confucian philosopher who lived during the Warring States Period. Like other Confucians, his philosophy is pragmatic, in that it aims to give its students directions on how to live, rather than engaging in metaphysical speculation, as the Daoists do. Unlike Confucius and Mencius, however, Hsün Tzu attributes to human beings an evil or selfish and aggressive nature. While human's are by nature evil, though, they can be taught to abide by moral rules with a firm authoritative hand of the ruler and the use of ritual to constrain the passions and force them to conform with social norms.

This authoritarian strain in Hsün Tzu's thought developed into the School of Legalism in the hands of his disciples, Han Fei and Li Ssu, who became very prominent scholars and the latter the Premier of the Ch'in dynasty (221–207 BCE). The Ch'in dynasty under the influence of Legalism, however, led to the downfall of philosophical and particularly Confucian thought. Legalism holds that the people could not be led by the example of a virtuous leader, but only by a firm, authoritarian hand, guided by the rule of law, which was designed for the benefit of the ruler.

Hsün Tzu's description of human nature is echoed by that of the modern philosopher Thomas Hobbes. Whereas, Hobbes comes to conclusions about the legitimacy of the sovereign that are similar to the Legalists, Hsün Tzu himself argued for a more Confucian vision of the ruler.

STUDY QUESTIONS:

1. What does Hsün Tzu mean by evil when he says that human nature is evil?

2. Why does Hsün Tzu object to the philosophy of Mencius?

3. What is the proper function of government?

That the Nature Is Evil

Translated by James Legge

The nature of man is evil; the good which it shows is factitious. There belongs to it, even at his birth, the love of gain, and as actions are in accordance with this, contentions and robberies grow up, and self-denial and yielding to others are not to be found; there belong to it envy and dislike, and as actions are in accordance with these, violence and injuries spring up, and self-devotedness and faith are not to be found; there belong to it the desires of the ears and the eyes, leading to the love of sound and beauty, and as the actions are in accordance with these, lewdness and disorder spring up, and righteousness and propriety, with their various orderly displays, are not to be found. It thus appears, that to follow man's nature and yield obedience to its feelings will assuredly conduct to contentions and robberies, to the violation of the duties belonging to everyone's lot, and the confounding of all distinctions, till the issue will be in a state of savagism; and that there must be the influence of teachers and laws, and the guidance of propriety and righteousness, from which will spring self-denial, yielding to others, and an observance of the well-ordered regulations of conduct, till the issue will be a state of good government.—From all this it is plain that the nature of man is evil; the good which it shows is factitious.

To illustrate.—A crooked stick must be submitted to the pressing-frame to soften and bend it, and then it becomes straight; a blunt knife must be submitted to the grindstone and whetstone, and then it becomes sharp: so, the nature of man, being evil, must be submitted to teachers and laws, and then it becomes correct; it must be submitted to propriety and righteousness, and then it comes under government. If men were without teachers and laws their condition would be one of deflection and insecurity, entirely incorrect; if they were without propriety and righteousness, their condition would be one of rebellious disorder, rejecting all government. The sage kings of antiquity, understanding that the nature of man was thus evil, in a state of hazardous defection, and incorrect, rebellious and disorderly, and refusing to be governed, set up the principles of righteousness and propriety, and framed laws and regulations to straighten and ornament the feelings of that nature and correct them, to tame and change those same feelings and guide them, so that they might all

From *The Chinese Classics*, VOLUME II, James Legge, translator, Oxford: The Clarendon Press, 1895.

go forth in the way of moral government and in agreement with reason. Now, the man who is transformed by teachers and laws, gathers on himself the ornament of learning, and proceeds in the path of propriety and righteousness is a superior man; and he who gives the reins to his nature and its feelings, indulges its resentments, and walks contrary to propriety and righteousness is a mean man. Looking at the subject in this way, we see clearly that the nature of man is evil; the good which it shows is factitious.

Mencius said, "Man has only to learn, and his nature appears to be good"; but I reply,—It is not so. To say so shows that he had not attained to the knowledge of man's nature, nor examined into the difference between what is natural in man and what is factitious. The natural is what the constitution spontaneously moves to:—it needs not to be learned, it needs not to be followed hard after; propriety and righteousness are what the sages have given birth to:—it is by learning that men become capable of them, it is by hard practice that they achieve them. That which is in man, not needing to be learned and striven after, is what I call natural; that in man which is attained to by learning, and achieved by hard striving, is what I call factitious. This is the distinction between those two. By the nature of man, the eyes are capable of seeing, and the ears are capable of hearing. But the power of seeing is inseparable from the eyes, and the power of hearing is inseparable from the ears;—it is plain that the faculties of seeing and hearing do not need to be learned. Mencius says, "The nature of man is good, but all lose and ruin their nature, and therefore it becomes bad"; but I say that this representation is erroneous. Man being born with his nature, when he thereafter departs from its simple constituent elements, he must lose it. From this consideration we may see clearly that man's nature is evil. What might be called the nature's being good, would be if

there were no departing from its simplicity to beautify it, no departing from its elementary dispositions to sharpen it. Suppose that those simple elements no more needed beautifying, and the mind's thoughts no more needed to be turned to good, than the power of vision which is inseparable from the eyes, and the power of hearing which is inseparable from the ears, need to be learned, *then we might say that the nature is good, just as* we say that the eyes see and the ears hear. It is the nature of man, when hungry, to desire to be filled; when cold, to desire to be warmed; when tired, to desire rest:—these are the feelings and nature of man. But now, a man is hungry, and in the presence of an elder he does not dare to eat before him:—he is yielding to that elder; he is tired with labour, and he does not dare to ask for rest:—he is working for some one. A son's yielding to his father and a younger brother to his elder, a son's labouring for his father and a younger brother for his elder:—these two instances of conduct are contrary to the nature and against the feelings; but they are according to the course laid down for a filial son, and to the refined distinctions of propriety and righteousness. It appears that if there were an accordance with the feelings and the nature, there would be no self-denial and yielding to others. Self-denial and yielding to others are contrary to the feelings and the nature. In this way we come to see how clear it is that the nature of man is evil; the good which it shows is factitious.

An inquirer will ask, "If man's nature be evil, whence do propriety and righteousness rise?" I reply:—All propriety and righteousness are the artificial production of the sages, and are not to be considered as growing out of the nature of man. It is just as when a potter makes a vessel from the clay;—the vessel is the product of the workman's art, and is not to be considered as growing out of his nature. Or it is as when another workman cuts and hews a vessel out of wood;—it is the product of his art, and is not to be considered as growing out of his nature. The sages pondered long in thought and gave themselves to practice, and so they succeeded in producing propriety and righteousness, and setting up laws and regulations. Thus it is that propriety and righteousness, laws and regulations, are the artificial product of the sages, and are not to be considered as growing properly from the nature of man.

If we speak of the fondness of the eyes for beauty, or of the mouth for *pleasant* flavours, or of the mind for gain, or the bones and skin for the enjoyment of ease;—all these grow out of the natural feelings of man. The object is presented and the desire is felt; there needs no effort to produce it. But when the object is presented, and the affection does not move till after hard effort, I say that this effect is factitious. Those cases prove the difference between what is produced by nature and what is produced by art.

Thus the sages transformed their nature, and commenced their artificial work. Having commenced this work with their nature, they produced propriety and righteousness. When propriety and righteousness were produced, they proceeded to frame laws and regulations. It appears, therefore, that propriety and righteousness, laws and regulations, are given birth to by the sages. Wherein they agree with all other men and do not differ from them, is their nature; wherein they differ from and exceed other men, is this artificial work.

Now to love gain and desire to get;—this is the natural feeling of men. Suppose the case that there is an amount of property or money to be divided among brothers, and let this natural feeling to love gain and to desire to get come into play;—why, then the brothers will be opposing, and snatching from, one another. But where the changing influence of propriety and righteousness, with their refined distinctions, has taken effect, a man will give up to

any other man. Thus it is that if they act in accordance with their natural feelings, brothers will quarrel together; and if they have come under the transforming influence of propriety and righteousness, men will give up to other men, to say nothing of brothers. *Again*, the fact that men WISH to do what is good, is because their nature is bad. The thin wishes to be thick; the ugly wish to be beautiful; the narrow wishes to be wide; the poor wish to be rich; the mean wish to be noble:—when anything is not possessed in one's self, he seeks for it outside himself. But the rich do not wish for wealth; the noble do not wish for position:—when anything is possessed by one's self, he does not need to go beyond himself for it. When we look at things in this way, we perceive that the fact of men's WISHING to do what is good is because their nature is evil. It is the case indeed, that man's nature is without propriety and benevolence:—he therefore studies them with vigorous effort and seeks to have them. It is the case that by nature he does not know propriety and righteousness:—he therefore thinks and reflects and seeks to know them. Speaking of man, therefore, as he is by birth simply, he is without propriety and righteousness, without the knowledge of propriety and righteousness. Without propriety and righteousness, man must be all confusion and disorder; without the knowledge of propriety and righteousness, man must be all confusion and disorder; without the knowledge of propriety and righteousness, there must ensue all the manifestations of disorder. Man, as he is born, therefore, has in him nothing but the elements of disorder, passive and active. It is plain from this view of the subject that the nature of man is evil; the good which it shows is factitious.

When Mencius says that "Man's nature is good," I affirm that it is not so. In ancient times and now, throughout the kingdom, what is meant by good is a condition of correctness, regulation, and happy government; and what is meant by evil, is a condition of deflection, insecurity, and refusing to be under government:—in this lies the distinction between being good and being evil. And now, if man's nature be really so correct, regulated, and happily governed in itself, where would be the use for sage kings? where would be the use for propriety and righteousness? Although there were the sage kings, propriety, and righteousness, what could they add to the nature so correct, regulated, and happily ruled in itself? But it is not so; the nature of man is bad. It was on this account, that anciently the sage kings, understanding that man's nature was bad, in a state of deflection and insecurity, instead of being correct; in a state of rebellious disorder, instead of one of happy rule, set up therefore the majesty of princes and governors to awe it; and set forth propriety and righteousness to change it; and framed laws and statutes of correctness to rule it; and devised severe punishments to restrain it: so that its outgoings might be under the dominion of rule, and in accordance with what is good. This is *the true account of* the governance of the sage kings, and the transforming power of propriety and righteousness. Let us suppose a state of things in which there shall be no majesty of rulers and governors, no influence of propriety and righteousness, no rule of laws and statutes, no restraints of punishment:—what would be the relations of men with one another, all under heaven? The strong would be injuring the weak, and spoiling them; the many would be tyrannizing over the few, and hooting them; a universal disorder and mutual destruction would speedily ensue. When we look at the subject in this way, we see clearly that the nature of man is evil; the good which it shows is factitious.

He who would speak well of ancient times must have undoubted references in the present; he who would speak well of Heaven must

substantiate what he says from *the state of* man. In discourse and argument it is an excellent quality when the divisions which are made can be brought together like the halves of a token. When it is so, the arguer may sit down, and discourse of his principles; and he has only to rise up, and they may be set forth and displayed and carried into action. When Mencius says that the nature of man is good, there is no bringing together in the above manner of his divisions. He sits down and talks, but there is no getting up to display and set forth his principles, and put them in operation:—is not his error very gross? To say that the nature is good does away with the sage kings, and makes an end of propriety and righteousness; to say that the nature is bad exalts the sage kings, and dignifies propriety and righteousness. As the origin of the pressing-boards is to be found in the crooked wood, and the origin of the carpenter's marking-line is to be found in things not being straight; so the rise of princes and governors, and the illustration of propriety and righteousness, are to be traced to the badness of the nature. It is clear from this view of the subject that the nature of man is bad; the good which it shows is factitious.

A straight piece of wood does not need the pressing-boards to make it straight;—it is so by its nature. A crooked piece of wood must be submitted to the pressing-boards to soften and straighten it, and then it is straight; it is not straight by its nature. So it is that the nature of man, being evil, must be submitted to the rule of these kings, and to the transforming influence of propriety and righteousness, and then its outgoings are under the dominion of rule, and in accordance with what is good. This shows clearly that the nature of man is bad; the good which it shows is factitious.

An inquirer may say *again*, "Propriety and righteousness, though seen in an accumulation of factitious deeds, do yet belong to the nature of man; and thus it was that the sages were able to produce them." I reply:—It is not so. A potter takes a piece of clay, and produces an earthen dish from it; but are that dish and clay the nature of the potter? A carpenter plies his tools upon a piece of wood, and produces a vessel; but are that vessel and wood the nature of the carpenter? So it is with the sages and propriety and righteousness; they produced them, just as the potter works with the clay. It is plain that there is no reason for saying that propriety and righteousness, and the accumulation of their factitious actions, belong to the proper nature of man. Speaking of the nature of man, it is the same in all,—the same in Yâo and Shun and in Chieh and the robber Chih, the same in the superior man and in the mean man. If you say that propriety and righteousness, with the factitious actions accumulated from them, are the nature of man, on what ground do you proceed to ennoble Yâo and Yü, to ennoble *generally* the superior man? The ground on which we ennoble Yâo, Yü, and the superior man, is their ability to change the nature, and to produce factitious conduct. That factitious conduct being produced, out of it there are brought propriety and righteousness. The sages stand indeed in the same relation to propriety and righteousness, and the factitious conduct resulting from them, as the potter does to his clay:—we have a product in either case. This representation makes it clear that propriety and righteousness, with their factitious results, do not properly belong to the nature of man. *On the other hand,* that which we consider mean in Chieh, the robber Chih, and the mean man generally, is that they follow their nature, act in accordance with its feelings, and indulge its resentments, till all its outgoings are a greed of gain, contentions, and rapine.—It is plain that the nature of man is bad; the good which it shows is factitious.

Heaven did not make favourites of Tsăng *Shăn, Min* Tsze-ch'ien, and Hsiâochi, and deal unkindly with the rest of men. How then was it that they alone were distinguished by the greatness of their filial deeds, that all which the name of filial piety implies was complete in them? The reason was that they were entirely subject to the restraints of propriety and righteousness.

Heaven did not make favourites of the people of Ch'i and Lû, and deal unkindly with the people of Ch'in. How then was it that the latter were not equal to the former in the rich manifestation of the filial piety belonging to the righteousness of the relation between father and son, and the respectful observance of the proprieties belonging to the separate functions of husband and wife? The reason was that the people of Ch'in followed the feelings of their nature, indulged its resentments, and condemned propriety and righteousness. We are not to suppose that they were different in their nature.

What is the meaning of the saying, that "Any traveller on the road may become like Yü?" I answer:—All that made Yü what he was, was his practice of benevolence, righteousness, and his observance of laws and rectitude. But benevolence, righteousness, laws, and rectitude are all capable of being known and being practiced. Moreover, any traveller on the road has the capacity of knowing these, and the ability to practise them:—it is plain that he may become like Yü. If you say that benevolence, righteousness, laws, and rectitude are not capable of being known and practiced, then Yü himself could not have known, could not have practiced them. If you will have it that any traveller on the road is really without the capacity of knowing these things, and the ability to practise them, then, in his home, it will not be competent for him to know the righteousness that should rule between father and son, and, abroad, it will not be competent for him to know the rectitude that should rule between sovereign and minister. But it is not so. There is no one who travels along the road, but may know both that righteousness and that rectitude:—it is plain that the capacity to know and the ability to practise belong to every traveller on the way. Let him, therefore, with his capacity of knowing and ability to practise, take his ground on the knowableness and practicableness of benevolence and righteousness;—and it is clear that he may become like Yü. Yea, let any traveller on the way addict himself to the art of learning with all his heart and the entire bent of his will, thinking, searching, and closely examining;—let him do this day after day, through a long space of time, accumulating what is good, and he will penetrate as far as a spiritual Intelligence, he will become a ternion with Heaven and Earth. It follows that *the characters of* the sages were what any man may reach by accumulation.

It may be said:—"To be sage may thus be reached by accumulation;—why is it that all men cannot accumulate *to this extent?*" I reply:—They may do so, but they cannot be made to do so. The mean man might become a superior man, but he is not willing to be a superior man. The superior man might become a mean man, but he is not wiling to be a mean man. It is not that the mean man and the superior man may not become the one the other; their not becoming the one the other is because it is a thing which may be, but cannot be made to be. Any traveller on the road may become like Yü:—the case is so; that any traveller on the road can really become like Yü:—this is not a necessary conclusion. Though any one, however, cannot really become like Yü, that is not contrary at all to the truth that he may become so. One's feet might travel all over the world but there was never one who was really able to travel all over the world. There is noth-

ing to prevent the mechanic, the farmer, and the merchant from practising each the business of the others, but there has never been a case when it has really been done. Looking at the subject in this way, we see that what may be need not really be; and although it shall not really be, that is not contrary to the truth that it might be. It thus appears that the difference is wide between what is really done or not really done, and what may be or may not be. It is plain that these two cases may not become the one the other.

Yâo asked Shun what was the character of the feelings proper to man. Shun replied, "The feelings proper to man are very unlovely; why need you ask about them? When a man has got a wife and children, his filial piety withers away; under the influence of lust and gratified desires, his good faith to his friends withers away; when he is full of dignities and emoluments, his loyalty to his sovereign withers away. The natural feelings of man! The natural feelings of man! They are very unlovely. Why need you ask about them? It is only in the case of men of the highest worth that it is not so."

There is a knowledge characteristic of the sage; a knowledge characteristic of the scholar and superior man; a knowledge characteristic of the mean man; and a knowledge characteristic of the mere servant. In much speech to show his cultivation and maintain consistency, and though he may discuss for a whole day the reasons of a subject, to have a unity pervading the ten thousand changes of discourse:—this is the knowledge of the sage. To speak seldom, and in a brief and sparing manner, and to be orderly in his reasoning, as if its parts were connected with a string:—this is the knowledge of the scholar and superior man. Flattering words and disorderly conduct, with undertakings often followed by regrets:— these mark the knowledge of the mean man. Hasty, officious, smart, and swift, but without consistency; versatile, able, of extensive capabilities, but without use; decisive in discourse, rapid, exact, but the subject unimportant; regardless of right and wrong, taking no account of crooked and straight, to get the victory over others the guiding object:—this is the knowledge of the mere servant.

There is bravery of the highest order; bravery of the middle order; bravery of the lowest order. Boldly to take up his position in the place of the universally acknowledged Mean; boldly to carry into practice his views of the doctrines of the ancient kings; in a high situation, not to defer to a bad sovereign, and in a low situation not to follow the current of a bad people; to consider that there is no poverty where there is virtue, and no wealth or honour where virtue is not; when appreciated by the world, to stand up grandly alone between heaven and earth, and have no fears:—this is the bravery of the highest order. To be reverently observant of propriety, and sober-minded; to attach importance to adherence to fidelity, and set little store by material wealth; to have the boldness to push forward men of worth and exalt them, to hold back undeserving men, and get them deposed:—this is the bravery of the middle order. To be devoid of self-respect and set a great value on wealth; to feel complacent in calamity, and always have plenty to say for himself; saving himself in any way, without regard to right and wrong; whatever be the real state of a case, making it his object to get the victory over others:—this is the bravery of the lowest order.

The *fan-zâo* and the *chü-shû* were the best bows of antiquity; but without their regulators, they could not adjust themselves. The *tsung* of duke Hwan, the *chüeh* of Tâi-Kung, and the *lû* of King Wăn, the *hû* of prince Chwang, the *kan-tsiang, mŏyê; chü-chüeh* and *p'i-lü* of Ho-

lü—these were the best swords of antiquity; but without the grindstone and whetstone they would not have been sharp; without the strength of the arms that wielded them they would not have cut anything.

The *hwâ-liû*, the *li-ch'i*, the *hsien-li*, and the *lü-r*—these were the best horses of antiquity; but there were still necessary for them the restraints in front of bit and bridle, the stimulants behind of whip and cane, and the skillful driving of a Tsâofû, and then they could accomplish a thousand *li* in one day.

So it is with man:—granted to him an excellent capacity of nature and the faculty of intellect, he must still seek for good teachers under whom to place himself, and make choice of friends with whom he may be intimate. Having got good masters and placed himself under them, what he will hear will be the doctrines of Yâo, Shun, Yü, and T'ang; having got good friends and become intimate with them, what he will see will be deeds of self-consecration, fidelity, reverence, and complaisance:—he will go on from day to day to benevolence and righteousness, without being conscious of it: a natural following of them will make him do so. On the other hand, if he live with bad men, what he will hear will be the language of deceit, calumny, imposture, and hypocrisy; what he will see will be conduct of filthiness, insolence, lewdness, corruptness and greed:—he will be going on from day to day to punishment and disgrace, without being conscious of it; a natural following of them will make him do so.

The Record says, "If you do not know your son, look at his friends; if you do not know your prince, look at his confidants." All is the influence of association! All is the influence of association!

Chuang Tzu

We know very little about Chuang Tzu's (369–286 BCE) life and are even uncertain about his dates but he was approximately the contemporary of Mencius (385–302 BCE). Chuang Tzu was a follower of Lao Tzu (sixth century BCE), to whom is attributed the well-known work *Tao-te-ching*, and together they gave rise to the two seminal works of Taoism. In both cases, however, like the works of Confucius and Mencius, the actual texts were assembled by later students.

Taoism, like Confucianism, is a comprehensive world view that is followed as a religion by many people in China today. It posits the idea of a primal oneness of all of nature, the Tao, that existed before all particular things came to be. Taoists seek harmony with nature by avoiding what is artificial and therefore superficial. They also seek to keep the natural principles of Yin and Yang in harmony. The Yin is associated with the female, and is the principle of passivity and darkness, while the Yang is associated with the male, and is the principle of activity and light. Neither is superior to the other, and both are necessary for wholeness.

Chuang Tzu held that human nature is neither good nor evil, but would be better characterized at its best as a sort of benevolent self-interest. Human nature cannot successfully be guided by social institutions; individuals will tend to follow their own hearts. Natural inequalities exist among humans, but these do not imply moral inequalities, in Chuang Tzu's view.

Chuang Tzu's political philosophy comes out of his views on human nature and can be summarized by the basic principle: Not-ruling is the only way to rule. Chuang Tzu is thus an anarchist. His view is that individuals should (and do) care only for themselves, and that rules and laws lead only to bad characters. Thus, no government, or rather nongovernment, is legitimate.

Finally, a note about method: Chuang Tzu does not argue in a modern style, nor does he put forward explicit principles like Confucius. Rather, he tells stories and sets puzzles for the student to work through to find their meanings. Some straightforward philosophical claims can be discerned, but it would be difficult to put this in premise-conclusion form without doing damage to the text. As you are reading, use interpretive skills that you have learned studying literature to construct interpretations and test them against the basic points in this introduction.

STUDY QUESTIONS:

1. Why does the Taoist elevate simplicity, indifference, and lack of purpose as human ideals?

2. How would you interpret the story of Chaos, the Ruler of the Centre?

3. How does Chuang Tzu criticize Confucius?

The Normal Course for Rulers and Kings

Translated by James Legge

1. Nieh Khüeh put four questions to Wang Î, not one of which did he know (how to answer). On this Nieh Khüeh leaped up, and in great delight walked away and informed Phû-î-dze of it, who said to him, 'Do you (only) now know it? He of the line of Yü was not equal to him of the line of Thâi. He of Yü still kept in himself (the idea of) benevolence by which to constrain (the submission of) men; and he did win men, but he had not begun to proceed by what did not belong to him as a man. He of the line of Thâi would sleep tranquilly, and awake in contented simplicity. He would consider himself now (merely) as a horse, and now (merely) as an ox. His knowledge was real and untroubled by doubts; and his virtue was very true:—he had not begun to proceed by what belonged to him as a man.

2. Kien Wû went to see the mad (recluse), Khieh-yü, who said to him, 'What did Zäh-kung Shih tell you?' The reply was, 'He told me that when rulers gave forth their regulations according to their own views and enacted righteous measures, no one would venture not to obey them, and all would be transformed.' Khieh-yd said, 'That is but the hypocrisy of virtue. For the right ordering of the world it would be like trying to wade through the sea and dig through the Ho, or employing a musquito to carry a mountain on its back. And when a sage is governing, does he govern men's outward actions? He is (himself) correct, and so (his government) goes on;—this is the simple and certain way by which he secures the success of his affairs. Think of the bird which flies high, to avoid being hurt by the dart on the string of the archer, and the little mouse which makes its hole deep under Shän-khiû to avoid the danger of being smoked or dug out;—are (rulers) less knowing than these two little creatures?'

3. Thien Kän, rambling on the south of (mount) Yin, came to the neighbourhood of the Liâo-water.

   Happening there to meet with the man whose name is not known, he put a question to him, saying, 'I beg to ask what should be done in order to (carry on) the

From the *Sacred Books of the East*, translated by James Legge, 1891.

government of the world.' The nameless man said, 'Go away; you are a rude borderer. Why do you put to me a question for which you are unprepared? I would simply play the part of the Maker of (all) things. When wearied, I would mount on the bird of the light and empty air, proceed beyond the six cardinal points, and wander in the region of nonentity, to dwell in the wilderness of desert space. What method have you, moreover, for the government of the world that you (thus) agitate my mind?' (Thien Kän), however, again asked the question, and the nameless man said, 'Let your mind find its enjoyment in pure simplicity; blend yourself with (the primary) ether in idle indifference; allow all things to take their natural course; and admit no personal or selfish consideration:—do this and the world will be governed.'

4. Yang Dze-kü, having an interview with Lao Tan, said to him, 'Here is a man, alert and vigorous in responding to all matters, clearsighted and widely intelligent, and an unwearied student of the Tâo;—can he be compared to one of the intelligent kings?' The reply was, 'Such a man is to one of the intelligent kings but as the bustling underling of a court who toils his body and distresses his mind with his various contrivances. And moreover, it is the beauty of the skins of the tiger and leopard which makes men hunt them; the agility of the monkey, or (the sagacity of) the dog that catches the yak, which make men lead them in strings; but can one similarly endowed be compared to the intelligent kings?'

Yang dze-kü looked discomposed and said, 'I venture to ask you what the government of the intelligent kings is.' Lâo Tan replied, 'In the governing of the intelligent kings, their services overspread all under the sky, but they did not seem to consider it as proceeding from themselves; their transforming influence reached to all things, but the people did not refer it to them with hope. No one could tell the name of their agency, but they made men and things be joyful in themselves. Where they took their stand could not be fathomed, and they found their enjoyment in (the realm of) nonentity.'

5. In Käng there was a mysterious wizard called Ki-hsien. He knew all about the deaths and births of men, their preservation and ruin, their misery and happiness, and whether their lives would be long or short, foretelling the year, the month, the decade and the day like a spirit. When the people of Käng saw him, they all ran out of his way. Lieh-dze went to see him, and was fascinated by him. Returning, he told Hû-dze of his interview, and said, 'I considered your doctrine, my master, to be perfect, but I have found another which is superior to it.' Hû-dze replied, 'I have communicated to you but the outward letter of my doctrine, and have not communicated its reality and spirit; and do you think that you are in possession of it? However many hens there be, if there be not the cock among them, how should they lay (real) eggs? When you confront the world with your doctrine, you are sure to show in your countenance (all that is in your mind), and so enable (this) man to succeed in interpreting your physiognomy. Try and come to me with him, that I may show myself to him.'

On the morrow, accordingly, Lieh-dze came with the man and saw Ha-dze. When they went out, the wizard said, 'Alas! your master is a dead man. He will not live;—not for ten days more! I saw something strange about him;—I saw the ashes (of his life) all slaked with water!' When Lieh-dze reentered, he wept till the front of his jacket was wet with his tears, and told Hû-dze what the man had said. Hû-dze said, 'I showed myself to him with the forms of (vegetation beneath) the earth. There were the sprouts indeed, but without (any appearance of) growth or regularity:—he seemed to see me with the springs of my (vital) power closed up. Try and come to me with him again.'

Next day, accordingly, Lieh-dze brought the man again and saw Hû-dze. When they went out, the man said, 'It is a fortunate thing for your master that he met with me. He will get better; he has all the signs of living! I saw the balance (of the springs of life) that had been stopped (inclining in his favour).' Lieh-dze went in, and reported these words to his master, who said, 'I showed myself to him after the pattern of the earth (beneath the) sky. Neither semblance nor reality entered (into my exhibition), but the springs (of life) were issuing from beneath my feet;—he seemed to see me with the springs of vigorous action in full play. Try and come with him again.'

Next day Lieh-dze came with the man again, and again saw Hû-dze with him. When they went out, the wizard said, 'Your master is never the same. I cannot understand his physiognomy. Let him try to steady himself, and I will again view him.' Lieh-dze went in and reported this to Hû-dze, who said, 'This time I showed myself to him after the pattern of the grand harmony (of the two elemental forces), with the superiority inclining to neither. He seemed to see me with the

springs of (vital) power in equal balance. Where the water wheels about from (the movements of) a dugong, there is an abyss; where it does so from the arresting (of its course), there is an abyss; where it does so, and the water keeps flowing on, there is an abyss. There are nine abysses with their several names, and I have only exhibited three of them. Try and come with him again.'

Next day they came, and they again saw Hû-dze. But before he had settled himself in his position, the wizard lost himself and ran away. 'Pursue him,' said Hû-dze, and Lieh-dze did so, but could not come up with him. He returned, and told Hû-dze, saying, 'There is an end of him; he is lost; I could not find him.' Hû-dze rejoined, 'I was showing him myself after the pattern of what was before I began to come from my author. I confronted him with pure vacancy, and an easy indifference. He did not know what I meant to represent. Now he thought it was the idea of exhausted strength, and now that of an onward flow, and therefore he ran away.

After this, Lieh-dze considered that he had not yet begun to learn (his master's doctrine). He returned to his house, and for three years did not go out. He did the cooking for his wife. He fed the pigs as if he were feeding men. He took no part or interest in occurring affairs. He put away the carving and sculpture about him, and returned to pure simplicity. Like a clod of earth he stood there in his bodily presence. Amid all distractions he was (silent) and shut up in himself. And in this way he continued to the end of his life.

6. Non-action (makes its exemplifier) the lord of all fame; non-action (serves him as) the treasury of all plans; non-action (fits him

for) the burden of all offices; non-action (makes him) the lord of all wisdom. The range of his action is inexhaustible, but there is nowhere any trace of his presence. He fulfils all that he has received from Heaven, but he does not see that he was the recipient of anything. A pure vacancy (of all purpose) is what characterises him. When the perfect man employs his mind, it is a mirror. It conducts nothing and anticipates nothing; it responds to (what is before it), but does not retain it. Thus he is able to deal successfully with all things, and injures none.

7. The Ruler of the Southern Ocean was Shû, the Ruler of the Northern Ocean was Hû, and the Ruler of the Centre was Chaos. Shû and Hû were continually meeting in the land of Chaos, who treated them very well. They consulted together how they might repay his kindness, and said, 'Men all have seven orifices for the purpose of seeing, hearing, eating, and breathing, while this (poor) Ruler alone has not one. Let us try and make them for him.' Accordingly they dug one orifice in him every day; and at the end of seven days Chaos died.

Letting Be, and Exercising Forbearance

Translated by James Legge

1. I have heard of letting the world be, and exercising forbearance; I have not heard of governing the world. Letting be is from the fear that men, (when interfered with), will carry their nature beyond its normal condition; exercising forbearance is from the fear that men, (when not so dealt with), will alter the characteristics of their nature. When all men do not carry their nature beyond its normal condition, nor alter its characteristics, the good government of the world is secured.

Formerly, Yâo's government of the world made men look joyful; but when they have this joy in their nature, there is a want of its (proper) placidity. The government of the world by Kieh, (on the contrary), made men look distressed; but when their nature shows the symptoms of distress, there is a want of its (proper) contentment. The want of placidity and the want of contentment are contrary to the character (of the nature); and where this obtains, it is impossible that any man or state should anywhere abide long. Are men exceedingly joyful?—the Yang or element of expansion in them is too much developed. Are they exceedingly irritated?—the Yin or opposite element is too much developed. When those elements thus predominate in men, (it is as if) the four seasons were not to come (at their proper times), and the harmony of cold and heat were not to be maintained;—would there not result injury to the bodies of men? Men's joy and dissatisfaction are made to arise where they ought not to do so; their movements are all uncertain; they lose the mastery of their thoughts; they stop short midway, and do not finish what they have begun. In this state of things the world begins to have lofty aims, and jealous dislikes, ambitious courses, and fierce animosities, and then we have actions like those of the robber Kih, or of Zäng (Shän) and Shih (Zhiû). If now the whole world were taken to reward the good it would not suffice, nor would it be possible with it to punish the bad. Thus the world, great as it is, not sufficing for rewards and punishments, from the time of the three dynasties downwards, there has been nothing but bustle and excitement. Always occupied with rewards and punishments, what leisure have men had to rest in the instincts of the nature with which they are endowed?

From the *Sacred Books of the East*, translated by James Legge, 1891.

2. Moreover, delight in the power of vision leads to excess in the pursuit of (ornamental) colours; delight in the power of hearing, to excess in seeking (the pleasures of) sound; delight in benevolence tends to disorder that virtue (as proper to the nature); delight in righteousness sets the man in opposition to what is right in reason; delight in (the practice of) ceremonies is helpful to artful forms; delight in music leads to voluptuous airs; delight in sageness is helpful to ingenious contrivances; delight in knowledge contributes to fault-finding. If all men were to rest in the instincts of their nature, to keep or to extinguish these eight delights might be a matter of indifference; but if they will not rest in those instincts, then those eight delights begin to be imperfectly and unevenly developed or violently suppressed, and the world is thrown into disorder. But when men begin to honour them, and to long for them, how great is the deception practised on the world! And not only, when (a performance of them) is once over, do they not have done with them, but they prepare themselves (as) with fasting to describe them, they seem to kneel reverentially when they bring them forward, and they go through them with the excitements of music and singing; and then what can be done (to remedy the evil of them)? Therefore the superior man, who feels himself constrained to engage in the administration of the world will find it his best way to do nothing [1]. In (that policy of) doing nothing, he can rest in the instincts of the nature with which he is endowed. Hence he who will administer (the government of) the world honouring it as he honours his own person, may have that government committed to him, and he who will administer it loving it as he loves his own person, may have it entrusted

to him [1]. Therefore, if the superior man will keep (the faculties lodged in) his five viscera unemployed, and not display his powers of seeing and hearing, while he is motionless as a representative of the dead, his dragon-like presence will be seen; while he is profoundly silent, the thunder (of his words) will resound, while his movements are (unseen) like those of a spirit, all heavenly influences will follow them; while he is (thus) unconcerned and does nothing, his genial influence will attract and gather all things round him:—what leisure has he to do anything more for the government of the world?

3. Zhui Khü asked Lâo Tan, saying, 'If you do not govern the world, how can you make men's minds good?' The reply was, 'Take care how you meddle with and disturb men's minds. The mind, if pushed about, gets depressed; if helped forward, it gets exalted. Now exalted, now depressed, here it appears as a prisoner, and there as a wrathful fury. (At one time) it becomes pliable and soft, yielding to what is hard and strong; (at another), it is sharp as the sharpest corner, fit to carve or chisel (stone or jade). Now it is hot as a scorching fire, and anon it is cold as ice. It is so swift that while one is bending down and lifting up his head, it shall twice have put forth a soothing hand beyond the four seas. Resting, it is still as a deep abyss; moving, it is like one of the bodies in the sky; in its resolute haughtiness, it refuses to be bound;—such is the mind of man!'

Anciently, Hwang-Tî was the first to meddle with and disturb the mind of man with his benevolence and righteousness. After him, Yâo and Shun wore their thighs bare and the hair off the calves of their legs, in their labours to nourish the bodies of the people. They toiled painfully with all the powers in their five viscera at the practice of their benevolence and righteousness; they tasked their blood and breath to make out a code of laws;—and after all they were unsuccessful. On this Yâo sent away Hwan Tâu to Khung hill, and (the Chiefs of) the Three Miâo to San-wei, and banished the Minister of Works to the Dark Capital; so unequal had they been to cope with the world. Then we are carried on to the kings of the Three (dynasties), when the world was in a state of great distraction. Of the lowest type of character there were Kieh and Kih; of a higher type there were Zäng (Shän) and Shih (Zhiû). At the same time there arose the classes of the Literati and the Mohists. Hereupon, complacency in, and hatred of, one another produced mutual suspicions; the stupid and the wise imposed on one another; the good and the bad condemned one another; the boastful and the sincere interchanged their recriminations;—and the world fell into decay. Views as to what was greatly virtuous did not agree, and the nature with its endowments became as if shrivelled by fire or carried away by a flood. All were eager for knowledge, and the people were exhausted with their searchings (after what was good). On this the axe and the saw were brought into play; guilt was determined as by the plumb-line and death inflicted; the hammer and gouge did their work. The world fell into great disorder, and presented the appearance of a jagged mountain ridge. The crime to which all was due was the meddling with and disturbing men's minds. The effect was that men of ability and worth lay concealed at the foot of the crags of mount Thâi, and princes of ten thousand chariots were anxious and terrified in their ancestral temples. In the pres-

ent age those Who have been put to death in various ways lie thick as if pillowed on each other; those who are wearing the cangue press on each other (on the roads); those who are suffering the bastinado can see each other (all over the land). And now the Literati and the Mohists begin to stand, on tiptoe and with bare arms, among the fettered and manacled crowd! Ah! extreme is their shamelessness, and their failure to see the disgrace! Strange that we should be slow to recognise their sageness and wisdom in the bars of the cangue, and their benevolence and righteousness in the rivets of the fetters and handcuffs! How do we know that Zäng and Shih are not the whizzing arrows of Kieh and Kih? Therefore it is said, 'Abolish sageness and cast away knowledge, and the world will be brought to a state of great order.'

4. Hwang-Tî had been on the throne for nineteen years, and his ordinances were in operation all through the kingdom, when he heard that Kwang Khäng-dze was living on the summit of Khung-thung, and went to see him. 'I have heard,' he said, 'that you, Sir, are well acquainted with the perfect Tâo. I venture to ask you what is the essential thing in it. I wish to take the subtlest influences of heaven and earth, and assist with them the (growth of the) five cereals for the (better) nourishment of the people. I also wish to direct the (operation of the) Yin and Yang, so as to secure the comfort of all living beings. How shall I proceed to accomplish those objects?' Kwang Khäng-dze replied, 'What you wish to ask about is the original substance of all things; what you wish to have the direction of is that substance as it was shattered and divided [1]. According to your government of the world, the vapours of the clouds, before they were collected, would descend

in rain; the herbs and trees would shed their leaves before they became yellow; and the light of the sun and moon would hasten to extinction. Your mind is that of a flatterer with his plausible words;—it is not fit that I should tell you the perfect Tâo.'

Hwang-Tî withdrew, gave up (his government of) the kingdom, built himself a solitary apartment, spread in it a mat of the white mâo grass, dwelt in it unoccupied for three months, and then went again to seek an interview with (the recluse). Kwang Khäng-dze was then lying down with his head to the south. Hwang-Tî, with an air of deferential submission, went forward on his knees, twice bowed low with his face to the ground, and asked him, saying, 'I have heard that you, Sir, are well acquainted with the perfect Tâo;—I venture to ask how I should rule my body, in order that it may continue for a long time.' Kwang Khäng-dze hastily rose, and said, 'A good question! Come and I will tell you the perfect Tâo. Its essence is (surrounded with) the deepest obscurity; its highest reach is in darkness and silence. There is nothing to be seen; nothing to be heard. When it holds the spirit in its arms in stillness, then the bodily form of itself will become correct. You must be still; you must be pure; not subjecting your body to toil, not agitating your vital force;—then you may live for long. When your eyes see nothing, your ears hear nothing, and your mind knows nothing, your spirit will keep your body, and the body will live long. Watch over what is within you, shut up the avenues that connect you with what is external;—much knowledge is pernicious. I (will) proceed with you to the summit of the Grand Brilliance, where we come to the source of the bright and expanding (element); I will enter with you the gate of the Deepest Obscurity, where we come to the source of the dark and repressing (element). There heaven and earth have their controllers; there the Yin and Yang have their Repositories. Watch over and keep your body, and all things will of themselves give it vigour. I maintain the (original) unity (of these elements), and dwell in the harmony of them. In this way 1 have cultivated myself for one thousand and two hundred years, and my bodily form has undergone no decay.' Hwang-Tî twice bowed low with his head to the ground, and said, 'In Kwang Khäng-dze we have an example of what is called Heaven.' The other said, 'Come, and I will tell you:— (The perfect Tâo) is something inexhaustible, and yet men all think it has an end; it is something unfathomable, and yet men all think its extreme limit can be reached. He who attains to my Tâo, if he be in a high position, will be one of the August ones, and in a low position, will be a king. He who fails in attaining it, in his highest attainment will see the light, but will descend and be of the Earth. At present all things are produced from the Earth and return to the Earth. Therefore I will leave you, and enter the gate of the Unending, to enjoy myself in the fields of the Illimitable. I will blend my light with that of the sun and moon, and will endure while heaven and earth endure. If men agree with my views, I will be unconscious of it; if they keep far apart from them, I will be unconscious of it; they may all die, and I will abide alone!'

5. Yün Kiang, rambling to the east, having been borne along on a gentle breeze, suddenly encountered Hung Mung, who was rambling about, slapping his buttocks and hopping like a bird. Amazed at the sight, Yün Kiang stood reverentially, and said

to the other, 'Venerable Sir, who are you? and why are you doing this?' Hung Mung went on slapping his buttocks and hopping like a bird, but replied, 'I am enjoying myself.' Yün Kiang said, 'I wish to ask you a question.' Hung Mung lifted up his head, looked at the stranger, and said, 'Pooh!' Yün Kiang, however, continued, 'The breath of heaven is out of harmony; the breath of earth is bound up; the six elemental influences do not act in concord; the four seasons do not observe their proper times. Now I wish to blend together the essential qualities of those six influences in order to nourish all living things;—how shall I go about it?' Hung Mung slapped his buttocks, hopped about, and shook his head, saying, 'I do not know; I do not know!'

Yün Kiang could not pursue his question; but three years afterwards, when (again) rambling in the east, as he was passing by the wild of Sung, he happened to meet Hung Mung. Delighted with the rencontre, he hastened to him, and said, 'Have you forgotten me, O Heaven? Have you forgotten me, O Heaven?' At the same time, he bowed twice with his head to the ground, wishing to receive his instructions. Hung Mung said, 'Wandering listlessly about, I know not what I seek; carried on by a wild impulse, I know not where I am going. I wander about in the strange manner (which you have seen), and see that nothing proceeds without method and order;—what more should I know?' Yün Kiang replied, 'I also seem carried on by an aimless influence, and yet the people follow me wherever I go. I cannot help their doing so. But now as they thus imitate me, I wish to hear a word from you (in the case).' The other said, 'What disturbs the regular method of Heaven, comes into collision with the nature of things, prevents the accomplishment of the mysterious (operation of) Heaven, scatters the herds of animals, makes the birds all sing at night, is calamitous to vegetation, and disastrous to all insects;—all this is owing, I conceive, to the error of governing men.' 'What then,' said Yün Kiang, 'shall I do?' 'Ah,' said the other, 'you will only injure them! I will leave you in my dancing way, and return to my place.' Yün Kiang rejoined, 'It has been a difficult thing to get this meeting with you, O Heaven! I should like to hear from you a word (more).' Hung Mung said, 'Ah! your mind (needs to be) nourished. Do you only take the position of doing nothing, and things will of themselves become transformed. Neglect your body; cast out from you your power of hearing and sight; forget what you have in common with things; cultivate a grand similarity with the chaos of the plastic ether; unloose your mind; set your spirit free; be still as if you had no soul. Of all the multitude of things every one returns to its root. Every one returns to its root, and does not know (that it is doing so). They all are as in the state of chaos, and during all their existence they do not leave it. If they knew (that they were returning to their root), they would be (consciously) leaving it. They do not ask its name; they do not seek to spy out their nature; and thus it is that things come to life of themselves.'

Yün Kiang said, 'Heaven, you have conferred on me (the knowledge of) your operation, and revealed to me the mystery of it. All my life I had been seeking for it, and now I have obtained it.' He then bowed twice, with his head to the ground, arose, took his leave, and walked away.

6. The ordinary men of the world all rejoice in men's agreeing with themselves, and dislike

---

men's being different from themselves. This rejoicing and this dislike arise from their being bent on making themselves distinguished above all others. But have they who have this object at heart so risen out above all others? They depend on them to rest quietly (in the position which they desire), and their knowledge is not equal to the multitude of the arts of all those others! When they wish again to administer a state for its ruler, they proceed to employ all the methods which the kings of the three dynasties considered profitable without seeing the evils of such a course. This is to make the state depend on the peradventure of their luck. But how seldom it is that that peradventure does not issue in the ruin of the state! Not once in ten thousand instances will such men preserve a state. Not once will they succeed, and in more than ten thousand cases will they ruin it. Alas that the possessors of territory,—(the rulers of states),—should not know the danger (of employing such men)! Now the possessors of territory possess the greatest of (all) things. Possessing the greatest of all things,—(possessing, that is, men),—they should not try to deal with them as (simply) things. And it is he who is not a thing (himself) that is therefore able to deal with (all) things as they severally require. When (a ruler) clearly understands that he who should so deal with all things is not a thing himself, will he only rule the kingdom? He will go out and in throughout the universe (at his pleasure); he will roam over the nine regions, alone in going, alone in coming. Him we call the sole possessor (of this ability); and the sole possessor (of this ability) is what is called the noblest of all.

The teaching of (this) great man goes forth as the shadow from the substance, as the echo responds to the sound. When questioned, he responds, exhausting (from his own stores) all that is in the (enquirer's) mind, as if front to front with all under heaven. His resting-place gives forth no sound; his sphere of activity has no restriction of place. He conducts every one to his proper goal, proceeding to it and bringing him back to it as by his own movement. His movements have no trace; his going forth and his re-enterings have no deviation; his course is like that of the sun without beginning (or ending).

If you would praise or discourse about his personality, he is united with the great community of existences. He belongs to that great community, and has no individual self. Having no individual self, how should he have anything that can be called his? If you look at those who have what they call their own, they are the superior men of former times; if you look at him who has nothing of the kind, he is the friend of heaven and earth.

7. Mean, and yet demanding to be allowed their free course;—such are Things. Low, and yet requiring to be relied on;—such are the People. Hidden (as to their issues), and yet requiring to be done;—such are Affairs. Coarse, and yet necessary to be set forth;—such are Laws. Remote, and yet necessary to have dwelling (in one's self);—such is Righteousness. Near, and yet necessary to be widely extended;—such is Benevolence. Restrictive, and yet necessary to be multiplied;—such are Ceremonies. Lodged in the centre, and yet requiring to be exalted;—such is Virtue. Always One, and yet requiring to be modified;—such is the Tâo. Spirit-like, and yet requiring to be exercised;—such is Heaven.

Therefore the sages contemplated Heaven, but did not assist It. They tried to perfect their virtue, but did not allow it to embarrass them. They proceeded according to the Tâo, but did not lay any plans. They associated benevolence (with all their doings), but did not rely on it. They pursued righteousness extensively, but did not try to accumulate it. They responded to ceremonies, but did not conceal (their opinion as to the troublesomeness of them). They engaged in affairs as they occurred, and did not decline them. They strove to render their laws uniform, but (feared that confusion) might arise from them. They relied upon the people, and did not set light by them. They depended on things as their instruments, and did not discard them.

They did not think things equal to what they employed them for, but yet they did not see that they could do without employing them. Those who do not understand Heaven are not pure in their virtue. Those who do not comprehend the Tâo have no course which they can pursue successfully. Alas for them who do not clearly understand the Tâo!

What is it that we call the Tâo? There is the Tâo, or Way of Heaven; and there is the Tâo, or Way of Man. Doing nothing and yet attracting all honour is the Way of Heaven; Doing and being embarrassed thereby is the Way of Man. It is the Way of Heaven that plays the part of the Lord; it is the Way of Man that plays the part of the Servant. The Way of Heaven and the Way of Man are far apart. They should be clearly distinguished from each other.

Ancient Chinese Schools of Political Thought

The following table compares the main schools of thought of ancient Chinese political philosophy.

	School of thought	Principles of ruling	Ruling techniques & Type of ruler
Government of Men	**Confucianism**	Benevolence and efficient administration	Nourishing and teaching
	Mohism	Universal love	Elevate the worthy; condemn partiality and offensive war
Government of Law	**Legalism**	Laws, power	Clearly articulated laws; strict regulations
Nongoverning	**Taoism**	Nonaction	Spontaneity and harmony with nature

REFERENCE

A History of Chinese Political Thought, vol. 1, by Kung-chuan Hsiao, translated by F.W. Mote. Princeton University Press, 1979, p. 41.

Modern Political Philosophy

The Modern period of Political Philosophy stretches from the 16th to the early 19th centuries in Europe. The two greatest influences on this period of Political Philosophy are the Enlightenment generally, and specifically the Intellectual Revolutions in science and politics. To help you place these readings in their proper intellectual perspectives, let's look at a time line for some of the most important events of science, religion, and politics, beginning with the 16th century scientist Copernicus and ending at the beginning of the 19th century with the great philosopher Immanuel Kant.

1473–1543	Copernicus (*De Revolutionibus*, 1543)
1517	Martin Luther's 95 Theses
1564–1642	Galileo
1588–1679	Hobbes (*Leviathan*, 1651)
1642–1648	English Civil War
1649	Monarchy abolished in England
1653	Institution of Cromwell as Lord Protector
1660	Restoration of the Crown, Charles II
1632–1704	Locke (*Second Treatise on Government,* 1690)
1642–1727	Newton (*Principia Mathematica*, 1687; *Opticks*, 1704)
1663	Founding of the Royal Society
1675	Founding of Greenwich Observatory
1711–1776	Hume (*Treatise of Human Nature*, 1739; *Dialogues Concerning Natural Religion*, 1779)
1776	Adam Smith (*Wealth of Nations*)
1776	Declaration of Independence
1775–1783	American Revolution
1787	United States Constitution
1724–1804	Kant (*Critique of Pure Reason*, 1781; *Perpetual Peace*, 1795)

The most basic change in thought that came about during the Enlightenment was that science rather than faith came to be seen as the proper means to formulate one's beliefs about the world. Religion was thereby confined to the sphere of the supernatural. The most important change in

Political Philosophy was the idea that legitimate governments require the consent of the governed. Thus, in religion, science, and politics, authority was questioned in the modern age as never before.

THOMAS HOBBES

Thomas Hobbes (1588–1679) was an English philosopher best known for his works in Political Philosophy. He was educated at Oxford (Magdalen College), and lived during a time of revolution in science and philosophy, and civil war in England. In his great work, the *Leviathan*, he attempted to make a mathematical, deductive science of human nature, and politics, to do for politics and morals what Galileo and Descartes had done for science, geometry, and epistemology. Hobbes was especially inspired by the mechanical model in physics and engineering.

Hobbes had a very stark view of human nature, from which he derives his views of the nature of thought, morality, and ultimately, legitimate governmental authority. Hobbes studied human psychology and physiology, and developed a mechanical picture of man and reason. His interesting insight was to see reasoning as a matter of addition and subtraction of ideas B an early version of what is now called the Computational Theory of the Mind.

Hobbes held a Subjectivist Theory of good and evil, which means that each particular subject determines for him or herself whether something is good or not. Hobbes thought that this was a matter of human physiology, and that what we will find to be good is what will enhance our vital motion or, in contemporary terms, our ability to survive. Furthermore, because of our physiology we must always want to increase our power. In his view, human nature is self-interested, but once we enter society we can develop an Objective Theory of Justice.

STUDY QUESTIONS:

1. How does Hobbes describe conditions in the State of Nature, and how do these arise out of Hobbes' Theory of Human Nature?

2. What does Hobbes think is necessary to do to avoid the war of all against all, where life is solitary, poor, nasty, brutish, and short?

3. What are the first two Laws of Nature according to Hobbes?

Leviathan, Thomas Hobbes

Chapters XIII, XIV and XVIII

—————————— ❧⊙❧ ——————————

OF THE NATURALL CONDITION OF MANKIND, AS CONCERNING THEIR FELICITY, AND MISERY

CHAP. XIII NATURE hath made men so equall, in the faculties of body, and mind; as that though there bee found one man some-

 Men by nature Equall

times manifestly stronger in body, or of quicker mind then another; yet when all is reckoned together, the difference between man, and man, is not so considerable, as that one man can thereupon claim to himselfe any benefit, to which another may not pretend, as well as he. For as to the strength of body, the weakest has strength enough to kill the strongest, either by secret machination, or by confederacy with others, that are in the same danger with himselfe.

And as to the faculties of the mind, (setting aside the arts grounded upon words, and especially that skill of proceeding upon generall, and infallible rules, called Science; which very few have, and but in few things; as being not a native faculty, born with us; nor attained, (as Prudence,) while we look after somewhat els,) I find yet a greater equality amongst men, than that of strength. For Prudence, is but Experi-

ence; which equall time, equally bestowes on all men, in [6I] those things they equally apply themselves unto. That which may perhaps make such equality incredible, is but a vain conceipt of ones owne wisdome, which almost all men think they have in a greater degree, than the Vulgar; that is, than all men but themselves, and a few others, whom by Fame, or for concurring with themselves, they approve. For such is the nature of men, that howsoever they may acknowledge many others to be more witty, or more eloquent, or more learned; Yet they will hardly believe there be many so wise as themselves: For they see their own wit at hand, and other mens at a distance. But this proveth rather that men are in that point equall, than unequall. For there is not ordinarily a greater signe of the equall distribution of any thing, than that every man is contented with his share.

From this equality of ability, ariseth equality of hope in the attaining of our Ends. And therefore if any two men desire the same thing, which never-thelesse they cannot both enjoy, they become enemies;

From Equality proceeds Diffidence

and in the way to their End, (which is principally their owne conservation, and sometimes

———————

From *Leviathan* by Thomas Hobbes, first published 1651.

their delectation only,) endeavour to destroy, or subdue one an other. And from hence it comes to passe, that *where an Invader hath no more to feare, than an other mans single power; if one plant, sow, build, or possesse a convenient Seat, others may probably be expected to come prepared with forces united, to dispossesse, and deprive him, not only of the fruit of his labour, but also of his life, or liberty. And the Invader again is in the like danger of another.*

And from this diffidence of one another, there is no way for any man to secure himselfe,

From Diffidence Warre

so reasonable, as Anticipation; that is, by force, or wiles, to master the persons of all men he can, so long, till he see no other power great enough to endanger him: And this is no more than his own conservation requireth, and is generally allowed. Also because there be some, that taking pleasure in contemplating their own power in the acts of conquest, which they pursue farther than their security requires; if others, that otherwise would be glad to be at ease within modest bounds, should not by invasion increase their power, they would not be able, long time, by standing only on their defence, to subsist. And by consequence, such augmentation of dominion over men, being necessary to a mans conservation, it ought to be allowed him.

Againe, men have no pleasure, (but on the contrary a great deale of griefe) in keeping company, where there is no power able to over-awe them all. For every man looketh that his companion should value him, at the same rate he sets upon himselfe: And upon all signes of contempt, or undervaluing, naturally endeavours, as far as he dares (which amongst them that have no common power, to keep them in quiet, is far enough to make them destroy each other,) to extort a greater value from his contemners, by dommage; and from others, by the example.

So that in the nature of man, we find three principall causes of quarrell. First, Competition; Secondly, Diffidence; Thirdly, Glory.

[62] The first, maketh men invade for Gain; the second, for Safety; and the third, for Reputation. The first use Violence, to make themselves Masters of other mens persons, wives, children, and cattell; the second, to defend them; the third, for trifles, as a word, a smile, a different opinion, and any other signe of undervalue, either direct in their Persons, or by reflexion in their Kindred, their Friends, their Nation, their Profession, or their Name.

Hereby it is manifest, that *during the time men live without a common Power to keep them all in awe, they are in that condition which is called Warre; and such a warre, as is of every man, against every man.* For *WARRE,*

Out of Civil States, there is always Warre of every one against every one

consisteth not in Battell onely, or the act of fighting; but in a tract of time, wherein the Will to contend by Battell is sufficiently known: and therefore the notion of Time, is to be considered in the nature of Warre; as it is in the nature of Weather. For as the nature of Foule weather, lyeth not in a showre or two of rain; but in an inclination thereto of many dayes together: So the nature of War, consisteth not in actuall fighting; but in the known disposition thereto, during all the time there is no assurance to the contrary. All other time is PEACE.

Whatsoever therefore is consequent to a time of Warre, where every man is Enemy to every man; the same is consequent to the time, wherein men live without other security, than what their own

The Incommodites of such a War

strength, and their own invention shall furnish them withall. In such condition, there is no place for Industry; because the fruit thereof is uncertain: and consequently no Culture of the Earth; no Navigation, nor use of the commodities that may be imported by Sea; no commodious Building; no Instruments of moving, and removing such things as require much force; no Knowledge of the face of the Earth; no account of Time; no Arts; no Letters; no Society; and which is worst of all, continuall feare, and danger of violent death; And the life of man, solitary, poore, nasty, brutish, and short.

It may seem strange to some man, that has not well weighed these things; that Nature should thus dissociate, and render men apt to invade, and destroy one another: and he may therefore, not trusting to this Inference, made from the Passions, desire perhaps to have the same confirmed by Experience. Let him therefore consider with himselfe, when taking a journey, he armes himselfe, and seeks to go well accompanied; when going to sleep, he locks his dores; when even in his house he locks his chests; and this when he knows there bee Lawes, and publike Officers, armed, to revenge all injuries shall bee done him; what opinion he has of his fellow subjects, when he rides armed; of his fellow Citizens, when he locks his dores; and of his children, and servants, when he locks his chests. Does he not there as much accuse mankind by his actions, as I do by my words? But neither of us accuse mans nature in it. *The Desires, and other Passions of man, are in themselves no Sin. No more are the Actions, that proceed from those Passions, till they know a Law that forbids them:* which till Lawes be made they cannot know: nor can any Law be made, till they have agreed upon the Person that shall make it.

[63] *It may peradventure be thought, there was never such a time, nor condition of warre as this; and I believe it was never generally so, over all the world: but there are many places, where they live so now.* For the savage people in many places of *America,* except the government of small Families, the concord whereof dependeth on naturall lust, have no government at all; and live at this day in that brutish manner, as I said before. Howsoever, *it may be perceived*

what manner of life there would be, where there were no common Power to feare; by the manner of life, which men that have formerly lived under a peacefull government, use to degenerate into, in a civill Warre.

But though there had never been any time, wherein particular men were in a condition of warre one against another; yet in all times, Kings, and Persons of Soveraigne authority, because of their Independency, are in continuall jealousies, and in the state and posture of Gladiators; having their weapons pointing, and their eyes fixed on one another; that is, their Forts, Garrisons, and Guns upon the Frontiers of their Kingdomes; and continuall Spyes upon their neighbours; which is a posture of War. But because they uphold thereby, the Industry of their Subjects; there does not follow from it, that misery, which accompanies the Liberty of particular men.

To this warre of every man against every man, this also is consequent; that nothing can be Unjust. *The notions of Right and Wrong, Justice and Injustice have there no place. Where there is no common Power, there is no Law: where no Law, no Injustice.* Force, and Fraud, are in warre the two Cardinall vertues. Justice, and Injustice are none of the Faculties neither of the Body, nor Mind. If they were, they might be in a man that were alone in the world, as well as his Senses, and Passions. They are Qualities, that relate to men in Society, not in Solitude. *It is consequent also to the same condition, that there be no Propriety, no Dominion, no Mine and Thine distinct; but onely that to be every mans that he can get; and for so long, as he can keep it.* And thus much for the ill condition, which man by meer Nature is actually placed in; though with a possiblity to come out of it, consisting partly in the Passions, partly in his Reason.

The Passions that encline men to Peace, are Feare of Death; Desire of such things as are necessary to

> In such a Warre, nothing is Unjust

commodious living; and a Hope by their Industry to obtain them. And Reason suggesteth convenient

The Passions that incline men to Peace

Articles of Peace, upon which men may be drawn to agreement. These Articles, are they, which otherwise are called the Lawes of Nature: whereof I shall speak more particularly, in the two following Chapters. [64]

CHAP. XIV

Of the first and second NATURALL LAWES, and of CONTRACTS

THE *RIGHT OF NATURE,* which Writers commonly call *Jus Naturale,* is the Liberty each

Right of Nature what

man hath, to use his own power, as he will himselfe, for the preservation of his own Nature; that is to say, of his own Life; and consequently, of doing any thing, which in his own Judgement, and Reason, hee shall conceive to be the aptest means thereunto.

By LIBERTY, is understood, according to the proper signification of the word, the absence of externall Impediments: which Impediments,

Liberty what

may oft take away part of a mans power to do what hee would; but cannot hinder him from using the power left him, according as his judgement, and reason shall dictate to him.

A LAW OF NATURE, (Lex Naturalis,) is a Precept, or generall Rule, found out by Reason,

A Law of Nature what

by which a man is forbidden to do, that, which is destructive of his life, or taketh away the means of preserving the same; and to omit, that, by which he thinketh it may be best preserved. For though they that speak of this subject, use to confound *Jus,* and *Lex, Right* and *Law*; yet they ought to be distinguished; because RIGHT, consisteth in liberty to do,

or to forbeare; Whereas LAW, determineth, and bindeth to one of them: so that Law, and Right, differ as much, as Obligation, and Liberty;

Difference of Right and Law

which in one and the same matter are inconsistent.

And because the condition of Man, (as hath been declared in the precedent Chapter) is a condition of Warre of every one against every one; in which case every one is governed by his own Reason; and there is nothing he can make use of, that may not be a

Naturally every man has Right to everything

help unto him, in preserving his life against his enemyes; It followeth, that in such a condition, every man has a Right to every thing; even to one anothers body. And therefore, as long as this naturall Right of every man to every thing endureth, there can be no security to any man, (how

The Fundamental Law of Nature

strong or wise soever he be,) of living out the time, which Nature ordinarily alloweth men to live. And consequently it is a precept, or generall rule of Reason, *That every man, ought to endeavour Peace, as farre as he has hope of obtaining it; and when he cannot obtain it, that he may seek, and use, all helps, and advantages of Warre.* The first branch of which Rule, containeth the first, and Fundamentall Law of Nature; which is, *to seek Peace, and follow it.* The Second, the summe of the Right of Nature; which is, *By all means we can, to defend our selves.*

From this Fundamentall Law of Nature, by which men are commanded to endeavour Peace, is derived this second Law; *That a man be willing, when others are so too, as farre-forth, as for*

The second Law of Nature

Peace, and [65] *defence of himselfe he shall think it necessary, to lay down this right to all things; and be contented with so much liberty against other men, as he would allow other men against himselfe.* For as long as every man holdeth this Right, of doing any thing he liketh; so long are all men in the condition of Warre. But if other men will not lay down their Right, as well as he; then there is no Reason for any one, to devest himselfe of his: For that were to expose himselfe to Prey, (which no man is bound to) rather than to dispose himselfe to Peace. This is that Law of the Gospell; *Whatsoever you require that others should do to you, that do ye to them.* And that Law of all men, *Quod tibi fieri non vis, alteri ne feceris.*

To *lay downe* a mans *Right* to any thing, is to *devest* himselfe of the *Liberty,* of hindring another of the benefit of his own Right to

| What it is to lay down a Right |

the same. For he that renounceth, or passeth away his Right, giveth not to any other man a Right which he had not before; because there is nothing to which every man had not Right by Nature: but onely standeth out of his way, that he may enjoy his own originall Right, without hindrance from him; not without hindrance from another. So that the effect which redoundeth to one man, by another mans defect of Right, is but so much diminution of impediments to the use of his own Right originall.

Right is layd aside, either by simply Renouncing it; or by Transferring it to another. By *Simply RENOUNCING;* when he cares

| Renouncing a Right what it is |

not to whom the benefit thereof redoundeth. By *TRANSFERRING; when he intendeth the benefit thereof to some certain person,* or persons. And when a man hath in either manner abandoned,

| Transferring Right what |

or granted away his Right; then is he said to be OBLIGED, or BOUND, not to hinder those, to whom such Right is granted, or abandoned, from the benefit of it:

and that he *Ought,* and it is his *DUTY, not to make voyd that voluntary act of his own: and that such hindrance* is *INJUS-TICE,* and INJURY, as being *Sine Jure;* the Right

| Obligation |

being before renounced, or transferred. So that *Injury,* or *Injustice,* in the controversies of the world, is somewhat like to that, which in the

| Duty |

disputations of Scholers is called *Absurdity.* For as it is there called an Absurdity, to contradict what one maintained in the Beginning: so in the world, it is called Injustice, and Injury, voluntarily to undo that, which from the beginning

| Injustice |

he had voluntarily done. The way by which a man either simply Renounceth, or Transferreth his Right, is a Declaration, or Signification, by some voluntary and sufficient signe, or signes, that he doth so Renounce, or Transferre; or hath so Renounced, or Transferred the same, to him that accepteth it. And these Signes are either Words onely, or Actions onely; or (as it happeneth most often) both Words and Actions. And the same are the BONDS, by which men are bound, and obliged: Bonds, that have their strength, not from their own Nature, (for nothing is more easily broken then a mans word,) but from Feare of some evil consequence upon the rupture.

Whensoever a man Transferreth his Right, or Renounceth it; it is either in consideration of some Right reciprocally transferred to [66] himselfe; or for some

| Not all Rights are alienable |

other good he hopeth for thereby. For it is a voluntary act: and of the voluntary acts of every man, the object is some *Good to himselfe.* And *therefore there be some Rights, which no man can be understood by any words, or other signes, to have abandoned, or transferred. As first a man cannot lay down the right of resisting them, that assault him by force, to take away his life;* because he cannot be understood to ayme thereby, at any Good to himselfe. The same may be sayd of Wounds, and Chayns, and Imprisonment; both because there is no benefit consequent to such patience; as there is to the patience of suffering another to be wounded, or imprisoned: as also because a man cannot tell, when he seeth men proceed against him by violence, whether they intend his death or not. And lastly the motive, and end for which this renouncing, and transferring of Right is introduced, is nothing else but the security of a mans person, in his life, and in the means of so preserving life, as not to be weary of it. And therefore if a man by words, or other signes, seem to despoyle himselfe of the End, for which those signes were intended; he is not to be understood as if he meant it, or that it was his will; but that he was ignorant of how such words and actions were to be interpreted.

The mutuall transferring of Right, is that which men call CONTRACT.

There is difference, between transferring of Right to the Thing; and transferring, or

| Contract what |

tradition, that is, delivery of the Thing it selfe. For the Thing may be delivered together with the Translation of the Right; as in buying and selling with ready mony; or exchange of goods, or lands: and it may be delivered some time after.

Again, *one of the Contractors, may deliver the Thing contracted for on his part, and leave the other to perform his part at some determinate time after,* and in the mean time be trusted; and then the Contract on his part, is called *PACT,*

| Covenant what |

or COVENANT: Or both parts may contract now, to performe hereafter: in which cases, he that is to performe in time to come, being trusted, his performance is called *Keeping of Promise,* or Faith; and the fayling of performance (if it be voluntary) *Violation of Faith.*

When the transferring of Right, is not mutuall; but one of the parties transferreth, in hope to gain thereby friendship, or service from another, or from his friends; or in hope to gain the reputation of Charity, or Magnanimity; or to deliver his mind from the pain of compassion; or in hope of reward

| Free-gift |

in heaven; This is not Contract, but GIFT, FREE-GIFT, GRACE: which words signifie one and the same thing.

Signes of Contract, are either *Expresse,* or *by Inference.* Expresse, are words spoken with understanding of what

| Signes of Contract Expresse |

they signifie: And such words are either of the time *Present,* or *Past; as, I Give, I Grant, I have Given, I have Granted, I will that this be yours:* Or of the future; as, *I will Give, I will Grant:* which words of the future, are called PROMISE.

Signes by Inference, are sometimes the consequence of Words; [67] sometimes the consequence of Silence; sometimes the consequence of Actions; sometimes the

| Signes of Contract by Inference |

consequence of Forbearing an Action: and generally a signe by Inference, of any Contract, is whatsoever sufficiently argues the will of the Contractor.

Words alone, if they be of the time to come, and contain a bare promise, are an insufficient signe of a Free-gift and therefore not obligatory. For if they be of the time

| Free gift passeth by words of the Present or Past |

to Come, as, *To morrow I will Give,* they are a signe I have not given yet, and consequently that my right is not transferred, but remaineth till I transferre it by some other Act. But if the words be of the time Present, or Past, as, *I have given, or do give to be delivered to morrow,* then is my to morrows Right given away to day; and that by the vertue of the words, though there were no other argument of my will. And there is a great difference in the signification of these words, *Volc hoc tuum esse cras,* and *Cras dabo;* that is, between *I will that this be thine to morrow,* and, *I will give it thee to morrow.* For the word *I will,* in the former manner of speech, signifies an act of the will Present; but in the later, it signifies a promise of an act of the will to Come: and therefore the former words, being of the Present, transferre a future right; the later, that be of the Future, transferre nothing. But if there be other signes of the Will to transferre a Right, besides Words; then, though the gift be Free, yet may the Right be understood to passe by words of the future: as if a man propound a Prize to him that comes first to the end of a race, The gift is Free; and though the words be of the Future, yet the Right passeth: for if he would not have his words so be understood, he should not have let them runne.

In Contracts, the right passeth, not onely where the words are of the time Present, or Past; but also where they are of the Future: because all Contract is mutuall translation, or change of Right; and therefore he that promiseth onely, because he hath already received the benefit for which he promiseth, is to be understood as if he intended the Right should passe: for unlesse he had been content to have his words so understood, the other would not have performed his part first. And for that cause, in buying, and selling, and other acts of Contract, *a Promise is equivalent to a Covenant; and therefore obligatory.*

Signes of Contract are words both of the Past, Present, and Future

He that performeth first in the case of a Contract, is said to MERIT that which he is to receive by the performance of the other; and he hath it as *Due.* Also when a Prize is propounded to many, which is to be given to him onely that winneth; or mony is thrown amongst many, to be enjoyed by them that catch it; though this be a Free gift; yet so to Win, or so to Catch, is

Merit what

to *Merit,* and to have it as DUE. For the Right is transferred in the Propounding of the Prize, and in throwing down the mony; though it be not determined to whom, but by the Event of the contention. But there is between these two sorts of Merit, this difference, that In Contract, I Merit by vertue of my own power, and the Contractors need; but in this case of Free gift, I am enabled to Merit onely by the benignity of the Giver: In Contract, I merit at the Contractors hand that hee [68] should depart with his right; In this case of Gift, I Merit not that the giver should part with his right; but that when he has parted with it, it should be mine, rather than anothers. And this I think to be the meaning of that distinction of the Schooles, between *Meritum congrui,* and *Meritum condigni.* For God Almighty, having promised Paradise to those men (hoodwinkt with carnall desires,) that can walk through this world according to the Precepts, and Limits prescribed by him; they say, he that shall so walk, shall Merit Paradise *Ex congruo.* But because no man can demand a right to it, by his own Righteousnesse, or any other power in himselfe, but by the Free Grace of God onely; they say, no man can Merit Paradise *ex condigno.* This I say, I think is the meaning of that distinction; but because Disputers do not agree upon the signification of their own termes of Art, longer than it serves their turn; I will not affirme anything of their meaning: onely this I say; when a gift is given indefinitely, as a prize to be contended for, he that winneth Meriteth, and may claime the Prize as Due.

If a Covenant be made, wherein neither of the parties performe presently, but trust one another; in the condition of meer Nature, (which is a condition of Warre of every man against every

Coventants of Mutuall trust, when Invalid

man,) *upon any reasonable suspition, it is Voyd: But if there be a common Power set over them* both, *with right and force sufficient to compell performance; it is not Voyd.* For he that performeth first, has no assurance the other will performe after; because the bonds of words are too weak to bridle mens ambition, avarice, anger, and other Passions, without the feare of some coerceive Power; which in the condition of meer Nature, where all men are equall, and judges of the justnesse of their own fears cannot possibly be supposed. And therefore he which performeth first, does but betray himselfe to his enemy; contrary to the Right (he can never abandon) of defending his life, and means of living.

But in a civill estate, where there is a Power set up to constrain those that would otherwise violate their faith, that feare is no more reasonable; and for that cause, he which by the Covenant is to perform first, is obliged so to do.

The cause of feare, which maketh such a Covenant invalid, must be always something arising after the Covenant made; as some new fact, or other signe of the Will not to performe: else it cannot make the Covenant voyd. For that which could not hinder a man from promising, ought not to be admitted as a hindrance of performing.

He that transferreth any Right, transferreth the Means of enjoying it, as farre as lyeth in his power. As he that selleth Land, is understood to transferre the Herbage, and whatsoever growes upon it; Nor

Right to the End, Containeth Right to the Means

can he that sells a Mill turn away the Stream that drives it. And they that give to a man the Right of government in Soveraignty, are understood to give him the right of levying mony to maintain Souldiers; and of appointing Magistrates for the administration of Justice.

To make Covenant with bruit Beasts, is impossible; because not understanding our speech, they understand not, nor accept of any [69] translation of Right; nor can translate any Right to another:

No Covenant with Beasts

and without *mutuall acceptation*, there is no Covenant.

To make Covenant with God, is impossible, but by Mediation of such as God speaketh to, either by Revelation supernaturall, or by his Lieutenants that govern under him, and in his Name: For otherwise we know not whether our Covenants be accepted, or not. And therefore they that Vow any thing contrary to any law of Nature, Vow in vain; as being a thing unjust to pay such Vow. And if it be a thing commanded by the Law of Nature, it is not the Vow, but the Law that binds them.

The matter, or subject of *a Covenant, is always something that falleth under deliberation;* (For to Covenant, is an act of the Will; that is to say an act, and the last act, of deliberation;) and is therefore always understood to be something to

No Covenant, but of Possible and Future

come; and which is judged Possible for him that Covenanteth, to performe.

And therefore, to promise that which is known to be Impossible, is no Covenant. But if that prove impossible afterwards, which before was thought possible, the Covenant is valid, and bindeth, (though not to the thing it selfe,) yet to the value; or, if that also be impossible, to the unfeigned endeavour of performing as much as is possible: for to more no man can be obliged.

Men are freed of their Covenants two wayes; by Performing; or by being Forgiven. For Performance, is the naturall end of obligation; and Forgivenesse,

Covenants how made voyd

the restitution of liberty; as being a retransferring of that Right, in which the obligation consisted.

Covenants entred into by fear, in the condition of meer Nature, are obligatory. For example, if I Covenant to pay a ransome, or service for my life, to an enemy; I am bound by it. For it is a Contract, wherein one receiveth the benefit of life; the other is to receive mony, or service for it; and consequently, where no other Law (as in the condition, of meer Nature) forbiddeth the performance, the Covenant is valid.

| Covenants extorted by feare are valide |

Therefore Prisoners of warre, if trusted with the payment of their Ransome, are obliged to pay it: And if a weaker Prince, make a disadvantageous peace with a stronger, for feare; he is bound to keep it; unlesse (as hath been sayd before) there ariseth some new, and just cause of feare, to renew the war. And even in Commonwealths, if I be forced to redeem my selfe from a Theefe by promising him mony, I am bound to pay it, till the Civill Law discharge me. For whatsoever I may lawfully do without Obligation, the same I may lawfully Covenant to do through feare: and what I lawfully Covenant, I cannot lawfully break.

A former Covenant, makes voyd a later. For a man that hath passed away his Right to one man to day, hath it not to passe to morrow to another: and therefore the later promise passeth no Right, but is null.

| The former Covenant to one, makes voyd the later to another |

A Covenant not to defend my selfe from force, by force, is always voyd. For (as I have shewed before) no man can transferre, or lay down his Right to save himselfe from Death, Wounds, and Imprisonment, (the avoyding whereof is the onely End of laying [70] down any Right, and therefore the promise of not resisting force, in no Covenant transferreth any right; nor is obliging. For though a man may Covenant thus, *Unlesse I do so, or so, kill me;* he cannot Covenant thus, *Unlesse I do so, or so, I*

| A mans Covenant not to defend himselfe, is voyd |

will not resist you, when you come to kill me. For man by nature chooseth the lesser evill, which is danger of death in resisting; rather than the greater, which is certain and present death in not resisting. And this is granted to be true by all men, in that they lead Criminals to Execution, and Prison, with armed men notwithstanding that such Criminals have consented to the Law, by which they are condemned.

A Covenant to accuse ones selfe, without assurance of pardon, is likewise invalid. For in the condition of Nature, where every man is Judge, there is no place for Accusation: and in the Civill State, the Accusation is followed with Punishment; which being Force, a man is not obliged not to resist. The same is also true, of the Accusation of those, by whose Condemnation a man falls into misery; as of a Father, Wife, or Benefactor. For the Testimony of such an Accuser, if it be not willingly given, is præsumed to be corrupted by Nature; and therefore not to be received: and *where a mans Testimony is not to be credited, he is not bound to give it.* Also Accusations upon Torture, are not to be reputed as Testimonies. For Torture is to be used but as means of conjecture, and light, in the further examination, and search of truth: and what is in that case confessed, tendeth to the ease of him that is Tortured; not to the informing of the Torturers: and therefore ought not to have the credit of a sufficient Testimony: for whether he deliver himselfe by true, or false Accusation, he does it by the Right of preserving his own life.

| No man obliged to accuse himselfe |

The force of Words, being (as I have formerly noted) too weak to hold men to the performance of their Covenants; there are in mans nature, but two imaginable helps to strengthen it. And those are either a Feare of the consequence of breaking their word; or a Glory, or Pride in appearing

| The End of an Oath |

not to need to breake it. This later is a Generosity too rarely found to be presumed on, especially in the pursuers of Wealth, Command, or sensuall Pleasure; which are the greatest part of Mankind. The Passion to be reckoned upon, is Fear; whereof there be two very generall Objects: one, The Power of Spirits Invisible; the other, The Power of those men they shall therein Offend. Of these two, though the former be the greater Power, yet the feare of the later is commonly the greater Feare. The Feare of the former is in every man, his own Religion: which hath place in the nature of man before Civill Society. The later hath not so; at least not place enough, to keep men to their promises; because in the condition of meer Nature, the inequality of Power is not discerned, but by the event of Battell. So that before the time of Civill Society, or in the interruption thereof by Warre, there is nothing can strengthen a Covenant of Peace agreed on, against the temptations of Avarice, Ambition, Lust, or other strong desire, but the feare of that Invisible Power, which they every one Worship as God; and Feare as a Revenger of their perfidy. All therefore that can be done [71] between two men not subject to Civill Power, is to put one another to swear by the God he feareth:

Which *Swearing,* or OATH, is a *Forme of Speech, added to a Promise; by which he that*

| The forme of an Oath | *promiseth, signifieth, that unlesse he performe, he* |

renounceth the mercy of his God, or calleth to him for vengeance on himselfe. Such was the Heathen Forme, *Let* Jupiter *kill me else, as I kill this Beast.* So is our Forme, *I shall do thus, and thus, so help me God.* And this, with the Rites and Ceremonies, which every one useth in his own Religion, that the feare of breaking faith might be the greater.

By this it appears, that an Oath taken according to any other Forme, or Rite, then his, that sweareth, is in vain; and no Oath: And that there is no Swearing by any thing which the Swearer thinks not God. For though men have sometimes used to swear by their Kings, for feare, or flattery; yet they

| | No Oath, but by God |

would have it thereby understood, they attributed to them Divine honour. And that Swearing unnecessarily by God, is but prophaning of his name: and Swearing by other things, as men do in common discourse, is not Swearing, but an impious Custome, gotten by too much vehemence of talking.

It appears also, that the Oath addes nothing to the Obligation. For a Covenant, if lawfull, binds in the sight of God, without the Oath, as much as with it: if unlawfull, bindeth not at all;

| | An Oath addes nothing to the Obligation |

though it be confirmed with an Oath.

CHAP. XVIII

Of the RIGHTS *of Soveraignes by Institution*

A *Common-wealth* is said to be *Instituted,* when a *Multitude* of men do Agree, and *Covenant, every one, with every one,* that to whatsoever *Man,* or *Assembly of Men,* shall be given by the major part, the *Right* to *Present* the Person of them all, (that is to say, to be their *Representative;*)

| | The act of Instituting a Common-wealth, what |

every one, as well he that *Voted for it,* as he that *Voted against it,* shall *Authorise* all the Actions and Judgements, of that Man, or Assembly of men, in the same manner, as if they were his own, to the end, to live peaceably amongst themselves, and be protected against other men.

From this Institution of a Common-wealth are derived all the *Rights, and Facultyes of him,* or them, on whom *the Soveraigne Power* is conferred by the consent of the People assembled.

First, because they Covenant, it is to be understood, they are not obliged by former Covenant to any thing repugnant hereunto. And Consequently they that have already Instituted a Commonwealth, being thereby bound by Covenant, to own the Actions, and Judgements of one, cannot lawfully make a new Covenant, amongst themselves, to be obedient to any other, in any thing whatsoever, without his permission. And therefore, they that are subjects to a Monarch, *cannot without his leave cast off Monarchy*, and return to the confusion of a disunited Multitude;

> *The Consequences to such Institution, are I. The Subjects cannot change the forme of government*

nor transferre their Person from him that beareth it, to another Man, or other Assembly of men: for they [89] are bound, every man to every man, to Own, and be reputed Author of all, that he that already is their Soveraigne, shall do, and judge fit to be done: so that any one man dissenting, all the rest should break their Covenant made to that man, which is injustice: and they have also every man given the Soveraignty to him that beareth their Person; and therefore *if they depose him, they take from him that which is his own, and so again it is injustice.* Besides, if he that attempteth to depose his Soveraign, be killed, or punished by him for such attempt, he is author of his own punishment, as being by the Institution, Author of all his Soveraign shall do: And because it is injustice for a man to do any thing, for which he may be punished by his own authority, he is also upon that title, unjust. And whereas some men have pretended for their disobedience to their Soveraign, a new Covenant, made, not with men, but with God; this also is unjust: for there is no Covenant with God, but by mediation of some body that representeth Gods Person; which none doth but Gods Lieutenant, who hath the Soveraignty under God. But this pretence of Covenant with God, is so evident a lye, even in the pretenders own consciences, that it is not onely an act of an unjust, but also of a vile, and unmanly disposition.

Secondly, Because the Right of bearing the Person of them all, is given to him they make Soveraigne, *by Covenant onely of one to another, and not of him to any of them*; there can happen no breach of Covenant on the part of the Soveraigne; and consequently none of his Subjects, by any pretence of forfeiture, can

> *2. Soveraigne Power cannot be forfeited*

be freed from his Subjection. *That he which is made Soveraigne maketh no Covenant with his Subjects beforehand, is manifest; because either he must make it with the whole multitude, as one party to the Covenant; or he must make a severall Covenant with every man. With the whole, as one party, it is impossible; because as yet they are not one Person: and if he make so many severall Covenants as there be men, those Covenants after he hath the Soveraignty are voyd*, because what act soever can be pretended by any one of them for breach thereof, is the act both of himselfe, and of all the rest, because done in the Person, and by the Right of every one of them in particular. Besides, if any one, or more of them, pretend a breach of the Covenant made by the Soveraigne at his Institution; and others, or one other of his Subjects, or himselfe alone, pretend there was no such breach, there is in this case, no Judge to decide the controversie: it returns therefore to the Sword again; and every man recovereth the right of Protecting himselfe by his own strength, contrary to the designe they had in the Institution. It is therefore in vain to grant Soveraignty by way of precedent Covenant. The opinion that any Monarch receiveth his Power by Covenant, that is to say on Condition, proceedeth from want of understanding this easie truth, that Covenants being but words, and breath, have no force to oblige, contain, constrain, or protect any man, but what it has from the publique Sword; that is from the untyed hands of that Man, or Assembly of men that hath the Soveraignty, and whose actions are avouched by them [90] all, and performed by the strength of them all, in him united. But *when an Assembly of men is made Soveraigne; then no man imagineth any such Covenant to have past in the Institution; for no man is so dull as to say, for example, the People of Rome, made a Covenant with the Romans, to hold the Soveraignty on such or such conditions; which not performed, the Romans might lawfully depose the Roman People.* That men see not the reason to be alike in a Monarchy, and in a Popular Government, proceedeth from the ambition of some, that are kinder to the government of an Assembly, whereof they may hope to participate, than of Monarchy, which they despair to enjoy.

Regress org.

Soo is not a contracting party.

Thirdly, because the major part hath by consenting voices declared a Soveraigne; he that dissented must now consent with the rest; that is, be contented to avow all the actions he shall do, or else justly be destroyed by the rest. For if he voluntarily entered into the Congre-

> **3. No man can without injustice protest against the Institution of the Soveraigne declared by the major part**

gation of them that were assembled, he sufficiently declared thereby his will (and therefore *tacitely covenanted*) to stand to what the major part should ordayne: and therefore if he refuse to stand thereto, or make Protestation against any of their Decrees, he does contrary to his Covenant, and therefore unjustly. And whether he be of the Congregation, or not; and whether his consent be asked, or not, he must either submit to their decrees, or be left in the condition of warre he was in before; wherein he

might without injustice be destroyed by any man whatsoever.

Fourthly, because every Subject is by this Institution Author of all the Actions, and Judgments of the Soveraigne Instituted; it followes, that whatsoever he doth, it can be no injury to any of his Subjects; nor

> **4. The Soveraigns Actions cannot be justly accused by the Subject**

ought he to be by any of them accused of Injustice. For he that doth any thing by authority from another, doth therein no injury to him by whose authority he acteth: But by this Institution of a Common-wealth, every particular man is Author of all the Soveraigne doth; and consequently he that complaineth of injury from his Soveraigne, complaineth of that whereof he himselfe is Author; and therefore ought not to accuse any man but himselfe; no nor himselfe of injury; because to do injury to ones selfe, is impossible. It is true that they that have Soveraigne power, may commit Iniquity; but not Injustice, or Injury in the proper signification.

Fiftly, and consequently to that which was sayd last, no man that hath Soveraigne power can justly be put to death, or otherwise in any manner by his Subjects

> **5. What soever the Soveraigne doth, is unpunishable by the Subject**

punished. For seeing every Subject is Author of the actions of his Soveraigne; he punisheth another, for the actions committed by himselfe.

And because the End of this Institution, is the Peace and Defence of them all; and whosoever has right to the End, has right to the Means; it belongeth of Right, to whatsoever Man, or Assembly that hath the Soveraignty, to be Judge both of the meanes of Peace and Defence; and also of the hindrances, and disturbances of the

> **6. The Soveraigne is judge of what is necessary for the Peace and Defence of his Subjects**

same; and to do whatsoever he shall think necessary to be done, both before hand, for the preserving of Peace and Security, by prevention of Discord at home and [91] Hostility from abroad; and, when Peace and Security are lost, for the recovery of the same. And therefore.

Sixtly, it is annexed to the Soveraignty, to be Judge of what Opinions and Doctrines are averse, and what conducing to Peace; and consequently, on what occasions, how farre, and what, men are to be trusted withall, in speaking to Multitudes of people; and who shall examine the Doctrines of all bookes before they be published. For the

> And Judge of what Doctrines are fit to be taught them

Actions of men proceed from their Opinions; and in the welgoverning of Opinions, consisteth the well governing of mens Actions, in order to their Peace, and Concord. And though in matter of Doctrine, nothing ought to be regarded but the Truth; yet this is not repugnant to regulating of the same by Peace. For Doctrine repugnant to Peace, can no more be True, than Peace and Concord can be against the Law of Nature. It is true, that in a Common-wealth, where by the negligence, or unskilfullnesse of Governours, and Teachers, false Doctrines are by time generally received; the contrary Truths may be generally offensive: Yet the most sudden, and rough busling in of a new Truth, that can be, does never breake the Peace, but only sometimes awake the Warre. For those men that are so remissely governed, that they dare take up Armes, to defend, or introduce an Opinion, are still in Warre; and their condition not Peace, but only a Cessation of Armes for feare of one another; and they live as it were, in the procincts of battaile continually. It belongeth therefore to him that hath the Soveraign Power, to be Judge, or constitute all Judges of Opinions and Doctrines, as a thing necessary to Peace, thereby to prevent Discord and Civill Warre.

Seventhly, is annexed to the Soveraigntie, the whole power of prescribing the Rules, whereby every man may know, what Goods he may enjoy and what Actions he may doe, without being molested by any of his fellow Subjects: And this is it men call *Propriety*. For before constitution of Soveraign Power (as hath already been shewn) all men had right to all things; which neces-

> 7. The Right of making Rules, whereby the Subjects may every man know what is so his owne, as no other Subject can without injustice take it from him

sarily causeth Warre: and therefore this Proprietie, being necessary to Peace, and depending on Soveraign Power, is the Act of that Power, in order to the publique peace. These Rules of Propriety (or *Meum* and *Tuum*) and of *Good*, *Evill*, *Lawfull*, and *Unlawfull* in the actions of Subjects, are the Civill Lawes, that is to say, the Lawes of each Common-wealth in particular; though the name of Civill Law be now restrained to the antient Civill Lawes of the City of *Rome*; which being the head of a great part of the World, her Lawes at that time were in these parts the Civill Law.

Eightly, is annexed to the Soveraigntie, the Right of Judicature; that is to say, of hearing and deciding all Controversies, which may arise concerning Law, either Civill, or Naturall, or concerning Fact. For without the decision of Controversies, there is no protection of one

> 8. To him also belongeth the Right of all Judicature and decision of Controversies:

Subject, against the injuries of another; the Lawes concerning *Meum* and *Tuum* are in vaine; and to every man remaineth, from the naturall and necessary appetite of his own conservation, the right of protecting himselfe by his private strength, which is the condition [92] of Warre; and contrary to the end for which every Common-wealth is instituted.

Ninthly, is annexed to the Soveraignty, the Right of making Warre, and Peace with other Nations, and Common-wealths; that is to say,

9. And of making War, and Peace, as he shall think best:

of Judging when it is for the publique good, and how great forces are to be assembled, armed, and payd for that end; and to levy mony upon the Subjects, to defray the expenses thereof. For the Power by which the people are to be defended, consisteth in their Armies; and the strength of an Army, in the union of their strength under one Command; which Command the Soveraign Instituted, therefore hath; because the command of the *Militia*, without other Institution, maketh him that hath it Soveraign. And therefore whosoever is made Generall of an Army, he that hath the Soveraign Power is always Generallissimo.

Tenthly, is annexed to the Soveraignty, the choosing of all Councellours, Minis-

10. And of choosing all Counsellours, and Ministers, both of Peace, and Warre:

ters, Magistrates, and Officers, both in Peace, and War. For seeing the Soveraign is charged with the End, which is the common Peace and Defence; he is understood to have Power to use such Means, as he shall think most fit for his discharge.

Eleventhly, to the Soveraign is committed the Power of Rewarding with riches, or honour;

11. And of Rewarding, and Punishing, and that (where no former Law hath determined the measure of it) arbitrary:

and of Punishing with corporall, or pecuniary punishment, or with ignominy every Subject according to the Law he hath formerly made; or if there be no Law made, according as he shall judge most to conduce to the encouraging of men to serve the Common-wealth, or deterring of them from doing dis-service to the same.

Lastly, considering what values men are naturally apt to set upon themselves; what respect they look for from others; and how little they value other

12. And of Honour and Order

men; from whence continually arise amongst them, Emulation, Quarrells, Factions, and at last Warre, to the destroying of one another, and diminution of their strength against a Common Enemy; It is necessary that there be *Lawes of Honour*, and a publique rate of the worth of such men as have deserved, or are able to deserve well of the Common-wealth; and that there be force in the hands of some or other, to put those Lawes in execution. But it hath already been shewn, that not onely the whole *Militia*, or forces of the Common-wealth; but also the Judicature of all Controversies, is annexed to the Soveraignty. To the Soveraign therefore it belongeth also to give titles of Honour; and to appoint what Order of place, and dignity, each man shall hold; and what signes of respect, in publique or private meetings, they shall give to one another.

These are the Rights, which make the Essence of Soveraignty; and which are the markes, whereby a man may discern in what Man, or Assembly of men, the Soveraign Power is

These Rights are indivisible

placed, and resideth. For these are incommunicable, and inseparable. *The Power to coyn Mony; to dispose of the estate and persons of Infant heires; to have præemption in Markets; and all other Statute Prærogatives, may be transferred by the Soveraign; and yet the Power to protect his Subjects be retained.* But if he transferre the *Militia*, he retains the Ju[93]dicature in vain, for want of execution of the Lawes: Or if he grant away the Power of raising Mony; the *Militia* is in vain: or if he give away the government of Doctrines, men will be frighted into rebellion with the feare of Spirits. And so if we consider any one of the said Rights, we shall presently see, that the holding of all the rest, will produce no effect, in the conservation of Peace and Justice, the end for which all Common-wealths are Instituted. And this division is it, whereof it is said, *a Kingdome divided in it selfe cannot stand:* For unless this division precede, division into opposite Armies can never happen. If there had not first been an opinion received of the greatest part of *England,* that these Powers were divided between the King, and the Lords, and the House of Commons, the people had never been divided, and fallen into this Civill Warre; first between those that disagreed in Politiques; and after between the Dissenters about the liberty of Religion; which have so instructed men in this point of Soveraign Right, that there be few now (in *England,*) that do not see, that these Rights are inseparable, and will be so generally acknowledged, at the next return of Peace; and so continue, till their miseries are forgotten; and no longer, except the vulgar be better taught than they have hetherto been.

And because they are essentiall and inseparable Rights, it follows necessarily, that in whatsoever, words any of them seem to be

> And can by no Grant passe away without direct renouncing of the Soveraign Power

granted away, yet if the Soveraign Power it selfe be not in direct termes renounced, and the name of Soveraign no more given by the Grantees to him that Grants them, the Grant is voyd: for when he has granted all he can, if we grant back the Soveraignty, all is restored, as inseparably annexed thereunto.

This great Authority being Indivisible, and inseparably annexed to the Soveraignty, there

> The Power and Honour of Subjects vanisheth in the presence of the Power Sovereign

is little ground for the opinion of them, that say of Soveraign Kings, though they be *singulis majores,* of greater Power than every one of their Subjects, yet they be *Universis minores,* of lesse power than them all together. For if by *all together,* they mean not the collective body as one person, then *all together,* and *every one,* signifie the same; and the speech is absurd. But if by *all together,* they understand them as one Person (which person the Soveraign bears,) then the power of all together, is the same with the Soveraigns power; and so again the speech is absurd: which absurdity they see well enough, when the Soveraignty is in an Assembly of the people; but in a Monarch they see it not; and yet the power of Soveraignty is the same in whomsoever it be placed.

And as the Power, so also the Honour of the Soveraign, ought to be greater, than that of any, or all the Subjects. For in the Soveraignty is the fountain of Honour. The dignities of Lord, Earle, Duke, and Prince are his Creatures. As in the presence of the Master, the Servants are equall, and without any honour at all; So are the Subjects, in the presence of the Soveraign. And though they shine some more, some lesse, when they are out of his sight; yet in his presence, they shine no more than the Starres in presence of the Sun.

[94] *But a man may here object, that the Condition of Subjects is very miserable; as being obnoxious to the lusts, and other irregular passions of him, or them that have so unlimited a Power in their hands.* And commonly they that live under a Monarch, think it the fault of Monarchy; and they that live under the government of Democracy, or other

> Soveraigne Power not so hurtfull as the want of it, and the hurt proceeds for the greatest part from not submitting readily, to a lesse.

Soveraign Assembly, attribute all the inconvenience to that forme of Common-wealth; whereas the Power in all formes, if they be perfect enough to protect them is the same; not considering that the estate of Man can never be without some incommodity or other; and that *the greatest, that in any forme of Government can possibly happen to the people in generall, is scarce sensible, in respect of the miseries, and horrible calamities, that accompany a Civill Warre; or that dissolute condition of masterlesse men, without subjection to Lawes, and a coërcive Power to tye their hands from rapine, and revenge:* nor considering that the greatest pressure of Soveraign Governours, proceedeth not from any delight, or profit they can expect in the dammage, or weakening of their Subjects, in whose vigor, consisteth their own strength and glory; but in the restiveness of themselves, that unwillingly contributing to their own defence, make it necessary for their Governours to draw from them what they can in time of Peace, that they may have means on any emergent occasion, or sudden need, to resist, or take advantage on their Enemies. For all men are by nature provided of notable multiplying glasses, (that is their Passions and Self-love,) through which, every little payment appeareth a great grievance; but are destitute of those prospective glasses, (namely Morall and Civill Science,) to see a farre off the miseries that hang over them, and cannot without such payments beavoyded.

John Locke

John Locke (1632–1704) was born in a well-to-do family in England, but was influenced by the fact that his parents were Puritans rather than members of the State Church of England. He was educated at Oxford, where he concentrated on medicine and philosophy, taught philosophy, and took a medical degree. Locke is considered as an important philosopher not only for his political philosophy, but also for his metaphysics and epistemology. His *Essay Concerning Human Understanding* (1690) is one of the most important works of the Period of Thought known as British Empiricism, particularly for its views of substance and personal identity.

Locke's Second Treatise of Government and *Letter Concerning Toleration* (1689) which argues for religious freedom, are two of the most influential documents for the founding of the United States, and therefore in the history of Political Thought. As you read the Declaration of Independence it is easy to hear echoes of Locke.

The Second Treatise of Government is the second of the *Two Treatises of Government* (1689), the first of which is an argument against the divine right of kings, particularly against the argument for that view put forward by a contemporary of John Locke named Sir Robert Filmer. The Second Treatise sets out the argument for the origin and the legitimacy of civil government. In short, Locke argues that legitimate government can only be instituted by the consent of the people, and that there are limits on the kinds of government that people will/should consent to.

STUDY QUESTIONS:

1. How is Locke's version of the State of Nature differ from that of Hobbes?

2. What causes humans to want to enter into political society according to Locke?

3. What is Locke's Principle of Legitimacy?

Second Treatise of Government

Chapters II, VIII, IX and XI

§. 4. TO understand political power right, and derive it from its original, we must consider, what state all men are naturally in, and that is, *a state of perfect freedom* to order their actions, and dispose of their possessions and persons, as they think fit, within the bounds of the law of nature, without asking leave, or depending upon the will of any other man.

A *state also of equality*, wherein all the power and jurisdiction is reciprocal, no one having more than another; there being nothing more evident, than that creatures of the same species and rank, promiscuously born to all the same advantages of nature, and the use of the same faculties, should also be equal one amongst another without subordination or subjection, unless the lord and master of them all should, by any manifest declaration of his will, set one above another, and confer on him, by an evident and clear appointment, an undoubted right to dominion and sovereignty.

§. 5. This *equality* of men by nature, the judicious *Hooker* looks upon as so evident in itself, and beyond all question, that he makes it the foundation of that obligation to mutual love amongst men, on which he builds the duties they owe one another, and from whence he derives the great maxims *of justice* and *charity*. His words are,

The like natural inducement hath brought men to know that it is no less their duty, to love others than themselves; for seeing those things which are equal, must needs all have one measure; if I cannot but wish to receive good, even as much at every man's hands, as any man can wish unto his own soul, how should I look to have any part of my desire herein satisfied, unless myself be careful to satisfy the like desire, which is undoubtedly in other men, being of one and the same nature? To have any thing offered them repugnant to this desire, must needs in all respects grieve them as much as me; so that if I do harm, I must look to suffer, there being no reason that others should shew greater measure of love to me, than they have by me shewed unto them: my desire therefore to be loved of my equals in nature, as much as possible may be, imposeth upon me a natural duty of bearing to them-ward fully the like affection; from which relation of equality between ourselves and them that are as ourselves, what several rules and canons natural reason hath drawn, for direction of life, no man is ignorant, Eccl. Pol. Lib. 1.

§. 6. But though this be a *state of liberty*, yet *it is not a state of licence:* though man in that

---

From *Second Treatise of Government* by John Locke. First published 1690.

state have an uncontroulable liberty to dispose of his person or possessions, *yet he has not liberty to destroy himself,* or so much as any creature in his possession, but where some nobler use than its bare preservation calls for it. The *state of nature* has a law of nature to govern it, which obliges every one: and reason, which is that law, teaches all mankind, who will but consult it, *that being all equal and independent,* no one ought to *harm another in his life, health, liberty, or possessions: for men being all the workmanship of one omnipotent, and infinitely wise maker; all the servants of one sovereign master, sent into the world by his order, and about his business; they are his property, whose workmanship they are, made to last during his, not one another's pleasure*: and being furnished with like faculties, sharing all in one community of nature, there cannot be supposed any such *subordination* among us, that may authorize us to destroy one another, as if we were made for one another's uses, as the inferior ranks of creatures are for our's. *Every one, as he is bound to preserve himself,* and not to quit his station wilfully, *so by the like reason, when his own preservation comes not in competition, ought he, as much as he can, to preserve the rest of mankind,* and may not, unless it be to do justice on an offender, take away, or impair the life, or what tends to the preservation of the life, the liberty, health, limb, or goods of another.

§. 7. And that all men may be restrained from invading others rights, and from doing hurt to one another, and the law of nature be observed, which willeth the peace and *preservation of all mankind,* the *execution* of the law of nature is, in that state, put into every man's hands, whereby every one has a right to punish the transgressors of that law to such a degree, as may hinder its violation: for the *law of nature* would, as all other laws that concern men in this world, be in vain, if there were no body that in the state of nature had a *power to execute*

that law, and thereby preserve the innocent and restrain offenders. And if any one in the state of nature may punish another for any evil he has done, every one may do so: for in that *state of perfect equality,* where naturally there is no superiority or jurisdiction of one over another, what any may do in prosecution of that law, every one must needs have a right to do.

§. 8. And thus, in the state of nature, *one man comes by a power over another;* but yet no absolute or arbitrary power, to use a criminal, when he has got him in his hands, according to the passionate heats, or boundless extravagancy of his own will; but only to retribute to him, so far as calm reason and conscience dictate, what is proportionate to his transgression, which is so much as may serve for *reparation and restraint: for these two are the only reasons, why one man may lawfully do harm to another,* which is that we call *punishment.* In transgressing the law of nature, the offender declares himself to live by another rule than that of reason and common equity, which is that measure God has set to the actions of men, for their mutual security; and so he becomes dangerous to mankind, the tye, which is to secure them from injury and violence, being slighted and broken by him. Which being a trespass against the whole species, and the peace and safety of it, provided for by the law of nature, every man upon this score, by the right he hath to preserve mankind in general, may restrain, or where it is necessary, destroy things noxious to them, and so may bring such evil on any one, who hath transgressed that law, as may make him repent the doing of it, and thereby deter him, and by his example others, from doing the like mischief. And in the case, and upon this ground, *every man hath a right to punish the offender, and be executioner of the law of nature.*

§. 9. I doubt not but this will seem a very strange doctrine to some men: but before they condemn it, I desire them to resolve me, by what right any prince or state can put to death, or *punish an alien,* for any crime he commits in their country. It is certain their laws, by virtue of any sanction they receive from the promulgated will of the legislative, reach not a stranger: they speak not to him, nor, if they did, is he bound to hearken to them. The legislative authority, by which they are in force over the subjects of that common-wealth, hath no power over him. Those who have the supreme power of making laws in *England, France or Holland,* are to an *Indian,* but like the rest of the world, men without authority: and therefore, if by the law of nature every man hath not a power to punish offences against it, as he soberly judges the case to require, I see not how the magistrates of any community can *punish an alien* of another country; since, in reference to him, they can have no more power than what every man naturally may have over another.

§. 10. Besides the crime which consists in violating the law, and varying from the right rule of reason, whereby a man so far becomes degenerate, and declares himself to quit the principles of human nature, and to be a noxious creature, there is commonly *injury* done to some person or other, and some other man receives damage by his transgression: in which case *he who hath received any damage, has, besides the right of punishment common to him with other men, a particular right to seek reparation from him that has done it:* and any other person, who finds it just, may also join with him that is injured, and assist him in recovering from the offender so much as may make satisfaction for the harm he has suffered.

§. 11. From these *two distinct rights,* the one of *punishing* the crime *for restraint,* and preventing the like offence, which right of punishing is in every body; the other of taking *reparation,* which belongs only to the injured party, comes it to pass that the magistrate, who by being magistrate hath the common right of

punishing put into his hands, can often, where the public good demands not the execution of the law, *remit* the punishment of criminal offences by his own authority, but yet cannot *remit* the satisfaction due to any private man for the damage he has received. That, he who has suffered the damage has a right to demand in his own name, and he alone can remit: the damnified person has this power of appropriating to himself the goods or service of the offender, *by right of self-preservation,* as every man has a power to punish the crime, to prevent its being committed again, *by the right he has of preserving all mankind,* and doing all reasonable things he can in order to that end: and thus it is, that every man, in the state of nature, has a power to kill a murderer, both *to deter* others from doing the like injury, which no reparation can compensate, by the example of the punishment that attends it from every body, and also to secure men from the attempts of a criminal, who having renounced reason, the common rule and measure God hath given to mankind, hath, by the unjust violence and slaughter he hath committed upon one, declared war against all mankind, and therefore may be destroyed as a *lion* or a *tyger,* one of those wild savage beasts, with whom men can have no society nor security: and upon this is grounded that great law of nature, *Whoso sheddeth man's blood, by man shall his blood be shed.* And *Cain* was so fully convinced, that every one had a right to destroy such a criminal, that after the murder of his brother, he cries out, *Every one that findeth me, shall slay me;* so plain was it writ in the hearts of all mankind.

§. 12. By the same reason may a man in the state of nature *punish the lesser breaches* of that law. It will perhaps be demanded, with death? I answer, each transgression may be *punished* to that *degree,* and with so much *severity,* as will suffice to make it an ill bargain to the offender, give him cause to repent, and terrify others from doing the like. Every offence, that can be committed in the state of nature, may in the state of nature be also punished equally, and as far forth as it may, in a common-wealth: for though it would be besides my present purpose, to enter here into the particulars of the law of nature, or its *measures of punishment;* yet, it is certain there is such a law, and that too, as intelligible and plain to a rational creature, and a studier of that law, as the positive laws of common-wealths; nay, possibly plainer; as much as reason is easier to be understood, than the fancies and intricate contrivances of men, following contrary and hidden interests put into words; for so truly are a great part of the *municipal laws* of countries, which are only so far right, as they are founded on the law of nature, by which they are to be regulated and interpreted.

§. 13. To this strange doctrine, *viz.* That *in the state of nature every one has the executive power* of the law of nature, I doubt not but it will be objected, that it is unreasonable for men to be judges in their own cases, that self-love will make men partial to themselves and their friends: and on the other side, that ill nature, passion and revenge will carry them too far in punishing others; and hence nothing but confusion and disorder will follow, and that therefore God hath certainly appointed government to restrain the partiality and violence of men. I easily grant, that *civil government* is the proper remedy for the inconveniencies of the state of nature, which must certainly be great, where men may be *judges in their own case*, since it is easy to be imagined, that he who was so unjust as to do his brother an injury, will scarce be so just as to condemn himself for it; but I shall desire those who make this objection, to remember, that *absolute monarchs* are but men; and if government is to be the remedy of those evils, which necessarily follow from men's being judges in their own cases, and the state of

nature is therefore not to be endured, I desire to know what kind of government that is, and how much better it is than the state of nature, where one man, commanding a multitude, has the liberty to be judge in his own case, and may do to all his subjects whatever he pleases, without the least liberty to any one to question or controul those who execute his pleasure? and in whatsoever he doth, whether led by reason, mistake or passion, must be submitted to? much better it is in the state of nature, wherein men are not bound to submit to the unjust will of another: and if he that judges, judges amiss in his own, or any other case, he is answerable for it to the rest of mankind.

§. 14. It is often asked as a mighty objection, *where are,* or ever were there any *men in such a state of nature?* To which it may suffice as an answer at present, that since all princes and rulers of *independent* governments all through the world, are in a state of nature, it is plain the world never was, nor ever will be, without numbers of men in that state. I have named all governors of *independent communities,* whether they are, or are not, in league with others: for it is not every compact that puts an end to the state of nature between men, but only this one of agreeing together mutually to enter into one community, and make one body politic; other promises, and compacts, men may make one with another, and yet still be in the state of nature. The promises and bargains for truck, *&c.* between the two men in the desert island, mentioned by *Garcilasso de la Vega,* in his history of *Peru;* or between a *Swiss* and an *Indian,* in the woods of *America,* are binding to them, though they are perfectly in a state of nature, in reference to one another: for truth and keeping of faith belongs to men, as men, and not as members of society.

§. 15. *To those that say, there were never any men in the state of nature, I will not only oppose the authority of the judicious Hooker,*

Eccl. Pol. lib. i. sect. 10. where he says, The laws which have been hitherto mentioned, i. e. the laws of nature, *do bind men absolutely, even as they are men, although they have never any settled fellowship, never any solemn agreement amongst themselves what to do, or not to do: but forasmuch as we are not by ourselves sufficient to furnish ourselves with competent store of things, needful for such a life as our nature doth desire, a life fit for the dignity of man; therefore to supply those defects and imperfections which are in us, as living single and solely by ourselves, we are naturally induced to seek communion and fellowship with others: this was the cause of men's uniting themselves at first in politic societies.* But I moreover affirm, that all men are naturally in that state, and remain so, till by their own consents they make themselves members of some politic society; and I doubt not in the sequel of this discourse, to make it very clear.

CHAP. VIII

Of the Beginning of Political Societies

§. 95. Men being, as has been said, by nature, all free, equal, and independent, no one can be put out of this estate, and subjected to the political power of another, without his own consent. The only way whereby any one divests himself of his natural liberty, and puts on the *bonds of civil society,* is by agreeing with other men to join and unite into a community for their comfortable, safe, and peaceable living one amongst another, in a secure enjoyment of their properties, and a greater security against any, that are not of it. This any number of men may do, because it injures not the freedom of the rest; they are left as they were in the liberty of the state of nature. When any number of men have so *consented to make one community or government,* they are thereby presently incorporated, and make *one body politic,* wherein the *majority* have a right to act and conclude the rest.

§. 96. For when any number of men have, by the consent of every individual, made a *community,* they have thereby made that *community* one body, with a power to act as one body, which is only by the will and determination of the *majority:* for that which acts any community, being only the consent of the individuals of it, and it being necessary to that which is one body to move one way; it is necessary the body should move that way whither the greater force carries it, which is the *consent of the majority:* or else it is impossible it should act or continue one body, *one community,* which the consent of every individual that united into it, agreed that it should; and so every one is bound by that consent to be concluded by the *majority.* And therefore we see, that in assemblies, impowered to act by positive laws, where no number is set by that positive law which impowers them, the *act of the majority* passes for the act of the whole, and of course determines, as having, by the law of nature and reason, the power of the whole.

§. 97. And thus every man, by consenting with others to make one body politic under one government, puts himself under an obligation, to every one of that society, to submit to the determination of the *majority,* and to be concluded by it; or else this *original compact,* whereby he with others incorporates into *one society,* would signify nothing, and be no compact, if he be left free, and under no other ties than he was in before in the state of nature. For what appearance would there be of any compact? What new engagement if he were no farther tied by any decrees of the society, than he himself thought fit, and did actually consent to? This would be still as great a liberty, as he himself had before his compact, or any one else in the state of nature hath, who may submit himself, and consent to any acts of it he thinks fit.

§. 98. For *if the consent of the majority* shall not, in reason, be received as *the act of the whole,* and conclude every individual; nothing but the consent of every individual can make any thing to be the act of the whole: but such a consent is next to impossible ever to be had, if we consider the infirmities of health, and avocations of business, which in a number, though much less than that of a common-wealth, will necessarily keep many away from the public assembly. To which if we add the variety of opinions, and contrariety of interests, which unavoidably happen in all collections of men, the coming into society upon such terms would be only like *Cato's* coming into the theatre, only to go out again. Such a constitution as this would make the mighty *Leviathan* of a shorter duration, than the feeblest creatures, and not let it outlast the day it was born in: which cannot be supposed, till we can think, that rational creatures should desire and constitute societies only to be dissolved: for where the *majority* cannot conclude the rest, there they cannot act as one body, and consequently will be immediately dissolved again.

§. 99. Whosoever therefore out of a state of nature unite into a *community*, must be understood to give up all the power, necessary to the ends for which they unite into society, to the *majority* of the community, unless they expresly agreed in any number greater than the majority. And this is done by barely agreeing to *unite into one political society*, which is *all the compact* that is, or needs be, between the individuals, that enter into, or make up a *commonwealth*. And thus that, which begins and actually *constitutes any political society*, is nothing but the consent of any number of freemen capable of a majority to unite and incorporate into such a society. And this is that, and that only, which did, or could give beginning to any *lawful government* in the world.

§. 100. To this I find two objections made.

First, *That there are no instances to be found in story, of a company of men independent, and equal one amongst another, that met together, and in this way began and set up a government.*

Secondly, *It is impossible of right, that men should do so, because all men being born under government, they are to submit to that, and are not at liberty to begin a new one.*

§. 101. To the first there is this to answer, That it is not at all to be wondered, that *history* gives us but a very little account of *men, that lived together in the state of nature*. The inconveniences of that condition, and the love and want of society, no sooner brought any number of them together, but they presently united and incorporated, if they designed to continue together. And if we may not suppose *men* ever to have been *in the state of nature*, because we hear not much of them in such a state, we may as well suppose the armies of *Salmanasser* or *Xerxes* were never children, because we hear little of them, till they were men, and imbodied in armies. Government is every where antecedent to records, and letters seldom come in amongst a people till a long continuation of civil society has, by other more necessary arts, provided for their safety, ease, and plenty: and then they begin to look after the history of their founders, and search into their *original*, when they have outlived the memory of it: for it is with *common-wealths* as with particular persons, they are commonly *ignorant of their own births and infancies*: and if they know any thing of their *original*, they are beholden for it, to the accidental records that others have kept of it. And those that we have, of the beginning of any polities in the world, excepting that of the *Jews*, where God himself immediately interposed, and which favours not at all paternal dominion, are all either plain instances of such a beginning as I have mentioned, or at least have manifest footsteps of it.

˙At first, when some certain kind of regiment was once approved, it may be nothing was then farther thought upon for the manner of governing, but all permitted unto their wisdom and discretion which were to rule, till by experience they found this for all parts very inconvenient, so as the thing which they had devised for a remedy, did indeed but increase the sore which it should have cured. They saw, that to live by one man's will, became the cause of all men's misery. This constrained them to come unto laws wherein all men might see their duty before hand, and know the penalties of transgressing them. *Hooker's Eccl. Pol. l.* i. *sect.* 10.

§. 113. *That all men being born under government, some or other, it is impossible any of them should ever be free, and at liberty to unite together, and begin a new one, or ever be able to erect a lawful government.*

If this argument be good; I ask, how came so many lawful monarchies into the world? for if any body, upon this supposition, can shew me any one man in any age of the world *free* to begin a lawful monarchy, I will be bound to shew him ten other *free men* at liberty, at the same time to unite and begin a new government under a regal, or any other form; it being demonstration, that if any one, *born under the dominion* of another, may be so *free* as to have a right to command others in a new and distinct empire, every one that is *born under the dominion* of another may be so free too, and may become a ruler, or subject, of a distinct separate government. And so by this their own principle, either all men, however *born*, are *free*, or else there is but one lawful prince, one lawful government in the world. And then they have nothing to do, but barely to shew us which that is; which when they have done, I doubt not but all mankind will easily agree to pay obedience to him.

§. 114. Though it be a sufficient answer to their objection, to shew that it involves them in the same difficulties that it doth those they use it against; yet I shall endeavour to discover the weakness of this argument a little farther.

All men, say they, *are born under government, and therefore they cannot be at liberty to begin a new one. Every one is born a subject to his father, or his prince, and is therefore under the perpetual tie of subjection and allegiance.* It is plain mankind never owned nor considered any such natural *subjection that they were born in*, to one or to the other that tied them, without their own consents, to a subjection to them and their heirs.

§. 115. For there are no examples so frequent in history, both sacred and profane, as those of men withdrawing themselves, and their obedience, from the jurisdiction they were born under, and the family or community they were bred up in, and *setting up new governments* in other places; from whence sprang all that number of petty common-wealths in the beginning of ages, and which always multiplied, as long as there was room enough, till the stronger, or more fortunate, swallowed the weaker; and those great ones again breaking to pieces, dissolved into lesser dominions. All which are so many testimonies against paternal sovereignty, and plainly prove, that it was not the natural right of the *father* descending to his heirs, that made governments in the beginning, since it was impossible, upon that ground, there should have been so many little kingdoms; all must have been but only one universal monarchy, if men had not been at *liberty to separate* themselves from their families, and the government, be it what it will, that was set up in it, and go and make distinct common-wealths and other governments, as they thought fit.

§. 116. This has been the practice of the world from its first beginning to this day; nor is it now any more hindrance to the freedom of mankind, that they are *born under constituted and ancient polities,* that have established laws, and set forms of government, than if they were born in the woods, amongst the unconfined inhabitants, that run loose in them: for those, who would persuade us, that *by being born under any government, we are naturally subjects to it,* and have no more any title or pretence to the freedom of the state of nature, have no other reason (bating that of paternal power, which we have already answered) to produce for it, but only, because our fathers or progenitors passed away their natural liberty, and thereby bound up themselves and their posterity to a perpetual subjection to the government, which they themselves submitted to. It is true, that whatever engagements or promises any one has made for himself, he is under the obligation of them, but *cannot, by any compact* whatsoever, *bind his children or posterity:* for his son, when a man, being altogether as free as the father, any *act of the father can no more give away the liberty of the son,* than it can of any body else: he may indeed annex such conditions to the land, he enjoyed as a subject of any common-wealth, as may oblige his son to be of that community, if he will enjoy those possessions which were his father's; because that estate being his father's property, he may dispose, or settle it, as he pleases.

§. 117. And this has generally given the occasion to mistake in this matter; because common-wealths not permitting any part of their dominions to be dismembered, nor to be enjoyed by any but those of their community, the son cannot ordinarily enjoy the possessions of his father, but under the same terms his father did, by becoming a member of the society; whereby he puts himself presently under the government he finds there established, as much as any other subject of that common-wealth. And thus *the consent of freemen, born under government,* which only *makes them members of it,* being given separately in their turns, as each comes to be of age, and not in a multitude together; people take no notice of it, and thinking it not done at all, or not necessary, conclude they are naturally subjects as they are men.

§. 118. But, it is plain, *governments* themselves understand it otherwise; they claim *no power over the son, because of that they had over the father;* nor look on children as being their subjects, by their fathers being so. If a subject of *England* have a child, by an *English* woman in *France,* whose subject is he? Not the king of *England's*; for he must have leave to be admitted to the privileges of it: nor the king of *France's*; for how then has his father a liberty to bring him away, and breed him as he pleases? and who ever was judged as a *traytor or deserter,* if he left, or warred against a country, for being barely born in it of parents that were aliens there? It is plain then, by the practice of governments themselves, as well as by the law of right reason, that *a child is born a subject of no country or government.* He is under his father's tuition and authority, till he comes to age of discretion; and then he is a freeman, at liberty what government he will put himself under, what body politic he will unite himself to: for if an *Englishman's* son, born in *France,* be at liberty, and may do so, it is evident there is no tie upon him by his father's being a subject of this kingdom; nor is he bound up by any compact of his ancestors. And why then hath not his son, by the same reason, the same liberty, though he be born any where else? Since the power that a father hath naturally over his children, is the same, where-ever they be born, and the ties of natural obligations, are not bounded by the positive limits of kingdoms and common-wealths.

§. 119. *Every man* being, as has been shewed, *naturally free,* and nothing being able to put him into subjection to any earthly power, but only his own *consent*; it is to be considered, *what shall be understood to be a sufficient declaration of a man's consent, to make him subject to the laws of any government.* There is a common distinction of an express and a tacit consent, which will concern our present case. No body doubts but an express *consent*, of any man entering into any society, makes him a perfect member of that society, a subject of that government. The difficulty is, what ought to be looked upon as a *tacit consent*, and how far it binds, *i.e.* how far any one shall be looked on to have consented, and thereby submitted to any government, where he has made no expressions of it at all. And to this I say, that every man, that hath any possessions, or enjoyment, of any part of the dominions of any government, doth thereby give his *tacit consent*, and is as far forth obliged to obedience to the laws of that government, during such enjoyment, as any one under it; whether this his possession be of land, to him and his heirs for ever, or a lodging only for a week; or whether it be barely travelling freely on the highway; and in effect, it reaches as far as the very being of any one within the territories of that government.

§. 120. To understand this the better, it is fit to consider, that every man, when he at first incorporates himself into any common-wealth, he, by his uniting himself thereunto, annexed also, and submits to the community, those possessions, which he has, or shall acquire, that do not already belong to any other government: for it would be a direct contradiction, for any one to enter into society with others for the securing and regulating of property; and yet to suppose his land, whose property is to be regulated by the laws of the society, should be exempt from the jurisdiction of that government, to which he himself, the proprietor of the land, is a subject. By the same act therefore, whereby any one unites his person, which was before free, to any common-wealth, by the same he unites his possessions, which were before free, to it also; and they become both of them, person and possession, subject to the government and dominion of that common-wealth, as long as it hath a being. Whoever therefore, from thenceforth, by inheritance,

purchase, permission, or otherways, *enjoys any part of the land*, so annexed to, and under the government *of that common-wealth, must take it with the condition* it is under; that is, *of submitting to the government of the common-wealth*, under whose jurisdiction it is, as far forth as any subject of it.

§. 121. But since the government has a direct jurisdiction only over the land, and reaches the possessor of it, (before he has actually incorporated himself in the society) only as he dwells upon, and enjoys that; the obligation any one is under, by virtue of such enjoyment, to *submit to the government, begins and ends with the enjoyment*; so that whenever the owner, who has given nothing but such a *tacit consent* to the government, will, by donation, sale, or otherwise, quit the said possession, he is at liberty to go and incorporate himself into any other common-wealth; or to agree with others to begin a new one, *in vacuis locis*, in any part of the world, they can find free and unpossessed: whereas he, that has once, by actual agreement, and any *express* declaration, given his *consent* to be of any common-wealth, is perpetually and indispensibly obliged to be, and remain unalterably a subject to it, and can never be again in the liberty of the state of nature; unless, by any calamity, the government he was under comes to be dissolved; or else by some public act cuts him off from being any longer a member of it.

§. 122. But submitting to the laws of any country, living quietly, and enjoying privileges and protection under them, *makes not a man a member of that society*: this is only a local protection and homage due to and from all those, who, not being in a state of war, come within the territories belonging to any government, to all parts whereof the force of its laws extends. But this no more *makes a man a member of that society*, a perpetual subject of that common-wealth, than it would make a man a subject to another, in whose family he found it convenient to abide for some time; though, whilst he continued in it, he were obliged to comply with the laws, and submit to the government he found there. And thus we see, that *foreigners*, by living all their lives under another government, and enjoying the privileges and protection of it, though they are bound, even in conscience, to submit to its administration, as far forth as any denison; yet do not thereby come to be *subjects or members of that common-wealth*. Nothing can make any man so, but his actually entering into it by positive engagement, and express promise and compact. This is that, which I think, concerning the beginning of political societies, and that *consent which makes any one a member* of any common-wealth.

CHAP. IX

Of the Ends of Political Society and Government

§. 123. If man in the state of nature be so free, as has been said; if he be absolute lord of his own person and possessions, equal to the greatest, and subject to no body, why will he part with his freedom? why will he give up this empire, and subject himself to the dominion and controul of any other power? To which it is obvious to answer, that though in the state of nature he hath such a right, yet the enjoyment of it is very uncertain, and constantly exposed to the invasion of others: for all being kings as much as he, every man his equal, and the greater part no strict observes of equity and justice, the enjoyment of the property he has in this state is very unsafe, very unsecure. This makes him willing to quit a condition, which, however free, is full of fears and continual dangers: and it is not without reason, that he seeks out, and is willing to join in society with others, who are already united, or have a mind to unite, for the mutual *preservation* of their lives, liberties

and estates, which I call by the general name, *property.*

§. 124. The great and *chief end*, therefore, of men's uniting into common-wealths, and putting themselves under government, *is the preservation of their property*. To which in the state of nature there are many things wanting.

First, There wants an *established*, settled, known *law*, received and allowed by common consent to be the standard of right and wrong, and the common measure to decide all controversies between them: for though the law of nature be plain and intelligible to all rational creatures; yet men being biassed by their interest, as well as ignorant for want of study of it, are not apt to allow of it as a law binding to them in the application of it to their particular cases.

§. 125. *Secondly In the state of nature there wants a known and indifferent judge*, with authority to determine all differences according to the established law: for every one in that state being both judge and executioner of the law of nature, men being partial to themselves, passion and revenge is very apt to carry them too far, and with too much heat, in their own cases; as well as negligence, and unconcernedness, to make them too remiss in other men's.

§. 126. *Thirdly, In the state of nature there often wants power to back and support the sentence when right, and to give it due executive.* They who by any injustice offended, will seldom fail, where they are able, by force to make good their injustice; such resistance many times makes the punishment dangerous, and frequently destructive, to those who attempt it.

§. 127. Thus mankind, notwithstanding all the privileges of the state of nature, being but in an ill condition, while they remain in it, are quickly driven into society. Hence it comes to pass, that we seldom find any number of men live any time together in this state. The inconveniencies that they are therein exposed to, by the irregular and uncertain exercise of the power every man has of punishing the transgressions of others, make them take sanctuary under the established laws of government, and therein seek *the preservation of their property*. It is this makes them so willingly give up every one his single power of punishing, to be exercised by such alone, as shall be appointed to it amongst them; and by such rules as the community, or those authorized by them to that purpose, shall agree on. And in this we have the original *right and rise of both the legislative and executive power*, as well as of the governments and societies themselves.

§. 128. *For in the state of nature, to omit the liberty he has of innocent delights, a man has two powers.*

The first is to do whatsoever he thinks fit for the preservation of himself, and others within the permission of the *law of nature*: by which law, common to them all, he and all the rest of *mankind are one community*, make up one society, distinct from all other creatures. And were it not for the corruption and vitiousness of degenerate men, there would be no need of any other; no necessity that men should separate from this great and natural community, and by positive agreements combine into smaller and divided associations.

The other power a man has in the state of nature, is the *power to punish the crimes* committed against that law. Both these he gives up, when he joins in a private, if I may so call it, or particular politic society, and incorporates into any common-wealth, separate from the rest of mankind.

§. 129. The first *power, viz. of doing whatsoever he thought for the preservation of himself*, and the rest of mankind, *he gives up* to be regulated by laws made by the society, so far forth as the preservation of himself, and the rest of that society shall require; which laws of the society in many things confine the liberty he had by the law of nature.

§. 130. *Secondly*, The *power of punishing he wholly gives up*, and engages his natural force, (which he might before employ in the execution of the law of nature, by his own single authority, as he thought fit) *to assist the executive power of the society*, as the law thereof shall require: for being now in a new state, wherein he is to enjoy many conveniencies, from the labour, assistance, and society of others in the same community, as well as protection from its whole strength; he is to part also with as much of his natural liberty, in providing for himself, as the good, prosperity, and safety of the society shall require; which is not only necessary, but just, since the other members of the society do the like.

§. 131. But though men, when they enter into society, give up the equality, liberty, and executive power they had in the state of nature, into the hands of the society, to be so far disposed of by the legislative, as the good of the society shall require; yet it being only with an intention in every one the better to preserve himself, his liberty and property; (for no rational creature can be supposed to change his condition with an intention to be worse) the power of the society, or *legislative* constituted by them, can *never be supposed to extend farther, than the common good*; but is obliged to secure every one's property, by providing against those three defects above mentioned, that made the state of nature so unsafe and uneasy. And so whoever has the legislative or supreme power of any common-wealth, is bound to govern by established *standing laws*, promulgated and known to the people, and not by extemporary decrees; by *indifferent* and upright *judges*, who are to decide controversies by those laws; and to employ the force of the community at home, *only in the execution of such laws*, or abroad to prevent or redress foreign injuries, and secure the community from inroads and invasion. And all this to be directed to no other *end*, but the *peace, safety, and public good* of the people.

CHAP. X

Of the Forms of a Common-wealth

§. 132. The majority having, as has been shewed, upon men's first uniting into society, the whole power of the community naturally in them, may employ all that power in making laws for the community from time to time, and executing those laws by officers of their own appointing; and then the *form* of the government is a perfect *democracy*: or else may put the power of making laws into the hands of a few select men, and their heirs or successors; and then it is an *oligarchy*: or else into the hands of one man, and then it is a *monarchy*: if to him and his heirs, it is an *hereditary monarchy*: if to him only for life, but upon his death the power only of nominating a successor to return to them; an *elective monarchy*. And so accordingly of these the community may make compounded and mixed forms of government, as they think good. And if the legislative power be at first given by the majority to one or more persons only for their lives, or any limited time, and then the supreme power to revert to them again; when it is so reverted, the community may dispose of it again anew into what hands they please, and so constitute a new form of government: for the *form of government depending upon the placing the* supreme power, which is *the legislative*, it being impossible to conceive that an inferior power should prescribe to a superior, or any but the supreme make laws, according as the power of making laws is placed, such is the *form of the common-wealth*.

§. 133. By *common-wealth*, I must be understood all along to mean, not a democracy, or any form of government, but *any independent community*, which the *Latines* signified by the word *civitas*, to which the word which best answers in our language, is *common-wealth*, and most properly expresses such a society of men, which community or city in *English* does not; for there may be subordinate communities in a government; and city amongst us has a quite different notion from common-wealth: and therefore, to avoid ambiguity, I crave leave to use the word *common-wealth* in that sense, in which I find it used by king *James the first*; and I take it to be its genuine signification; which if any body dislike, I consent with him to change it for a better.

CHAP. XI

Of the Extent of the Legislative Power

§. 134. The great end of men's entering into society, being the enjoyment of their properties in peace and safety, and the great instrument and means of that being the laws established in that society; the *first and fundamental positive law* of all common-wealths *is the establishing of the legislative* power; as the *first and fundamental natural law*, which is to govern even the legislative itself, *is the preservation of the society*, and (as far as will consist with the public good) of every person in it. This *legislative* is not only *the supreme power* of the common-wealth, but sacred and unalterable in the hands where the community have once placed it; nor can any edict of any body else, in what form soever conceived, or by what power soever backed, have the force and obligation of a *law*, which has not its *sanction from* that *legislative* which the public has chosen and appointed: for without this the law could not have that, which is absolutely necessary to its being a *law*, *the consent of the society*, over whom no body can have a power to make laws, but by their own consent, and by authority received from them; and therefore all the *obedience*, which by the most solemn ties any one can be obliged to pay, ultimately terminates in this *supreme power*, and is directed by those laws which it enacts: nor can any oaths to any foreign power whatsoever, or any domestic subordinate power, discharge any member of the society from his *obedience to the legislative*, acting pursuant to their trust; nor oblige him to any obedience contrary to the laws so enacted, or farther than they do allow; it being ridiculous to imagine one can be tied ultimately to *obey* any *power* in the society, which is not the *supreme.*

§. 135. *Though the legislative, whether placed in one or more, whether it be always in being, or only by intervals, though it be the supreme power in every common-wealth; yet,*

First, It is *not,* nor can possibly be absolutely *arbitrary* over the lives and fortunes of the people: for it being but the joint power of every member of the society given up to that person, or assembly, which is legislator; it can be no more than those persons had in a state of nature before they entered into society, and gave up to the community: for no body can transfer to another more power than he has in himself; and no body has an absolute arbitrary power over himself, or over any other, to destroy his own life, or take away the life or property of another. A man, as has been proved, cannot subject himself to the arbitrary power of another; and having in the state of nature no arbitrary power over the life, liberty, or possession of another, but only so much as the law of nature gave him for the preservation of himself, and the rest of mankind; this is all he doth, or can give up to the common-wealth, and by it to the *legislative power,* so that the legislative can have no more than this. Their power, in the utmost bounds of it, is *limited to the public good* of the society. It is a power, that hath no other end but preservation, and therefore can never* have a right to destroy, enslave, or designedly to impoverish the subjects. The obligations of the law of nature cease not in society, but only in many cases are drawn closer, and have by human laws known penalties annexed to them, to inforce their observation.

Thus the law of nature stands as an eternal rule to all men, *legislators* as well as others. The *rules* that they make for other men's actions, must, as well as their own and other men's actions, be conformable to the law of nature, *i. e.* to the will of God, of which that is a declaration, and the *fundamental law of nature being the preservation of mankind,* no human sanction can be good, or valid against it.

§. 136. *Secondly,* *The *legislative* or supreme authority, cannot assume to its self a power to rule by extemporary arbitrary decrees, but *is bound to dispense justice,* and decide the rights of the subject *by promulgated standing laws, and known authorized judges*: for the law of nature being unwritten, and so no where to be found but in the minds of men, they who through passion or interest shall miscite, or misapply it, cannot so easily be convinced of their mistake where there is no established judge: and so it serves not, as it ought, to determine the rights, and fence the properties of those that live under it, especially where every one is judge, interpreter, and executioner of it too, and that in his own case: and he that has right on his side, having ordinarily but his own single strength, hath not force enough to defend himself from injuries, or to punish delinquents. To avoid these inconveniences, which disorder men's properties in the state of nature, men unite into societies, that they may have the united strength of the whole society to secure and defend their properties, and may have *standing rules* to bound it, by which every one may know what is his. To this end it is that men give up all their natural power to the society which they enter into, and the community put the legislative power into such hands as they think fit, with this trust, that they shall be governed by *declared laws,* or else their peace, quiet, and property will still be at the same uncertainty, as it was in the state of nature.

§. 137. Absolute arbitrary power, or governing without *settled standing laws,* can neither of them consist with the ends of society and government, which men would not quit the freedom of the state of nature for, and tie themselves up under, were it not to preserve their lives, liberties and fortunes, and by *stated rules* of right and property to secure their peace and quiet. It cannot be supposed that they should intend, had they a power so to do, to give to any one, or more, an *absolute arbitary power* over their persons and estates, and put a force into the magistrate's hand to execute his unlimited will arbitrarily upon them. This were to put themselves into a worse condition than the state of nature, wherein they had a liberty to defend their right against the injuries of others, and were upon equal terms of force to maintain it, whether invaded by a single man, or many in combination. Whereas by supposing they have given up themselves to the *absolute arbitrary power* and will of a legislator, they have disarmed themselves, and armed him, to make a prey of them when he pleases; he being in a much worse condition, who is exposed to the arbitrary power of one man, who has the command of 100,000, than he that is exposed to the arbitrary power of 100,000 single men; no body being secure, that his will, who has such a command, is better than that of other men, though his force be 100,000 times stronger. And therefore, whatever form the common-wealth is under, the ruling power ought to govern by *declared* and *received laws*, and not by extemporary dictates and undetermined resolutions: for then mankind will be in a far worse condition than in the state of nature, if they shall have armed one, or a few men with the joint power of a multitude, to force them to obey at pleasure the exorbitant and unlimited decrees of their sudden thoughts, or unrestrained, and till that moment unknown wills, without having any measures set down which may guide and justify their actions: for all the power the government has, being only for the good of the society, as it ought not to be *arbi-*

trary and at pleasure, so it ought to be exercised by *established and promulgated laws*; that both the people may know their duty, and be safe and secure within the limits of the law; and the rulers too kept within their bounds, and not be tempted, by the power they have in their hands, to employ it to such purposes, and by such measures, as they would not have known, and own not willingly.

§. 138. *Thirdly*, The *supreme power cannot take* from any man any part of his *property* without his own consent: for the preservation of property being the end of government, and that for which men enter into society, it necessarily supposes and requires, that the people should *have property*, without which they must be supposed to lose that, by entering into society, which was the end for which they entered into it; too gross an absurdity for any man to own. *Men* therefore *in society having property*, they have such a right to the goods, which by the law of the community are their's, that no body hath a right to take their substance or any part of it from them, without their own consent: without this they have no *property* at all; for I have truly no *property* in that, which another can by right take from me, when he pleases, against my consent. Hence it is a mistake to think, that the *supreme or legislative power* of any commonwealth, can do what it will, and dispose of the estates of the subject *arbitrarily*, or take any part of them at pleasure. This is not much to be feared in governments where the *legislative* consists, wholly or in part, in assemblies which are variable, whose members, upon the dissolution of the assembly, are subjects under the common laws of their country, equally with the rest. But in governments, where the *legislative* is in one lasting assembly always in being, or in one man, as in absolute monarchies, there is danger still, that they will think themselves to have a distinct interest from the rest of the community; and so will be apt to increase their own riches and power, by taking what they think fit from the people: for a man's *property* is not at all secure, tho' there be good and equitable laws to set the bounds of it between him and his fellow subjects, if he who commands those subjects have power to take from any private man, what part he pleases of his *property*, and use and dispose of it as he thinks good.

§. 139. But *government*, into whatsoever hands it is put, being, as I have before shewed, intrusted with this condition, and *for this end*, that men might have and secure their *properties*: the prince, or senate, however it may have power to make laws, for the regulating of *property* between the subjects one amongst another, yet can never have a power to take to themselves the whole, or any part of the subjects *property*, without their own consent: for this would be in effect to leave them no *property* at all. And to let us see, that even *absolute power*, where it is necessary, is *not arbitrary* by being absolute, but is still limited by that reason, and confined to those ends, which required it in some cases to be absolute, we need look no farther than the common practice of martial discipline: for the preservation of the army, and in it of the whole common-wealth, requires an *absolute obedience* to the command of every superior officer, and it is justly death to disobey or dispute the most dangerous or unreasonable of them; but yet we see, that neither the serjeant, that could command a soldier to march up to the mouth of a cannon, or stand in a breach, where he is almost sure to perish, can command that soldier to give him one penny of his money; nor the *general*, that can condemn him to death for deserting his post, or for not obeying the most desperate orders, can yet, with all his *absolute power* of life and death, dispose of one farthing of that soldier's estate, or seize one jot of his goods; whom yet he can command any thing, and hang for the least disobedience; because such a blind obedience is necessary to that end,

for which the commander has his power, *viz.* the preservation of the rest; but the disposing of his goods has nothing to do with it.

§. 140. It is true, governments cannot be supported without great charge, and it is fit every one who enjoys his share of the protection, should pay out of his estate his proportion for the maintenance of it. But still it must be with his own consent, *i.e.* the consent of the majority, giving it either by themselves, or their representatives chosen by them: for if any one shall claim a *power to lay* and levy *taxes* on the people, by his own authority, and without such consent of the people, he thereby invades the *fundamental law of property*, and subverts the end of government: for what property have I in that, which another may by right take, when he pleases, to himself?

§. 141. *Fourthly,* The *legislative cannot transfer the power of making laws* to any other hands: for it being but a delegated power from the people, they who have it cannot pass it over to others. The people alone can appoint the form of the common-wealth, which is by constituting the legislative, and appointing in whose hands that shall be. And when the people have said, We will submit to rules, and be governed by *laws* made by such men, and in such forms, no body else can say other men shall make *laws* for them; nor can the people be bound by any *laws,* but such as are enacted by those whom they have chosen, and authorized to make *laws* for them. The power of the *legislative*, being derived from the people by a positive voluntary grant and institution, can be no other than what that positive grant conveyed, which being only to make *laws*, and not to make *legislators*, the *legislative* can have no power to transfer their authority of making laws, and place it in other hands.

§. 142. These are the *bounds* which the trust, that is put in them by the society, and the law of God and nature, have *set to the legislative* power of every common-wealth, in all forms of government.

First, They are to govern by *promulgated established laws,* not to be varied in particular cases, but to have one rule for rich and poor, for the favourite at court, and the country man at plough.

Secondly, These *laws* also ought to be designed *for* no other end ultimately, but *the good of the people.*

Thirdly, They must *not raises taxes* on the *property of the people, without the consent of the people,* given by themselves, or their deputies. And this properly concerns only such governments where the *legislative* is always in being, or at least where the people have not reserved any part of the legislative to deputies, to be from time to time chosen by themselves.

Fourthly, The *legislative* neither must *nor can transfer the power of making laws* to any body else, or place it any where, but where the people have.

*The lawful power of making laws to command whole politic societies of men, belonging so properly unto the same intire societies, that for any prince or potentate of what kind soever upon earth, to exercise the same of himself, and not by express commission immediately and personally received from God, or else by authority derived at the first from their consent, upon whose persons they impose laws, it is no better than mere tyranny. Laws they are not therefore which public approbation hath not made so. *Hooker's Eccl. Pol. l.* i. *sect.* 10. Of this point therefore we are to note, that sith men naturally have no full and perfect power to command whole politic multitudes of men, therefore utterly without our consent, we could in such sort be at no man's commandment living. And to be commanded we do consent,

when that society, whereof we be a part, hath at any time before consented, without revoking the same after by the like universal agreement.

Laws therefore human, of what kind so ever, are available by consent. *Ibid.*

*Two foundations there are which bear up public societies; the one a natural inclination, whereby all men desire sociable life and fellowship; the other an order, expresly or secretly agreed upon, touching the manner of their union in living together: the latter is that which we call the law of a common-weal, the very soul of a politic body, the parts whereof are by law animated, held together, and set on work in such actions as the common good requireth. Laws politic, ordained for external order and regiment amongst men, are never framed as they should be, unless presuming the will of man to be inwardly obstinate, rebellious, and averse from all obedience to the sacred laws of his nature; in a word, unless presuming man to be, in regard of his depraved mind, little better than a wild beast, they do accordingly provide, notwithstanding, so to frame his outward actions, that they be no hindrance unto the common good, for which societies are instituted. Unless they do this, they are not perfect. *Hooker's Eccl. Pol. l.* i. *sect.* 10.

*Human laws are measures in respect of men whose actions they must direct, howbeit such measures they are as have also their higher rules to be measured by, which rules are two, the law of God, and the law of nature; so that laws human must be made according to the general laws of nature, and without contradiction to any positive law of scripture, otherwise they are ill made. *Hooker's Eccl. Pol. l.* iii. *sect. 9.*

To constrain men to any thing inconvenient doth seem unreasonable. *Ibid. l.* i. sect. 10.

Theories of Human Nature, Governmental Authority, and Political Legitimacy

overnmental Authority can be exercised only if the form of government and its techniques for governing are capable of motivating people to accept or at least obey the government. If there is a fixed human nature, then this nature has to be taken into account in formulating a philosophy of Governmental Authority. The philosophers we have read to this point hold different views of human nature, and these differences imply differences in their Theories of Authority. A philosopher's Theory of Human Nature also determines whether and how governmental authority can be legitimate or justified. The Theory of Governmental Authority espoused by a philosopher can be summarized by a principle of government summarizing the most important rules or virtues of the ruler. Likewise, the Theory of Legitimacy can be summarized by a Principle of Legitimacy that specifies the conditions, which

a Governmental Authority must meet to be justified in its use of coercive force to guide the people's behavior.

Consider the philosophers we have read to this point and how their views of human nature have influenced their views of authority and legitimacy of government. Do the Theories of Government they propose follow from or conflict with their views of human nature? Do their views of human nature seem correct to you? Because these philosophers offer different Theories of Governmental Authority and Legitimacy, at least some of them must be mistaken. If you reject any of the views of government, is that because of a faulty (in your view) Theory of Human Nature? The following table compares views of human nature (HN) and the resulting principles of government and of legitimacy among the Chinese and the Western philosophers we have read.

Philosopher	Theory of Human Nature	Principle of Government	Legitimation Principle
Confucius/Mencius	HN is good; inequality of ability	Benevolence; ruler sets example	Prosperity, tradition
Mo Tzu	HN potentially good; equality of ability	Authoritarian rule; universal love	Satisfaction of basic needs of greatest number
Hsun Tzu	HN is evil; inequality of ability	Authoritarian rule by the virtuous	Secure virtue in the masses
Chuang Tzu	HN is benevolent, but unchangeable; self-interested	Nongovernment; anarchism	No legitimate government
Hobbes	HN is selfish	Authoritarian rule by self-interested	Maintain power; keep peace
Locke	HN is benevolent self-interested	Liberalism	Consent of governed

The Declaration of Independence

IN CONGRESS, July 4, 1776

THE UNANIMOUS DECLARATION OF THE THIRTEEN UNITED STATES OF AMERICA

When in the Course of human events, it becomes necessary for one people to dissolve the political bands which have connected them with another, and to assume among the powers of the earth, the separate and equal station to which the Laws of Nature and of Nature's God entitle them, a decent respect to the opinions of mankind requires that they should declare the causes which impel them to the separation.

We hold these truths to be self-evident, that all men are created equal, that they are endowed by their Creator with certain unalienable Rights, that among these are Life, Liberty and the pursuit of Happiness.—That to secure these rights, Governments are instituted among Men, deriving their just powers from the consent of the governed, —That whenever any Form of Government becomes destructive of these ends, it is the Right of the People to alter or to abolish it, and to institute new Government, laying its foundation on such principles and organizing its powers in such form, as to them shall seem most likely to effect their Safety and Happiness. Prudence, indeed, will dictate that Governments long established should not be changed for light and transient causes; and accordingly all experience hath shewn, that mankind are more disposed to suffer, while evils are sufferable, than to right themselves by abolishing the forms to which they are accustomed. But when a long train of abuses and usurpations, pursuing invariably the same Object evinces a design to reduce them under absolute Despotism, it is their right, it is their duty, to throw off such Government, and to provide new Guards for their future security.—Such has been the patient sufferance of these Colonies; and such is now the necessity which constrains them to alter their former Systems of Government. The history of the present King of Great Britain is a history of repeated injuries and usurpations, all having in direct object the establishment of an absolute Tyranny over these States. To prove this, let Facts be submitted to a candid world.

He has refused his Assent to Laws, the most wholesome and necessary for the public good.

He has forbidden his Governors to pass Laws of immediate and pressing importance, unless suspended in their operation till his Assent should be obtained; and when so suspended, he has utterly neglected to attend to them.

He has refused to pass other Laws for the accommodation of large districts of people, unless those people would relinquish the right of Representation in the Legislature, a right inestimable to them and formidable to tyrants only.

He has called together legislative bodies at places unusual, uncomfortable, and distant from the depository of their public Records, for the sole purpose of fatiguing them into compliance with his measures.

He has dissolved Representative Houses repeatedly, for opposing with manly firmness his invasions on the rights of the people.

He has refused for a long time, after such dissolutions, to cause others to be elected; whereby the Legislative powers, incapable of Annihilation, have returned to the People at large for their exercise; the State remaining in the mean time exposed to all the dangers of invasion from without, and convulsions within.

He has endeavoured to prevent the population of these States; for that purpose obstructing the Laws for Naturalization of Foreigners; refusing to pass others to encourage their migrations hither, and raising the conditions of new Appropriations of Lands.

He has obstructed the Administration of Justice, by refusing his Assent to Laws for establishing Judiciary powers.

He has made Judges dependent on his Will alone, for the tenure of their offices, and the amount and payment of their salaries.

He has erected a multitude of New Offices, and sent hither swarms of Officers to harrass our people, and eat out their substance.

He has kept among us, in times of peace, Standing Armies without the Consent of our legislatures.

He has affected to render the Military independent of and superior to the Civil power.

He has combined with others to subject us to a jurisdiction foreign to our constitution, and unacknowledged by our laws; giving his Assent to their Acts of pretended Legislation:

For Quartering large bodies of armed troops among us:

For protecting them, by a mock Trial, from punishment for any Murders which they should commit on the Inhabitants of these States:

For cutting off our Trade with all parts of the world:

For imposing Taxes on us without our Consent:

For depriving us in many cases, of the benefits of Trial by Jury:

For transporting us beyond Seas to be tried for pretended offences

For abolishing the free System of English Laws in a neighbouring Province, establishing therein an Arbitrary government, and enlarging its Boundaries so as to render it at once an example and fit instrument for introducing the same absolute rule into these Colonies:

For taking away our Charters, abolishing our most valuable Laws, and altering fundamentally the Forms of our Governments:

For suspending our own Legislatures, and declaring themselves invested with power to legislate for us in all cases whatsoever.

He has abdicated Government here, by declaring us out of his Protection and waging War against us.

He has plundered our seas, ravaged our Coasts, burnt our towns, and destroyed the lives of our people.

He is at this time transporting large Armies of foreign Mercenaries to compleat the works of death, desolation and tyranny, already begun with circumstances of Cruelty & perfidy scarcely paralleled in the most barbarous ages, and totally unworthy the Head of a civilized nation.

He has constrained our fellow Citizens taken Captive on the high Seas to bear Arms against their Country, to become the executioners of their friends and Brethren, or to fall themselves by their Hands.

He has excited domestic insurrections amongst us, and has endeavoured to bring on the inhabitants of our frontiers, the merciless Indian Savages, whose known rule of warfare, is an undistinguished destruction of all ages, sexes and conditions.

In every stage of these Oppressions We have Petitioned for Redress in the most humble terms: Our repeated Petitions have been answered only by repeated injury. A Prince whose character is thus marked by every act which may define a Tyrant, is unfit to be the ruler of a free people.

Nor have We been wanting in attentions to our Brittish brethren. We have warned them from time to time of attempts by their legislature to extend an unwarrantable jurisdiction over us. We have reminded them of the circumstances of our emigration and settlement here. We have appealed to their native justice and magnanimity, and we have conjured them by the ties of our common kindred to disavow these usurpations, which, would inevitably interrupt our connections and correspondence. They too have been deaf to the voice of justice and of consanguinity. We must, therefore, acquiesce in the necessity, which denounces our Separation, and hold them, as we hold the rest of mankind, Enemies in War, in Peace Friends.

We, therefore, the Representatives of the united States of America, in General Congress, Assembled, appealing to the Supreme Judge of the world for the rectitude of our intentions, do, in the Name, and by Authority of the good People of these Colonies, solemnly publish and declare, That these United Colonies are, and of Right ought to be Free and Independent States; that they are Absolved from all Allegiance to the British Crown, and that all political connection between them and the State of Great Britain, is and ought to be totally dissolved; and that as Free and Independent States, they have full Power to levy War, conclude Peace, contract Alliances, establish Commerce, and to do all other Acts and Things which Independent States may of right

do. And for the support of this Declaration, with a firm reliance on the protection of divine Providence, we mutually pledge to each other our Lives, our Fortunes and our sacred Honor.

The 56 signatures on the Declaration appear in the positions indicated:

Column 1

Georgia
   Button Gwinnett
   Lyman Hall
   George Walton

Column 2

North Carolina
   William Hooper
   Joseph Hewes
   John Penn

South Carolina
   Edward Rutledge
   Thomas Heyward, Jr.
   Thomas Lynch, Jr.
   Arthur Middleton

Column 3

Massachusetts
   John Hancock

Maryland
   Samuel Chase
   William Paca
   Thomas Stone
   Charles Carroll of Carrollton

Virginia
   George Wythe
   Richard Henry Lee
   Thomas Jefferson
   Benjamin Harrison
   Thomas Nelson, Jr.
   Francis Lightfoot Lee
   Carter Braxton

Column 4

Pennsylvania
Robert Morris
Benjamin Rush
Benjamin Franklin
John Morton
George Clymer
James Smith
George Taylor
James Wilson
George Ross

Delaware
Caesar Rodney
George Read
Thomas McKean

Column 5

New York
William Floyd
Philip Livingston
Francis Lewis
Lewis Morris

New Jersey
Richard Stockton
John Witherspoon
Francis Hopkinson
John Hart
Abraham Clark

Column 6

New Hampshire
Josiah Bartlett
William Whipple

Massachusetts
Samuel Adams
John Adams
Robert Treat Paine
Elbridge Gerry

Rhode Island
Stephen Hopkins
William Ellery

Connecticut
Roger Sherman
Samuel Huntington
William Williams
Oliver Wolcott

New Hampshire
Matthew Thornton

John Stuart Mill

John Stuart Mill (1806-1873) was born in London and educated privately by his father, the economist James Mill, and his friend the moral and legal philosopher Jeremy Bentham. The elder Mill and Bentham made an experiment of John Stuart, in order to prove their Progressive Theory that anyone could be made into a genius with the correct upbringing. John Stuart Mill claimed in his autobiography that he learned to write and was beginning to translate Greek and Latin by age three. In addition to classical literature and philosophy, he was taught mathematics and philosophy of Utilitarianism, which was founded by Bentham. The fact that the younger Mill did, indeed, turn out to be a genius, however, cannot be taken to prove their theory, because the sample size of one could hardly constitute such proof. Being a guinea pig for his father's experiment was not altogether healthy for John Stuart, for when he was 18 years old he became depressed because, he explained, his education and training had focused on rational analysis to the exclusion of emotion, sympathy, or art. He brought himself out of it by reading Romantic literature and poetry, a kind of indulgence of which his father disapproved. John Stuart Mill was the companion and later the husband of Harriet Taylor, with whom he formulated many of his ideas. *On Liberty* is in some sense their joint product, as they discussed and edited the work together, and he published it shortly after her sudden death.

Mill propounded three main theses in moral and political philosophy. The first of these, Utilitarianism, he expounded in his book entitled *Utilitarianism* (1861), holds that the moral action in each case is that action that brings the greatest good for the greatest number, where good is measured subjectively, by what brings pleasure to individuals. He appeals to this principle in *On Liberty*, but as he says there he means utility in the larger sense of utility of man as a progressive being. His second main thesis is feminism, that men and women are morally equal and that the inequalities of the sexes are unjust and largely of social origin. His great feminist work is *The Subjection of Women* (1858). In *On Liberty*, Mill expounds the third of his main theses: Liberalism. Liberalism in the modern sense of the term is the Theory of Political Authority that prizes individual liberty above all other values. Liberals are not anarchists, however, because they do not think that individual liberty is maximized in the absence of a political state. Rather, law is needed to keep individuals from interfering with each other's liberty, but the power of the state must also be carefully circumscribed.

STUDY QUESTIONS:

1. How does Mill employ the utilitarian principle to argue for Liberalism?

2. Mill argues that there are some cases where the state may restrict an individual's liberty when the individual is harming herself. What are those cases?

3. Why does Mill think that there should be religious freedom?

On Liberty

Chapter IV Of the Limits to the Authority of Society Over the Individual

What, then, is the rightful limit to the sovereignty of the individual over himself? Where does the authority of society begin? How much of human life should be assigned to individuality, and how much to society?

Each will receive its proper share if each has that which more particularly concerns it. To individuality should belong the part of life in which it is chiefly the individual that is interested; to society, the part which chiefly interests society.

Though society is not founded on a contract, and though no good purpose is answered by inventing a contract in order to deduce social obligations from it, everyone who receives the protection of society owes a return for the benefit, and the fact of living in society renders it indispensable that each should be bound to observe a certain line of conduct toward the rest. *This conduct consists, first, in not injuring the interests of one another, or rather certain interests which, either by express legal provision or by tacit understanding, ought to be considered as rights; and secondly, in each person's bearing his share (to be fixed on some equitable principle) of the labors and sacrifices incurred for defending the society or its members from injury and molestation.* These conditions society is justified in enforcing at all costs to those who endeavor to withhold fulfillment. Nor is this all that society may do. The acts of an individual may be hurtful to others or wanting in due consideration for their welfare, without going to the length of violating any of their constituted rights. The offender may then be justly punished by opinion, though not by law. As soon as any part of a person's conduct affects prejudicially the interests of others, society has jurisdiction over it, and the question whether the general welfare will or will not be promoted by interfering with it becomes open to discussion. But there is no room for entertaining any such question when a person's conduct affects the interests of no persons besides himself, or needs not affect them unless they like (all the persons concerned being of full age and the ordinary amount of understanding). In all such cases, there should be perfect freedom, legal and social, to do the action and stand the consequences.

From *On Liberty* by John Stuart Mill. First published in 1859.

It would be a great misunderstanding of this doctrine to suppose that it is one of selfish indifference which pretends that human beings have no business with each other's conduct in life, and that they should not concern themselves about the well-doing or well-being of one another, unless their own interest is involved. *Instead of any diminution, there is need of a great increase of disinterested exertion to promote the good of others.* But disinterested benevolence can find other instruments to persuade people to their good than whips and scourges, either of the literal or the metaphorical sort. I am the last person to undervalue the self-regarding virtues; they are only second in importance, if even second, to the social. It is equally the business of education to cultivate both. But even education works by conviction and persuasion as well as by compulsion, and it is by the former only that, when the period of education is passed, the self-regarding virtues should be inculcated. Human beings owe to each other help to distinguish the better from the worse, and encouragement to choose the former and avoid the latter. They should be forever stimulating each other to increased exercise of their higher faculties and increased direction of their feelings and aims toward wise instead of foolish, elevating instead of degrading, objects and contemplations. But neither one person, nor any number of persons, is warranted in saying to another human creature of ripe years that he shall not do with his life for his own benefit what he chooses to do with it. He is the person most interested in his own well-being: the interest which any other person, except in cases of strong personal attachment, can have in it is trifling compared with that which he himself has; the interest which society has in him individually (except as to his conduct to others) is fractional and altogether indirect, while with respect to his own feelings and circumstances the most ordinary *man or woman has means of*

knowledge immeasurably surpassing those that can be possessed by anyone else. The interference of society to overrule his judgment and purposes in what only regards himself must be grounded on general presumptions which may be altogether wrong and, even if right, are as likely as not to be misapplied to individual cases, by persons no better acquainted with the circumstances of such cases than those are who look at them merely from without. In this department, therefore, of human affairs, individuality has its proper field of action. In the conduct of human beings toward one another it is necessary that general rules should for the most part be observed in order that people may know what they have to expect; but in each person's own concerns his individual spontaneity is entitled to free exercise. *Considerations to aid his judgment, exhortations to strengthen his will may be offered to him, even obtruded on him, by others; but he himself is the final judge. All errors which he is likely to commit against advice and warning are far outweighed by the evil of allowing others to constrain him to what they deem his good.*

I do not mean that the feelings with which a person is regarded by others ought not to be in any way affected by his self-regarding qualities or deficiencies. This is neither possible nor desirable. If he is eminent in any of the qualities which conduce to his own good, he is, so far, a proper object of admiration. He is so much the nearer to the ideal perfection of human nature. If he is grossly deficient in those qualities, a sentiment the opposite of admiration will follow. There is a degree of folly, and a degree of what may be called (though the phrase is not unobjectionable) lowness or depravation of taste, which, though it cannot justify doing harm to the person who manifests it, renders him necessarily and properly a subject of distaste, or, in extreme cases, even of contempt: a person could not have the opposite qualities in due strength without entertaining these feelings.

Though doing no wrong to anyone, a person may so act as to compel us to judge him, and feel to him, as a fool or as a being of an inferior order; and since this judgment and feeling are a fact which he would prefer to avoid, it is doing him a service to warn him of it before-hand, as of any other disagreeable consequence to which he exposes himself. It would be well, indeed, if this good office were much more freely rendered than the common notions of politeness at present permit, and if one person could honestly point out to another that he thinks him in fault, without being considered unmannerly or presuming. We have a right, also, in various ways, to act upon our unfavorable opinion of anyone, not to the oppression of his individuality, but in the exercise of ours. We are not bound, for example, to seek his society; we have a right to avoid it (though not to parade the avoidance), for we have a right to choose the society most acceptable to us. We have a right, and it may be our duty, to caution others against him if we think his example or conversation likely to have a pernicious effect on those with whom he associates. We may give others a preference over him in optional good offices, except those which tend to his improvement. In these various modes a person may suffer very severe penalties at the hands of others for faults which directly concern only himself; but he suffers these penalties only in so far as they are the natural and, as it were, the spontaneous consequences of the faults themselves, not because they are purposely inflicted on him for the sake of punishment. A person who shows rashness, obstinacy, self-conceit—who cannot live within moderate means; who cannot restrain himself from hurtful indulgence; who pursues animal pleasures at the expense of those of feeling and intellect—must expect to be lowered in the opinion of others, and to have a less share of their favorable sentiments; but of this he has no right to complain unless he has merited their favor by special excellence in his social relations and has thus established a title to their good offices, which is not affected by his demerits toward himself.

What I contend for is that the inconveniences which are strictly inseparable from the unfavorable judgment of others are the only ones to which a person should ever be subjected for that portion of his conduct and character which concerns his own good, but which does not affect the interest of others in their relations with him. *Acts injurious to others require a totally different treatment. Encroachment on their rights; infliction on them of any loss or damage not justified by his own rights; falsehood or duplicity in dealing with them; unfair or ungenerous use of advantages over them; even selfish abstinence from defending them against injury—these are fit objects of moral reprobation and, in grave cases, of moral retribution and punishment.* And not only these acts, but the dispositions which lead to them, are properly immoral and fit subjects of disapprobation which may rise to abhorrence. Cruelty of disposition; malice and ill-nature; that most antisocial and odious of all passions, envy; dissimulation and insincerity, irascibility on insufficient cause, and resentment disproportioned to the provocation; the love of domineering over others; the desire to engross more than one's share of advantages (the *pleonexia*[1] of the Greeks); the pride which derives gratification from the abasement of others; the egotism which thinks self and its concerns more important than everything else, and decides all doubtful questions in its own favor—these are moral vices and constitute a bad and odious moral character; unlike the self-regarding faults previously mentioned, which are not properly immoralities and, to whatever pitch they may be carried, do not constitute wickedness. They may be proofs of any amount of folly or want of personal dignity and self-respect, but they are only a subject of moral reprobation when they involve a breach of duty to others, for whose sake the individual is bound to have care for himself. What are called duties to ourselves are not socially obligatory unless circumstances render them at the same time duties to others. *The term duty to oneself, when it means anything more than prudence, means self-respect or self-development, and for none of these is anyone accountable to his fellow creatures, because for none of them is it for the good of mankind that he be held accountable to them.*

The distinction between the loss of consideration which a person may rightly incur by defect of prudence or of personal dignity, and the reprobation which is due to him for an offense against the rights of others, is not a merely nominal distinction. It makes a vast difference both in our feelings and in our conduct toward him whether he displeases us in things in which we think we have a right to control him or in things in which we know that we have not. If he displeases us, we may express our distaste, and we may stand aloof from a person as well as from a thing that displeases us; but we shall not therefore feel called on to make his life uncomfortable. We shall reflect that he already bears, or will bear, the whole penalty of his error; *if he spoils his life by mismanagement, we shall not, for that reason, desire to spoil it still further; instead of wishing to punish him, we shall rather endeavor to alleviate his punishment by showing him how he may avoid or cure the evils his conduct tends to bring upon him.* He may be to us an object of pity, perhaps of dislike, but not of anger or resentment; we shall not treat him like an enemy of society; the worst we shall think ourselves justified in doing is leaving him to himself, if we do not interfere benevolently by showing interest or concern for him. It is far otherwise if he has infringed the rules necessary for the protection of his fellow creatures, individually or collectively. The evil consequences of his acts do not then fall on himself, but on

others; and society, as the protector of all its members, must retaliate on him, must inflict pain on him for the express purpose of punishment, and must take care that it be sufficiently severe. In the one case, he is an offender at our bar, and we are called on not only to sit in judgment on him, but, in one shape or another, to execute our own sentence; in the other case, it is not our part to inflict any suffering on him, except what may incidentally follow from our using the same liberty in the regulation of our own affairs which we allow to him in his.

The distinction here pointed out between the part of a person's life which concerns only himself and that which concerns others, many persons will refuse to admit. *How (it may be asked) can any part of the conduct of a member of society be a matter of indifference to the other members?* No person is an entirely isolated being; it is impossible for a person to do anything seriously or permanently hurtful to himself without mischief reaching at least to his near connections, and often far beyond them. If he injures his property, he does harm to those who directly or indirectly derived support from it, and usually diminishes, by a greater or less amount, the general resources of the community. *If he deteriorates his bodily or mental faculties*, he not only brings evil upon all who depended upon him for any portion of their happiness, but disqualifies himself for rendering the services which he owes to his fellow creatures generally, perhaps becomes a burden on their affection or benevolence; and if such conduct were very frequent hardly any offense that is committed would detract more from the general sum of good. Finally, if by his vices or follies a person does no direct harm to others, he is nevertheless (it may be said) injurious by his example, and ought to be compelled to control himself for the sake of those whom the sight or knowledge of his conduct might corrupt or mislead.

And even (it will be added) if the consequences of misconduct could be confined to the vicious or thoughtless individual, ought society to abandon to their own guidance those who are manifestly unfit for it? If protection against themselves is confessedly due to children and persons under age, is not society equally bound to afford it to persons of mature years who are equally incapable of self-government? If gambling, or drunkenness, or incontinence, or idleness, or uncleanliness are as injurious to happiness, and as great a hindrance to improvement, as many or most of the acts prohibited by law, why (it may be asked) should not law, so far as is consistent with practicability and social convenience, endeavor to repress these also? And as a supplement to the unavoidable imperfections of law, ought not opinion at least to organize a powerful police against these vices and visit rigidly with social penalties those who are known to practice them? There is no question here (it may be said) about restricting individuality, or impeding the trial of new and original experiments in living. The only things it is sought to prevent are things which have been tried and condemned from the beginning of the world until now—things which experience has shown not to be useful or suitable to any person's individuality. There must be some length of time and amount of experience after which a moral or prudential truth may be regarded as established; and it is merely desired to prevent generation after generation from falling over the same precipice which has been fatal to their predecessors.

I fully admit that the mischief which a person does to himself may seriously affect, both through their sympathies and their interests, those nearly connected with him and, in a minor degree, society at large. *When, by conduct of this sort, a person is led to violate a distinct and assignable obligation to any other person or persons, the case is taken out of the self-regarding class and becomes amenable to moral disapprobation in the proper sense of the term.* If, for example, a man, through intemperance or extravagance, becomes *unable to pay his debts, or, having undertaken the moral responsibility of a family, becomes from the same cause incapable of supporting or educating them,* he is deservedly reprobated and might be justly punished; *but it is for the breach of duty to his family or creditors, not for the extravagance.* If the resources which ought to have been devoted to them had been diverted from them for the most prudent investment, the moral culpability would have been the same. George Barnwell[2] murdered his uncle to get money for his mistress, but if he had done it to set himself up in business, he would equally have been hanged. Again, in the frequent case of a man who causes grief to his family by addiction to bad habits, he deserves reproach for his unkindness or ingratitude; but so he may for cultivating habits not in themselves vicious, if they are painful to those with whom he passes his life, or who from personal ties are dependent on him for their comfort. Whoever fails in the consideration generally due to the interests and feelings of others, not being compelled by some more imperative duty, or justified by allowable self-preference, is a subject of moral disapprobation for that failure, but not for the cause of it, nor for the errors, merely personal to himself, which may have remotely led to it. In like manner, when a person disables himself, by conduct purely self-regarding, from the performance of some definite duty incumbent on him to the public, he is guilty of a social offense. No person ought to be punished simply for being drunk; but a soldier or policeman should be punished for being drunk on duty. Whenever, in short, there is a definite damage, or a definite risk of damage, either to an individual or to the public, the case is taken out of the province of liberty and placed in that of morality or law.

But with regard to the merely contingent or, as it may be called, constructive injury which a person causes to society by *conduct which neither violates any specific duty to the public,* nor occasions perceptible hurt to *any assignable individual except himself,* the inconvenience is one which society can afford to bear, for the sake of the greater good of human freedom. If grown persons are to be punished for not taking proper care of themselves, I would rather it were for their own sake than under pretense of preventing them from impairing their capacity or rendering to society benefits which society does not pretend it has a right to exact. But I cannot consent to argue the point as if society had no means of bringing its weaker members up to its ordinary standard of rational conduct, except waiting till they do something irrational, and then punishing them, legally or morally, for it. Society has had absolute power over them during all the early portion of their existence; it has had the whole period of childhood and nonage in which to try whether it could make them capable of rational conduct in life. The existing generation is master both of the training and the entire circumstances of the generation to come; it cannot indeed make them perfectly wise and good, because it is itself so lamentably deficient in goodness and wisdom; and its best efforts are not always, in individual cases, its most successful ones; but it is perfectly well able to make the rising generation, as a whole, as good as, and a little better than, itself. If society lets any considerable number of its members grow up mere children, incapable of being acted on by rational consideration of distant motives, society has itself to blame for the consequences. Armed not only with all the powers of education, but with the ascendency which the authority of a received opinion always exercises over the minds who are least fitted to judge for themselves, and aided by the *natural* penalties which cannot be

prevented from falling on those who incur the distaste or the contempt of those who know them—let not society pretend that it needs, besides all this, the power to issue commands and enforce obedience in the personal concerns of individuals in which, on all principles of justice and policy, the decision ought to rest with those who are to abide the consequences. Nor is there anything which tends more to discredit and frustrate the better means of influencing conduct than a resort to the worse. If there be among those whom it is attempted to coerce into prudence or temperance any of the material of which vigorous and independent characters are made, they will infallibly rebel against the yoke. No such person will ever feel that others have a right to control him in his concerns, such as they have to prevent him from injuring them in theirs; and it easily comes to be considered a mark of spirit and courage to fly in the face of such usurped authority and do with ostentation the exact opposite of what it enjoins, as in the fashion of grossness which succeeded, in the time of Charles II, to the fanatical moral intolerance of the Puritans. With respect to what is said of the necessity of protecting society from the bad example set to others by the vicious or the self-indulgent, it is true that bad example may have a pernicious effect, especially the example of doing wrong to others with impunity to the wrongdoer. But we are now speaking of conduct which, while it does no wrong to others, is supposed to do great harm to the agent himself; and I do not see how those who believe this can think otherwise than that the example, on the whole, must be more salutary than hurtful, since, if it displays the misconduct, it displays also the painful or degrading consequences which, if the conduct is justly censured, must be supposed to be in all or most cases attendant on it.

But the strongest of all the arguments against the interference of the public with purely personal conduct is that, when it does interfere, the odds are that it interferes wrongly and in the wrong place. *On questions of social morality of duty to others, the opinion of the public, that is, of an overruling majority, though often wrong, is likely to be still oftener right,* because on such questions they are only required to judge of their own interests, of the manner in which some mode of conduct, if allowed to be practiced, would affect themselves. But the opinion of a similar majority, imposed as a law on the minority, on questions of self-regarding conduct is quite as likely to be wrong as right, for in these cases public opinion means, at the best, some people's opinion of what is good or bad for other people, while very often it does not even mean that—the public, with the most perfect indifference, passing over the pleasure or convenience of those whose conduct they censure and considering only their own preference. There are many who consider as an injury to themselves any conduct which they have a distaste for, and resent it as an outrage to their feelings; as a religious bigot, when charged with disregarding the religious feelings of others, has been known to retort that they disregard his feelings by persisting in their abominable worship or creed. But there is no parity between the feeling of a person for his own opinion and the feeling of another who is offended at his holding it, no more than between the desire of a thief to take a purse and the desire of the right owner to keep it. And a person's taste is as much his own peculiar concern as his opinion or his purse. It is easy for anyone to imagine an ideal public which leaves the freedom and choice of individuals in all uncertain matters undisturbed and only requires them to abstain from modes of conduct which universal experience has condemned. But where has there been seen a public which set any such limit to its censorship? Or when does the public trouble itself about universal experience? In

its interferences with personal conduct it is seldom thinking of anything but the enormity of acting or feeling differently from itself; and this standard of judgment, thinly disguised, is held up to mankind as the dictate of religion and philosophy by nine-tenths of all moralists and speculative writers. These teach that things are right because they are right; because we feel them to be so. They tell us to search in our own minds and hearts for laws of conduct binding on ourselves and on all others. What can the poor public do but apply these instructions and make their own personal feelings of good and evil, if they are tolerably unanimous in them, obligatory on all the world?

The evil here pointed out is not one which exists only in theory; and it may perhaps be expected that I should specify the instances in which the public of this age and country improperly invests its own preferences with the character of moral laws. I am not writing an essay on the aberrations of existing moral feeling. That is too weighty a subject to be discussed parenthetically, and by way of illustration. Yet examples are necessary to show that the principle I maintain is of serious and practical moment, and that I am not endeavoring to erect a barrier against imaginary evils. And it is not difficult to show, by abundant instances, that to extend the bounds of what may be called moral police until it encroaches on the most unquestionably legitimate liberty of the individual is one of the most universal of all human propensities.

As a first instance, consider the antipathies which men cherish on no better grounds than that persons whose religious opinions are different from theirs do not practice their religious observances, especially their religious abstinences. To cite a rather trivial example, nothing in the creed or practice of Christians does more to envenom the hatred of Mohammedans against them than the fact of their eating pork. There are few acts which Christians and Europeans regard with more unaffected disgust than Mussulmans regard this particular mode of satisfying hunger. It is in the first place, an offense against their religion; but this circumstance by no means explains either the degree or the kind of their repugnance; for wine also is forbidden by their religion, and to partake of it is by all Mussulmans accounted wrong, but not disgusting. Their aversion to the flesh of the "unclean beast" is, on the contrary, of that peculiar character, resembling an instinctive antipathy, which the idea of uncleanness, when once it thoroughly sinks into the feelings, seems always to excite even in those whose personal habits are anything but scrupulously cleanly, and of which the sentiment of religious impurity, so intense in the Hindus, is a remarkable example, Suppose now that in a people of whom the majority were Mussulmans, that majority should insist upon not permitting pork to be eaten within the limits of the country. This would be nothing new in Mohammedan countries.* Would it be a legitimate exercise of the moral authority of public opinion, and if not, why not? The practice is really revolting to such a public. They also sincerely think that it is forbidden and abhorred by the Deity. Neither could the prohibition be censured as religious persecution. It might be religious in its origin, but it would not be persecution for religion, since nobody's religion makes it a duty to eat pork. The only tenable ground of condemnation would be that with the personal tastes and self-regarding concerns of individuals the public has no business to interfere.

To come somewhat nearer home: the majority of Spaniards consider it a gross impiety, offensive in the highest degree to the Supreme Being, to worship him in any other manner than the Roman Catholic; and no other public worship is lawful on Spanish soil. The people of all southern Europe look upon a married clergy

as not only irreligious, but unchaste, indecent, gross, disgusting. What do Protestants think of these perfectly sincere feelings, and of the attempt to enforce them against non-Catholics? Yet, if mankind are justified in interfering with each other's liberty in things which do not concern the interests of others, on what principle is it possible consistently to exclude these cases? Or who can blame people for desiring to suppress what they regard as a scandal in the sight of God and man? No stronger case can be shown for prohibiting anything which is regarded as a personal immorality than is made out for suppressing these practices in the eyes of those who regard them as impieties; and unless we are willing to adopt the logic of persecutors, and to say that we may persecute others because we are right, and that they must not persecute us because they are wrong, we must beware of admitting a principle of which we should resent as a gross injustice the application to ourselves.

The preceding instances may be objected to, although unreasonably, as drawn from contingencies impossible among us—opinion, in this country, not being likely to enforce abstinence from meats or to interfere with people for worshiping and for either marrying or not marrying, according to their creed or inclination. The next example, however, shall be taken from an interference with liberty which we have by no means passed all danger of. Wherever the Puritans have been sufficiently powerful, as in New England, and in Great Britain at the time of the Commonwealth, they have endeavored, with considerable success, to put down all public, and nearly all private, amusements: especially music, dancing, public games, or other assemblages for purpose of diversion, and the theater. There are still in this country large bodies of persons by whose notions of morality and religion these recreations are condemned; and those persons belonging chiefly to the middle class, who are the ascendant power in the present social and political condition of the kingdom, it is by no means impossible that persons of these sentiments may at some time or other command a majority in Parliament. How will the remaining portion of the community like to have the amusements that shall be permitted to them regulated by the religious and moral sentiments of the stricter Calvinists and Methodists? Would they not, with considerable peremptoriness, desire these intrusively pious members of society to mind their own business? This is precisely what should be said to every government and every public who have the pretension that no person shall enjoy any pleasure which they think wrong. But if the principle of the pretension be admitted, no one can reasonably object to its being acted on in the sense of the majority, or other preponderating power in the country; and all persons must be ready to conform to the idea of a Christian commonwealth as understood by the early settlers in New England, if a religious profession similar to theirs should ever succeed in regaining its lost ground, as religions supposed to be declining have so often been known to do.

To imagine another contingency, perhaps more likely to be realized than the one last mentioned. There is confessedly a strong tendency in the modern world toward a democratic constitution of society, accompanied or not by popular political institutions. It is affirmed that in the country where this tendency is most completely realized—where both society and the government are most democratic: the United States—the feeling of the majority, to whom any appearance of a more showy or costly style of living than they can hope to rival is disagreeable, operates as a tolerably effectual sumptuary law[3], and that in many parts of the Union it is really difficult for a person possessing a very large income to find any mode of spending it which will not

incur popular disapprobation. Though such statements as these are doubtless much exaggerated as a representation of existing facts, the state of things they describe is not only a conceivable and possible, but a probable result of democratic feeling combined with the notion that the public has a right to veto on the manner in which individuals shall spend their incomes. We have only further to suppose a considerable diffusion of Socialist opinions, and it may become infamous in the eyes of the majority to possess more property than some very small amount, or any income not earned by manual labor. Opinions similar in principle to these already prevail widely among the artisan class and weigh oppressively on those who are amenable to the opinion chiefly of that class, namely, its own members. It is known that the bad workmen who form the majority of the operatives in many branches of industry are decidedly of opinion that bad workmen ought to receive the same wages as good, and that no one ought to be allowed, through piecework or otherwise, to earn by superior skill or industry more than others can without it. And they employ a moral police, which occasionally becomes a physical one, to deter skillful workmen from receiving, and employers from giving, a larger remuneration for a more useful service. If the public have any jurisdiction over private concerns, I cannot see that these people are in fault, or that any individual's particular public can be blamed for asserting the same authority over his individual conduct which the general public asserts over people in general.

But, without dwelling upon supposititious cases, there are, in our own day, gross usurpations upon the liberty of private life actually practiced, and still greater ones threatened with some expectation of success, and opinions propounded which assert an unlimited right in the public not only to prohibit by law everything which it thinks wrong, but, in order to get at what it thinks wrong, to prohibit a number of things which it admits to be innocent.

Under the name of preventing intemperance, the people of one English colony, and of nearly half the United States, have been interdicted by law[4] from making any use whatever of fermented drinks, except for medical purposes, for prohibition of their sale is in fact, as it is intended to be, prohibition of their use. And though the impracticability of executing the law has caused its repeal in several of the States which had adopted it, including the one from which it derives its name, an attempt has notwithstanding been commenced, and is prosecuted with considerable zeal by many of the professed philanthropists, to agitate for a similar law in the country. The association, or "Alliance," as it terms itself, which has been formed for this purpose, has acquired some notoriety through the publicity given to a correspondence between its secretary and one of the very few English public men who hold that a politican's opinions ought to be founded on principles. Lord Stanley's[5] share in this correspondence is calculated to strengthen the hopes already built on him by those who know how rare such qualities as are manifested in some of his public appearances unhappily are among those who figure in political life. The organ of the Alliance, who would "deeply deplore the recognition of any principle which could be wrested to justify bigotry and persecution," undertakes to point out the "broad and impassable barrier" which divides such principles from those of the association. "All matters relating to thought, opinion, conscience, appear to me," he says, "to be without the sphere of legislation; all pertaining to social act, habit, relation, subject only to a discretionary power vested in the State itself, and not in the individual, to be within it." No mention is made of a third class, different from either of these, viz., acts and habits which are not social, but individual; although it is to this

class, surely that the act of drinking fermented liquors belongs. Selling fermented liquors, however, is trading, and trading is a social act. But the infringement complained of is not on the liberty of the seller, but on that of the buyer and consumer; since the State might just as well forbid him to drink wine as purposely make it impossible for him to obtain it. The secretary, however, says, "I claim, as a citizen, a right to legislate whenever my social rights are invaded by the social act of another." And now for the definition of these "social rights": "If anything invades my social rights, certainly the traffic in strong drink does. It destroys my primary right of security by constantly creating and stimulating social disorder. It invades my right of equality by deriving a profit from the creation of a misery I am taxed to support. It impedes my right to free moral and intellectual development by surrounding my path with dangers and by weakening and demoralizing society, from which I have a right to claim mutual aid and intercourse." A theory of "social rights" the like of which probably never before found its way into distinct language: being nothing short of this—that it is the absolute social right of every individual that every other individual shall act in every respect exactly as he ought; that whosoever fails thereof in the smallest particular violates my social right and entitles me to demand from the legislature the removal of the grievance. So monstrous a principle is far more dangerous than any single interference with liberty; there is no violation of liberty which it would not justify; it acknowledges no right to any freedom whatever, except perhaps to that of holding opinions in secret, without ever disclosing them; for the moment an opinion which I consider noxious passes anyone's lips, it invades all the "social rights" attributed to me by the Alliance. The doctrine ascribes to all mankind a vested interest in each other's moral, intellectual, and even physical perfection, to be defined by each claimant according to his own standard.

Another important example of illegitimate interference with the rightful liberty of the individual, not simply threatened, but long since carried into triumphant effect, is Sabbatarian legislation. Without doubt, abstinence on one day in the week, so far as the exigencies of life permit, from the usual daily occupation, though in no respect religiously binding on any except Jews, is a highly beneficial custom. And inasmuch as this custom cannot be observed without a general consent to that effect among the industrious classes, therefore, in so far as some persons by working may impose the same necessity on others, it may be allowable and right that the law should guarantee to each the observance by others of the custom, by suspending the greater operations of industry on a particular day. But this justification, grounded on the direct interest which others have in each individual's observance of the practice, does not apply to the self-chosen occupations in which a person may think fit to employ his leisure, nor does it hold good, in the smallest degree, for legal restrictions on amusements. It is true that the amusement of some is the day's work of others; but the pleasure, not to say the useful recreation, of many is worth the labor of a few, provided the occupation is freely chosen and can be freely resigned. The operatives are perfectly right in thinking that if all worked on Sunday, seven days' work would have to be given for six days' wages; but so long as the great mass of employments are suspended, the small number who for the enjoyment of others must still work obtain a proportional increase of earnings; and they are not obliged to follow those occupations if they prefer leisure to emolument. If a further remedy is sought, it might be found in the establishment by custom of a holiday on some other day of the week for those particular classes of persons. The only ground, therefore, on which restrictions on Sunday amusements can be defended must be that they are religiously wrong–a motive of legislation which can never be too earnestly protested against. *"Deorum injuriae Diis curae."* [6] It remains to be proved that society or any of its officers holds a commission from on high to avenge any supposed offense to Omnipotence which is not also a wrong to our fellow creatures. The notion that it is one man's duty that another should be religious was the foundation of all the religious persecutions ever perpetrated, and, if admitted, would fully justify them. Though the feeling which breaks out in the repeated attempts to stop railway traveling on Sunday, in the resistance to the opening of museums, and the like, has not the cruelty of the old persecutors, the state of mind indicated by it is fundamentally the same. It is a determination not to tolerate others in doing what is permitted by their religion, because it is not permitted by the persecutor's religion. It is a belief that God not only abominates the act of the misbeliever, but will not hold us guiltless if we leave him unmolested.

I cannot refrain from adding to these examples of the little account commonly made of human liberty the language of downright persecution which breaks out from the press of this country whenever it feels called on to notice the remarkable phenomenon of Mormonism. Much might be said on the unexpected and instructive fact that an alleged new revelation and a religion founded on it–the product of palpable imposture, not even supported by the *prestige* of extraordinary qualities in its founder– is believed by hundreds of thousands, and has been made the foundation of a society in the age of newspapers, railways, and the electric telegraph. What here concerns us is that this religion, like other and better religions, has its martyrs: that its prophet and founder was, for his teaching, put to death by a mob; that others of its adherents lost their lives by the same lawless violence; that they were forcibly expelled, in a body, from the country in which they first grew up, while, now that they have been chased into a solitary recess in the midst of a desert, many in this country openly declare that it would be right (only that it is not convenient) to send an expedition against them and compel them by force to conform to the opinions of other people. The article of the Mormonite doctrine which is the chief provocative to the antipathy which thus breaks through the ordinary restraints of religious tolerance is its sanction of *polygamy*; which, though permitted to Mohammedans, and Hindus, and Chinese, seems to excite unquenchable animosity when practiced by persons who speak English and profess to be a kind of Christians. No one has a deeper disapprobation than I have of this Mormon institution; both for other reasons and because, far from being in any way countenanced by the principle of liberty, it is a direct infraction of that principle, being a mere riveting of the chains of one half of the community, and an emancipation of the other from reciprocity of obligation toward them. Still, it must be remembered that this relation is as much voluntary on the part of the women concerned in it, and who may be deemed the sufferers by it, as is the case with any other form of the marriage institution; and however surprising this fact may appear, it has its explanation in the common ideas and customs of the world, which, teaching women to think marriage the one thing needful, make it intelligible that many a woman should prefer being one of several wives to not being a wife at all. Other countries are not asked to recognize such unions, or release any portion of their inhabitants from their own laws on the score of Mormonite opinions. But when the dissentients have conceded to the hostile sentiments of others far more than could justly be demanded; when they have left the countries to which their doctrines were unacceptable and established themselves in a remote corner of the earth, which they have been the first to render habitable to human beings, it is difficult to see on what principles but those of tyranny they can be prevented from living there under what laws they please, provided they commit no aggression on other nations and allow perfect freedom of departure to those who are dissatisfied with their ways. A recent writer, in some respects of considerable merit, proposes (to use his own words) not a crusade, but a *civilizade*, against this polygamous community, to put an end to what seems to him a retrograde step in civilization. It also appears so to me, but I am not aware that any community has a right to force another to be civilized. So long as the sufferers by the bad law do not invoke assistance from other communities, I cannot admit that persons entirely unconnected with them ought to step in and require that a condition of things with which all who are directly interested appear to be satisfied should be put an end to because it is a scandal to persons some thousands of miles distant who have no part or concern in it. Let them send missionaries, if they please, to preach against it; and let them, by any fair means (of which silencing the teachers is not one), oppose the progress of similar doctrines among their own people. If civilization has got the better of barbarism when barbarism had the world to itself, it is too much to profess to be afraid lest barbarism, after having been fairly got under, should revive and conquer civilization. A civilization that can thus succumb to its vanquished enemy must first have become so degenerate that neither its appointed priests and teachers, nor anybody else, has the capacity, or will take the trouble, to stand up for it. If this be so, the sooner such a civilization receives notice to quit, the better. It can only go on from bad to worse until destroyed and regenerated (like the Western Empire) by energetic barbarians.

*The case of the Bombay Parsees is a curious instance in point. When this industrious and enterprising tribe, the descendants of the Persian fire-worshipers, flying from their native country before the Caliphs, arrived in western India, they were admitted to toleration by the Hindu sovereigns, on condition of not eating beef. When those regions afterward fell under the dominion of Mohammedan conquerors, the Parsees obtained from them a continuance of indulgence, on condition of refraining from pork. What was at first obedience to authority became a second nature, and the Parsees to this day abstain both from beef and pork. Though not required by their religion, the double abstinence has had time to grow into a custom of their tribe; and custom, in the East, is a religion.

NOTES

1 Greed.

2 *The London Merchant: or, the History of George Barnwell* was a melodrama by George Lillo.

3 Medieval laws which regulated sale and consumption to prevent overindulgence in the fleshly pleasures. "Blue law" is the modern term.

4 A precursor of prohibition, called the Maine Law, after the state that first adopted it in 1815.

5 Edward Henry Stanley (1826–1893) had a long and distinguished career in the foreign service and diplomacy.

6 A quotation from Tacitus, which translates as "leave offenses against the gods to the care of the gods."

Karl Marx and Friedrich Engels

Karl Marx (1818–1833) and Friedrich Engels (1820–1895) were both born in Germany within 100 miles of each other; Marx in Trier and Engels in Barmen. While Marx earned a Doctorate in Philosophy and then attempted to make a living as a journalist, Engels, who was born into a wealthy family of textile manufacturers, went into the family business. Both were very concerned about poverty, and devoted their lives to changing social conditions for the poor. Marx's particular concern began with the peasantry, while Engels saw urban poverty up close in his family's business. This led them both to critique the increasingly Capitalist production system of their time. Marx and Engels collaborated on a number of works, including the Communist Manifesto (1848).

While Marx is regarded as the better philosopher, Engels's writing is very clear and this excerpt provides us a good overview of their philosophy of history, called Historical Materialism, and of Socialism. Although there were other forms of Socialism and Communism around at the time, Marx and Engels were concerned with what they called Scientific Socialism, which was a Political Theory grounded in the science of Historical Materialism.

Historical Materialism holds that historical change is motivated by changing material circumstances, which are the resources and technologies that the society has for making use of them, along with the kinds of social relationships through which individuals interact to produce their livelihood. Marx developed this view in opposition to the idealist view of famous German philosopher Hegel, who held that historical change comes about as a result of the development of social, political, and religious ideas. Marx and Engels thought that Hegel had the matter backwards, that instead political and social ideas be the ideological superstructure of the society—to develop in response to changes in the material base of the society.

Each stage of material development, or epoch, has its own class structure that supports the means of production that prevails in that epoch. The epochs of European development were (and will be) Slavery, Feudalism, Capitalism, (and Socialism). There are characteristic social classes and means of production that go along with each of these epochs. In the epoch of *slavery,* the slaves are the producers for all the free persons in society. The slaves produce for nothing and are themselves owned by others, and the society is engaged in relatively primitive agriculture. During *Feudalism,* serfs live on land owned by feudal lords. The serfs produce to support both their families and the lords. This epoch is characterized by more advanced agriculture, along with the beginnings of towns and guild-based production. Under *Capitalism,* workers (the proletariat) work for wages, which are paid by the owners of the means of production, the Capitalists (bourgeoisie). Capitalism brought many changes in how people could live; some good, some bad. In this reading, Engels shows how Socialism will be the inevitable result of Capitalist development.

STUDY QUESTIONS:

1. What material conditions are necessary for Socialism to arise, according to Engels?

2. Why does Engels think that state ownership of the means of production is not by itself the solution to the crises of Capitalism?

3. Why will the state wither away under Socialism?

Socialism: Utopian and Scientific, 1880

PART III

The materialist conception of history starts from the proposition that the production of the means to support human life and, next to production, the exchange of things produced, is the basis of all social structure; that in every society that has appeared in history, the manner in which wealth is distributed and society divided into classes or orders is dependent upon what is produced, how it is produced, and how the products are exchanged. From this point of view the final causes of all social changes and political revolutions are to be sought, not in men's brains, not in men's better insight into eternal truth and justice, but in changes in the modes of production and exchange. They are to be sought not in the philosophy, but in the economics of each particular epoch. The growing perception that existing social institutions are unreasonable and unjust, that reason has become unreason and right wrong,[1] is only proof that in the modes of production and exchange changes have silently taken place with which the social order, adapted to earlier economic conditions, is no longer in keeping. From this it also follows that the means of getting rid of the incongruities that have been brought to light must also be present, in a more or less developed condition, within the changed modes of production

themselves. These means are not to be invented by deduction from fundamental principles, but are to be discovered in the stubborn facts of the existing system of production.

What is, then, the position of modern socialism in this connection?

The present structure of society-this is now pretty generally conceded-is the creation of the ruling class of today, of the bourgeoisie. The mode of production peculiar to the bourgeoisie, known, since Marx, as the capitalist mode of production, was incompatible with the feudal system, with the privileges it conferred upon individuals, entire social ranks and local corporations, as well as with the hereditary ties of subordination which constituted the framework of its social organisation. The bourgeoisie broke up the feudal system and built upon its ruins the capitalist order of society, the kingdom of free competition, of personal liberty, of the equality, before the law, of all commodity owners, of all the rest of the capitalist blessings. Thenceforward the capitalist mode of production could develop in freedom. Since steam, machinery, and the making of machines by machinery transformed the older manufacture into modern industry, the productive forces evolved under the guidance of the bourgeoisie developed with a rapidity and in a degree

From *Marx-Engles Reader*

unheard of before. But just as the older manu-facture, in its time, and handicraft, becoming more developed under its influence, had come into collision with the feudal trammels of the guilds, so now modern industry, in its more complete development, comes into collision with the bounds within which the capitalistic mode of production holds it confined. The new productive forces have already outgrown the capitalistic mode of using them. And this conflict between productive forces and modes of production is not a conflict engendered in the mind of man, like that between original sin and divine justice. It exists, in fact, objec-tively, outside us, independently of the will and actions even of the men that have brought it on. Modern socialism is nothing but the reflex, in thought, of this conflict in fact; its ideal reflec-tion in the minds, first, of the class directly suffering under it, the working class.

Now, in what does this conflict consist?

Before capitalistic production, i.e., in the Middle Ages, the system of petty industry obtained generally, based upon the private prop-erty of the labourers in their means of production; in the country, the agriculture of the small peas-ant, freeman or serf; in the towns, the handicrafts organised in guilds. The instruments of labour-land, agricultural implements, the workshop, the tool-were the instruments of labour of single indi-viduals, adapted for the use of one worker, and, therefore, of necessity, small, dwarfish, circum-scribed. But, for this very reason they belonged, as a rule, to the producer himself. To concentrate these scattered, limited means of production, to enlarge them, to turn them into the powerful levers of production of the present day-this was precisely the historic role of capitalist produc-tion and of its upholder, the bourgeoisie. In the fourth section of *Capital*[2] Marx has explained in detail how since the fifteenth century this has been historically worked out through the three phases of simple co-operation, manufacture

and modern industry. But the bourgeoisie, as is also shown there, could not transform these puny means of production into mighty produc-tive forces without transforming them, at the same time, from means of production of the individual into *social* means of production only workable by a collectivity of men. The spinning-wheel, the hand-loom, the blacksmith's hammer, were replaced by the spinning-machine, the power-loom, the steam-hammer; the individual workshop, by the factory implying the co-opera-tion of hundreds and thousands of workmen. In like manner, production itself changed from a series of individual into a series of social acts, and the products from individual to social products. The yarn, the cloth, the metal articles that now came out of the factory, were the joint product of many workers, through whose hands they had successively to pass before they were ready. No one person could say of them; "I made that; this is *my* product."

But where, in a given society, the funda-mental form of production is that spontaneous division of labour which creeps in gradually and not upon any preconceived plan, there the products take on the form of *commodi-ties,* whose mutual exchange, buying and sell-ing, enable the individual producers to satisfy their manifold wants. And this was the case in the Middle Ages. The peasant, e.g., sold to the artisan agricultural products and bought from him the products of handicraft. Into this society of individual producers, of commodity producers, the new mode of production thrust itself. In the midst of the old division of labour, grown up spontaneously and upon *no definite plan,* which had governed the whole of society, now arose division of labour upon a *definite* plan, as organised in the factory; side by side with *individual* production appeared *social* production. The products of both were sold in the same market, and, therefore, at prices at least approximately equal. But organisation upon a definite plan was stronger than sponta-neous division of labour. The factories working with the combined social forces of a collectiv-ity of individuals produced their commodities far more cheaply than the individual small producers. Individual production succumbed in one department after another. Socialised production revolutionised all the old methods of production. But its revolutionary character was, at the same time, so little recognised that it was, on the contrary, introduced as a means of increasing and developing the produc-tion of commodities. When it arose, it found ready-made, and made liberal use of, certain machinery for the production and exchange of commodities: merchants' capital, handi-craft, wage-labour. Socialised production thus introducing itself as a new form of the produc-tion of commodities, it was a matter of course that under it the old forms of appropriation remained in full swing, and were applied to its products as well.

In the mediaeval stage of evolution of the production of commodities, the question as to the owner of the product of labour could not arise. The individual producer, as a rule, had, from raw material belonging to himself, and generally his own handiwork, produced it with his own tools, by the labour of his own hands or of his family. There was no need for him to appropriate the new product. It belonged wholly to him, as a matter of course. His property in the product was, therefore, based *upon his own labour.* Even where exter-nal help was used, this was, as a rule, of little importance, and very generally was compen-sated by something other than wages. The apprentices and journeymen of the guilds worked less for board and wages than for education, in order that they might become master craftsmen themselves.

Then came the concentration of the means of production and of the producers in large workshops and manufactories, their transformation into actual socialised means of production and socialised producers. But the socialised producers and means of production and their products were still treated, after this change, just as they had been before, i.e., as the means of production and the products of individuals. Hitherto, the owner of the instruments of labour had himself appropri-ated the product, because, as a rule, it was his own product and the assistance of others was the exception. Now the owner of the instruments of labour always appropriated to himself the product, although it was no longer *his* product but exclusively the prod-uct of the *labour of others.* Thus, the products now produced socially were not appropriated by those who had actually set in motion the means of production and actually produced the commodities, but by the *capitalists.* The means of production, and production itself, had become in essence socialised. But they were subjected to a form of appropriation which presupposes the private production of individuals, under which, therefore, everyone owns his own product and brings it to market. The mode of production is subjected to this form of appropriation, although it abolishes the conditions upon which the latter rates.[3]

This contradiction, which gives to the new mode of production its capitalistic charac-ter, *contains the germ of the whole of the social antagonisms of today.* The greater the mastery obtained by the new mode of production over all important fields of production and in all manufacturing countries, the more it reduced individual production to an insignificant residuum, *the more clearly was brought out the incompatibility of socialised production with capitalistic appropriation.*

The first capitalists found, as we have said, alongside of other forms of labour, wage-labour ready-made for them on the market. But it was exceptional, complementary, accessory, transitory wage-labour. The agricultural labourer, though, upon occasion, he hired himself out by the day, had a few acres of his own land on which he could at all events live at a pinch. The guilds were so organized that the journeyman of today became the master of tomorrow. But all this changed as soon as the means of production became socialised and concentrated in the hands of capitalists. The means of production, as well as the product, of the individual producer became more and more worthless; there was nothing left for him but to turn wage-worker under the capitalist. Wage-labour, aforetime the exception and accessory, now became the rule and basis of all production; aforetime complementary, it now became the sole remaining function of the workers. The wage-worker for a time became a wage-worker for life. The number of these permanent wage-workers was further enormously increased by the breaking-up of the feudal system that occurred at the same time, by the disbanding of the retainers of the feudal lords, the eviction of the peasants from their homesteads, etc. The separation was made complete between the means of production concentrated in the hands of the capitalists, on the one side, and the producers, possessing nothing but their labour-power, on the other. *The contradiction between socialised production and capitalistic appropriation manifested itself as the antagonism of proletariat and bourgeoisie.*

We have seen that the capitalistic mode of production thrust its way into a society of commodity-producers, of individual producers, whose social bond was the exchange of their products. But every society based upon the production of commodities has this peculiarity: that the producers have lost control over their own social interrelations. Each man produces for himself with such means of production as he may happen to have, and for such exchange as he may require to satisfy his remaining wants. No one knows how much of his particular article is coming on the market, nor how much of it will be wanted. No one knows whether his individual product will meet an actual demand, whether he will be able to make good his costs of production or even to sell his commodity at all. *Anarchy reigns in socialised production.*

But the production of commodities, like every other form of production, has its peculiar, inherent laws inseparable from it; and these laws work, despite anarchy, in and through anarchy. They reveal themselves in the only persistent form of social inter-relations, i.e., in exchange, and here they affect the individual producers as compulsory laws of competition. They are, at first, unknown to these producers themselves, and have to be discovered by them gradually and as the result of experience. They work themselves out, therefore, independently of the producers, and in antagonism to them, as inexorable natural laws of their particular form of production. The product governs the producers.

In mediaeval society, especially in the earlier centuries, production was essentially directed towards satisfying the wants of the individual. It satisfied, in the main, only the wants of the producer and his family. Where relations of personal dependence existed, as in the country, it also helped to satisfy the wants of the feudal lord. In all this there was, therefore, no exchange; the products, consequently, did not assume the character of commodities. The family of the peasant produced almost everything they wanted: clothes and furniture, as well as means of subsistence. Only when it began to produce more than was sufficient to supply its own wants and the payments in kind to the feudal lord, only then did it also produce commodities. This surplus, thrown into socialised exchange and offered for sale, became commodities.

The artisans of the towns, it is true, had from the first to produce for exchange. But they, also, themselves supplied the greatest part of their own individual wants. They had gardens and plots of land. They turned their cattle out into the communal forest, which, also, yielded them timber and firing. The women spun flax, wool, and so forth. Production for the purpose of exchange, production of commodities, was only in its infancy. Hence, exchange was restricted, the market narrow, the methods of production stable; there was local exclusiveness without, local unity within; the Mark in the country; in the town, the guild.

But with the extension of the production of commodities, and especially with the introduction of the capitalist mode of production, the laws of commodity production, hitherto latent, came into action more openly and with greater force. The old bonds were loosened, the old exclusive limits broken through, the producers were more and more turned into independent, isolated producers of commodities. It became apparent that the production of society at large was ruled by absence of plan, by accident, by anarchy; and this anarchy grew to greater and greater height. But the chief means by aid of which the capitalist mode of production intensified this anarchy of socialised production was the exact opposite of anarchy. It was the increasing organisation of production, upon a social basis, in every individual productive establishment. By this, the old, peaceful, stable condition of things was ended. Wherever this organisation of production was introduced into a branch of industry, it brooked no other method of production by its side. The field of labour became a battle-ground. The great geographical discoveries, and the colonisation following upon them, multiplied markets and quickened the transformation of handicraft into manufacture. The war did not simply break out between the individual producers of particular localities. The local struggles begot in their turn national conflicts, the commercial wars of the seventeenth and eighteenth centuries.

Finally, modern industry and the opening of the world market made the struggle universal, and at the same time gave it an unheard-of virulence. Advantages in natural or artificial conditions of production now decide the existence or non-existence of individual capitalists, as well as of whole industries and countries. He that falls is remorselessly cast aside. It is the Darwinian struggle of the individual for existence transferred from Nature to society with intensified violence. The conditions of existence natural to the animal appear as the final term of human development. *The contradiction between socialised production and capitalistic appropriation now presents itself as an antagonism between the organisation of production in the individual workshop and the anarchy of production in society generally.*

The capitalistic mode of production moves in these two forms of the antagonism immanent to it from its very origin. It is never able to get out of that "vicious circle" which Fourier had already discovered. What Fourier could not, indeed, see in his time is that this circle is gradually narrowing; that the movement becomes more and more a spiral, and must come to an end, like the movement of the planets, by collision with the centre. It is the compelling force of anarchy in the production of society at large that more and more completely turns the great majority of men into proletarians; and it is the masses of the proletariat again who will finally put an end to anarchy in production. *It is the compelling force of anarchy in social production that turns the limitless perfectibility of machinery under modern industry into a compulsory law by which every individual industrial capitalist must perfect his machinery more and more, under penalty of ruin.*

But the perfecting of machinery is making human labour superfluous. If the introduction and increase of machinery means the displacement of millions of manual by a few machine-workers, improvement in machinery means the displacement of more and more of the machine-workers themselves. It means, in the last instance, the production of a number of available wage-workers in excess of the average needs of capital, the formation of a complete industrial reserve army, as I called it in 1845, available at the times when industry is working at high pressure, to be cast out upon the street when the inevitable crash comes, a constant dead weight upon the limbs of the working class in its struggle for existence with capital, a regulator for the keeping of wages down to the low level that suits the interests of capital. Thus it comes about, to quote Marx, that machinery becomes the most powerful weapon in the war of capital against the working class; that the instruments of labour constantly tear the means of subsistence out of the hands of the labourer; that the very product of the worker is turned into an instrument for his subjugation. Thus it comes about that the economising of the instruments of labour becomes at the same time, from the outset, the most reckless waste of labour power, and robbery based upon the normal conditions under which labour functions; that machinery, "the most powerful instrument for shortening labour time, becomes the most unfailing means for placing every moment of the labourer's time and that of his family at the disposal of the capitalist for the purpose of expanding the value of his capital." (*Capital*, English edition, p. 406.)[4] Thus it comes about that the overwork of some becomes the preliminary condition for the idleness of others, and that modern industry, which hunts after new consumers over the whole world, forces the consumption of the masses at home down to a starvation minimum, and in doing thus destroys its own home market. "The law that always equilibrates the relative surplus population, or industrial reserve army, to the extent and energy of accumulation, this law rivets the labourer to capital more firmly than the wedges of Vulcan did Prometheus to the rock. It establishes an accumulation of misery, corresponding with accumulation of capital. Accumulation of wealth at one pole is, therefore, at the same time, accumulation of misery, agony of toil, slavery, ignorance, brutality, mental degradation, at the opposite pole, i.e. on the side of the class that produces *its own product in the form of capital.*" (*Capital*, p. 661.)[5] And to expect any other division of the products from the capitalistic mode of production is the same as expecting the electrodes of a battery not to decompose acidulated water, not to liberate oxygen at the positive, hydrogen at the negative pole, so long as they are connected with the battery.

We have seen that the ever-increasing perfectibility of modern machinery is, by the anarchy of social production, turned into a compulsory law that forces the individual industrial capitalist always to improve his machinery, always to increase its productive force. The bare possibility of extending the field of production is transformed for him into a similar compulsory law. The enormous expansive force of modern industry, compared with which that of gases is mere child's play, appears to us now as a *necessity* for expansion, both qualitative and quantitative, that laughs at all resistance. Such resistance is offered by consumption, by sales, by the markets for the products of modern industry. But the capacity for extension, extensive and intensive, of the markets is primarily governed by quite different laws that work much less energetically. The extension of the markets cannot keep pace with the extension of production. The collision becomes inevitable, and as this cannot produce any real solution so long as it does not break in pieces the capitalist mode of production, the collisions become periodic. Capitalist production has begotten another "vicious circle."

As a matter of fact, since 1825, when the first general crisis broke out, the whole industrial and commercial world, production and exchange among all civilised peoples and their more or less barbaric hangers-on, are thrown out of joint about once every ten years. Commerce is at a standstill, the markets are glutted, products accumulate, as multitudinous as they are unsaleable, hard cash disappears, credit vanishes, factories are closed, the mass of the workers are in want of the means of subsistence, because they have produced too much of the means of subsistence; bankruptcy follows upon bankruptcy, execution upon execution. The stagnation lasts for years; productive forces and products are wasted and destroyed wholesale, until the accumulated mass of commodities finally filters off, more or less depreciated in value, until production and exchange gradually begin to move again. Little by little the pace quickens. It becomes a trot. The industrial trot breaks into a canter, the canter in turn grows into the headlong gallop of a perfect steeple-chase of industry, commercial credit, and speculation which finally, after breakneck leaps, ends where it began-in the ditch of a crisis. And so over and over again. We have now, since the year 1825, gone through this five times, and at the present moment (1877) we are going through it for the sixth time. And the character of these crises is so clearly defined that Fourier hit all of them off when he described the first as *"crise pléthorique,"* a crisis from plethora.

In these crises, the contradiction between socialised production and capitalist appropriation ends in a violent explosion. The circulation of commodities is, for the time being, stopped. Money, the means of circulation, becomes a hindrance to circulation. All the laws of production and circulation of commodities are turned upside down. The economic collision has reached its apogee. *The mode of production is in rebellion against the mode of exchange.*

The fact that the socialised organisation of production within the factory has developed so far that it has become incompatible with the anarchy of production in society, which exists side by side with and dominates it, is brought home to the capitalists themselves by the violent concentration of capital that occurs during crises, through the ruin of many large, and a still greater number of small, capitalists. The whole mechanism of the capitalist mode of production breaks down under the pressure of the productive forces, its own creations. It is no longer able to turn all this mass of means of production into capital. They lie fallow, and for that very reason the industrial reserve army must also lie fallow. Means of production, means of subsistence, available labourers, all the elements of production and of general wealth, are present in abundance. But "abundance becomes the source of distress and want" (Fourier), because it is the very thing that prevents the transformation of the means of production and subsistence into capital. For in capitalistic society the means of production can only function when they have undergone a preliminary transformation into capital, into the means of exploiting human labour power. The necessity of this transformation into capital of the means of production and subsistence stands like a ghost between these and the workers. It alone prevents the coming together of the material and personal levers of production; it alone forbids the means of production to function, the workers to work and live. On the one hand, therefore, the capitalistic mode of production stands convicted of its own incapacity to further direct these productive forces. On the other, these productive forces themselves, with increasing energy, press forward to the removal of the existing contradiction to the abolition of their quality as capital, to the *practical recognition of their character as social productive forces.*

This rebellion of the productive forces, as they grow more and more powerful, against their quality as capital, this stronger and stronger command that their social character shall be recognised, forces the capitalist class itself to treat them more and more as social productive forces, so far as this is possible under capitalist conditions. The period of industrial high pressure, with its unbounded inflation of credit, not less than the crash itself, by the collapse of great capitalist establishments, tends to bring about that form of the socialisation of great masses of means of production which we meet with in the different kinds of joint-stock companies. Many of these means of production and of distribution are, from the outset, so colossal that, like the railways, they exclude all other forms of capitalistic exploitation. At a further stage of evolution this form also becomes insufficient. The producers on a large scale in a particular branch of industry in a particular country unite in a trust, a union for the purpose of regulating production. They determine the total amount to be produced, parcel it out among themselves, and thus enforce the selling price fixed beforehand. But trusts of this kind, as soon as business becomes bad, are generally liable to break up, and on this very account compel a yet greater concentration of association. The whole of the particular industry is turned into one gigantic joint-stock company; internal competition gives place to the internal monopoloy of this one company. This has happened in 1890 with the English alkali production, which is now, after the fusion of 48 large works, in the hands of one company, conducted upon a single plan, and with a capital of £6,000,000.

In the trusts, freedom of competition changes into its very opposite-into monopoly; and the production without any definite plan of capitalistic society capitulates to the production upon a definite plan of the invading socialistic society. Certainly this is so far still to the benefit and advantage of the capitalists. But in this case the exploitation is so palpable that it must break down. No nation will put up with production conducted by trusts, with so barefaced an exploitation of the community by a small band of dividend-mongers.

In any case, with trusts or without, the official representative of capitalist society-the state-will ultimately have to undertake the direction of production.[6] This necessity for conversion into state property is felt first in the great institutions for intercourse and communication-the post office, the telegraphs, the railways.

If the crises demonstrate the incapacity of the bourgeoisie for managing any longer modern productive forces, the transformation of the great establishments for production and distrubution into joint-stock companies, trusts and state property shows how unnecessary the bourgeoisie are for that purpose. All the social functions of the capitalist are now performed by salaried employees. The capitalist has no further social function than that of pocketing dividends, tearing off coupons, and gambling on the Stock Exchange, where the different capitalists despoil one another of their capital. At first the capitalistic mode of production forces out the workers. Now it forces out the capitalists, and reduces them, just as it reduced the workers, to the ranks of the surplus population, although not immediately into those of the industrial reserve army.

But the transformation, either into joint-stock companies and trusts, or into state ownership, does not do away with the capitalistic nature of the productive forces. In the joint-stock companies and trusts this is obvious. And the modern state, again, is only the organisation that bourgeois society takes on in order to support the external conditions of the capitalist mode of production against the encroachments as well of the workers as of individual capitalists. The modern state, no matter what its form, is essentially a capitalist machine, the state of the capitalists, the ideal personification of the total national capital. The more it proceeds to the taking over of productive forces, the more does it actually become the national capitalist, the more citizens does it exploit. The workers remain wage-workers-proletarians. The capitalist relation is not done away with. It is rather brought to a head. But, brought to a head, it topples over. *State ownership of the productive forces is not the solution of the conflict, but concealed within it are the technical conditions that form the elements of that solution.*

This solution can only consist in the practical recognition of the social nature of the modern forces of production, and therefore in the harmonising of the modes of production, appropriation, and exchange with the socialised character of the means of production. And this can only come about by society openly and directly taking possession of the productive forces which have outgrown all control except that of society as a whole. The social character of the means of production and of the products today reacts against the producers, periodically distrupts all production and exchange, acts only like a law of Nature working blindly, forcibly, destructively. But with the taking over by society of the productive forces, the social character of the means of production and of the products will be utilised by the producers with a perfect understanding of its nature, and instead of being a source of disturbance and periodical collapse, will become the most powerful lever of production itself.

Active social forces work exactly like natural forces: blindly, forcibly, destructively, so long as we do not understand, and reckon with, them. But when once we understand them, when once we grasp their action, their direction, their effects, it depends only upon ourselves to subject them *more and more to our own will, and by means of them to reach our own ends.* And this holds quite especially of the mighty productive forces of today. As long as we obstinately refuse to understand the nature and the character of these social means of action-and this understanding goes against the grain of the capitalist mode of production and its defenders-so long these forces are at work in spite of us, in opposition to us, so long they master us, as we have shown above in detail.

But when once their nature is understood, they can, in the hands of the producers working together, be transformed from master demons into willing servants. The difference is as that between the destructive force of electricity in the lightning of the storm, and electricity under command in the telegraph and the voltaic arc; the difference between a conflagration, and fire working in the service of man. *With this recognition, at last, of the real nature of the productive forces of today, the social anarchy of production gives place to a social regulation of production upon a definite plan, according to the needs of the community and of each individual. Then the capitalist mode of appropriation, in which the product enslaves first the producer and then the appropriator, is replaced by the mode of appropriation of the products that is based upon the nature of the modern means of production; upon the one hand, direct social appropriation, as means to the maintenance and extension of production-on the other, direct individual appropriation, as means of subsistence and of enjoyment.*

Whilst the capitalist mode of production more and more completely transforms the great majority of the population into proletarians, it creates the power which, under penalty of its own destruction, is forced to accomplish this revolution. Whilst it forces on more and more the transformation of the vast means of production, already socialised, into state property, it shows itself the way to accomplishing this revolution. *The proletariat seizes political power and turns the means of production into state property.*

But, in doing this, it abolishes itself as proletariat, abolishes all class distinctions and class antagonisms, abolishes also the state as state. Society thus far, based upon class antagonisms, had need of the state. That is, of an organisation of the particular class which was *pro tempore* the exploiting class, an organisation for the purpose of preventing any interference from without with the existing conditions of production, and, therefore, especially, for the purpose of forcibly keeping the exploited classes in the condition of oppression corresponding with the given mode of production (slavery, serfdom, wage-labour). *The state was the official representative of society as a whole; the gathering of it together into a visible embodiment. But it was this only in so far as it was the state of that class which itself represented, for the time being, society as a whole*: in ancient times, the state of slaveowning citizens; in the Middle Ages, the feudal lords; in our own time, the bourgeoisie. When at last it becomes the real representative of the whole of society, it renders itself unnecessary. As soon as there is no longer any social class to be held in subjection; as soon as class rule, and the individual struggle for existence based upon our present anarchy in production, with the collisions and excesses arising from these, are removed, nothing more remains to be repressed, and a special repressive force, *a state, is no longer necessary.* The first act by virtue of which the state really constitutes itself the representative of the whole of society-this is, at the same time, its last independent act as a state. State interference in social relations becomes, in one domain after another, superfluous, and then dies out of itself; the government of persons is replaced by the administration of things, and by the conduct of processes of production. The state is not

"abolished." *It dies out.* This gives the measure of the value of the phrase *"a free state,"* both as to its justifiable use at times by agitators, and as to its ultimate scientific insufficiency; and also of the demands of the so-called anarchists for the abolition of the state out of hand.

Since the historical appearance of the capitalist mode of production, the appropriation by society of all the means of production has often been dreamed of, more or less vaguely, by individuals, as well as by sects, as the ideal of the future. But it could become possible, could become a historical necessity, only when the actual conditions for its realisation were there. Like every other social advance, it becomes practicable, not by men understanding that the existence of classes is in contradiction to justice, equality, etc., not by the mere willingness to abolish these classes, but by virtue of certain new economic conditions. The separation of society into an exploiting and an exploited class, a ruling and an oppressed class, was the necessary consequence of the deficient and restricted development of production in former times. So long as the total social labour only yields a product which but slightly exceeds that barely necessary for the existence of all; so long, therefore, as labour engages all or almost all the time of the great majority of the members of society-so long, of necessity, this society is divided into classes. Side by side with the great majority, exclusively bond slaves to labour, arises a class freed from directly productive labour, which looks after the general affairs of society: the direction of labour, state business, law, science, art, etc. It is, therefore, the law of division of labour that lies at the basis of the division into classes. But this does not prevent this division into classes from being carried out by means of violence and robbery, trickery and fraud. It does not prevent the ruling class, once having the upper hand, from consolidating its power at the expense of the working class, from turning its social leadership into an intensified exploitation of the masses.

But if, upon this showing, division into classes has a certain historical justification, it has this only for a given period, only under given social conditions. It was based upon the insufficiency of production. It will be swept away by the complete development of modern productive forces. And, in fact, the abolition of classes in society presupposes a degree of historical evolution at which the existence, not simply of this or that particular ruling class, but of any ruling class at all, and, therefore, the existence of class distinction itself has become an obsolete anachronism. It presupposes, therefore, the development of production carried out to a degree at which appropriation of the means of production and of the products, and, with this, of political domination, of the monopoly of culture, and of intellectual leadership by a particular class of society, has become not only superfluous but economically, politically, intellectually, a hindrance to development.

This point is now reached. Their political and intellectual bankruptcy is scarcely any longer a secret to the bourgeoisie themselves. Their economic bankruptcy recurs regularly every ten years. In every crisis, society is suffocated beneath the weight of its own productive forces and products, which it cannot use, and stands helpless, face to face with the absurd contradiction that the producers have nothing to consume, because consumers are wanting. The expansive force of the means of production bursts the bonds that the capitalist mode of production had imposed upon them. Their deliverance from these bonds is the one precondition for an unbroken, constantly accelerated development of the productive forces, and there-with for a practically unlimited increase of production itself. Nor is this all. The socialised appropriation of the means of production does away, not only with the present artificial restrictions upon production, but also with the positive waste and devastation of productive forces and products that are at the present time the inevitable concomitants of production, and that reach their height in the crises. Further, it sets free for the community at large a mass of means of production and of products, by doing away with the senseless extravagance of the ruling classes of today and their political representatives. The possibility of securing for every member of society, by means of socialised production, an existence not only fully sufficient materially, and becoming day by day more full, but an existence guaranteeing to all the free development and exercise of their physical and mental faculties-this possibility is now for the first time here, but *it is here*.[7]

With the seizing of the means of production by society, production of commodities is done away with, and, simultaneously, the mastery of the product over the producer. Anarchy in social production is replaced by systematic, definite organisation. The struggle for individual existence disappears. Then for the first time man, in a certain sense, is finally marked off from the rest of the animal kingdom, and emerges from mere animal conditions of existence into really human ones. The whole sphere of the conditions of life which environ man, and which have hitherto ruled man, now comes under the dominion and control of man, who for the first time becomes the real, conscious lord of Nature, *because he has now become master of his own social organisation. The laws of his own social action, hitherto standing face to face with man as laws of Nature foreign to, and dominating him, will then be used with full understanding, and so mastered by him. Man's own social organisation, hitherto confronting him as a necessity imposed by Nature and history, now becomes the result of his own free action. The extraneous objective forces that have hitherto governed history pass under the control of man himself.* Only from that time will man himself, more and more consciously, make his own history-only from that time will the social causes set in movement by him have, in the main and in a constantly growing measure, the results intended by him. It is the ascent of man from the kingdom of necessity to the kingdom of freedom.

Let us briefly sum up our sketch of historical evolution.

I. *Mediaeval Society.* Individual production on a small scale. Means of production adapted for individual use; hence primitive, ungainly, petty, dwarfed in action. Production for immediate consumption, either of the producer himself or of his feudal lord. Only where an excess of production over this consumption occurs is such excess offered for sale, enters into exchange. Production of commodities, therefore, only in its infancy. But already it contains within itself, in embryo, *anarchy in the production of society at large.*

II. *Capitalist Revolution.* Transformation of industry, at first by means of simple co-operation and manufacture. Concentration of the means of production, hitherto scattered, into great workshops. As a consequence, their transformation from individual to social means of production-a transformation which does not, on the whole, affect the form of exchange. The old forms of appropriation remain in force. The capitalist appears. In his capacity as owner of the means of production, he also appropriates the products and turns them into commodities. Production has become a *social* act. Exchange and appropriation continue to be *individual* acts, the acts of individuals. *The social product is appropriated by the individual capitalist.* Fundamental contradiction, whence arise all the contradictions in which our present-day society moves, and which modern industry brings to light.

A. Severance of the producer from the means of production. Condemnation of the worker to wage-labour for life. *Antagonism between the proletariat and the bourgeoisie.*

B. Growing predominance and increasing effectiveness of the laws governing the production of commodities. Unbridled competition. *Contradiction between socialised organisation in the individual factory and social anarchy in production as a whole.*

C. On the one hand, perfecting of machinery, made by competition compulsory for each individual manufacturer, and complemented by a constantly growing displacement of labourers. *Industrial reserve army.* On the other hand, unlimited extension of production, also compulsory under competition, for every manufacturer. On both sides, unheard-of development of productive forces, excess of supply over demand, over-production, glutting of the markets, crises every ten years, the vicious circle: excess here, of means of production and products-excess there, of labourers, without employment and without means of existence. But these two levers of production and of social well-being are unable to work together, because the capitalist form of production prevents the productive forces from working and the products from circulating, unless they are first turned into capital-which their very superabundance prevents. The contradiction has grown into an absurdity. *The mode of production rises in rebellion against the form of exchange.*

The bourgeoisie are convicted of incapacity further to manage their own social productive forces.

D. Partial recognition of the social character of the productive forces forced upon the capitalists themselves. Taking over of the great institutions for production and communication, first by jointstock companies, later on by trusts, then by the state. The bourgeoisie demonstrated to be a superfluous class. All its social functions are now performed by salaried employees.

III. *Proletarian Revolution.* Solution of the contradictions. The proletariat seizes the public power, and by means of this transforms the socialised means of production, slipping from the hands of the bourgeoisie, into public property. By this act, the proletariat frees the means of production from the character of capital they have thus far borne, and gives their socialised character complete freedom to work itself out. Socialised production upon a predetermined plan becomes henceforth possible. The development of production makes the existence of different classes of society thenceforth an anachronism. In proportion as anarchy in social production vanishes, the political authority of the state dies out. Man, at last the master of his own form of social organisation, becomes at the same time the lord over Nature, his own master-free.

To accomplish this act of universal emancipation is the historical mission of the modern proletariat. To thoroughly comprehend the historical conditions and thus the very nature of this act, to impart to the new oppressed proletarian class a full knowledge of the conditions and of the meaning of the momentous act it is called upon to accomplish, this is the task of the theoretical expression of the proletarian movement, scientific socialism.

NOTES

[1]Mephistopheles, in Goethe's *Faust.*

[2]See pp. 384-403, above. [*R. T.*]

[3]It is hardly necessary in this connection to point out that, even if the *form* of appropriation remains the same, the *character* of the appropriation is just as much revolutionised as production is by the changes described above. It is, of course, a very different matter whether I appropriate to myself my own product or that of another. Note in passing that wage-labour, which contains the whole capitalistic mode of production in embryo, is very ancient; in a sporadic, scattered form it existed for centuries alongside of slave-labour. But the embryo could duly develop into the capitalistic mode of production only when the necessary historical preconditions had been furnished. [*Engels*]

[4]See p. 406, above. [*R. T.*]

[5]See p. 431, above, [*R. T.*]

[6]I say "have to." For only when the means of production and distribution have *actually* outgrown the form of management by jointstock companies, and when, therefore, the taking them over by the state has become *economically* inevitable, only then-even if it is the state of today that effects this-is there an economic advance, the attainment of another step preliminary to the taking over of all productive forces by society itself. But of late, since Bismarck went in for state ownership of industrial establishments, a kind of spurious socialism has arisen, degenerating, now and again, into something of flunkeyism, that without more ado declares *all* state ownership, even of the Bismarckian sort, to

be socialistic. Certainly, if the taking over by the state of the tobacco industry is socialistic, then Napoleon and Metternich must be numbered among the founders of socialism. If the Belgian state, for quite ordinary political and financial reasons, itself constructed its chief railway lines; if Bismarck, not under any economic compulsion, took over for the state the chief Prussian lines, simply to be the better able to have them in hand in case of war, to bring up the railway employees as voting cattle for the government, and especially to create for himself a new source of income independent of parliamentary votes-this was, in no sense, a socialistic measure, directly or indirectly, consciously or unconsciously. Otherwise, the Royal Maritime Company, the Royal porcelain manufacture, and even the regimental tailor shops of the Army would also be socialistic institutions, or even, as was seriously proposed by a sly dog in Frederick William III's reign, the taking over by the state of the brothels. [*Engels*]

[7]A few figures may serve to give an approximate idea of the enormous expansive force of the modern means of production, even under capitalist pressure. According to Mr. Giffen, the total wealth of Great Britain and Ireland amounted, in round numbers in 1814 to £2,200,000,000. 1865 to £6,100,000,000. 1875 to £8,500,000,000.

As an instance of the squandering of means of production and of products during a crisis, the total loss in the German iron industry alone, in the crisis 1873-78, was given at the second German Industrial Congress (Berlin, February 21, 1878) as £22, 750, 000. [*Engels*]

Mao Tse-tung

Mao Tse-tung (1893–1976) was born in the Hunan province of China to an upwardly mobile peasant family. Mao was not educated abroad, nor did he know other languages. He served as a soldier in the 1911 Revolution that ousted the last of the Feudal Aristocracy, and installed Sun Yat-Sen as the first president of the Republic of China. Mao began working with the fledgling Communist Party, however, after the revolution the Communist Party was purged by the Kuomintang Party in 1927 and continued to be persecuted for many more years. Mao became the head of the Communist Party in 1935, and at that time Mao began serious study of Marxism-Leninism.

During the war against the invading Japanese Army, Communists and Kuomintang cooperated. But after World War II, Mao ended the Communist Revolution by ousting the Kuomintang Party and its leader Chaing Kai Chek, who retreated to Taiwan. Mao was the leader throughout the Communist Revolution, and became the official head of New People's Republic in 1949. His system of economic and political reform failed, and to hold onto political power, he purged many of the other Chinese Communist Party members in the Cultural Revolution, begun in 1966 and ended in 1969, in an attempt to deflect blame for the failure from himself.

The essay On Coalition Government, written at the end of the Communist Revolution, set out Mao's two phase program for bringing about Socialism in China. He subscribes to the basic principles of Historical Materialism, and recognized that at that time the level of economic development in the society was not where it needed to be to bring about a successful Proletarian Revolution. Thus, there needed to be an intermediate stage. The intermediate state was to be New Democracy, a United-Front Democratic Alliance based on the overwhelming majority of the people under the leadership of the working class.

The essay On the People's Democratic Dictatorship, which was written in 1949 after Mao had become the dictator of China, displays a sharply different tone. It argues for the right to persecute Mao's political enemies.

STUDY QUESTIONS:

1. Why is an intermediate stage necessary for China between the stage before Mao and the Communist future he envisions?

2. What does Mao mean by a Coalition Government?

3. How does the definition of the people differ in the two essays, and how does this help Mao to justify persecution of those who disagree with him?

On Coalition Government

OUR GENERAL PROGRAMME

An agreed common programme is urgently needed by the Chinese people, the Chinese Communist Party and all the anti-Japanese democratic parties for the purpose of mobilizing and uniting all the anti-Japanese forces of the Chinese people, completely wiping out the Japanese aggressors and building a new China that is independent, free, democratic, united, prosperous and powerful.

Such a common programme may be divided into two parts, the general and the specific. Let us consider first the general and then the specific programme.

On the major premise that the Japanese aggressors must be completely destroyed and a new China must be built, we Communists and the overwhelming majority of the population are agreed on the following fundamental propositions at the present stage of China's development. First, China should not have a feudal, fascist and anti-popular state system under the dictatorship of the big landlords and big bourgeoisie, because eighteen years of government by the chief ruling clique of the Kuomintang have already proved its complete bankruptcy. Second, China cannot possibly establish the old type of democratic dictatorship—a purely national-bourgeois state—and therefore should not attempt to do so, because on the one

hand the Chinese national bourgeoisie has proved itself very flabby economically and politically, and on the other, for a long time now a new factor has been present, namely, the awakened Chinese proletariat with its leader, the Chinese Communist Party, which has demonstrated great capacity in the political arena and assumed leadership of the peasant masses, the urban petty bourgeoisie, the intelligentsia and other democratic forces. Third, it is likewise impossible for the Chinese people to institute a socialist state system at the present stage when it is still their task to fight foreign and feudal oppression and the necessary social and economic conditions for a socialist state are still lacking.

What then do we propose? We propose the establishment, after the thorough defeat of the Japanese aggressors, of a state system which we call New Democracy, namely, a united-front democratic alliance based on the overwhelming majority of the people, under the leadership of the working class.

It is this kind of state system that truly meets the demands of the overwhelming majority of the Chinese population, because it can win and indeed has been winning the approval, first, of millions of industrial workers and tens of millions of handicraftsmen and farm labourers, second, of the peasantry, which constitutes 80 per cent of China's population, i.e., 360 million out of a population of 450 million, and third, of the large numbers of the urban petty bourgeoisie as well as the national bourgeoisie, the enlightened gentry and other patriots.

Of course, there are still contradictions among those classes, notably the contradiction between labour and capital, and consequently each has its own particular demands. It would be hypocritical and wrong to deny the existence of these contradictions and differing demands. But throughout the stage of New Democracy, these contradictions, these differing demands, will not grow and transcend the demands which all have in common and should not be allowed to do so; they can be adjusted. Given such adjustment, these classes can together accomplish the political, economic and cultural tasks of the new-democratic state.

The politics of New Democracy which we advocate consists in the overthrow of external oppression and of internal feudal and fascist oppression, and then the setting up not of the old type of democracy but of a political system which is a united front of all the democratic classes. These views of ours are completely in accord with the revolutionary views of Dr. Sun Yat sen. In the Manifesto of the First National Congress of the Kuomintang, Dr. Sun wrote:

The so-called democratic system in modern states is usually monopolized by the bourgeoisie and has become simply an instrument for oppressing the common people. On the other hand, the Kuomintang's Principle of Democracy means a democratic system shared by all the common people and not privately owned by the few.

This is a great political injunction of Dr. Sun's. The Chinese people, the Chinese Communist Party and all other democrats must respect it, firmly put it into practice and wage a determined fight against all individuals and groups that violate or oppose it, and so defend and develop this perfectly correct political principle of New Democracy.

The organizational principle of the new democratic state should be democratic centralism, with the people's congresses determining the major policies and electing the governments at the various levels. It is at once democratic and centralized, that is, centralized on the basis of democracy and democratic under centralized guidance. This is the only system that can give full expression to democracy with full powers vested in the people's congresses at all levels and, at the same time, guarantee centralized administration with the governments at each level exercising centralized management of all the affairs entrusted to them by the people's congresses at the corresponding level and safeguarding whatever is essential to the democratic life of the people.

The army and the other armed forces constitute an important part of the apparatus of the new-democratic state power, without which the state cannot be defended. As with all other organs of power, the armed forces of the new-democratic state belong to the people and protect the people; they have nothing in common with the army, police, etc. of the old type which belong to the few and oppress the people.

The economy of New Democracy which we advocate is likewise in accord with Dr. Sun's principles. On the land question, Dr. Sun championed "land to the tiller". On the question of industry and commerce, Dr. Sun stated in the Manifesto quoted above:

Enterprises, such as banks, railways and airlines, whether Chinese-owned or foreign owned, which are either monopolistic in character or too big for private management, shall be operated and administered by the state, so that private capital cannot dominate the livelihood of the people: this is the main principle of the regulation of capital.

In the present stage, we fully agree with these views of Dr. Sun's on economic questions.

Some people suspect that the Chinese Communists are opposed to the development of individual initiative, the growth of private capital and the protection of private property, but they are mistaken. It is foreign oppression and feudal oppression that cruelly fetter the development of the individual initiative of the Chinese people, hamper the growth of private capital and destroy the property of the people. It is the very task of the New Democracy we advocate to remove these fetters and stop this destruction, to guarantee that the people can freely develop their individuality within the framework of society and freely develop such private capitalist economy as will benefit and not "dominate the livelihood of the people", and to protect all appropriate forms of private property.

In accordance with Dr. Sun's principles and the experience of the Chinese revolution, China's national economy at the present stage should be composed of the state sector, the private sector and the co operative sector. But the state here must certainly not be one "privately owned by the few", but a new democratic state "shared by all the common people" under the leadership of the proletariat.

The culture of New Democracy should likewise be "shared by all the common people", that is, it should be a national, scientific and mass culture, and must under no circumstances be a culture "privately owned by the few".

Such is the general or fundamental programme which we Communists advocate

for the present stage, the entire stage of the bourgeois-democratic revolution. This is our minimum programme as against our future or maximum programme of socialism and communism. Its realization will carry the Chinese state and Chinese society a step forward, from a colonial, semi colonial and semi feudal to a new democratic state and society.

The political leadership of the proletariat and the proletarian-led state and co-operative sectors of the economy required by our programme are socialist factors. Yet the fulfilment of this programme will not turn China into a socialist society.

We Communists do not conceal our political views. Definitely and beyond all doubt, our future or maximum programme is to carry China forward to socialism and communism. Both the name of our Party and our Marxist world outlook unequivocally point to this supreme ideal of the future, a future of incomparable brightness and splendour. On joining the Party, every Communist has two clearly-defined objectives at heart, the new-democratic revolution now and socialism and communism in the future, and for these he will fight despite the animosity of the enemies of communism and their vulgar and ignorant calumny, abuse and ridicule, which we must firmly combat. As for the well-meaning sceptics, we should explain things to them with goodwill and patience and not attack them. All this is very clear, definite and unequivocal.

But all Communists and sympathizers with communism in China must struggle to achieve the objective of the present stage; they must struggle against foreign and feudal oppression to deliver the Chinese people from their miserable colonial, semi-colonial and semi-feudal plight and establish a proletarian-led new-democratic China whose main task is the liberation of the peasantry, a China of the revolutionary Three

People's Principles of Dr. Sun Yat-sen, a China which is independent, free, democratic, united, prosperous and powerful. This is what we have actually been doing. Together with the masses of the Chinese people, we Communists have been fighting heroically for this objective for the past twenty-four years.

If any Communist or Communist sympathizer talks about socialism and communism but fails to fight for this objective, if he belittles this bourgeois-democratic revolution, relaxes or slows down ever so slightly and shows the least disloyalty and coolness or is reluctant to shed his blood or give his life for it, then wittingly or unwittingly, such a person is betraying socialism and communism to a greater or lesser extent and is certainly not a politically conscious and staunch fighter for communism. It is a law of Marxism that socialism can be attained only via the stage of democracy. And in China the fight for democracy is a protracted one. It would be a sheer illusion to try to build a socialist society on the ruins of the colonial, semi colonial and semi-feudal order without a united new-democtatic state, without the development of the state sector of the new-democratic economy, of the private capitalist and the co operative sectors, and of a national, scientific and mass culture, i.e., a new-democratic culture, and without the liberation and the development of the individuality of hundreds of millions of people—in short, without a thoroughgoing bourgeois-democratic revolution of a new type led by the Communist Party.

Some people fail to understand why, so far from fearing capitalism, Communists should advocate its development in certain given conditions. Our answer is simple. The substitution of a certain degree of capitalist development for the oppression of foreign imperialism and domestic feudalism is not only an advance but an unavoidable process. It benefits the proletariat as well as the bourgeoisie, and

the former perhaps more. It is not domestic capitalism but foreign imperialism and domestic feudalism which are superfluous in China today; indeed, we have too little of capitalism. Strangely enough, some spokesmen of the Chinese bourgeoisie fight shy of openly advocating the development of capitalism, but refer to it obliquely. There are other people who flatly deny that China should permit a necessary degree of capitalist development and who talk about reaching socialism in one stride and "accomplishing at one stroke" the tasks of the Three People's Principles and socialism. Obviously, these opinions either reflect the weakness of the Chinese national bourgeoisie or are a demagogic trick on the part of the big landlords and the big bourgeoisie. From our knowledge of the Marxist laws of social development, we Communists clearly understand that under the state system of New Democracy in China it will be necessary in the interests of social progress to facilitate the development of the private capitalist sector of the economy (provided it does not dominate the livelihood of the people) besides the development of the state sector and of the individual and co-operative sectors run by the labouring people. We Communists will not let empty talk or deceitful tricks befuddle us.

There are some people who doubt whether we Communists are sincere when we declare that "the Three People's Principles being what China needs today, our Party is ready to fight for their complete realization". This is the result of their failure to understand that the basic tenets of the Three People's Principles, which Dr. Sun Yat-sen enunciated in the Manifesto of the First National Congress of the Kuomintang in 1924 and which we have accepted, coincide with certain basic tenets of our Party's programme for the present stage, that is, of our minimum programme. It should be pointed out that these Three People's Principles of Dr. Sun Yat-sen coincide with our Party's programme for the present stage only in certain basic tenets and not in everything. Our Party's programme of New Democracy is of course much more comprehensive than Dr. Sun's principles, particularly as our Party's theory, programme and practice of New Democracy have greatly developed with the development of the Chinese revolution in the twenty years since Dr. Sun's death, and will develop still further. In essence, however, these Three People's Principles are a programme of New Democracy, as distinguished from the previous, old Three People's Principles; naturally they are "what China needs today" and naturally "our Party is ready to fight for their complete realization". To us Chinese Communists, the struggle for our Party's minimum programme and the struggle for Dr. Sun's revolutionary, or new, Three People's Principles are basically (though not in every respect) one and the same thing. Therefore, as in the past and the present, the Chinese Communists will prove to be the most sincere and thoroughgoing executors of the revolutionary Three People's Principles in the future as well.

Some people are suspicious and think that once in power, the Communist Party will follow Russia's example and establish the dictatorship of the proletariat and a one-party system. Our answer is that a new-democratic state based on an alliance of the democratic classes is different in principle from a socialist state under the dictatorship of the proletariat. Beyond all doubt, our system of New Democracy will be built under the leadership of the proletariat and of the Communist Party, but throughout the stage of New Democracy China cannot possibly have a one-class dictatorship and one-party government and therefore should not attempt it. We have no reason for refusing to co-operate with all political parties, social groups and individuals, provided their attitude to the Communist Party is cooperative and not hostile. The Russian system has been shaped

by Russian history; in Russia the exploitation of man by man has been abolished as a social system, the political, economic and cultural system of the newest type of democracy, i.e. socialism, has been put into effect, and the people support the Bolshevik Party alone, having discarded all the anti-socialist parties. All this has shaped the Russian system, which is perfectly necessary and reasonable there. But even in Russia, where the Bolshevik Party is the sole political party, the system practised in the organs of state power is still one of an alliance of workers, peasants and intellectuals and an alliance of Party members and non-Party people, and not a system in which the working class and the Bolsheviks alone may work in the organs of government. The Chinese system for the present stage is being shaped by the present stage of Chinese history, and for a long time to come there will exist a special form of state and political power, a form that is distinguished from the Russian system but is perfectly necessary and reasonable for us, namely, the new-democratic form of state and political power based on the alliance of the democratic classes.

OUR SPECIFIC PROGRAMME

Our Party must also have a specific programme for each period based on this general programme. Our general programme of New Democracy will remain unchanged throughout the stage of the bourgeois-democratic revolution, that is, for several decades. But from phase to phase during this stage, conditions have changed or are changing and it is only natural that we have to change our specific programme accordingly. For example, our general programme of New Democracy has remained the same throughout the periods of the Northern Expedition, the Agrarian Revolutionary War and the War of Resistance Against Japan, but there have been changes in our specific programme, because our friends and enemies have not remained the same in the three periods.

The Chinese people now find themselves in the following situation:

1. the Japanese aggressors have not yet been defeated;
2. the Chinese people urgently need to work together for a democratic change in order to achieve national unity, rapidly mobilize and unite all anti-Japanese forces, and defeat the Japanese aggressors in co-operation with the allies; and
3. the Kuomintang government is disrupting national unity and obstructing such a democratic change.

What is our specific programme in the circumstances or, in other words, what are the immediate demands of the people?

We consider the following to be appropriate and minimum demands:

- Mobilize all available forces for the thorough defeat of the Japanese aggressors and the establishment of international peace in co-operation with the allies;
- Abolish the Kuomintang one party dictatorship and establish a democratic coalition government and a joint supreme command;
- Punish the pro Japanese elements, fascists and defeatists who are opposing the people and disrupting national unity, and so help to build national unity;
- Punish the reactionaries who are creating the danger of civil war, and so help to ensure internal peace;
- Punish the traitors, take punitive action against officers who surrender to the enemy, and punish the agents of the Japanese;
- Liquidate the reactionary secret service and all its repressive activities and abolish the concentration camps;

- Revoke all reactionary laws and decrees aimed at suppressing the people's freedom of speech, press, assembly, association, political conviction and religious belief and freedom of the person, and guarantee full civil rights to the people;
- Recognize the legal status of all democratic parties and groups;
- Release all patriotic political prisoners;
- Withdraw all troops encircling and attacking China's Liberated Areas and dispatch them to the anti-Japanese front;
- Recognize the anti-Japanese armed forces and popularly elected governments of China's Liberated Areas;
- Consolidate and expand the Liberated Areas and their armed forces, and recover all lost territory;
- Help the people in the Japanese-occupied areas to organize underground armed forces for armed uprisings;
- Allow the Chinese people to arm themselves and defend their homes and their country;
- Bring about the political and military transformation of those armies directly under the Kuomintang supreme command, which constantly lose battles, oppress the people and discriminate against armies not directly under it, and punish the commanders who are responsible for disastrous defeats;
- Improve the recruiting system and the living conditions of the officers and men;
- Give preferential treatment to the families of the soldiers fighting in the anti-Japanese war, so that the officers and men at the front are free from domestic worries;
- Provide preferential treatment for disabled soldiers and for the families of the soldiers who give their lives for the country, and help demobilized soldiers to settle down and earn a living;

- Develop war industries to facilitate the prosecution of the war;
- Distribute the military and financial aid received from the allies impartially to all the armies fighting in the War of Resistance;
- Punish corrupt officials and institute clean government;
- Improve the pay of the middle and lower grade government employees;
- Give the Chinese people democratic rights;
- Abolish the oppressive pao-chia system;
- Provide the war refugees and the victims of natural disasters with relief;
- Appropriate substantial funds after the recovery of China's lost territory for the extensive relief of people who have suffered under enemy occupation;
- Abolish exorbitant taxes and miscellaneous levies and establish a consolidated progressive tax;
- Introduce rural reforms, reduce rent and interest, provide suitable safeguards for the rights of tenants, grant low-interest loans to impoverished peasants and help the peasants to organize, in order to facilitate the expansion of agricultural production;
- Outlaw bureaucrat capital;
- Abolish the present policy of economic controls;
- Check the unbridled inflation and rocketing prices;
- Assist private industry and provide it with facilities for obtaining loans, purchasing raw materials and marketing its products;
- Improve the livelihood of the workers, provide relief for the unemployed and help the workers to organize, in order to facilitate the expansion of industrial production;
- Abolish Kuomintang indoctrination in education and promote a national, scientific and mass culture and education;
- Guarantee the livelihood of the teachers and other staff members of educational institutions and guarantee academic freedom;
- Protect the interests of the youth, women and children—provide assistance to young student refugees, help the youth and women to organize in order to participate on an equal footing in all work useful to the war effort and to social progress, ensure freedom of marriage and equality as between men and women, and give young people and children a useful education;
- Give the minority nationalities in China better and grant them autonomous rights;
- Protect the interests of the overseas Chinese and assist those who have returned to the motherland;
- Protect foreign nationals who have fled to China from the Japanese oppression and support their struggle against the Japanese aggressors;
- Improve Sino-Soviet relations.

To achieve these demands, the most important thing is the immediate abolition of the Kuomintang one party dictatorship and the establishment of a democratic provisional central government, a coalition government enjoying nation-wide support and including representatives of all the anti-Japanese parties and people without party affiliation. Without this prerequisite it is impossible to make any genuine change in the Kuomintang areas, and therefore in the country as a whole.

These demands voice the desires of the Chinese masses and also of broad sections of democratic public opinion in the allied countries. A minimum specific programme which is agreed upon by all the anti-Japanese democratic parties is absolutely indispensable, and we are prepared to consult with them on the basis of the programme outlined above. Different parties may have different demands, but all should reach agreement on a common programme.

As far as the Kuomintang areas are concerned, such a programme is still at the stage of being a demand of the people; as far as the Japanese-occupied areas are concerned, it is a programme whose fulfilment must await their recovery, except for the item on the organization of underground forces for armed uprisings; as far as the Liberated Areas are concerned, it is a programme which has already been, is being and should continue to be, put into practice.

The immediate demands or specific programme of the Chinese people outlined above involve many vital war-time and post-war problems which require further elucidation. In explaining these problems below we shall criticize some of the wrong viewpoints held by the chief ruling clique of the Kuomintang and at the same time answer some questions raised by other people.

On the People's Democratic Dictatorship

...[Our opponents charge:] "You are dictatorial." My dear sirs, you are right, that is just what we are. All the experience the Chinese people have accumulated through several decades teaches us to enforce the people's democratic dictatorship, that is, to deprive the reactionaries of the right to speak and let the people alone have that right.

Who are the people? At the present stage in China, they are the working class, the peasantry, the urban petty bourgeoisie and the national bourgeoisie. These classes, led by the working class and the Communist Party, unite to form their own state and elect their own government; they enforce their dictatorship over the running dogs of imperialism—the landlord class and bureaucrat—bourgeoisie, as well as the representatives of those classes, the Kuomintang reactionaries and their accomplices—suppress them, allow them only to behave themselves and not to be unruly in word or deed. If they speak or act in an unruly way, they will be promptly stopped and punished. Democracy is practiced within the ranks of the people, who enjoy the rights of freedom of speech, assembly, association and so on. The right to vote belongs only to the people, not to the reactionaries. The combination of these two aspects, democracy for the people and dictatorship over the reactionaries, is the people's democratic dictatorship.

Why must things be done this way? The reason is quite clear to everybody. If things were not done this way, the revolution would fail, the people would suffer, the country would be conquered.

[Our opponents ask:] "Don't you want to abolish state power?" Yes, we do, but not right now; we cannot do it yet. Why? Because imperialism still exists, because domestic reaction still exists, because classes still exist in our country. Our present task is to strengthen the people's state apparatus—mainly the people's army, the people's police and the people's courts—in order to consolidate national defence and protect the people's interests. Given this condition, China can develop steadily, under the leadership of the working class and the Communist Party, from an agricultural into an industrial country and from a new democratic into a socialist and communist society, can abolish classes and realize the Great Harmony. The state apparatus, including the army, the police and the courts, is the instrument by which one class oppresses another. It is an instrument for the oppression of antagonistic classes, it is violence and not "benevolence". "You are not benevolent!" Quite so. We definitely do not apply a policy of benevolence to the reactionaries and towards the reactionary activities of the reactionary classes. Our policy of benevolence is applied only within the ranks of the people, not beyond them to the reactionaries or to the reactionary activities of reactionary classes.

The people's state protects the people. Only when the people have such a state can they educate and remould themselves by democratic methods on a country wide scale, with everyone taking part, and shake off the influence of domestic and foreign reactionaries (which is still very strong, will survive for a long time and cannot be quickly destroyed), rid themselves of the bad habits and ideas acquired in the old society, not allow themselves to be led astray by the reactionaries, and continue to advance to advance towards a socialist and communist society.

Here, the method we employ is democratic, the method of persuasion, not of compulsion. When anyone among the people breaks the law, he too should be punished, imprisoned or even sentenced to death; but this is a matter of a few individual cases, and it differs in principle from the dictatorship exercised over the reactionaries as a class.

As for the members of the reactionary classes and individual reactionaries, so long as they do not rebel, sabotage or create trouble after their political power has been overthrown, land and work will be given to them as well in order to allow them to live and remould themselves through labour into new people. If they are not willing to work, the people's state will compel them to work. Propaganda and educational work will be done among them too and will be done, moreover, with as much care and thoroughness as among the captured army officers in the past. This, too, may be called a "policy of benevolence" if you like, but it is imposed by us on the members of the enemy classes and cannot be mentioned in the same breath with the work of self education which we carry on within the ranks of the revolutionary people.

Such remoulding of members of the reactionary classes can be accomplished only by a state of the people's democratic dictatorship under the leadership of the Communist Party. When it is well done, China's major exploiting classes, the landlord class and the bureaucrat-bourgeoisie (the monopoly capitalist class), will be eliminated for good. There remain the national bourgeoisie; at the present stage, we can already do a good deal of suitable educational work with many of them. When the time comes to realize socialism, that is, to nationalize private enterprise, we shall carry the work of educating and remoulding them a step further. The people have a powerful state apparatus in their hands—there is no need to fear rebellion by the national bourgeoisie.

Colonialism

Colonialism can be understood in at least two different senses. In what I will call the narrow sense "colonialism" refers to the legalized, violently enforced, domination of one nation or people by another. In the first of the readings here, E. Chukwudi Eze means "colonialism" in a broader sense, which also includes many of the effects of this domination, especially neo-colonialism. Neo-colonialism is the common result of colonialism that occurs after the colonial power has officially or formally left the country, but unofficially or through non-legal means the old power continues to control the affairs of the formerly colonized nation. Eze argues that colonialism and neo-colonialism are the inevitable results of the modern social and political philosophies of western Europeans, which included their view of Africans as inferior peoples. Thus, Eze's article can be read as a critique of modern political philosophy by revealing its dark side.

Dinesh D'Souza, a neo-conservative pundit and fellow of the Hoover Institution at Stanford University, argues in the second of these readings that colonialism brought mainly good things to India. Thus he urges us to focus not on the racism or greed that motivated colonial intervention, but rather on the effects of the social, political, and intellectual legacy of Western imperialism.

STUDY QUESTIONS:

1. How does Eze think that racism is connected to modern political philosophy?
2. Why did *Bantu Philosophy* make such an important contribution to Africans, according to Eze?
3. What are the three big ideas that have enriched the West, according to D'Souza?

Modern Western Philosophy and African Colonialism

E. Chukwudi Eze

By "colonialism" we should understand the indescribable crisis disproportionately suffered and endured by the African peoples in their tragic encounter with the European world, from the beginning of the fifteenth century through the end of the nineteenth into the first half of the twentieth. This is a period marked by the horror and violence of the transatlantic slave trade, the imperial occupation of most parts of Africa and the forced administrations of its peoples, and the resilient and enduring ideologies and practices of European cultural superiority (ethnocentrism) and "racial" supremacy (racism). In vain do we seek to limit the colonial period to the "brief" 70 years between the 1884 Berlin Conference that partitioned and legitimized European occupation of Africa and the early 1960s when most African countries attained constitutional decolonization.[1]

The beginnings of colonialism need to be traced to both the sporadic and the systematic maritime commercial incursions into Africa by European fortune seekers which began in the mid-fifteenth century. These commercial interests, individual as well as institutional,

were aimed at the extraction and trading of gold, ivory, and other natural resources and raw materials, but it quickly expanded into the exportation of able-bodied Africans and their children as slaves to the Americas and other parts of the world. It was the wealth and capital, accumulated by European merchants and institutions (Barclays, Lloyds, etc.) in the Triangular Trade that financed technological innovations in arms and other sailing equipment. These, in turn, made possible subsequent large-scale military expeditions that eventually "pacified" African kingdoms. Most of these trading companies kept salaried armies, or financed, through taxes, the (European) governmental administrations of the conquered territories. Aijaz Ahmad's observation about Britain, in this regard, is accurate:

> commercial developers and adventurers like Cecil Rhodes in Southern Africa, Frederick Luggard in Nigeria, and Hugh Cholmondeley Delamere in Kenya, played important roles in later British colonization on the African continent. Although the British

government initially kept a safe distance from these adventurers and their questionable aims and practices, it later adopted many of their early dreams and ambitions to justify colonial expansion . . . And the English government in most cases provided the companies with protection to ensure free trading rights. Eventually the government took the natural step of establishing administrative, colonial control over those areas in which British trading companies were involved.[2]

With respect to Africa, then, I use the term "colonialism" as a clustered concept to designate the historical realities of: (a) the European imperial incursions into Africa, which began in the late fifteenth and early sixteenth centuries and grew into the massive transatlantic slave trade; (b) the violent conquest and occupation of the various parts of the continent by diverse European powers which took place in the late nineteenth and early twentieth centuries; (c) the forced administration of African lands and peoples which followed this conquest, and lasted into the years of independence in the 1950s and 1960s and—in case of Zimbabwe and South Africa—into the 1980s and the 1990s. Slave trade, conquest, occupation, and forced administration of peoples, in that order, were all part of an unfolding history of colonialism.

PHILOSOPHY, MODERNITY, AND COLONIALISM

The "colonial period," in a larger sense, should then be understood to cover, roughly, what Cornel West has correctly characterized as "the Age of Europe." This, according to West, is the period "[b]etween 1492 and 1945," a period that was marked by "European breakthroughs in oceanic transportation, agricultural production, state consolidation, bureaucratization, industrialization, urbanization and *imperial dominion* [that] shaped the makings of the modern world."[3] And since the imperial and the colonial domination of Africa were, at root, constitutive elements in the historical formation of the economic, political, and cultural expressions of the Age of Europe, including the Enlightenment, it is imperative that when we study the nature and the dynamic of European modernity, we examine the intellectual and the philosophical productions of the time in order to understand how, in too many cases, they justified imperialism and colonialism. Significant aspects of the philosophies produced by Hume, Kant, Hegel, and Marx have been shown to originate in, and to be intelligible only when understood as, an organic development within larger socio-historical contexts of European colonialism and the ethnocentric idea: Europe is *the* model of humanity, culture, and history in itself. It is precisely this critical (re)examination of the colonial intentions organic to Western modern philosophy that animates at least one wing of contemporary African/a Philosophy. It is a philosophical project aptly captured by Serequeberhan's phrase, "the critique of Eurocentrism."

Basil Davidson, in *Africa: History of a Continent* and in his recent *The African Genius* (as well as in his other numerous publications on African history), points out that the earliest recorded encounters between Europeans and African kingdoms in the beginning of the fifteenth century reveal remarkable accounts of relationships between equals: the exchange of diplomatic counsels was routine, and glowing European accounts of the thriving and vibrant nations of Bini, Dahomey, Ashanti, etc. whose organizational powers and influence were constantly favorably compared by the Europeans to that of the Roman papacy. However, as the plantations in the Americas developed and Afro-European trade demands shifted from raw material to human labor, there was also a shift in the European literary, artistic, and philosophical characterizations of Africans. Specifically within philosophy, Africans became identified as a subhuman "race" and speculations about the "savage" and "inferior" nature of "the African" and "the African mind" became widespread and intertextually entrenched within the *univers de discours* of the French, British, and German Enlightenment thinkers. David Hume, for example, who at one time served in the British colonial office, wrote in the famous footnote to his essay, "On National Character":

> I am apt to suspect the Negroes to be naturally inferior to the whites. There scarcely ever was a civilized nation of that complexion, nor even any individual eminent in action or speculation. No ingenious manufacturers amongst them, no arts, no sciences. On the other hand, the most rude and barbarous of the whites, such as the ancient GERMANS, the present TARTARS, have still something eminent about them . . . Such a uniform and constant difference could not happen . . . if nature had not made original distinction betwixt these breeds of men.[4]

What is philosophically significant here, I think, is Hume's casting of the "difference" between Europeans and Africans, "white" and "negroes" (*negre,* black), as a "constant" (read: permanent) and "original distinction" established by "nature." It is this form of "natural" philosophical casting of racial differences that framed the African outside of "proper" (read: European) humanity. And since, for the Enlightenment philosophers, European humanity was not only universal but was the embodiment of, and coincident with, humanity as such, the framing of the African as being

of a different, sub-human, species therefore philosophically and anthropologically sanctioned the exploitation of Africans in barbaric ways that were not allowed for Europeans.

Such formulations of philosophical prejudices against Africa and Africans (and other non-European peoples generally) were easily circulated and recycled among modern European philosopher—with little originality. In his essay "On the Varieties of the Different Races of Man," Immanuel Kant amplified and completed the remarks he had made about "the Negro" elsewhere (*Observations On the Feeling of the Beautiful and Sublime*) with the following hierarchical chart on the different "races."

STEM GENUS: *white brunette*
First race, very blond (northern Europe)
Second race, Copper-Red (America)
Third race, Black (Senegambia)
Fourth race, Olive-Yellow (Indians)[5]

As in Hume, the assumption behind this arrangement and this order is precisely skin color: white, black, red, yellow; and the ideal skin tone is the "white"—the *white brunette*—to which others are superior or inferior as they approximate the "white." It is therefore not unfair to point once again to Kant's statement: "This man was black from head to toe, *a clear proof* that what he said was stupid" as clear proof that Kant ascribed to skin color (White or black) the evidence of rational (and therefore, human) capacity—or the lack of it. But when he needs to justify his statement and his positions on this issue, Kant directly appealed to Hume's footnote, already cited.[6]

If the trade and practices of transatlantic slavery were carefully philosophically constructed on the alleged sub-humanity of the African "race," the practice of colonialism was parallely predicated on a metaphysical denial of the historicity of African existence. Nowhere is this line of modern European thought as evident as in Hegel's twin treatise:

Lectures on Philosophy of History and Lectures on the Philosophy of Right. In the former, Hegel positions Africa *outside* of History, as the absolute, non-historical beginning of the movement of Spirit. Accordingly, Africans are depicted as incapable of rational thought or ethical conduct. They therefore have no laws, religion, and political order. Africa, in human terms, is, for Hegel a wasteland filled with "lawlessness," "fetishism," and "cannibalism"—waiting for European soldiers and missionaries to conquer it and impose "order" and "morality."[7] For Hegel, the African deserved to be enslaved. Besides, slavery to Europeans, Hegel argued, benefited the African, as it provided him/her with moral "education"! Accordingly, colonialism was also a benefit to Africa because Europe inseminated it with its reason, ethic, culture, and mores, and thereby historicized it.

Although he is already quite aware of the colonial phenomenon in the *Philosophy of History*,[8] it is not until the *Philosophy of Right* that Hegel elaborately lays out the theoretical structures that at once directly justify and explain colonialism—as the inevitable logic of the unfolding of Spirit in (European) history. Building upon the metaphysical schemes laid out in the *Logic* and in the *Philosophy of History*, Hegel in the *Philosophy of Right* accurately and painstakingly explains why and how the modern capitalist organization of state and economy in Europe necessarily leads to imperialism and colonialism.

For Hegel, the imperial and the colonial expansion of Europe is the necessary and *logical* outlet for resolving the problem of poverty inherent to capitalism. When the capitalist division of labor and trade that was meant to satisfy the "system of wants" of a civil society generates at the same time a class of paupers and disenfranchised segments of the population,

there are, for Hegel, only two ways of resolving this contradiction. The first option is welfare, while the second is more jobs. The consequences of both options, however, violate what Hegel considered the basic tenets of the civil society. Welfare deprives the individual [the poor] of initiative and self-respect and independence, while the second—the creation of more jobs – according to Hegel, would cause over-production of goods and services in proportion to available market. This is how Hegel stages the scenario:

> *When the masses begin to decline into poverty, (a) the burden of maintaining them at their ordinary standards of living might be directly laid on the wealthier class [higher taxes, for example], or they might receive the means of livelihood directly from other public sources of wealth . . . In either case, however, the needy would receive subsistence directly, not by means of their work, and this would violate the principle of civil society and the feeling of individual independence and self-respect . . . (b) As an alternative, they might be given subsistence indirectly through being given work, i.e., opportunity to work. In this event the volume of production would be increased, but the evil consists precisely in an excess of production and in the lack of a proportionate number of consumers . . . It hence becomes apparent that despite an excess of wealth civil society is not rich enough, i.e., its own resources are insufficient to check excessive poverty and the creation of a penurious rabble.*[9]

In order, then, to resolve the problem of the poverty of the "penurious rabble" which results from the unequal distribution of wealth inherent to modern European capitalist societies, the solution, Hegel recommends, is the generation of more wealth for Europe from outside of

Europe, through expansion of the market for European goods as well as through colonist and colonialist expansions. Poverty and the need for market, Hegel says,

> drives it [the capitalistically "mature" European society] to push beyond its own limits and seek markets and so its necessary means of subsistence, in other lands which are either deficient in the goods it overproduced, or else generally backward in industry.[10]

Colonial and capitalist expansions are therefore a logical necessity for the realization of the obviously universal European Idea, and by labeling the non-European territories and people as "backward" in "industry," they become legitimate prey for colonial and colonialist activities. According to Hegel: "All great peoples . . . press onward to the sea," because

> the sea affords the means for the colonizing activity—sporadic or systematic—to which the mature civil society is driven and by which it supplies to part of its population a return to life on the family basis in a new land and so also supplies itself with a new demand and field for its industry.[11]

In this articulation of Europe's rush for wealth and for territory in other lands, Hegel does not raise any ethical questions or moral consideration precisely because, in addition to Hume and Kant, Hegel himself had declared the African sub-human: the African lacked reason and therefore moral and ethical content. This philosophically articulated "natural" status of the African automatically precludes the possibility that the relationship between Europe and Africa, the European and the African, the colonizer and the colonized, may be governed or regulated by any sort of law or ethics. In Hegel's words (*Philosophy of Right*):

> The civilized nation [Europe] is conscious that the rights of the barbarians [Africans, for example] are unequal to its own and treats their autonomy as only a formality.[12]

It is clear, then, that nowhere is the *direct* conjunction/intersection of the philosophical and the political and economic interests in the European denigration and exploitation of Africans so evident and shameless as in Hegel. Since Africa, for Hegel, "Is the Gold-land compressed within itself," the continent *and* its peoples become, all at once, a treasure island and a *terra nulla*, a virgin territory brimming with natural and human raw-material passively waiting for Europe to exploit and turn it into mini-European territories.[13]

It is for good reasons then that "the critique of Eurocentrism" has become a significant, if "negative," moment in the practice of African Philosophy.[14] For it is with the authorities of Hume, Kant, Hegel, and Marx behind them, and with the enduring image of "the African" as "black," "savage," "primitive," and so forth, in conjunction with clearly articulated political and economic colonial interests, that nineteenth- and twentieth-century European anthropologists descended upon Africa. And *quelle surprise!*: the Lévy-Bruhls and the Evans-Pritchards report that the "African mind" is "pre-logical," "mystical," and "irrational." These anthropological productions, often commissioned after military invasion of an African territory or after a rebellion against occupying European powers,[15] were intended to provide the European administrations and missionary-cultural workers with information about the "primitive" to guarantee both efficient administration as well as provide knowledge of the "African mentality" so that, while demonizing and repressing African practices, the "superior" European values and attitudes could be effectively inculcated into the African conscience. From the transformations in the African economies and politics to religion and the educational institutions, the goal was to maximize European profit, secure the total domination and subjection of the colonial territory to the metropole, and reproduce Europe and European values not only in the material lives but also in the cultural and spiritual lives and expressions of the African.

AFRICAN PHILOSOPHY AS COUNTER-COLONIAL PRACTICE

(a) It is within the colonial context that we must explore the significance of a book which, more than any other, influenced, at the continental level, the development and self-understanding of twentieth-century history of African philosophy. I am speaking of Father Placide Tempels' *Bantu Philosophy* (1945). As stated by the author, the aim of the book is to serve the European colonialist as a handbook on indigenous African "philosophy." According to the argument of the book, the European needed to understand the African worldviews and belief systems so that the missionary message and "civilizationary" projects could be implanted in the vital nodes of the structures of faith and the existential interiority of the African. Thus, colonization could succeed, and succeed in a self-sustaining manner. Tempels' work is therefore predominantly an exposition of the ontological systems of the Baluba, an ethnic group in Zaire where Tempels, a Belgian missionary, worked for many years. Tempels believed that the Baluba ontology grounded and regulated the daily ethical, political, and economic existence of the African. In order to elevate the "pagan" existence of the African to "civilization," one must work through this ontological system which grounds the subjectivity of the Bantu.

But the volcanic historical significance of Tempels' work is not necessarily located in its intentions. It is located elsewhere—in the title of the book; specifically the author's explicit use of the term "philosophy" to characterize an intellectual product associated with the African. Whereas the anthropologist spoke of "savage mentality," or "primitive thought," Tempels spoke of *philosophy*; and because philosophy, to the Western mind, is the honorific term symbolizing the highest exercise of the faculty of reason, the book's title amounted to an admission of the existence of an African philosophy, the existence of African reason, and hence—following this logocentric European logic—African humanity. This notion flew in the face of the entire intellectual edifice of slavery and colonialism which was built precisely on the negation of this possibility.

Tempels' book, then, became inadvertently fruitfully ambiguous. The author intended it as a "handbook" for the missionary-cultural worker: a plea to the European colonialist administrator or missionary that the African's "philosophy" and culture ought to be understood and respected in order for the "civilizing" mission to succeed. But the ambiguous conjunction of "philosophy" as an implicit ontological system which underlies and sustains an African communal worldview, and the honorific notion of "philosophy" in the West as the highest rational (human) achievement was not lost on the African intelligentsia engaged in anti-colonial projects. Tempels' book, for them had collapsed the ideological scaffold that had supported and sustained racism and colonialism, and the book became for these Africans a manual for cultural and political revolt.[16]

With the "discovery" of Bantu philosophy in Africa and the emergence in the United States of the Harlem Renaissance—with its philosophers and intellectuals: Alain Locke, Claude McKay, W. E. B. Dubois and others—where

Africans in the Diaspora were already engaged in the critique of African colonialism and the racism of the New World, a third moment in the history of African philosophy was born: Négritude.[17] As a literary, artistic, and philosophical movement originated in Paris by African and Afro-Caribbean students, Négritude, through Aimé Césaire and Leopold Sedar Senghor, found in *Bantu Philosophy* and in the pluralist anthropologies of Frobenius, Herskovits, and Delafosse, and in the cultural movements of the Harlem Renaissance, renewed energy and resources for a continuing struggle against European denigration and depravation of Africans, on the continent and in Europe. The idea of "African philosophy" as a field of inquiry thus has its contemporary roots in the effort of African thinkers to combat political and economic exploitations, and to examine, question, and contest identities imposed upon them by Europeans. The claims and counter-claims, justifications and alienations that characterize such historical and conceptual protests and contestations indelibly mark the discipline of African philosophy.

(b) A major and continuing dilemma for African philosophy, then, is its attempt to understand and articulate Africa's experience of the "Age of Europe." How, it is asked, could the same European modernity and Enlightenment that promoted "precious ideals like the dignity of persons" and "democracy" also be so intimately and inextricably implicated in slavery and the colonial projects?

Confronted with this duplicity at the heart of European modernity—the subscription to the ideals of universal humanity and democracy on the one hand, and the imperial and colonial subjugation of non-European peoples and racism on the other, some critics are satisfied to attribute the contradictions,—as Cornel West suggests, to an inevitable "discrepancy between sterling rhetoric and lived reality," between "glowing principles and actual practices."[18] Abiola Irele, for example, while recognizing that "many have been betrayed by . . . the Enlightenment ideals of universal reason and universal equality . . . by the difference between word and deed," recommends that we "separate" the ideal from the real, holding on to one while rejecting the other. According to Irele:

> *Africans have suffered greatly from the derogatory insults of the Enlightenment. I believe we must separate the ideals of universal reason and equality from their historical implementation. We must, as it were, trust the tale and not the teller, for though the messenger be tainted, the message need not be.*[19]

But how does one, even conceptually, nicely and neatly separate the "ideals" of European modernity, the Age of Europe, from its concreteness or "historical implementation"? Were the European philosophers' ideas about "humanity" and "freedom" pure and "sterling" and perfect as this argument presumes—in which case it is only in the "implementation" that imperfections (racism, colonialism, etc.) arose? Is it not evident that these "imperfections" were conceptualized as integral and as constitutive of the logic of capitalist and ethnocentric and racist modernity?

Irele's exhortation that "we must separate the [European] ideals of universal reason" from the imperfect "historical implementation" operates a false dichotomy that may mislead one to believe that we can clearly separate the "ideal" from the "real" (the tale from the teller, the message from the messenger, etc.) How do we know what constitutes "ideal" except in/through the way it was and has been practiced? Furthermore, to speak of ideals or ideas as universally neutral schemes or models which we historically perfectly or imperfectly implement obscures the fact that these ideals and ideas and models are always already part and parcel of, i.e., always already infused with historical practices and intentions out of which ideals are, in the first place, constituted as such—and judged worthy of pursuit. Ideals do not have meaning in a historical vacuum.

It is more appropriate I think, to consider Africa's experience of the "Age of Europe" as the *cost* of Occidental modernity. This idea of "cost," introduced but left undeveloped by the West, is to be understood literally, as that which had to be *sacrificed* in order to purchase, or pursue, European modernity's "order," "progress," "culture," "civilization," etc. By *negating* Africa, Europe was able to posit and represent itself and its contingent historicity as the ideal culture, the ideal humanity, and ideal history. While "reason" and "humanity" and "light" remained in Europe, "irrationality" and "savagery," and "darkness" were conveniently— and perhaps unconsciously—projected unto Africa, the Big, Bad, Primeval Evil, the "Dark Continent." The very condition of the possibility of European modernity as an Idea was the explicit metaphysical negation and theoretical exclusion of Africa and the African, archetypally frozen as "savage" and "primitive".

To gain a general understanding of the historical scope of this "Africa" in the European imaginary, one has only to carefully study V. Y. Mudimbe's most recent works: *The Invention of Africa* and the sequel, *The Idea of Africa*.[20] But to appreciate its continuing depth and endurance within professional European philosophy, one could easily point to the works of those who claim to be the most radical critics of modernity, for example, Martin Heidegger or the critical-reformist philosopher of European modernity, Jürgen Habermas. Consider Heidegger's very recent comments, to this effect: "Nature has its history. But then *Negroes* would also have history. Or does nature then have no history? It

can enter into the past as something transitory, but not everything that fades away enters into history."[21] Or Habermas' willful typologies of Africa and the African worldview in his two-volume *Theory of Communicative Actions*.[22] The aims and intentions, the questions and the problems, that preoccupy twentieth-century African philosophy are stalked by a singular and incisive Occidental model of man.

When Western philosophy speaks of "reason," it is not just speaking of "science" and "knowledge" and "method," and "critique," or even "thought." In and through these codes it is more fundamentally the question of the "anthropos," of the human, that is at stake, for questions of knowledge and identity, logos and anthropos, always hang together. It is within this background of *anthropos* as *logikos*, the interlacing of human understanding and the understanding of the human, that Europeans originally introduced the notion of a *difference in kind* between themselves and Africans as a way of justifying unspeakable exploitation and denigration of Africans.

PHILOSOPHY AND THE (POST)COLONIAL

African Philosophy labors under this yet-to-end exploitation and denigration of African humanity. It challenges the long-standing exclusion of Africa, or more accurately, its inclusion as the negative "other" of reason and of the western world in the major traditions of modern Western philosophy. And because this is an ongoing task, as well as in light of many other factors not unconnected with the colonial and neo-colonial nature of Africa's relationship with the West, the "post" of the "postcolonial" African philosophy has to be written under erasure, or—more conveniently—in brackets. Scribing the "post" of the postcolonial under erasure or brackets serves as signal and pointer to the unfulfilled dreams of the independence achievements of the 1960s.

It also highlights the paradoxical—and productively "deconstructive"—nature of a self-conscious (post)colonial critical philosophical work. For, to borrow an eloquent passage from Gayatri Spivak:

> Postcoloniality—the heritage of imperialism in the rest of the globe—is a deconstructive case. As follows: Those of us from formerly colonized countries are able to communicate with each other and with the metropolis to exchange and to establish sociality and transnationality, because we have had access to the culture of imperialism. Shall we then assign to that culture, in the words of the ethical philosopher Bernard Williams, a measure of "moral luck"? I think there can be no question that the answer is "no". This impossible "no" to a structure which one critiques, yet inhabits intimately, is the deconstructive philosophical position, and the everyday here and now of "post-coloniality" is a case of it.[23]

Spivak's "impossible 'no'" confirms what I have always known from an enduring truth of the Igbo proverb: *Okuko bere na ngugu na-azo isi, na-azokwa odu.* Like this Igbo proverbial hen, on a rope minding both its head and tale, distrustful of one-dimensional vision, the "(post)colonial" in philosophy, historically, is also a place of dangerous potency, and as critical project, it must necessarily remain a project in double-gesture.[24]

We know that the earliest Africans in America and Europe were largely forcefully brought there through slavery, and that the succeeding generation who came after the abolition of slave trade came largely to learn the ways of the West in preparation for the revolutions that would crystallize in constitutional de-colonization (Kwame Nkrumah, Nnamdi Azikiwe, Senghor, etc.). Today, however, for the first time in known history, Africans come to Europe and America to find—ironically—a place of refuge, a refuge always precarious because of racism and discriminatory immigration laws. This sad and ironic recent development results from the fact that Africa's transition from colony to nation-states has failed to translate into freedom. A commentator recently stated:

> The oppressive class configuration which colonialism epitomized, in essence, remains intact, as direct colonial presence was effectively replaced with indigenous clones. Not only did strife ensue, thanks in part to the conceited manner of colonial withdrawal, repression returned and [political] opposition was once more anathematized, often with a crudity and brutality equaling the barbarism of colonialism.[25]

With migration and instability as chronic elements in modern history of African, African/a philosophy must find ways to make sense, and speak of, the multiplicities and the pluralisms of these historical "African" experiences.

"The African experience," however, has never really been a monolith, on the continent or abroad. From Amo to Nkrumah to Du Bois; from Equiano to Locke to Senghor; continental and Diaspora modern Africans found a "language"—largely based upon their awareness of a collective entanglement with the history of the modern West, their objectification and "thingfication" by this West, and so have also always individually and collectively struggled in multi-faceted and pluralistic ways against the oppressive tendencies within European capitalist cultures, and the illegitimate colonial structures that crush African initiatives on the continent.

NOTES

1 Ali Mazrui refers to this point of view as the "episodic" theory of African colonialism. This theory "asserts that the European [occupation] of Africa has been shallow rather than deep, transitional rather than long-lasting." As proof, the theorists argue: "It is not often realized how brief the colonial period was," and offer, as examples, "When Jomo Kenyatta was born, Kenya was not yet a crown colony. Kenyatta lived right through the period of British rule and outlasted British rule by fifteen years." Conclusion: "if the entire period of colonialism could be compressed into the life-span of a single individual, how deep was the impact?" See: Mazrui, *The African: A Triple Heritage* (Boston: Little, Brown and Company, 1986), p. 14. The position I take, and my arguments, are against this "theory".

2 "The Politics of Literary Postcoloniality," *Race and Class*, vol. 36, no. 3, 1995, p. 7. Italics are mine.

3 Cornel West, *Keeping Faith: Philosophy and Race in America* (New York: Routledge, 1993), p. 5; my emphasis.

4 I am quoting from a later version of this statement which incorporated corrections Hume had made to it in response to criticisms and objections raised against the original by James Beatie (*An Essay on the Nature and Immutability of Truth in Opposition to Sophistry and Skepticism* 1770). For a detailed discussion of the differences between the earlier and the later versions, see my editorial notes in *Racist Enlightenment* (forthcoming from Blackwell); or my essay, "The Idea of 'Race' in Hume's Social Philosophy and Its Impact on Eighteen-Century America," included in Dorothy Coleman, ed. *Hume and Eighteenth-Century America*, forthcoming.

5 The most extensive discussion of the role the idea of "race" plays in Kant's thought is probably my essay, "The Color of Reason: The Idea of 'race' in Kant's Anthropology," in *Anthropology and the German Enlightenment*, ed. Katherine Faull (London: Bucknell and Associated University Presses, 1994), pp. 201–41. (Partially reprinted in SAPINA: *Bulletin of Society for African Philosophy in North America*, vol. 8, nos. 1–2, Jan.–July, 1995, pp. 53–78. Other valuable sources are: Christian Neugebauer, "The Racism of Kant and Hegel," in Odera Oruka, ed., *Sage Philosophy: Indigenous Thinkers and Modern Debate on African Philosophy* (New York: Brill, 1990), pp. 259–72; Ronald Judy, "Kant and the Negro," SAPINA, Jan.–July, 1991.

6 According to Kant: "Mr Hume challenges anyone to cite a simple example in which a Negro has shown talents, and asserts that among the hundreds of thousands of black. . .not a single one was ever found who presented anything great in art or science. . . So fundamental is the difference between the two races of man, and it appears to be great in regard to mental capacities as in color." *Observations*, trans. John T. Goldthwait (Berkeley: University of California Press, 1960), pp. 110–11.

7 Within a few pages of *Philosophy of History*, Hegel has used the following terms to describe African peoples: "barbarism and savagery," "barbarous ferocity," "terrible hordes," "barbarity," "animal man," "savagery and lawlessness," "primitive," "animality," "the most terrible manifestation of human nature," "wild confusion," and "Unhistorical, Undeveloped Spirit." A first-year Bucknell student, Sean Gray, who researched this language as part of an assignment for my course, "Hegel,

Modernity and the African World," had this to say: "This [Hegel's] language is argumentative in nature, attempting to shock the reader into following what he said. These words show up way before Hegel provides specific accounts of any historical African peoples. By formulating such steep language ahead of time, the reader is psychologically set to look for the worst and so won't be shocked by whatever fantasies or exaggerations about Africa Hegel chooses to provide." (Sean Gray: "The Notions of Barbarism and Savagery in Hegel's Treatment of Africa.") Critical literature on Hegel's ideas about Africa include Serequeberhan, "The Idea of Colonialism in Hegel's Philosophy of Right," in *International Philosophical Quarterly*, vol no. 3, Sept. 29, 1989, pp. 302–18; Robert Bernasconi, "Hegel at the Court of the Ashanti," forthcoming. I also examined Hegel's *Philosophy of History* and *Philosophy of Right* in the second chapter of my 1993 dissertation, "Rationality and the Debates about African Philosophy," and will expand this study in a volume, *Racist Enlightenment*, under preparation for Blackwell Publishers.

8   Hegel, for example, writes in this volume that "the North American states . . . were entirely *colonized* [emphasis in the original] by the Europeans." *Lectures on the Philosophy of World History*, trans. H. B. Nisbet (Cambridge: Cambridge University Press, 1993), p. 167

9   Hegel, *Philosophy of Right*, trans. T. M. Knox (Oxford: Oxford University Press, 1967) p. 150.

10   Hegel, *The Essential Writings*, ed. F. Weiss (New York: Harper Books, 1974), pp. 282–3.

11   Ibid. Italics are mine.

12   Knox trans., par. 351, p. 219.

13   As we know, subsequent major European philosophers re-inscribed these Hegelian colonialist intentions on Africa into their own philosophical systems. Edward Said pointed out in *Orientalism* that although Marx may have "turned Hegel on his head," his views on European colonization of India and Africa were no different.

14   It is, however, only a "negative" moment in a qualified sense. Positively, it is a way of de-blocking African philosophical consciousness clouded over by Eurocentric and racist writings, a way of critiquing in order to reject the pernicious parts of the philosophical traditions we ambiguously inherit from European modernity, because we recognize human and humane elements in them that may also speak cross-culturally and with less exploitation, less racism, and less ethnocentrism.

15   See the excellent volume edited by Tala Asad: *Anthropology and the Colonial Encounter* (London: Ithaca Press, 1973); also some choice essays in Chinua Achebe, *Hopes and Impediments* (New York: Doubleday, 1988).

16   It was not until much later that African philosophers such as Aimé Césaire (*Discourse on Colonialism*, trans. J. Pinkham (New York: Monthly Review Press, 1972)) and Frantz Fanon started to focus negative-critical attention explicitly and publicly on the colonialist and ideological intentions of Tempels' *Bantu Philosophy*. The more widespread immediate response was similar to that of Aléxis Kagamé and a host of others now identified in the "ethno-philosophy" schools: they revised and expanded but continued Tempels' major methodological orientation, namely, the documentation and analysis of evidence of philosophical thought in African languages and in the unwritten traditions of various African peoples.

17   I do not intend to make Tempels, or the three "moments" I discuss here, the absolute

beginning for African philosophical practice. In addition to philosophical works in the "oral" traditions (for example, the "Ifa" [or "Afa"] Corpus among the Yorubas and the Igbos of West Africa), there are bodies of written anti-slavery and anti-colonial philosophical works that date back to the sixteenth century. On the continent, the rational hermeneutics of the Abyssinian Zera Yecob (1599–1692), for example, was concerned with the question of the nature of reason and faith in the context of the acute crisis of Abyssinian cultural, and political integrity, "In confrontation with the subversive work of Jesuit missionaries and aggressive Catholicism" (Tsenay Serequeberhan, *The Hermeneutics of African Philosophy*, New York: Routledge, 1994, p. 18). In the Diaspora, in 1732, William Amo, a native of a little town in present Ghana, at age 27 received what is today called a doctorate degree in Philosophy from the University of Wittenberg. He taught at the universities of Halle and Jena, and, in addition to extant works on epistemology and philosophical psychology, also wrote and, perhaps, published a lost work entitled *On the Freedom of Africans in Europe*. Amo returned to Ghana in 1747 and lived there as a hermit for the rest of his life (his date of death is unknown). Likewise, the autobiography of the Igbo gentleman Olaudah Equiano, although written from the point of view of his involvement in abolitionist movements in eighteenth- and nineteenth-century England, is an excellent document of the racist and colonialist social and political thinking of Europeans on Africa in modern Europe. The examples of Amo and Equiano only alert us to Leonard Harris's landmark collection, *Philosophy Born of Struggle* (Dubuque, Iowa: Kendall/Hunt, 1983) which chronicles the enormous wide-ranging philosophical productivity in Afro-America from the beginning of our century. Today, as we know, African and African-Diasporic men and women of letters: Chinua Achebe, Wole Soyinka, Toni Morrison, Cheikh Amidoukane, etc.—in addition to the efforts of those whose professional vocation is more strictly "Philosophy"—are producing literary resources of unsurpassed philosophical depths that powerfully articulate and chronicles our contemporary experiences. Finally, we should specifically mention the numerous successful attempts by Osabutey (1936), G. James (1954), Diop (1974), Henry Olela (1980) Onyenwuenyi (1994), Th. Obenga (1973; 1990), and Martin Bernal (1991) to (re)write the history of the African origins of Greek and European philosophy. Regardless of the admittedly ideological functions of *some* of these works, others are needed antidotes to racist inanities that have been spouted for too long about a supposedly a-historical "Greek miracle," as a way of marginalizing or suppressing African and Semitic contributions to ancient philosophy.

[18] *Keeping Faith*, p. 6.

[19] Abiola Irele, "Contemporary Thought in French Speaking Africa," in Albert Moseley, ed., *African Philosophy: Selected Readings* (Englewood Cliffs, NJ: Prentice Hall, 1995), p. 296.

[20] Both published by Indiana University Press, 1988 and 1994.

[21] Heidegger went on to illustrate his assertion with the following example: "When an airplane's propeller turns, then nothing actually 'occurs.' Conversely, when the same airplane takes the Führer to Mussolini, then history occurs." We wish this plane would make a return trip for Abacha and Mobutu and Idi Amin and Emperor Bokassa—so that "history" will truly fully "occur"!

22 See especially the first chapters of volume I subtitled *Reason and the Rationalization of Society*, trans. Thomas McCarthy (Boston: Beacon Press, 1984).

23 *Outside in the Teaching Machine* (London: Routledge, 1993).

24 Outlaw's "African Philosophy: Deconstructive and Reconstructive Challenges" is an elaborate case of this; Serequeberhan's *The Hermeneu-tics of African Philosophy* and Amilcar Cabral's *Return to the Source* are exemplary in terms of working with colonial "tools" to dismantle the house that colonialism built for the sake of a (re)new(ed) sense of humanity and values in the social order.

25 Olu Oguibe, ed., *Sojourners: New Writings by Africans in Britain* (London: Africa Refugee Publishing Collective, 1994) pp. xiv–xv.

Two Cheers for Colonialism

Dinesh D'souza

Colonialism has gotten a bad name in recent decades. Anticolonialism was one of the dominant political currents of the 20th century, as dozens of European colonies in Asia and Africa became free. Today we are still living with the aftermath of colonialism. Apologists for terrorism, including Osama bin Laden, argue that terrorist acts are an understandable attempt on the part of subjugated non-Western peoples to lash out against their longtime Western oppressors. Activists at last year's World Conference on Racism, including the Rev. Jesse Jackson, have called on the West to pay reparations for slavery and colonialism to minorities and natives of the third world.

These justifications of violence, and calls for monetary compensation, rely on a large body of scholarship that has been produced in the Western academy. That scholarship, which goes by the name of anticolonial studies, postcolonial studies, or subaltern studies, is now an intellectual school in itself, and it exercises a powerful influence on the humanities and social sciences. Its leading Western scholars include Edward Said, Gayatri Spivak, Walter Rodney, and Samir Amin. Their arguments are supported by the ideas of third-world intellectuals like Wole Soyinka, Chinweizu, Ashis

Nandy, and, perhaps most influential of all, Frantz Fanon.

The assault against colonialism and its legacy has many dimensions, but at its core it is a theory of oppression that relies on three premises: First, colonialism and imperialism are distinctively Western evils that were inflicted on the non-Western world. Second, as a consequence of colonialism, the West became rich and the colonies became impoverished; in short, the West succeeded at the expense of the colonies. Third, the descendants of colonialism are worse off than they would be had colonialism never occurred.

In a widely used text, How Europe Underdeveloped Africa, the Marxist scholar Walter Rodney accuses European colonialism of "draining African wealth and making it impossible to develop more rapidly the resources of the continent." The African writer Chinweizu strikes a similar note in his influential book The West and the Rest of Us. He offers the following explanation for African poverty: "White hordes have sallied forth from their Western homelands to assault, loot, occupy, rule, and exploit the world. Even now the fury of their expansionist assault on the rest of us has not abated." In his classic work The Wretched of the Earth, Fanon

"Two Cheers for Colonialism" originally appeared in *The Chronicle of Higher Education*, Volume 48, issue 35. Reprinted by permission of the author Dinesh D'Souza.

writes, "European opulence has been founded on slavery. The well-being and progress of Europe have been built up with the sweat and the dead bodies of Negroes, Arabs, Indians, and the yellow races."

Those notions are pervasive and emotionally appealing. By suggesting that the West became dominant because it is oppressive, they provide an explanation for Western global dominance without encouraging white racial arrogance. They relieve the third world of blame for its wretchedness. Moreover, they imply politically egalitarian policy solutions: The West is in possession of the "stolen goods" of other cultures, and it has a moral and legal obligation to make some form of repayment. I was raised to believe in such things, and among most third-world intellectuals they are articles of faith. The only problem is that they are not true.

There is nothing uniquely Western about colonialism. My native country of India, for example, was ruled by the British for more than two centuries, and many of my fellow Indians are still smarting about that. What they often forget, however, is that before the British came, the Indians had been invaded and conquered by the Persians, the Afghans, Alexander the Great, the Mongols, the Arabs, and the Turks. Depending on how you count, the British were preceded by at least six colonial powers that invaded and occupied India since ancient times. Indeed, ancient India was itself settled by the Aryan people, who came from the north and subjugated the dark-skinned indigenous people.

Those who identify colonialism and empire only with the West either have no sense of history or have forgotten about the Egyptian empire, the Persian empire, the Macedonian empire, the Islamic empire, the Mongol empire, the Chinese empire, and the Aztec and Inca empires in the Americas. Shouldn't the Arabs be paying reparations for their destruction of the Byzantine and Persian empires? Come to think of it, shouldn't the Byzantine and Persian people be paying reparations to the descendants of the people they subjugated? And while we're at it, shouldn't the Muslims reimburse the Spaniards for their 700-year rule?

As the example of Islamic Spain suggests, the people of the West have participated in the game of conquest not only as the perpetrators, but also as the victims. Ancient Greece, for example, was conquered by Rome, and the Roman Empire itself was destroyed by invasions of Huns, Vandals, Lombards, and Visigoths from northern Europe. America, as we all know, was itself a colony of England before its war of independence; England, before that, had been subdued and ruled by Normans from France. Those of us living today are taking on a large project if we are going to settle on a rule of social justice based on figuring out whose ancestors did what to whom.

The West did not become rich and powerful through colonial oppression. It makes no sense to claim that the West grew rich and strong by conquering other countries and taking their stuff. How did the West manage to do that? In the late Middle Ages, say 1500, the West was by no means the world's most affluent or most powerful civilization. Indeed, those of China and of the Arab-Islamic world exceeded the West in wealth, in knowledge, in exploration, in learning, and in military power. So how did the West gain so rapidly in economic, political, and military power that, by the 19th century, it was able to conquer virtually all of the other civilizations? That question demands to be answered, and the oppression theorists have never provided an adequate explanation.

Moreover, the West could not have reached its current stage of wealth and influence by stealing from other cultures, for the simple reason that there wasn't very much to take. "Oh yes there was," the retort often comes. "The Europeans stole the raw material to build their civilization. They took rubber from Malaya, cocoa from West Africa, and tea from India." But as the economic historian P.T. Bauer points out, before British rule, there were no rubber trees in Malaya, no cocoa trees in West Africa, no tea in India. The British brought the rubber tree to Malaya from South America. They brought tea to India from China. And they taught the Africans to grow cocoa, a crop the native people had never heard of. None of this is to deny that when the colonialists could exploit native resources, they did. But that larceny cannot possibly account for the enormous gap in economic, political, and military power that opened up between the West and the rest of the world.

What, then, is the source of that power? The reason the West became so affluent and dominant in the modern era is that it invented three institutions: science, democracy, and capitalism. All those institutions are based on universal impulses and aspirations, but those aspirations were given a unique expression in Western civilization.

Consider science. It is based on a shared human trait: the desire to know. People in every culture have tried to learn about the world. Thus the Chinese recorded the eclipses, the Mayans developed a calendar, the Hindus discovered the number zero, and so on. But science—which requires experiments, laboratories, induction, verification, and what one scholar has called "the invention of invention," the scientific method—that is a Western institution. Similarly, tribal participation is universal, but democracy—which involves free elections, peaceful transitions of power, and separation of powers—is a Western idea. Finally, the impulse to trade is universal, and there is nothing Western about the use of money, but capitalism—which requires property rights, contracts, courts to enforce them, limited-liability corporations, stock

exchanges, patents, insurance, double-entry bookkeeping—this ensemble of practices was developed in the West.

It is the dynamic interaction among these three Western institutions—science, democracy, and capitalism—that has produced the great wealth, strength, and success of Western civilization. An example of this interaction is technology, which arises out of the marriage between science and capitalism. Science provides the knowledge that leads to invention, and capitalism supplies the mechanism by which the invention is transmitted to the larger society, as well as the economic incentive for inventors to continue to make new things.

Now we can understand better why the West was able, between the 16th and 19th centuries, to subdue the rest of the world and bend it to its will. Indian elephants and Zulu spears were no match for British rifles and cannonballs. Colonialism and imperialism are not the cause of the West's success; they are the result of that success. The wealth and power of European nations made them arrogant and stimulated their appetite for global conquest. Colonial possessions added to the prestige, and to a much lesser degree the wealth, of Europe. But the primary cause of Western affluence and power is internal—the institutions of science, democracy, and capitalism acting together. Consequently, it is simply wrong to maintain that the rest of the world is poor because the West is rich, or that the West grew rich off stolen goods from Asia, Africa, and Latin America. The West created its own wealth, and still does.

The descendants of colonialism are better off than they would be if colonialism had never happened. I would like to illustrate this point through a personal example. While I was a young boy, growing up in India, I noticed that my grandfather, who had lived under British colonialism, was instinctively and habitually antiwhite. He wasn't just against the English; he was generally against white people. I realized that I did not share his antiwhite animus. That puzzled me: Why did he and I feel so differently?

Only years later, after a great deal of reflection and a fair amount of study, did the answer finally hit me. The reason for our difference of perception was that colonialism had been pretty bad for him, but pretty good for me. Another way to put it was that colonialism had injured those who lived under it, but paradoxically it proved beneficial to their descendants. Much as it chagrins me to admit it—and much as it will outrage many third-world intellectuals for me to say it—my life would have been much worse had the British never ruled India.

How is that possible? Virtually everything that I am, what I do, and my deepest beliefs, all are the product of a worldview that was brought to India by colonialism. I am a writer, and I write in English. My ability to do this, and to reach a broad market, is entirely thanks to the British. My understanding of technology, which allows me, like so many Indians, to function successfully in the modern world, was largely the product of a Western education that came to India as a result of the British. So also my beliefs in freedom of expression, in self-government, in equality of rights under the law, and in the universal principle of human dignity—they are all the products of Western civilization.

I am not suggesting that it was the intention of the colonialists to give all those wonderful gifts to the Indians. Colonialism was not based on philanthropy; it was a form of conquest and rule. The British came to India to govern, and they were not primarily interested in the development of the natives, whom they viewed as picturesque savages. It is impossible to measure, or overlook, the pain and humiliation that the British inflicted during their long period of occupation. Understandably, the Indians chafed under that yoke. Toward

the end of the British reign in India, Mahatma Gandhi was asked, "What do you think of Western civilization?" He replied, "I think it would be a good idea."

Despite their suspect motives and bad behavior, however, the British needed a certain amount of infrastructure to effectively govern India. So they built roads, shipping docks, railway tracks, irrigation systems, and government buildings. Then they realized that they needed courts of law to adjudicate disputes that went beyond local systems of dispensing justice. And so the British legal system was introduced, with all its procedural novelties, like "innocent until proven guilty." The British also had to educate the Indians, in order to communicate with them and to train them to be civil servants in the empire. Thus Indian children were exposed to Shakespeare, Dickens, Hobbes, and Locke. In that way the Indians began to encounter words and ideas that were unmentioned in their ancestral culture: "liberty," "sovereignty," "rights," and so on.

That brings me to the greatest benefit that the British provided to the Indians: They taught them the language of freedom. Once again, it was not the objective of the colonial rulers to encourage rebellion. But by exposing Indians to the ideas of the West, they did. The Indian leaders were the product of Western civilization. Gandhi studied in England and South Africa; Nehru was a product of Harrow and Cambridge. That exposure was not entirely to the good; Nehru, for example, who became India's first prime minister after independence, was highly influenced by Fabian socialism through the teachings of Harold Laski. The result was that India had a mismanaged socialist economy for a generation. But my broader point is that the champions of Indian independence acquired the principles, the language, and even the strategies of liberation from the civilization of their oppressors. This was true not just of India but also of other Asian and African countries that broke free of the European yoke.

My conclusion is that against their intentions, the colonialists brought things to India that have immeasurably enriched the lives of the descendants of colonialism. It is doubtful that non-Western countries would have acquired those good things by themselves. It was the British who, applying a universal notion of human rights, in the early 19th century abolished the ancient Indian institution of suttee—the custom of tossing widows on their husbands' funeral pyres. There is no reason to believe that the Indians, who had practiced suttee for centuries, would have reached such a conclusion on their own. Imagine an African or Indian king encountering the works of Locke or Madison and saying, "You know, I think those fellows have a good point. I should relinquish my power and let my people decide whether they want me or someone else to rule." Somehow, I don't see that as likely.

Colonialism was the transmission belt that brought to Asia, Africa, and South America the blessings of Western civilization. Many of those cultures continue to have serious problems of tyranny, tribal and religious conflict, poverty, and underdevelopment, but that is not due to an excess of Western influence; rather, it is due to the fact that those countries are insufficiently Westernized. Sub-Saharan Africa, which is probably in the worst position, has

been described by U.N. Secretary General Kofi Annan as "a cocktail of disasters." That is not because colonialism in Africa lasted so long, but because it lasted a mere half-century. It was too short a time to permit Western institutions to take firm root. Consequently, after their independence, most African nations have retreated into a kind of tribal barbarism that can be remedied only with more Western influence, not less. Africa needs more Western capital, more technology, more rule of law, and more individual freedom.

The academy needs to shed its irrational prejudice against colonialism. By providing a more balanced perspective, scholars can help to show the foolishness of policies like reparations as well as justifications of terrorism that are based on anticolonial myths. None of this is to say that colonialism by itself was a good thing, only that bad institutions sometimes produce good results. Colonialism, I freely acknowledge, was a harsh regime for those who lived under it. My grandfather would have a hard time giving even one cheer for colonialism. As for me, I cannot manage three, but I am quite willing to grant two. So here they are: two cheers for colonialism! Maybe you will now see why I am not going to be sending an invoice for reparations to Tony Blair.

Dinesh D'Souza is a fellow at the Hoover Institution at Stanford University and the author, most recently, of What's So Great About America, to be published this month by Regnery.

Plato, *Crito*, 4th century BCE

Plato (428–348, BCE) was the most famous student of Socrates (479–399 BCE) and the teacher of Aristotle. Plato wrote many philosophical works in the form of dialogues, like the following selection. In each of them he explores a virtue, such as justice or courage, or a concept, such as knowledge, love, virtue itself, or truth. His early dialogues place Socrates in the role of protagonist, as this one, the *Crito*, does. This dialogue is the third of a series of four dialogues chronicling the trial and the death of Socrates. In the first, the *Euthyphro*, Socrates is indicted for the crime of corrupting the youth. In the second, the *Apology*, Socrates presents his defense to the jury, is convicted, and sentenced to death. In the last dialogue, the *Phaedro*, Socrates is put to death after a long discussion of the soul and the afterlife.

In the *Crito*, Socrates' argues that he ought to obey the law even when it is going to put him to death for a crime he did not commit, (or if he did corrupt the youth it was surely not wrong of him to do so as he did, namely by talking philosophy with them). At the beginning of the dialogue Crito is waiting for Socrates to awaken in his jail cell. Crito has just heard that the ship that was on a religious mission is about to return to Athens, signaling that executions can again take place in the city, and so that Socrates will soon die. Crito intends to try to persuade Socrates to escape into exile rather than submit to punishment that both feel is undeserved.

STUDY QUESTIONS:

1. How does Crito try to persuade Socrates that he should escape from jail? Why does Socrates reject these arguments?

2. Whose voice does Socrates take during the long monologue in which the main argument for accepting punishment is given?

3. Does Socrates' argument rule out acts of civil disobedience?

Crito

Translated by G.M.A. Grube

About the time of Socrates' trial, a state galley had set out on an annual religious mission to Delos and while it was away no execution was allowed to take place. So it was that Socrates was kept in prison for a month after the trial. The ship has now arrived at Cape Sunium in Attica and is thus expected at the Piraeus momentarily. So Socrates' old and faithful friend, Crito, makes one last effort to persuade him to escape into exile, and all arrangements for this plan have been made. It is this conversation between the two old friends that Plato professes to report in this dialogue. It is, as Crito plainly tells him, his last chance, but Socrates will not take it, and he gives his reasons for his refusal. Whether this conversation took place at this particular time is not important, for there is every reason to believe that Socrates' friends tried to plan his escape, and that he refused. Plato more than hints that the authorities would not have minded much, as long as he left the country.

SOCRATES: Why have you come so early, Crito? Or is it not still early?

CRITO: It certainly is.

S: How early?

C: Early dawn.

S: I am surprised that the warder was willing to listen to you.

C: He is quite friendly to me by now, Socrates. I have been here often and I have given him something.

S: Have you just come, or have you been here for some time?

C: A fair time.

S: Then why did you not wake me right away but sit there in silence?

C: By Zeus no, Socrates. I would not myself want to be in distress and awake so long. I have been surprised to see you so peacefully asleep. It was on purpose that I did not wake you, so that you should spend your time most agreeably. Often in the past throughout my life, I have considered the way you live happy, and especially so now that you bear your present misfortune so easily and lightly.

S: It would not be fitting at my age to resent the fact that I must die now.

C: Other men of your age are caught in such misfortunes, but their age does not prevent them resenting their fate.

S: That is so. Why have you come so early?

C: I bring bad news, Socrates, not for you, apparently, but for me and all your friends the news is bad and hard to bear. Indeed, I would count it among the hardest.

S: What is it? Or has the ship arrived from Delos, at the arrival of which I must die?

C: It has not arrived yet, but it will, I believe, arrive today, according to a message brought by some men from Sunium, where they left it. This makes it obvious that it will come today, and that your life must end tomorrow.

S: May it be for the best. If it so please the gods, so be it. However, I do not think it will arrive today.

C: What indication have you of this?

S: I will tell you. I must die the day after the ship arrives.

C: That is what those in authority say.

S: Then I do not think it will arrive on this coming day, but on the next. I take to witness of this a dream I had a little earlier during this night. It looks as if it was the right time for you not to wake me.

C: What was your dream?

S: I thought that a beautiful and comely woman dressed in white approached me. She called me and said: "Socrates, may you arrive at fertile Phthia[1] on the third day."

C: A strange dream, Socrates.

S: But it seems clear enough to me, Crito.

C: Too clear it seems, my dear Socrates, but listen to me even now and be saved. If you die, it will not be a single misfortune for me. Not only will I be deprived of a friend, the like of whom I shall never find again, but many people who do not know you or me very well will think that I could have saved you if I were willing to spend money, but that I did not care to do so. Surely there can be no worse reputation than to be thought to value money more highly than one's friends, for the majority will not believe that you yourself were not willing to leave prison while we were eager for you to do so.

S: My good Crito, why should we care so much for what the majority think? The most reasonable people, to whom one should pay more attention, will believe that things were done as they were done.

C: You see, Socrates, that one must also pay attention to the opinion of the majority. Your present situation makes clear that the majority can inflict not the least but pretty well the greatest evils if one is slandered among them.

S: Would that the majority could inflict the greatest evils, for they would then be capable of the greatest good, and that would be fine, but now they cannot do either. They cannot make a man either wise or foolish, but they inflict things haphazardly.

C: That may be so. But tell me this, Socrates, are you anticipating that I and your other friends would have trouble with the informers if you escape from here, as having stolen you away, and that we should be compelled to lose all our property or pay heavy fines and suffer other punishment besides? If you have any such fear, forget it. We would be justified in running this risk to save you, and worse, if necessary. Do follow my advice, and do not act differently.

S: I do have these things in mind, Crito, and also many others.

C: Have no such fear. It is not much money that some people require to save you and get you out of here. Further, do you not see that those informers are cheap, and that not much money would be needed to deal with them? My money is available and is, I think, sufficient. If, because of your affection for me, you feel you should not spend any of mine, there are those strangers here ready to spend money. One of them, Simmias the Theban, has brought enough for this very purpose. Cebes, too, and a good many others. So, as I say, do not let this fear make you hesitate to save yourself, nor let what you said in court trouble you, that you would not know what to do with yourself if you left Athens, for you would be welcomed in many places to which you might go. If you want to go to Thessaly, I have friends there who will greatly appreciate you and keep you safe, so that no one in Thessaly will harm you.

Besides, Socrates, I do not think that what you are doing is right, to give up your life when you can save it, and to hasten your fate as your enemies would hasten it, and indeed have hastened it in their wish to destroy you. Moreover, I think you are betraying your sons by going away and leaving them, when you could bring them up and educate them. You thus show no concern for what their fate may be. They will probably have the usual fate of orphans. Either one should not have children, or one should share with them to the end the toil of upbringing and education. You seem to me to choose the easiest path, whereas one should choose the path a good and courageous man would choose, particularly when one claims throughout one's life to care for virtue.

I feel ashamed on your behalf and on behalf of us, your friends, lest all that has happened to you be thought due to cowardice on our part: the fact that your trial came to court when it need not have done so, the handling of the trial itself, and now this absurd ending which will be thought to have got beyond our control through some cowardice and unmanliness on our part, since we did not save you, or you save yourself, when it was possible and could be done if we had been of the slightest use. Consider, Socrates, whether this is not only evil, but shameful, both for you and for us. Take counsel with yourself, or rather the time for counsel is past and the decision should have been taken, and there is no further opportunity, for this whole business must be ended tonight. If we delay now, then it will no longer be possible, it will be too late. Let me persuade you on every count, Socrates, and do not act otherwise.

S: My dear Crito, your eagerness is worth much if it should have some right aim; if not, then the greater your keenness the more difficult it is to deal with. We must therefore examine whether we should act in this way or not, as not only now but at all times I am the kind of man who listens only to the argument that on reflection seems best to me. I cannot, now that this fate has come upon me, discard the arguments I used; they seem to me much the same. I value and respect the same principles as before, and if we have no better arguments to bring up at this moment, be sure that I shall not agree with you, not even if the power of the majority were to frighten us with more bogeys, as if we were children, with threats of incarcerations and executions and confiscation of property. How should we examine this matter most reasonably? Would it be by taking up first your argument about the opinions of men, whether it is sound in every case that one should pay attention to some opinions, but not to others? Or was that well-spoken before the necessity to die came upon me, but now it is clear that this was said in vain for the sake of argument, that it was in truth play and nonsense?

I am eager to examine together with you, Crito, whether this argument will appear in any way different to me in my present circumstances, or whether it remains the same, whether we are to abandon it or believe it. It was said on every occasion by those who thought they were speaking sensibly, as I have just now been speaking, that one should greatly value some people's opinions, but not others. Does that seem to you a sound statement?

You, as far as a human being can tell, are exempt from the likelihood of dying tomorrow, so the present misfortune is not likely to lead you astray. Consider then, do you not think it a sound statement that one must not value all the opinions of men, but some and not others, nor the opinions of all men, but those of some and not of others? What do you say? Is this not well said?

C: It is.

S: One should value the good opinions, and not the bad ones?

C: Yes.

S: The good opinions are those of wise men, the bad ones those of foolish men?

C: Of course.

S: Come then, what of statements such as this: Should a man professionally engaged in physical training pay attention to the praise and blame and opinion of any man, or to those of one man only, namely a doctor or trainer?

C: To those of one only.

S: He should therefore fear the blame and welcome the praise of that one man, and not those of the many?

C: Obviously.

S: He must then act and exercise, eat and drink in the way the one, the trainer and the one who knows, thinks right, not all the others?

C: That is so.

S: Very well. And if he disobeys the one, disregards his opinion and his praises while valuing those of the many who have no knowledge, will he not suffer harm?

C: Of course.

S: What is that harm, where does it tend, and what part of the man who disobeys does it affect?

C: Obviously the harm is to his body, which it ruins.

S: Well said. So with other matters, not to enumerate them all, and certainly with actions just and unjust, shameful and beautiful, good and bad, about which we are now deliberating, should we follow the opinion of the many and fear it, or that of the one, if there is one who has knowledge of these things and before whom we feel fear and shame more than before all the others. If we do not follow his directions, we shall harm and corrupt that part of ourselves that is improved by just actions and destroyed by unjust actions. Or is there nothing in this?

C: I think there certainly is, Socrates.

S: Come now, if we ruin that which is improved by health and corrupted by disease by not following the opinions of those who know, is life worth living for us when that is ruined? And that is the body, is it not?

C: Yes.

S: And is life worth living with a body that is corrupted and in bad condition?

C: In no way.

S: And is life worth living for us with that part of us corrupted that unjust action harms and just action benefits? Or do we think that part of us, whatever it is, that is concerned with justice and injustice, is inferior to the body?

C: Not at all.

S: It is more valuable?

C: Much more.

S: We should not then think so much of what the majority will say about us, but what he will say who understands justice and injustice, the one, that is, and the truth itself. So that, in the first place, you were wrong to believe that we should care for the opinion of the many about what is just, beautiful, good, and their opposites. "But," someone might say "the many are able to put us to death."

C: That too is obvious, Socrates, and someone might well say so.

S: And, my admirable friend, that argument that we have gone through remains, I think, as before. Examine the following statement in turn as to whether it stays the same or not, that the most important thing is not life, but the good life.

C: It stays the same.

S: And that the good life, the beautiful life, and the just life are the same; does that still hold, or not?

C: It does hold.

S: As we have agreed so far, we must examine next whether it is right for me to try to get out of here when the Athenians have not acquitted me. If it is seen to be right, we will try to do so; if it is not, we will abandon the idea. As for those questions you raise about money, reputation, the upbringing of children, Crito, those considerations in truth belong to those people who easily put men to death and would bring them to life again if they could, without thinking; I mean the majority of men. For us, however, since our argument leads to this, the only valid consideration, as we were saying just now, is whether we should be acting rightly in giving money and gratitude to those who will lead me out of here, and ourselves helping with the escape, or whether in truth we shall do wrong in doing all this. If it appears that we shall be acting unjustly, then we have no need at all to take into account whether we shall have to die if we stay here and keep quiet, or suffer in another way, rather than do wrong.

C: I think you put that beautifully, Socrates, but see what we should do.

S: Let us examine the question together, my dear friend, and if you can make any objection while I am speaking, make it and I will listen to you, but if you have no objection to make, my dear Crito, then stop now from saying the same thing so often, that I must leave here against the will of the Athenians. I think it important to persuade you before I act, and not to act against your wishes. See whether the start of our enquiry is adequately stated, and try to answer what I ask you in the way you think best.

C: I shall try.

S: Do we say that one must never in any way do wrong willingly, or must one do wrong in one way and not in another? Is to do wrong never good or admirable, as we have agreed in the past, or have all these former agreements been washed out during the last few days? Have we at our age failed to notice for some time that in our serious discussions we were no different from children? Above all, is the truth such as we used to say it was, whether the majority agree or not, and whether we must still suffer worse things than we do now, or will be treated more gently, that nonetheless, wrongdoing

is in every way harmful and shameful to the wrongdoer? Do we say so or not?

C: We do.

S: So one must never do wrong.

C: Certainly not.

S: Nor must one, when wronged, inflict wrong in return, as the majority believe, since one must never do wrong.

C: That seems to be the case.

S: Come now, should one injure anyone or not, Crito?

C: One must never do so.

S: Well then, if one is oneself injured, is it right, as the majority say, to inflict an injury in return, or is it not?

C: It is never right.

S: Injuring people is no different from wrongdoing.

C: That is true.

S: One should never do wrong in return, nor injure any man, whatever injury one has suffered at his hands. And Crito, see that you do not agree to this, contrary to your belief. For I know that only a few people hold this view or will hold it, and there is no common ground between those who hold this view and those who do not, but they inevitably despise each other's views. So them consider very carefully whether we have this view in common, and whether you agree, and let this be the basis of our deliberation, that neither to do wrong or to return a wrong is ever right, not even to injure in return for an injury received. Or do you disagree and do not share this view as a basis for discussion? I have held it for a long time and still hold it now, but if your think other- wise, tell me now. If, however, you stick to our former opinion, then listen to the next point.

C: I stick to it and agree with you. So say on.

S: Then I state the next point, or rather I ask you: when one has come to an agreement that is just with someone, should one fulfill it or cheat on it?

C: One should fulfill it.

S: See what follows from this: if we leave here without the city's permission, are we injuring people whom we should least injure? And are we sticking to a just agreement, or not?

C: I cannot answer your question, Socrates. I do not know.

S: Look at it this way. If, as we were planning to run away from here, or whatever one should call it, the laws and the state came and confronted us and asked: "Tell me, Socrates, what are you intending to do? Do you not by this action you are attempting intend to destroy us, the laws, and indeed the whole city, as far as you are concerned? Or do you think it possible for a city not to be destroyed if the verdicts of its courts have no force but are nullified and set at naught by private individuals?" What shall we answer to this and other such arguments? For many things could be said, especially by an orator on behalf of this law we are destroying, which orders that the judgments of the courts shall be carried out. Shall we say in answer, "The city wronged me, and its decision was not rights." Shall we say that, or what?

C: Yes, by Zeus, Socrates, that is our answer.

S: Then what if the laws said: "Was that the agreement between us, Socrates, or was it to respect the judgments that the city came to?" And if we wondered at their words, they would perhaps add: "Socrates, do not wonder at what we say but answer, since you are accustomed to proceed by question and answer. Come now, what accusation do you bring against us and the city, that you should try to destroy us? Did we not, first, bring you to birth, and was it not through us that your father married your mother and begat you? Tell us, do you find anything to criticize in those of us who are concerned with marriage?" And I would say that I do not criticize them. "Or in those of us concerned with the nurture of babies and the education that you too received? Were those assigned to that subject not right to instruct your father to educate you in the arts and in physical culture?" And I would say that they were right. "Very well," they would continue, "and after you were born and nurtured and educated, could you, in the first place, deny that you are our offspring and servant, both you and your forefathers? If that is so, do you think that we are on an equal footing as regards the right, and that whatever we do to you it is right for you to do to us? You were not on an equal footing with your father as regards the right, nor with your master if you had one, so as to retaliate for anything they did to you, to revile them if they reviled you, to beat them if they beat you, and so with many other things. Do you think you have this right to retaliation against your country and its laws? That it we undertake to destroy you and think it right to do so, you can undertake to destroy us, as far as you can, in return? And will you say that you are right to do so, you who truly care for virtue? Is your wisdom such as not to realize that your country is to be honoured more than your mother, your father and all your ancestors, that it is more to be revered and more sacred, and that it counts for more among the gods and sensible men, that you must worship it, yield to it and placate its anger more than your father's? you must either persuade it or obey its orders, and endure in silence whatever it instructs you to endure, whether blows or bonds, and if it leads you into war to be wounded or killed, you must obey. To do so is right, and one must not give way or retreat or leave one's post, but both in war and in courts and everywhere else, one must obey the commands of one's city and country, or persuade it as to the nature of justice. It is impious to bring violence to bear against your mother or father, it is much more so to use it against your country." What shall we say in reply, Crito, that the laws speak the truth, or not?

C: I think they do.

S: "Reflect now, Socrates," the laws might say "that if what we say is true, you are not treating us rightly by planning to do what you are planning. We have given you birth, nurtured you, educated you, we have given you and all other citizens a share of all the good things we could. Even so, by giving every Athenian the opportunity, after he has reached manhood and observed the affairs of the city and us the laws, we proclaim that if we do not please him, he can take his possessions and go wherever he pleases. Not one of our laws raises any obstacle or forbids him, if he is not satisfied with us or the city, if one of you wants to go and live in a colony or wants to go anywhere else, and keep his property. We say, however, that whoever of you remains, when he sees how we conduct our trials and manage the city in other ways, has in fact come to an agreement with us to obey our instructions. We say that the one who disobeys does wrong in three ways, first because in us he disobeys his parents, also those who brought him up, and because, in spite of his agreement, he neither obeys us nor, if we do something wrong, does he try to persuade us to do better. Yet we only propose things, we do not issue savage commands to do whatever we order; we give two alternatives, either to persuade us or do what we say. He does neither. We do say that you too, Socrates, are open to those charges if you do what your have in mind; you would be among, not the least, but the most guilty of the Athenians." And if I should say "Why so?" they might well be right to upbraid me and say that I am among the Athenians who most definitely came to that agreement with them. They might well say: "Socrates, we have convincing proofs that we and the city were congenial to you. You would not have dwelt here most consistently of all the Athenians if the city had not been exceedingly pleasing to you. You have never left the city, even to see a festival, nor for any other reason except military service; you have never gone to stay in any other city, as people do; you have had no desire to know another city or other laws; we and our city satisfied you.

"So decisively did you choose us and agree to be a citizen under us. Also, you have had children in this city, thus showing that it was congenial to you. Then at your trial you could have assessed your penalty at exile if you wished, and you are now attempting to do against the city's wishes what you could then have done with her consent. Then you prided yourself that you did not resent death, but you chose, as you said, death in preference to exile. Now, however, those words do not make you ashamed, and you pay no heed to us, the laws, as you plan to destroy us, and you act like the meanest type of slave by trying to run away, contrary to your undertakings and your agreement to live as a citizen under us. First then, answer us on this very point, whether we speak the truth when we say that you agreed, not only in words but by your deeds, to live in accordance with us." What are we to say to that, Crito? Must we not agree?

C: We must, Socrates.

S: "Surely," they might say, "you are breaking the undertakings and agreements that you made with us without compulsion or deceit, and under no pressure of time for deliberation. You have had seventy years during which you could have gone away if you did not like us, and if you though our agreements unjust. You did not choose to go to Sparta or to Crete, which you are always saying are well governed, nor to any other city, Greek or foreign. You have been away from Athens less than the lame or the blind or other handicapped people. It is clear that the city has been outstandingly more congenial to you than to other Athenians, and so have we, the laws, for what city can please without laws? Will you then not now stick to our agreements? You will, Socrates, if we can persuade you, and not make yourself a laughing-stock by leaving the city.

"For consider what good you will do yourself or your friends by breaking our agreements and committing such a wrong? It is pretty obvious that your friends will themselves be in danger of exile, disfranchisement and loss of property. As for yourself, if you go to one of the nearby cities - Thebes or Megara, both are well governed - you will arrive as an enemy to their government; all who care for their city will look on you with suspicion, as a destroyer of the laws. You will also strengthen the conviction of the jury that they passed the right sentence on you, for anyone who destroys the laws could easily be though to corrupt the young and the ignorant. Or will you avoid cities that are well governed and men who are civilized? if you do this, will your life be worth living? Will you have social intercourse with them and not be ashamed to talk to them? And what will you say? The same as you did here, that virtue and justice are man's most precious possession, along with lawful behaviour and the laws? Do you not think that Socrates would appear to be an unseemly kind of person? One must think so. Or will you leave those places and go to Crito's friends in Thessaly? There you will find the greatest license and disorder, and they may enjoy hearing from you how absurdly you escaped from prison in some disguise, in a leather jerkin or some other things in which escapees wrap themselves, thus altering your appearance. Will there be no one to say that you, likely to live but a short time more, were so greedy for life that you transgressed the most important laws? Possibly, Socrates, if you do not annoy anyone, but if you do, many disgraceful things will be said about you.

"You will spend your time ingratiating yourself with all men, and be at their beck and call. What will you do in Thessaly but feast, as if you had gone to a banquet in Thessaly? As for those conversations of yours about justice and the rest of virtue, where will they be? You say you want to live for the sake of your children, that you may bring them up and educate them. How so? Will you bring them up and educate them by taking them to Thessaly and making strangers of them, that they may enjoy that too? Or not so, but they will be better brought up and educated here, while you are alive, though absent? Yes, your friends will look after them. Will they look after them if you go and live in Thessaly, but not if you go away to the underworld? If those who profess themselves your friends are any good at all, one must assume that they will.

"Be persuaded by us who have brought you up, Socrates. Do not value either your children or your life or anything else more than goodness, in order that when you arrive in Hades you may have all this as your defence before the rulers there. If you do this deed, you will not think it better or more just or more pious here, nor will any one of your friends, nor will it be better for you when you arrive yonder. As it is, you depart, if you depart, after being wronged not by us, the laws, but by men; but if you depart after shamefully returning wrong for wrong and injury for injury, after breaking your agreement and contract with us, after injuring those you should injure least—yourself, your friends, your country and us - we shall be angry with you while you are still alive, and our brothers, the laws of the underworld, will not receive you kindly, knowing that you tried to destroy us as far as you could. Do not let Crito persuade you, rather than us, to do what he says."

Crito, my dear friend, be assured that these are the words I seem to hear, as the Corybants seem to hear the music of their flutes, and the echo of these words resounds in me, and makes it impossible for me to hear anything else. As far as my present beliefs go, if you speak in opposition to them, you will speak in vain. However, if you think you can accomplish anything, speak.

C: I have nothing to say, Socrates.

S: Let it be then, Crito, and let us act in this way, since this is the way the god is leading us.

NOTE

[1] A quotation from the ninth book of the Iliad (363). Achilles has rejected all the presents of Agamemnon for him to return to the battle, and threatens to go home. He says his ships will sail in the morning, and with good weather he might arrive on the third day "in fertile Phthia" (which is his home). The dream means, obviously, that on the third day Socrates' soul, after death, will find its home. As always, counting the first member of a series, the third day is the day after tomorrow.

Frederick Douglass

F rederick Douglass (1818–1895) was born Frederick Baily, a slave, in February 1818 near the town of Easton on Maryland's Eastern Shore. In September 1838, he escaped to New York City, married his fiancée, a free black woman named Anna Murray, and changed his name to Frederick Douglass to begin his new life as a freeman. However, he was still in danger of being captured by slave catchers who patrolled for fugitive slaves to gain rewards from the slave owners. Douglass lived as a fugitive becoming a leader in the Abolitionist Movement until 1846, when his English admirers bought his freedom from his former owner. In 1847 he moved his family to Rochester and founded a weekly antislavery newspaper, *The North Star,* whose masthead read: "Right is of no sex—Truth is of no color—God is the Father of us all, and we are all Brethren." Douglass was not only a fierce opponent of slavery, but also a strong supporter of equal rights for women, and was one of the main speakers at the Women's Suffrage Convention in Seneca Falls in 1848 at which the *Declaration of Sentiments,* a document demanding women's freedom from oppression, was issued. Frederick Douglass wrote voluminously, including three volumes of autobiography, and numerous essays that were published in newspapers, such as the current selection.

This essay was written for a Boston newspaper in 1851. The Fugitive Slave Bill, which was passed by Congress to appease the South in 1850, gave slave owners the right to organize a posse at any point in the United States to aid in recapturing runaway slaves. Courts and police everywhere in the United States were obligated to assist them. Slave catchers were allowed to use force to capture and return runaway slaves. Even private citizens were obligated to assist in the recapture of runaways. People who were caught helping slaves served jail time and were forced to pay fines and restitution to the slave owner.

Under these circumstances, an escaped slave named Anthony Burns was arrested and jailed. While in jail, a Deputy U.S. Marshal named James Batchelder, attempting to resist a group who were intent on freeing Burns, was shot and killed. In this essay Douglass argues that the actions of Batchelder were seriously immoral, and that his killing was justified under the circumstances.

STUDY QUESTIONS:

1. Why is it Right to kill the kidnapper (i.e., Batchelder), according to Douglass?

2. Do you think that Batchelder's actions could have justified his killing?

3. Why does Douglass think it is wise for free Blacks to have killed Batchelder?

Is it Right and Wise to Kill a Kidnapper?

Akidnapper has been shot dead, while attempting to execute the fugitive slave bill in Boston. The streets of Boston in sight of Bunker Hill Monument, have been stained with the warm blood of a man in the act of perpetrating the most atrocious robbery which one man can possibly commit upon another—even the wresting from him his very person and natural powers. The deed of blood, as of course must have been expected, is making a tremendous sensation in all parts of the country, and calling forth all sorts of comments. Many are branding the deed as "murder," and would visit upon the perpetrator the terrible penalty attached to that dreadful crime. The occurrence naturally brings up the question of the reasonableness, and the rightfulness of killing a man who is in the act of forcibly reducing a brother man who is guilty of no crime, to the horrible condition of a slave. The question bids fair to be one of important and solemn interest, since it is evident that the practice of slave-hunting and slave-catching, with all their attendant enormities, will either be pursued, indefinitely, or abandoned immediately according to the decision arrived at by the community.

Cherishing a very high respect for the opinions of such of our readers and friends as hold to the inviolability of the human life, and differing from them on this vital question, we avail ourselves of the present excitement in the public mind, calmly to state our views and opinions, in reference to the case in hand, asking for them an attentive and candid perusal.

Our moral philosophy on this point is our own—never having read what others may have said in favor of the views which we entertain.

The shedding of human blood at first sight, and without explanation is, and must ever be, regarded with horror; and he who takes pleasure in human slaughter is very properly looked upon as a moral monster. Even the killing of animals produces a shudder in sensitive minds, uncalloused by crime; and men are only reconciled to it by being shown, not only its reasonableness, but its necessity. These tender feelings so susceptible to pain, are most wisely designed by the Creator, for the preservation of life. They are, especially, the affirmation of God, speaking through nature, and asserting man's right to live. Contemplated in the light of warmth of these feelings, it is in all cases, a crime to deprive a human being of life: but God has not left us solely to the guidance of our feelings, having endowed us with reason, as well as with feeling, and it is

From *The Life and Writings of Frederick Douglass*, Volume II.

in the light of reason that this question ought to be decided.

All will agree that human life is valuable or worthless, as to the innocent or criminal use that is made of it. Most evidently, also, the possession of life was permitted and ordained for beneficent ends, and not to defeat those ends, or to render their attainment impossible. Comprehensively stated, the end of man's creation is his own good, and the honor of his Creator. Life, therefore, is but a means to an end, and must be held in reason to be not superior to the purposes for which it was designed by the All-wise Creator. In this view there is no such thing as an absolute right to live; that is to say, the right to live, like any other human right, may be forfeited, and if forfeited, may be taken away. If the right to *life* stands on the same ground as the right to *liberty*, it is subject to all the exceptions that apply to the right to liberty. All admit that the right to enjoy *liberty* largely depends upon the use made of that liberty; hence Society has erected jails and prisons, with a view to deprive men of their liberty when they are so wicked as to abuse it by invading the liberties of their fellows. We have a right to arrest the locomotion of a man who insists upon walking and trampling on his brother man, instead of upon the highway. This right of society is essential to its preservations; without it a single individual would have it in his power to destroy the peace and the happiness of ten thousand otherwise right minded people. Precisely on the same ground, we hold that a man may, properly, wisely and even mercifully be deprived of life. Of course life being the most precious is the most sacred of all rights, and cannot be taken away, but under the direst necessity; and not until all reasonable modes had been adopted to prevent this necessity, and to spare the aggressor.

It is no answer to this view, to say that society is selfish in sacrificing the life of an individual, or of many individuals, to save the mass of mankind, or society at large. It is in accordance with nature, and the examples of the Almighty, in the execution of his will and beneficent laws. When a man flings himself from the top of some lofty monument, against a granite pavement, in that act he forfeits his *right* to live. He dies according to law, and however shocking may be the spectacle he presents, it is no argument against the beneficence of the law of gravitation, the suspension of whose operation must work ruin to the well-being of mankind. The observance of this law was necessary to his preservation; and his wickedness or folly, in violating it, could not be excused without imperilling those who are living in obedience to it. The atheist sees no benevolence in the law referred to; but to such minds we address not this article. It is enough for us that the All-Wise has established the law, and determined its character, and the penalty of its violation; and however we may deplore the mangled forms of the foolish and the wicked who transgress it, the beneficence of the law itself is fully vindicated by the security it gives to all who obey it.

We hold, then, in view of this great principle, or rule, in the physical world, we may properly infer that other law or principle of justice is the moral and social world, and vindicate its practical application to the preservation of the rights and liberties of the race, as against such exceptions furnished in the monsters who deliberately violate it by taking pleasure in enslaving, imbruting and murdering their fellow-men. As human life is not superior to the laws for the preservation of the physical universe, so, too, it is not superior to the eternal law of justice, which is essential to the preservation of the rights, and the security, and happiness of the race.

The argument thus far is to the point, that society has the right to preserve itself even at the expense of the life of the aggressor; and it may be said that, while what we allege may be right enough, as regards society, it is false as vested in an individual, such as the poor, powerless, and almost friendless wretch, now in the clutches of this proud and powerful republican government. But we take it to be a sound principle, that when government fails to protect the just rights of any individual man, either he or his friends may be held in the sight of God and man, innocent, in exercising any right for his preservation which society may exercise for its preservation. Such an individual is flung, by his untoward circumstances, upon his original right of self defence. We hold, therefore, that when James Batchelder, the truckman of Boston, abandoned his useful employment, as a common laborer, and took upon himself the revolting business of a kidnapper, and undertook to play the bloodhound on the track of his crimeless brother Burns, he labelled himself the common enemy of mankind, and his slaughter was as innocent, in the sight of God, as would be the slaughter of a ravenous wolf in the act of throttling an infant. We hold that he had forfeited his right to live, and that his death was necessary, as a warning to others liable to pursue a like course.

It may be said, that though the right to kill in defence of one's liberty be admitted, it is still unwise for the fugitive slave or his friends to avail themselves of this right; and that submission, in the circumstances, is far wiser than resistance. To this it is a sufficient answer to show that submission is valuable only so long as it has some chance of being recognized as a virtue. While it has this chance, it is well enough to practice it, as it may then have some moral effect in restraining crime and shaming aggression, but no longer. That submission on the part of the slave, has ceased to be a virtue, is very evident. While fugitives quietly cross their hands to be tied, adjust their ankles to be chained, and march off unresistingly to the hell of slavery, there will ever be fiends enough to hunt them and carry them back. Nor is this all nor the worst. Such submission, instead of being set to the credit of the poor sable ones, only creates contempt for them in the public mind, and becomes an argument in the mouths of the community, that Negroes are, by nature, only fit for slavery; that slavery is their normal condition. Their patient and unresisting disposition, their unwillingness to peril their own lives, by shooting down their pursuers, is already quoted against them, as marking them as an inferior race. This reproach must be wiped out, and nothing short of resistance on the part of colored men, can wipe it out. Every slavehunter who meets a bloody death in his infernal business, is an argument in favor of the manhood of our race. Resistance is, therefore, wise as well as just.

Part Two

Democracy

Political Philosophy and Democracy

Democracy means many things to many people. For some it is almost synonymous with freedom, and for others it implies mob rule. Still others, whose nations have been dominated, invaded, or occupied in the name of "Democracy" are understandably cynical about its promises. The term "Democracy" literally means "rule by the people," as opposed to Monarchy, Oligarchy, or Aristocracy, to name a few other possibilities, where the governing authority is constituted by a smaller group. But the definition of Democracy as rule by the people raises two immediate questions:

1. What does it mean for the people to rule?
2. Who are the people?

Traditionally it has been understood that the people rule only when they get to exercise the power to vote on issues. But this opens the question of: what issues do the people get to vote on? If they are limited by the kinds of decisions they can make, then we have a *Limited Democracy*. A Constitutional Democracy is an example of a Limited Democracy, where at least some of the limits are set by the constitution. But in assessing a particular government's claim to be the people we must ask who sets the agendas on which citizen's vote? If the people vote on each issue, then it is a *Direct Democracy*, whereas if the people vote for representatives who then decide on the issues we have an *Indirect* or *Representative Democracy*.

The question of who counts as 'the people' is also an important issue for Democracies. In some Democracies the people may include many more persons than voters. For example, at its founding, the United States was a Democracy in which most of the adult persons within the territory (e.g., women, poor white men, native people, and black slaves) did not have the right to vote. Some of these (white women, poor whites, and black slaves) were part of the People of the United States, but others (native people) were not. We have since come to see the idea of Democracy as requiring universal adult suffrage. However, noncitizen residents are not included among the people, and therefore not among those granted the vote. If the people is restricted to a small class of persons, or if universal adult suffrage is not practiced, then the claim of a nation to be a Democracy is put in question. For example, in the reading by Mao in the previous section, Mao did not include among the people the 'running dogs of imperialism', that is, his opponents. His state could for this reason among others make no claim to real Democracy. Likewise, any nation in which women are denied the right to vote could only cynically be classified as Democratic.

The first set of readings in this section concern a particular version of Democracy, that set out by the Founders of the United States. As you read them, you should keep in mind these two questions and the answers that the founders forged, and think about the ways in which you think their answers were good ones or bad ones, for their times and for now. The first reading comes from the *Federalist Papers*, published as a series of articles in the newspapers of New York City in 1787–1788 by Alexander Hamilton, James Madison, and John Jay (writing under the pseudonym Publius) as the United States Constitution was being debated. George Clinton, then governor of New York strongly opposed the Federalism in the Constitution. The Federalist Papers are the strongest case for the Constitution and a republican, federalist government. James Madison was the author of the Constitution, and of the particular the three selections of the Federalist Papers that are included here.

Following the Constitution and its amendments, two articles raise questions about how well the rules for voting and electing our President suit our nation today. Sanford Levinson's 2006 article argues for amending the Constitution to improve the Democracy, while Lani Guinier's article, written in the time between the November 2000 Presidential election and the January 2001 conclusion to the election, argues for a number of ways that elections might be improved in the interest of greater Democratic Participation.

STUDY QUESTIONS:

1. What is the problem of factions that Madison raises in Federalist #10?

2. How does Madison think that the design of the United States federal republic solves the problem of factions?

3. What were the competing sides of the argument over the question of how slaves should be represented in the United States Congress?

4. What are the flaws of the United States Constitution that Levinson thinks should be remedied?

5. Why does Guinier think that some votes do not count in federal elections?

Federalist No. 10

James Madison

To the People of the State of New York:

Among the numerous advantages promised by a wellconstructed Union, none deserves to be more accurately developed than its tendency to break and control the violence of faction. The friend of popular governments never finds himself so much alarmed for their character and fate, as when he contemplates their propensity to this dangerous vice. He will not fail, therefore, to set a due value on any plan which, without violating the principles to which he is attached, provides a proper cure for it. The instability, injustice, and confusion introduced into the public councils, have, in truth, been the mortal diseases under which popular governments have everywhere perished; as they continue to be the favorite and fruitful topics from which the adversaries to liberty derive their most specious declamations. The valuable improvements made by the American constitutions on the popular models, both ancient and modern, cannot certainly be too much admired; but it would be an unwarrantable partiality, to contend that they have as effectually obviated the danger on this side, as was wished and expected. Complaints are everywhere heard from our most considerate and virtuous citizens, equally the friends of public and private faith, and of public and personal liberty, that our governments are too unstable, that the public good is disregarded in the conflicts of rival parties, and that measures are too often decided, not according to the rules of justice and the rights of the minor party, but by the superior force of an interested and overbearing majority. However anxiously we may wish that these complaints had no foundation, the evidence, of known facts will not permit us to deny that they are in some degree true. It will be found, indeed, on a candid review of our situation, that some of the distresses under which we labor have been erroneously charged on the operation of our governments; but it will be found, at the same time, that other causes will not alone account for many of our heaviest misfortunes; and, particularly, for that prevailing and increasing distrust of public engagements, and alarm for private rights, which are echoed from one end of the continent to the other. These must be chiefly, if not wholly, effects of the unsteadiness and injustice with which a factious spirit has tainted our public administrations.

The Federalist Papers, 1787, 1788.

By a faction, I understand a number of citizens, whether amounting to a majority or a minority of the whole, who are united and actuated by some common impulse of passion, or of interest, adversed to the rights of other citizens, or to the permanent and aggregate interests of the community.

There are two methods of curing the mischiefs of faction: the one, by removing its causes; the other, by controlling its effects.

There are again two methods of removing the causes of faction: the one, by destroying the liberty which is essential to its existence; the other, by giving to every citizen the same opinions, the same passions, and the same interests.

It could never be more truly said than of the first remedy, that it was worse than the disease. Liberty is to faction what air is to fire, an aliment without which it instantly expires. But it could not be less folly to abolish liberty, which is essential to political life, because it nourishes faction, than it would be to wish the annihilation of air, which is essential to animal life, because it imparts to fire its destructive agency.

The second expedient is as impracticable as the first would be unwise. As long as the reason of man continues fallible, and he is at liberty to exercise it, different opinions will be formed. As long as the connection subsists between his reason and his self-love, his opinions and his passions will have a reciprocal influence on each other; and the former will be objects to which the latter will attach themselves. The diversity in the faculties of men, from which the rights of property originate, is not less an insuperable obstacle to a uniformity of interests. The protection of these faculties is the first object of government. From the protection of different and unequal faculties of acquiring property, the possession of different degrees and kinds of property immediately results; and from the influence of these on the sentiments and views of the respective proprietors, ensues a division of the society into different interests and parties.

The latent causes of faction are thus sown in the nature of man; and we see them everywhere brought into different degrees of activity, according to the different circumstances of civil society. A zeal for different opinions concerning religion, concerning government, and many other points, as well of speculation as of practice; an attachment to different leaders ambitiously contending for pre-eminence and power; or to persons of other descriptions whose fortunes have been interesting to the human passions, have, in turn, divided mankind into parties, inflamed them with mutual animosity, and rendered them much more disposed to vex and oppress each other than to co-operate for their common good. So strong is this propensity of mankind to fall into mutual animosities, that where no substantial occasion presents itself, the most frivolous and fanciful distinctions have been sufficient to kindle their unfriendly passions and excite their most violent conflicts. But the most common and durable source of factions has been the various and unequal distribution of property. Those who hold and those who are without property have ever formed distinct interests in society. Those who are creditors, and those who are debtors, fall under a like discrimination. A landed interest, a manufacturing interest, a mercantile interest, a moneyed interest, with many lesser interests, grow up of necessity in civilized nations, and divide them into different classes, actuated by different sentiments and views. The regulation of these various and interfering interests forms the principal task of modern legislation, and involves the spirit of party and faction in the necessary and ordinary operations of the government.

No man is allowed to be a judge in his own cause, because his interest would certainly bias his judgment, and, not improbably, corrupt his integrity. With equal, nay with greater reason, a body of men are unfit to be both judges and parties at the same time; yet what are many of the most important acts of legislation, but so many judicial determinations, not indeed concerning the rights of single persons, but concerning the rights of large bodies of citizens? And what are the different classes of legislators but advocates and parties to the causes which they determine? Is a law proposed concerning private debts? It is a question to which the creditors are parties on one side and the debtors on the other. Justice ought to hold the balance between them. Yet the parties are, and must be, themselves the judges; and the most numerous party, or, in other words, the most powerful faction must be expected to prevail. Shall domestic manufactures be encouraged, and in what degree, by restrictions on foreign manufactures? are questions which would be differently decided by the landed and the manufacturing classes, and probably by neither with a sole regard to justice and the public good. The apportionment of taxes on the various descriptions of property is an act which seems to require the most exact impartiality; yet there is, perhaps, no legislative act in which greater opportunity and temptation are given to a predominant party to trample on the rules of justice. Every shilling with which they overburden the inferior number, is a shilling saved to their own pockets.

It is in vain to say that enlightened statesmen will be able to adjust these clashing interests, and render them all subservient to the public good. Enlightened statesmen will not always be at the helm. Nor, in many cases, can such an adjustment be made at all without taking into view indirect and remote considerations, which will rarely prevail over the immediate interest which one party may find in disregarding the rights of another or the good of the whole.

The inference to which we are brought is, that the CAUSES of faction cannot be removed, and that relief is only to be sought in the means of controlling its EFFECTS.

If a faction consists of less than a majority, relief is supplied by the republican principle, which enables the majority to defeat its sinister views by regular vote. It may clog the administration, it may convulse the society; but it will be unable to execute and mask its violence under the forms of the Constitution. When a majority is included in a faction, the form of popular government, on the other hand, enables it to sacrifice to its ruling passion or interest both the public good and the rights of other citizens. To secure the public good and private rights against the danger of such a faction, and at the same time to preserve the spirit and the form of popular government, is then the great object to which our inquiries are directed. Let me add that it is the great desideratum by which this form of government can be rescued from the opprobrium under which it has so long labored, and be recommended to the esteem and adoption of mankind.

By what means is this object attainable? Evidently by one of two only. Either the existence of the same passion or interest in a majority at the same time must be prevented, or the majority, having such coexistent passion or interest, must be rendered, by their number and local situation, unable to concert and carry into effect schemes of oppression. If the impulse and the opportunity be suffered to coincide, we well know that neither moral nor religious motives can be relied on as an adequate control. They are not found to be such on the injustice and violence of individuals, and lose their efficacy in proportion to the number combined together, that is, in proportion as their efficacy becomes needful.

From this view of the subject it may be concluded that a pure democracy, by which I mean a society consisting of a small number of citizens, who assemble and administer the government in person, can admit of no cure for the mischiefs of faction. A common passion or interest will, in almost every case, be felt by a majority of the whole; a communication and concert result from the form of government itself; and there is nothing to check the inducements to sacrifice the weaker party or an obnoxious individual. Hence it is that such democracies have ever been spectacles of turbulence and contention; have ever been found incompatible with personal security or the rights of property; and have in general been as short in their lives as they have been violent in their deaths. Theoretic politicians, who have patronized this species of government, have erroneously supposed that by reducing mankind to a perfect equality in their political rights, they would, at the same time, be perfectly equalized and assimilated in their possessions, their opinions, and their passions.

A republic, by which I mean a government in which the scheme of representation takes place, opens a different prospect, and promises the cure for which we are seeking. Let us examine the points in which it varies from pure democracy, and we shall comprehend both the nature of the cure and the efficacy which it must derive from the Union.

The two great points of difference between a democracy and a republic are: first, the delegation of the government, in the latter, to a small number of citizens elected by the rest; secondly, the greater number of citizens, and greater sphere of country, over which the latter may be extended.

The effect of the first difference is, on the one hand, to refine and enlarge the public views, by passing them through the medium of a chosen body of citizens, whose wisdom may best discern the true interest of their country, and whose patriotism and love of justice will be least likely to sacrifice it to temporary or partial considerations. Under such a regulation, it may well happen that the public voice, pronounced by the representatives of the people, will be more consonant to the public good than if pronounced by the people themselves, convened for the purpose. On the other hand, the effect may be inverted. Men of factious tempers, of local prejudices, or of sinister designs, may, by intrigue, by corruption, or by other means, first obtain the suffrages, and then betray the interests, of the people. The question resulting is, whether small or extensive republics are more favorable to the election of proper guardians of the public weal; and it is clearly decided in favor of the latter by two obvious considerations:

In the first place, it is to be remarked that, however small the republic may be, the representatives must be raised to a certain number, in order to guard against the cabals of a few; and that, however large it may be, they must be limited to a certain number, in order to guard against the confusion of a multitude. Hence, the number of representatives in the two cases not being in proportion to that of the two constituents, and being proportionally greater in the small republic, it follows that, if the proportion of fit characters be not less in the large than in the small republic, the former will present a greater option, and consequently a greater probability of a fit choice.

In the next place, as each representative will be chosen by a greater number of citizens in the large than in the small republic, it will be more difficult for unworthy candidates to practice with success the vicious arts by which elections are too often carried; and the suffrages of the people being more free, will be more likely to centre in men who possess the most attractive merit and the most diffusive and established characters.

It must be confessed that in this, as in most other cases, there is a mean, on both sides of which inconveniences will be found to lie. By enlarging too much the number of electors, you render the representatives too little acquainted with all their local circumstances and lesser interests; as by reducing it too much, you render him unduly attached to these, and too little fit to comprehend and pursue great and national objects. The federal Constitution forms a happy combination in this respect; the great and aggregate interests being referred to the national, the local and particular to the State legislatures.

The other point of difference is, the greater number of citizens and extent of territory which may be brought within the compass of republican than of democratic government; and it is this circumstance principally which renders factious combinations less to be dreaded in the former than in the latter. The smaller the society, the fewer probably will be the distinct parties and interests composing it; the fewer the distinct parties and interests, the more frequently will a majority be found of the same party; and the smaller the number of individuals composing a majority, and the smaller the compass within which they are placed, the more easily will they concert and execute their plans of oppression. Extend the sphere, and you take in a greater variety of parties and interests; you make it less probable that a majority of the whole will have a common motive to invade the rights of other citizens; or if such a common motive exists, it will be more difficult for all who feel it to discover their own strength, and to act in unison with each other. Besides other impediments, it may be remarked that, where there is a consciousness of unjust or dishonorable purposes, communication is always checked by distrust in proportion to the number whose concurrence is necessary.

Hence, it clearly appears, that the same advantage which a republic has over a democracy, in controlling the effects of faction, is enjoyed by a large over a small republic,—is enjoyed by the Union over the States composing it. Does the advantage consist in the substitution of representatives whose enlightened views and virtuous sentiments render them superior to local prejudices and schemes of injustice? It will not be denied that the representation of the Union will be most likely to possess these requisite endowments. Does it consist in the greater security afforded by a greater variety of parties, against the event of any one party being able to outnumber and oppress the rest? In an equal degree does the increased variety of parties comprised within the Union, increase this security. Does it, in fine, consist in the greater obstacles opposed to the concert and accomplishment of the secret wishes of an unjust and interested majority? Here, again, the extent of the Union gives it the most palpable advantage.

The influence of factious leaders may kindle a flame within their particular States, but will be unable to spread a general conflagration through the other States. A religious sect may degenerate into a political faction in a part of the Confederacy; but the variety of sects dispersed over the entire face of it must secure the national councils against any danger from that source. A rage for paper money, for an abolition of debts, for an equal division of property, or for any other improper or wicked project, will be less apt to pervade the whole body of the Union than a particular member of it; in the same proportion as such a malady is more likely to taint a particular county or district, than an entire State.

In the extent and proper structure of the Union, therefore, we behold a republican remedy for the diseases most incident to republican government. And according to the degree of pleasure and pride we feel in being republicans, ought to be our zeal in cherishing the spirit and supporting the character of Federalists.

Federalist No. 51

James Madison

To the People of the State of New York:

To What expedient, then, shall we finally resort, for maintaining in practice the necessary partition of power among the several departments, as laid down in the Constitution? The only answer that can be given is, that as all these exterior provisions are found to be inadequate, the defect must be supplied, by so contriving the interior structure of the government as that its several constituent parts may, by their mutual relations, be the means of keeping each other in their proper places. Without presuming to undertake a full development of this important idea, I will hazard a few general observations, which may perhaps place it in a clearer light, and enable us to form a more correct judgment of the principles and structure of the government planned by the convention.

In order to lay a due foundation for that separate and distinct exercise of the different powers of government, which to a certain extent is admitted on all hands to be essential to the preservation of liberty, it is evident that each department should have a will of its own; and consequently should be so constituted that the members of each should have as little agency as possible in the appointment of the members of the others. Were this principle rigorously adhered to, it would require that all the appointments for the supreme executive, legislative, and judiciary magistracies should be drawn from the same fountain of authority, the people, through channels having no communication whatever with one another. Perhaps such a plan of constructing the several departments would be less difficult in practice than it may in contemplation appear. Some difficulties, however, and some additional expense would attend the execution of it. Some deviations, therefore, from the principle must be admitted. In the constitution of the judiciary department in particular, it might be inexpedient to insist rigorously on the principle: first, because peculiar qualifications being essential in the members, the primary consideration ought to be to select that mode of choice which best secures these qualifications; secondly, because the permanent tenure by which the appointments are held in that department, must soon destroy all sense of dependence on the authority conferring them.

The Federalist Papers, 1787, 1788.

It is equally evident, that the members of each department should be as little dependent as possible on those of the others, for the emoluments annexed to their offices. Were the executive magistrate, or the judges, not independent of the legislature in this particular, their independence in every other would be merely nominal.

But the great security against a gradual concentration of the several powers in the same department, consists in giving to those who administer each department the necessary constitutional means and personal motives to resist encroachments of the others. The provision for defense must in this, as in all other cases, be made commensurate to the danger of attack. Ambition must be made to counteract ambition. The interest of the man must be connected with the constitutional rights of the place. It may be a reflection on human nature, that such devices should be necessary to control the abuses of government. But what is government itself, but the greatest of all reflections on human nature? If men were angels, no government would be necessary. If angels were to govern men, neither external nor internal controls on government would be necessary. In framing a government which is to be administered by men over men, the great difficulty lies in this: you must first enable the government to control the governed; and in the next place oblige it to control itself. A dependence on the people is, no doubt, the primary control on the government; but experience has taught mankind the necessity of auxiliary precautions.

This policy of supplying, by opposite and rival interests, the defect of better motives, might be traced through the whole system of human affairs, private as well as public. We see it particularly displayed in all the subordinate distributions of power, where the constant aim is to divide and arrange the several offices in such a manner as that each may be a check on the other that the private interest of every individual may be a sentinel over the public rights. These inventions of prudence cannot be less requisite in the distribution of the supreme powers of the State.

But it is not possible to give to each department an equal power of self-defense. In republican government, the legislative authority necessarily predominates. The remedy for this inconveniency is to divide the legislature into different branches; and to render them, by different modes of election and different principles of action, as little connected with each other as the nature of their common functions and their common dependence on the society will admit. It may even be necessary to guard against dangerous encroachments by still further precautions. As the weight of the legislative authority requires that it should be thus divided, the weakness of the executive may require, on the other hand, that it should be fortified. An absolute negative on the legislature appears, at first view, to be the natural defense with which the executive magistrate should be armed. But perhaps it would be neither altogether safe nor alone sufficient. On ordinary occasions it might not be exerted with the requisite firmness, and on extraordinary occasions it might be perfidiously abused. May not this defect of an absolute negative be supplied by some qualified connection between this weaker department and the weaker branch of the stronger department, by which the latter may be led to support the constitutional rights of the former, without being too much detached from the rights of its own department?

If the principles on which these observations are founded be just, as I persuade myself they are, and they be applied as a criterion to the several State constitutions, and to the federal Constitution it will be found that if the latter does not perfectly correspond with them, the former are infinitely less able to bear such a test.

There are, moreover, two considerations particularly applicable to the federal system of America, which place that system in a very interesting point of view.

First. In a single republic, all the power surrendered by the people is submitted to the administration of a single government; and the usurpations are guarded against by a division of the government into distinct and separate departments. In the compound republic of America, the power surrendered by the people is first divided between two distinct governments, and then the portion allotted to each subdivided among distinct and separate departments. Hence a double security arises to the rights of the people. The different governments will control each other, at the same time that each will be controlled by itself.

Second. It is of great importance in a republic not only to guard the society against the oppression of its rulers, but to guard one part of the society against the injustice of the other part. Different interests necessarily exist in different classes of citizens. If a majority be united by a common interest, the rights of the minority will be insecure. There are but two methods of providing against this evil: the one by creating a will in the community independent of the majority that is, of the society itself; the other, by comprehending in the society so many separate descriptions of citizens as will render an unjust combination of a majority of the whole very improbable, if not impracticable. The first method prevails in all governments possessing an hereditary or self-appointed authority. This, at best, is but a precarious security; because a power independent of the society may as well espouse the unjust views of the major, as the rightful interests of the minor party, and may possibly be turned against both parties. The

second method will be exemplified in the federal republic of the United States. Whilst all authority in it will be derived from and dependent on the society, the society itself will be broken into so many parts, interests, and classes of citizens, that the rights of individuals, or of the minority, will be in little danger from interested combinations of the majority. In a free government the security for civil rights must be the same as that for religious rights. It consists in the one case in the multiplicity of interests, and in the other in the multiplicity of sects. The degree of security in both cases will depend on the number of interests and sects; and this may be presumed to depend on the extent of country and number of people comprehended under the same government. This view of the subject must particularly recommend a proper federal system to all the sincere and considerate friends of republican government, since it shows that in exact proportion as the territory of the Union may be formed into more circumscribed Confederacies, or States oppressive combinations of a majority will be facilitated: the best security, under the republican forms, for the rights of every class of citizens, will be diminished: and consequently the stability and independence of some member of the government, the only other security, must be proportionately increased. Justice is the end of government. It is the end of civil society. It ever has been and ever will be pursued until it be obtained, or until liberty be lost in the pursuit. In a society under the forms of which the stronger faction can readily unite and oppress the weaker, anarchy may as truly be said to reign as in a state of nature, where the weaker individual is not secured against the violence of the stronger; and as, in the latter state, even the stronger individuals are prompted, by the uncertainty of their condition, to submit to a government which may protect the weak as well as themselves; so, in the former state, will the more powerful factions or parties be gradnally induced, by a like motive, to wish for a government which will protect all parties, the weaker as well as the more powerful. It can be little doubted that if the State of Rhode Island was separated from the Confederacy and left to itself, the insecurity of rights under the popular form of government within such narrow limits would be displayed by such reiterated oppressions of factious majorities that some power altogether independent of the people would soon be called for by the voice of the very factions whose misrule had proved the necessity of it. In the extended republic of the United States, and among the great variety of interests, parties, and sects which it embraces, a coalition of a majority of the whole society could seldom take place on any other principles than those of justice and the general good; whilst there being thus less danger to a minor from the will of a major party, there must be less pretext, also, to provide for the security of the former, by introducing into the government a will not dependent on the latter, or, in other words, a will independent of the society itself. It is no less certain than it is important, notwithstanding the contrary opinions which have been entertained, that the larger the society, provided it lie within a practical sphere, the more duly capable it will be of self-government. And happily for the REPUBLICAN CAUSE, the practicable sphere may be carried to a very great extent, by a judicious modification and mixture of the FEDERAL PRINCIPLE.

Federalist No. 54

James Madison

To the People of the State of New York:

The next view which I shall take of the House of Representatives relates to the appointment of its members to the several States which is to be determined by the same rule with that of direct taxes.

It is not contended that the number of people in each State ought not to be the standard for regulating the proportion of those who are to represent the people of each State. The establishment of the same rule for the appointment of taxes, will probably be as little contested; though the rule itself in this case, is by no means founded on the same principle. In the former case, the rule is understood to refer to the personal rights of the people, with which it has a natural and universal connection. In the latter, it has reference to the proportion of wealth, of which it is in no case a precise measure, and in ordinary cases a very unfit one. But notwithstanding the imperfection of the rule as applied to the relative wealth and contributions of the States, it is evidently the least objectionable among the practicable rules, and had too recently obtained the general sanction of America, not to have found a ready preference with the convention.

All this is admitted, it will perhaps be said; but does it follow, from an admission of numbers for the measure of representation, or of slaves combined with free citizens as a ratio of taxation, that slaves ought to be included in the numerical rule of representation? Slaves are considered as property, not as persons. They ought therefore to be comprehended in estimates of taxation which are founded on property, and to be excluded from representation which is regulated by a census of persons. This is the objection, as I understand it, stated in its full force. I shall be equally candid in stating the reasoning which may be offered on the opposite side.

"We subscribe to the doctrine," might one of our Southern brethren observe, "that representation relates more immediately to persons, and taxation more immediately to property, and we join in the application of this distinction to the case of our slaves. But we must deny the fact, that slaves are considered merely as property, and in no respect whatever as persons. The true state of the case is, that they partake of both these qualities: being considered by our laws, in some respects, as persons, and in other respects as property. In being compelled to labor, not for himself, but for a master; in being vendible by one master to another master; and in being subject at all times to be restrained in his liberty and chastised in his body, by the capricious will of another, the slave may appear to be degraded from the human rank, and classed with those irrational animals which fall under the legal denomination of property. In being protected, on the other hand, in his life and in his limbs, against the violence of all others, even the master of his labor and his liberty; and in being punishable himself for all violence committed against others, the slave is no less evidently regarded by the law as a member of the society, not as a part of the irrational creation; as a moral person, not as a mere article of property. The federal Constitution, therefore, decides with great propriety on the case of our slaves, when it views them in the mixed character of persons and of property. This is in fact their true character. It is the character bestowed on them by the laws under which they live; and it will not be denied, that these are the proper criterion; because it is only under the pretext that the laws have transformed the negroes into subjects of property, that a place is disputed them in the computation of numbers; and it is admitted, that if the laws were to restore the rights which have been taken away, the negroes could no longer be refused an equal share of representation with the other inhabitants.

This question may be placed in another light. It is agreed on all sides, that numbers are the best scale of wealth and taxation, as they are the only proper scale of representation. Would the convention have been impartial or consistent, if they had rejected the slaves from the list of inhabitants, when the shares of representation were to be calculated, and inserted them on the lists when the tariff of contributions was to be adjusted? Could it be reasonably expected, that the Southern States would concur in a system, which considered their slaves in some degree as men, when burdens were to be imposed, but refused to consider them in the same light, when advantages were to be conferred? Might not some surprise also be expressed, that those who reproach the Southern States with the barbarous policy of considering as property a part of their human brethren, should themselves contend, that the government to which all the States are to be parties, ought to consider this unfortunate race more completely in the unnatural light of property, than the very laws of which they complain?

It may be replied, perhaps, that slaves are not included in the estimate of representatives in any of the States possessing them. They neither vote themselves nor increase the votes of their masters. Upon what principle, then, ought they to be taken into the federal estimate of representation? In rejecting them altogether, the Constitution would, in this respect, have followed the very laws which have been appealed to as the proper guide.

This objection is repelled by a single observation. It is a fundamental principle of the proposed Constitution, that as the aggregate number of representatives allotted to the several States is to be determined by a federal rule, founded on the aggregate number of inhabitants, so the right of choosing this allotted number in each State is to be exercised by such part of the inhabitants as the State itself may designate. The qualifications on which the right of suffrage depend are not, perhaps, the same in any two States. In some of the States the difference is very material. In every State, a certain proportion of inhabitants are deprived of this right by the constitution of the State, who will be included in the census by which the federal Constitution apportions the representatives. In this point of view the Southern States might retort the complaint, by insisting that the principle laid down by the convention required that no regard should be had to the policy of particular States towards their own inhabitants; and consequently, that the slaves, as inhabitants, should have been admitted into the census according to their full number, in like manner with other inhabitants, who, by the policy of other States, are not admitted to all the rights of citizens. A rigorous adherence, however, to this principle, is waived by those who would be gainers by it. All that they ask is that equal moderation be shown on the other side. Let the case of the slaves be considered, as it is in truth, a peculiar one. Let the compromising expedient of the Constitution be mutually adopted, which regards them as inhabitants, but as debased by servitude below the equal level of free inhabitants, which regards the SLAVE as divested of two fifths of the MAN.

After all, may not another ground be taken on which this article of the Constitution will admit of a still more ready defense? We have hitherto proceeded on the idea that representation related to persons only, and not at all to property. But is it a just idea? Government is instituted no less for protection of the property, than of the persons, of individuals. The one as well as the other, therefore, may be considered as represented by those who are charged with the government. Upon this principle it is, that in several of the States, and particularly in the State of New York, one branch of the government is intended more especially to be the guardian of property, and is accordingly elected by that part of the society which is most interested in this object of government. In the federal Constitution, this policy does not prevail. The rights of property are committed into the same hands with the personal rights. Some attention ought, therefore, to be paid to property in the choice of those hands.

For another reason, the votes allowed in the federal legislature to the people of each State, ought to bear some proportion to the comparative wealth of the States. States have not, like individuals, an influence over each other, arising from superior advantages of fortune. If the law allows an opulent citizen but a single vote in the choice of his representative, the respect and consequence which he derives from his fortunate situation very frequently guide the votes of others to the objects of his choice; and through this imperceptible channel the rights of prop-

erty are conveyed into the public representation. A State possesses no such influence over other States. It is not probable that the richest State in the Confederacy will ever influence the choice of a single representative in any other State. Nor will the representatives of the larger and richer States possess any other advantage in the federal legislature, over the representatives of other States, than what may result from their superior number alone. As far, therefore, as their superior wealth and weight may justly entitle them to any advantage, it ought to be secured to them by a superior share of representation. The new Constitution is, in this respect, materially different from the existing Confederation, as well as from that of the United Netherlands, and other similar confederacies. In each of the latter, the efficacy of the federal resolutions depends on the subsequent and voluntary resolutions of the states composing the union. Hence the states, though possessing an equal vote in the public councils, have an unequal influence, corresponding with the unequal importance of these subsequent and voluntary resolutions. Under the proposed Constitution, the federal acts will take effect without the necessary intervention of the individual States. They will depend merely on the majority of votes in the federal legislature, and consequently each vote, whether proceeding from a larger or smaller State, or a State more or less wealthy or powerful, will have an equal weight and efficacy: in the same manner as the votes individually given in a State legislature, by the representatives of unequal counties or other districts, have each a precise equality of value and effect; or if there be any difference in the case, it proceeds from the difference in the personal character of the individual representative, rather than from any regard to the extent of the district from which he comes.

Such is the reasoning which an advocate for the Southern interests might employ on this subject; and although it may appear to be a little strained in some points, yet, on the whole, I must confess that it fully reconciles me to the scale of representation which the convention have established.

In one respect, the establishment of a common measure for representation and taxation will have a very salutary effect. As the accuracy of the census to be obtained by the Congress will necessarily depend, in a considerable degree on the disposition, if not on the co-operation, of the States, it is of great importance that the States should feel as little bias as possible, to swell or to reduce the amount of their numbers. Were their share of representation alone to be governed by this rule, they would have an interest in exaggerating their inhabitants. Were the rule to decide their share of taxation alone, a contrary temptation would prevail. By extending the rule to both objects, the States will have opposite interests, which will control and balance each other, and produce the requisite impartiality.

The Constitution of the United States of America

We the People of the United States, in Order to form a more perfect Union, establish Justice, insure domestic Tranquility, provide for the common defence, promote the general Welfare, and secure the Blessings of Liberty to ourselves and our Posterity, do ordain and establish this Constitution for the United States of America.

ARTICLE I

Section 1

All legislative Powers herein granted shall be vested in a Congress of the United States, which shall consist of a Senate and House of Representatives.

Section 2

The House of Representatives shall be composed of Members chosen every second Year by the People of the several States, and the Electors in each State shall have the Qualifications requisite for Electors of the most numerous Branch of the State Legislature.

No Person shall be a Representative who shall not have attained to the Age of twenty five Years, and been seven Years a Citizen of the United States, and who shall not, when elected, be an Inhabitant of that State in which he shall be chosen.

Representatives and direct Taxes shall be apportioned among the several States which may be included within this Union, according to their respective Numbers, which shall be determined by adding to the whole Number of free Persons, including those bound to Service for a Term of Years, and excluding Indians not taxed, three fifths of all other Persons. The actual Enumeration shall be made within three Years after the first Meeting of the Congress of the United States, and within every subsequent Term of ten Years, in such Manner as they shall by Law direct. The Number of Representatives shall not exceed one for every thirty Thousand, but each State shall have at Least one Representative; and until such enumeration shall be made, the State of New Hampshire shall be entitled to chuse three, Massachusetts eight, Rhode-Island and Providence Plantations one, Connecticut five, New-York six, New Jersey four, Pennsylvania eight, Delaware one, Maryland six, Virginia ten, North Carolina five, South Carolina five, and Georgia three.

When vacancies happen in the Representation from any State, the Executive Authority thereof shall issue Writs of Election to fill such Vacancies.

The House of Representatives shall chuse their Speaker and other Officers; and shall have the sole Power of Impeachment.

Section 3

The Senate of the United States shall be composed of two Senators from each State, chosen by the Legislature thereof for six Years; and each Senator shall have one Vote.

Immediately after they shall be assembled in Consequence of the first Election, they shall be divided as equally as may be into three Classes. The Seats of the Senators of the first Class shall be vacated at the Expiration of the second Year, of the second Class at the Expiration of the fourth Year, and of the third Class at the Expiration of the sixth Year, so that one third may be chosen every second Year; and if Vacancies happen by Resignation, or otherwise, during the Recess of the Legislature of any State, the Executive thereof may make temporary Appointments until the next Meeting of the Legislature, which shall then fill such Vacancies.

No Person shall be a Senator who shall not have attained to the Age of thirty Years, and been nine Years a Citizen of the United States, and who shall not, when elected, be an Inhabitant of that State for which he shall be chosen.

The Vice President of the United States shall be President of the Senate, but shall have no Vote, unless they be equally divided.

The Senate shall chuse their other Officers, and also a President pro tempore, in the Absence of the Vice President, or when he shall exercise the Office of President of the United States.

The Senate shall have the sole Power to try all Impeachments. When sitting for that Purpose, they shall be on Oath or Affirmation. When the President of the United States is tried, the Chief Justice shall preside: And no Person shall be convicted without the Concurrence of two thirds of the Members present.

Judgment in Cases of Impeachment shall not extend further than to removal from Office, and disqualification to hold and enjoy any Office of honor, Trust or Profit under the United States: but the Party convicted shall nevertheless be liable and subject to Indictment, Trial, Judgment and Punishment, according to Law.

Section 4

The Times, Places and Manner of holding Elections for Senators and Representatives, shall be prescribed in each State by the Legislature thereof; but the Congress may at any time by Law make or alter such Regulations, except as to the Places of chusing Senators.

The Congress shall assemble at least once in every Year, and such Meeting shall be on the first Monday in December, unless they shall by Law appoint a different Day.

Section 5

Each House shall be the Judge of the Elections, Returns and Qualifications of its own Members, and a Majority of each shall constitute a Quorum to do Business; but a smaller Number may adjourn from day to day, and may be authorized to compel the Attendance of absent Members, in such Manner, and under such Penalties as each House may provide.

Each House may determine the Rules of its Proceedings, punish its Members for disorderly Behaviour, and, with the Concurrence of two thirds, expel a Member.

Each House shall keep a Journal of its Proceedings, and from time to time publish the same, excepting such Parts as may in their Judgment require Secrecy; and the Yeas and Nays of the Members of either House on any question shall, at the Desire of one fifth of those Present, be entered on the Journal.

Neither House, during the Session of Congress, shall, without the Consent of the other, adjourn for more than three days, nor to any other Place than that in which the two Houses shall be sitting.

Section 6

The Senators and Representatives shall receive a Compensation for their Services, to be ascertained by Law, and paid out of the Treasury of the United States. They shall in all Cases, except Treason, Felony and Breach of the Peace, be privileged from Arrest during their Attendance at the Session of their respective Houses, and in going to and returning from the same; and for any Speech or Debate in either House, they shall not be questioned in any other Place.

No Senator or Representative shall, during the Time for which he was elected, be appointed to any civil Office under the Authority of the United States, which shall have been created, or the Emoluments whereof shall have been encreased during such time; and no Person holding any Office under the United States, shall be a Member of either House during his Continuance in Office.

Section 7

All Bills for raising Revenue shall originate in the House of Representatives; but the Senate may propose or concur with Amendments as on other Bills.

Every Bill which shall have passed the House of Representatives and the Senate, shall, before it become a Law, be presented to the President of the United States: If he approve he shall sign it, but if not he shall return it, with his Objections to that House in which it shall have originated, who shall enter the Objections at large on their Journal, and proceed to reconsider it. If after such Reconsideration two thirds of that House shall agree to pass the Bill, it shall be sent, together with the Objections, to the other House, by which it shall likewise be reconsidered, and

if approved by two thirds of that House, it shall become a Law. But in all such Cases the Votes of both Houses shall be determined by yeas and Nays, and the Names of the Persons voting for and against the Bill shall be entered on the Journal of each House respectively. If any Bill shall not be returned by the President within ten Days (Sundays excepted) after it shall have been presented to him, the Same shall be a Law, in like Manner as if he had signed it, unless the Congress by their Adjournment prevent its Return, in which Case it shall not be a Law.

Every Order, Resolution, or Vote to which the Concurrence of the Senate and House of Representatives may be necessary (except on a question of Adjournment) shall be presented to the President of the United States; and before the Same shall take Effect, shall be approved by him, or being disapproved by him, shall be repassed by two thirds of the Senate and House of Representatives, according to the Rules and Limitations prescribed in the Case of a Bill.

Section 8

The Congress shall have Power To lay and collect Taxes, Duties, Imposts and Excises, to pay the Debts and provide for the common Defence and general Welfare of the United States; but all Duties, Imposts and Excises shall be uniform throughout the United States;

To borrow Money on the credit of the United States;

To regulate Commerce with foreign Nations, and among the several States, and with the Indian Tribes;

To establish an uniform Rule of Naturalization, and uniform Laws on the subject of Bankruptcies throughout the United States;

To coin Money, regulate the Value thereof, and of foreign Coin, and fix the Standard of Weights and Measures;

To provide for the Punishment of counter-feiting the Securities and current Coin of the United States;

To establish Post Offices and post Roads;

To promote the Progress of Science and useful Arts, by securing for limited Times to Authors and Inventors the exclusive Right to their respective Writings and Discoveries;

To constitute Tribunals inferior to the supreme Court;

To define and punish Piracies and Felonies committed on the high Seas, and Offences against the Law of Nations;

To declare War, grant Letters of Marque and Reprisal, and make Rules concerning Captures on Land and Water;

To raise and support Armies, but no Appropriation of Money to that Use shall be for a longer Term than two Years;

To provide and maintain a Navy;

To make Rules for the Government and Regulation of the land and naval Forces;

To provide for calling forth the Militia to execute the Laws of the Union, suppress Insurrections and repel Invasions;

To provide for organizing, arming, and disciplining, the Militia, and for governing such Part of them as may be employed in the Service of the United States, reserving to the States respectively, the Appointment of the Officers, and the Authority of training the Militia according to the discipline prescribed by Congress;

To exercise exclusive Legislation in all Cases whatsoever, over such District (not exceeding ten Miles square) as may, by Cession of particular States, and the Acceptance of Congress, become the Seat of the Government of the United States, and to exercise like Authority over all Places purchased by the Consent of the Legislature of the State in which the Same shall be, for the Erection of Forts, Magazines, Arsenals, dock-Yards, and other needful Buildings;–And

To make all Laws which shall be necessary and proper for carrying into Execution the foregoing Powers, and all other Powers vested by this Constitution in the Government of the United States, or in any Department or Officer thereof.

Section 9

The Migration or Importation of such Persons as any of the States now existing shall think proper to admit, shall not be prohibited by the Congress prior to the Year one thousand eight hundred and eight, but a Tax or duty may be imposed on such Importation, not exceeding ten dollars for each Person.

The Privilege of the Writ of Habeas Corpus shall not be suspended, unless when in Cases of Rebellion or Invasion the public Safety may require it.

No Bill of Attainder or ex post facto Law shall be passed.

No Capitation, or other direct, Tax shall be laid, unless in Proportion to the Census or enumeration herein before directed to be taken.

No Tax or Duty shall be laid on Articles exported from any State.

No Preference shall be given by any Regulation of Commerce or Revenue to the Ports of one State over those of another; nor shall Vessels bound to, or from, one State, be obliged to enter, clear, or pay Duties in another.

No Money shall be drawn from the Treasury, but in Consequence of Appropriations made by Law; and a regular Statement and Account of the Receipts and Expenditures of all public Money shall be published from time to time.

No Title of Nobility shall be granted by the United States: And no Person holding any Office of Profit or Trust under them, shall, without the Consent of the Congress, accept of any present, Emolument, Office, or Title, of any kind whatever, from any King, Prince, or foreign State.

Section 10

No State shall enter into any Treaty, Alliance, or Confederation; grant Letters of Marque and Reprisal; coin Money; emit Bills of Credit; make any Thing but gold and silver Coin a Tender in Payment of Debts; pass any Bill of Attainder, ex post facto Law, or Law impairing the Obligation of Contracts, or grant any Title of Nobility.

No State shall, without the Consent of the Congress, lay any Imposts or Duties on Imports or Exports, except what may be absolutely necessary for executing it's inspection Laws: and the net Produce of all Duties and Imposts, laid by any State on Imports or Exports, shall be for the Use of the Treasury of the United States; and all such Laws shall be subject to the Revision and Controul of the Congress.

No State shall, without the Consent of Congress, lay any Duty of Tonnage, keep Troops, or Ships of War in time of Peace, enter into any Agreement or Compact with another State, or with a foreign Power, or engage in War, unless actually invaded, or in such imminent Danger as will not admit of delay.

ARTICLE II

Section 1

The executive Power shall be vested in a President of the United States of America. He shall hold his Office during the Term of four Years, and, together with the Vice President, chosen for the same Term, be elected, as follows:

Each State shall appoint, in such Manner as the Legislature thereof may direct, a Number of Electors, equal to the whole Number of Senators and Representatives to which the State may be entitled in the Congress: but no Senator or Representative, or Person holding an Office of Trust or Profit under the United States, shall be appointed an Elector.

The Electors shall meet in their respective States, and vote by Ballot for two Persons, of whom one at least shall not be an Inhabitant of the same State with themselves. And they shall make a List of all the Persons voted for, and of the Number of Votes for each; which List they shall sign and certify, and transmit sealed to the Seat of the Government of the United States, directed to the President of the Senate. The President of the Senate shall, in the Presence of the Senate and House of Representatives, open all the Certificates, and the Votes shall then be counted. The Person having the greatest Number of Votes shall be the President, if such Number be a Majority of the whole Number of Electors appointed; and if there be more than one who have such Majority, and have an equal Number of Votes, then the House of Representatives shall immediately chuse by Ballot one of them for President; and if no Person have a Majority, then from the five highest on the List the said House shall in like Manner chuse the President. But in chusing the President, the Votes shall be taken by States, the Representation from each State having one Vote; A quorum for this purpose shall consist of a Member or Members from two thirds of the States, and a Majority of all the States shall be necessary to a Choice. In every Case, after the Choice of the President, the Person having the greatest Number of Votes of the Electors shall be the Vice President. But if there should remain two or more who have equal Votes, the Senate shall chuse from them by Ballot the Vice President.

The Congress may determine the Time of chusing the Electors, and the Day on which they shall give their Votes; which Day shall be the same throughout the United States.

No Person except a natural born Citizen, or a Citizen of the United States, at the time of the Adoption of this Constitution, shall be eligible to the Office of President; neither shall any Person be eligible to that Office who shall not have attained to the Age of thirty five Years, and been fourteen Years a Resident within the United States.

In Case of the Removal of the President from Office, or of his Death, Resignation, or Inability to discharge the Powers and Duties of the said Office, the Same shall devolve on the Vice President, and the Congress may by Law provide for the Case of Removal, Death, Resignation or Inability, both of the President and Vice President, declaring what Officer shall then act as President, and such Officer shall act accordingly, until the Disability be removed, or a President shall be elected.

The President shall, at stated Times, receive for his Services, a Compensation, which shall neither be increased nor diminished during the Period for which he shall have been elected, and he shall not receive within that Period any other Emolument from the United States, or any of them.

Before he enter on the Execution of his Office, he shall take the following Oath or Affirmation:—"I do solemnly swear (or affirm) that I will faithfully execute the Office of President of the United States, and will to the best of my Ability, preserve, protect and defend the Constitution of the United States."

Section 2

The President shall be Commander in Chief of the Army and Navy of the United States, and of the Militia of the several States, when called into the actual Service of the United States; he may require the Opinion, in writing, of the principal Officer in each of the executive Departments, upon any Subject relating to the Duties of their respective Offices, and he shall have Power to grant Reprieves and Pardons for Offences against the United States, except in Cases of Impeachment.

He shall have Power, by and with the Advice and Consent of the Senate, to make Treaties, provided two thirds of the Senators present concur; and he shall nominate, and by and with the Advice and Consent of the Senate, shall appoint Ambassadors, other public Ministers and Consuls, Judges of the supreme Court, and all other Officers of the United States, whose Appointments are not herein otherwise provided for, and which shall be established by Law: but the Congress may by Law vest the Appointment of such inferior Officers, as they think proper, in the President alone, in the Courts of Law, or in the Heads of Departments.

The President shall have Power to fill up all Vacancies that may happen during the Recess of the Senate, by granting Commissions which shall expire at the End of their next Session.

Section 3

He shall from time to time give to the Congress Information of the State of the Union, and recommend to their Consideration such Measures as he shall judge necessary and expedient; he may, on extraordinary Occasions, convene both Houses, or either of them, and in Case of Disagreement between them, with Respect to the Time of Adjournment, he may adjourn them to such Time as he shall think proper; he shall receive Ambassadors and other public Ministers; he shall take Care that the Laws be faithfully executed, and shall Commission all the Officers of the United States.

Section 4

The President, Vice President and all civil Officers of the United States, shall be removed from Office on Impeachment for, and Conviction of, Treason, Bribery, or other high Crimes and Misdemeanors.

ARTICLE III

Section 1

The judicial Power of the United States shall be vested in one supreme Court, and in such inferior Courts as the Congress may from time to time ordain and establish. The Judges, both of the supreme and inferior Courts, shall hold their Offices during good Behaviour, and shall, at stated Times, receive for their Services a Compensation, which shall not be diminished during their Continuance in Office.

Section 2

The judicial Power shall extend to all Cases, in Law and Equity, arising under this Constitution, the Laws of the United States, and Treaties made, or which shall be made, under their Authority;—to all Cases affecting Ambassadors, other public Ministers and Consuls;—to all Cases of admiralty and maritime Jurisdiction;—to Controversies to which the United States shall be a Party;—to Controversies between two or more States;—between a State and Citizens of another State;—between Citizens of different States;—between Citizens of the same State claiming Lands under Grants of different States, and between a State, or the Citizens thereof, and foreign States, Citizens or Subjects.

In all Cases affecting Ambassadors, other public Ministers and Consuls, and those in which a State shall be Party, the supreme Court shall have original Jurisdiction. In all the other Cases before mentioned, the supreme Court shall have appellate Jurisdiction, both as to Law and Fact, with such Exceptions, and under such Regulations as the Congress shall make.

The Trial of all Crimes, except in Cases of Impeachment, shall be by Jury; and such Trial shall be held in the State where the said Crimes shall have been committed; but when not committed within any State, the Trial shall be at such Place or Places as the Congress may by Law have directed.

Section 3

Treason against the United States, shall consist only in levying War against them, or in adhering to their Enemies, giving them Aid and Comfort. No Person shall be convicted of Treason unless on the Testimony of two Witnesses to the same overt Act, or on Confession in open Court.

The Congress shall have Power to declare the Punishment of Treason, but no Attainder of Treason shall work Corruption of Blood, or Forfeiture except during the Life of the Person attainted.

ARTICLE IV

Section 1

Full Faith and Credit shall be given in each State to the public Acts, Records, and judicial Proceedings of every other State. And the Congress may by general Laws prescribe the Manner in which such Acts, Records and Proceedings shall be proved, and the Effect thereof.

Section 2

The Citizens of each State shall be entitled to all Privileges and Immunities of Citizens in the several States.

A Person charged in any State with Treason, Felony, or other Crime, who shall flee from Justice, and be found in another State, shall on Demand of the executive Authority of the State from which he fled, be delivered up, to be removed to the State having Jurisdiction of the Crime.

No Person held to Service or Labour in one State, under the Laws thereof, escaping into another, shall, in Consequence of any Law or Regulation therein, be discharged from such

Service or Labour, but shall be delivered up on Claim of the Party to whom such Service or Labour may be due.

Section 3

New States may be admitted by the Congress into this Union; but no new State shall be formed or erected within the Jurisdiction of any other State; nor any State be formed by the Junction of two or more States, or Parts of States, without the Consent of the Legislatures of the States concerned as well as of the Congress.

The Congress shall have Power to dispose of and make all needful Rules and Regulations respecting the Territory or other Property belonging to the United States; and nothing in this Constitution shall be so construed as to Prejudice any Claims of the United States, or of any particular State.

Section 4

The United States shall guarantee to every State in this Union a Republican Form of Government, and shall protect each of them against Invasion; and on Application of the Legislature, or of the Executive (when the Legislature cannot be convened), against domestic Violence.

ARTICLE V

The Congress, whenever two thirds of both Houses shall deem it necessary, shall propose Amendments to this Constitution, or, on the Application of the Legislatures of two thirds of the several States, shall call a Convention for proposing Amendments, which, in either Case, shall be valid to all Intents and Purposes, as Part of this Constitution, when ratified by the Legislatures of three fourths of the several States, or by Conventions in three fourths thereof, as the one or the other

Mode of Ratification may be proposed by the Congress; Provided that no Amendment which may be made prior to the Year One thousand eight hundred and eight shall in any Manner affect the first and fourth Clauses in the Ninth Section of the first Article; and that no State, without its Consent, shall be deprived of its equal Suffrage in the Senate.

ARTICLE VI

All Debts contracted and Engagements entered into, before the Adoption of this Constitution, shall be as valid against the United States under this Constitution, as under the Confederation.

This Constitution, and the Laws of the United States which shall be made in Pursuance thereof; and all Treaties made, or which shall be made, under the Authority of the United States, shall be the supreme Law of the Land; and the Judges in every State shall be bound thereby, any Thing in the Constitution or Laws of any State to the Contrary notwithstanding.

The Senators and Representatives before mentioned, and the Members of the several State Legislatures, and all executive and judicial Officers, both of the United States and of the several States, shall be bound by Oath or Affirmation, to support this Constitution; but no religious Test shall ever be required as a Qualification to any Office or public Trust under the United States.

ARTICLE VII

The Ratification of the Conventions of nine States, shall be sufficient for the Establishment of this Constitution between the States so ratifying the Same.

The Word, "the," being interlined between the seventh and eighth Lines of the first Page, the Word "Thirty" being partly written on an

Erazure in the fifteenth Line of the first Page, The Words "is tried" being interlined between the thirty second and thirty third Lines of the first Page and the Word "the" being interlined between the forty third and forty fourth Lines of the second Page.

Attest William Jackson Secretary

Done in Convention by the Unanimous Consent of the States present the Seventeenth Day of September in the Year of our Lord one thousand seven hundred and Eighty seven and of the Independence of the United States of America the Twelfth In witness whereof We have hereunto subscribed our Names,

G. Washington
President and deputy from Virginia

‹As shown›Delaware
Geo: Read
Gunning Bedford jun
John Dickinson
Richard Bassett
Jaco: Broom

Maryland
James McHenry
Dan of St Thos. Jenifer
Danl. Carroll

Virginia
John Blair—
James Madison Jr.

North Carolina
Wm. Blount
Richd. Dobbs Spaight
Hu Williamson

South Carolina
J. Rutledge
Charles Cotesworth Pinckney
Charles Pinckney
Pierce Butler

Georgia
William Few
Abr Baldwin

New Hampshire
John Langdon
Nicholas Gilman

Massachusetts
Nathaniel Gorham
Rufus King

Connecticut
Wm. Saml. Johnson
Roger Sherman

New York
Alexander Hamilton

New Jersey
Wil: Livingston
David Brearley
Wm. Paterson
Jona: Dayton

Pennsylvania
B Franklin
Thomas Mifflin
Robt. Morris
Geo. Clymer
Thos. FitzSimons
Jared Ingersoll
James Wilson
Gouv Morris

The Bill of Rights

The Preamble to The Bill of Rights

Congress of the United States begun and held at the City of New-York, on Wednesday the fourth of March, one thousand seven hundred and eighty nine.

THE Conventions of a number of the States, having at the time of their adopting the Constitution, expressed a desire, in order to prevent misconstruction or abuse of its powers, that further declaratory and restrictive clauses should be added: And as extending the ground of public confidence in the Government, will best ensure the beneficent ends of its institution.

RESOLVED by the Senate and House of Representatives of the United States of America, in Congress assembled, two thirds of both Houses concurring, that the following Articles be proposed to the Legislatures of the several States, as amendments to the Constitution of the United States, all, or any of which Articles, when ratified by three fourths of the said Legislatures, to be valid to all intents and purposes, as part of the said Constitution; viz.

ARTICLES in addition to, and Amendment of the Constitution of the United States of America, proposed by Congress, and ratified by the Legislatures of the several States, pursuant to the fifth Article of the original Constitution.

Note: The following text is a transcription of the first ten amendments to the Constitution in their original form. These amendments were ratified December 15, 1791, and form what is known as the "Bill of Rights."

AMENDMENT I

Congress shall make no law respecting an establishment of religion, or prohibiting the free exercise thereof; or abridging the freedom of speech, or of the press; or the right of the people peaceably to assemble, and to petition the Government for a redress of grievances.

AMENDMENT II

A well regulated Militia, being necessary to the security of a free State, the right of the people to keep and bear Arms, shall not be infringed.

AMENDMENT III

No Soldier shall, in time of peace be quartered in any house, without the consent of the Owner, nor in time of war, but in a manner to be prescribed by law.

AMENDMENT IV

The right of the people to be secure in their persons, houses, papers, and effects, against unreasonable searches and seizures, shall not be violated, and no Warrants shall issue, but upon probable cause, supported by Oath or affirmation, and particularly describing the place to be searched, and the persons or things to be seized.

AMENDMENT V

No person shall be held to answer for a capital, or otherwise infamous crime, unless on a presentment or indictment of a Grand Jury, except in cases arising in the land or naval forces, or in the Militia, when in actual service in time of War or public danger; nor shall any person be subject for the same offence to be twice put in jeopardy of life or limb; nor shall be compelled in any criminal case to be a witness against himself, nor be deprived of life, liberty, or property, without due process of law; nor shall private property be taken for public use, without just compensation.

AMENDMENT VI

In all criminal prosecutions, the accused shall enjoy the right to a speedy and public trial, by an impartial jury of the State and district wherein the crime shall have been committed, which district shall have been previously ascertained by law,

and to be informed of the nature and cause of the accusation; to be confronted with the witnesses against him; to have compulsory process for obtaining witnesses in his favor, and to have the Assistance of Counsel for his defence.

AMENDMENT VII

In Suits at common law, where the value in controversy shall exceed twenty dollars, the right of trial by jury shall be preserved, and no fact tried by a jury, shall be otherwise re-examined in any Court of the United States, than according to the rules of the common law.

AMENDMENT VIII

Excessive bail shall not be required, nor excessive fines imposed, nor cruel and unusual punishments inflicted.

AMENDMENT IX

The enumeration in the Constitution, of certain rights, shall not be construed to deny or disparage others retained by the people.

AMENDMENT X

The powers not delegated to the United States by the Constitution, nor prohibited by it to the States, are reserved to the States respectively, or to the people.

The Constitution: Amendments 11–27

AMENDMENT XI

Passed by Congress March 4, 1794. Ratified February 7, 1795.

Note: Article III, section 2, of the Constitution was modified by amendment 11.

The Judicial power of the United States shall not be construed to extend to any suit in law or equity, commenced or prosecuted against one of the United States by Citizens of another State, or by Citizens or Subjects of any Foreign State.

AMENDMENT XII

Passed by Congress December 9, 1803. Ratified June 15, 1804.

Note: A portion of Article II, section 1, of the Constitution was superseded by the 12th amendment.

The Electors shall meet in their respective states and vote by ballot for President and Vice-President, one of whom, at least, shall not be an inhabitant of the same state with themselves; they shall name in their ballots the person voted for as President, and in distinct ballots the person voted for as Vice-President, and they shall make distinct lists of all persons voted for as President, and of all persons voted for as Vice-President, and of the number of votes for each, which lists they shall sign and certify, and transmit sealed to the seat of the government of the United States, directed to the President of the Senate;—the President of the Senate shall, in the presence of the Senate and House of Representatives, open all the certificates and the votes shall then be counted;—The person having the greatest number of votes for President, shall be the President, if such number be a majority of the whole number of Electors appointed; and if no person have such majority, then from the persons having the highest numbers not exceeding three on the list of those voted for as President, the House of Representatives shall choose immediately, by ballot, the President. But in choosing the President, the votes shall be taken by states, the representation from each state having one vote; a quorum for this purpose shall consist of a member or members from two-thirds of the states, and a majority of all the states shall be necessary to a choice. [And if the House of Representatives shall not choose a President whenever the right of choice shall devolve upon them, before the fourth day of March next following, then the Vice-President shall act as President, as in case of the death or other constitutional disability of the President.—]* The person having the greatest number of votes as Vice-President, shall be the Vice-President, if such number be a majority of the whole number of Electors appointed, and if no person have a majority, then from the two highest numbers on the list, the Senate shall choose the Vice-President; a quorum for the purpose shall consist of two-thirds of the whole number of Senators, and a majority of the whole number shall be necessary to a choice. But no person constitutionally ineligible to the office of President shall be eligible to that of Vice-President of the United States.

Superseded by section 3 of the 20th amendment.

AMENDMENT XIII

Passed by Congress January 31, 1865. Ratified December 6, 1865.

Note: A portion of Article IV, section 2, of the Constitution was superseded by the 13th amendment.

Section 1

Neither slavery nor involuntary servitude, except as a punishment for crime whereof the party shall have been duly convicted, shall exist within the United States, or any place subject to their jurisdiction.

Section 2

Congress shall have power to enforce this article by appropriate legislation.

AMENDMENT XIV

Passed by Congress June 13, 1866. Ratified July 9, 1868.

Note: Article I, section 2, of the Constitution was modified by section 2 of the 14th amendment.

Section 1

All persons born or naturalized in the United States, and subject to the jurisdiction thereof, are citizens of the United States and of the State wherein they reside. No State shall make or enforce any law which shall abridge the privileges or immunities of citizens of the United States; nor shall any State deprive any person of life, liberty, or property, without due process of law; nor deny to any person within its jurisdiction the equal protection of the laws.

Section 2

Representatives shall be apportioned among the several States according to their respective numbers, counting the whole number of persons in each State, excluding Indians not taxed. But when the right to vote at any election for the choice of electors for President and Vice-President of the United States, Representatives in Congress, the Executive and Judicial officers of a State, or the members of the Legislature thereof, is denied to any of the male inhabitants of such State, being twenty-one years of age,* and citizens of the United States, or in any way abridged, except for participation in rebellion, or other crime, the basis of representation therein shall be reduced in the proportion which the number of such male citizens shall bear to the whole number of male citizens twenty-one years of age in such State.

Section 3

No person shall be a Senator or Representative in Congress, or elector of President and Vice-President, or hold any office, civil or military, under the United States, or under any State, who, having previously taken an oath, as a member of Congress, or as an officer of the United States, or as a member of any

State legislature, or as an executive or judicial officer of any State, to support the Constitution of the United States, shall have engaged in insurrection or rebellion against the same, or given aid or comfort to the enemies thereof. But Congress may by a vote of two-thirds of each House, remove such disability.

Section 4

The validity of the public debt of the United States, authorized by law, including debts incurred for payment of pensions and bounties for services in suppressing insurrection or rebellion, shall not be questioned. But neither the United States nor any State shall assume or pay any debt or obligation incurred in aid of insurrection or rebellion against the United States, or any claim for the loss or emancipation of any slave; but all such debts, obligations and claims shall be held illegal and void.

Section 5

The Congress shall have the power to enforce, by appropriate legislation, the provisions of this article.

*Changed by section 1 of the 26th amendment.

AMENDMENT XV

Passed by Congress February 26, 1869. Ratified February 3, 1870.

Section 1

The right of citizens of the United States to vote shall not be denied or abridged by the United States or by any State on account of race, color, or previous condition of servitude—

Section 2

The Congress shall have the power to enforce this article by appropriate legislation.

AMENDMENT XVI

Passed by Congress July 2, 1909. Ratified February 3, 1913.

Note: Article I, section 9, of the Constitution was modified by amendment 16.

The Congress shall have power to lay and collect taxes on incomes, from whatever source derived, without apportionment among the several States, and without regard to any census or enumeration.

AMENDMENT XVII

Passed by Congress May 13, 1912. Ratified April 8, 1913.

Note: Article I, section 3, of the Constitution was modified by the 17th amendment.

The Senate of the United States shall be composed of two Senators from each State, elected by the people thereof, for six years; and each Senator shall have one vote. The electors in each State shall have the qualifications requisite for electors of the most numerous branch of the State legislatures.

When vacancies happen in the representation of any State in the Senate, the executive authority of such State shall issue writs of election to fill such vacancies: *Provided*, That the legislature of any State may empower the executive thereof to make temporary appointments until the people fill the vacancies by election as the legislature may direct.

This amendment shall not be so construed as to affect the election or term of any Senator chosen before it becomes valid as part of the Constitution.

AMENDMENT XVIII

Passed by Congress December 18, 1917. Ratified January 16, 1919. Repealed by amendment 21.

Section 1

After one year from the ratification of this article the manufacture, sale, or transportation of intoxicating liquors within, the importation thereof into, or the exportation thereof from the United States and all territory subject to the jurisdiction thereof for beverage purposes is hereby prohibited.

Section 2

The Congress and the several States shall have concurrent power to enforce this article by appropriate legislation.

Section 3

This article shall be inoperative unless it shall have been ratified as an amendment to the Constitution by the legislatures of the several States, as provided in the Constitution, within seven years from the date of the submission hereof to the States by the Congress.

AMENDMENT XIX

Passed by Congress June 4, 1919. Ratified August 18, 1920.

The right of citizens of the United States to vote shall not be denied or abridged by the United States or by any State on account of sex.

Congress shall have power to enforce this article by appropriate legislation.

AMENDMENT XX

Passed by Congress March 2, 1932. Ratified January 23, 1933.

Note: Article I, section 4, of the Constitution was modified by section 2 of this amendment. In addition, a portion of the 12th amendment was superseded by section 3.

Section 1

The terms of the President and the Vice President shall end at noon on the 20th day of January, and the terms of Senators and Representatives at noon on the 3d day of January, of the years in which such terms would have ended if this article had not been ratified; and the terms of their successors shall then begin.

Section 2

The Congress shall assemble at least once in every year, and such meeting shall begin at noon on the 3d day of January, unless they shall by law appoint a different day.

Section 3

If, at the time fixed for the beginning of the term of the President, the President elect shall have died, the Vice President elect shall become President. If a President shall not have been chosen before the time fixed for the beginning of his term, or if the President elect shall have failed to qualify, then the Vice President elect shall act as President until a President shall have qualified; and the Congress may by law provide for the case wherein neither a President elect nor a Vice President shall have qualified, declaring who shall then act as President, or the manner in which one who is to act shall be selected, and such person shall act accordingly until a President or Vice President shall have qualified.

Section 4

The Congress may by law provide for the case of the death of any of the persons from whom the House of Representatives may choose a President whenever the right of choice shall have devolved upon them, and for the case of the death of any of the persons from whom the Senate may choose a Vice President whenever the right of choice shall have devolved upon them.

Section 5

Sections 1 and 2 shall take effect on the 15th day of October following the ratification of this article.

Section 6

This article shall be inoperative unless it shall have been ratified as an amendment to the Constitution by the legislatures of three-fourths of the several States within seven years from the date of its submission.

AMENDMENT XXI

Passed by Congress February 20, 1933. Ratified December 5, 1933.

Section 1

The eighteenth article of amendment to the Constitution of the United States is hereby repealed.

Section 2

The transportation or importation into any State, Territory, or Possession of the United States for delivery or use therein of intoxicating liquors, in violation of the laws thereof, is hereby prohibited.

Section 3

This article shall be inoperative unless it shall have been ratified as an amendment to the Constitution by conventions in the several States, as provided in the Constitution, within seven years from the date of the submission hereof to the States by the Congress.

AMENDMENT XXII

Passed by Congress March 21, 1947. Ratified February 27, 1951.

Section 1

No person shall be elected to the office of the President more than twice, and no person who has held the office of President, or acted as President, for more than two years of a term to which some other person was elected President shall be elected to the office of President more than once. But this Article shall not apply to any person holding the office of President when this Article was proposed by Congress, and shall not prevent any person who may be holding the office of President, or acting as President, during the term within which this Article becomes operative from holding the office of President or acting as President during the remainder of such term.

Section 2

This article shall be inoperative unless it shall have been ratified as an amendment to the Constitution by the legislatures of three-fourths of the several States within seven years from the date of its submission to the States by the Congress.

AMENDMENT XXIII

Passed by Congress June 16, 1960. Ratified March 29, 1961.

Section 1

The District constituting the seat of Government of the United States shall appoint in such manner as Congress may direct:

A number of electors of President and Vice President equal to the whole number of Senators and Representatives in Congress to which the District would be entitled if it were a State, but in no event more than the least populous State; they shall be in addition to those appointed by the States, but they shall be considered, for the purposes of the election of President and Vice

President, to be electors appointed by a State; and they shall meet in the District and perform such duties as provided by the twelfth article of amendment.

Section 2

The Congress shall have power to enforce this article by appropriate legislation.

AMENDMENT XXIV

Passed by Congress August 27, 1962. Ratified January 23, 1964.

Section 1

The right of citizens of the United States to vote in any primary or other election for President or Vice President, for electors for President or Vice President, or for Senator or Representative in Congress, shall not be denied or abridged by the United States or any State by reason of failure to pay poll tax or other tax.

Section 2

The Congress shall have power to enforce this article by appropriate legislation.

AMENDMENT XXV

Passed by Congress July 6, 1965. Ratified February 10, 1967.

Note: Article II, section 1, of the Constitution was affected by the 25th amendment.

Section 1

In case of the removal of the President from office or of his death or resignation, the Vice President shall become President.

Section 2

Whenever there is a vacancy in the office of the Vice President, the President shall nominate a Vice President who shall take office upon confirmation by a majority vote of both Houses of Congress.

Section 3

Whenever the President transmits to the President pro tempore of the Senate and the Speaker of the House of Representatives his written declaration that he is unable to discharge the powers and duties of his office, and until he transmits to them a written declaration to the contrary, such powers and duties shall be discharged by the Vice President as Acting President.

Section 4

Whenever the Vice President and a majority of either the principal officers of the executive departments or of such other body as Congress may by law provide, transmit to the President pro tempore of the Senate and the Speaker of the House of Representatives their written declaration that the President is unable to discharge the powers and duties of his office, the Vice President shall immediately assume the powers and duties of the office as Acting President.

Thereafter, when the President transmits to the President pro tempore of the Senate and the Speaker of the House of Representatives his written declaration that no inability exists, he shall resume the powers and duties of his office unless the Vice President and a majority of either the principal officers of the executive department or of such other body as Congress may by law provide, transmit within four days to the President pro tempore of the Senate and the Speaker of the House of Representatives their written declaration that the President is unable to discharge the powers and duties of his office. Thereupon Congress shall decide the issue, assembling within forty-eight hours for that purpose if not in session. If the Congress, within twenty-one days after receipt of the latter written declaration, or, if Congress is not in session, within twenty-one days after Congress is required to assemble, determines by two-thirds vote of both Houses that the President is unable to discharge the powers and duties of his office, the Vice President shall continue to discharge the same as Acting President; otherwise, the President shall resume the powers and duties of his office.

AMENDMENT XXVI

Passed by Congress March 23, 1971. Ratified July 1, 1971.

Note: Amendment 14, section 2, of the Constitution was modified by section 1 of the 26th amendment.

Section 1

The right of citizens of the United States, who are eighteen years of age or older, to vote shall not be denied or abridged by the United States or by any State on account of age.

Section 2

The Congress shall have power to enforce this article by appropriate legislation.

AMENDMENT XXVII

Originally proposed Sept. 25, 1789. Ratified May 7, 1992.

No law, varying the compensation for the services of the Senators and Representatives, shall take effect, until an election of representatives shall have intervened.

It Is Time to Repair the Constitution's Flaws

Sanford Levinson

In 1987 I went to a marvelous exhibit in Philadelphia commemorating the bicentennial of the drafting of the U.S. Constitution. The exhibit concluded with two scrolls, each with the same two questions: First, "Will You Sign This Constitution?" And then, "If you had been in Independence Hall on September 17, 1787, would you have endorsed the Constitution?" The second question emphasized that we were being asked to assess the 1787 Constitution. That was no small matter inasmuch as the document did not include *any* of the subsequent amendments, including the Bill of Rights. Moreover, the viewer had been made aware in the course of the exhibit that the Constitution included several terrible compromises with slavery.

Even in 1987, because of those compromises I tended to regard the original Constitution as what the antislavery crusader William Lloyd Garrison so memorably called "a covenant with death and an agreement with hell." So why did I choose to sign the scroll? I was impressed that Frederick Douglass, the great black abolitionist, after an initial flirtation

with Garrison's rejectionism, endorsed even the antebellum Constitution. He argued that, correctly understood, it was deeply antislavery at its core.

The language of the Constitution—including, most importantly, its magnificent preamble—allows us to mount a critique of slavery, and much else, from within. The Constitution offers us a language by which we can protect those rights that we deem important. We need not reject the Constitution in order to carry on such a conversation. If the Constitution, at the present time, is viewed as insufficiently protective of such rights, that is because of the limited imagination of those interpreters with the most political power, including members of the Supreme Court. So I added my signature to the scroll endorsing the 1787 Constitution.

On July 3, 2003, I was back in Philadelphia to participate in the grand opening of the National Constitution Center. The exhibit culminated in Signers' Hall, which featured life-size (and lifelike) statues of each of the delegates to the constitutional convention. As one

Introduction, pp. 3–9 "It is time to repair the constitution flaws" from *Our Undemocratic Constitution* by Sanford Levinson, Oxford University Press, 2007. Reprinted by permission.

walked through the hall and brushed against James Madison, Alexander Hamilton, and other giants of our history, one could almost feel the remarkable energy that must have impressed itself on those actually in Independence Hall.

As was true in 1987, the visitor was invited to join the signers by adding his or her own signature to the Constitution. Indeed, the center organized a major project during September 2003 called "I Signed the Constitution." Sites in all 50 states were available for such a signing. Both the temporary 1987 exhibit and the permanent one that remains at the National Constitution Center leave little doubt about the proper stance that a citizen should take toward our founding document.

This time, however, I rejected the invitation to re-sign the Constitution. I had not changed my mind that in many ways it offers a rich, even inspiring, language to envision and defend a desirable political order. Nor did my decision necessarily mean that I would have preferred that the Constitution go down to defeat in the ratification votes of 1787–88. Rather, I treated the center as asking me about my level of support for the Constitution *today* and, just as important, whether I wished to encourage my fellow citizens to reaffirm it in a relatively thoughtless manner. As to the first, I realized that I had, between 1987 and 2003, become far more concerned about the inadequacies of the Constitution. As to the second, I had come to think that it is vitally important to engage in a national conversation about its adequacy rather than automatically to assume its fitness for our own times.

My concern is only minimally related to the formal rights protected by the Constitution. Even if, as a practical matter, the Supreme Court reads the Constitution less protectively with regard to certain rights than I do, the proper response is not to reject the Constitution but to work within it by trying to persuade fellow Americans to share our views of constitutional possibility and by supporting presidential candidates who will appoint (and get through the Senate) judges who will be more open to better interpretations. Given that much constitutional interpretation occurs outside the courts, one also wants public officials at all levels to share one's own visions of constitutional possibility—as well, of course, as of constitutional constraints. And that is true even for readers who disagree with me on what specific rights are most important.

So what accounts for my change of views since 1987? The brief answer is that I have become ever more despondent about many structural provisions of the Constitution that place almost insurmountable barriers in the way of any acceptable contemporary notion of democracy. I put it that way to acknowledge that "democracy" is most certainly what political theorists call an "essentially contested concept." It would be tendentious to claim that there is only one understanding—such as "numerical majorities always prevail"—that is consistent with "democracy." Liberal constitutionalists, for example, would correctly place certain constraints on what majorities can do to vulnerable minorities.

That being said, I believe that it is increasingly difficult to construct a theory of democratic constitutionalism, *applying our own 21st-century norms*, that vindicates the Constitution under which we are governed today. Our 18th-century ancestors had little trouble integrating slavery and the rank subordination of women into their conception of a "republican" political order. *That* vision of politics is blessedly long behind us, but the Constitution is not. It does not deserve rote support from Americans who properly believe that majority rule, even if tempered by the recognition of minority rights, is integral to "consent of the governed."

I invite you to ask the following questions:

1. Even if you support having a Senate in addition to a House of Representatives, do you support as well giving Wyoming the same number of votes as California, which has roughly 70 times the population? To the degree that Congress is in significant ways *unrepresentative*, we have less reason to respect it. It is not a cogent response, incidentally, to say that any such inequalities are vitiated by the fact that the House of Representatives is organized on the basis of population, putting to one side issues raised by partisan gerrymandering. The very nature of our particular version of bicameralism, after all, requires that both houses assent to any legislation. By definition, that means that *the Senate can exercise the equivalent of an absolute veto power* on majoritarian legislation passed by the House that is deemed too costly to the interests of the small states that are over-represented in the Senate, especially those clustered together in the Rocky Mountain area and the upper Midwest.

2. Are you comfortable with an Electoral College that, among other things, has since World War II placed in the White House five candidates—Truman, Kennedy, Nixon (1968), Clinton (1992 and 1996), and Bush (2000)—who did not get a majority of the popular vote? In at least two of those elections—in 1960, for which evidence exists that Nixon would have won a recount, and in 2000—the winners did not even come in first in the popular vote. The fact is that presidential candidates and their campaign managers are not necessarily trying to win the popular vote, except as an afterthought. Instead they are dedicated to putting together a coalition of states that will provide a majority of the electoral votes.

3. Are you concerned that the president might have too much power, whether to spy on Americans without any Congressional or judicial authorization or to frustrate the will of a majority of both houses of Congress by vetoing legislation with which he disagrees on political, as distinguished from constitutional, grounds? At the very least, it should be clear from recent controversies that the present Constitution does not offer a clear understanding of the limits of presidential power, particularly during times of presidentially perceived emergencies.

4. Are you concerned about whether the country is well served by the extended hiatus between election day and the presidential inauguration some 10 weeks later, during which lame-duck presidents retain full legal authority to make often controversial decisions? Imagine if John Kerry had won the 2004 election, and President Bush had continued to make decisions about policy on Iraq, Iran, and North Korea that would have greatly affected his administration. Much of the hiatus is explicable only with regard to the need for the Electoral College to operate (which serves as an additional reason to eliminate that dysfunctional institution).

5. Are you satisfied with a Constitution that, in effect, maximizes the baleful consequences of certain kinds of terrorist attacks on the United States? If a successor to United Flight 93 were to succeed in a catastrophic attack on the House of Representatives and the Senate, we could find ourselves in a situation where neither institution could operate—because the Constitution makes it impossible to replace disabled (as distinguished from dead) senators or to fill House vacancies

by any process other than an election. That would contribute to the overwhelming likelihood of a presidential dictatorship. The Constitution is written for what is termed "retail" vacancies, which occur only occasionally and are easily subject to being handled by the existing rules. Should "wholesale" vacancies occur, however, the present Constitution is nothing less than a ticking time bomb.

6. Do you really want justices on the Supreme Court to serve up to four decades and, among other things, to be able to time their resignations to mesh with their own political preferences as to their successors?

7. Finally, do you find it "democratic" that 13 legislative houses in as many states can block constitutional amendments desired by the overwhelming majority of Americans as well as, possibly, 86 out of the 99 legislative houses in the American states? No other country—nor, for that matter, any of the 50 American states—makes it so difficult to amend its constitution. Article V of our Constitution constitutes an iron cage with regard to changing some of the most important aspects of our political system. But almost as important is the way that it also constitutes an iron cage with regard to our imagination. Because it is so difficult to amend the Constitution—it seems almost utopian to suggest the possibility, with regard to anything that is truly important—citizens are encouraged to believe that change is almost never desirable, let alone necessary.

One might regard those questions as raising only theoretical, perhaps even "aesthetic," objections to our basic institutional structures *if* we feel truly satisfied by the outcomes generated by our national political institutions. But

that is patently not the case. Consider the results when samples of Americans are asked whether they believe the country is headed in the right or the wrong direction. In April 2005, a full 62 percent of the respondents to a CBS poll indicated that they believed that the country was headed in "the wrong direction." A year later, a similar CBS poll found that 71 percent of the respondents said that the country was "on the wrong track," with unfavorable ratings for Congress and the president, and only a slim majority approving of the Supreme Court. Surely that comprehensive sense of dissatisfaction is related for most Americans to a belief that our political institutions are *not* adequately responding to the issues at hand. Serious liberals and conservatives increasingly share an attitude of profound disquiet about the capacity of our institutions to meet the problems confronting us as a society.

To be sure, most Americans still seem to approve of their particular members of Congress. The reason for such approval, alas, may be the representatives' success in bringing home federally financed pork, which scarcely relates to the great national and international issues that we might hope that Congress could confront effectively. In any event, we should resist the temptation simply to criticize specific inhabitants of national offices. An emphasis on the deficiencies of particular officeholders suggests that the cure for what ails us is simply to win some elections and replace those office-holders with presumptively more virtuous officials. But we are deluding ourselves if we believe that winning elections is enough to overcome the deficiencies of the American political system.

We must recognize that substantial responsibility for the defects of our polity lies in the Constitution itself. A number of wrong turns were taken at the time of the initial drafting of the Constitution, even if for the best of reasons given the political realities of 1787. Even the most skilled and admirable leaders may not be able to overcome the barriers to effective government constructed by the Constitution. In many ways, we are like the police officer in Edgar Allen Poe's classic *The Purloined Letter*, unable to comprehend the true importance of what is clearly in front of us.

If I am correct that the Constitution is both insufficiently democratic, in a country that professes to believe in democracy, *and* significantly dysfunctional, in terms of the quality of government that we receive, then it follows that we should no longer express our blind devotion to it. It is not, as Thomas Jefferson properly suggested, the equivalent of the Ark of the Covenant. It is a human creation open to criticism and even to rejection. You should join me in supporting the call for a new constitutional convention.

Sanford Levinson is a professor of law at the University of Texas Law School. This essay is adapted from Our Undemocratic Constitution: Where the Constitution Goes Wrong (And How We the People Can Correct It).

Making Every Vote Count

Lani Guinier

For years many of us have called for a national conversation about what it means to be a multiracial democracy. We have enumerated the glaring flaws inherent in our winner-take-all form of voting, which has produced a steady decline in voter participation, underrepresentation of racial minorities in office, lack of meaningful competition and choice in most elections, and the general failure of politics to mobilize, inform and inspire half the eligible electorate. But nothing changed. Democracy was an asterisk in political debate, typically encompassed in a vague reference to "campaign finance reform." Enter Florida.

The fiasco there provides a rare opportunity to rethink and improve our voting practices in a way that reflects our professed desire to have "every vote count." This conversation has already begun, as several highly educated communities in Palm Beach experienced the same sense of systematic disfranchisement that beset the area's poorer and less-educated communities of color. "It felt like Birmingham last night," Mari Castellanos, a Latina activist in Miami, wrote in an e-mail describing a mammoth rally at the 14,000-member New Birth Baptist Church, a primarily African-American congregation in Miami.

"The sanctuary was standing room only. So were the overflow rooms and the school hall, where congregants connected via large TV screens. The people sang and prayed and listened. Story after story was told of voters being turned away at the polls, of ballots being destroyed, of NAACP election literature being discarded at the main post office, of Spanish-speaking poll workers being sent to Creole precincts and vice-versa.... Union leaders, civil rights activists, Black elected officials, ministers, rabbis and an incredibly passionate and inspiring Marlene Bastiene—president of the Haitian women's organization—spoke for two or three minutes each, reminding the assembly of the price their communities had paid for the right to vote and vowing not to be disfranchised ever again."

We must not let this once-in-a-generation moment pass without addressing the basic questions these impassioned citizens are raising: Who votes, how do they vote, whom do they vote for, how are their votes counted and what happens after the voting? These questions go to the very legitimacy of our democratic procedures, not just in Florida but nationwide—and the answers could lead to profound but eminently achievable reforms.

"Making Every Vote Count: by Lani Guinier from the December 4, 2000 issue of *The Nation*. Used with permission.

§ *Who votes—and doesn't?* As with the rest of the nation, in Florida only about half of all adults vote, about the same as the national average. Even more disturbing, nonvoters are increasingly low-income, young and less educated. This trend persists despite the Voting Rights Act, which since 1970 has banned literacy tests nationwide as prerequisites for voting—a ban enacted by Congress and unanimously upheld by the Supreme Court.

We are a democracy that supposedly believes in universal suffrage, and yet the differential turnout between high-income and low-income voters is far greater than in Europe, where it ranges from 5 to 10 percent. More than two-thirds of people in America with incomes greater than $50,000 vote, compared with one-third of those with incomes under $10,000. Those convicted of a felony are permanently banned from voting in Florida and twelve other states. In Florida alone, this year more than 400,000 ex-felons, about half of them black, were denied the opportunity to vote. Canada, on the other hand, takes special steps to register former prisoners and bring them into full citizenship.

§ *How do they vote?* Florida now abounds with stories of long poll lines, confusing ballots and strict limitations on how long voters could spend in the voting booth. The shocking number of invalid ballots—more ballots were "spoiled" in the presidential race than were cast for "spoiler" Ralph Nader—are a direct result of antiquated voting mechanics that would shame any nation, let alone one of the world's oldest democracies. Even the better-educated older voters of Palm Beach found, to their surprise, how much they had in common with more frequently disfranchised populations. Given how many decisions voters are expected to make in less than five minutes in the polling booth, it is common sense that the polls should be open over a weekend, or at least for twenty-four hours, and that Election Day should be a national holiday. By highlighting our wretched record on voting practices, Florida raises the obvious question: Do we really want large voter participation?

§ *Whom do they vote for?* Obviously, Florida voters chose among Al Gore, George Bush and a handful of minor-party candidates who, given their status as unlikely to win, were generally ignored and at best chastised as spoilers. But as many voters are now realizing, in the presidential race they were voting not for the candidates whose name they selected (or attempted to select) but for "electors" to that opaque institution, the Electoral College. Our constitutional framers did some things well—chiefly dulling the edge of winner-take-all elections through institutions that demand coalition-building, compromise and recognition of certain minority voices—but the Electoral College was created on illegitimate grounds and has no place in a modern democracy.

As Yale law professor Akhil Reed Amar argues, the Electoral College was established as a device to boost the power of Southern states in the election of the President. The same "compromise" that gave Southern states more House members by counting slaves as three-fifths of a person for purposes of apportioning representation (while giving them none of the privileges of citizenship) gave those states Electoral College votes in proportion to their Congressional delegation. This hypocrisy enhanced the Southern states' Electoral College percentage, and as a result, Virginia slaveowners controlled the presidency for thirty-two of our first thirty-six years.

Its immoral origins notwithstanding, the Electoral College was soon justified as a deliberative body that would choose among several candidates and assure the voice of small geographic areas. But under the Electoral College, voters in small states have more than just a voice; indeed their say often exceeds that of voters in big states. In Wyoming one vote in the Electoral College corresponds to 71,000 voters; in Florida, one electoral vote corresponds to 238,000 voters. At minimum we should eliminate the extra bias that adding electors for each of two senators gives our smallest states. As Robert Naiman of the Center for Economic and Policy Research reports, allowing each state only as many electors as it has members in the House of Representatives would mean, for example, that even if Bush won Oregon and Florida, he would have 216 and Gore would have 220 electoral votes.

Today its backers still argue that the Electoral College is necessary to insure that small states are not ignored by the presidential candidates. Yet the many states—including small ones—that weren't close in this election were neglected by both campaigns. Some of the nation's biggest states, with the most people of color, saw very little presidential campaigning and get-out-the-vote activity. Given their lopsided results this year, we can expect California, Illinois, New York, Texas and nearly all Southern states to be shunned in the 2004 campaign.

§ *How are their votes counted?* The presidency rests on a handful of votes in Florida because allocation of electoral votes is winner-take-all—if Gore wins by ten votes out of 6 million, he will win 100 percent of the state's twenty-five electoral votes. The ballots cast for a losing candidate are always "invalid" for the purposes of representation; only those cast for the winner actually "count." Thus winner-take-all elections underrepresent the voice of the minority and exaggerate the power of one state's razor-thin majority. Winner-take-all is the great barrier to representation of political and racial minorities at both the federal and the state level. No blacks or Latinos serve in the US Senate or in any governor's mansion. Third-party candidates did not win a single state legislature race except for a handful in Vermont.

Given the national questioning of the Electoral College sparked by the anomalous gap between the popular vote and the college's vote in the presidential election, those committed to real representative democracy now have a chance to shine a spot-light on the glaring flaws and disfranchisement inherent in winner-take-all practices and to propose important reforms.

What we need are election rules that encourage voter turnout rather than suppress it. A system of proportional representation—which would allocate seats to parties based on their proportion of the total vote—would more fairly reflect intense feeling within the electorate, mobilize more people to participate and even encourage those who do participate to do so beyond just the single act of voting on Election Day. Most democracies around the world have some form of proportional voting and manage to engage a much greater percentage of their citizens in elections. Proportional representation in South Africa, for example, allows the white Afrikaner parties and the ANC to gain seats in the national legislature commensurate with the total number of votes cast for each party. Under this system, third parties are a plausible alternative. Moreover, to allow third parties to run presidential candidates without being "spoilers," some advocate instant-runoff elections in which voters would rank their choices for President. That way, even voters whose top choice loses the election could influence the race among the other candidates.

Winner-take-all elections, by contrast, encourage the two major parties to concentrate primarily on the "undecideds" and to take tens of millions of dollars of corporate and special-interest contributions to broadcast ads on the public airwaves appealing to the center of the political spectrum. Winner-take-all incentives discourage either of the two major parties from trying to learn, through organizing and door-knocking, how to mobilize the vast numbers of disengaged poor and working-class voters. Rather than develop a vision, they produce a product and fail to build political capacity from the ground up.

§ *What happens after the voting?* Our nation is more focused on elections now than it has been for decades; yet on any given Sunday, more people will watch professional football than voted this November. What democracy demands is a system of elections that enables minor parties to gain a voice in the legislature and encourages the development of local political organizations that educate and mobilize voters.

Between elections, grassroots organizations could play an important monitoring role now unfulfilled by the two major parties. If the Bush campaign is right that large numbers of ballots using the same butterfly format were thrown out in previous elections in Palm Beach, then something is wrong with more than the ballot. For those Democratic senior citizens in Palm Beach, it was not enough that their election supervisor was a Democrat. They needed a vibrant local organization that could have served as a watchdog, alerting voters and election officials that there were problems with the ballot. No one should inadvertently vote for two candidates; the same watchdog organizations should require ballot-counting machines like those in some states that notify the voter of such problems before he or she leaves the booth. Voters should be asked, as on the popular TV quiz show, "Is that your final answer?" And surely we cannot claim to be a functioning democracy when voters are turned away from the polls or denied assistance in violation of both state and federal law.

Before the lessons of Florida are forgotten, let us use this window of opportunity to forge a strong pro-democracy coalition to rally around "one vote, one value." The value of a vote depends on its being fairly counted but also on its counting toward the election of the person the voter chose as her representative. This can happen only if we recognize the excesses of winner-take-all voting and stop exaggerating the power of the winner by denying the loser any voice at all.

Lani Guinier is a professor of law at Harvard Law School. Her latest book is the forthcoming The Miner's Canary: Rethinking Race and Power *(Harvard). Rob Richie of the Center for Voting and Democracy (www.fairvote.org) provided invaluable assistance in the preparation of this essay.*

Minorities and Democratic Representation

What does it mean for one person to represent another or a group of persons? In Federalist #10, Madison argued that a Representative Democracy would be more likely to solve the problem of factions, or the tyranny of the majority, but leading voters to consider the interest of the whole people rather than their own special interest. But while Representative Democracy does seem to widen the view of persons somewhat beyond their own individual interest, there is still a tendency for voters to elect persons who represent their group interests in some sense that is narrower than that of the whole of the nation. The Constitution acknowledges the legitimacy of one particular narrow group interest, that of states, but not groups defined by race or sex.

The two articles in this section raise issues about whether there is need to be guaranteed representation for women and for racial minorities as there now exists for geographically defined groups. Anne Phillips, a professor of political science at the London School of Economics, examines the issue of how our representatives can and should represent us. Bernard Boxill, an African-American professor of philosophy at the University of North Carolina, argues for a voting scheme that would enable cultural minorities to ensure that they have a representative in Congress.

STUDY QUESTIONS:

1. What is the argument from justice for gender parity in representation?

2. What is the argument from interest for gender parity in representation?

3. What is a Majoritarian Democracy?

4. Why is Majoritarianism particularly problematic for a *cultural* minority?

5. How would the single, transferable vote scheme work?

Democracy and Representation: Or, Why Should it Matter Who our Representatives Are?

Anne Phillips

Though the overall statistics on women in politics continue to tell their dreary tale of under-representation, this under-representation is now widely regarded as a problem, and a significant number of political parties have adopted measures to raise the proportion of women elected. That the issue is even discussed marks a significant change. Even more remarkable is that growing support for a variety of *enabling* devices (day-schools, for example, to encourage potential women candidates) now combines with some minority backing for measures that *guarantee* parity between women and men. Parties in the Nordic countries took the lead in this, introducing gender quotas for the selection of parliamentary candidates from the mid-1970s onwards, but a quick survey across Europe throws up a number of parallel developments. Positive action to increase the proportion of women elected is now on the political agenda. It has become one of the issues on which politicians disagree.

In some ways, indeed, this is an area where those engaged in the practice of politics have edged ahead of those engaged in its theory. Gatherings of party politicians are significantly more likely to admit the problem of women's under-representation than gatherings of political scientists, for while the former remain deeply divided over the particular measures they will support, most can manage at least a lukewarm expression of 'regret' that so few women are elected. The pressures of party competition weigh heavily on their shoulders. In an era of increased voter volatility, they cannot afford to disparage issues that competitors might turn to electoral advantage. Hence the cumulative effect noted in Norwegian politics, where the Socialist Left Party first adopted gender quotas in the 1970s; this was followed in the 1980s by similar initiatives from the Labour and Centre Parties; and was accompanied by substantial increases in the number of women selected by the Conservative Party as well (Skjeie 1991). Hence the impact of the German Green Party, which decided to alternate women and men on its list for the 1986 election; the threat of this small—but at

Originally published in Schweizerisches Jahrbuch fur Politische Wissenschaften and reprinted in the *Feminism and Politics* reader. Used with permission of Anne Phillips.

the time, rapidly growing—party contributed to the Christian Democrats' adoption of a voluntary quota, and the Social Democrat's conversion to a formal one (Chapman 1993: ch. 9). Hence the otherwise surprising consensus that has emerged among Britain's major political parties—at central office level if not yet in local constituencies—in favour of selecting a higher proportion of women candidates (Lovenduski and Norris 1989). None of this would have happened without vigorous campaigning inside the political parties, but the campaigns have proved particularly effective where parties were already worried about their electoral appeal.

This pragmatically driven conversion contrasts with a more tough-minded resistance inside the political science community, where arguments range from a supposed lack of evidence that sex affects policy decisions, to a distaste with what is implied in saying that it should. Women's under-representation in politics is in one sense just empirical fact: they are not present in elected assemblies in the same proportions as they are present in the electorate. But the characteristics of those elected may diverge in any number of ways from the characteristics of those who elect them, and this is not always seen as a matter of democratic consequence. In a much cited article on representation, A. Phillips Griffiths (1960: 190) argued that some divergences are regarded as positively beneficial. We do not normally consider the interests of lunatics as best represented by people who are mad, and 'while we might well wish to complain that there are not enough representative members of the working class among Parliamentary representatives, we would not want to complain that the large class of stupid or maleficent people have too few representatives in Parliament: quite the contrary'. Feminists may find the implied parallels unconvincing, especially when we recall the

many decades in which women were classified with children and the insane as ineligible for the right to a vote; but the general point remains. Establishing an empirical under-representation of certain categories of people does not in itself add up to a normative case for their equal or proportionate presence. It may alert us to overt forms of discrimination that are keeping certain people out, but does not yet provide the basis for radical change.

The contemporary version of 'Phillips Griffiths' argument takes the form of the notorious 'slippery slope': if measures are proposed for achieving a fair 'representation' of the proportion of women in the electorate, why not also of homosexuals, of pensioners, of the unemployed, of people with blue eyes and red hair? Though usually raised with deliberately facetious intent, such questions combine with more serious work on representation which has tended to dismiss ideals of 'descriptive' or 'mirror' representation as a nostalgic yearning for direct democracy. In her influential work on *The Concept of Representation*, Hanna Pitkin (1967: 86) suggests that the metaphors of descriptive representation are most commonly found among those who regard representative democracy as a poor second-best, and who therefore look to more 'accurate' or pictorial representation of the electorate as a way of approximating the old citizen assemblies. Yet representatives, she argues, are supposed to act—what would be the point of a system of representation that involved no responsibility for delivering policy results?—and too much emphasis on who is present may divert us from the more urgent questions of what the representatives actually do. 'Think of the legislature as a pictorial representation or a representative sample of the nation, and you will almost certainly concentrate on its composition rather than its activities' (1967: 226). In Pitkin's preferred version, it is the activities rather than the characteristics that matter, and what happens after the action rather than before it that counts. Representing 'means acting in the interests of the represented, in a manner responsive to them' (1967: 209). Fair representation cannot be guaranteed in advance; it is achieved in more continuous process, which depends on a (somewhat unspecified) level of responsiveness to the electorate. The representatives may and almost certainly will differ from those they act for, not only in their social and sexual characteristics, but also in their understanding of where the 'true' interests of their constituents lie. What renders this representative is the requirement for responsiveness. 'There need not be a constant activity of responding, but there must be a constant condition of responsi*veness*, of potential readiness to respond' (1967: 233).

Radicals may challenge this resolution as allowing too much independence of judgement and action to the representatives, but the direction their criticisms take also lends little support to arguments for gender parity. The most radical among them will scorn what they see as a reformist preoccupation with the composition of political élites—and they may express some dismay that a once obsessively democratic women's movement could retreat to such limited ambitions. Others will give more serious consideration to reforms that increase the representative nature of existing national assemblies, but they will prefer mechanisms of accountability that minimize the significance of the individuals elected. The shift from direct to representative democracy has shifted the emphasis from *who* the politicians are to *what* (policies, preferences, ideas) they represent, and in doing so, has made accountability to the electorate the pre-eminent concern. We may no longer have much hope of sharing in the activities of government, but we can at least demand that our politicians do what they promised to do. The quality of representation is

then thought to depend on tighter mechanisms of accountability that bind politicians more closely to the opinions they profess to represent. Where such processes are successful, they reduce the discretion and autonomy of individual representatives; in the process, they seem to minimize the importance of whether these individuals are women or men.

Consider, in this context, the guidelines that were introduced by the US Democrats in the early 1970s, to make their National Convention (which carries the crucial responsibility of deciding on the presidential candidate) more representative of the party rank and file. Dismay at the seemingly undemocratic nature of the 1968 Convention prompted the formation of a Commission on Party Structure and Delegate Selection, which recommended more extensive participation by party members in the selection of delegates, as well as quota guidelines to increase the proportion of delegates who were female, black, and young. As a result of this, the composition of the 1972 Convention was markedly more 'descriptive' of Party members than previous ones had been: 40 per cent of the delegates were women, 15 per cent were black, and 21 per cent were aged between 18 and 30. But the reforms pointed in potentially contradictory directions, for they simultaneously sought to increase rank and file participation in the selection of delegates, to bind delegates more tightly to the preferences of this rank and file, and to ensure a more descriptive representation according to age, gender, and race. As Austin Ranney (1982: 196)—one of the members of the Commission—later noted, the success of the first two initiatives undermined the importance of the third. By 1980, the overwhelming majority of delegates were being chosen in party primaries which bound them to cast their votes for one particular candidate; they became in consequence mere ciphers, who were there to register preferences already expressed. 'If that is the case,' Ranney argues, then it really doesn't matter very much who the delegates are.' The more radical the emphasis on accountability, the less significance attaches to who does the work of representation.

Those engaged in campaigns for gender quotas have worked with some success on the electoral sensitivities of party politicians, but have made less headway among the tough-minded theorists of representation. My concern here is to address the latter, and to create maximum difficulties for myself I will focus on the stronger claim of gender parity, rather than the more modest claim for some more women elected.[1] This reflects what may be a naïve confidence on my part: that no one who seriously considers the matter could regard the current balance between the sexes as a fair process of representation. At the lowest points of women's under-representation (it was only in 1987 for example, that the British House of Commons lifted itself above the 5 per cent mark), one need only reverse the position of the sexes to demonstrate the democratic deficit. What would men think of a system of political representation in which they were outnumbered nineteen to one? At such gross levels of gender imbalance, rhetorical devices are all that we need—one would have to be a pretty determined patriarch to defend this as an appropriate state of affairs. But recent initiatives have raised the stakes considerably higher, insisting on positive action as a condition for effective change, and aiming at fifty/fifty parity, or a 40 per cent minimum for either sex. What are the arguments for this more radical position, and how do they engage with current conventions of accountability and representation?

Arguments for raising the proportion of women elected fall broadly into four groups. There are those that dwell on the role model successful women politicians offer; those that appeal to principles of justice between the sexes; those that identify particular interests of women that would be otherwise overlooked; and those that point towards a revitalized democracy that bridges the gap between representation and participation. The least interesting of these, from my point of view, is the role model. When more women candidates are elected, their example is said to raise women's self-esteem, encourage others to follow in their footsteps, and dislodge deep-rooted assumptions on what is appropriate to women and men. I leave this to one side, for I see it as an argument that has no particular purchase on politics *per se*. Positive role models are certainly beneficial, but I want to address arguments that engage more directly with issues of democracy and representation.

One final preamble. Though I deal here only with general issues of justification, there is a second order question, which is how legitimate objectives can be best achieved. The emphasis on quota mechanisms and other such guarantees has aroused strong resistance even among those who claim to share the ultimate goal of women's equality in politics, and while some of this can be discounted as intellectual or political dishonesty, much of it relates to pragmatic judgements of what is possible in any particular context. The potential backlash against women is one consideration here, as are the difficulties some political parties claim to experience in finding enough women candidates. Some of the resistance depends on more general arguments against positive action; some of it reflects still unresolved tensions between gender and class; some relates to a familiar problem in political argument, which is that mechanisms proposed for achieving one desired goal can conflict with other desirable ends. Considerations of space prevent me dealing with this second order question, and I will merely note that there *are* pragmatic judgements to be made, which do not flow simply from the conclusions on general objectives. But if gender parity can be shown to matter, and existing structures can be shown to discourage it, this constitutes a case for positive action.

I. THE CASE FOR GENDER PARITY: THE JUSTICE ARGUMENT

One of the most powerful arguments for gender parity is simply in terms of justice: that it is patently and grotesquely unfair for men to monopolize representation. If there were no obstacles operating to keep certain groups of people out of political life, then we would expect positions of political influence to be randomly distributed between both sexes and across all the ethnic groups that make up the society. There might be some minor and innocent deviations, but any more distorted distribution of political office is evidence of intentional or structural discrimination (Phillips 1991). In such contexts (that is, most contexts!) women are being denied rights and opportunities that are currently available to men. There is a *prima facie* case for action.

There are three things to be said about this argument. One is that it relies on a strong position on the current sexual division of labour as inequitable and 'unnatural'. Consider the parallel under-representation of the very young and very old in politics. Most people will accept this as part of a normal and natural life-cycle, in which the young have no time for conventional politics, and the old have already contributed their share; and since each in principle has a chance in the middle years of life, this under-representation does not strike us as particularly unfair. The consequent 'exclusion' of certain views or experiences may be said to pose a problem. But however much people worry about this, they rarely argue for proportionate representation for the over-70s and the under-25s.2 The situation of women

looks more obviously unfair, in that women will be under-represented throughout their entire lives, but anyone wedded to the current division of labour can treat it as a parallel case. A woman's life-cycle typically includes a lengthy period of caring for children, and another lengthy period of caring for parents as they grow old. It is hardly surprising, then, that fewer women come forward as candidates, or that so few women are elected. Here, too, there may be an under-representation of particular experiences and concerns, but since this arises quite 'naturally' from particular life-cycles it is not at odds with equality or justice.

I do not find the parallel convincing, but my reasons lie in a feminist analysis of the sexual division of labour as 'unnatural' and unjust. The general argument from equal rights or opportunities only translates into a specific case for gender parity in politics when it is combined with some such analysis; failing this, it engages merely with the more overt forms of discrimination that exclude women from political office, and cannot deliver any stronger conclusion. Justice requires us to eliminate discrimination (this is already implied in the notion of justice), but the argument for women's equal representation in politics depends on that further ingredient which establishes structural discrimination. Feminists will have no difficulty adding this. This first point then helps clarify what is involved in moving from a description of women's under-representation to an analysis of its injustice.

The second and third points are more intrinsically problematic, and relate to the status of representation as a political act. If we treat the under-representation of women in politics as akin to their under-representation in management or the professions, we seem to treat being a politician as on a continuum with all those other careers that should be opened up equally to women. In each case, there is disturbing evidence of sexual inequality; in each case, there should be positive action for change. The argument appeals to our sense of justice, but it does so at the expense of an equally strong feeling that being a politician is not just another kind of job. 'Career politician' is still—and rightly—a term of abuse; however accurately it may describe people's activities in politics, it does not capture our political ideals. If political office has been reduced to yet another favourable and privileged position, then there is a clear argument from justice for making such office equally available to women. Most democrats, however, will want to resist pressures to regard political office in this way. So while men have no 'right' to monopolize political office, there is something rather unsatisfying in basing women's claim to political equality on an equal right to an interesting job.

An alternative and more promising formulation considers the under-representation of women in elected assemblies as analogous to their under-representation in the membership of political parties or the attendance at political meetings, and thus treats the equal right to be an elected representative as part of an equal right to political participation. This provides a more theoretically satisfying foundation, for equality in participation is one of the criteria by which democracies are judged, and the systematic under-participation of particular social groups is normally regarded as a political problem (Verba, Nie, and Kim 1978; Parry, Moyser, and Day 1992). This is not to say that everyone must be equally enthralled by the political process: the interest in politics is unevenly distributed, as is the interest in sport or in jazz. But when the distribution coincides too neatly with divisions by class or gender or ethnicity, political participation is by definition unequal and political influence as a consequence skewed. The principle of a rough equality between various social groups

is already implicit in our idea of participation, and too marked a deviation from this is already regarded as a political failing. Once gender is admitted as an additional and relevant imbalance, it is easy enough to argue for equal participation between women and men.

As applied to representation, however, the argument seems to assert what has still to be established: that representation is just another aspect of participation, to be judged by the same criteria. Yet many theorists of democracy proceed from just the opposite direction, and they have based much of their critique of direct or participatory democracy on precisely what differentiates representation from participation. Participation implies activity, and yet activity is always a minority affair. By setting the requirements for participation impossibly high, theorists of participatory democracy are said to promote a politics that becomes 'unrepresentative' and unequal, for while most citizens can manage an occasional foray into the polling booth, few are willing or able to take on more continuous engagement, and the power then slips into the hands of those who most love politics. Representative democracy claims to solve this conundrum by removing the requirement for physical presence. As long as there is a minimal level of equality in the act of voting, then the representation can be said to be equal; we do not have to commit ourselves additionally to the hard labour of the political life.

Equality of presence—a rough approximation to the social groups that make up the society—is already implicit in the notion of participation. But it is not so obviously implicit in the notion of representation, which was, if anything, dreamt up to get round this bothersome condition. The two are, of course, related, for a society that provided genuinely equal access to participation in meetings and pressure groups and parties would almost certainly produce the same kind of equality among the people elected. In principle, however, they are separate, for in distancing itself from participating democracy representative democracy has distanced itself from physical presence as the measure of political equality. Representative democracy claims, for example, to represent the competing interests of capital and labour by giving each of us an equal right to vote, and this is said to encourage a variety of parties to emerge that will speak to our different concerns. But representative democracy makes no claims about achieving a proportionate representation of working class people inside the legislative assemblies: workers, should be equally represented, but not necessarily by workers themselves. So while we can readily appeal to existing understandings of democracy as the basis for women's equal participation, the case for gender parity among elected representatives moves onto more unchartered ground.

What we can perhaps do is turn the argument around, and ask by what 'natural' superiority of talent or experience men could claim a right to dominate assemblies? The burden of proof then shifts to the men, who would have to establish either some genetic distinction which makes them better at understanding problems and taking decisions, or some more socially derived advantage which enhances their political skills. Neither of these looks particularly persuasive: the first has never been successfully established; and the second is no justification if it depends on structures of discrimination. There is no argument from justice that can defend the current state of affairs; and in this more negative sense, there is an argument from justice for parity between women and men. But there is still a troubling sense in which the argument overlooks what is peculiar to representation as a political act. When democracy has become largely a matter of representing particular policies or programmes or ideas, this

leaves a question-mark over why the sex of the representatives should matter.

II. THE CASE FOR GENDER PARITY: WOMEN'S INTERESTS

The second way of arguing for gender parity is in terms of the interests that would be otherwise discounted: this is an argument from political realism. In the heterogeneous societies contained by the modern nation state, there is no transparently obvious 'public interest', but rather a multiplicity of different and potentially conflicting interests which must be acknowledged and held in check. Our political representatives are only human, and as such they cannot pretend to any greater generosity of spirit than those who elected them to office. There may be altruists among them, but it would be unwise to rely on this in framing our constitutional arrangements. Failing Plato's solution to the intrusion of private interest (a class of Guardians with no property or family of their own) we must look to other ways of limiting tyrannical tendencies, and most of these will involve giving all interests their legitimate voice.

This, in essence, was James Mill's case for representative government and an extended franchise, though he notoriously combined this with the argument that women could 'be struck off without inconvenience' from the list of potential claimants, because they had no interests not already included in those of their fathers or husbands. (He also thought we could strike off 'young' men under forty years of age.) Part of the argument for increasing women's political representation looks like a feminist rewrite and extension of this. Women occupy a distinct position within society: they are typically concentrated, for example, in lower-paid jobs; and they carry the primary responsibility for the unpaid work of caring for others. There are particular needs, interests, and concerns that arise from women's experience, and these will be inadequately addressed in a politics that is dominated by men. Equal rights to a vote have not proved strong enough to deal with this problem; there must also be equality among those elected to office.

At an intuitive level, this is hard to fault. It takes what is a widely accepted element in our understanding of democracy and applies it to women's situation. Looked at more closely, however, the argument from women's interests or women's concerns seems to rest on three conditions: that women have a distinct and separate interest as women; that this interest cannot be adequately represented by men; and that the election of women ensures its representation. As critics of gender quotas will be quick to point out, each condition is vulnerable to attack. The notion that women have at least some interests distinct from and even in conflict with men's is relatively straightforward (we can all think of appropriate examples), but this falls a long way short of establishing a set of interests shared by all women. If interests are understood in terms of what women express as their priorities and goals, there is considerable disagreement among women, and while attitude surveys frequently expose a 'gender gap' between women and men, the more striking development over recent decades has been the convergence in the voting behaviour of women and men. There may be more mileage in notions of a distinct woman's interest if this is understood in terms of some underlying but as yet unnoticed 'reality', but this edges uncomfortably close to notions of 'false consciousness', which most feminists would prefer to avoid. Indeed the presumption of a clearly demarcated 'woman's interest' which holds true for all women in all classes and all countries has been one of the casualties of recent feminist critique, and the exposure of multiple

differences between women has undermined more global understandings of women's interests and concerns (see, for example, Mohanty 1992). If there is no clearly agreed and recognized 'women's interest', does it really matter if the representatives are predominantly men?

Definitive as this might seem, it does not seriously undermine the claim to gender parity; if anything, it can be said to strengthen it. Consider, in this context, Edmund Burke's rather odd understanding of interests as reflecting 'an objective, impersonal, unattached reality', which can then be represented by any sufficiently competent and honest individual (Pitkin 1967: 168). Odd as this is, it conveys a partial truth. The more fixed the interests, or the more definite and easily defined, the less significance attaches to who does the work of representation. So if women's interests were transparently obvious to any intelligent observer, there might be no particular case—beyond the perennial one of trust—for insisting on representatives who also happen to be women. We might feel that men will be less diligent in pressing women's interests or concerns, but if we all know what these are, it will be correspondingly easy to tell whether they are being adequately pursued. If, however, the interests are varied, unstable, perhaps still in the process of formation, it will be far more difficult to separate out what is to be represented from who is to do the representation. The greater problems arise, that is, where interests are not so precisely delineated, where the political agenda has been constructed without reference to certain areas of concern, or where much fresh thinking is necessary to work out the appropriate policies. To this extent, the very difficulties in defining what are in women's interests strengthen the case for more women as representatives.

The more decisive problem lies in the third condition. Does the election of more women then ensure their representation? Again, at an intuitive level, an increase in the number of women elected seems likely to change both the practices and the priorities of politics, increasing the attention given to matters of childcare, for example, or ensuring that women's poor position in the labour market is more vigorously addressed. This intuition is already partially confirmed by the experience of those countries which have changed the gender composition of their elected assemblies. But what does this mean in terms of political representation? Elections are typically organized by geographical constituencies, which sometimes coincide with concentrations of particular ethnic or religious groups, or concentrations of certain social classes, but which never coincide with concentrations of women or men. Elections typically take place through the medium of political parties, each of which produces candidates who are said to represent that party's policies and programmes and goals. In what sense can we say that the women elected through this process carry an additional responsibility to represent women? In the absence of mechanisms to establish accountability, the equation of more women with more adequate representation of women's interests looks suspiciously undemocratic. How do the women elected know what the women who elected them want? By what right do they claim responsibility to represent women's concerns?

Though this is rarely stated in the literature, the argument from women's interests implies that representatives will have considerable autonomy: that they do have currently, and by implication, that this ought to continue. Women's exclusion from politics is said to matter precisely because politicians do not abide by pre-agreed policies and goals. As any observer of the political process knows, policy decisions are *not* settled in advance by party programmes, for new problems and issues emerge alongside unanticipated constraints, and in the subsequent weighing of interpretations and priorities, it matters immensely who the representatives are. Feminists have much experience of this, gained through painful years of watching hard won commitments to sexual equality drop off the final agenda. When there is a significant under-representation of women at the point of final decision, this can and does have serious consequences, and it is partly in reflection of this that feminists have shifted their attention from the details of policy commitments to the composition of the decision-making group. Political experience tells us that all male or mostly male assemblies will be poor judges of women's interests and priorities and concerns, and that trying to shore up this judgement by pre-agreed programmes has only limited effect. There is a strong dose of political realism here. Representatives *do* have considerable autonomy, which is why it matters who those representatives are.

It is worth dwelling on this point, for it highlights a divergence between current feminist preoccupations and what has long been the main thrust in radical democracy. Radical democrats distrust the wayward autonomy of politicians and the way they concentrate power around them, and they typically work to combat these tendencies by measures that will bind politicians more tightly to their promises, and disperse over-centralized power. Feminists have usually joined forces in support of the second objective: feminism is widely associated with bringing politics closer to home; and women are often intensely involved in local and community affairs. But when feminists insist that the sex of the representatives matters, they are expressing a deeper ambivalence towards the first objective. The politics of binding mandates, for example, turns the representatives into glorified messengers: it puts all the emphasis onto the content of the messages, and makes it irrelevant who the messengers are. In contesting the sex of the representatives, feminists are querying this version of democratic accountability.

The final point about the argument from interests is that it may not of itself justify equal or proportionate presence. In a recent discussion of demands for group representation in Canada, Will Kymlicka (1993) makes a useful distinction between arguments for equal or proportionate presence (where the number of women or aboriginal Indians or francophone Canadians in any legislative assembly would correspond to their proportion in the citizenry as a whole), and the case for a threshold presence (where the numbers would reach the requisite level that ensured each group's concerns were adequately addressed). When the group in question is a numerically small minority, the threshold might prove larger than their proportion in the population as a whole; when the group composes half the population, the threshold might be considerably lower. On this basis, there might be an argument for greater than proportionate representation of Indians, for example, but less than proportionate representation of women: not that women would be formally restricted to 25 or 30 per cent of the seats, but that they might not require any more than this in order to change the political agenda. It is the argument from justice that most readily translates into strict notions of equality; the argument from women's interests need not deliver such strong results.

III. THE CASE FOR GENDER PARITY: TOWARDS A REVITALISED DEMOCRACY

The third argument is less developed, and I offer it here as a way of dealing with some of the problems I identify above. The argument form justice works well enough on the limited ground that treats being a politician like any other kind of job, or on the negative ground that denies any just basis for male monopoly. The argument from women's interests works well enough as a case for a threshold, but not necessarily equal, presence, but is best understood in terms of a realistic assessment of how rarely politicians abide by their pre-agreed programmes. These are powerful arguments, but they art not, on the whole, the kinds of arguments that feminists most admire: they are too much grounded in an impoverished experience of democracy to bear the full weight of feminist ambition. And they leave unresolved that recurrent radical concern about controlling wayward politicians. Apart from the argument that women should get an equal chance at a political career (which is a fair enough argument, but not intrinsically about democracy), we can only believe that the sex of the representatives matters if we think it will change what the representatives do. In saying this, we seem to be undermining accountability through party programmes. We are saying we expect our representatives to do more—or other—than they promised in the election campaign.

There is often an expectation, for example, that women politicians will operate on a cross-party basis, forging alliances to press for improvements in childcare provision or changes in the abortion laws. In her study of Norwegian representatives, Hege Skjeie (1991) records a number of such initiatives, but she notes that it is the priorites of their party that finally dictate the way women politicians vote. If we are either surprised or disappointed by this, it must be because we see an increase in the number of women politicians as challenging the dominance of the party system or the tradition of voting along party lines. Those who feel that the tighter controls of party discipline have discouraged serious discussion and debate may be happy enough with this conclusion. But in the absence of alternative mechanisms of consultation or accountability, it does read like a recipe for letting representatives do what they choose to do.

What makes sense of this, I believe, is an additional presumption that is implicit in most feminist arguments, a conviction that changing the composition of existing elected assemblies is only part of a wider project of increasing and enhancing democracy. When the argument for gender parity is taken out of this context, it has to rely more heavily on arguments from political realism, and while these are powerful enough arguments in themselves, they fall short on some key concerns. Put back into its context, the argument often reveals a more ambitious programme of dispersing power through a wider range of decision-making assemblies, and changing the balance between participation and representation.

We might think here of the further initiatives that are so typical of women in politics: the use of the open forum, for example, as a way of consulting women in a local community; the report back to women's sections or women's conferences; or just the extraordinary energy so many women politicians devote to what they see as their responsibilities for representing women. Even among those most committed to party politics (and many women deliberately stay outside, in the more amorphous politics of women's movement groups and compaigns), the political party is frequently viewed as an inadequate vehicle for representation. In 1980s Britain, for example, there was a flowering of women's committees within the frame work of local government (usually associated with more left-wing Labour councils), and these made extensive use of co-option or the open forum as a way of consulting women outside the political parties. Now you could think of this as a short term compensation for women's current under-representation among elected councillors, but there is little

to support this view. More commonly, those associated with the development of women's committees saw the additional mechanisms of consultation and participation as always and everywhere desirable—even under some future scenario where women might hold 50 per cent of council seats. The women involved were querying the exclusive emphasis on the party as the vehicle for representation; they were pursuing complementary (sometimes conflicting) ways of empowering women to make their needs better known.

The case for gender parity in politics should, I believe, be understood within this broader context, and to this extent, it confirms Hanna Pitkin's intuition. The argument for more 'descriptive' or 'mirror' representation does move in close parallel with arguments for a more participatory form of democracy; and those concerned with the under-representation of women in politics do look to additional mechanisms of consultation and accountability and participation that would complement our occasional vote. We do not need this additional ammunition to argue for more women in politics; there are arguments enough from justice or interests that provide a basis for substantial change. But as a more profound set of issues about democracy and representation, the case for gender parity is at its strongest when it is associated with the larger dream.

NOTES

[1] I use the term parity to indicate a rough equality between the proportion of women and men elected. My use of this term should not be confused with the arguments that have recently surfaced within the Council of Europe for so-called parity democracy. See Outshoorn (1993) for a critical review of this literature.

[2] There *are* parties which operate quotas for youth—as with my own example of the 1972 Democratic National Convention—but when it comes to parliamentary candidatures, few people worry about the paucity of those under 25.

REFERENCES

Chapman, Jenny (1993), Politics, Feminism, and the Reformation of Gender (London: Routledge).

Grofman, B., Lijphart, A., Mckay, R. B., Scarrow, H.A. (eds.) (1982), Representation and Redistricting Issues (Lexington, Mass.: D. C. Health and Co.).

Kymlicka, Will (1993), 'Group Representation in Canadian Politics'. Paper prepared for IRPP project on 'Communities, the Charter and Interest Advocacy'.

Lovenduski, Joni and Norris, Pippa (1989), 'Selecting Women Candidates: Obstacles to the Feminisation of the House of Commons', European Journal of Political Research, 17, 533–63.

Mohanty, Chandra (1993), 'Feminist Encounters: Locating the Politics of Experience', in Michèle Barrett and Anne Phillips (eds.), Destabilizing Theory: Contemporary Feminist Debates (Cambridge: Polity Press),74–92.

Outshoorn, Joyce (1993), 'Parity Democracy: A Critical Look at a "New" Strategy', paper prepared for workshop on 'Citizenship and Plurality', European Consortium for Political Research, Leiden.

Parry, Geraint, Moyser, George, and Day, Neil (1992), Political Participation and Democracy in Britain (Cambridge: Cambridge University Press).

Phillips, Anne (1991) Engendering Democracy (Cambridge: Polity Press).

Phillips Griffiths, A. (1960), 'How Can One Person Represent Another?' Aristotelian Society, Supplementary vol. xxxiv, 187–208.

Pitkin, Hanna F. (1967), The Concept of Representation (Berkeley: University of California Press).

Ranney, Austin (1982), 'Comments on Representation Within the Political Party System', in Grofman et al. (1982), 193–7.

Skjeie, Hege (1991), 'The Rhetoric of Difference: On Women's Inclusion into Political Elites', Politics and Society, 19/2, 233–63.

Verba, Sidney, Nie, Norman H., and Kim, Jae-on (1978), Participation and Political Equality: A Seven National Comparison (Cambridge: Cambridge University Press).

Majoritarian Democracy and Cultural Minorities

Bernard Boxill

The classic problem of majoritarian democracy is that it enables the majority to tyrannize minorities. This problem is less serious if different majorities tend to form on different issues, for in that case no minority is likely to be a permanent minority. It is more serious in culturally plural societies where one of the cultural groups is an absolute majority. The cultural ties binding the members of such a majority will incline them to stand together on many different issues, to use the principle of majority rule to secure their interests at the expense of the minority cultures, and to impose their values and way of life on them.

Members of the majority culture may claim that they should be free to impose their values and way of life on minorities. To support this claim they may appeal to the dangers of culturally plural societies and to the benefits of culturally homogeneous societies. Culturally plural societies are said to be prone to murderous conflict, and culturally homogeneous societies are said to contribute to community, fraternity, and a sense of belonging. But even if these claims are true, a cultural majority may act wrongly in imposing its values and way of life on cultural minorities. People may have rights to retain their culture and to pass it on to their children, which forbid their forcible acculturation, even if that would make the society culturally homogeneous and a better society.

Democracies have standardly tried to solve the problem of the tyranny of the majority by enshrining certain rights in a constitution that can be changed only by an overwhelming majority. This device can be applied to the particular problem of a majority culture trying to impose its values and way of life on minorities. But it is not altogether satisfactory. For one thing, even rights enshrined in a constitution can be revoked if the majority that wants them revoked is large and determined enough. More importantly, the device only forces the majority to tolerate minorities. It may prevent a majority from violating minorities' most basic interests, but it need not give minorities opportunity to flourish or to contribute to the society. In this essay I develop this objection to majoritarian democracy and suggest briefly one possible solution to the problem it points to.

I begin with the argument that the usual rights enshrined in the Constitution for the protection of minorities need not give them an opportunity to flourish. My argument is based on an argument proposed by Mill in *Representative Government*. In that book Mill argued that "true" democracy required provisions to ensure that minorities were represented in the legislative body. Since the usual systems of majoritarian rule keep minorities out of the legislative body, Mill called them "false" democracy and argued that their "inevitable consequence" was the "complete disfranchisement of minorities" even if they had the vote.[1] Mill's conclusion is too strong. Although he was right that the usual systems of majoritarian rule do not ensure that minorities are represented in legislative bodies, he was wrong to conclude that they lead to the disfranchisement of minorities. People are not disfranchised because their favorite candidate for office is not elected, they are disfranchised when their right to vote is violated; but the usual systems of majoritarian rule guarantee minorities the right to vote. Still, there is something to Mill's complaint about majoritarian democracy. Part of this, I argue, is that majoritarian democracy may not give cultural minorities an equal opportunity to flourish.

I assume that Mill's claim about majoritarian democracy and minorities in general implies a similar claim about majoritarian democracy and cultural minorities. That claim, that majoritarian democracy keeps members of cultural minorities out of legislative bodies, is the main premise of my argument. It does not imply by itself that majoritarian democracies do not give people of minority cultures an equal opportunity to flourish; arguably, to flourish in such democracies people must be represented by politicians who pass legislation to help them flourish, and such politicians may be drawn from the majority culture. My argument therefore appeals to two further considerations: first, that, given the usual assumptions of majoritarian democracy, politicians will normally be reluctant to pass legislation specifically to enable people of minority cultures to advance; second, that politicians who care about such people's interests and understand the kind of legislation necessary to enable them to thrive will probably share their culture.

Despite some utopian thinkers, it may not be possible to design policies that enable all cultural groups to advance and to do so at the same rate. In particular, legislation that enables people of minority cultures to advance may very well slow the advance of those of the majority culture. Further, because human beings usually seem to want to have others to feel superior to, people of the majority culture often feel threatened by legislation that would only enable people of minority cultures to gain on them. Since voters do not support politicians who introduce legislation they see as threatening and politicians want voters' support, politicians usually do not even discuss legislation that would obviously enable people of minority cultures to advance.

It is an invidious assumption that people from the majority culture cannot care about the interests of those in minority cultures and cannot possibly understand and devise the kind of legislation that would enable them to thrive. But two considerations suggest that, all else equal, people of minority cultures are more likely to be well represented by those who share their culture than by others. First, people who share their culture are more likely to identify with them, and consequently to love and care for them, than are outsiders. Supposing that this is usually the case, politicians from a minority culture are likely to be more strongly motivated to design and pass legislation aimed at helping their cultural group advance than are politicians from the majority culture.

The second argument that people of minority cultures are better represented by those who share their culture than by outsiders is that people who share their culture are likely to better understand their culture than outsiders, and consequently likely to better understand what legislation will help them to thrive. This may seem false on the ground that an outsider, standing outside a culture, may better understand a culture's strengths and weaknesses than does a cultural insider. I grant that one must be able to stand outside a culture in order to appreciate its strengths and weaknesses. But politicians from the minority culture will often be able to stand outside their own culture, because they live in a society dominated by the majority culture and are therefore often compelled to step outside their own culture and to operate in the majority culture. Consequently, they will be able to gain the perspective necessary to assessing its strengths and weaknesses. Assuming that they are likely to be among their culture's more mobile and energetic members, they will be especially able to have an informed outsider's view of it, although most members of the culture will enjoy this advantage to some degree. Further, standing outside a culture enables one to appreciate its strengths and weaknesses only if one knows the culture intimately. But politicians from the majority are not likely to know the minority culture intimately. Their culture dominates the society and they do not need to know much about minority cultures. Consequently, unlike politicians from minority cultures, they are unlikely to have an informed outsider's view of minority cultures.

It may be objected that minority cultures do not have to be represented by people who understand their peculiarities and who care about them specifically. I will be reminded of the Japanese and Jews, who have done remarkably well in the United States although they are usually represented by Caucasians and Christians who neither understand them nor particularly care for them. These cases, and others that could be cited, show that it is not a necessary condition that a cultural minority be represented by its members, or even those who understand and care about it, in order to thrive. The cultural minority may feel itself invisible or may believe that the majority will not take the trouble to devise legislation detrimental to it; or it may have qualities that enable it to advance, given the legislation that the politicians elected by the majority pass, even if this legislation is not passed in order to enable it to advance. Considerations such as these probably account for the success of the Japanese and Jews, though it is arguable that the Japanese might have avoided some disasters—I have in mind their internment during the Second World War—if they had not kept such a low political profile. But we cannot generalize from these exceptional cases and conclude that cultural minorities ordinarily do not need to represent themselves politically in order to flourish. In many cases a cultural minority's qualities will not enable it to advance given the legislation that the politicians elected by the majority pass. Normally, to thrive it must be represented by those who understand and care about it, and usually such people will come from its own ranks. This is the basic point about political life that the American revolutionaries learned, and that justified their separation from Great Britain; and it explains why cultural groups invariably seek political representation and power as soon as they become too numerous or too successful to be invisible.

My argument that the usual apparatus of democratic procedures need not give minority cultures opportunity to thrive assumes that members of minority cultures will not be elected to office. This is a reasonable assumption, given the principle of majoritarian democracy that the candidate elected to office gets the most votes and that people tend to vote for candidates from their own cultural group. But it is not always true. A cultural group can constitute a majority in several voting districts even if it is a small minority in the country as a whole. In these districts it will probably be represented by those who share its culture, precisely because people tend to vote for candidates of their own cultural groups, and the candidates elected to office are those who get the most votes.

Such representation is better than no representation. It gives the minority culture some measure of self-government and ensures that its representatives have an opportunity to urge policies for its advancement in legislatures made up of representatives of many voting districts, even if the policies they urge are unlikely to be adopted, given that the principle of majority rule holds in the legislature as well as in the competition for office. Nevertheless, requiring cultural groups to segregate themselves in particular voting districts in order to make themselves majorities in those district has unacceptable consequences. The segregation involved is not likely to be only the innocent result of likeminded people freely choosing to live together. It will probably also require coercion. In order to remain, or to become, a majority in a voting district, a cultural group may have to prevent those of different cultures from moving into the district, or even compel them to leave if they are already there. Since this is unjust and likely to lead to conflict between cultural groups, representation achieved by cultural segregation probably comes at too high a price.

I now take up the argument that majoritarian democracies also fail to give people of minority cultures an equal opportunity to contribute to their societies by taking part directly in legislation. This does not mean, of course, that majoritarian democracies altogether prevent members of cultural minorities

from contributing to their societies. There are ways to contribute to one's society besides being elected to office.

The argument that majoritarian democracies do not give members of minority cultures an equal opportunity to contribute directly to the legislation of their society is in a sense a trivial implication of the fact, already established, that majoritarian democracies give members of minority cultures little opportunity to be elected to office. But members of cultural minorities who are excluded from political office by the mechanisms of majoritarian democracy are not likely to feel that their exclusion is trivial. Elected officials design and pass legislation and consequently are able to contribute to their societies in peculiarly powerful and effective ways.

I also want to make the stronger point that members of minority cultures may have something to contribute to legislation in their society that members of the majority culture may not be able to contribute. It relies on the kind of considerations that John Stuart Mill used to justify his claim that society should value freethinkers, eccentrics, and intellectuals. Mill did not simply urge mechanisms and policies—like systems of entrenched rights—that would help to prevent the majority from overwhelming freethinkers, eccentrics, and intellectuals. More generally, he did not want the majority only to tolerate these minorities. He believed that it should *value* them because they could have something to teach it. His best-known argument is stated in *On Liberty*. In that work Mill maintains that unless people harm others they should be allowed to live as they decide. Some of his arguments for this claim justify only toleration. I have in mind where he argues that a person's "own mode of laying out his existence is best, not because it is best in itself, but because it is his own mode."[2] But other arguments stress that allowing others to live as they please can contribute to the discovery of ways to live that are objectively best. This is the well-known "experiments in living" argument. Mill's idea was that people who try unconventional ways of living may well hit on practices that the majority can learn from and adopt to its benefit. As he wrote, "It is important to give the freest scope possible to uncustomary things, in order that it may in time appear which of these are fit to be converted into customs."[3]

If Mill's argument is sound, valuable and useful ideas about how to live probably derive from all cultures, and consequently from minority cultures. I believe this to be the case because cultures are experiments in living.

People do not normally think of their own culture as an experiment in living. They do not suppose that their culture's mores and practices are hypotheses about how life should be lived and that in following these mores and practices they are behaving somewhat like scientists subjecting hypotheses to empirical tests. Normally they act as their culture dictates because they don't think about it, or because they believe that alternatives are wrong, or sometimes because they cannot conceive of alternatives. Still a culture is an experiment in living in the sense that things happen as a result of people following its mores and practices, and people do learn from how and why these things happen. This is why cultures change. People see what the consequences of living according to the mores and practices of their culture are, and as a result some of the more sensitive or imaginative or daring among them are moved from time to time to do things differently themselves or to urge their fellows to do things differently. When their example is followed, or their suggestions are accepted—and only rarely does either happen quickly—their culture slowly changes.

I say "changes" advisedly, and not "improves." An enterprising knave may hit on a way to circumvent an important cultural convention for his personal advantage. If others follow his example, the overall result could be retrogression. Of course, in time people will learn from that "experiment," and some of them may introduce reforms, though again we cannot conclude that these reforms will be altogether successful or that they will not have unforeseen and undesirable side effects. Still, if Mill is right that a majority may stand to learn from the experiments in living of freethinkers and eccentrics, it probably stands to learn much more from the experiments in living of minority cultures. The experiments in living of freethinkers and eccentrics are usually conducted on a small scale and for a short time. This should make a large society that wants to reproduce itself extremely wary of taking them seriously, however attractive they may seem. A culture, on the other hand, is always the result of an exceedingly long series of related experiments in living in which each experiment is designed in the light of what was learned in earlier experiments. More than that, it is also partly a series of interrelated reflections on the series of experiments in living. People do not only learn from their mores and practices; they also reflect on what they have learned, on the possibilities and impossibilities it reveals to them, and consequently on what they can and cannot reasonably hope to achieve. Each of these reflections is made in the light of previous reflections and influences the direction the series of experiments in living takes. As a result the experiments in living of a culture become an attempt to work out a point of view of how to live, and every culture contains a commentary on the difficulties and possibilities of working out that point of view. Now it is highly unlikely that every culture has the same point of view on how to live and the same commentary on the difficulties and possibilities of working it out. The protean nature of human inventiveness and the variety of circumstances in which cultures evolves ensure this. Assuming that the majority has not discovered all there is to know about how to live, and that minorities have not gotten it all wrong, I conclude that minority cultures may well contain moral and political ideas that would help legislatures make better laws if they were presented there.

The main conclusion of the preceding sections is that the classic problem of majoritarian democracy, the "tyranny of the majority," is likely to be especially pertinent and costly in culturally plural societies where one of the cultural groups is an absolute majority. In such societies, majoritarian democracy denies cultural minorities opportunities to flourish and to contribute directly to legislation. Since people feel alienated from their societies when they are denied such opportunities, it is hardly surprising that the standard democratic apparatus of measures and provisions often fails to foster a sense of community and belonging in culturally plural societies.

This suggests that culturally plural societies should begin to consider seriously alternatives to the standard procedures of majoritarian democracy. One alternative is especially attractive because it has much to recommend it apart from the fact that it seems a promising way to correct the tendency of majoritarian democracy to exclude cultural minorities from public office. This is Thomas Hare's system of the single transferable vote, which Mill hailed as "among the greatest improvements yet made in the theory and practice of governments." [4] Mill was enthusiastic about Hare's system because it ensured that his favorite minorities—freethinkers and intellectuals—would get represented in proportion to their numbers without having to live in any particular part of the country. But it would also ensure that cultural minorities were represented in proportion to their numbers without having to segregate themselves in particular voting districts. [5] Majoritarians have strongly criticized the single transferable vote system and have questioned Mill's motives for endorsing it. [6] These criticisms have to be taken seriously. But the single transferable vote system seems a good place to start the search for a way to avoid the weakness of majoritarian democracy in culturally plural societies.

NOTES

[1] John Stuart Mill, *Utilitarianism, On Liberty and Representative Government* (New York: Dutton, 1951), 345.

[2] Mill, 167.

[3] Mill, 167.

[4] Mill, 354.

[5] Arthur Lewis made this point when he recommended proportional representation to the culturally plural societies of West Africa. See his *Politics in West Africa* (New York: Oxford University Press, 1965).

[6] See, for example, Paul B. Kern, "Universal Suffrage Without Democracy: Thomas Hare and John Stuart Mill," *Review of politics* 34 (1972): 306–22; and Gideon Doron and Richard Kronick, "Single Transferable Vote: An Example of a Perverse Social Choice Function," *American Journal of Political Science* 21 (1977): 303–11.

Democratic Values

We often hear our leaders say, and we often assume with them, that Democracy is special, that it is the best, and perhaps the only legitimate, form of governmental rule. But what makes Democracy special, if indeed it is special? In this section, the reading by Brian Barry, a British political philosopher at Oxford, considers whether the simple fact of majority rule makes Democracy uniquely good. The second reading in the section by Chenyang Li, a Chinese-born United States political philosopher, considers whether Democracy requires liberal values, or whether it could be made compatible with Confucian values. The next two readings continue to question the compatibility of Democracy with particular other sets of values. William Galston, a political theorist at the University of Maryland and former domestic policy advisor to President Clinton, takes up the question of whether and how Islam and Democracy could be made compatible. Carole Pateman, a British born political scientist at UCLA, discusses the demands that taking women seriously as citizens makes on Democracy.

The final reading of this section is by the most important political philosopher of the 20th century, the late John Rawls of Harvard. In this essay Rawls discusses the kind of reasoning that Democracy requires its citizens to engage in, namely not those inspired by their particular metaphysical beliefs but rather reasons that are shared by all in the demos.

STUDY QUESTIONS:

1. What argument can be given for the legitimacy of majority rule?

2. What are the liberal values typically associated with Democracy today?

3. What are the Confucian values that conflict with those liberal values?

4. What features of Islam does Galston think are more likely to lead Islamist states to be aggressive and less likely to be Democratic?

5. Why does Pateman think that formal equality among citizens is not sufficient for Democracy?

6. What is public reason?

7. Why should we use public reason and not private reasons in Democratic debate and voting?

Is Democracy Special?

Brian Barry

thers (the essence of the Rawlsian sense of 'justice as fairness'). There are also often reasons for disobeying it, of which personal advantage is the most obvious. In addition it seems plausible that approval of the content of the law makes the case for obeying it stronger than it would otherwise be, while disapproval makes it weaker. 'Approval' and 'disapproval', however, are anodyne generic terms, which conceal a range of relevantly different responses. It seems on the face of it reasonable to say, for example, that equally strong disapproval of two laws, one on the basis of its imprudence or inefficiency, the other on the basis of its injustice or immorality, should have different implications.

Exactly how and why all these factors provide reasons in favour of obedience or reasons telling against it is by no means straightforward. Nor, I am sure, would everyone agree that all of them should be reckoned as reasons at all. For the purpose of this paper, however, I shall simply assume that at least some of these factors, and perhaps others like them, provide reasons for obeying or disobeying laws. My question then is whether an entirely different sort of consideration, namely the procedure by which the law was enacted, or, in the case

of long-standing laws, the procedure by which it might have been repealed and has not been, should be a reason for obeying a law.

More specifically, the question I wish to raise is whether or not a law's having been enacted (or not repealed) by a democratic procedure adds a reason for obeying it to whatever reasons exist independently of that. By a democratic procedure I mean a method of determining the content of laws (and other legally binding decisions) such that the preferences of the citizens have some formal connection with the outcome in which each counts equally. Let me make four comments on this definition.

First, I follow here those who insist that 'democracy' is to be understood in procedural terms. That is to say, I reject the notion that one should build into 'democracy' any constraints on the content of the outcomes produced, such as substantive equality, respect for human rights, concern for the general welfare, personal liberty or the rule of law. The only exceptions (and these are significant) are those required by democracy itself as a procedure. Thus, some degree of freedom of communication and organization is a necessary condition of the formation, expression and aggregation of political preferences. And in a state (as against a small

From *Philosophy, Politics & Society*, edited by James S. Fishkin and Peter Laslett. Reprinted by permission of Yale University Press.

commune, say) the only preferences people can have are preferences for general lines of policy. There are not going to be widely-held preferences about whether or not Mr Jones should be fined £10 for speeding or Mrs Smith should get supplementary benefit payments of £3.65 per week. At most there can be preferences for a speeding tariff or for general rules about eligibility for supplementary benefit. If magistrates or civil servants are arbitrary or capricious, therefore, they make democracy impossible.

Second, I require that there should be a formal connection between the preferences of the citizens and the outcomes produced. My intention in specifying a formal connection is to rule out cases where the decision-making process is *de facto* affected by the preferences of the citizens but not in virtue of any constitutional rule. Thus, eighteenth century England has been described as 'oligarchy tempered by riot'.[1] But however efficacious the rioters might be I would not say that their ability to coerce the government constituted a democratic procedure. In the concluding words of the judge appointed to enquire into riots in West Pakistan in 1953: 'But if democracy means the subordination of law and order to political ends—then Allah knoweth best and we end the report.'[2]

Third, by 'some formal connection' I intend deliberately to leave open a variety of possible ways in which democratic procedures might be implemented. In particular, I wish to include both voting on laws by the citizens at large and voting for representatives who exercise the law-making function. I shall take either of these to constitute 'some formal connection with the outcome' in the sense required by the definition: in the first case the citizens choose the laws and in the second they choose the law-makers (in both cases, of course, within the limits of the choice presented to them).

Finally, the phrase 'each counts equally' has to be read in conjunction with the preceding phrase 'some formal connection with the outcome'. That is to say, nothing is suggested by the definition of democratic procedure about equality of actual influence on outcomes. The equality is in the formal aspect: each adult citizen is to have a vote (only minor exceptions covering a tiny proportion of those otherwise eligible being allowed) and there are to be no 'fancy franchises' giving extra votes to some.

What about the notion that each vote should have an 'equal value'? This is valid if we construe it as a formal requirement. If there are two constituencies each of which returns one representative, the value of a vote is obviously unequal if one constituency contains more voters than another.[3] To talk about 'equal value' except in this *a priori* sense is, in my view, sheer muddle. In recent years, for example, supporters of systems of proportional representation in Britain have succeeded in scoring something of a propaganda victory by pressing the idea that the vote for a candidate who comes third (or lower) in a plurality system is 'wasted' and the people who vote for the candidate are 'effectively disfranchised'. But then why stop there? The only way of making sense of this argument is by postulating that anyone who voted for a candidate other than the actual winner—even the runner—up-was 'effectively disfranchised'; and it was not long before some academics stumbled on this amazing theoretical breakthrough.[4] I do not think that anyone of ordinary intelligence would be found saying of an election for, say, the post of president of a club: 'I didn't vote for the winning candidate. In other words my vote didn't help elect anybody. And that means I was effectively disfranchised'. It is a little alarming that such palpably fallacious reasoning should have the power to impose on people when the context is a parliamentary election.

II

There is one simple, and, on the face of it, attractive, reason for giving special weight to laws arrived at by democratic procedures, namely that, on any given question about which opinion is divided, the decision must, as a matter of logic, accord with either the preferences of the majority or the preferences of the minority. And, by something akin to the rule of insufficient reason, it seems difficult to say why the decision should go in the way wanted by the minority rather than in the way wanted by the majority.

Obviously, even if the majority principle were accepted, there would still be a gap between the majority principle and democratic procedures as I have defined them. The implication of the majority principle is, fairly clearly, that the best form of democratic procedure is that which permits a vote on issues by referendum. There is no guarantee that elected representatives will on every issue vote in such a way that the outcome preferred by a majority of citizens will be the one chosen. However much we cry up the effects of electoral competition in keeping representatives in line, there is no theoretical reason for expecting that a party or coalition of parties with a majority will always do what a majority of voters want, (Persistent non-voters will in any case have their preferences disregarded by competitive parties-though it may be noted that this is equally so in a referendum.) Even a purely opportunistic party would not necessarily be well-advised to back the side on every issue that the majority supports, as Anthony Downs pointed out.[5] And in practice no party is purely opportunistic-indeed a purely opportunistic party would in most circumstances be an electoral failure because it would be too unpredictable. The party or parties with a legislative majority are therefore always liable to have a package of policies approved of by a majority and policies opposed by a majority. (On many other issues, there may be no single policy with majority support, but that is a complication in the specification of the majority principle that I shall discuss below.)

All this, however, is not as damaging for democratic procedures as might be supposed. For it may surely be said that no method for selecting law-makers and governments that was *not* democratic (in the sense defined) could provide a better long-run prospect of producing outcomes in accord with the majority principle. However disappointed an adherent of the majority principle might be in the actual working of democratic procedures, it is hard to see what he or she would stand to gain by helping to secure their overthrow. In principle, of course, this majoritarian might assist the rise to power of a group of dedicated majoritarians who would be committed to acting in accord with majority preferences as ascertained, say, by sophisticated opinion polling. But once in power what reason would there be for confidence in the good faith of these people, or, even more perhaps, of their successors?

I think, therefore, that an adherent of the majority principle would be prepared to disobey laws that were enacted (or not repealed) in the face of clear majority sentiment. But he or she would not take part in any activity either designed for or having the predictable consequence of bringing about the collapse of democratic procedures, because in the long run democratic procedures are more likely to produce majoritarian outcomes than are alternative procedures. Of course, it does not follow that a majoritarian who is satisfied that there is a clear majority against a piece of legislation is thereby committed to disobeying it. All the reasons for not breaking the law that I mentioned at the beginning of this paper may still apply. The only thing that the absence of majority support does for a majoritarian is to remove one (conclusive) reason for obedience.

Can an adherent of the majority principle break the law in an attempt to get the majority to change its mind? I think that this may be done consistently with the principle if it is formulated so that not just any majority counts but only one based on a serious and informed consideration of the issue. Thus, on the facts as stated by him, Bertrand Russell's campaign against nuclear weapons could be consistent with a majoritarian standpoint.[6] But it is essential to the honesty of such a position that one must be prepared to specify what would constitute a fair test of 'real' majority opinion in a way that does not fall back on the proposition that 'No majority can *really* be in favour of X'.

I have suggested, then, that the majority principle provides fairly strong backing for democratic procedures. What now has to be asked, of course, is whether there is any reason for accepting the majority principle. The view that there is something natural and inevitable about it was expressed forcefully by John Locke in paragraphs 95–9 of the *Second Treatise*. The argument is tied up with Locke's consent theory of political authority but can, I think, be detached from it. The nub is that if there is going to be a body capable of making binding decisions then it 'must move one way' and 'it is necessary the Body should move that way whither the greater force carries it, which is the *consent of the majority*'. Locke adds that 'therefore we see that in Assemblies impowered to act by positive Laws where no number is set by that positive Law which impowers them, the *act of the Majority* passes for the act of the whole, and of course determines, as having by the Law of Nature and Reason, the power of the whole'.[7]

In my first book, *Political Argument*, I put forward the example of 'five people in a railway compartment which the railway opera-

tor has omitted to lable either "smoking" or "no-smoking"' each of whom 'either wants to smoke or objects to others smoking in the vicinity'.[8] (I should have added that the carriage should be understood as one of the sort that does not have a corridor, so the option of changing compartments is not open.) I still think that the example was a good one. Unless all five can reach agreement on some general substantive principle—that in the absence of positive regulation there is a 'natural right' to smoke or a 'natural right' for any one person to veto smoking—it is difficult to see any plausible alternative to saying that the outcome should correspond to majority preference.

The position of someone who is outvoted but refuses to accept the decision is difficult to maintain. As I have suggested, quite persuasive arguments can be made for saying that the decision should not simply reflect the number of people who want to smoke as against the number who dislike being in the presence of smokers. But, since opposing principles can be advanced, the existence of relevant principles does not seem to offer a sound basis for resistance to a majority decision. Or suppose that one of the travellers happens to be the Archbishop of Canterbury. He might claim the right to decide the smoking question on the basis either of his social position or on the basis of his presumptive expertise in casuistry. If his claim is accepted by all the other passengers, no decision-making problem arises because there is agreement. If not all the fellow-passengers accept his claim, however, it again seems difficult to see how the question can be settled except by a vote. And if he finds himself in the minority it must be because he has failed to convince the others (or more than one of them) of his claim to authority. He may continue to maintain that it should have been accepted, just as a believer in the natural right to smoke may continue to maintain that the others should have accepted that principle. But in the face of actual non-acceptance, the case for bowing to the majority decision looks strong.

On further analysis, however, we have to recognize that the 'naturalness' of the majority principle as a way of settling the dispute rests on several features of the particular example which are not commonly found together. I am therefore now inclined to say that it was a good example in the sense that it illustrated well the case for the majority principle but that it was in another sense a bad example because of its special features. I shall single out four, the first three of which make the majority principle determinate while the fourth makes it acceptable. First, we implicitly assume that the people in the compartment have to make only this one decision. Second, only two alternatives are envisaged: smoking or nonsmoking. Third, the decision-making constituency is not open to doubt. And fourth, nothing has been said to suggest that the outcome on the issue is of vital importance for the long-term well-being of any of those involved.

To begin with, then, let us retain the feature from the original case that the decisions to be made are dichotomous (that is to say, there are only two alternatives to choose between) but now say that several different decisions have to be taken. In addition to the question whether to permit smoking the passengers also have to decide whether to allow the playing of transistor radios.

Suppose that a vote is taken on each question and there is a majority against each. It may be that a majority of the passengers would neverthe-less prefer permitting both to prohibiting both, if they were given a choice in those terms.

Let us assign the following symbols: W is no smoking, X is smoking allowed; Y is no playing of radios, Z is playing allowed. The preferences of the five passengers (A, B, C, D and E) are in descending order as in Table 1.[9]
Table 1

In a straight vote A, B, D and E all prefer W to X, and C, D and E prefer Y to Z, so the outcome would be W and Y. But the pair WY is less well liked than the opposite pair XZ by A, B and C.

We now ask: what does the majority prin-ciple prescribe in a situation like this? Are we committed to the view that neither smoking nor playing radios should be allowed, because there is a majority against each? Or can we take account of the fact that there is a majority in favour of overturning the result of the two sepa-rate votes and substituting their opposites?

The case just presented is consistent with each person's preferences on smoking being independent of what is decided about radio playing, and vice versa. But, in most politi-cal matters, this assumption of 'separability' does not hold. What we favour on one issue depends on how other issues are settled. Some things are complementary: we don't want to

Rank order	A	B	C	D	E
1	WZ	WZ	XY	WY	WY
2	XZ	XZ	XZ	WZ	XY
3	WY	WY	WY	XY	WZ
4	XY	XY	WZ	XZ	XZ

Table 1

vote for buying the land unless there is going to be a majority for spending money on the building that is proposed to go on the land. Others are competitive: if expensive project X is going to be funded, we don't want to vote for expensive project Y as well, but if project X is going to be defeated, we would favour project Y. In such a case, the whole concept of a majority on a single issue becomes indeterminate, because each person's preference depends on his or her expectations about the way the other relevant issues are going to be decided. And the outcome if issues are packaged together depends on the way the packaging is done.

A further difficulty is that as soon as we aggregate two or more dichotomous decisions we get a choice between more than two outcomes, and there is then the possibility that no one is capable of getting a majority over each of the others in a pair-wise vote. (In the jargon of collective choice theory, there is no Condorcet winner among the alternatives.) Thus, in the example I set out, I pointed out that A, B and C prefer XZ to WY. But I could have gone on to say that C, D and E prefer XY to XZ, that A, B and D prefer WZ to XY, and that C, D and E prefer WY to WZ. Since, as we already know, A, B and C prefer XZ to WY, it is clear that we have here a cycle including all four possible combinations. No outcome is capable of getting a majority over each of the others and so the majority principle offers no guidance.

The simplest way of generating a situation in which there are cyclical majorities is to have a choice between three possible outcomes. Suppose that our passengers consider three candidates for a binding rule about smoking: X (no smoking), Y (smoking but only of cigarettes) and Z (smoking of pipes and cigars as well as cigarettes). There may, of course, be an outright majority for one outcome. And, even if there is not, there may be a majority for some outcome over each of the others. Thus, suppose

Preference ranking	A, B	C	D, E
1	X	Y	Z
2	Y	Z	Y
3	Z	X	X

Table 2

the preferences lie as in Table 2. Then Y gets a majority over X (C, D and E prefer it) and also a majority over Z (A, B and C prefer it).

A sufficient (though not necessary) condition of there being an outcome that is preferred by a majority to any other is that preferences should be what is called 'single peaked'.[10] All this means is that it should be possible to arrange the alternative outcomes along a single line in such a way that, when we draw for each of the people involved a curve whose height represents their relative preference for each outcome, we get a curve with a single peak for each. Thus, in the present case we can easily see that the preferences satisfy the condition of single-peakedness. (C's preferences could instead have the order YXZ and still be consistent with single-peakedness).

When preferences take a single-peaked form, as in Figure 8.1, it is normally possible to discern an underlying dimension from which the orderings derive. (I have here labelled it pro-smoking/anti-smoking.) But the existence of a majority winner is established if we can arrange the outcomes on a line so as to be compatible with single-peaked preferences—even if we as analysts have trouble assigning a label to the line.

When preferences are single-peaked we know not only that a majority winner exists but we also know how to find it easily. The simple rule is that the outcome that is most preferred by the median person is the outcome that is preferred by a majority to any other. The median person is the one (for an odd number of participants) who has exactly as many others on one side as on the other. If there are n people (n being an odd number) whose preferences are to be taken into account, we should start counting at one end (it doesn't matter which since the answer will be the same) and stop when we get to $1/2(n + 1)$. This will be the median person. In our example of five people $1/2(n + 1) = 3$ and it will be seen that we get to C's most preferred position by counting to three from either end. Where there is an even number of people, there is no unique median but the people at $1/2 n$ and $(1/2 n) + 1$ (again counting from either end) occupy positions each of which is capable of gaining a majority against any other position. These two positions have an equal number of supporters when matched against each other so on the majority principle they may be regarded as equally good.

The trouble is that there may not be any outcome that is capable of getting majority support against any other (or, in the case of even numbers, two that are equally good in the sense just specified). Thus, suppose now that D and E do not like to smoke cigarettes and, if they cannot smoke their pipes, would prefer a smoke-free environment to one contaminated by C's cigarette smoke. Then the preference matrix becomes as in Table 3. We now pit each possible outcome against each other in a series of three pairwise comparisons and get the result that X beats Y (A, B, D and E prefer it), Z beats X (C, D and E prefer it) and Y beats Z (A, B and C prefer it). Thus, a quite plausible

distribution of preferences generates a 'paradox of voting' in which the majorities arising from pairwise comparisons form a cycle.

The two sources of indeterminacy in the majority principle that I have so far been pointing out may be considered rather dull and technical, incapable of arousing political passions. This is by no means true. Consider, for example, the importance that both sympathizers of President Allende and apologists for the coup that overthrew him and the regime have attached in their polemics to the question whether or not he had majority support for his policies. Given a political setup with three blocs, Allende was able to come into power as President on a bare plurality; and the Popular Unity Coalition that supported him never achieved a majority of votes cast. It was on the basis of these facts that the junta claimed legitimacy in terms of the majority principle for overthrowing the constitutional government. On the other side, however, it may be argued that 'one cannot infer that those who opposed Allende necessarily supported a military coup, especially the bloody one that ensued following his overthrow. Thus there is little evidence that a majority of Chileans wanted Allende overthrown by the military'.[11]

It is not my intention to join in this debate, merely to point out that, where the majority principle is indeterminate, generals find it worth appealing to it and scholars find it worth rebutting that appeal. However, if we measure the importance of a question by the blood spilt over it (and I find it hard to think of a better criterion) the importance of the third reason for the indeterminacy of the majority principle can hardly be denied. The question is the deceptively innocent one: majority of *what*?

In the railway carriage example this is not a problem. If the decision about permitting or prohibiting smoking is to be made according to majority preference there can be no doubt that

Rankorder	A and B	C	D and E
1	X	Y	Z
2	Y	Z	X
3	Z	X	Y

Table 3

the people whose preferences should be taken into account are the five people in the railway carriage who will be affected by the decision. But when the question is the boundaries of political entities—empires, supranational organizations, federations, nation states, provinces or other sub-divisions—and their respective decision-making powers, the question 'who is included?' is an explosive one.

There is no need to labour the point. The briefest survey is enough. In Western Europe, after centuries of wars between states, civil wars, and heavy-handed centralizing government, Northern Ireland is paralyzed by conflict, Scottish nationalism is a powerful force, the centralized Belgian state has been virtually partitioned, unfinished business from the nineteenth century still hangs over the Swiss Jura and the Alto Adige, while in Spain Basque and Catalan separatism are stirring again after the long freeze. In Eastern Europe almost every state has claims on the territory of at least one other. Order, of a kind, is maintained by the Soviet Union, which is itself a patchwork of nationalities held together by coercion. And nobody is taking bets on the existence of Yugoslavia in ten years time. In North America, Quebec has a separatist government, and the unity of the country is in question. In the Middle East three wars have been fought over the boundaries of Israel and no end is in sight. In Africa, the boundaries bequeathed by the colonial powers, after a period of surprising stability (interrupted only by the Biafran and Katagan secessions) are coming under pressure in the Horn of Africa, and the trouble looks as if it may well spread further in coming years. The Indian subcontinent has seen first the convulsion of the creation of Pakistan and then the almost equally bloody process of its splitting into two; while in India the states have had to be reconstituted, amid a good deal of disorder, in an attempt to satisfy the aspirations of linguistic groups. There are few parts of the world where boundaries are not a potential source of serious conflict, and where we do not hear that they are (e.g. China) this is as likely to reflect our ignorance as the absence of potential conflict.

The only thing that has to be established, beyond the existence of conflicts over boundaries, is that the majority principle has no way of solving them, either in practice or in theory. In practice, the majority principle, so far from alleviating conflicts over boundaries, greatly exacerbates them. It may be tolerable to be ruled over by a cosmopolitan autocracy, like the Austrian empire, or a more or less even-handed colonial power like the British in India. But to be subject to a majority of different language, religion or national identity is far more threatening. In an area where nationalities are intermingled, like the Balkans, every move to satisfy majority aspirations leaves the remaining minorities even more vulnerable.

On a theoretical level, any use of the majority principle in order to establish boundaries must involve begging the question. Locke, to do him credit, saw that the majority principle could come into play only after the constituency has been identified, but he finessed the problem by resorting to the fiction that those who are to form 'one body' all individually agree to do so. This approach obviously fails to provide any guidance in any situation where it is actually needed, that is to say where people are disagreeing about the 'body' they want to be members of.

The so-called 'principle of national self-determination' espoused by the Versailles Treaty of 1919 says, in effect, that if a minority within a state wishes to secede and the majority does not wish them to secede the minority should win—provided the minority is a 'nation'. As it stands, this is both question-begging (since the crucial judgement is packed into the question whether the would-be secessionists constitute a 'nation') and contrary to the majority principle. But the attempt to reformulate it so as to derive it from the majority principle simply begs the question in a different way.

Suppose we say: the majority in any given territorial area should decide on the political status of that area. Then the question is thrown back one stage further. What is the relevant territorial area within which to count preferences? Consider, for example, the Irish question as it stood between 1918 and 1922. Simplifying somewhat, there was (probably) a majority in the U.K. as a whole (i.e. the British Isles) for the maintenance of the union; within Ireland (i.e. the whole island) there was a majority in favour of independence for the whole of Ireland; within the six provinces that became Northern Ireland there was a majority for partition as a second best to union; but within two of those six counties there was a majority for unification with the south as a second best to independence for the whole of Ireland. But why stop at counties? Counties could have been further divided and some areas within them would have had one sort of majority and others other sorts.

A contemporary puzzle of the same sort is offered by Gibraltar: 'London insists that it will respect the wishes of the 25,000 Gibraltarians, a mixture of people who, for the most part, tend to favour retaining their colonial connection with Britain. Madrid insists on regaining sovereignty over what a broad spectrum of Spanish opinion considers a usurped segment of national territory'.[12] Is the majority of Gibraltarians the relevant one, or the majority of people in Spain plus Gibraltar?

It seems clear that the majority principle can offer no guidance. If we feel that (within limits of contiguity and feasibility) the right answer is to try to satisfy the wishes of as many people as possible to form a polity with those they wish to have in it and only those, we are moving beyond the majority principle to another, and

in my view more defensible, notion. This is that what matters is not to satisfy the preferences of a majority but to respect the interests of all. I shall argue in the next section that democratic procedures, can, under some conditions, be defended in terms of that conception.

Meanwhile, it should be noted that the upshot of the discussion is that any attempt to justify boundaries by appealing to the majority principle must be void. You can have as many referenda as you like, and show every time that over half of the people within the existing boundaries approve of them, but you cannot use that to prove to a minority that wants to secede that they ought to acquiesce in the *status quo*. If their loyalty is to be awakened, other and better arguments—backed by deeds rather than votes—are needed.

Suppose, however, that the composition of the group that is to be subject to a common policy is not at issue, and that the two more technical sources of indeterminacy are absent, does that make the majority principle unassailable? Of course not. The fourth and last of the special features of the railway carriage case that I singled out was that, as the story had been told, we had no reason to suppose that the question of smoking or not smoking was of vital importance to any of the people involved. (It might be said that smoking is inherently a vital interest in that being smoked at lowers one's expectation of life; but, if we put it as a question of interests, is a few minutes more life a greater interest than the freedom of the addict from withdrawal symptoms?) Suppose, however, that one of the passengers suffers from severe asthma or emphysema, and that being subjected to tobacco smoke is liable to precipitate a dangerous attack. No doubt one would hope that this fact, when explained, would lead the others to agree not to smoke, however many of them would like to. But say that it does not. It seems clear to me that the person at risk would be behaving with an almost insane disregard for his or her interests in accepting a majority decision to allow smoking. The obvious recourse would be, I presume, to pull the communication cord and bring the train to a grinding halt.

It might be argued that nothing said here shows that the majority principle lacks universality; it still applies but in some cases the reason it provides for obedience is overridden by a more pressing consideration, such as self-protection against a risk of substantial harm. However, it does not seem to me that this is a correct representation of the position. Where the decision is sufficiently threatening to the vital interests of (some of) those affected by it, its pedigree is neither here nor there.

Take for example a group of youths like those in *The Clockwork Orange* who beat up strangers for fun. Would we be inclined to say 'Well, at least there's one redeeming feature: they choose their victims by majority vote'? I think not. This example of course raises the question of constituency, since the victim is outside the decision-making group. But if we modify it so that the members of a group decide by majority vote to beat up one of their own number I still do not think that the chosen victim has less reason to resist or escape than he would if the decision were taken by a strong-arm leader. I do not see any significant respect in which my modified example of the railway passengers differs from that. I suppose that someone might adduce the difference between deliberately causing harm and doing something whose known but unintended consequences are harmful, but that is not in my view a morally relevant distinction.

The political parallels hardly need to be filled in. No minority can be, or should be, expected to acquiesce in the majority's trampling on its vital interests. Unfortunately the parallel to pulling the communication cord—bringing the state, or that part of its policy that is objectionable, to a

grinding halt—is a much more messy business and carries the risk of incurring costs much higher than a £25 fine. But the principle is clear enough. Nobody but a moral imbecile would really be prepared to deliver himself over body and soul to the majority principle.

NOTES

[1] W. J. M. Mackenzie, *Power, Violence, Decision* (Harmondsworth: Penguin, 1975), p. 151.

[2] Quoted in Hugh Tinker, *Ballot Box and Bayonet: People and Government in Emergent Asian Countries* (Chatham House Essays, 5; London: Oxford University Press, 1964), p. 83.

[3] This is, it may be noted, the line taken by the U.S. Supreme Court in its decision requiring redistricting to secure approximately equal constituencies, (The leading case is Reynolds *v.* Sims, 377 U.S. 533 (1964).)

[4] An analysis with whose general line I concur is Paul E. Meehl, 'The Selfish Voter Paradox and the Thrown-Away Vote Argument', *The American Political Science Review* LXXI (1977): pp. 11–30.

[5] A. Downs, *An Economic Theory of Democracy* (New York: Harper and Brothers, 1957), pp. 55–60.

[6] 'Long and frustrated experience has proved, to those among us who have endeavoured to make unpleasant facts [about nuclear weapons] known, that orthodox methods, alone, are insufficient. By means of civil disobedience a certain kind of publicity becomes possible.... Many people are roused into inquiry into inquiry into questions which they had been willing to ignore.... It seems not unlikely that, in the end, an irresistible popular movement of protest will compel governments to allow their subjects to continue to

exist.' Bertrand Russell, 'Civil Disobedience and the Threat of Nuclear Warfare', in Hugo Adam Bedau (ed.), *Civil Disobedience: Theory and Practice* (New York: Pegasus, 1969), pp, 153–9 at p. 157.

7 John Locke, *Two Treatises of Government*, ed. Peter Laslett (New York: The New American Library, Mentor Book, 1965), pp. 375–6.

8 B. M. Barry, *Political Argument* (London: Routledge and Kegan Paul, 1965), p. 312.

9 Adapted from Appendix, Example 1 (p. 69) of Nicholas R. Miller, 'Logrolling, Vote trading, and the Paradox of Voting: A Game-Theoretical Overview', *Public Choice 30* (1977): pp. 49–75.

10 The *locus classicus* is Duncan Black, *The Theory of Committees and Elections* (Cambridge: Cambridge University Press, 1963).

11 James Petras and Morris Morley, 'Chilean Destabilisation and Its Aftermath', *Politics* XI (1976) pp. 140–8 at p. 145.

12 James M. Markham, 'Talks on Gibraltar Due in October', *The New York Times*, Sept. 25, 1977, p. 4.

Confucian Value and Democratic Value

Chenyang Li

INTRODUCTION

Samuel P. Huntington asserts that the world is now entering an age of "the clash of civilizations."[1] Specifically, the clash is between democratic Western civilization and undemocratic civilizations in the rest of the world, Confucian and Islamic civilizations in particular. Huntington also suggests that in order for democracy to take roots in a Confucian society, undemocratic elements in Confucianism must be superseded by democratic elements.[2] The purpose of this essay is to examine the future relationship between democracy and Confucianism in the part of the world where they are most likely to clash, namely, China.

1. What democracy is and what China needs

The word "democracy" has been used in so many ways that people today often disagree about exactly what it means. Many controversies about democracy concern whether it is merely a procedural method for political decisions or something more substantive that has value content.[3] Joseph Schumpeter, for example, has proposed as a minimal definition of democracy:

the democratic method is that institutional arrangement for arriving at political decisions in which individuals acquire the power to decide by means of a competitive struggle for the people's vote.[4]

His use of "democratic method," instead of "democracy," indicates that he takes democracy primarily as a procedural form.

Francis Fukuyama has recently argued that the consolidation of democracy must occur on four levels: ideology, institutions, civil society, and finally, culture. He regards culture as the "deepest level" of democracy.[5] Many people would agree with Fukuyama in as much as democracy penetrates culture and is therefore value-loaded. Jürgen Domes, for instance, also defines democracy primarily as a value-loaded political system. In addition to its formal dimension, Domes characterizes democracy specifically by three principles: liberty, equality, and pluralism.[6] This is sometimes said to characterize liberal democracy.

Without a context, it makes little sense to ask whose definition is right. The question we should ask here is, what kind of democracy does China need? I believe the answer is the kind of democracy with the values of individual liberty, equality, and pluralism. These values, as I will show, make the clash between democracy and Confucianism possible. Confucianism is no longer an institutional arrangement, and such a clash cannot take place anywhere but on the dimension of value.

Without the values of individual liberty, equality, and pluralism, democracy as a mere procedure is merely a technique or formality. This technique has been and continues to be misused in China. Unless we make explicit the values found in democracy, the misuse is likely to continue. For example, within the Chinese Communist Party (CCP), democracy as a voting procedure has been practiced. Missing, however, is the value of individual liberty. Within the CCP, members can vote, but the party leadership demands absolute loyalty. The value of loyalty takes the place of individual liberty in the current mainland Chinese version of democracy. Even when the voting procedure is carried through, the outcome has almost always been a unanimous decision. In *Democracy in America* Alexis de Tocqueville wrote:

> if a democratic republic, similar to that of the United States, were ever founded in a country where the power of a single individual had previously subsisted, and the effects of a centralized administration had sunk deep into the habits and the laws of the people, I do not hesitate to assert, that in that country a more insufferable despotism would prevail than any which now exists in the monarchical states of Europe; or indeed than any which could be found on this side of the confines of Asia.[7]

When democracy is taken to be merely a voting procedure, it can be counterproductive in countries like China where people have formed the habits of following a centralized administration which they may have mistakenly identified as representing their own interest and to which

they habitually render unconditional loyalty. Unless individual liberty is valued, voters will not realize that they ought to feel free in choosing their representatives; and unless voters can freely choose to vote for their candidates, there cannot be true democracy. Here "free choice" does not merely mean choice without external coercion. It also means choosing candidates on the basis of individual liberty. Imagine a people in whom loyalty to their leader is such an overwhelming value that no matter what happens they will always cast their votes for their own leader. Such a so-called democracy would be no better than a tyranny. This form of government is not worth fighting for, except perhaps as a mere preliminary step from totalitarianism to real democracy. What China needs is democracy with the value of individual liberty, equality, and pluralism.[8]

While acknowledging that democracy has institutional forms, I will focus on democracy on a cultural level and consider democracy mainly as a value system which is centered on the rights of individual liberty and equality. In that value system, pluralism is also an important element. If we recognize that democracy is value-loaded, then no matter how we think about democracy and Confucianism, we have to think about how values from both sides interact.[9]

2. Is Confucianism democratic?

Among influential Confucian thinkers Mencius had a thought which is probably closest to one that might be considered democratic and is most often cited by those looking for democratic elements in traditional Chinese thought.[10] Mencius said: "(In a state) the people are the most important; the spirits of the land and grain (guardians of territory) are the next; the ruler is of slight importance."[11] This thought is often called the thought of *min-ben*, or people-rootedness. Some people think this is the model for Chinese democracy. For example, Sun Yat-sen said that Confucius and Mencius more than two thousand years ago already advocated democracy because they advocated the common good and emphasized the importance of the people.[12]

However, Mencius' thought is not democracy as defined by individual liberty and equality. First of all, Mencius' thought does not exclude having a king as the sole decision maker for social affairs. As Shu-hsien Liu properly pointed out, Mencius' idea of people-rootedness and the idea of having a good king mutually depend on each other.[13] When a king makes a decision, he should consider the well-being of the people first.[14] It would be unreasonable if we were to look for a form of government without a king in Mencius. The point here is that Mencius' form of government is what Lin Yutang has called "parental government."[15] It requires a king to treat people as he treats his children *ai min ru zi*. But even though a king considers the well-being of the people first, the form of government is not democratic. For even if a parent has the children's well-being in mind, the parent is the sole decision-maker. As the decision-making power of a parent does not come from children, a king's power comes from Heaven, not from popular free choice. In this picture there is no room for individual liberty and equality, both of which are essential for democracy. This kind of government is at most, in the phrasing of Lincoln, "for the people." It is highly questionable whether it is "of the people." It is clearly not "by the people."

Secondly, the question of whose well-being should be put first has little to do with democracy. A dictator might put the people's well-being first. The Confucian concept of government is government by gentlemen and governance by moral force. But gentlemen may be mistaken in believing that they make decisions on behalf of the people and in their best interests; or they may really represent the best interests of the people, without the people, due to lack of knowledge or wisdom, wanting them to do so. In each case the Confucian form of government would not be democratic.

Among prominent classic Confucian philosophers, Mencius' thought is considered the closest to the idea of democracy.[16] If his idea is not that of real democracy, we can conclude that democracy is not an influential value in traditional Confucianism.

While there may be practical reasons for Confucians today to make Confucianism look democratic, the claim that Confucianism is democratic is seriously flawed and, as I will show later, the move to make Confucianism democratic is misguided.

3. Are Confucianism and democracy compatible?

If democracy has not been at the heart of traditional Chinese culture, are democracy and Confucianism compatible? Liang Shuming, for example, thought that there is no room in Chinese culture for democracy. He wrote that, "it is not that China has not entered democracy, it is rather that China cannot enter democracy."[17] He believed that traditional Chinese value systems alone provide a solid foundation for a good civil society. Mou Tsung-san, a prominent contemporary New-Confucian, sees the inadequacy of traditional Confucianism and believes that through a transformation of the Confucian moral subjectivity into a cognitive subjectivity, Confucianism will provide an adequate foundation for democracy. But it is not clear how such a transformation can actually take place.[18] Mou includes liberty, equality, and human rights in democracy.[19] It is doubtful that these values can be integrated into Confucianism. Shu-heien Liu, in contrast, sees many difficulties in grafting democracy onto Confucianism and maintains that unless politics is separated from morals, democracy will not find a home in China.[20] Liu is certainly right in thinking that democracy must take the political realm as a social institution. But what about the value content of democracy? If democratic values are to enter the culture, then we cannot ignore the relationship between democratic values and Confucian values.

There are fundamentally conflicting values between democracy and Confucianism. Democracy, as we have seen, presupposes the concept of rights. A democratic society is one in which individual rights are recognized and respected. This requires the recognition that some basic rights of individuals are inalienable. Confucianism, at least in the traditional form, has no place for the concept of rights.[21] It is, however, a serious mistake to think that Confucius left out the concept of rights by negligence. In the ideal society that Confucius envisioned, there is just supposed to be no need for rights. On the issue of whether human nature is good or bad, rights-based theories typically lean toward the view that human nature is bad or flawed. Rights are viewed as the basis for individuals to stand up for themselves. When others impose on someone, the person can stand on a right. The Confucian social ideal is one of *jen*, which signifies humanity, compassion, and benevolence. Unlike rights-based social theories, which tend to regulate society by giving weapons to the weak to protect themselves, Confucian theory promotes the view that *jen* regulates society and protects the weak by placing moral restraints on the strong and powerful. If all people are to embody *jen* as Confucius wished, no one would inflict pain on others unjustly and everyone would be taken care of.

In Confucianism the primary concern for individuals has to do with duty, not liberty. The Confucian motto is "to return to the observance of the rites through overcoming the self constitutes benevolence (*jen*)."[22] Overcoming ourselves implies suppressing our desires of self-interest, including the desire for individual liberty. For Confucians the first order of a person's social life concerns family life, where liberty is typically not a primary concern.[23] In a family model of society, people are defined by their social roles that come with responsibilities. In Confucianism responsibilities override liberty.

Closely connected to duty is the Confucian notion of loyalty (*zhong*). Loyalty is not only a virtue of the subject to the ruler, but also a virtue among people in general. Replying to Fan Chi's question on the meaning of *jen*, Confucius said: "Be respectful in private life, be serious (*ching*) in handling affairs, and be loyal in dealing with others."[24] In a broad sense, a child's filial piety to parents and trust between friends are also forms of loyalty. Loyalty implies being bound to other people. As long as people have to be loyal to others, they are not really free in the liberal sense. Thus, there is an essential tension between loyalty and liberty as two values. Of course someone can freely *choose* to be loyal. But that does not mean that liberty and loyalty, as primary virtues, point in the same direction. Someone can freely choose to be a slave too.

Confucian loyalty becomes even more binding when it is coupled with another cardinal Confucian value, *yi*. Usually translated in English as "righteousness," *yi* has more than one meaning. In a primary sense, *yi* requires that we do not abandon friends when they are in trouble or in need of our help and that we do not let friends down even under extreme circumstances. Heavy emphasis on loyalty and *yi* as central Confucian virtues can be seen throughtout history. For instance, in 1948 after Chiang Kaishek was forced to resign from the presidency of the Republic of China, he still had almost full control of the government. The acting president, Li Tsung-jen, formally in the post, was simply unable to perform his duties without having his own people in the government. A main reason for this was that people in the government had an overwhelmingly strong sense of duty of loyalty to Chiang. The kind of loyalty he felt is almost incomprehensible to many Westerners. In contrast, a democratic society such as the United States characteristically lacks for loyalty. Voters are willing to readily withdraw their support from a leader and turn to someone else at almost any time. Elected officials simply cannot count on loyalty from their voters.

As we have seen, a fundamental value for democracy is equality, whereas in Confucianism equality receives only minimal recognition. In Confucianism, while people may have equal opportunities for laboring through the role of an obedient young person to become a respected old person, there is little hope for submissive ministers to rule. Confucians believe that we are what we make ourselves to be. While everyone has the potential to make themselves a sage or superior person (jun zi), in practice because people are inevitably at different stages of this process, they are not on the same footing. Therefore they are not equal. To add the value of equality to Confucianism would inevitably undermine the Confucian ideal of superior person which is at its core.

Confucianism is characteristically paternalistic. Paternalism may be seen as a necessary consequence of the lack of equality within the tradition, a natural extension from the concept of jen, and a corollary of the Confucian ideal of meritocracy. Confucius said: "the character of a ruler (jun zi) is like wind and that of the people is like grass. In whatever direction the wind blows, the grass always bends."[25] Mencius advocated that those who use their minds should rule those who use their muscles.[26] A cardinal Confucian virtue for the able and

wise is to direct and take care of the less able and wise. For example, it is the inescapable duty of Confucian intellectuals to speak on behalf of the masses. In contrast, in democracy, the concepts of liberty and individual rights assure that individuals are entitled to make choices for themselves even if they are wrong or unwise.[27] For that, Confucianism leaves little room. In Confucianism, under the name of common good, paternalism prevails over individual liberty and individual autonomy.

Confucians place a strong value on unity (da yi tong), not plurality. "Unity" here means not only political and territorial unity, but also unity in thought and ideology.[28] Confucius placed paramount importance on following the way of the Chou dynasty and thereby excluded other options.[29] While Mencius believed that the only way to settle the empire was through unity, Xun Zi advocated the idea of using a unitary principle in deciding world-affairs. The Confucian classic Li Ji states: "Today throughout the empire carts all have wheels with the same gauge; all writing is with the same character; and for conduct there exist the same rules."[30] This is stated with enthusiastic approval. The Kung-Yang School Confucianism almost took unity to be the only manifestation of Tao or the Way. In this tradition pluralism has no place.

The problem between Confucian and democratic values is that both sets of values are worthwhile. On the one hand, such democratic values as liberty, equality, and pluralism are desirable; and on the other, so are Confucian values like the family, duty, loyalty, and unity. Confucian values are as cherishable as democratic values. Traditional Confucian virtues such as loyalty, filial piety, paternalism, and unity are good values and ought to be retained. Just because Confucian virtues are in conflict with some democratic values, that does not mean they are less good or less valuable. The real strength of Confucianism is not in being or becoming democratic, but in the traditional virtues that are not democratic. It is a simple-minded fallacious inference that, since democracy is good, anything that is undemocratic must be bad. An argument can be made that in the United States and throughout the democratic West, healthy society has been threatened precisely by the diminishing of traditional values similar to these undemocratic Confucian values. Scholars like Samuel Huntington have made much the same mistake in thinking that because democratic values are good, undemocratic or non-democratic Confucian values must be abandoned or superseded.

At this historically critical and conceptually perplexing point, where ought China to go? Or, as the Confucian would ask, what ought Chinese intellectuals to advocate?

4. Democracy as an independent value system in China

Since Confucianism is the predominant value system in China and is not compatible with democracy in one integrated value system, will the two value systems clash with one another as democracy enters China? There are at least four possible answers to this question.

Let us call the first answer "Confucianism but not democracy." Among its proponents, besides those outrightly rejecting democracy, I include people who would want China to have minimal democracy, or democracy without pluralism or rights to individual liberty and equality. Liang Shu-ming outrightly rejected democracy. Recently Western scholars such as Henry Rosemont, Jr. also have appeared to favor the alternative of minimal democracy in China.[31] Yet since the May Fourth Movement of 1919 some people have chosen the opposing view of complete Westernization in China. Westernization may include democratization. Therefore this view may be called "democracy but not Confucianism."

Samuel Huntington provides a third answer. Pointing out the impending clash between democracy and some traditional cultures in some parts of the world, Huntington writes:

> Great historic cultural traditions, such as Islam and Confucianism, are highly complex bodies of ideas, beliefs, doctrines, assumptions, writings, and behavior patterns. Any major culture, including even Confucianism, has some elements that are compatible with democracy, just as Protestantism and Catholicism have elements that are clearly undemocratic. Confucian democracy may be a contradiction in terms, but democracy in a Confucian society need not be. The question is: What elements in Islam and Confucianism are favorable to democracy, and how and under what circumstances can these supersede the undemocratic elements in those cultural traditions?[32]

Huntington is evidently applying a Western hierarchical model of thinking here. For him, Confucianism can survive democratization by superseding or abandoning its undemocratic values. Admittedly, this option is not entirely impossible, just as a China with only residual Confucian values is not entirely impossible. But is that too great a price for Confucianism to pay? Can Confucianism do better than that?

I propose a fourth answer: that Confucianism and democracy independently co-exist in China. I believe that China needs both democratic and Confucian values. Because of essential tensions between democratic values and some undemocratic Confucian values, the two value systems cannot be integrated into a single system without undermining their integrity. Therefore the only way out has to be for democracy to exist in China independently of Confucianism. Chinese should not pursue a single integrated system of values, whether it is called "democratic Confucianism" or "Confucian democracy."

Because of the tensions between democratic values and some undemocratic Confucian values, the two sets of values cannot be integrated into one coherent value system without substantially sacrificing either democratic or Confucian values. Unfortunately some New-Confucians try to do just that. Any attempt to make Confucianism democratic will only make it nondescript. As a value system, Confucianism is not unchangeable. It has changed in many ways since Confucius' time, and it needs to change further. To some extent the vitality of Confucianism lies in its potentialities for change. But it does have some elements which are so central to Confucianism that it cannot survive substantially without them. Features like its emphasis on the family, filial piety, and self-cultivation and self-constraint are an indispensable part of Confucianism. Since Confucian emphases lead away from individual liberty and equality, if the emphases were to shift, how Confucian would a democratic Confucianism be? Any attempt to democratize Confucianism by superseding its traditional values would jeopardize the integrity of Confucianism. The inevitable result would be a loss of the real value of Confucianism. This kind of integration, if applied to all the non-Western world, would indeed lead to "the end of history."[33]

China should become democratic and retain its Confucian heritage. The coexistence of two value systems cannot be that of institutional Confucianism with democracy as a social institution. Confucianism as a social institution no longer exists. As value systems, democracy and Confucianism may influence each other, even as they remain independent. Confucianism and democracy may coexist in two ways. Some people are more Confucian than democratic, and value Confucian values more than democratic values, while others are more democratic than Confucian, and value democratic values more than Confucian values. Perhaps more importantly,

the values of Confucianism and democracy may co-exist in the same individual. Various values that are not consistent with each other may be worth pursuing. Where that is the case, we need to achieve a delicate balance among them.

History hints at how to balance the values. The three major existing value systems in China, Confucianism, Taoism, and Buddhism, have co-existed for a long time. As Wing-Tsit Chan observed: "most Chinese follow the three systems of Confucianism, Taoism, and Buddhism, and usually take a multiple approach to things."[34] Tao Yuanming was a Taoist and a Confucian at the same time; the so-called last Confucian, Liang Shuming, remained a Buddhist throughout his life.

Thinking is not a linear process that always follows a consistent pattern. In the West, people tend to overlook this by overemphasizing a unitary rationality. People have different values, desires, and needs which can be alternately pursued. A Confucian scholar once said that Buddhism is like floating on the water, drifting wherever the current takes you, and Confucianism is like having a rudder in the boat to guide it in a certain direction. This analogy was meant to show the advantage of Confucianism over Buddhism. But if we read it from a different perspective, we can find new meanings. Is it always so bad to drift along the current? Perhaps it is better to drift for a while before using the rudder again. Sometimes it may be better to follow both ways at different times. Reading the analogy this way may help us understand how someone can adopt Confucianism along with Buddhism.[35]

Democracy may enter China similarly. The Confucian, the Taoist, and the Buddhist, who have been engaged in a dialogue for an extended period of time, may invite another participant, the democrat, to join them. Then we will see the four different value systems side by side. The primary characteristic of the dialogue should be one of harmony. When one party is too loud, it is time to shift attention to another party. For instance, the concept of rights should be voiced when there is too much emphasis on paternalism and the paternalistic practice has become oppressive; but Confucianism, Taoism, and perhaps Buddhism should be voiced when rights-based talk has aroused too much individualism. Thus, despite tensions between Confucianism and democracy, the four systems can nevertheless keep themselves in balance and harmony in the same land.[36]

NOTES

1 Samuel P. Huntington, "The clash of civilizations," *Foreign Affairs*, 72:3 (Summer 1993), pp. 22–49.

2 Ibid.

3 For different versions of democracy, see C.B. Macpherson, *The Real World of Democracy* (New York: Oxford University Press, 1972).

4 Joseph A. Schumpeter, *Capitalism, Socialism, and Democracy*, 2nd edn. (New York: Harper, 1947), p. 269.

5 Francis Fukuyama, "The primacy of culture," *Journal of Democracy*, 6:1 (January 1995), pp. 7–14.

6 Jürgen Domes, "China's Modernization and the Doctrine of Democracy," in *Sun Yat-Sen's Doctrine in the Modern World*, ed. Chu-yuan Cheng (Boulder, Colo.: Westview Press, 1989), pp. 201–224.

7 Alexis de Tocqueville, *Democracy in America*, vol. 1 (New York: Schocken Books, 1974), p. 320.

8 For some liberal views on what kind of democracy China needs, see Hua Shiping, "All roads lead to democracy: A critical analysis of the writings of three Chinese reformist intellectuals," *Bulletin of Concerned Asian Scholars*, (January–March 1992), pp. 43–58; and Yu-sheng Lin, "Reluctance to modernize: The influence of Confucianism on China's search for political modernity," in *Confucianism and Modernization: A Symposium*, ed. Joseph P.L. Jiang (Taipei, Freedom Council, 1987), pp. 21–33.

9 The relation between democracy on the one hand and Taoism and Buddhism on the other is complex and cannot be adequately dealt with in this essay. Confucianism, the predominant value system in Chinese culture, is my main concern here.

10 For the view that Confucianism is democratic, see Leonard Shihlien Hsü, *The Political Philosophy of Confucianism* (New York: Harper & Row, 1975), particularly Chapter IX: Democracy and Representation, pp. 174–197; Huang Chun-chieh and Wu Kuangming, "Taiwan and the Confucian aspiration: Toward the twenty-first century," in *Cultural Change in Postwar Taiwan*, ed. Stevan Harrell and Huang Chun-chieh (Boulder, Colo.: Westview Press, 1994), pp. 69–87; and more recently, Lee Teng-hui, "Chinese culture and political renewal," *The Journal of Democracy*, 6:4 (October 1995), pp. 3–8.

11 Wing-Tsit Chan, *A Source Book in Chinese Philosophy* (Princeton, N.J.: Princeton University Press, 1963), p. 81.

12 Sun Yat-sen, "First lecture on democracy," in *The Teachings of the Nation-Founding Father* [*Guo Fu Yi Jiao*] (Taiwan: Cultural Book Inc., 1984), Section 3, p. 70.

13 Shu-hsien Liu, *Confucianism and Modernization* [*Ru Jia Si Xiang Yu Xian Dai Hua*], ed. Jing Hai-Feng (Beijing: Chinese Broadcasting and TV Publishing House, 1992), p. 19.

14 Female monarchs were evidently not a possibility at Mencius's time.

[15] Lin Yutang, *My Country and My People* (New York: The John Day Company Books, 1939), p. 206.

[16] Other liberal Confucian philosophers like Huang Zongxi (1610–1695) were much less influential in the society. For some marginal liberal elements in Confucian tradition, see Wm. Theodore de Barry, *The Liberal Tradition in China* (Hong Kong: The Chinese University Press and New York: Columbia University Press, 1983), and his "Neo-Confucianism and human rights," in *Human Rights and the World's Religions*, ed. Leroy S. Rouner (Notre Dame, Ind.: University of Notre Dame Press, 1988), pp. 183–198

[17] Liang Shu-ming, "Elements of Chinese culture [*Zhong Guo Wen Hua Yao Yi*]," Chapter 2, Section 5; in *Collected Works of Liang Shu-ming*, vol. 3 (Jinan, China: Shandoing People's Publishing House, 1990), p. 48.

[18] Mou Tsung-san, "Preface to *Philosophy of History*," in *Reconstruction of Moral Idealism*, ed. Zheng Jiadong (Beijing: China Broadcasting TV Publishing House, 1992), pp. 128–132.

[19] Ibid., p. 15.

[20] Shu-hsien Liu, op. cit., pp. 17–40.

[21] See Henry Rosemont Jr., "Why take rights seriously? A Confucian critique," in *Human Rights and the World Religions*, ed. Leroy Rouner (Notre Dame Ind.: University of Notre Dame Press, 1988), pp. 167–182.

[22] Confucius, *Analects*, 12:1, trans. D.C. Lau (New York: Penguin Books, 1979), p. 112.

[23] See Fung Yu-lan, "China's road to freedom [*Xin Shi Lun*]," Chapter 4: On The Family and State, in *Collected Work of Fung Yu-lan*, ed. Huang Kejian and Wu Xiaolong (Beijing: Qun-Yan Publishers, 1993), pp. 270–280. Also Liang Shu-min, op. cit., pp. 19–24.

[24] Wing-Tsit Chan, op. cit., p. 41.

[25] Ibid., p. 40.

[26] Ibid., p. 69.

[27] See Michael Walzer, "Philosophy and democracy," *Political Theory*, 9:3 (August 1981), pp. 379–399.

[28] See Yu Rubo, "On the Confucian thought of Great Unity [*Rujia Da Yitong Sixiang Jianyi*], "*The Academic Journal of Qilu [Qilu Xuekan]*, No. 1 (1995), pp. 51–54.

[29] Confucius, *Analects* 3:14, op. cit., p. 69.

[30] Quoted from Fung Yu-lan's *A History of Chinese Philosophy* vol. 1 (Princeton: Princeton University Press, 1952), p. 370.

[31] Henry Rosement, Jr., *A Chinese Mirror: Moral Reflections on Political Economy and Society* (La Salle, Ill.: Open Court, 1991).

[32] Samuel P. Huntington, *The Third Wave: Democratization in the Late Twentieth Century* (Norman, Okla.: University of Oklahoma Press, 1991), p. 310.

[33] Francis Fukuyama, "The end of history?," *The National Interest*, 16 (Summer 1989), pp. 3–18.

[34] Wing-Tsit Chan, op. cit., pp. 184–185.

[35] For a detailed account of how a person can incorporate different values, see my "How can one be a Taoist-Buddhist-Confucian?," *International Review of Chinese Religion and Philosophy*, 1 (March 1996), pp. 29–66.

[36] An earlier version of this paper was presented at the Seventh East-West Philosophers' Conference at the East-West Center and the University of Hawaii. I would like to thank Joel Kupperman, Charles Hayford, Craig Ihara, Ira Smolensky, Walter Benesch, Ruiping Fan, and Qingjie Wang for reading previous drafts of the paper, and the Midwest Faculty Seminar, the Center for East Asian Studies of the University of Chicago, the Center for Chinese Studies of the University of Michigan, and Monmouth College for their generous support.

Religious Violence or Religious Pluralism: Islam's Essential Choice

William A. Galston

INTRODUCTION

The question of the hour is whether traditional Islam is compatible with democracy. Though important, that question is subordinate to another: whether Islamic traditionalists can make their peace with religious pluralism, whether their efforts to impose their practices on Muslims who reject them will engender unending conflict.

It is natural for Western observers to believe that the "irrationality" of religious violence is the problem and that rationality (or at least reasonableness) is the solution. I want to suggest a somewhat different approach. The diminution of religious violence in the West, I shall argue, is the product not so much of ideas as of concrete historical experiences that made populations more receptive to the reality of religious pluralism and the necessity of tolerance. These practices, in turn, lent support to the theory and institutions of liberal constitutionalism. The real issue today, therefore, is whether there are concrete processes underway within Islam that may

over time make the politics of pluralism more acceptable and attractive, even to traditionalist Muslims unsympathetic to Western liberalism.

POLITICS, RELIGION, PLURALISM

Speaking broadly and schematically, there are three possible relations between political and religious authority. First, political authority may be comprehensively dominant over religion, which is seen as serving state power (and for this reason is often called "civil"). One of many difficulties with this position is that it subordinates the religious content of faith—its theological claims—to its civil consequences. Recent controversies in France over religious garb and symbols in public schools reveal the continuing compatibility between the civic republican tradition and the consignment of religion to civil status.

Second, and conversely, religious authority may coincide with, or comprehensively dominate, political authority, yielding some version

From *Philosophy & Public Policy* Quarterly, V. 25, No. 3, Summer, 2005 by William G. Galston. Copyright © 2005 by The Institute for Philosophy & Public Policy. Reprinted by permission.

of theocracy. This stance invariably represents the dominance of particular faith at the expense of all others.

Third, political and religious authority may coexist without either enjoying a comprehensive dominance. One version of this position seeks to divide social life into different spheres, dominated by either politics or faith. (Maxims such as "Render unto Caesar what is Caesar's . . ." provide the basis for such an understanding.) It is hard to come by such neat surgical divisions, however. More typically, the coexistence model implies overlapping and conflicting claims, generating the need for both theoretical clarification and legal adjudication.

Few individual believers or faith communities can be satisfied with the civic republican approach, which embodies an ordering of values antithetical to most religious commitments. As the history of European nations such as France and Italy with deep civic republican traditions shows, the effort to demote religion to purely civil status is bound to spark political conflict and, on occasion, actual violence.

The theocratic option fares no better. Whatever may be the case for homogeneous communities espousing a single faith (few of any size do so), the theocratic impulse creates grave difficulties for societies with multiple faith communities. In circumstances of diversity, a serious religious establishment (as distinguished from, say, the increasingly symbolic role of the Church of England) will inevitably use legal coercion to impose its views on faith communities that conscientiously reject them. Here again, political conflict will tend to spill over into episodes of violent resistance.

That leaves the coexistence model, a mode of pluralism that implies horizontal rather than hierarchical relations, not only between political and religious authority claims, but also among faith communities. By definition, this option is bound to leave both theocrats and

civic totalists dissatisfied, but it holds out the hope of reducing coercion to a manageable minimum. The problem of religiously related violence can be addressed best, not through secularism, but rather through institutionalized pluralism.

Compared to the sixteenth and seventeenth centuries, the level of religious violence originating in the West is low. It is natural for those who applaud this change to wonder how it happened, and whether it can serve as a template for reform in regions where religiously inspired violence remains high. And it is reasonable to conjecture that ways of thinking now pervasive in the West helped shape that template.

One might speculate that there exists a relationship between the pluralist approach, the reduction of religious violence, and Enlightenment. For the purposes of this essay, I will presuppose what many deny—namely, that religion often serves as an independent source of conflict rather than as a rhetorical screen for violent antipathies spawned by oppression, deprivation, the memory of colonialism, or a deep sense of humiliation—not to mention very specific complaints. It is more gratifying and convenient for Americans to believe that we were attacked on September 11 because our adversaries "have freedom" than because they oppose the presence of our troops in Saudi Arabia. At the least, we should remain aware of the possibility that our current concerns about religious terrorism reflect tensions considerably less exalted than faith-based disputes over the content of God's law.

One might speculate that there exists a relationship between the pluralist approach, the reduction of religious violence, and the Enlightenment.

It is a mistake, I believe, to think of the Enlightenment (even in Europe, leaving aside the encounters of Christianity, Judaism, and Islam with Greek philosophy) as a single, unified historical phenomenon. We may identify a *radical* Enlightenment, atheistic in theory and aggressively secularist in practice. The early days of the French Revolution revealed what the politics of radical Enlightenment actually meant, leading many who initially sympathized with the revolutionary impulse to recoil.

But there was also a moderate Enlightenment that wished to open a social space for free inquiry and religious diversity without denigrating or expunging specific faiths. The majority of the American founders fell in this category; those who did not (think of Thomas Paine) tended to stand out.

I would argue that the proponents of moderate Enlightenment were in fact pluralists, even though they did not use the term. For example, James Madison's depiction of right of religious conscience, which became canonical for American political thought and eventually American jurisprudence as well, rested explicitly on the coexistence of two different kinds of authority, neither of which straightforwardly trumps the other.

It is also a mistake to trace the reduction of religious violence in the West solely to the Enlightenment, however understood. Consider the theocratic argument, stripped to its essentials. IF (1) revealed religion X is true; and (2) to secure spiritual perfection or salvation, individuals and communities must live in accordance with that truth; and (3) law backed by coercive force is a permissible means of overcoming the inevitable resistance to living in that manner, THEN there is no objection in principle to establishing and enforcing religion X. But while a handful of daring Enlightenment thinkers such as Benedict Spinoza and Pierre Bayle were offering critiques of this argument's first two premises, the most effectual response focused on the third premise, for reasons that had little to do with the Enlightenment.

By 1640, a century of religious conflict had left Europe exhausted and disillusioned.

Ordinary people as well as distinguished thinkers were moving toward the conclusion that coercion in matters of religion was unacceptable, even in the name of saving souls. Their experience had led them to an historic judgment: violence in the name of religion was a greater problem than the political, moral, and spiritual ills it purported to cure. Modern scholars as diverse as political theorists Judith Shklar and Leo Strauss have documented how European attitudes shifted against what Machiavelli was the first to call "pious cruelty."

This judgment sparked the development of new conceptions of religious toleration. Some argued that coercion in matters of faith was a contradiction in terms and therefore bound to fail. Others contended that Christianity, rightly understood, precluded such coercion. A few brave souls even speculated that precisely because it is given to mortals to see the divine only through a glass, darkly, there was more than one path to God and that religious controversies over which so much blood had been spilled should be regarded as matters of "indifference."

We should remain aware of the possibility that our current concerns about religious terrorism reflect tensions considerably less exalted than faith-based disputes over the content of God's law.

This thesis could, and did, verge on an approach to religion that reflected more directly the influence of the Enlightenment—the idea of "natural theology," or (in the title of Kant's notable contribution to the genre) religion within the limits of reason alone. But while this approach might vindicate the god and cosmos of the philosophers, it was bound to leave out most of what bound the pious to their particular faiths. Worse, it denied, tacitly if not explicitly, the core claim of most actual religions—that miraculous events of revelation or incarnation had pierced the barrier between God and man, making known truths beyond the bounds of reason. Even Kant felt impelled to remark that his famous critique of pure reason had limited reason's reach in order to make room for faith. It seems safest to say that while philosophy can try to understand the conflict between faith and reason, it cannot surmount or abolish that conflict. Because there is no final solution, any viable political response must somehow embody this tension without overcoming it. This is what liberal constitutionalism at its pluralist best is able to achieve.

"RELIGION" AND "VIOLENCE": SOME DISTINCTIONS

Up to now, I have conjured with "religion" and "violence" as undifferentiated concepts. At this stage of my argument, I need to offer some distinctions.

Religion

For my purposes, I want to propose three dimensions of variation among religions. (1) Religions differ in their basic structure. Some focus on inward states, while others give greater emphasis to external behavior, in the form of worship rituals as well as laws governing daily life. (2) Religions differ in the share of human existence over which they claim primary jurisdiction. Some view their domain as partial (Render unto Caesar what is Caesar's . . .), while others make totalizing claims to direct every aspect of life. (3) Some religions make universalistic claims, to be the one true faith for all human beings whoever and wherever they might be, while others are more particularistic.

My suggestion is that each of these dimensions bears on the ability of a specific religion to live with moral and religious plurality. In the first place, acceptance of pluralism comes more easily to religions that emphasize inner conviction, because they need ask little of politics beyond being left alone. By contrast, religions

that take the form of law, as do traditional forms of Judaism and Islam, are forced to take seriously the content of public law. The terms of engagement between religious law and public law then become critical.

Second, religions that view their domain of jurisdiction as restricted are likely to coexist more comfortably with pluralism than are those with unlimited claims. Practitioners of a religion in which everything matters, from the consumption of food to the organization of politics, will feel compelled to use public power to mandate, or at least protect, their preferred practices. And this is bound to repress free expression and free exercise for other believers, not to mention nonbelievers, within that political community.

The difficulties for plurality engendered by comprehensive faith claims are deepened whenever a religion propounds the seamless unity of all existence. According to a leading traditionalist scholar of Islam, Seyyed Hossein Nasr, Islam rejects the distinction (characteristic of Christianity) between the religious and the secular, or the sacred and the profane: "In the unitary perspective of Islam, all aspects of life...are governed by a single principle." From this standpoint, the idea of a secular realm of freedom and plurality, independent of religion, is a leading modern example of the "mortal threat of 'polytheism'" against which Islam has struggled since its inception.

Finally, universalistic religions are likely to have a less accommodating stance toward plurality, wherever it may appear. At the very least, they will proselytize, raising the hackles of religious communities subjected to their messengers. And if they view the use of more forceful modes of conversion as limited only by prudential considerations rather than moral norms, then universalistic claims can be (and during the past two millennia, have been) translated into outright coercion.

My hypothesis is this: the more a religion expresses itself in external law, the more extensive its scope, and the more universalistic its claims, the less accommodating will be its stance toward plurality, and the more likely it will be to resort to violence to overcome or eliminate plurality. Thus, the universalism of many Protestant denominations is counterbalanced by their inward focus, and in some cases by more than prudential restraints on religious coercion as well. While classical rabbinic Judaism emphasizes external observance (and must therefore engage with public law), its claims are particularistic and (as we shall see) partial as well. Of all the "Abrahamic" faiths, my hypothesis suggests that Catholicism and Islam should have had a much harder time accepting plurality and eschewing violence; Islam the hardest of all, in that it holds *Shari'ah* to express the direct, unalterable will of God to a greater extent than does civil or canon law for Catholics.

The more a religion expresses itself in external law, the more extensive its scope, and the more universalistic its claims, the less accommodating will be its stance toward plurality, and the more likely it will be to resort to violence to overcome or eliminate plurality.

Violence

The distinctions between restricted and unlimited domains, and between particularist and universalistic faiths, allow us to distinguish between religious violence that is essentially *defensive* in nature and violence that is *offensive*.

Particularist faith with limited domains are content to withdraw from the arena of power, or to participate in it on equal terms with others, so long as they are free to practice their faith. They may not accept other faiths as equal to their own. They may not accept other faiths as equal to their own. They may deplore the copresence of "foreign" or "strange" gods within their political community. But they are prepared to accept competing practices, out of necessity, as the price for being left alone. They will resort to violence only to defend themselves against other religious communities or public power seeking to restrict the free exercise of their faith.

Offensive religions, by contrast, seek and use power to impose their way on others. Four characteristics render them especially dangerous: their outlook is intolerant; their stance, uncompromising; their aspirations, totalist; their tactics, coercive when necessary. These are the faiths that pluralist societies and those seeking to build such societies have good reason to fear.

There is another distinction that I introduce more tentatively. Some religious violence is *instrumental*—that is, consciously and deliberately chosen as the most effective way of advancing the one true faith. By contrast, another kind of religious violence is *instinctive*, when believers spontaneously lash out at practices they experience as degraded or disgusting.

My speculation is that it is easier to deter instrumental violence (through incentives and disincentives that rational actors must consider) than to restrain instinctive violence. Religions that experience diverse practices—for example, in gender relations—as impure and defiling are especially likely to be violence-prone. Consider the case of Sayyid Qutb, arguably the father of modern Islamist fundamentalism. As a graduate student at the University of Northern Colorado, he was revolted by what he felt to be the licentiousness of relations between young American men and women—a wanton intermingling (while dancing, for example) rather than the strict division ordained by God. Describing his US experiences years later, his prose remains suffused with disgust. Radically divergent visions of gender relations may be close to the heart of the conflict between traditionalist Islam and social forces (within as well as outside the Islamic world) that have been influenced by Western modernity.

Those who believe that there are many paths to God, or that it is not given to finite humans to know which is the right path to the Infinite God, will find it relatively easy to embrace religious pluralism.

PLURALISM AND RELIGIOUS VIOLENCE IN TRADITIONALIST ISLAM

At the outset of this essay, I suggested that more than ideas (let alone something as diffuse as the Enlightenment) it is concrete historical experiences that prepare the ground for religious pluralism and tolerance. In this concluding section of my essay, I offer the case of traditionalist Islam to illustrate this thesis.

Those who believe that there are many paths to God, or that it is not given to finite humans to know which is the right path to the Infinite God, will find it relatively easy to embrace religious pluralism. Islamic traditionalists cannot accept either of these beliefs. They may, however, believe that other faiths are on the same (right) path although they cannot reach the end—the one true faith. They may also believe that it is wrong to use coercion as an instrument of religious conversion.

Each of these beliefs finds textual support as well as opposition within Islam. For example, in the Koran we find the following: "Verily, those who believe and those who are Jews and Christians and Sabians, whoever believes in Allah and the Last day and do righteous good deeds shall have their reward with their Lord; on them shall be no fear, nor shall they grieve." And even more famously, the Koran declares that "There can be no compulsion in religion." In a recent article, Reza Aslan argues that

Islam is and always has been a religion of diversity. The [Wahhabist] notion that there

was once an original, unadulterated Islam that was shattered into heretical sects and schisms is a historical fiction. Both Shiism and Sufism in all their wonderful manifestations represent trends of thought that have existed from the very beginning of Islam, and both find their inspiration in the words and deeds of the Prophet. God may be One, but Islam most definitely is not.

Much depends on the ability of the proponents of a genuinely Islamic pluralism to broaden public support for a generous and accommodating interpretation of their shared tradition.

This will not be easy, in part because there are important historical differences between Judaism and Islam that make traditionalist Muslims more receptive to theocratic claims than are most traditionalist Jews. Throughout the medieval and early modern periods, Jewish populations sought to maximize communal autonomy and to minimize conflict between the law of secular authorities and the commandments of the Torah. Efforts to enforce the fundamentals of the religion were invariably *defensive*, never offensive. And when, after World War II, Israel was established, it was barely thinkable that the religious law developed over centuries of political marginality in the diaspora could serve as civil legislation for the new state. For the most part, Orthodox communities and political parties in Israel ranked other goals ahead of the aspiration to rest civil legislation on Torah law, in part because applying it to political power wielded by a Jewish majority might well require sweeping revisions in the content of that law.

Much depends on the ability of the proponents of a genuinely Islamic pluralism to broaden public support for a generous and accommodating interpretation of their shared tradition.

In contrast to Talmudic law, *Shari'ah* (Muslim religious law founded on the Koran and the conduct and statements of the Prophet) developed in an extended period during which

Muslims wielded political power, often over populations that were overwhelmingly Muslim. The structure of that law thus reflects the expectation that it would have political as well as communal authority. The idea of a secular state in which *Shari'ah* is both distinct from and subordinate to political authority stands in uneasy relation to this ideal, and many Muslims experience that idea as an alien (Western) imposition.

For example, in 1959, Iraq's new revolutionary ruler, General Abd al-Karim Qasim, promulgated a Code of Personal Status that contradicted *Shari'ah* in areas such as polygamy and inheritance. Clerical resistance to the Code helped undermine General Qasim's regime, and the repeal of the Code was among the first acts of the new government that took power in 1963 following a successful coup. (After taking power, Saddam Hussein instated a code that contradicted *Shari'ah* and permitted a substantial degree of gender equality.)

In the wake of the recent Iraqi elections, the new Shia majority is pushing for the restoration of *Shari'ah*-based codes, especially in the area of family law. "Our position on the family status law is non-negotiable. It will be based on *Shari'ah*," said Sheikh Kashef al Gatta, an influential Shiite politician who is expected to play a central role in drafting a new permanent constitution for Iraq. If this happens, traditionalist religious courts will make most decisions concerning marriage, divorce, inheritance, child custody, and the status of women. In this event, US policy makers would be faced with an unpalatable choice between honoring the results of a democratic election and defending what most Americans regard as basic human rights. Said one US official when asked about the possible majoritarian imposition of *Shari'ah*, "There is a vision of where we want Iraq to be that would make sense in terms of the resources we've put into this place and our overarching goal for democracy." The official's

clear implication was that a coercive, theocratic family code would fail that test.

It would be too hasty to conclude, however, that Islamic traditionalism must entail some form of theocracy or always take a violent and intolerant form. One might well imagine an Islamic version of the Netherlands, a state in which a number of different faiths enjoy public funding and public standing, especially in the arena of education. Another possibility is a new version of the multi-confessional structure of the Ottoman Empire (reproduced to some degree in Israel), in which a dominant religious group shares civic space with other faiths that enjoy substantial autonomy and authority, especially over family law.

In short, there is no reason in principle why a moderate official "establishment" of Islam need eventuate in religious persecution and repression. As Noah Feldman, author of *After Jihad: America and the Struggle for Islamic Democracy*, has written:

If many in the West cannot imagine democracy without separation of church and state, many in the Muslim world find it impossible to imagine legitimate democracy with it. Fortunately, democracy does not require an absolute divide between religion and political authority. Liberty of conscience is an indispensable requirement of free government—but an established religion that does not coerce religious belief and that treats religious minorities as equals may be perfectly compatible with democracy.

Feldman is right, at least in principle. The most effectual cure for religious violence within Islam (or any other faith tradition, for that matter) is not grafting on some external concept of enlightenment, but rather mobilizing the resources within the faith that can open up social space for religious pluralism. But as the experience of early modern Europe shows, it can take a very long time indeed before the combatants conclude that the costs of religious violence exceed its benefits. In the process, instability reigns, and blood spills in profusion. It is not yet clear that the brave proponents of pluralism within Islam are speaking for anyone except themselves.

William A. Galston

Sources: Seyyed Hossein Nasr, *Islamic Life and Thought* (Chicago: ABC International Group, 2001). Reza Aslan, "From Islam Pluralist Democracies Will Surely Grow," *Chronicle of Higher Education* (March 11, 2005). For the quote of the US official asked about the possible majoritarian imposition of *Shari'ah*, see Farnaz Fassihi, "Iraqi Shiite Women Push Islamic Law on Gender Roles," *Wall Street Journal* (March 9, 2005).

Feminism and Democracy

Carole Pateman

A feminist might dispose briskly of the subject of this essay. For feminists, democracy has never existed; women have never been and still are not admitted as full and equal members and citizens in any country known as a 'democracy'. A telling image that recurs throughout the history of feminism is of liberal society as a series of male clubs—usually, as Virginia Woolf points out in *Three Guineas*, distinguished by their own costumes and uniforms—that embrace parliament, the courts, political parties, the military and police, universities, workplaces, trade unions, public (private) schools, exclusive Clubs and popular leisure clubs, from all of which women are excluded or to which they are mere auxiliaries. Feminists will find confirmation of their view in academic discussions of democracy which usually take it for granted that feminism or the structure of the relationship between the sexes are irrelevant matters. The present volume at least acknowledges that feminism might have something significant to say to democratic theorists or citizens, albeit in a token paper by a token woman writer. In the scope of a short essay it is hardly possible to demolish the assumption of two thousand years that there is no incompatibility between 'democracy' and the subjection of women or their exclusion from full and equal participation in political life. Instead, I shall indicate why feminism provides democracy—whether in its existing liberal guise or in the form of a possible future participatory or self-managing democracy—with its most important challenge and most comprehensive critique.

The objection that will be brought against the feminists is that after a century or more of legal reforms and the introduction of universal suffrage women are now the civil and political equals of men, so that feminism today has little or nothing to contribute to democratic theory and practice. This objection ignores much that is crucial to an understanding of the real character of liberal democratic societies. It ignores the existence of wide-spread and deeply held convictions, and of social practices that give them expression, that contradict the (more or less) formally equal civic status of women. The objection is based on the liberal argument that social inequalities are irrelevant to political equality. Thus, it has to ignore the problems that have arisen from the attempt to universalize liberal principles by extending them to women while at the same time maintaining the division between private and political life which is central to liberal democracy, and is also a division between women and men. If liberal theorists of democracy are content to avoid these questions, their radical critics, along with advocates of participatory democracy, might have been expected to confront them enthusiastically. However, although they have paid a good deal of attention to the class structure of liberal democracies and the way in which class inequality undercuts formal political equality, they have rarely examined the significance of sexual inequality and the patriarchal order of the liberal state for a democratic transformation of liberalism. Writers on democracy, whether defenders or critics of the status quo, invariably fail to consider, for example, whether their discussions of freedom or consent have any relevance to women. They implicitly argue as if 'individuals' and 'citizens' are men.

It is frequently overlooked how recently democratic or universal suffrage was established. Political scientists have remained remarkably silent about the struggle for womanhood suffrage (in England there was a continuous organized campaign for 48 years from 1866 to 1914) and the political meaning and consequence of enfranchisement. Women's position as voters also appears to cause some difficulty for writers on democracy. Little comment is excited, for example, by Schumpeter's explicit statement, in his extremely influential revisionist text, that the exclusion of women from the franchise does not invalidate a polity's claim to be a 'democracy'. In Barber's fascinating account of direct democracy in a Swiss canton, womanhood suffrage (gained only in 1971) is treated very equivocally. Barber emphasizes that women's enfranchisement was 'just and equitable'—but the cost was 'participation and community'. Assemblies grew unwieldy and participation diminished, atomistic

individualism gained official recognition and the ideal of the citizen-soldier could no longer be justified. The reader is left wondering whether women should not have sacrificed their just demand for the sake of men's citizenship. Again, in Verba, Nie and Kim's recent cross-national study of political participation it is noted, in a discussion of the change in Holland from compulsory to voluntary voting, that 'voting, rights were universal'. The footnote, on the same page, says that in both electoral systems there was 'a one man one vote system'. Did women vote? Unrecognized historical ironies abound in discussions of democracy. Feminists are frequently told today that we must not be offended by masculine language because 'man' really means 'human being', although when, in 1867 in support of the first women's suffrage bill in Britain, it was argued that 'man' (referring to the householder) was a generic term that included women the argument was firmly rejected. Another recent example of the way in which women can be written out of democratic political life can be found in Margolis' *Viable Democracy*. He begins by presenting a history of 'Citizen Brown', who is a man and who, we learn, in 1920 obtained 'his latest major triumph, the enfranchisement of women'. Thus the history of women's democratic struggles disappears and democratic voting appears as the sole creation—or gift—of men.

Such examples might be amusing if they were not symptomatic of the past and present social standing of women. Feminism, liberalism and democracy (that is, a political order in which citizenship is universal, the right of each adult individual member of the community) share a common origin. Feminism, a general critique of social relationships of sexual domination and subordination and a vision of a sexually egalitarian future, like liberalism and democracy, emerges only when individualism, or the idea that individuals are by nature free and equal to each other, has developed as a universal theory of social organization. However, from the time, three hundred years ago, when the individualist social contract theorists launched the first critical attack on patriarchalism the prevailing approach to the position of women can be exemplified by the words of Fichte who asks:

> Has woman the same rights in the state which man has? This question may appear ridiculous to many. For if the only ground of all legal rights is reason and freedom, how can a distinction exist between two sexes which possess both the same reason and the same freedom?

He replies to this question as follows:

> Nevertheless, it seems that, so long as men have lived, this has been differently held, and the female sex seems not to have been placed on a par with the male sex in the exercise of its rights. *Such a universal sentiment must have a ground, to discover which was never a more urgent problem than in our days.*

The anti-feminists and anti-democrats have never found this 'urgent problem' difficult to solve. Differential rights and status have been and are defended by appeal to the 'natural' differences between the sexes, from which it is held to follow that women are subordinate to their fathers or husbands and that their proper place is in domestic life. The argument from nature stretches back into mythology and ancient times (and today often comes dressed up in the scientific garb of sociobiology) and its longevity appears to confirm that it informs us of an eternal and essential part of the human condition. But, far from being timeless, the argument has specific formulations in different historical epochs and, in the context of the development of liberal-capitalist

society, it appears in a form which obscures the patriarchal structure of liberalism beneath the ideology of individual freedom and equality.

It is usually assumed that the social contract theorists, and Locke in particular, provided the definitive counter to the patriarchal thesis that paternal and political power are one and the same, grounded in the natural subjection of sons to fathers. Locke certainly drew a sharp distinction between natural or familial ties and the conventional relations of political life, but although he argued that sons, when adult, were as free as their fathers and equal to them, and hence could only justifiably be governed with their own consent, it is usually 'forgotten' that he excluded women (wives) from this argument. His criticism of the patriarchalists depends upon the assumption of natural individual freedom and equality, but only men count as 'individuals'. Women are held to be born to subjection. Locke takes it for granted that a woman will, through the marriage contract, always agree to place herself in subordination to her husband. He agrees with the patriarchalists that wifely subjection has 'a Foundation in Nature' and argues that in the family the husband's will, as that of the 'abler and the stronger', must always prevail over 'that of his wife in all things of their common Concernment'. The contradiction between the premise of individual freedom and equality, with its corollary of the conventional basis of authority, and the assumption that women (wives) are naturally subject has since gone unnoticed. Similarly, there has been no acknowledgement of the problem that if women are naturally subordinate, or born into subjection, then talk of their consent or agreement to this status is redundant. Yet this contradiction and paradox lie at the heart of democratic theory and practice. The continuing silence about the status of wives is testament to the strength of the union of a transformed patriarchalism with liberalism. For the first time in history, liberal individualism promised women an equal social standing with men as naturally free individuals, but at the same time socio-economic developments ensured that the subordination of wives to husbands continued to be seen as natural, and so outside the domain of democratic theorists or the political struggle to democratize liberalism.

The conviction that a married woman's proper place is in the conjugal home as a servant to her husband and mother to her children is now so widespread and well established that this arrangement appears as a natural feature of human existence rather than historically and culturally specific. The history of the development of the capitalist organization of production is also the history of the development of a particular form of the sexual division of labour (although this is not the history to be found in most books). At the time when the social contract theorists attacked the patriarchal thesis of a natural hierarchy of inequality and subordination, wives were not their husband's equals, but nor were they their economic dependants. Wives, as associates and partners in economic production, had an independent status. As production moved out of the household, women were forced out of the trades they controlled and wives became dependent on their husbands for subsistence or competed for individual wages in certain areas of production. Many working-class wives and mothers have had to continue to try to find paid employment to ensure the survival of their families, but by the mid-nineteenth century the ideal, the natural and respectable, mode of life had come to be seen as that of the middle-class, breadwinning paterfamilias and his totally dependent wife. By then the subjection of wives was complete; with no independent legal or civil standing they had been reduced to the status of property, as the nineteenth-century feminists emphasized in their comparisons

of wives to the slaves of the West Indies and American South. Today, women have won an independent civil status and the vote; they are, apparently, 'individuals' as well as citizens— and thus require no special attention in discussions of democracy. However, one of the most important consequences of the institutionalization of liberal individualism and the establishment of universal suffrage has been to highlight the practical contradiction between the formal political equality of liberal democracy and the social subordination of women, including their subjection as wives within the patriarchal structure of the institution of marriage.

It is indicative of the attitude of democratic theorists (and political activists) towards feminism that John Stuart Mill's criticism of the argument from (women's) nature, and the lessons to be learned from it, are so little known. The present revival of the organized feminist movement has begun to rescue *The Subjection of Women* from the obscurity into which Mill's commentators have pushed it, although it provides a logical extension of the arguments of his academically acceptable *On Liberty*. The *Subjection* is important for its substantive argument, but also because the ultimately contradictory position that Mill takes in the essay illustrates just how radical feminist criticism is, and how the attempt to universalize liberal principles to both sexes pushes beyond the confines of liberal democratic theory and practice.

In *The Subjection* Mill argues that the relation between women and men, or, more specifically, between wives and husbands, forms an unjustified exception to the liberal principles of individual rights, freedom and choice, to the principles of equality of opportunity and the allocation of occupational positions by merit that, he believes, now govern other social and political institutions. In the modern world, consent has supplanted force and the principle of achievement has replaced that of ascription—except where women are concerned. Mill writes that the conjugal relation is an example of 'the primitive state of slavery lasting on, . . . It has not lost the taint of its brutal origin' (p. 130). More generally, the social subordination of women is 'a single relic of an old world of thought and practice, exploded in everything else' (p. 146). Mill opens the *Subjection* with some pertinent comments on the difficulty feminists face in presenting an intellectually convincing case. Domination by men is rooted in long-standing customs, and the idea that male supremacy is the proper order of things derives from deep feelings and sentiments rather than rationally tested beliefs (and, it might be added, men have a lot to lose by being convinced). Thus feminists must not expect their opponents to 'give up practical principles in which they have been born and bred and which are the basis of much of the existing order of the world, at the first argumentative attack which they are not capable of logically resisting' (p. 128). Mill is very conscious of the importance of the appeal to nature. He notes that it provides no criterion to differentiate the subordination of women from other forms of domination because all rulers have attempted to claim a grounding in nature for their position. He also argues that nothing at all can be said about the respective natures of women and men because we have only seen the sexes in an unequal relationship. Any differences in their moral and other capacities will become known when men and women can interact as independent and equal rational beings.

However, despite Mill's vigorous attack on the appeal to custom and nature he ultimately falls back on the very argument that he has carefully criticized. His failure consistently to apply his principles to domestic life has been noted by recent feminist critics, but it is less often pointed out that his inconsistency undermines his defence of womanhood suffrage

and equal democratic citizenship. The central argument of *The Subjection* is that husbands must be stripped of their legally-sanctioned despotic powers over their wives. Most of the legal reforms of the marriage law that Mill advocated have now been enacted (with the significant exception of marital rape, to which I shall return), and the implications of his unwillingness to extend his criticism to the sexual division of labour within the home are now fully revealed. Mill argues that because of their upbringing, lack of education and legal and social pressures, women do not have a free choice whether or not to marry: 'wife' is the only occupation open to them. But although he also argues that women must have equal opportunity with men to obtain a proper education that will enable them to support themselves, he assumes that, if marriage were reformed, most women would *not* choose independence.

Mill states that it is generally understood that when a woman marries she has chosen her career, like a man when he chooses a profession. When a woman becomes a wife, 'she makes choice of the management of a household, and the bringing up of a family, as the first call on her exertions, . . . she renounces, . . . all [occupations] not consistent with the requirement of this' (p. 179). Mill is reverting here to ascriptive arguments and the belief in women's natural place and occupation. He is falling back on the ancient tradition of patriarchal political theory that, as Susan Okin has shown in *Women in Western Political Thought* (Princeton, 1979), asserts that whereas men are, or can be, many things, women are placed on earth to fulfil one function only; to bear and rear children. Mill neatly evades the question of how, if women's task is prescribed by their sex, they can be said to have a real choice of occupation, or why equal opportunity is relevant to women if marriage itself is a 'career'. Mill compares an egalitarian marriage to a business partnership in which the partners are free to negotiate their own terms of association, but he relies on some very weak arguments, which run counter to liberal principles, to support his view that equality will not disturb the conventional domestic division of labour. He suggests that the 'natural arrangement' would be for wife and husband each to be 'absolute in the executive branch of their own department . . . any change of system and principle requiring the consent of both' (p. 169). He also suggests that the division of labour between the spouses could be agreed in the marriage contract—but he assumes that wives will be willing to accept the 'natural' arrangement. Mill notes that duties are already divided 'by consent . . . and general custom' (p.170) modified in individual cases; but it is exactly 'general custom', as the bulwark of male domination, that he is arguing against in the body of the essay. He forgets this when he suggests that the husband will generally have the greater voice in decisions as he is usually older. Mill adds that this is only until the time of life when age is irrelevant; but when do husbands admit that this has arrived? He also forgets his own arguments when he suggests that more weight will be given to the views of the partner who brings the means of support, disingenuously adding 'whichever this is' when he has already assumed that wives will 'choose' to be dependent by agreeing to marry.

Anti-feminist movements and propagandist in the 1980s also claim that the domestic division of labour supported by Mill is the only natural one. They would not be disturbed by the implications of this arrangement for the citizenship of women but advocates of democracy should be. Mill championed womanhood suffrage for the same reasons that he supported votes for men; because it was necessary for self-protection or the protection of individual interests and because political participation would enlarge the capacities of individual women.

The obvious problem with his argument is that women as wives will largely be confined to the small circle of the family and its daily routines and so will find it difficult to use their vote effectively as a protective measure. Women will not be able to learn what their interest are without experience outside domestic life. This point is even more crucial for Mill's arguments about political development and education through participation. He writes (p. 237) in general terms of the elevation of the individual 'as a moral, spiritual and social being' that occurs under free government, but this is a large claim to make for the periodic casting of a vote (although the moral transformation of political life through enfranchisement was a central theme of the womanhood suffrage movement). Nor did Mill himself entirely believe that this 'elevation' would result from the suffrage alone. He writes that 'citizenship', and here I take him to be referring to universal suffrage, 'fills only a small place in modern life, and does not come near the daily habits or inmost sentiments' (p. 174). He goes on to argue that the family, 'justly constituted', would be the 'real school of the virtues of freedom'. However, this is as implausible as the claim about the consequences of liberal democratic voting. A patriarchal family with the despotic husband at its head is no basis for democratic citizenship; but nor, *on its own*, is an egalitarian family. Mill argues in his social and political writings that only participation in a wide variety of institutions, especially the workplace, can provide the political education necessary for active, democratic citizenship. Yet how can wives and mothers, who have 'chosen' domestic life, have the opportunity to develop their capacities or learn what it means to be a democratic citizen? Women will therefore exemplify the selfish, private beings, lacking a sense of justice or public spirit, that result when an individual is confined to the narrow sphere of everyday family life. Mill's failure to question the apparently natural division of labour within the home means that his arguments for democratic citizenship apply only to men.

It might be objected that it is unreasonable and anachronistic to ask of Mill, writing in the 1860s, that he criticize the accepted division of labour between husband and wife when only very exceptional feminists in the nineteenth century were willing to question the doctrine of the separate spheres of the sexes. But if that objection is granted, it does not excuse the same critical failure by contemporary democratic theorists and empirical investigators. Until the feminist movement began, very recently, to have an impact on academic studies not only has the relation between the structure of the institution of marriage and the formal equality of citizenship been ignored, but women citizens have often been excluded from empirical investigations of political behaviour and attitudes or merely referred to briefly in patriarchal not scientific terms. A reading of *The Subjection* should long ago have placed these matters in the forefront of discussions of democracy. Perhaps the appearance of empirical findings showing, for example, that even women active in local politics are inhibited from running for office because of their responsibility for childcare and a belief that office-holding is not a proper activity for women, will be taken more seriously than the feminist writings of even eminent philosophers.

The problems surrounding women's citizenship in the liberal democracies may have been sadly neglected, but the failure of democratic theorists to confront the woman and wife question runs much deeper still. Democratic citizenship, even if interpreted in the minimal sense of universal suffrage in the context of liberal civil rights, presupposes the solid foundation of a practical, universal recognition that all members of the polity are social equals and independent 'individuals', having all the capacities implied by this status. The most serious failure of contemporary democratic theory and its language of freedom, equality, consent, and of the individual, is that women are so easily and inconspicuously excluded from references to the 'individual'. Thus the question never arises whether the exclusion reflects social and political realities. One reason why there is no consciousness of the need to ask this question is that democratic theorists conventionally see their subject-matter as encompassing the political or public sphere, which for radical theorists includes the economy and the workplace. The sphere of personal and domestic life—the sphere that is the 'natural' realm of women—is excluded from scrutiny. Despite the central role that consent plays in their arguments democratic theorists pay no attention to the structure of sexual relations between men and women and, more specifically, to the practice of rape and the interpretation of consent and non-consent which define it as a criminal offence. The facts about rape are central to the social realities which are reflected in and partly constituted by our use of the term 'individual'.

Among Mill's criticism of the despotic powers of nineteenth-century husbands is a harsh reminder that a husband had the legal right to rape his wife. Over a century later a husband still has that right in most legal jurisdictions. Locke excludes women from the status of 'free and equal individual' by his agreement with the patriarchal claim that wives were subject to their husbands by nature; the content of the marriage contract confirms that, today, this assumption still lies at the heart of the institution of marriage. The presumed consent of a woman, in a free marriage contract, to her subordinate status gives a voluntarist gloss to an essentially ascribed status of 'wife'. If the assumption of natural subjection did not still hold, liberal democratic theorists would long ago have begun to ask why it is that an ostensibly free and equal individual should *always* agree to enter a contract which subordinates her to another such individual. They would long ago have begun to question the character of an institution in which the initial agreement of a wife deprives her of the right to retract her consent to provide sexual services to her husband, and which gives him the legal right to force her to submit. If contemporary democratic theorists are to distance themselves from the patriarchal assumptions of their predecessors they must begin to ask whether a person can be, at one and the same time, a free democratic citizen and a wife who gives up a vital aspect of her freedom and individuality, the freedom to refuse consent and say 'no' to the violation of the integrity of her person.

A woman's right of refusal of consent is also a matter of more general importance. Outside of marriage rape is a serious criminal offence, yet the evidence indicates that the majority of offenders are not prosecuted. Women have exemplified the beings whom political theorists have regarded as lacking the capacities to attain the status of individual and citizen or to participate in the practice of consent, but women have, simultaneously, been perceived as beings who, in their personal lives, always consent, and whose explicit refusal of consent can be disregarded and reinterpreted as agreement. This contradictory perception of women is a major reason why it is so difficult for a woman who has been raped to secure the conviction of her attacker(s). Public opinion, the police and the courts are willing to identify enforced submission with consent, and the reason why this identification is possible is that it is widely believed that if a woman says 'no' her words have no meaning, since she 'really' means 'yes'. It is widely regarded as perfectly reasonable for a man to reinterpret explicit rejection of his advances as consent. Thus women find that their speech is persistently and systematically invalidated. Such invalidation would be incomprehensible if the two sexes actually shared the same status as 'individuals'. No person with a secure, recognized standing as an 'individual' could be seen as someone who consistently said the opposite of what they meant and who, therefore, could justifiably have their words reinterpreted by others. On the other hand, invalidation and reinterpretation are readily comprehensible parts of a relationship in which one person is seen as a natural subordinate and thus has an exceedingly ambiguous place in social practices (held to be) grounded in convention, in free agreement and consent.

Political theorists who take seriously the question of the conceptual foundations and social conditions of democracy can no longer avoid the feminist critique of marriage and personal life. The critique raises some awkward and often embarrassing questions, but questions that have to be faced if 'democracy' is to be more than a men's club writ large and the patriarchal structure of the liberal democratic state is to be challenged. The assumptions and practices which govern the everyday, personal lives of women and men, including their sexual lives, can no longer be treated as matters remote from political life and the concerns of democratic theorists. Women's status as 'individuals' pervades the whole of their social life, personal and political. The structure of everyday life, including marriage, is constituted by beliefs and practices which presuppose that women are naturally subject to men—yet writers on democracy continue to assert that women and men can and will freely interact as equals in their capacity as enfranchised democratic citizens.

The preceding argument and criticism is relevant to discussions of both liberal democracy and participatory democracy, but particularly to the latter. Liberal theorists continue to claim that the structure of social relations and social inequality is irrelevant to political equality and democratic citizenship, so they are no more likely to be impressed by feminists than by any other radical critics. Advocates of participatory democracy have been reluctant to take feminist arguments into account even though these arguments are, seen in one light, an extension of the participatory democratic claim that 'democracy' extends beyond the state to the organization of society. The resistance to feminism is particularly ironical because the contemporary feminist movement has, under a variety of labels attempted to put participatory democratic organization into practice. The movement is decentralized, anti-hierarchical and tries to ensure that its members collectively educate themselves and gain independence through consciousness-raising, participatory decision-making and rotation of tasks and offices.

Feminists deny the liberal claim that private and public life can be understood in isolation from each other. One reason for the neglect of J.S. Mill's feminist essay is that his extension of liberal principles to the institution of marriage breaches the central liberal separation, established by Locke, between paternal and political rule; or between the impersonal, conventional public sphere and the family, the sphere of natural affection and natural relations. Proponents of participatory democracy have, of course, been willing to challenge commonplace conceptions of the public and the private in their discussions of the workplace, but this challenge ignores the insights of feminism. It is rarely appreciated that the feminists and participatory democrats see the division between public and private very differently. From the feminist perspective participatory democratic arguments remain within the patriarchal-liberal separation of civil society and state; domestic life has an exceedingly ambiguous relation to this separation, which is a division within public life itself. In contrast, feminists see domestic life, the 'natural' sphere of women, as private, and thus as divided from a public realm encompassing both economic and political life, the 'natural' arenas of men.

By failing to take into account the feminist conception of 'private' life, by ignoring the family, participatory democratic arguments for the democratization of economic life have neglected a crucial dimension of democratic social transformation (and I include my *Participation and Democratic Theory* here). It is difficult to find any appreciation of the significance of the integral relation between the domestic division of labour and economic life, or the sexual division of labour in the workplace, let alone any mention of the implications of the deeper matters touched on in this essay, in writings on industrial democracy. It is the feminists, not the advocates of workplace democracy, who have investigated the very different position of women workers, especially married women workers, from that of male employees. Writers on democracy have yet to digest the now large body of feminist research on women and paid employment or to acknowledge that unless it is brought into the centre of reflection, debate and political action, women will remain as peripheral in a future participatory 'democracy' as they are at present in liberal democracies.

I have drawn attention to the problem posed by the assumption that women's natural place is a private one, as wife and mother in the home, for arguments about the educative and developmental consequences of political participation. It might be argued that this problem is much less pressing today than in Mill's time because many married women have now entered the public world of paid employment and so they, if not housewives, already have their horizons widened and will gain a political education if enterprises are democratized. In Australia, for example, in 1977 women formed 35% of the labour force and 63% of these women were married. The reality behind the statistics, however, is that women's status as workers is as uncertain and ambiguous as our status as citizens and both reflect the more fundamental problem of our status as 'individuals'. The conventional but implicit assumption is that 'work' is undertaken in a workplace, not within the 'private' home, and that a 'worker' is male—someone who has his need for a clean place of relaxation, clean clothes, food and care of his children provided for him by his wife. When a wife enters paid employment it is significant for her position as 'worker' that no one asks who performs these services for her. In fact, married women workers do two shifts, one in the office or factory, the other at home. A large question arises here why members of enterprises who are already burdened with two jobs should be eager to take on the new responsibilities, as well as exercise the opportunities, that democratization would bring.

The relative importance of the two components of the wife's double day, and so the evaluation of women's status as workers, is reflected, as Eisenstein notes, in the popular use of 'the term "working mother" which simultaneously asserts women's first responsibility to motherhood and her secondary status as worker'. Again, the question has to be asked how workers of secondary status could, without some very large changes being made, take their place as equal participants in a democratized workplace. The magnitude of the changes required can be indicated by brief reference to three features of women's (paid) worklife. The sexual harassment of women workers is still a largely unacknowledged practice but it reveals the extent to which the problem of sexual relations, consent and women's status as

'individuals' is also a problem of the economic sphere. Secondly, women still have to win the struggle against discrimination by employers and unions before they can participate as equals. Finally, it has to be recognized that the workplace is structured by a sexual division of labour which poses still further complex problems for equality and participation. Women are segregated into certain occupational categories ('women's work') and they are concentrated in non-supervisory and low-skilled and low-status jobs. It is precisely workers in such jobs that empirical research has shown to be the least likely to participate.

The example of the workplace, together with the other examples discussed in this essay, should be sufficient to show the fundamental importance to democratic theory and practice of the contemporary feminist insistence that personal and political life are integrally connected. Neither the equal opportunity of liberalism nor the active, participatory democratic citizenship of *all* the people can be achieved without radical changes in personal and domestic life. The struggles of the organized feminist movement of the last 150 years have achieved a great deal. An exceptional woman can now become Prime Minister—but that particular achievement leaves untouched the structure of social life of unexceptional women, of women as a social category. They remain in an uncertain position as individuals, workers and citizens, and popular opinion echoes Rousseau's pronouncement that 'nature herself has decreed that women, . . . should be at the mercy of man's judgement'. The creation of a free and egalitarian sexual and personal life is the most difficult to achieve of all the changes necessary to build a truly democratic society precisely because it is not something remote from everyday life that can be applauded in abstract slogans while life, and the subjection of women, goes on as usual. Democratic ideals and politics have to be put into practice in the kitchen, the nursery and the bedroom; they come home, as J.S. Mill wrote (p. 136) 'to the person and hearth of every male head of a family, and of everyone who looks forward to being so'. It is a natural biological fact of human existence that only women can bear children, but that fact gives no warrant whatsoever for the separation of social life into two sexually defined spheres of private (female) existence and (male) public activity. This separation is ultimately grounded in the mistaken extension of the argument from natural necessity to child-rearing. There is nothing in nature that prevents fathers from sharing equally in bringing up their children, although there is a great deal in the organization of social and economic life that works against it. Women cannot win an equal place in democratic productive life and citizenship if they are deemed destined for a one ascribed task, but nor can fathers take an equal share in reproductive activities without a transformation in our conception of 'work' and of the structure of economic life.

The battle joined three hundred years ago when the social contract theorists pitted conventionalist arguments against the patriarchalists' appeal to nature is far from concluded, and a proper, democratic understanding of the relation of nature and convention is still lacking. The successful conclusion of this long battle demands some radical reconceptualization to provide a comprehensive theory of a properly democratic practice. Recent feminist theoretical work offers new perspectives and insights into the problem of democratic theory and practice, including the question of individualism and participatory democracy, and an appropriate conception of 'political' life. It has been hard to imagine what a democratic form of social life might look like for much of the past century. Male-dominated political parties, sects and their theoreticians have attempted to bury the old 'utopian' political movements which are part of the history of the struggle for democracy and women's emancipation, and which argued for prefigurative forms of political organization and activity. The lesson to be learnt from the past is that a 'democratic' theory and practice that is not at the same time feminist merely serves to maintain a fundamental form of domination and so makes a mockery of the ideals and values that democracy is held to embody.

The Idea of Public Reason[1]

John Rawls

A political society, and indeed every reasonable and rational agent, whether it be an indi vidual, or a family or an association, or even a confederation of political societies, has a way of formulating its plans, of putting its ends in an order of priority and of making its decisions accordingly. The way a political society does this is its reason; its ability to do these things is also its reason, though in a different sense: it is an intellectual and moral power, rooted in the capacities of its human members.

Not all reasons are public reasons, as there are the nonpublic reasons of churches and universities and of many other associations in civil society. In aristocratic and autocratic regimes, when the good of society is considered, this is done not by the public, if it exists at all, but by the rulers, whoever they may be. Public reason is characteristic of a democratic people: it is the reason of its citizens, of those sharing the status of equal citizenship. The subject of their reason is the good of the public: what the political conception of justice requires of society's basic structure of institutions, and of the purposes and ends they are to serve. Public reason, then, is public in

three ways: as the reason of citizens as such, it is the reason of the public; its subject is the good of the public and matters of fundamental justice; and its nature and content is public, being given by the ideals and principles expressed by society's conception of political justice, and conducted open to view on that basis.

That public reason should be so understood and honored by citizens is not, of course, a matter of law. As an ideal conception of citizenship for a constitutional democratic regime, it presents how things might be, taking people as a just and well-ordered society would encourage them to be. It describes what is possible and can be, yet may never be, though no less fundamental for that.

§ 1. THE QUESTIONS AND FORUMS OF PUBLIC REASON

1. The idea of public reason has been often discussed and has a long history, and in some form it is widely accepted.[2] My aim here is to try to express it in an acceptable way as part of a political conception of justice that is broadly speaking liberal.[3]

To begin: in a democratic society public reason is the reason of equal citizens who, as a collective body, exercise final political and coercive power over one another in enacting laws and in amending their constitution. The first point is that the limits imposed by public reason do not apply to all political questions but only to those involving what we may call "constitutional essentials" and questions of basic justice. (These are specified in §5.) This means that political values alone are to settle such fundamental questions as: who has the right to vote, or what religions are to be tolerated, or who is to be assured fair equality of opportunity, or to hold property. These and similar questions are the special subject of public reason.

Many if not most political questions do not concern those fundamental matters, for example, much tax legislation and many laws regulating property; statutes protecting the environment and controlling pollution; establishing national parks and preserving wilderness areas and animal and plant species; and laying aside funds for museums and the arts. Of course, sometimes these do involve fundamental matters. A full account of public reason would take up these other questions and explain in more detail than I can here how they differ from constitutional essentials and questions of basic justice and why the restrictions imposed by public reason may not apply to them; or if they do, not in the same way, or so strictly.

Some will ask: why not say that all questions in regard to which citizens exercise their final and coercive political power over one another are subject to public reason? Why would it ever be admissible to go outside its range of political values? To answer: my aim is to consider first the strongest case where the political questions concern the most fundamental matters. If we should not honor the limits of public reason here, it would seem we need not honor them anywhere. Should they hold here, we can

then proceed to other cases. Still, I grant that it is usually highly desirable to settle political questions by invoking the values of public reason. Yet this may not always be so.

2. Another feature of public reason is that its limits do not apply to our personal deliberations and reflections about political questions, or to the reasoning about them by members of associations such as churches and universities, all of which is a vital part of the background culture. Plainly, religious, philosophical, and moral considerations of many kinds may here properly play a role. But the ideal of public reason does hold for citizens when they engage in political advocacy in the public forum, and thus for members of political parties and for candidates in their campaigns and for other groups who support them. It holds equally for how citizens are to vote in elections when constitutional essentials and matters of basic justice are at stake. Thus the ideal of public reason not only governs the public discourse of elections insofar as the issues involve those fundamental questions, but also how citizens are to cast their vote on these questions (§2.4). Otherwise, public discourse runs the risks of being hypocritical: citizens talk before one another one way and vote another.

We must distinguish, however, between how the ideal of public reason applies to citizens and how it applies to various officers of the government. It applies in official forums and so to legislators when they speak on the floor of parliament, and to the executive in its public acts and pronouncements. It applies also in a special way to the judiciary and above all to a supreme court in a constitutional democracy with judicial review. This is because the justices have to explain and justify their decisions as based on their understanding of the constitution and relevant statutes and precedents. Since acts of the legislative and the executive need not be justified in this way, the court's special role makes it the exemplar of public reason (§6).

§ 2. PUBLIC REASON AND THE IDEAL OF DEMOCRATIC CITIZENSHIP

1. I now turn to what to many is a basic difficulty with the idea of public reason, one that makes it seem paradoxical. They ask: why should citizens in discussing and voting on the most fundamental political questions honor the limits of public reason? How can it be either reasonable or rational, when basic matters are at stake, for citizens to appeal only to a public conception of justice and not to the whole truth as they see it? Surely, the most fundamental questions should be settled by appealing to the most important truths, yet these may far transcend public reason!

I begin by trying to dissolve this paradox and invoke a principle of liberal legitimacy as explained in IV:1.2–3. Recall that this principle is connected with two special features of the political relationship among democratic citizens:

First, it is a relationship of persons within the basic structure of the society into which they are born and in which they normally lead a complete life.

Second, in a democracy political power, which is always coercive power, is the power of the public, that is, of free and equal citizens as a collective body.

As always, we assume that the diversity of reasonable religious, philosophical, and moral doctrines found in democratic societies is a permanent feature of the public culture and not a mere historical condition soon to pass away.

Granted all this, we ask: when may citizens by their vote properly exercise their coercive political power over one another when fundamental questions are at stake? Or in the light of what principles and ideals must we exercise that power if our doing so is to be justifiable to others as free and equal? To this question political liberalism replies: our exercise of political power is proper and hence justifiable only when it is exercised in accordance with a constitution the essentials of which all citizens may reasonably be expected to endorse in the light of principles and ideals acceptable to them as reasonable and rational. This is the liberal principle of legitimacy. And since the exercise of political power itself must be legitimate, the ideal of citizenship imposes a moral, not a legal, duty—the duty of civility—to be able to explain to one another on those fundamental questions how the principles and policies they advocate and vote for can be supported by the political values of public reason. This duty also involves a willingness to listen to others and a fairmindedness in deciding when accommodations to their views should reasonably be made.[4]

2. Some might say that the limits of public reason apply only in official forums and so only to legislators, say, when they speak on the floor of parliament, or to the executive and the judiciary in their public acts and decisions. If they honor public reason, then citizens are indeed given public reasons for the laws they are to comply with and for the policies society follows. But this does not go far enough.

Democracy involves, as I have said, a political relationship between citizens within the basic structure of the society into which they are born and within which they normally lead a complete life; it implies further an equal share in the coercive political power that citizens exercise over one another by voting and in other ways. As reasonable and rational, and knowing that they affirm a diversity of reasonable religious and philosophical doctrines, they should be ready to explain the basis of their actions to one another in terms each could reasonably expect that others might endorse as consistent with their freedom and equality.

Trying to meet this condition is one of the tasks that this ideal of democratic politics asks of us. Understanding how to conduct oneself as a democratic citizen includes understanding an ideal of public reason.

Beyond this, the political values realized by a well-ordered constitutional regime are very great values and not easily overridden and the ideals they express are not to be lightly abandoned. Thus, when the political conception is supported by an overlapping consensus of reasonable comprehensive doctrines, the paradox of public reason disappears. The union of the duty of civility with the great values of the political yields the ideal of citizens governing themselves in ways that each thinks the others might reasonably be expected to accept; and this ideal in turn is supported by the comprehensive doctrines reasonable persons affirm. Citizens affirm the ideal of public reason, not as a result of political compromise, as in a modus vivendi, but from within their own reasonable doctrines.

3. Why the apparent paradox of public reason is no paradox is clearer once we remember that there are familiar cases where we grant that we should not appeal to the whole truth as we see it, even when it might be readily available. Consider how in a criminal case the rules of evidence limit the testimony that can be introduced, all this to insure the accused the basic right of a fair trial. Not only is hearsay evidence excluded but also evidence gained by improper searches and seizures, or by the abuse of defendants upon arrest and failing to inform them of their rights. Nor can defendants be forced to testify in their own defense. Finally, to mention a restriction with a quite different ground, spouses cannot be required to testify against one another, this to protect the great good of family life and to show public respect for the value of bonds of affection.

It may be objected that these examples are quite remote from the limits involved in relying solely on public reason. Remote perhaps but the idea is similar. All these examples are cases where we recognize a duty not to decide in view of the whole truth so as to honor a right or duty, or to advance an ideal good, or both. The examples serve the purpose, as many others would, of showing how it is often perfectly reasonable to forswear the whole truth and this parallels how the alleged paradox of public reason is resolved. What has to be shown is either that honoring the limits of public reason by citizens generally is required by certain basic rights and liberties and their corresponding duties, or else that it advances certain great values, or both. Political liberalism relies on the conjecture that the basic rights and duties and values in question have sufficient weight so that the limits of public reason are justified by the overall assessments of reasonable comprehensive doctrines once those doctrines have adapted to the conception of justice itself.[5]

4. On fundamental political questions the idea of public reason rejects common views of voting as a private and even personal matter. One view is that people may properly vote their preferences and interests, social and economic, not to mention their dislikes and hatreds. Democracy is said to be majority rule and a majority can do as it wishes. Another view, offhand quite different, is that people may vote what they see as right and true as their comprehensive convictions direct without taking into account public reasons.

Yet both views are similar in that neither recognizes the duty of civility and neither respects the limits of public reason in voting on matters of constitutional essentials and questions of basic justice. The first view is guided by our preferences and interests, the second view by what we see as the whole truth. Whereas public reason with its duty of civility gives a view about voting on fundamental questions in some ways reminiscent of Rousseau's *Social Contract.* He saw voting as ideally expressing our opinion as to which of the alternatives best advances the common good.[6]

§ 3. NONPUBLIC REASONS

1. The nature of public reason will be clearer if we consider the differences between it and nonpublic reasons. First of all, there are many nonpublic reasons and but one public reason. Among the nonpublic reasons are those of associations of all kinds: churches and universities, scientific societies and professional groups. As we have said, to act reasonably and responsibly, corporate bodies, as well as individuals, need a way of reasoning about what is to be done. This way of reasoning is public with respect to their members, but nonpublic with respect to political society and to citizens generally. Nonpublic reasons comprise the many reasons of civil society and belong to what I have called the "background culture," in contrast with the public political culture. These reasons are social, and certainly not private.[7]

Now all ways of reasoning—whether individual, associational, or political—must acknowledge certain common elements: the concept of judgment, principles of inference, and rules of evidence, and much else, otherwise they would not be ways of reasoning but perhaps rhetoric or means of persuasion. We are concerned with reason, not simply with discourse. A way of reasoning, then, must incorporate the fundamental concepts and principles of reason, and include standards of correctness and criteria of justification. A capacity to master these ideas is part of common human reason. However, different procedures and methods are appropriate to different conceptions of themselves held by individuals and corporate bodies, given the different conditions under which their reasoning is carried out, as well as the different constraints to which their reasoning is subject. These constraints may arise from the necessity to protect certain rights or to achieve certain values.

To illustrate: the rules for weighing evidence in a court of law—the rules relating to hearsay evidence in a criminal trial and requiring that the defendant be shown guilty beyond a reasonable doubt—are suited to the special role of courts and needed to protect the right of the accused to a fair trial. Different rules of evidence are used by a scientific society; and different authorities are recognized as relevant or binding by different corporate bodies. Consider the different authorities cited in a church council discussing a point of theological doctrine, in a university faculty debating educational policy, and in a meeting of a scientific association trying to assess the harm to the public from a nuclear accident. The criteria and methods of these nonpublic reasons depend in part on how the nature (the aim and point) of each association is understood and the conditions under which it pursues its ends.

2. In a democratic society nonpublic power, as seen, for example, in the authority of churches over their members, is freely accepted. In the case of ecclesiastical power, since apostasy and heresy are not legal offenses, those who are no longer able to recognize a church's authority may cease being members without running afoul of state power.[8] Whatever comprehensive religious, philosophical, or moral views we hold are also freely accepted, politically speaking; for given liberty of conscience and freedom of thought, we impose any such doctrine on ourselves. By this I do not mean that we do this by an act of free choice, as it were, apart from all prior loyalties and commitments, attachments, and affections. I mean that, as free and equal citizens, whether we affirm these views is regarded as within our political competence

specified by basic constitutional rights and liberties.

By contrast, the government's authority cannot be evaded except by leaving the territory over which it governs, and not always then. That its authority is guided by public reason does not change this. For normally leaving one's country is a grave step: it involves leaving the society and culture in which we have been raised, the society and culture whose language we use in speech and thought to express and understand ourselves, our aims, goals, and values; the society and culture whose history, customs, and conventions we depend on to find our place in the social world. In large part we affirm our society and culture, and have an intimate and inexpressible knowledge of it, even though much of it we may question, if not reject.

The government's authority cannot, then, be freely accepted in the sense that the bonds of society and culture, of history and social place of origin, begin so early to shape our life and are normally so strong that the right of emigration (suitably qualified) does not suffice to make accepting its authority free, politically speaking, in the way that liberty of conscience suffices to make accepting ecclesiastical authority free, politically speaking. Nevertheless, we may over the course of life come freely to accept, as the outcome of reflective thought and reasoned judgment, the ideals, principles, and standards that specify our basic rights and liberties, and effectively guide and moderate the political power to which we are subject. This is the outer limit of our freedom.[9]

§ 4. THE CONTENT OF PUBLIC REASON

1. I now turn to the content of public reason, having considered its nature and sketched how the apparent paradox of honoring its limits may be dissolved. *This content is formulated by what I have called a "political conception of justice," which I assume is broadly liberal in character. By this I mean three things: first, it specifies certain basic rights, liberties, and opportunities* (of the kind familiar from constitutional democratic regimes); *second, it assigns a special priority* to these rights, liberties, and opportunities, especially with respect to claims of the general good and of perfectionist values; and third, it affirms measures assuring all citizens adequate all-purpose means to make *effective use of their basic liberties and opportunities*. The two principles stated in I:1.1–2 fall under this general description. But each of these elements can be seen in different ways, so there are many liberalisms.

In saying a conception of justice is political I also mean three things (I:2): that it is framed to apply solely to the basic structure *of society*, its main political, social, and economic institutions as *a unified scheme of social cooperation; that it is presented independently of any wider comprehensive religious or philosophical doctrine;* and that it is elaborated in terms of fundamental political ideas viewed as implicit in the public political culture of a democratic society.

2. Now it is essential that a liberal political conception include, *besides its* principles of justice, guidelines of inquiry that specify *ways of reasoning* and criteria for the kinds of information relevant for political questions. Without such guidelines substantive principles cannot be applied and this leaves the political conception incomplete and fragmentary. That conception has, then, two parts:

a. first, substantive principles of justice for the basic structure; and

b. second, guidelines of inquiry: principles of reasoning and rules of evidence in the light of which citizens are to decide whether substantive principles properly apply and to identify laws and policies that best satisfy them.

Hence liberal political values are likewise of two kinds:

a. The first kind—the values of political justice—fall under the principles of justice for the basic structure: the values of equal political and civil liberty; equality of opportunity; the values of social equality and economic reciprocity; and let us add also values of the common good as well as the various necessary conditions for all these values.

b. The second kind of political values—the values of public reason—fall under the guidelines for public inquiry, which make that inquiry free and public. Also included here are such political virtues as reasonableness and a readiness to honor the (moral) duty of civility, which as virtues of citizens help to make possible reasoned public discussion of political questions.

3. As we have said, on matters of constitutional essentials and basic justice, the basic structure and its public policies are to be justifiable to all citizens, as the principle of political legitimacy requires. We add to this that in making these justifications we are to appeal only to presently accepted general beliefs and forms of reasoning found in common sense, and the methods and conclusions of science *when* these are not controversial. The liberal principle of legitimacy makes this the most appropriate, if not the only, way to specify the guidelines of public inquiry. What other guidelines and criteria have we for this case?

This means that in discussing constitutional essentials and matters of basic justice we are not to appeal to comprehensive religious and philosophical doctrines—to what we as individuals or members of associations see as the whole truth—nor to elaborate economic theories of

general equilibrium, say, if these are in dispute. As far as possible, the knowledge and ways of reasoning that ground our affirming the principles of justice and their application to constitutional essentials and basic justice are to rest on the plain truths now widely accepted, or available, to citizens generally. Otherwise, the political conception would not provide a public basis of justification.

As we consider later in §5, we want the substantive content and the guidelines of inquiry of a political conception, when taken together, to be complete. This means that the values specified by that conception can be suitably balanced or combined, or otherwise united, as the case may be, so that those values alone give a reasonable public answer to all, or to nearly all, questions involving the constitutional essentials and basic questions of justice. For an account of public reason we must have a reasonable answer, or think we can in due course find one, to all, or nearly all, those cases. I shall say a political conception is complete if it meets this condition.

4. In justice as fairness, and I think in many other liberal views, the guidelines of inquiry of public reason, as well as its principle of legitimacy, have the same basis as the substantive principles of justice. This means in justice as fairness that the parties in the original position, in adopting principles of justice for the basic structure, must also adopt guidelines and criteria of public reason for applying those norms. The argument for those guidelines, and for the principle of legitimacy, is much the same as, and as strong as, the argument for the principles of justice themselves. In securing the interests of the persons they represent, the parties insist that the application of substantive principles be guided by judgment and inference, reasons and evidence that the persons they represent can reasonably be expected to endorse. Should the parties fail to insist on this, they would not

act responsibly as trustees. Thus we have the principle of legitimacy.

In justice as fairness, then, the guidelines of public reason and the principles of justice have essentially the same grounds. They are companion parts of one agreement. There is no reason why any citizen, or association of citizens, should have the right to use state power to decide constitutional essentials as that person's, or that association's, comprehensive doctrine directs. When equally represented, no citizen could grant to another person or association that political authority. Any such authority is, therefore, without grounds in public reason, and reasonable comprehensive doctrines recognize this.

5. Keep in mind that political liberalism is a kind of view. It has many forms, depending on the substantive principles used and how the guidelines of inquiry are set out. These forms have in common substantive principles of justice that are liberal and an idea of public reason. Content and idea may vary within these limits.

Accepting the idea of public reason and its principle of legitimacy emphatically does not mean, then, accepting a particular liberal conception of justice down to the last details of the principles defining its content. We may differ about these principles and still agree in accepting a conception's more general features. We agree that citizens share in political power as free and equal, and that as reasonable and rational they have a duty of civility to appeal to public reason, yet we differ as to which principles are the most reasonable basis of public justification. The view I have called "justice as fairness" is but one example of a liberal political conception; its specific content is not definitive of such a view.

The point of the ideal of public reason is that citizens are to conduct their fundamental discussions within the framework of what each regards as a political conception of justice based on values that the others can reasonably be expected to endorse and each is, in good faith, prepared to defend that conception so understood. This means that each of us must have, and be ready to explain, a criterion of what principles and guidelines we think other citizens (who are also free and equal) may reasonably be expected to endorse along with us. We must have some test we are ready to state as to when this condition is met. I have elsewhere suggested as a criterion the values expressed by the principles and guidelines that would be agreed to in the original position. Many will prefer another criterion.

Of course, we may find that actually others fail to endorse the principles and guidelines our criterion selects. That is to be expected. The idea is that we must have such a criterion and this alone already imposes very considerable discipline on public discussion. Not any value is reasonably said to meet this test, or to be a political value; and not any balance of political values is reasonable. It is inevitable and often desirable that citizens have different views as to the most appropriate political conception; for the public political culture is bound to contain different fundamental ideas that can be developed in different ways. An orderly contest between them over time is a reliable way to find which one, if any, is most reasonable.

§5. THE IDEA OF CONSTITUTIONAL ESSENTIALS

1. We said above (§4.3) that to find a complete political conception we need to identify a class of fundamental questions for which the conception's political values yield reasonable answers. As these questions I propose the constitutional essentials and questions of basic justice. To explain:

There is the greatest urgency for citizens to reach practical agreement in judgment about the constitutional essentials. These are of two kinds:

a. fundamental principles that specify the general structure of government and the political process: the powers of the legislature, executive and the judiciary; the scope of majority rule; and

b. equal basic rights and liberties of citizenship that legislative majorities are to respect: such as the right to vote and to participate in politics, liberty of conscience, freedom of thought and of association, as well as the protections of the rule of law.

§ 6. THE SUPREME COURT AS EXEMPLAR OF PUBLIC REASON

1. At the beginning (§1.2) I remarked that in a constitutional regime with judicial review, public reason is the reason of its supreme court.[11] I now sketch two points about this: first, that public reason is well suited to be the court's reason in exercising its role as the highest judicial interpreter but not the final interpreter of the higher law;[12] and second, that the supreme court is the branch of government that serves as the exemplar of public reason. To clarify these points, I mention briefly five principles of constitutionalism.[13]

The first principle is Locke's distinction in the *Two Treatises* between the people's constituent power to establish a new regime and the ordinary power of officers of government and the electorate exercised in day-to-day politics. That constituent power of the people (II:134, 141) sets up a framework to regulate ordinary power, and it comes into play only when the existing regime has been dissolved.

The second distinction is between higher and ordinary law. Higher law is the expression of the people's constituent power and has the

higher authority of the will of We the People, whereas ordinary legislation has the authority, and is the expression of, the ordinary power of Congress and of the electorate. Higher law binds and guides this ordinary power.

As a third principle, a democratic constitution is a principled expression in higher law of the political ideal of a people to govern itself in a certain way. The aim of public reason is to articulate this ideal. Some of the ends of political society may be stated in a preamble—to establish justice and to promote the general welfare—and certain constraints are found in a bill of rights or implied in a framework of government—due process of law and equal protection of the laws. Together they fall under political values and its public reason. This principled expression of higher law is to be widely supported and for this and other reasons it is best not to burden it with many details and qualifications. It should also be possible to make visible in basic institutions its essential principles.[14]

A fourth principle is that by a democratically ratified constitution with a bill of rights, the citizen body fixes once and for all certain constitutional essentials, for example, the equal basic political rights and liberties, and freedom of speech and association, as well as those rights and liberties guaranteeing the security and independence of citizens, such as freedom of movement and choice of occupation, and the protections of the rule of law. This ensures that ordinary laws are enacted in a certain way by citizens as free and independent. It is through these fixed procedures that the people can express, even if they do not, their reasoned democratic will, and indeed without those procedures they can have no such will.

Fifth and last, in constitutional government the ultimate power cannot be left to the legislature or even to a supreme court, which is only the highest judicial interpreter of the constitution. Ultimate power is held by the three branches in a duly specified relation with one another with each responsible to the people.[15]

Now admittedly, in the long run a strong majority of the electorate can eventually make the constitution conform to its political will. This is simply a fact about political power as such. There is no way around this fact, not even by entrenchment clauses that try to fix permanently the basic democratic guarantees. No institutional procedure exists that cannot be abused or distorted to enact statutes violating basic constitutional democratic principles.[16] The idea of right and just constitutions and basic laws is always ascertained by the most reasonable political conception of justice and not by the result of an actual political process. I return to a question this raises below (§6.4).

2. Thus, constitutional democracy is dualist: it distinguishes constituent power from ordinary power as well as the higher law of the people from the ordinary law of legislative bodies. Parliamentary supremacy is rejected.

A supreme court fits into this idea of dualist constitutional democracy as one of the institutional devices to protect the higher law.[17] By applying public reason the court is to prevent that law from being eroded by the legislation of transient majorities, or more likely, by organized and well-situated narrow interests skilled at getting their way. If the court assumes this role and effectively carries it out,[18] it is incorrect to say that it is straightforwardly antidemocratic. It is indeed antimajoritarian with respect to ordinary law, for a court with judicial review can hold such law unconstitutional. Nevertheless, the higher authority of the people supports that. The court is not antimajoritarian with respect to higher law when its decisions reasonably accord with the constitution itself and with its amendments and politically mandated interpretations.

Suppose we agree that the three most innovative periods of our constitutional history are the founding, Reconstruction, and the New Deal.[19] Here it is important that all three seem to rely on, and only on, the political values of public reason. The constitution and its amendment process, the Reconstruction amendments that sought to remove the curse of slavery, and the modern activist so-called welfare state of the New Deal, all seem to fit that description, though it would take some time to show this. Yet accepting this as correct, and seeing the Court as the highest judicial though not the final interpreter of this body of higher law, the point is that the political values of public reason provide the Court's basis for interpretation. A political conception of justice covers the fundamental questions addressed by higher law and sets out the political values in terms of which they can be decided.[20]

Some will say, certainly, that parliamentary supremacy with no bill of rights at all is superior to our dualist regime. It offers firmer support for the values that higher law in the dualist scheme tries to secure. On the other hand, some may think it better that a constitution entrench a list of basic rights, as the German constitution does. It places those rights beyond amendment, even by the people and the German supreme court, and in enforcing those rights can be said to be undemocratic. Entrenchment has that consequence. Judged by the values of a reasonable political conception of justice, these regimes may be superior to a dualist regime in which these basic questions are settled by the higher law of We the People.[21]

Political liberalism as such, it should be stressed, does not assert or deny any of these claims and so we need not discuss them. Our point here is simply that, however these questions are decided, the content of a political conception of justice includes the values of public reason by appeal to which the merits of the three kinds of regime are to be judged.

3. Now I turn to a second point: the court's role is not merely defensive but to give due and continuing effect to public reason by serving as its institutional exemplar.[22] This means, first, that public reason is the sole reason the court exercises. It is the only branch of government that is visibly on its face the creature of that reason and of that reason alone. Citizens and legislators may properly vote their more comprehensive views when constitutional essentials and basic justice are not at stake; they need not justify by public reason why they vote as they do or make their grounds consistent and fit them into a coherent constitutional view over the whole range of their decisions. The role of the justices is to do precisely that and in doing it they have no other reason and no other values than the political. Beyond that they are to go by what they think the constitutional cases, practices, and traditions, and constitutionally significant historical texts require.

To say that the court is the exemplar of public reason also means that it is the task of the justices to try to develop and express in their reasoned opinions the best interpretation of the constitution they can, using their knowledge of what the constitution and constitutional precedents require. Here the best interpretation is the one that best fits the relevant body of those constitutional materials, and justifies it in terms of the public conception of justice or a reasonable variant thereof. In doing this it is expected that the justices may and do appeal to the political values of the public conception whenever the constitution itself expressly or implicitly invokes those values, as it does, for example, in a bill of rights guaranteeing the free exercise of religion or the equal protection of the laws. The court's role here is part of the publicity of reason and is an aspect of the wide, or educative, role of public reason.

The justices cannot, of course, invoke their own personal morality, nor the ideals and virtues of morality generally. Those they must view as irrelevant. Equally, they cannot invoke their or other people's religious or philosophical views. Nor can they cite political values without restriction. Rather, they must appeal to the political values they think belong to the most reasonable understanding of the public conception and its political values of justice and public reason. These are values that they believe in good faith, as the duty of civility requires, that all citizens as reasonable and rational might reasonably be expected to endorse.[23]

But, as I have said (§4.5), the idea of public reason does not mean that judges agree with one another, any more than citizens do, in the details of their understanding of the constitution. Yet they must be, and appear to be, interpreting the same constitution in view of what they see as the relevant parts of the political conception and in good faith believe it can be defended as such. The court's role as the highest judicial interpreter of the constitution supposes that the political conceptions judges hold and their views of constitutional essentials locate the central range of the basic freedoms in more or less the same place. In these cases at least its decisions succeed in settling the most fundamental political questions.

5. Finally, the court's role as exemplar of public reason has a third aspect: to give public reason vividness and vitality in the public forum; this it does by its authoritative judgments on fundamental political questions. The court fulfills this role when it clearly and effectively interprets the constitution in a reasonable way; and when it fails to do this, as ours often has, it stands at the center of a political controversy the terms of settlement of which are public values.

The constitution is not what the Court says it is. Rather, it is what the people acting constitutionally through the other branches eventually allow the Court to say it is. A particular understanding of the constitution may be mandated to the Court by amendments, or by a wide and continuing political majority, as it was in the case of the New Deal.[24] This raises the question whether an amendment to repeal the First Amendment, say, and to make a particular religion the state religion with all the consquences of that, or to repeal the Fourteenth Amendment with its equal protection of the laws, must be accepted by the Court as a valid amendment.[25] It is truistic to say, as I said above, that if the people act constitutionally such amendments are valid. But is it sufficient for the validity of an amendment that it be enacted by the procedure of Article V?[26] What reasons could the Court or the executive have (assuming the amendment was over its veto) for counting invalid an enactment meeting that condition?

Consider the following reasons: an amendment is not merely a change. One idea of an amendment is to adjust basic constitutional values to changing political and social circumstances, or to incorporate into the constitution a broader and more inclusive understanding of those values. The three amendments related to the Civil War all do this, as does the Nineteenth Amendment granting women the vote; and the Equal Rights Amendment attempted the same. At the Founding there was the blatant contradiction between the idea of equality in the Declaration of Independence and the Constitution and chattel slavery of a subjugated race; there were also property qualifications for voting and women were denied the suffrage altogether. Historically those amendments brought the Constitution more in line with its original promise.[27] Another idea of amendment is to adapt basic institutions in order to remove weaknesses that come to light in subsequent constitutional practice. Thus, with the exception of the Eighteenth, the other amendments concern either the institutional design of government, witness the Twenty-second, which allows the president to serve only two terms; or certain basic matters of policy, witness the Sixteenth, which grants Congress the power to levy income taxes. Such has been the role of amendments.

The Court could say, then that an amendment to repeal the First Amendment and replace it with its opposite fundamentally contradicts the constitutional tradition of the oldest democratic regime in the world. It is therefore invalid. Does this mean that the Bill of Rights and the other amendments are entrenched? Well, they are entrenched in the sense of being validated by long historical practice. They may be amended in the ways mentioned above but not simply repealed and reversed. Should that happen, and it is not inconceivable that the exercise of political power might take that turn, that would be constitutional breakdown,[28] or revolution in the proper sense, and not a valid amendment of the constitution. The successful practice of its ideas and principles over two centuries place restrictions on what can now count as an amendment, whatever was true at the beginning.

Thus, in the midst of any great constitutional change, legitimate or otherwise, the Court is bound to be a center of controversy. Often its role forces political discussion to take a principled form so as to address the constitutional question in line with the political values of justice and public reason. Public discussion becomes more than a contest for power and position. This educates citizens to the use of public reason and its value of political justice by focusing their attention on basic constitutional matters.

To conclude these remarks on the Supreme Court in a constitutional regime with judicial review, I emphasize that they are not intended as a defense of such review, although it can perhaps be defended given certain historical circumstances and conditions of political culture. Rather, my aim has been to elaborate the idea of public reason, and in order to make this idea more definite, I have looked at the way in which the Court may serve as its exemplar. And while the Court is special in this respect, the other branches of government can certainly, if they would but do so, be forums of principle along with it in debating constitutional questions.[29]

NOTES

[1] Two lectures on this topic were first given at the University of California at Irvine in late February and early March of 1990 to inaugurate the Melden Lectures, named in honor after A. I. Melden. While much revised, this lecture greatly benefits from discussion then with Sharon Lloyd, Gerasimos Santas, Lawrence Solum, Gary Watson, and Paul Weithman. I have gained much since from many conversations with Samuel Freeman, Peter de Marneffe, and David Estlund.

[2] The title is suggested by Kant's distinction between public and private reason in "What is Enlightenment?" (1784), although his distinction is different from the one used here. There are other relevant discussions in Kant's works, for example, *Critique of Pure Reason*, B767–97. For a valuable account, see Onora O'Neill, *Constructions of Reason*, (Cambridge: Cambridge University Press, 1989), chap. 2, "The Public Use of Reason." See also her recent essay, "Vindicating Reason," in *The Cambridge Companion to Kant*, edited by Paul Guyer (Cambridge: Cambridge University Press, 1992).

[3] For some recent views that are roughly speaking liberal though importantly different, see David Lyons, *Ethics and the Rule of Law* (Cambridge: Cambridge University Press, 1984), with a clear statement, p. 190f.; Ronald Dworkin, "The Forum of Principle," in *A Matter of Principle*, pp. 33–71; Charles Larmore, *Patterns of Moral Complexity* and "Political Liberalism," *Political Theory* 18 (August 1990); Thomas Nagel, *Equality and Partiality* (New York: Oxford University Press, 1991), chap. 14. For a valuable discussion of the idea of deliberative democracy, see Joshua Cohen, "Deliberation and Democratic Legitimacy," in *The Good Polity*, edited by Alan Hamlin (Oxford: Basil Blackwell, 1989). For the bearing of religion on public reason, see Kent Greenawalt's *Religious Conviction and Political Choice*, esp. chaps. 8 and 12; Robert Audi, "The Separation of Church and State and the Obligations of Citizenship," *Philosophy and Public Affairs* 18 (Summer 1989) and Paul Weithman's "The Separation of Church and State: Some Questions for Professor Audi," *Philosophy and Public Affairs* 20 (Winter 1991), with Audi's reply in the same issue; and finally, Lawrence Solum's instructive "Faith and Justice," *DePaul Law Review* 39 (Summer 1990).

[4] On this last, see the instructive discussion by Amy Gutmann and Dennis Thompson in their "Moral Conflict and Political Consensus," *Ethics* 101 (October 1990): 76–86.

[5] The process of adaptation was described in IV:6–7.

[6] *The Social Contract*, bk. IV, chap. II, para. 8.

[7] The public vs. nonpublic distinction is not the distinction between public and private. This latter I ignore: there is no such thing as private reason. There is social reason—the many reasons of associations in society which make up the background culture; there is also, let us say, domestic reason—the reason of families as small groups in society—and this contrasts both with public and social

reason. As citizens, we participate in all these kinds of reason and have the rights of equal citizens when we do so.

8 In this case we think of liberty of conscience as protecting the individual against the church. This is an example of the the protection that basic rights and liberties secure for individuals generally. But equally, liberty of conscience and other liberties such as freedom of association protect churches from the intrusions of government and from other powerful associations. Both associations and individuals need protection, and so do families need protection from associations and government, as do the individual members of families from other family members (wives from their husbands, children from their parents). It is incorrect to say that liberalism focuses solely on the rights of individuals; rather, the rights it recognizes are to protect associations, smaller groups, and individuals, all from one another in an appropriate balance specified by its guiding principles of justice.

9 Here I accept the Kantian (not Kant's) view that what we affirm on the basis of free and informed reason and reflection is affirmed freely; and that insofar as our conduct expresses what we affirm freely, our conduct is free to the extent it can be. Freedom at the deepest level calls upon the freedom of reason, both theoretical and practical, as expressed in what we say and do. Limits on freedom are at bottom limits on our reason: on its development and education, its knowledge and information, and on the scope of the actions in which it can be expressed, and therefore our freedom depends on the nature of the surrounding institutional and social context.

11 This is not a definition. I assume that in a well-ordered society the two more or less

overlap. I am grateful to James Fleming for valuable guidance in formulating many points in this section.

12 Here I have found particularly helpful: Bruce Ackerman, "Constitutional Politics/ Constitutional Law," *Yale Law Journal* 99 (December 1989), as well as his recent *We The People: Foundations* (Cambridge, Mass.: Harvard University Press, 1991), vol. I.

13 Here I draw upon John Agresto, *The Supreme Court and Constitutional Democracy* (Ithaca: Cornell University Press, 1984), esp. pp. 45–55; Stephen Holmes, "Gag Rules or the Politics of Omission," and "Precommitment and the Paradox of Democracy," both in *Constitutionalism and Democracy*, edited by Jon Elster and Rune Slagstad (Cambridge: Cambridge University Press, 1987); Jon Elster, *Ulysses and the Sirens* (Cambridge: Cambridge University Press, 1979), pp. 81–86, 88–103. There is nothing at all novel in my account.

14 For these reasons, among others, I suppose that the principle of fair equality of opportunity and the difference principle are not constitutional essentials, though, as I have said, in justice as fairness they are matters of basic justice (§5.3).

15 In saying this I follow what I understand to be Lincoln's view as expressed in his remarks about Dred Scott (1857) in his speeches and in his debates with Douglas in *Lincoln: Speeches and Writings*, edited by Don Fehrenbacher (New York: Library of America, 1989), pp. 392f., 450ff., 524ff., 714–17, 740f.; and in his First Inaugural (1861), ibid., vol. 2, pp. 220f. For accounts of Lincoln's view see Alexander Bickel, *The Least Dangerous Branch* (New York: Bobbs-Merrill, 1962), pp. 65–69; 259–69; Agresto, *The Supreme Court*, esp. pp. 86–95, 105, 128f.; and Don Fehrenbacher, *Lincoln: In Text and Context* (Stanford: Stanford University Press, 1987),

esp. pp. 20–23, 125ff., and 293.

16 Similarly, there is no procedure of inquiry, not even that of the investigations of science and scholarship that can be guaranteed in the long run to uncover the truth. As we commented at the end of III:8, we cannot define truth as given by the beliefs that would stand up even in an idealized consensus, however far extended.

17 See Ackerman, "Constitutional Politics/ Constitutional Law," pp. 464f. and *We the People*, pp. 6–10.

18 It must be said that historically the court has often failed badly in this role. It upheld the Alien and Sedition Acts of 1798 and one need only mention Dred Scott (1857). It emasculated the Reconstruction amendments by interpreting them as a charter of capitalist liberty rather than the liberty of the freed slaves; and from Lochner (1905) through the early New Deal years it did much the same.

19 Here I follow Ackerman's account in "Constitutional Politics/Constitutional Law," at essentially pp. 486–515, and *We the People*, chaps. 3–6 passim.

20 See Samuel Freeman, "Original Meaning, Democratic Interpretation, and the Constitution," *Philosophy and Public Affairs* 21 (Winter 1992), pp. 26f. and 36f., where these matters are discussed.

21 Robert Dahl, in his *Democracy and Its Critics* (New Haven: Yale University Press, 1989), discusses the relative merits of these forms of democratic institutions. He is in some ways critical of the British parliamentary system (the "Westminster model") (pp. 156–57), and although he is also critical of judicial review (pp. 187–91), he thinks there is no one universally best way to solve the problem of how to protect fundamental rights and interests. He says: "In the absence of a universally best solution, specific solutions need to be adapted to the historical conditions and experiences, political culture, and concrete political institutions of a particular country" (p. 192). I incline to agree with this and thank Dennis Thompson for correcting my earlier misunderstanding of Dahl's view.

22 The judiciary with a supreme court is not the only institution that does this. It is essential that other social arrangements also do the same, as is done for example by an orderly public financing of elections and constraints on private funding that achieves the fair value of the political liberties, or at least significantly move the political process in that direction. See *Theory*, pp. 224–27 and VIII:7, 12 at pp. 324–31 and 356–63, respectively.

23 This account of what the justices are to do seems to be the same as Ronald Dworkin's view as stated say in "Hard Cases" in *Taking Rights Seriously* (Cambridge, Mass.: Harvard University Press, 1978) or in *Law's Empire* (Cambridge, Mass.: Harvard University Press, 1986), chap. 7, except for possibly one proviso. I have said that the justices in interpreting the constitution are to appeal to the political values covered by the public political conception of justice, or at least by some recognizable variant thereof. The values the justices can invoke are restricted to what is reasonably believed to be covered by that conception or its variants, and not by a conception of morality as such, not even of political morality. The latter I think too broad. Thus, though an appeal to a social minimum specified by basic needs is appropriate (accepting Frank Michelman's view as stated in "Welfare Rights and Constitutional Democracy," *Washington University Law Quarterly* 1979 (Summer 1979), an appeal cannot be made to the difference principle

unless it appears as a guideline in a statute (§5.3). I believe Dworkin thinks that his requirement of fit alone leads to roughly the same conclusion, as he takes the requirement of fit to distinguish interpretation from invention and that a reasonable interpretation suffices to show what is already implicit in the law as articulated within the political conception, or one of its recognizable variants. He may be correct about this but I am unsure. I incline to require, in addition to fit, that in order for the court's decisions to be properly judicial decisions of law, that the interpretation fall within the public political conception of justice or a recognizeable variant thereof. I doubt that this view differs in substance from Dworkin's.

24 See Ackerman, "Constitutional Politics/Constitutional Law," pp. 510–15 and *We the People,* chap 5.

25 Ackerman suggests that a commitment to dualist democracy implies that the Court must accept the amendment as valid, whereas I want to deny this. While Ackerman says he would be proud to belong to the generation that entrenched the Bill of Rights, as that would give a more ideal regime, entrenchment, he thinks, is contrary to the idea of our dualist democracy. *We the People,* pp. 319–22.

26 I am indebted to Stephen Macedo for valuable discussion that led me to take up this question. See his *Liberal Virtues* (Oxford: Clarendon Press, 1990), pp. 182f. What I say is similar to what he says there.

27 See the late Judith Shklar's lucid brief account of this history in her *American Citizenship: The Quest for Inclusion* (Cambridge, Mass.: Harvard University Press, 1991).

28 This is the term Samuel Freeman uses in his "Original Meaning, Democratic Interpretation, and the Constitution," pp. 41f., where he contrasts his view with Ackerman's. I am indebted to his discussion.

29 For this last aspect, see Dworkin, "The Forum of Principle," in *A Matter of Principle* (Cambridge: Harvard University Press, 1985), pp. 70f.

Part Three

Rights

Rights

Rights are claims on others' behavior; they trump others' abilities to do as they please. Rights imply obligations: if I have a right to x, you have an obligation to give me x or to allow me to enjoy x, regardless of your preferences. In the context of our discussion of governmental authority, having a right to free speech, for instance, gives one a right against governmental interference with one's speech. In this section, the readings introduce the subject of natural rights and human rights. To frame these readings, consider these three big questions regarding rights:

1. What justifies a claim that someone has a right to something?
2. What rights are we justified in claiming that persons in fact have?
3. Are human rights universal or are they relative to time or place?

The first of these questions asks for a normative theory about the foundation of rights. The second asks what rights can be derived from that normative foundation. The third question asks whether that normative foundation can be seen as applying to all humans regardless of what country or historical time period they exist in.

The history of the idea of rights, and the liberal foundation of rights in the United States Constitution, owes much to Locke's discussion of property rights, and so we begin this section with his chapter on Property Rights from the *Second Treatise of Government*. Locke argues for the claim that we can come to have a natural right to own property. He assumes, unlike his adversary at the time, Robert Filmer who argued for the natural rights of kings, that the earth and its fruits were given to humanity by God, and that they hold them *in common*. His aim is to show how people can come to own things individually without any agreement on the part of all the other people. The argument turns on the fact that one owns one's own body, and therefore its labor. (Please see the introduction to the eighth reading for more on Locke's life and work.) Natural rights theories provide a universal foundation for rights.

The second reading by the German born political philosopher, Thomas Pogge appeals to the list of human rights in the Universal Declaration of Human Rights and addresses the issue of universality. He argues for a strong obligation to help provide worldwide support of human rights. The third reading in this section is by Malcolm X, the Black Muslim leader who was murdered in 1965. His essay was written during the Civil Rights Movement in the United States and reminds us that respect for human rights often require appeal beyond national borders. This section also includes two important rights documents: the Universal Declaration of Human Rights, originally drafted by the Commission on Human Rights chaired by Eleanor Roosevelt at the founding of the United Nations, and the Convention on Elimination of All forms of Discrimination Against Women, adopted in 1979 by the United Nations General Assembly.

STUDY QUESTIONS:

1. How much does the argument for property rights rely on the existence of a benevolent God with a purpose for humanity?

2. What are the restrictions Locke places on the right to own property?

3. What are the five features of human rights according to Pogge?

4. Explain how the international borrowing and natural resource privileges obligate Developed Nations to uphold human rights in Developing Countries.

5. How does Malcolm X distinguish civil rights from human rights?

Second Treatise of Government

Chapter V

John Locke

CHAP. V

§. 25. Whether we consider natural *reason,* which tells us, that men, being once born, have a right to their preservation, and consequently to meat and drink, and such other things as nature affords for their subsistence: or *revelation,* which gives us an account of those grants God made of the world to *Adam,* and to *Noah,* and his sons, it is very clear, that God, as king *David* says, *Psal.* cxv. 16. *has given the earth to the children of men;* given it to mankind in common. But this being supposed, it seems to some a very great difficulty, how any one should ever come to have a *property* in any thing: I will not content myself to answer, that if it be difficult to make out *property,* upon a supposition that God gave the world to *Adam,* and his posterity in common, it is impossible that any man, but one universal monarch, should have any *property* upon a supposition, that God gave the world to *Adam,* and his heirs in succession, exclusive of all the rest of his posterity. But I shall endeavour to shew, how men might come to have a *property* in several parts of that which God gave

to mankind in common, and that without any express compact of all the commoners.

§. 26. God, who hath given the world to men in common, hath also given them reason to make use of it to the best advantage of life, and convenience. The earth, and all that is therein, is given to men for the support and comfort of their being. And tho' all the fruits it naturally produces, and beasts it feeds, belong to mankind in common, as they are produced by the spontaneous hand of nature; and no body has originally a private dominion, exclusive of the rest of mankind, in any of them, as they are thus in their natural state: yet being given for the use of men, there must of necessity be *a means to appropriate* them some way or other, before they can be of any use, or at all beneficial to any particular man. The fruit, or venison, which nourishes the wild *Indian,* who knows no inclosure, and is still a tenant in common, must be his, and so his, *i. e.* a part of him, that another can no longer have any right to it, before it can do him any good for the support of his life.

From *Second Treatise of Government* by John Locke. First published 1690.

§. 27. Though the earth, and all inferior creatures, be common to all men, yet every man has a *property* in his own *person:* this no body has any right to but himself. The *labour* of his body, and the *work* of his hands, we may say, are properly his. Whatsoever then he removes out of the state that nature hath provided, and left it in, he hath mixed his *labour* with, and joined to it something that is his own, and thereby makes it his *property.* It being by him removed from the common state nature hath placed it in, it hath by this *labour* something annexed to it, that excludes the common right of other men: for this *labour* being the unquestionable property of the labourer, no man but he can have a right to what that is once joined to, at least where there is enough, and as good, left in common for others.

§. 28. He that is nourished by the acorns he picked up under an oak, or the apples he gathered from the trees in the wood, has certainly appropriated them to himself. No body can deny but the nourishment is his. I ask then, when did they begin to be his? when he digested? or when he eat? or when he boiled? or when he brought them home? or when he picked them up? and it is plain, if the first gathering made them not his, nothing else could. *That labour* put a distinction between them and common: that added something to them more than nature, the common mother of all, had done; and so they became his private right. And will any one say, he had no right to those acorns or apples, he thus appropriated, because he had not the consent of all mankind to make them his? Was it a robbery thus to assume to himself what belonged to all in common? If such a consent as that was necessary, man had starved, notwithstanding the plenty God had given him. We see in *commons,* which remain so by compact, that it is the taking any part of what is common, and removing it out of the state nature leaves it in, which *begins the*

property; without which the common is of no use. And the taking of this or that part, does not depend on the express consent of all the commoners. Thus the grass my horse has bit; the turfs my servant has cut; and the ore I have digged in any place, where I have a right to them in common with others, become my *property,* without the assignation or consent of any body. The *labour* that was mine, removing them out of that common state they were in, hath *fixed* my *property* in them.

§. 29. By making an explicit consent of every commoner, necessary to any one's appropriating to himself any part of what is given in common, children or servants could not cut the meat, which their father or master had provided for them in common, without assigning to every one his peculiar part. Though the water running in the fountain be every one's, yet who can doubt, but that in the pitcher is his only who drew it out? His *labour* hath taken it out of the hands of nature, where it was common, and belonged equally to all her children, and *hath* thereby *appropriated* it to himself.

§. 30. Thus this law of reason makes the deer that *Indian's* who hath killed it; it is allowed to be his goods, who hath bestowed his labour upon it, though before it was the common right of every one. And amongst those who are counted the civilized part of mankind, who have made and multiplied positive laws to determine *property,* this original law of nature, for the *beginning of property,* in what was before common, still takes place; and by virtue thereof, what fish any one catches in the ocean, that great and still remaining common of mankind; or what ambergrise any one takes up here, is by the *labour* that removes it out of that common state nature left it in, *made* his *property,* who takes that pains about it. And even amongst us, the hare that any one is hunting, is thought his who pursues her during the chase: for being a beast that is still looked upon as common, and no man's private possession; whoever has employed so much *labour* about any of that kind, as to find and pursue her, has thereby removed her from the state of nature, wherein she was common, and hath *begun a property.*

§. 31. It will perhaps be objected to this, that if gathering the acorns, or other fruits of the earth, &c. makes a right to them, then any one may *ingross* as much as he will. To which I answer, Not so. The same law of nature, that does by this means give us property, does also *bound* that *property* too. *God has given us all things richly,* 1 Tim. vi. 12. is the voice of reason confirmed by inspiration. But how far has he given it us? *To enjoy.* As much as any one can make use of to any advantage of life before it spoils, so much he may by his labour fix a property in: whatever is beyond this, is more than his share, and belongs to others. Nothing was made by God for man to spoil or destroy. And thus, considering the plenty of natural provisions there was a long time in the world, and the few spenders; and to how small a part of that provision the industry of one man could extend itself, and ingross it to the prejudice of others; especially keeping within the *bounds,* set by reason, of what might serve for his *use;* there could be then little room for quarrels or contentions about property so established.

§. 32. But the *chief matter of property* being now not the fruits of the earth, and the beasts that subsist on it, but *the earth itself;* as that which takes in and carries with it all the rest; I think it is plain, that *property* in that too is acquired as the former. *As much land* as a man tills, plants, improves, cultivates, and can use the product of, so much is his *property.* He by his labour does, as it were, inclose it from the common. Nor will it invalidate his right, to say every body else has an equal title to it; and therefore he cannot appropriate, he cannot inclose, without the consent

of all his fellow-commoners, all mankind. God, when he gave the world in common to all mankind, commanded man also to labour, and the penury of his condition required it of him. God and his reason commanded him to subdue the earth *i.e.* improve it for the benefit of life, and therein lay out something upon it that was his own, his labour. He that in obedience to this command of God, subdued, tilled and sowed any part of it, thereby annexed to it something that was his *property,* which another had no title to, nor could without injury take from him.

§. 33. Nor was this *appropriation* of any parcel of *land,* by improving it, any prejudice to any other man, since there was still enough, and as good left; and more than the yet unprovided could use. So that, in effect, there was never the less left for others because of his inclosure for himself: for he that leaves as much as another can make use of, does as good as take nothing at all. No body could think himself injured by the drinking of another man, though he took a good draught, who had a whole river of the same water left him to quench his thirst: and the case of land and water, where there is enough of both, is perfectly the same.

§. 34. God gave the world to men in common; but since he gave it them for their benefit, and the greatest conveniencies of life they were capable to draw from it, it cannot be supposed he meant it should always remain common and uncultivated. He gave it to the use of the industrious and rational, (and *labour* was to be *his title* to it;) not to the fancy or covetousness of the quarrelsome and contentious. He that had as good left for his improvement, as was already taken up, needed not complain, ought not to meddle with what was already improved by another's labour: if he did, it is plain he desired the benefit of another's pains, which he had no right to, and not the ground which God had given him in common with others to labour on, and whereof there was as good left, as that already possessed, and more than he knew what to do with, or his industry could reach to.

§. 35. It is true, in *land* that is *common* in *England,* or any other country, where there is plenty of people under government, who have money and commerce, no one can inclose or appropriate any part, without the consent of all his fellow-commoners; because this is left common by compact, *i.e.* by the law of the land, which is not to be violated. And though it be common, in respect of some men, it is not so to all mankind; but is the joint property of this country, or this parish. Besides, the remainder, after such inclosure, would not be as good to the rest of the commoners, as the whole was when they could all make use of the whole; whereas in the beginning and first peopling of the great common of the world, it was quite otherwise. The law man was under, was rather for appropriating. God commanded, and his wants forced him to *labour.* That was his *property* which could not be taken from him whereever he had fixed it. And hence subduing or cultivating the earth, and having dominion, we see are joined together. The one gave title to the other. So that God, by commanding to subdue, gave authority so far to *appropriate:* and the condition of human life, which requires labour and materials to work on, necessarily introduces private possessions.

§. 36. The *measure of property* nature has well set by the extent of men's *labour and the conveniencies of life:* no man's labour could subdue, or appropriate all; nor could his enjoyment consume more than a small part; so that it was impossible for any man, this way, to intrench upon the right of another, or acquire to himself a property, to the prejudice of his neighbour, who would still have room for as good, and as large a possession (after the other had taken out his) as before it was appropriated.

This *measure* did confine every man's *possession* to a very moderate proportion, and such as he might appropriate to himself, without injury to any body, in the first ages of the world, when men were more in danger to be lost, by wandering from their company, in the then vast wilderness of the earth, than to be straitened for want of room to plant in. And the same *measure* may be allowed still without prejudice to any body, as full as the world seems: for supposing a man, or family, in the state they were at first peopling of the world by the children of *Adam,* or *Noah;* let him plant in some in-land, vacant places of *America,* we shall find that the *possessions* he could make himself, upon the *measures* we have given, would not be very large, nor, even to this day, prejudice the rest of mankind, or give them reason to complain, or think themselves injured by this man's incroachment, though the race of men have now spread themselves to all the corners of the world, and do infinitely exceed the small number was at the beginning. Nay, the extent of *ground* is of so little value, *without labour,* that I have heard it affirmed, that in *Spain* itself a man may be permitted to plough, sow and reap, without being disturbed, upon land he has no other title to, but only his making use of it. But, on the contrary, the inhabitants think themselves beholden to him, who, by his industry on neglected, and consequently waste land, has increased the stock of corn, which they wanted. But be this as it will, which I lay no stress on; this I dare boldly affirm, that the same *rule of propriety, (viz.)* that every man should have as much as he could make use of, would hold still in the world, without straitening any body; since there is land enough in the world to suffice double the inhabitants, had not the *invention of money,* and the tacit agreement of men to put a value on it, introduced (by consent) larger possessions, and a right to them; which, how it has done, I shall by and by shew more at large.

§. 37. This is certain, that in the beginning, before the desire of having more than man needed had altered the intrinsic value of things, which depends only on their usefulness to the life of man; or had *agreed, that a little piece of yellow metal,* which would keep without wasting or decay, should be worth a great piece of flesh, or a whole heap of corn; though men had a right to appropriate, by their labour, each one of himself, as much of the things of nature, as he could use: yet this could not be much, nor to the prejudice of others, where the same plenty was still left to those who would use the same industry. To which let me add, that he who appropriates land to himself by his labour, does not lessen, but increase the common stock of mankind: for the provisions serving to the support of human life, produced by one acre of inclosed and cultivated land, are (to speak much within compass) ten times more than those which are yielded by an acre of land of an equal richness lying waste in common. And therefore he that incloses land, and has a greater plenty of the conveniencies of life from ten acres, than he could have from an hundred left to nature, may truly be said to give ninety acres to mankind: for his labour now supplies him with provisions out of ten acres, which were but the product of an hundred lying in common. I have here rated the improved land very low, in making its product but as ten to one, when it is much nearer an hundred to one: for I ask, whether in the wild woods and uncultivated waste of *America,* left to nature, without any improvement, tillage or husbandry, a thousand acres yield the needy and wretched inhabitants as many conveniencies of life, as ten acres of equally fertile land do in *Devonshire,* where they are well cultivated?

Before the appropriation of land, he who gathered as much of the wild fruit, killed, caught, or tamed, as many of the beasts, as he could; he that so imployed his pains about any of the spontaneous products of nature, as any way to alter them from the state which nature put them in, *by* placing any of his *labour* on them, did thereby *acquire a propriety in them:* but if they perished, in his possession, without their due use; if the fruits rotted, or the venison putrified, before he could spend it, he offended against the common law of nature, and was liable to be punished; he invaded his neighbour's share, for he had *no right, farther than his use* called for any of them, and they might serve to afford him conveniencies of life.

§. 38. The same *measures* governed the *possession of land* too: whatsoever he tilled and reaped, laid up and made use of, before it spoiled, that was his peculiar right; whatsoever he enclosed, and could feed, and make use of, the cattle and product was also his. But if either the grass of his inclosure rotted on the ground, or the fruit of his planting perished without gathering, and laying up, this part of the earth, notwithstanding his inclosure, was still to be looked on as waste, and might be the possession of any other. Thus, at the beginning, *Cain* might take as much ground as he could till, and make it his own land, and yet leave enough to *Abel's* sheep to feed on; a few acres would serve for both their possessions. But as families increased, and industry inlarged their stocks, their *possessions inlarged* with the need of them; but yet it was commonly *without any fixed property in the ground* they made use of, till they incorporated, settled themselves together, and built cities; and then, by consent, they came in time, to set out the *bounds of their distinct territories,* and agree on limits between them and their neighbours; and by laws within themselves, settled the *properties* of those of the same society: for we see, that in that part of the world which was first inhabited, and therefore like to be best peopled, even as low down as *Abraham's* time, they wandered with their flocks, and their herds, which was their substance, freely up and down; and this *Abraham* did, in a country where he was a stranger. Whence it is plain, that at least a great part of the *land lay in common;* that the inhabitants valued it not, nor claimed property in any more than they made use of. But when there was not room enough in the same place, for their herds to feed together, they by consent, as *Abraham* and *Lot* did, *Gen.* xiii. 5. separated and inlarged their pasture, where it best liked them. And for the same reason *Esau* went from his father, and his brother, and planted in *mount Seir, Gen.* xxxvi. 6.

§. 39. And thus, without supposing any private dominion, and property in *Adam,* over all the world, exclusive of all other men, which can no way be proved, nor any one's property be made out from it; but supposing the *world* given, as it was, to the children of men *in common,* we see how *labour* could make men distinct titles to several parcels of it, for their private uses; wherein there could be no doubt of right, no room for quarrel.

§. 40. Nor is it so strange, as perhaps before consideration it may appear, that the *property of labour* should be able to over-balance the community of land: for it is *labour* indeed that *puts the difference of value* on every thing; and let any one consider what the difference is between an acre of land planted with tobacco or sugar, sown with wheat or barley, and an acre of the same land lying in common, without any husbandry upon it, and he will find, that the improvement of *labour makes* the far greater part of the value. I think it will be but a very modest computation to say, that of the *products* of the earth useful to the life of man nine tenths are the *effects of labour:* nay, if we will rightly estimate things as they come to our use, and cast up the several expences about them, what in them is purely owing to *nature,* and what to *labour,* we shall find, that in most of them ninety-nine hundredths are wholly to be put on the account of *labour.*

§. 41. There cannot be a clearer demonstration of any thing, than several nations of the *Americans* are of this, who are rich in land, and poor in all the comforts of life; whom nature having furnished as liberally as any other people, with the materials of plenty, *i. e.* a fruitful soil, apt to produce in abundance, what might serve for food, raiment, and delight; yet for *want of improving it by labour,* have not one hundredth part of the conveniencies we enjoy: and a king of a large and fruitful territory there, feeds, lodges, and is clad worse than a day-labourer in *England.*

§. 42. To make this a little clearer, let us but trace some of the ordinary provisions of life, through their several progresses, before they come to our use, and see how much they receive of their *value from human industry.* Bread, wine and cloth, are things of daily use, and great plenty; yet notwithstanding, acorns, water and leaves, or skins, must be our bread, drink and cloathing, did not *labour* furnish us with these more useful commodities: for whatever *bread* is more worth than acorns, wine than water, and *cloth* or *silk,* than leaves, skins or moss, that is wholly *owing to labour* and *industry;* the one of these being the food and raiment which unassisted nature furnishes us with; the other, provisions which our industry and pains prepare for us, which how much they exceed the other in value, when any one hath computed, he will then see how much *labour makes the far greatest part of the value* of things we enjoy in this world: and the ground which produces the materials, is scarce to be reckoned in, as any, or at most, but a very small part of it; so little, that even amongst us, land that is left wholly to nature, that hath no improvement of pasturage, tillage, or planting, is called, as indeed it is, *waste;* and we shall find the benefit of it amount to little more than nothing.

This shews how much numbers of men are to be preferred to largeness of dominions; and that the increase of lands, and the right employing of them, is the great art of government: and that prince, who shall be so wise and godlike, as by established laws of liberty to secure protection and encouragement to the honest industry of mankind, against the oppression of power and narrowness of party, will quickly be too hard for his neighbours: but this by the by. To return to the argument in hand,

§. 43. An acre of land, that bears here twenty bushels of wheat, and another in *America*, which, with the same husbandry, would do the like, are, without doubt, of the same natural intrinsic value: but yet the benefit mankind receives from the one in a year, is worth 5*l.* and from the other possibly not worth a penny, if all the profit an *Indian* received from it were to be valued, and sold here; at least, I may truly say, not one thousandth. It is *labour* then which *puts the greatest part of value upon land*, without which it would scarcely be worth any thing: it is to that we owe the greatest part of all its useful products; for all that the straw, bran, bread, of that acre of wheat, is more worth than the product of an acre of as good land, which lies waste, is all the effect of labour: for it is not barely the plough-man's pains, the reaper's and thresher's toil, and the baker's sweat, is to be counted into the *bread* we eat; the labour of those who broke the oxen, who digged and wrought the iron and stones, who felled and framed the timber employed about the plough, mill, oven, or any other utensils, which are a vast number, requisite to this corn, from its being feed to be sown to its being made bread, must all be *charged on* the account of labour, and received as an effect of that: nature and the earth furnished only the almost worthless materials, as in themselves. It would be a strange *catalogue of things, that industry provided and made use of, about every loaf of bread*, before it came to our use, if we could trace them; iron, wood, leather, bark, timber, stone, bricks, coals, lime, cloth, dying drugs, pitch, tar, masts, ropes, and all the

materials made use of in the ship, that brought any of the commodities made use of by any of the workmen, to any part of the work; all which it would be almost impossible, at least too long, to reckon up.

§. 44. From all which it is evident, that though the things of nature are given in common, yet man, by being master of himself, and *proprietor of his own person, and the actions or labour of it, had still in himself the great foundation of property*; and that which made up the great part of what he applied to the support or comfort of his being, when invention and arts had improved the conveniencies of life, was perfectly his own, and did not belong in common to others.

§. 45. Thus *labour*, in the beginning, *gave a right of property*, wherever any one was pleased to employ it upon what was common, which remained a long while the far greater part, and is yet more than mankind makes use of. Men, at first, for the most part, contented themselves with what unassisted nature offered to their necessities: and though afterwards, in some parts of the world, (where the increase of people and stock, with the *use of money*, had made land scarce, and so of some value) the several *communities* settled the bounds of their distinct territories, and by laws within themselves regulated the properties of the private men of their society, and so, *by compact* and agreement, *settled the property* which labour and industry began; and the leagues that have been made between several states and kingdoms, either expresly or tacitly disowning all claim and right to the land in the others possession, have, by common consent, given up their pretences to their natural common right, which originally they had to those countries, and so have, by *positive agreement, settled a property* amongst themselves, in distinct parts and parcels of the earth; yet there are still *great tracts of ground* to be found, which (the inhabitants thereof not having joined with the rest of mankind, in the consent of the use of their common money) *lie waste*, and are more than the people who dwell on it do, or can make use of, and so still lie in common; tho' this can scarce happen amongst that part of mankind that have consented to the use of money.

§. 46. The greatest part of *things really useful* to the life of man, and such as the necessity of subsisting made the first commoners of the world look after, as it doth the *Americans* now, *are* generally things of *short duration*; such as, if they are not consumed by use, will decay and perish of themselves: gold, silver and diamonds, are things that fancy or agreement hath put the value on, more than real use, and the necessary support of life. Now of those good things which nature hath provided in common, every one had a right (as hath been said) to as much as he could use, and *property* in all that he could effect with his labour; all that his *industry* could extend to, to alter from the state nature had put it in, was his. He that *gathered* a hundred bushels of acorns or apples, had thereby a *property* in them, they were his goods as soon as gathered. He was only to look, that he used them before they spoiled, else he took more than his share, and robbed others. And indeed it was a foolish thing, as well as dishonest, to hoard up more than he could make use of. If he gave away a part to any body else, so that it perished not uselesly in his possession, these he also made use of. And if he also bartered away plums, that would have rotted in a week, for nuts that would last good for his eating a whole year, he did no injury; he wasted not the common stock; destroyed no part of the portion of goods that belonged to others, so long as nothing perished uselesly in his hands. Again, if he would give his nuts for a piece of metal, pleased with its colour; or exchange his sheep for shells, or wool for a sparkling pebble or a diamond, and keep those by him all his life, he invaded not the

right of others, he might heap up as much of these durable things as he pleased; the *exceeding of the bounds of his just property* not lying in the largeness of his possession, but the perishing of any thing uselesly in it.

§. 47. And thus *came in the use of money*, some lasting thing that men might keep without spoiling, and that by mutual consent men would take in exchange for the truly useful, but perishable supports of life.

§. 48. And as different degrees of industry were apt to give men possessions in different proportions, so this *invention of money* gave them the opportunity to continue and enlarge them: for supposing an island, separate from all possible commerce with the rest of the world, wherein there were but an hundred families, but there were sheep, horses and cows, with other useful animals, wholsome fruits, and land enough for corn for a hundred thousand times as many, but nothing in the island, either because of its commonness, or perishableness, fit to supply the place of *money*; what reason could any one have there to enlarge his possessions beyond the use of his family, and a plentiful supply to its *consumption*, either in what their own industry produced, or they could barter for like perishable, useful commodities, with others? Where there is not some thing, both lasting and scarce, and so valuable to be hoarded up, there men will not be apt to enlarge their *possessions of land*, were it never so rich, never so free for them to take: for I ask, what would a man value ten thousand, or an hundred thousand acres of excellent *land*, ready cultivated, and well stocked too with cattle, in the middle of the inland parts of *America*, where he had no hopes of commerce with other parts of the world, to draw *money* to him by the sale of the product? It would not be worth the inclosing, and we should see him give up again to the wild common of nature, whatever was more than would supply the conveniencies of life to be had there for him and his family.

§. 49. Thus in the beginning all the world was *America*, and more so than that is now; for no such thing as *money* was any where known. Find out something that hath the *use and value of money* amongst his neighbours, you shall see the same man will begin presently to enlarge his possessions.

§. 50. But since gold and silver, being little useful to the life of man in proportion to food, raiment, and carriage, has its *value* only from the consent of men, whereof *labour* yet *makes*, in great part, *the measure*, it is plain, that men have agreed to a disproportionate and unequal *possession of the earth*, they having, by a tacit and voluntary consent, found out a way how a man may fairly possess more land than he himself can use the product of, by receiving in exchange for the overplus gold and silver, which may be hoarded up without injury to any one; these metals not spoiling or decaying in the hands of the possessor. This partage of things in an inequality of private possessions, men have made practicable out of the bounds of society, and without compact, only by putting a value on gold and silver, and tacitly agreeing in the use of money: for in governments, the laws regulate the right of property, and the possession of land is determined by positive constitutions.

§. 51 And thus, I think, it is very easy to conceive, without any difficulty, *how labour could at first begin a title of property* in the common things of nature, and how the spending it upon our uses bounded it. So that there could then be no reason of quarrelling about title, nor any doubt about the largeness of possession it gave. Right and conveniency went together; for as a man had a right to all he could employ his labour upon, so he had no temptation to labour for more than he could make use of. This left no room for controversy about the title, nor for incroachment on the right of others; what portion a man carved to himself, was easily seen; and it was useless, as well as dishonest, to carve himself too much, or take more than he needed.

Understanding Human Rights

Thomas Pogge

INTRODUCTION

"Everyone is entitled to a social and international order in which the rights and freedoms set forth in this Declaration can be fully realized." Thus reads Article 28 of the most important and most authoritative human rights document. My aim here is to explicate and to defend this Article, which may well be the most surprising and potentially most consequential sentence of the entire *Universal Declaration of Human Rights*.[1]

A conception of human rights may be factored into two main components:

- the *concept* of a human right used by this conception, or what one might also call its *understanding* of human rights, and
- the *substance* or content of the conception, the *objects* (goods) it singles out for protection by a set of human rights.

We face then two questions: What are human rights? And what human rights are there? This essay concentrates on the first of these topics.[2]

The opening of Article 28 sounds familiar from the preceding Articles and makes the reader expect that yet one more human right is about to be postulated. What follows, however, is not a new piece of content but a statement about how the contents already presented, "the rights and freedoms set forth in this Declaration," are to be understood. Article 28 does not add a further right to the list, but rather addresses the concept of a human right, the question what human rights are. It is then, on the one hand, consistent with any substantive account of the objects that a scheme of human rights ought to protect, but also clarifies, on the other hand, the meaning of any human rights postulated in the other Articles: They all are to be understood as claims on the institutional order of any comprehensive social systems. My goal is to develop and justify this institutional understanding of human rights suggested in Article 28.

The concept of a human right has six rather uncontroversial elements that any plausible understanding of human rights must incorporate. First, human rights express *ultimate moral* concerns: Agents have a moral duty to respect human rights, a duty that does not derive from a more general moral duty to comply with national or international laws. (In fact, the opposite may hold: Conformity with human rights is a moral requirement on

---

any legal order, whose capacity to create moral obligations depends in part on such conformity.) Second, human rights express **weighty** moral concerns, which normally override other normative considerations. Third, these moral concerns are focused on **human beings**, as all of them and they alone have human rights and the special moral status associated therewith. Fourth, with respect to these moral concerns, **all** human beings have **equal status**: They have exactly the same human rights, and the moral significance of these rights and of their fulfillment does not vary with whose human rights are at stake.[3] Fifth, human rights express moral concerns whose validity is **unrestricted**, i.e., they ought to be respected by all human agents irrespective of their particular epoch, culture, religion, moral tradition or philosophy. Sixth, these moral concerns are **broadly sharable**, that is, capable of being understood and appreciated by persons from different epochs and cultures as well as by adherents of a variety of different religions, moral traditions and philosophies. These last two elements of unrestrictedness and broad sharability are related in that we tend to feel more confident about conceiving of a moral concern as unrestricted when this concern is not parochial to some particular epoch, culture, religion, moral tradition or philosophy.[4]

My development of the institutional understanding of human rights suggested by Article 28 will take for granted these six elements of the concept of a human right. I will take for granted, that is, that any moral postulate can qualify as a human right only if it has each of the listed six features. The formulation of a complete conception of human rights involves then two further, more controversial tasks, namely: completing the explication of the concept of a human right (the task of the present essay) and defending a particular list of human rights.

THE INSTITUTIONAL UNDERSTANDING OF ARTICLE 28

Article 28 conceives human rights as being moral claims on any "social and international order." Any such institutional order is required, first and foremost, to be one "in which all human rights can be fully realized." Because any institutional order is created, maintained, and imposed by human agents, this requirement entails responsibilities for such agents to ensure that any institutional order they collaborate in upholding is one in which all human rights can be fully realized. So understood, your human rights are then not only moral claims on any institutional order imposed upon you, but also moral claims against those (especially: more influential and privileged) persons who contribute to its imposition.[5]

Viewing the full realization of human rights as a standard for judging any institutional order, how should such a standard be specified and applied? Let me suggest four plausible interpretive conjectures: (1) Alternative institutional orders that do not satisfy the requirement of Article 28 can be ranked by how close they come to fully realizing human rights: Social systems ought to be structured so that human rights can be realized in them as fully as possible. (2) How fully human rights **can** be realized in some institutional order is measured by how fully these human rights generally are, or (in the case of a hypothetical institutional order) generally would be, realized in it. (3) An institutional order **realizes** a human right insofar as (and fully if and only if) this human right is **fulfilled** for the persons upon whom this order is imposed. (4) A human right is fulfilled for some person if and only if this person enjoys **secure access to the object of this human right**. Here the **object** of a human right is whatever this human right is a right to—adequate nutrition, for example, or physical integrity. And what matters is **secure access** to such objects, rather than these objects themselves, because an institutional order is not morally problematic merely because some of its participants are choosing to fast or to compete in boxing matches.

Taking these four conjectures together, I thus read §28 as holding that the moral quality, or **justice**, of any institutional order depends primarily on its success in affording all its participants secure access to the objects of their human rights: Any institutional order is to be assessed and reformed principally by reference to its relative impact on the realization of the human rights of those on whom it is imposed.[6] Postulating a human right to X is then tantamount to declaring that every society and comparable social system ought to be so organized that, as far as possible, all its members enjoy secure access to X.

To be sure, no society can make the objects of all human rights **absolutely** secure for all. And making them as secure as possible would constitute a ludicrous drain on societal resources for what, at the margins, would be very minor increases in security. To be plausible, any conception of human rights employing the proposed concept must therefore incorporate an idea of reasonable security thresholds: Any human right of some person is **fulfilled** (completely) when its object is sufficiently secure—with the required degrees of security suitably adapted to the means and circumstances of the relevant social system. Thus, your human right to physical integrity (Article 3) is fulfilled by some institutional order, when it is sufficiently unlikely for you to suffer a violation of your physical integrity without your consent.[7] Of course, what is sufficiently unlikely, within a well-designed institutional order, may nevertheless happen. We should allow then for the possibility that a person is actually assaulted even while his human right is fulfilled (because

he is sufficiently secure from assault)—and also, conversely, for the possibility that someone's human right is not fulfilled (because his physical integrity is endangered) even though he never actually suffers an assault.

Given this understanding, a human right may be fulfilled for some and unfulfilled for other members of the same society. This is so because security of access to the object of some human right may vary across social groups. For example, only women may be facing a significant risk of assault, only rural dwellers may be in any real danger of hunger, or only persons of a certain skin color may be excluded from the franchise. Because an institutional order ought to be such that the human rights of all its participants are fulfilled, a human right is **fully realized** in some institutional order if and only if **all** of its participants have secure access to its object.

SOURCES OF THREATS

To realize human rights, a national institutional order must be such that the objects of all participants' human rights are secure against abuse by their government and its officials. But the danger of such abuse is merely one danger among others. An institutional order is also required to secure the objects of human rights against other social threats arising, for example, from death squads, criminals, domestic violence, or economic dependency.

The significance of this point becomes clearer when we contrast my understanding of human rights with another, more conventional understanding which presents a human right to X as a kind of meta-right—a moral right to an effective legal right to X. So understood, human rights demand their own juridification: The governments and citizens of every state ought to ensure that all human rights are incorporated into its fundamental legal texts and are observed and enforced within their state through an effective penal system.[8]

This understanding leads to demands that are, in my view, both too strong and too weak. That they are too strong can be shown by considering a human right to adequate nutrition (Article 25.1). A society may be so situated and organized that all its members have secure access to adequate nutrition, though not a legal right thereto. Would this be a human rights problem? I think not. Having the corresponding legal right in addition may be a good thing, but it is not so important that it must be built into the concept of a human right. Secure access is what really matters, and if this is achieved through a culture of solidarity among friends, relatives, neighbors, compatriots, then an additional legal right to adequate food when needed is not important. A conception of human rights should not then demand such additional legal rights, because it would thereby divert attention from its most important moral requirements.[9]

The demands entailed by this conventional understanding of human rights are also too weak, because legal and even constitutional rights, however conscientiously enforced, often do not suffice to ensure secure access. Here I am not merely thinking of the many showcase constitutions that detail a comprehensive list of strong protections but are widely ignored in governmental practice. It is likely that the proponents of the conventional understanding would not rest content with such "rights" either. I am mainly thinking of cases where, though legal rights are effectively enforced, poor and uneducated persons are nevertheless incapable of insisting on their rights, because they do not know what their legal rights are or lack either the knowledge or the economic independence necessary to have these rights enforced through the proper legal channels. Even if some state provides a legal path for domestic servants

to defend themselves against abuse by their employers, their human right to freedom from inhuman and degrading treatment (Article 5) may nevertheless remain unfulfilled for most of them.

Although any institutional order is required to secure the objects of its participants' human rights against all social threats, insecure access to these objects is nonetheless more serious when its source is official. It is, other things equal, more important that our laws and the agents and agencies of the state should not themselves endanger the objects of human rights than that they should protect these objects against other social dangers. The need for this differential weighing shows itself, for instance, in our attitudes toward the criminal law and the penal system.[10] The point can be communicated most quickly, perhaps, by distinguishing, in a preliminary way, six ways in which an institutional order may affect the lives of its participants. The following illustration uses six different scenarios, arranged in order of their intuitive injustice, in which, due to the prevailing institutional order, certain innocent persons are avoidably insecure in their access to some vital nutrients V (the vitamins contained in fresh fruit, say): First-class insecurities are **officially mandated**, paradigmatically by the law (legal restrictions prevent certain persons from buying foodstuffs containing V). Second-class insecurities arise from **legally authorized** conduct of private agents (sellers of foodstuffs containing V lawfully refuse to sell to certain persons). Third-class insecurities are **foreseeably engendered** through the uncoordinated conduct of agents under rules that do not specifically provide for these insecurities (certain persons, suffering severe poverty within an ill-conceived economic order, cannot afford to buy foodstuffs containing V). Fourth-class insecurities arise from private conduct that is **legally prohibited but generally tolerated** (sellers of foodstuffs containing V illegally refuse to sell to certain persons, but enforcement is lax and penalties are mild). Fifth-class insecurities arise from ***natural factors whose effects social rules avoidably leave unmitigated*** (certain persons are unable to metabolize V due to a treatable genetic defect but are not receiving the treatment that would correct their handicap). Sixth-class insecurities, finally, arise from ***self-caused factors whose effects social rules avoidably leave unmitigated*** (certain persons are unable to metabolize V due to a treatable self-caused disease[11] and are not receiving the treatment that would correct their ailment).

Behind the moral significance we attach to these distinctions lies the idea that an institutional order and the political and legal organs established through it should not merely ***serve*** justice, but also ***symbolize*** it. The point is important, because it undermines the plausibility of consequentialist (e.g., utilitarian) and hypothetical-contract (e.g., Rawlsian) moral conceptions which assess alternative institutional orders from the standpoint of prudent prospective participants who, of course, have no reason to care about this distinction among sources of threats.[12] A conception of human rights should avoid the mistake of such recipient-oriented approaches. To do so, it must, for each human right, distinguish and measure separately the different ways in which access to its object can be insecure; and it must then give more weight to first-class insecurities than to second-class insecurities, and so on.

THE GLOBAL NORMATIVE REACH OF HUMAN RIGHTS

Human rights are often said to be "universal"—a word also used in the title of the United Nations declaration. I have listed two respects in which human rights are universal among the uncontroversial elements of the concept of a human right: Human rights are equally possessed by, and are also equally binding upon, each and every human being. These two features are compatible with a nationalistic interpretation of human rights, according to which each person's responsibility for others' human rights is limited to his or her compatriots (cf. note 3). Yet Article 28 specifically excludes this interpretation by requiring that the ***international*** institutional order, as well, must be hospitable to the realization of human rights. This means that, in our time at least, human rights have global normative reach: Human rights give persons moral claims not merely on the institutional order of their own societies, which are claims against their fellow citizens, but also on the global institutional order, which are claims against their fellow human beings. Any national ***and any global*** institutional order is to be assessed and reformed principally by reference to its relative impact on the realization of the human rights of those on whom it is imposed. Human-rights based responsibilities arise from collaboration in the coercive imposition of any institutional order in which some persons avoidably lack secure access to the objects of their human rights. For persons collaborating in the coercive imposition of the global institutional order, these responsibilities extend worldwide.

Influential citizens and politicians in the wealthy countries nevertheless tend to regard the massive global underfulfillment of human rights with self-satisfied detachment. They are not unaware of the basic facts—for example, that about one third of all human beings or 18 million every year die of hunger and easily curable diseases,[13] that some 1.1 billion human beings, a quarter of humankind, live below the "$1 per day" international poverty line (typically on around $100 per person annually at official exchange rates, as compared to annual per capita GNI of $35,142 in the high-income countries),[14] and that hundreds of millions are oppressed by corrupt and undemocratic rulers, many of whom maintain themselves in power through violence and torture. But they do not view themselves as connected to, let alone responsible for, such suffering.

Such affluent persons might give three reasons for their supposed innocence. First, they might say that the massive underfulfillment of human rights is caused by a variety of local factors endemic to particular developing countries and is thus quite independent of the existing global institutional order.[15] Second, they might say that this global institutional order is so complex that it is impossible, even with the good will of the world's rich and mighty, to reform it in a way that would reliably improve human rights fulfillment. Third, they might say that this global institutional order is upheld by very many persons acting together so that the contribution of each of these persons is either negligible or even nonexistent.

The third of these reasons is a bad one. Even a very small fraction of responsibility for a very large harm can be quite large in absolute terms, and would be in the case before us.[16] Of course, nearly every influential and privileged person might say that he bears no responsibility at all because he alone is powerless to bring about any reform of our global institutional order. But this, too, is a poor argument. It would entail that each participant in a massacre is innocent provided any persons he killed would have been killed by others, had he abstained. It is true, of course, that the solution of a large problem requires many persons working together. But for such cooperation to occur, individuals must clearly indicate their willingness to participate, urge others to participate, and make efforts to facilitate cooperation. The number of citizens in the rich countries who are taking such steps toward solving the problem of world poverty is very small indeed.

The first two reasons are more difficult to disprove. It is quite true that national factors (political and economic system, culture, contingencies of history, population density, climate, soil conditions, and mineral wealth) significantly affect a society's levels of poverty and human rights fulfillment. Yet, it is also true that the existing global institutional order plays a profound role both in shaping many of these local factors and in influencing their effects. I can here only briefly illustrate this point by focusing on one consequential and reform-worthy feature of our global institutional order: Any group controlling a preponderance of the means of coercion within a country is internationally recognized as the legitimate government of this country's territory and people—regardless of how that group came to power, of how it exercises power, and of the extent to which it may be supported or opposed by the population it rules. That such a group exercising effective power receives international recognition means not merely that we are prepared to negotiate with it. It means also that we acknowledge this group's right to act for the people it rules, that we, most significantly, confer upon it the privileges freely to borrow in the country's name (international borrowing privilege) as well as freely to dispose of the country's natural resources (international resource privilege).

The *international borrowing privilege* includes the power to impose internationally valid legal obligations upon the country at large. Any successor government that refuses to honor debts incurred by an ever so corrupt, brutal, undemocratic, unconstitutional, repressive, unpopular predecessor will be severely punished by the banks and governments of other countries; at minimum it will lose its own borrowing privilege by being excluded from the international financial markets. Such refusals are therefore quite rare, as governments, even when newly elected after a dramatic break with the past, are compelled to pay the debts of their ever so awful predecessors.

The international borrowing privilege has three important negative effects on human rights fulfillment in the developing countries. First, this privilege facilitates borrowing by destructive governments. Such governments can borrow more money and can do so more cheaply than they could do if they alone, rather than the entire country, were obliged to repay. In this way, the borrowing privilege helps such governments maintain themselves in power even against near-universal popular discontent and opposition. Second, the international borrowing privilege imposes upon democratic successor regimes the often huge debts of their corrupt predecessors. It thereby saps the capacity of such democratic governments to implement institutional reforms and other political programs, thus rendering such governments less successful and less stable than they would otherwise be. Third, the international borrowing privilege provides incentives toward coup attempts: Whoever succeeds in bringing a preponderance of the means of coercion under his control gets the borrowing privilege as an additional reward.

The *international resource privilege* enjoyed by a group in power is much more than our mere acquiescence in its effective control over the natural resources of the country in question. This privilege includes the power to effect legally valid transfers of ownership rights in such resources. Thus a corporation that has purchased resources from the Saudi or Suharto families, or from Mobuto or Sani Abacha, has thereby become entitled to be—and actually *is*—recognized anywhere in the world as the legitimate owner of these resources. This is a remarkable feature of our global institutional order: A group that overpowers the guards and takes control of a warehouse may be able to give some of the merchandise to others, accepting money in exchange. But the fence who pays them becomes merely the possessor, not the owner, of the loot. Contrast this with a group that overpowers an elected government and takes control of a country. Such a group, too, can give away some of the country's natural resources, accepting money in exchange. In this case, however, the purchaser acquires not merely possession, but all the rights and liberties of ownership, which are supposed to be—and actually *are*—protected and enforced by all other states' courts and police forces. The international resource privilege, then, is the power to confer globally valid ownership rights in the country's resources.

The international resource privilege has disastrous effects on vast numbers of people, especially in developing countries in which the resource sector often constitutes a large segment of the national economy. Whoever can take power in such a country by whatever means can maintain his rule, even against widespread popular opposition, by buying the arms and soldiers he needs with (funds borrowed abroad in the country's name and) revenues from the export of natural resources. This fact in turn provides a strong incentive toward the undemocratic acquisition and unresponsive exercise of political power in these countries. And the international resources privilege also gives foreigners strong incentives to corrupt the officials of such countries who, no matter how badly they rule, continue to have resources to sell and money to spend. This shows how the local causal chain (persistent poverty caused by corrupt government caused by natural resource wealth) can itself be traced back to the international resource privilege, which makes it the case that resource-rich developing countries are more likely to experience coup attempts and civil wars and more likely also to be ruled by corrupt elites, so that—despite considerable natural wealth—poverty in these countries tends to decline only very slowly, if at all.[17]

These brief remarks about some effects of our current global institutional order show how one can refute the first two reasons that influential citizens and politicians in the wealthy countries might adduce in support of their innocence: The global institutional order they uphold does play a major role in causing the massive under-fulfillment of human rights today. It does so in four main ways: It crucially affects what sorts of persons shape national policy in the developing countries, what incentives these persons face, what options they have, and what impact the implementation of any of their options would have on domestic poverty and human rights fulfillment. Once the causal effects of specific global institutional arrangements (such as the two privileges I have discussed) are appreciated, it is not too difficult to formulate promising proposals for reform—though space constraints do not allow me to do this here.

THE NEED FOR ONE UNIVERSAL MORAL STANDARD

Many people see the fact that human rights are understood as universal as a strong reason for rejecting them. They view human rights as an outgrowth of a provincial morality whose pretension to universal validity is yet one more instance of European imperialism. They might say: "Non-European peoples have cultural traditions of their own from which they construct their own moral conceptions, perhaps wholly without the individualistic concept of a right. If you westerners want to make a conception of human rights the centerpiece of your political morality and want to realize it in your political system, then go ahead, by all means. But do leave other peoples the same freedom to define their values within the context of their own culture and national discourse."

Even if such admonitions are often put forward in bad faith,[18] they nevertheless require a reasoned response. The proposed interpretation of Article 28 makes available such a response: When human rights are understood as a standard for assessing only national institutional orders and governments, then it makes sense to envision a plurality of standards for states that differ in their history, culture, population size and density, natural environment, geopolitical context and stage of development. But when human rights are understood also as a standard for assessing the *global* institutional order, international diversity can no longer be accommodated in this way. There can be, at any given time, only *one* global institutional order. If it is to be possible to justify this global institutional order to persons in all parts of the world and also to reach agreement on how it should be adjusted and reformed in the light of new experience or changed circumstances, then we must aspire to a *single*, *universal* standard which all persons and peoples can accept as the basis for moral judgments about the global institutional order imposed on all of us.

Consider a domestic parallel. Imagine someone setting forth a moral conception of decent family life in the hope of achieving nationwide agreement. Our first reaction might be: We do not need such agreement, do not need such a shared conception. We can happily live together in one society even while we differ in many of our deepest aspirations, including those about family life. Having received this response, our interlocutor says that she meant to raise a quite different issue: The social rules of our society affect family life in countless ways. A few do so very directly—they define and limit the legal freedoms of spouses with regard to how they may treat each other and their children, how they may use and dispose of individually or jointly owned property, what kinds of education and medical care they may give to or withhold from their children, and so forth. Many other rules influence family life more indirectly, for example by affecting the economic burdens of child rearing, by shaping the physical and social environment within which families exist, or by determining the extent to which women are respected as the full equals of men, can successfully participate in the economy, and can present their concerns within the political process. Since a society's social rules are subject to intelligent (re)design and also have a great influence upon family life within this society, its citizens have a responsibility to bring their values concerning family life to bear upon the design of their shared institutional order. This, concludes our interlocutor, was her point in proposing a moral conception of decent family life.

Attaining a common standard for assessing a shared institutional order does not presuppose thoroughgoing agreement. Thus, our interlocutor in the domestic case need not decide what kinds of relationships among spouses and children are best. She may merely advocate certain constraints, insisting, for example, that wives must be secure from coercion by their husbands, which can be achieved by promoting through the education system equal respect and equal opportunities for women, by criminalizing inter-spousal rape, by safeguarding the voluntariness of religious practices, and by guaranteeing an economically safe option of divorce.

The analogous point holds for human rights as a moral standard for our global institutional order. This standard does not presuppose agreement on all or even most moral questions. It may merely demand that this global institutional order be so designed that, as far as possible, all persons have secure access to a few goods vital to all human beings. Now it is true that designing an institutional order with an eye to a few key values will have collateral

effects on the prevalence of other values. A solidly Catholic (or Muslim) family life may well be harder to sustain within a society that safeguards freedom of religion than in one in which Catholicism (Islam) is the official state religion. Similarly, the choice of a global institutional order designed to encourage the realization of human rights would have a differential impact on the cultures of various societies and on the popularity of various religions and ways of life. But such collateral effects are simply unavoidable: *Any* global (and national) institutional order can be criticized on the grounds that some values do not optimally thrive in it. So long as there is any global institutional order at all, this problem will necessarily persist.

Still, the problem can be mitigated by formulating a common moral standard so that the global institutional order it favors will allow a wide range of values to thrive locally. Human rights meet this condition, because they can be fully realized in a wide range of countries that differ greatly in their culture, traditions, and national institutional order.

The crucial thought here is this: Once human rights are understood as moral claims on our global institutional order, there simply is no attractive, tolerant and pluralistic alternative to conceiving them as valid universally. While the world can contain societies that are structured in a variety of ways (according to diverse, even incompatible values) it cannot itself be structured in a variety of ways. If the Iranians want their society to be organized as an Islamic state and we want ours to be a secular democracy, we can both have our way.[19] But if the Iranians wanted our *global* institutional order to be designed on the basis of the Koran while we want it to secure the objects of everyone's human rights, then we cannot both have our way. Our global institutional order cannot be designed so as to give all human beings the assurance that they will be able to meet their most basic needs **and** so as to give all governments maximal control over the lives and values of the peoples they rule **and** so as to ensure the fullest flourishing of Islam (etc.). Among competing plans for the future of our global institutional order, **one** will necessarily win out—through reason or through force. Neutrality is not an option here. The policies of the major societies will necessarily affect the outcome. It is, for the future of humankind, the most important and most urgent task of our time to set the development of our global institutional order upon an acceptable path. In order to do this together, peacefully, we need international agreement on a common moral standard for assessing the feasible alternatives. The best hope for such a common moral standard that is both plausible and capable of wide international acceptance today is a conception of human rights. At the very least, the burden now is on those who reject the very idea of human rights to formulate their own alternative moral vision for our common future.

MAKING HUMAN RIGHTS MORE BROADLY SHARABLE

In order to serve as a common moral standard, a conception of human rights must meet the sixth condition of broad sharability. Whether it does, depends not only on its content (the specific human rights it postulates), but also on the concept of a human right that it employs. Understanding human rights in the way I have proposed renders them significantly less vulnerable to critical doubts and hence more broadly sharable. Let me briefly indicate why this is so.

One important **communitarian** critique, often claimed to show that human rights are alien to communal cultures (for instance in Southeast Asia), asserts that human rights lead persons to view themselves as western-ers: as atomized, autonomous, secular, and

self-interested individuals ready to insist on their rights no matter what the cost may be to others or to society at large.[20] This critique may have some plausibility when human rights are understood as demanding their own juridifica-tion. But it has much less force when, as I have proposed, we avoid any conceptual connection of human rights with legal rights. We are then open to the idea that, in various economic and cultural contexts, secure access to the objects of human rights might be established in other ways. Yes, secure access to minimally adequate nutrition can generally be maintained through legal rights to food when needed. But it can also be maintained through other legal mecha-nisms—ones that keep land ownership widely dispersed, ban usury or speculative hoarding of basic staples, or provide child-care, education, retraining subsidies, unemployment benefits, or start-up loans. And non-legal practices—such as a culture of solidarity among friends, relatives, neighbors, compatriots—may also play an important role. Even those hostile to a legal-rights culture can, and often do, share the goal of establishing for all human beings secure access to certain vital goods (the objects of our human rights); and they may be quite will-ing to support a legally binding international commitment to shape national and interna-tional institutional arrangements so that all human beings can securely meet their most basic needs. We have reason then to conceive the realization of human rights in this broad way, rather than to insist on conceiving it narrowly as involving individual legal rights of matching content. We may feel strongly that such matching individual legal rights ought to exist in our own culture. But there is no good reason for requiring that secure access to the objects of human rights must be maintained in the same way everywhere on earth.

One important **libertarian** critique, which is often claimed to show that human rights are alien to individualist (esp. Anglo-American) cultures, asserts that human rights impose excessive restrictions on individual freedom by requiring all human agents to defend, as best they can, the objects of the human rights of any person anywhere.[21] Libertarians reject such a requirement not merely because it would be excessively burdensome in a world in which the human rights of so many remain unfulfilled, but mainly because they hold that all moral duties must be **negative** ones, that is, duties to refrain from harming others in certain ways. Libertarians may acknowledge that it is morally good to protect or to aid or to benefit others, but they deny that anyone has a moral duty to do such things. And since libertarians recognize no positive moral duties, they also deny the existence of any moral rights to be protected, aided, or benefited.

The proposed understanding of human rights can help accommodate this critique as well. It does not assume that agents have a human-rights based obligation merely by virtue of the fact that the human rights of some persons avoidably remain unfulfilled. Rather, such an obligation exists only for agents who significantly collaborate in imposing an institutional order that engenders this human-rights problem. Such agents must either stop contributing to this imposition or else compensate for this contribution by working toward appropriate institutional reforms and toward shielding the victims of injustice from the harms they help produce.[22] This is a **negative** duty on a par with the libertarians' favorite duty not to defraud others by breaking a contract or promise one has made. One can avoid all obligations arising from these duties by, respectively, not taking part in the coercive imposition of an unjust institutional order and not making any contracts or promises. But if one does contribute significantly to imposing an institutional order upon others, one is obligated to help ensure that it fulfills the human rights of these others as far as possible—just as, if one does make a promise, one is obligated to keep it.

RECONCILING CONFLICTING PRIORITIES AMONG HUMAN RIGHTS

The substance of a conception of human rights continues to be controversial. Prominent here is the debate between those who, like many western governments, emphasize civil and political rights and those who, like many socialist and developing states, emphasize social, economic, and cultural rights. I have shown already how my institutional concept of a human right can be detached from such controversies and defended with powerful, independent arguments. I will now show how its acceptance would also greatly reduce the significance of such controversies, which have occasioned much discord in the UN and elsewhere, and can thus facilitate agreement on the substance or content of our conception of human rights.

The institutional understanding does not lead to the idea that civil and political rights require only restraint, while social, economic, and cultural rights also demand positive efforts and costs. Rather, it emphasizes negative duties across the board: We are not to collaborate in the coercive imposition of any institutional order that avoidably fails to realize human rights. Moreover, there is no systematic correlation between categories of human rights, so understood, and effective institutional means for their realization, which may vary in time and place. Thus, in order to realize the classical civil right to freedom from inhuman and degrading treatment (Article 5), for instance, a state may have to do much more than create and enforce appropriate criminal statutes. It may also need to establish adequate social and economic safeguards, ensuring perhaps that domestic servants are literate, know about their rights and options, and have some economic security in case of job loss. Conversely, in order to realize a human right to adequate nutrition, perhaps all that is needed is an effective criminal statute against speculative hoarding of foodstuffs.

These considerations greatly narrow the *philosophical* gap between the friends of civil and political rights and the friends of social, economic, and cultural rights. Let me now show how my institutional understanding of human rights would also greatly reduce the *practical-political* significance of such controversies.

Suppose that only civil and political human rights are worthy of the name and that the social, economic, and cultural rights set forth in the *Universal Declaration* should therefore be repudiated. Conjoining this view with the institutional understanding of human rights yields the moral assertion that every human being is entitled to a national and global institutional order in which civil and political human rights can be fully realized. The existing global institutional order falls far short in this respect, and does so largely on account of the extreme poverty and inequality it reproduces: In most developing countries, the legal rights of ordinary citizens cannot be effectively enforced. Many of these countries are so poor that they cannot afford properly trained judges and police forces in sufficient numbers; and in many of them social institutions as well as politicians, officials and government agencies are in any case (partly through foreign influences) so thoroughly corrupted that the realization of civil and political human rights is not even seriously attempted. And even in those few countries where the legal rights of ordinary citizens can be effectively enforced, too many citizens are under too much economic pressure, too dependent on others, or too uneducated to effect the enforcement of their

rights. Thus, even the goal of realizing only the recognized civil and political human rights—if only they were interpreted in the light of Article 28—suffices to support the demand for global institutional reforms that would reduce global poverty and inequality.

Or suppose that only social, economic, and cultural human rights are worthy of the name. Conjoining this view with my reading of Article 28 yields the moral assertion that every human being is entitled to a national and global institutional order in which social, economic, and cultural human rights can be fully realized. The existing global institutional order falls far short in this respect as billions live in poverty, with little access to education and health care and in constant mortal danger from malnutrition and diseases that are easily controlled elsewhere. Their suffering is in large part due to the fact that the global poor live under governments that do little to alleviate their deprivations and often even contribute to them. The global poor are dispersed over some 150 countries, of which many are ruled not by general and public laws, but by powerful persons and groups (dictators, party bosses, military officers, landlords), often sponsored or assisted from abroad. In such societies, they are unable to organize themselves freely, to publicize their plight, or to work for reform through the political or legal system. Thus, even the goal of realizing only the usual social and economic human rights—if only they were interpreted in the light of Article 28—suffices to support the call for a global institutional order that would strongly encourage the incorporation of effective civil and political rights into national constitutions.[23]

I certainly did not mean to contend, in this section, that it makes no difference which rights we single out as human rights. I merely wanted to show that both the philosophical and the practical-political importance of the actual controversies about this question would diminish, if human rights were understood as Article 28 suggests: as moral claims on any institutional order. Even if we continue to disagree about which goods should be included in a conception of human rights, we will then—provided we really care about the realization of human rights rather than about ideological propaganda victories—work together on the same institutional reforms instead of arguing over how much praise or blame is deserved by this state or that.

CONCLUSION

In the aftermath of the second world war, a fledgling United Nations issued a ***Universal Declaration of Human Rights*** as the preeminent moral standard for all of humankind. This declaration, in its Article 28, specifically suggests that the realization of human rights will crucially depend on the achievement of a just global institutional order. In the intervening half century, the dominant powers, led by the US, have indeed created a far more comprehensive global order which severely constrains and conditions the political and economic institutions and policies of all national societies and governments. It is hardly surprising that these powers have tried to shape this order in their own interest. They have done so quite successfully, bringing peace and unprecedented prosperity to their populations. And yet, if we look at this global institutional order from a less parochial moral standpoint, which makes the worldwide realization of human rights the central concern, then we must conclude that this order is still deeply flawed and quite avoidably so. Yes, the last fifty years project a strong image of brisk progress from one declaration, summit, and convention to the next. There has been significant progress in formulations and ratifications of human rights documents,

in the gathering and publication of statistical information, and even in the realization of some human rights. But these fifty years have also culminated in a 200:1 income inequality between the most affluent tenth of humankind and the poorest quarter, those 1.5 billion persons subsisting below the international poverty line (*cf.* note 14). What makes this huge and steadily increasing inequality a monstrosity, morally, is the fact that the global poor are also so incredibly poor in absolute terms—lacking secure access to food, safe water, clothing, shelter, basic education, and also highly vulnerable to being deprived of the objects of their civil and political human rights by their governments as well as by private agents.

Since the features of the global institutional order are the decisive variable for the realization of human rights today, the primary moral responsibility for the realization of human rights must rest with those who shape and impose this order, with the governments and peoples of the most powerful and affluent countries. We lay down the fundamental rules governing internal and external sovereignty, trade, investments, loans, patents, trademarks, taxes, labor standards, environmental protection, use of seabed resources, and so on. And we enforce these rules through economic sanctions and occasional military interventions. These rules and their foreseeable effects are then our responsibility. And our failure to initiate meaningful institutional reforms that would drastically reduce global poverty is all the more appalling as the opportunity costs such reforms would impose upon ourselves have declined steeply with the end of the Cold War and the great economic and technological advances of the last decade.

Against this background I conclude, then, that the understanding of human rights and correlative human responsibilities which I have presented here in explication of Article 28 is compelling. It points us in the right direction: The key obstacle for the realization of human rights is the existing global economic and political order. Our preeminent moral task is to reshape this order so that all human beings have secure access to the basic goods they need to be full and respected members of their communities, societies, and of the wider world.

NOTES

¹ This **Universal Declaration** was adopted and proclaimed by the General Assembly of the United Nations on December 10, 1948, as resolution 217A(III). By drawing on this document for examples and illustrations, I do not endorse its particular list of human rights.

² A full understanding of the concept of a human right does not prejudge what human rights there are (or even whether there are any human rights at all). The fact that some formulated right has all the conceptual features of a human right does not entail that it exists (can be justified as such) any more than the fact that Hamlet as described has all the conceptual features of a human being entails that there was such a person. Settling what human rights there are requires not merely conceptual explication, but also substantive moral argument pro and con. It will be easier to engage in such substantive moral argument, however, once we will have a shared understanding of what human rights are and hence of what the assertion of some particular human right actually amounts to, especially in regard to correlative responsibilities.

³ This second component of equality is compatible with the view that the weight agents ought to give to the human rights of others varies with their relation to them—that agents have stronger moral reasons to

secure human rights in their own country, for example, than abroad—so long as this is not seen as being due to a difference in the moral significance of these rights, impersonally considered. (One can believe that the flourishing of all children is equally important even while one is also committed to showing greater concern for the flourishing of one's own children than for the flourishing of other children.)

⁴ These six central elements are discussed in greater detail in chapter 2 of my **World Poverty and Human Rights** (Cambridge: Polity Press 2002).

⁵ Participants in an institutional order will be differentially responsible for its moral quality, depending on how influential and privileged they are within it. Moreover, one must here distinguish responsibility from guilt and blame. Someone may contribute to an injustice and hence be partly responsible for it without being guilty or blameworthy on account of his conduct. For there might be applicable excuses such as, for instance, factual or moral error or ignorance.

⁶ "**Relative** impact," because a comparative judgment is needed about how much more or less fully human rights are realized in this institutional order than they would be realized in its feasible alternatives.

⁷ The task of specifying, for the object of each particular human right, acceptable probabilities for threats from various (official and nonofficial) sources belongs to the second, substantive component of a conception of human rights, which is not discussed in the present essay.

⁸ Thus, for example, Habermas: "The concept of human rights is not of moral origin, but . . . **by nature** juridical." Human rights "belong, through their structure, to a scheme of positive and coercive law which supports

justiciable subjective right claims. Hence it belongs to the meaning of human rights that they demand for themselves the status of constitutional rights." Jürgen Habermas: "Kants Idee des ewigen Friedens—aus dem historischen Abstand von 200 Jahren," *Kritische Justiz* 28 (1995) 3, 293–319. The quotes are from p.310 and p.312, italics are in the original, the translation is mine.

9 This is not to deny that some human rights may be difficult or impossible to realize without corresponding legal or even constitutional protections. This is clearly true, for example, of a human right to an effective remedy by the competent national tribunals for acts violating one's fundamental legal rights (Article 8). It is also hard to imagine a society under modern conditions whose members are secure in their property or have secure access to freedom of expression even while no legal right thereto exists.

10 We do not believe, for example, that the police should be authorized to beat up suspects in its custody if such authorization (by deterring criminal beatings) reduces the number of beatings overall.

11 This could have been caused, for instance, by their maintaining a long-term smoking habit in full knowledge of the medical dangers associated therewith.

12 My critique of such recipient-oriented moral conceptions is presented more fully in "Three Problems with Contractarian-Consequentialist Ways of Assessing Social Institutions," *Social Philosophy and Policy* 12 (1995), 241–266.

13 World Health Organization (WHO): *The World Health Report 2004,* Table 2 (also available at www.who.int/whr/2004).

14 See Shaohua Chen and Martin Ravallion: "How Have the World's Poorest Fared since the Early 1980s?," World Bank Research Observer, 19 (2004): 141–69, at 153; World Bank: *World Development Report 2007* (Washington: The World Bank 2006). Many economists reject such a comparison as misleading, claiming that the comparison should be made in terms of purchasing power parities (PPPs) rather than market exchange rates. However, market exchange rates are quite appropriate to highlight international inequalities in expertise and bargaining power as well as the increasing avoidability of poverty which is manifest in the fact that just one percent of the national incomes of the high-income countries would suffice to raise all 2,735 million now living below "$2 per day" up to this line.

15 A typical example is John Rawls, "The Law of Peoples" in *On Human Rights*, ed. Stephen Shute and Susan Hurley (New York, Basic Books 1993), 77: "the problem is commonly the nature of the public political culture and the religious and philosophical traditions that underlie its institutions. The great social evils in poorer societies are likely to be oppressive government and corrupt elites."

16 Cf. Derek Parfit, *Reasons and Persons* (Oxford, Oxford University Press 1984), Chapter 3 entitled "Five Mistakes in Moral Mathematics." Even if the world's privileged and influential persons each bear only one billionth of the responsibility for the avoidable underfulfillment of human rights caused by the existing global institutional order, the responsibility of each would still be quite substantial.

17 All this is confirmed by the—otherwise startling—empirical finding of a *negative* correlation between developing countries' resource endowments and their rates of economic growth, exemplified by the relatively low growth rates, over the past 40 years,

of resource-rich Nigeria, Kenya, Angola, Mozambique, Zaire, Venezuela, Brazil, Saudi Arabia, Burma, and the Philippines (Indonesia's growth was better, but poverty remains a great problem there). Cf. Ricky Lam and Leonard Wantchekon: "Dictatorships as a Political Dutch Disease," working paper (Yale University, January 19, 1999): "a one percentage increase in the size of the natural resource sector generates a decrease by half a percentage point in the probability of survival of democratic regimes" (35). The paper specifically supports the hypothesis that the causal connection between resource wealth and poor economic growth (the so-called "Dutch Disease") is mediated through reduced chances for democracy: "all petrostates or resource-dependent countries in Africa fail to initiate meaningful political reforms. . . . besides South Africa, transition to democracy has been successful only in resource-poor countries" (31).

18 For example, by westerners who benefit from or support sweat shops, child prostitution, or torture in developing countries and seek to defend their involvement in such practices against moral criticism from other westerners.

19 Mutual toleration with regard to this question is at least *possible*. This is not to say that we *ought* to tolerate the national institutional order of any other country no matter how unjust it may be.

20 This criticism has been voiced by Singapore's patriarch Lee Kuan Yew, by Mary Ann Glendon: *Rights Talk: The Impoverishment of Political Discourse* (New York, The Free Press 1991), and by many others as well.

21 This critique is provoked by an understanding of human rights that is suggested, for example, in David Luban's essay "Just War and Human Rights" in *International Ethics*, ed. Charles Beitz et al. (Princeton, Princeton University Press 1985), 209: "A human right, then, will be a right whose beneficiaries are all humans and whose obligors are all humans in a position to effect the right." Cf. also the view developed in Henry Shue, *Basic Rights* (Princeton, Princeton University Press 1980/1996), though Shue avoids the expression "human rights."

22 We might try to initiate appropriate changes in our global institutional order, for example, by publicizing its nature and effects and by formulating feasible paths of reform. And we might help preempt or undo some of the harms through volunteer work or contributions to effective relief organisations (such as UNICEF, Oxfam, or Amnesty International). How much should one contribute to such reform and protection efforts? In proportion to one's affluence and influence, at least as much as would suffice for the full realization of human rights if most similarly situated others followed suit. Thus, if one percent of the income of the most affluent tenth of humankind would suffice to eradicate world hunger within a few years, then we should give at least one percent of our incomes to fight hunger. For an extensive discussion of the fair distribution of demands, see Liam Murphy: *Moral Demands in Nonideal Theory* (New York: Oxford University Press 2000).

23 A global institutional order could give such encouragement through centrally determined economic (trade, loans, aid) and diplomatic privileges and penalties. Stronger sanctions, like embargoes and military interventions, should probably be triggered only in cases of extreme oppression.—Some of the governments that profess allegiance solely to social, economic, and cultural human rights maintain that certain prominent (legal) civil and political rights are currently unnecessary in their country: unhelpful, or even counter-

productive (distracting and expensive). But most of these governments would, I believe, concede that more extensive civil and political rights would often be helpful elsewhere or at other times. The Chinese government, for example, might maintain that instituting more extensive civil and political rights in China today would not work to the benefit of the Chinese poor, for whom the Party and the government are already doing all they can. But the same government might acknowledge that there are other regions today—Africa, perhaps, or Latin America, Eastern Europe, the former Soviet Union, Indonesia—where more extensive civil and political rights would help the poor and ethnic minorities to fend for themselves. Unofficially, some of its members would perhaps also acknowledge that the Chinese famine of 1958–61, whose staggering death toll of nearly 30 million has only recently become widely known, could not have occurred in a country with inde-

pendent mass media and a competitive political system. Compare an analogous domestic case. A decent police officer, who cares deeply about the suffering caused by crime, may see no good reason why she and her fellow officers at her station should not just do everything they can to nail a suspect they know to be guilty, without regard to procedural niceties. But would she also advocate a civil order in which the police in general can operate without procedural encumbrances? She must surely understand that not all officers would always use their greater powers in a decent, fair and judicious fashion, and also that some persons with criminal intentions would then have much greater incentives to try to join the police force. This example shows how one may consistently believe of certain safeguards that their observance should be strongly encouraged by social institutions and that they are unnecessary or even counterproductive in this or that particular case.

Universal Dimensions of Black Struggle II: Human Rights, Civil Rights

Malcolm X

[INTERVIEWER]: One question that I've wondered about—in several of your lectures you've stressed the idea that the struggle of your people is for human rights rather than civil rights. Can you explain a bit what you mean by that?

MALCOLM X: Civil rights actually keeps the struggle within the domestic confines of America. It keeps it under the jurisdiction of the American government, which means that as long as our struggle for what we're seeking is labeled civil rights, we can only go to Washington, DC, and then we rely upon either the Supreme Court, the President or the Congress or the senators. These senators—many of them are racists. Many of the congressmen are racists. Many of the judges are racists and oftentimes the president himself is a very shrewdly camouflaged racist. And so we really can't get meaningful redress for our grievances when we are depending upon these grievances being redressed just within the jurisdiction of the United States government.

On the other hand, human rights go beyond the jurisdiction of this government. Human rights are international. Human rights are something that a man has by dint of his having been born. The labeling of our struggle in this country under the title civil rights of the past 12 years has actually made it impossible for us to get outside help. Many foreign nations, many of our brothers and sisters on the African continent who have gotten their independence, have restrained themselves, have refrained from becoming vocally or actively involved in our struggle for fear that they would be violating US protocol, that they would be accused of getting involved in America's domestic affairs.

On the other hand, when we label it human rights, it internationalizes the problem and puts it at a level that makes it possible for any nation or any people anywhere on this earth to speak out in behalf of our human rights struggle.

So we feel that by calling it civil rights for the past 12 years, we've actually been barking up the wrong tree, that ours is a problem of *human* rights.

From Two Speeches of Malcolm X, 1965, 1990 by Betty Shabazz and Pathfinder Press. Reprinted with permission of Pathfinder Press.

Plus, if we have our human rights, our civil rights are automatic. If we're respected as a human being, we'll be respected as a citizen; and in this country the black man not only is not respected as a citizen, he is not even respected as a human being.

And the proof is that you find in many instances people can come to this country from other countries—they can come to this country from behind the Iron Curtain—and despite the fact that they come here from these other places, they don't have to have civil-rights legislation passed in order for their rights to be safeguarded.

No new legislation is necessary for foreigners who come here to have their rights safeguarded. The Constitution is sufficient, but when it comes to the black men who were born here—whenever we are asking for our rights, they tell us that new legislation is necessary.

Well, we don't believe that. The Organization of Afro-American Unity feels that as long as our people in this country confine their struggle within the limitations and under the jurisdiction of the United States government, we remain within the confines of the vicious system that has done nothing but exploit and oppress us ever since we've been here. So we feel that our only real hope is to make known that our problem is not a Negro problem or an American problem but rather, it has become a human problem, a world problem, and it has to be attacked at the world level, at a level at which all segments of humanity can intervene in our behalf.

Universal Declaration of
Human Rights

United Nations

Adopted and proclaimed by General Assembly resolution 217 A (III) of 10 December 1948

On December 10, 1948 the General Assembly of the United Nations adopted and proclaimed the Universal Declaration of Human Rights the full text of which appears in the following pages. Following this historic act the Assembly called upon all Member countries to publicize the text of the Declaration and "to cause it to be disseminated, displayed, read and expounded principally in schools and other educational institutions, without distinction based on the political status of countries or territories."

PREAMBLE

- Whereas recognition of the inherent dignity and of the equal and inalienable rights of all members of the human family is the foundation of freedom, justice and peace in the world,

- Whereas disregard and contempt for human rights have resulted in barbarous acts which have outraged the conscience of mankind, and the advent of a world in which human beings shall enjoy freedom of speech and belief and freedom from fear and want has been proclaimed as the highest aspiration of the common people,

- Whereas it is essential, if man is not to be compelled to have recourse, as a last resort, to rebellion against tyranny and oppression, that human rights should be protected by the rule of law,

- Whereas it is essential to promote the development of friendly relations between nations,

- Whereas the peoples of the United Nations have in the Charter reaffirmed their faith in fundamental human rights, in the dignity and worth of the human person and in the equal rights of men and women and have determined to promote social progress and better standards of life in larger freedom,

Universal Declaration of Human Rights, Adopted by General Assembly, December 10, 1948. Reprinted by permission of the United Nations.

- Whereas Member States have pledged themselves to achieve, in co-operation with the United Nations, the promotion of universal respect for and observance of human rights and fundamental freedoms,
- Whereas a common understanding of these rights and freedoms is of the greatest importance for the full realization of this pledge,

Now, Therefore THE GENERAL ASSEMBLY proclaims THIS UNIVERSAL DECLARATION OF HUMAN RIGHTS as a common standard of achievement for all peoples and all nations, to the end that every individual and every organ of society, keeping this Declaration constantly in mind, shall strive by teaching and education to promote respect for these rights and freedoms and by progressive measures, national and international, to secure their universal and effective recognition and observance, both among the peoples of Member States themselves and among the peoples of territories under their jurisdiction.

ARTICLE 1

All human beings are born free and equal in dignity and rights. They are endowed with reason and conscience and should act towards one another in a spirit of brotherhood.

ARTICLE 2

Everyone is entitled to all the rights and freedoms set forth in this Declaration, without distinction of any kind, such as race, colour, sex, language, religion, political or other opinion, national or social origin, property, birth or other status. Furthermore, no distinction shall be made on the basis of the political, jurisdictional or international status of the country or territory to which a person belongs, whether it be independent, trust, non-self-governing or under any other limitation of sovereignty.

ARTICLE 3

Everyone has the right to life, liberty and security of person.

ARTICLE 4

No one shall be held in slavery or servitude; slavery and the slave trade shall be prohibited in all their forms.

ARTICLE 5

No one shall be subjected to torture or to cruel, inhuman or degrading treatment or punishment.

ARTICLE 6

Everyone has the right to recognition everywhere as a person before the law.

ARTICLE 7

All are equal before the law and are entitled without any discrimination to equal protection of the law. All are entitled to equal protection against any discrimination in violation of this Declaration and against any incitement to such discrimination.

ARTICLE 8

Everyone has the right to an effective remedy by the competent national tribunals for acts violating the fundamental rights granted him by the constitution or by law.

ARTICLE 9

No one shall be subjected to arbitrary arrest, detention or exile.

ARTICLE 10

Everyone is entitled in full equality to a fair and public hearing by an independent and impartial tribunal, in the determination of his rights and obligations and of any criminal charge against him.

ARTICLE 11

1. Everyone charged with a penal offence has the right to be presumed innocent until proved guilty according to law in a public trial at which he has had all the guarantees necessary for his defence.
2. No one shall be held guilty of any penal offence on account of any act or omission which did not constitute a penal offence, under national or international law, at the time when it was committed. Nor shall a heavier penalty be imposed than the one that was applicable at the time the penal offence was committed.

ARTICLE 12

No one shall be subjected to arbitrary interference with his privacy, family, home or correspondence, nor to attacks upon his honour and reputation. Everyone has the right to the protection of the law against such interference or attacks.

ARTICLE 13

1. Everyone has the right to freedom of movement and residence within the borders of each state.
2. Everyone has the right to leave any country, including his own, and to return to his country.

ARTICLE 14

1. Everyone has the right to seek and to enjoy in other countries asylum from persecution.
2. This right may not be invoked in the case of prosecutions genuinely arising from non-political crimes or from acts contrary to the purposes and principles of the United Nations.

ARTICLE 15

1. Everyone has the right to a nationality.
2. No one shall be arbitrarily deprived of his nationality nor denied the right to change his nationality.

ARTICLE 16

1. Men and women of full age, without any limitation due to race, nationality or religion, have the right to marry and to found a family. They are entitled to equal rights as to marriage, during marriage and at its dissolution.
2. Marriage shall be entered into only with the free and full consent of the intending spouses.
3. The family is the natural and fundamental group unit of society and is entitled to protection by society and the State.

ARTICLE 17

1. Everyone has the right to own property alone as well as in association with others.
2. No one shall be arbitrarily deprived of his property.

ARTICLE 18

Everyone has the right to freedom of thought, conscience and religion; this right includes freedom to change his religion or belief, and freedom, either alone or in community with others and in public or private, to manifest his religion or belief in teaching, practice, worship and observance.

ARTICLE 19

Everyone has the right to freedom of opinion and expression; this right includes freedom to hold opinions without interference and to seek, receive and impart information and ideas through any media and regardless of frontiers.

ARTICLE 20

1. Everyone has the right to freedom of peaceful assembly and association.
2. No one may be compelled to belong to an association.

ARTICLE 21

1. Everyone has the right to take part in the government of his country, directly or through freely chosen representatives.
2. Everyone has the right of equal access to public service in his country.
3. The will of the people shall be the basis of the authority of government; this will shall be expressed in periodic and genuine elections which shall be by universal and equal suffrage and shall be held by secret vote or by equivalent free voting procedures.

ARTICLE 22

Everyone, as a member of society, has the right to social security and is entitled to realization, through national effort and international co-operation and in accordance with the organization and resources of each State, of the economic, social and cultural rights indispensable for his dignity and the free development of his personality.

ARTICLE 23

1. Everyone has the right to work, to free choice of employment, to just and favourable conditions of work and to protection against unemployment.
2. Everyone, without any discrimination, has the right to equal pay for equal work.
3. Everyone who works has the right to just and favourable remuneration ensuring for himself and his family an existence worthy of human dignity, and supplemented, if necessary, by other means of social protection.
4. Everyone has the right to form and to join trade unions for the protection of his interests.

ARTICLE 24

Everyone has the right to rest and leisure, including reasonable limitation of working hours and periodic holidays with pay.

ARTICLE 25

1. Everyone has the right to a standard of living adequate for the health and well-being of himself and of his family, including food, clothing, housing and medical care and necessary social services, and the right to security in the event of unemployment, sickness, disability, widowhood, old age or other lack of livelihood in circumstances beyond his control.
2. Motherhood and childhood are entitled to special care and assistance. All children, whether born in or out of wedlock, shall enjoy the same social protection.

ARTICLE 26

1. Everyone has the right to education. Education shall be free, at least in the elementary and fundamental stages. Elementary education shall be compulsory. Technical and professional education shall be made generally available and higher education shall be equally accessible to all on the basis of merit.

2. Education shall be directed to the full development of the human personality and to the strengthening of respect for human rights and fundamental freedoms. It shall promote understanding, tolerance and friendship among all nations, racial or religious groups, and shall further the activities of the United Nations for the maintenance of peace.

3. Parents have a prior right to choose the kind of education that shall be given to their children.

ARTICLE 27

1. Everyone has the right freely to participate in the cultural life of the community, to enjoy the arts and to share in scientific advancement and its benefits.

2. Everyone has the right to the protection of the moral and material interests resulting from any scientific, literary or artistic production of which he is the author.

ARTICLE 28

Everyone is entitled to a social and international order in which the rights and freedoms set forth in this Declaration can be fully realized.

ARTICLE 29

1. Everyone has duties to the community in which alone the free and full development of his personality is possible.

2. In the exercise of his rights and freedoms, everyone shall be subject only to such limitations as are determined by law solely for the purpose of securing due recognition and respect for the rights and freedoms of others and of meeting the just requirements of morality, public order and the general welfare in a democratic society.

3. These rights and freedoms may in no case be exercised contrary to the purposes and principles of the United Nations.

ARTICLE 30

Nothing in this Declaration may be interpreted as implying for any State, group or person any right to engage in any activity or to perform any act aimed at the destruction of any of the rights and freedoms set forth herein.

Convention on the Elimination of All Forms of Discrimination against Women

United Nations

INTRODUCTION

On 18 December 1979, the Convention on the Elimination of All Forms of Discrimination against Women was adopted by the United Nations General Assembly. It entered into force as an international treaty on 3 September 1981 after the twentieth country had ratified it. By the tenth anniversary of the Convention in 1989, almost one hundred nations have agreed to be bound by its provisions.

The Convention was the culmination of more than thirty years of work by the United Nations Commission on the Status of Women, a body established in 1946 to monitor the situation of women and to promote women's rights. The Commission's work has been instrumental in bringing to light all the areas in which women are denied equality with men. These efforts for the advancement of women have resulted in several declarations and conventions, of which the Convention on the Elimination of All Forms of Discrimination against Women is the central and most comprehensive document.

Among the international human rights treaties, the Convention takes an important place in bringing the female half of humanity into the focus of human rights concerns. The spirit of the Convention is rooted in the goals of the United Nations: to reaffirm faith in fundamental human rights, in the dignity, v and worth of the human person, in the equal rights of men and women. The present document spells out the meaning of equality and how it can be achieved. In so doing, the Convention establishes not only an international bill of rights for women, but also an agenda for action by countries to guarantee the enjoyment of those rights.

In its preamble, the Convention explicitly acknowledges that "extensive discrimination against women continues to exist", and emphasizes that such discrimination "violates the principles of equality of rights and respect for human dignity". As defined in article 1, discrimination is understood as "any distinction, exclusion or restriction made o.1 the basis of sex . . . in the political, economic, social, cultural, civil or any other field". The Convention gives positive affirmation to the principle of equality by requiring States parties to take "all appropriate measures, including legislation, to ensure the full development and advancement of women, for the purpose of guaranteeing them the exercise and enjoyment of human rights and fundamental freedoms on a basis of equality with men"(article 3).

The agenda for equality is specified in fourteen subsequent articles. In its approach, the Convention covers three dimensions of the situation of women. Civil rights and the legal status of women are dealt with in great detail. In addition, and unlike other human rights treaties, the Convention is also concerned with the dimension of human reproduction as well as with the impact of cultural factors on gender relations.

The legal status of women receives the broadest attention. Concern over the basic rights of political participation has not diminished since the adoption of the Convention on the Political Rights of Women in 1952. Its provisions, therefore, are restated in article 7 of the present document, whereby women are guaranteed the rights to vote, to hold public office and to exercise public functions. This includes equal rights for women to represent their countries at the international level (article 8). The Convention on the Nationality of Married Women—adopted in 1957—is integrated under article 9 providing for the statehood of women, irrespective of their marital status. The Convention, thereby, draws attention to the fact that often women's legal status has been linked to marriage, making them dependent on their husband's nationality rather than individuals in their own right. Articles 10, 11 and 13, respectively, affirm women's rights to non-discrimination in education, employment and economic and social activities. These demands are given special emphasis with regard to the situation of rural women, whose particular struggles and vital economic contributions, as noted in article 14, warrant more attention in policy planning. Article 15 asserts the full equality of women in civil and business matters, demanding that all instruments directed at restricting women's legal capacity "shall be deemed null and void". Finally, in article 16, the Convention returns to the issue of marriage and family relations, asserting the equal rights and obligations of women and men with regard to choice of spouse, parenthood, personal rights and command over property.

Aside from civil rights issues, the Convention also devotes major attention to a most vital concern of women, namely their reproductive rights. The preamble sets the tone by stating that "the role of women in procreation should not be a basis for discrimination". The link between discrimination and women's reproductive role is a matter of recurrent concern in the Convention. For example, it advocates, in article 5, "a proper understanding of maternity as a social function", demanding fully shared responsibility for child-rearing by both sexes. Accordingly, provisions for maternity protection and child-care are proclaimed as essential rights and are incorporated into all areas of the Convention, whether dealing with employment, family law, health core or education. Society's obligation extends to offering social services, especially child-care facilities, that allow individuals to combine family responsibilities with work and participation in public life. Special measures for maternity protection are recommended and "shall not be considered discriminatory". (article 4). "The Convention also affirms women's right to reproductive choice. Notably, it is the only human rights treaty to mention family planning. States parties are obliged to include advice on family planning in the education process (article 1 O.h) and to develop family codes that guarantee women's rights "to decide freely and responsibly on the number and spacing of their children and to hove access to the information, education and means to enable them to exercise these rights" (article 16.e).

The third general thrust of the Convention aims at enlarging our understanding of the concept of human rights, as it gives formal recognition to the influence of culture and tradition on restricting women's enjoyment of their fundamental rights. These forces take shape in stereotypes, customs and norms which give rise to the multitude of legal, political and economic constraints on the advancement of women. Noting this interrelationship, the preamble of the Convention stresses "that a change in the traditional role of men as well as the role of women in society and in the family is needed to achieve full equality of men and women". States parties are therefore obliged to work towards the modification of social and cultural patterns of individual conduct in order to eliminate "prejudices and customary and all other practices which are based on the idea of the inferiority or the superiority of either of the sexes or on stereotyped roles for men and women" (article 5). And Article 1O.c. mandates the revision of textbooks, school programmes and teaching methods with a view to eliminating stereotyped concepts in the field of education. Finally, cultural patterns which define the public realm as a man's world and the domestic sphere as women's domain are strongly targeted in all of the Convention's provisions that affirm the equal responsibilities of both sexes in family life and their equal rights with regard to education and employment. Altogether, the Convention provides a comprehensive framework for challenging the various forces that have created and sustained discrimination based upon sex.

The implementation of the Convention is monitored by the Committee on the Elimination of Discrimination against Women (CEDAW). The Committee's mandate and the administration of the treaty are defined in the Articles 17 to 30 of the Convention. The Committee is composed of 23 experts nominated by their Governments and elected by the States parties as individuals "of high moral standing and competence in the field covered by the Convention".

At least every four years, the States parties are expected to submit a national report to the Committee, indicating the measures they have adopted to give effect to the provisions of the Convention. During its annual session, the Committee members discuss these reports with the Government representatives and explore with them areas for further action by the specific country. The Committee also makes general recommendations to the States parties on matters concerning the elimination of discrimination against women.

The full text of the Convention is set out herein.

CONVENTION ON THE ELIMINATION OF ALL FORMS OF DISCRIMINATION AGAINST WOMEN

The States Parties to the present Convention,

Noting that the Charter of the United Nations reaffirms faith in fundamental human rights, in the dignity and worth of the human person and in the equal rights of men and women,

Noting that the Universal Declaration of Human Rights affirms the principle of the inadmissibility of discrimination and proclaims that all human beings are born free and equal in dignity and rights and that everyone is entitled to all the rights and freedoms set forth therein, without distinction of any kind, including distinction based on sex,

Noting that the States Parties to the International Covenants on Human Rights have the obligation to ensure the equal rights of men and women to enjoy all economic, social, cultural, civil and political rights,

Considering the international conventions concluded under the auspices of the United Nations and the specialized agencies promoting equality of rights of men and women,

Noting also the resolutions, declarations and recommendations adopted by the United Nations and the specialized agencies promoting equality of rights of men and women,

Concerned, however, that despite these various instruments extensive discrimination against women continues to exist,

Recalling that discrimination against women violates the principles of equality of rights and respect for human dignity, is an obstacle to the participation of women, on equal terms with men, in the political, social, economic and cultural life of their countries, hampers the growth of the prosperity of society and the family and makes more difficult the full development of the potentialities of women in the service of their countries and of humanity,

Concerned that in situations of poverty women have the least access to food, health, education, training and opportunities for employment and other needs,

Convinced that the establishment of the new international economic order based on equity and justice will contribute significantly towards the promotion of equality between men and women,

Emphasizing that the eradication of apartheid, all forms of racism, racial discrimination, colonialism, neo-colonialism, aggression, foreign occupation and domination and interference in the internal affairs of States is essential to the full enjoyment of the rights of men and women,

Affirming that the strengthening of international peace and security, the relaxation of international tension, mutual co-operation among all States irrespective of their social and economic systems, general and complete disarmament, in particular nuclear disarmament under strict and effective international control, the affirmation of the principles of justice, equality and mutual benefit in relations among countries and the realization of the right of peoples under alien and colonial domination and foreign occupation to self-determination and independence, as well as respect for national sovereignty and territorial integrity, will promote social progress and development and as a consequence will contribute to the attainment of full equality between men and women,

Convinced that the full and complete development of a country, the welfare of the world and the cause of peace require the maximum participation of women on equal terms with men in all fields,

Bearing in mind the great contribution of women to the welfare of the family and to the development of society, so far not fully recognized, the social significance of maternity and the role of both parents in the family and in the upbringing of children, and aware that the role of women in procreation should not be a basis for discrimination but that the upbringing of children requires a sharing of responsibility between men and women and society as a whole,

Aware that a change in the traditional role of men as well as the role of women in society and in the family is needed to achieve full equality between men and women,

Determined to implement the principles set forth in the Declaration on the Elimination of Discrimination against Women and, for that purpose, to adopt the measures required for the elimination of such discrimination in all its forms and manifestations,

Have agreed on the following:

PART I

Article 1

For the purposes of the present Convention, the term "discrimination against women" shall mean any distinction, exclusion or restriction made on the basis of sex which has the effect or purpose of impairing or nullifying the recognition, enjoyment or exercise by women, irrespective of their marital status, on a basis of equality of men and women, of human rights and fundamental freedoms in the political, economic, social, cultural, civil or any other field.

Article 2

States Parties condemn discrimination against women in all its forms, agree to pursue by all appropriate means and without delay a policy of eliminating discrimination against women and, to this end, undertake:

a. To embody the principle of the equality of men and women in their national constitutions or other appropriate legislation if not yet incorporated therein and to ensure, through law and other appropriate means, the practical realization of this principle;

b. To adopt appropriate legislative and other measures, including sanctions where appropriate, prohibiting all discrimination against women;

c. To establish legal protection of the rights of women on an equal basis with men and to ensure through competent national tribunals and other public institutions the effective protection of women against any act of discrimination;

d. To refrain from engaging in any act or practice of discrimination against women and to ensure that public authorities and institutions shall act in conformity with this obligation;

e. To take all appropriate measures to eliminate discrimination against women by any person, organization or enterprise;

f. To take all appropriate measures, including legislation, to modify or abolish existing laws, regulations, customs and practices which constitute discrimination against women;

g. To repeal all national penal provisions which constitute discrimination against women.

Article 3

States Parties shall take in all fields, in particular in the political, social, economic and cultural fields, all appropriate measures, including legislation, to en sure the full development and advancement of women, for the purpose of guaranteeing them the exercise and enjoyment of human rights and fundamental freedoms on a basis of equality with men.

Article 4

1. Adoption by States Parties of temporary special measures aimed at accelerating de facto equality between men and women shall not be considered discrimination as defined in the present Convention, but shall in no way entail as a consequence the maintenance of unequal or separate standards; these measures shall be discontinued when the objectives of equality of opportunity and treatment have been achieved.

2. Adoption by States Parties of special measures, including those measures contained in the present Convention, aimed at protecting maternity shall not be considered discriminatory.

Article 5

States Parties shall take all appropriate measures:

a. To modify the social and cultural patterns of conduct of men and women, with a view to achieving the elimination of prejudices and customary and all other practices which are based on the idea of the inferiority or the superiority of either of the sexes or on stereotyped roles for men and women;

b. To ensure that family education includes a proper understanding of maternity as a social function and the recognition of the common responsibility of men and women in the upbringing and development of their children, it being understood that the interest of the children is the primordial consideration in all cases.

Article 6

States Parties shall take all appropriate measures, including legislation, to suppress all forms of traffic in women and exploitation of prostitution of women.

PART II

Article 7

States Parties shall take all appropriate measures to eliminate discrimination against women in the political and public life of the country and, in particular, shall ensure to women, on equal terms with men, the right:

a. To vote in all elections and public referenda and to be eligible for election to all publicly elected bodies;

b. To participate in the formulation of government policy and the implementation thereof and to hold public office and perform all public functions at all levels of government;

c. To participate in non-governmental organizations and associations concerned with the public and political life of the country.

Article 8

States Parties shall take all appropriate measures to ensure to women, on equal terms with men and without any discrimination, the opportunity to represent their Governments at the international level and to participate in the work of international organizations.

Article 9

1. States Parties shall grant women equal rights with men to acquire, change or retain their nationality. They shall ensure in particular that neither marriage to an alien nor change of nationality by the husband during marriage shall automatically change the nationality of the wife, render her stateless or force upon her the nationality of the husband.

2. States Parties shall grant women equal rights with men with respect to the nationality of their children.

PART III

Article 10

States Parties shall take all appropriate measures to eliminate discrimination against women in order to ensure to them equal rights with men in the field of education and in particular to ensure, on a basis of equality of men and women:

a. The same conditions for career and vocational guidance, for access to studies and for the achievement of diplomas in educational establishments of all categories in rural as well as in urban areas; this equality shall be ensured in pre-school, general, technical, professional and higher technical education, as well as in all types of vocational training;

b. Access to the same curricula, the same examinations, teaching staff with qualifications of the same standard and school premises and equipment of the same quality;

c. The elimination of any stereotyped concept of the roles of men and women at all levels and in all forms of education by encouraging coeducation and other types of education which will help to achieve this aim and, in particular, by the revision of textbooks and school programmes and the adaptation of teaching methods;

d. The same opportunities to benefit from scholarships and other study grants;

e. The same opportunities for access to programmes of continuing education, including adult and functional literacy programmes, particulary those aimed at reducing, at the earliest possible time, any gap in education existing between men and women;

f. The reduction of female student drop-out rates and the organization of programmes for girls and women who have left school prematurely;

g. The same Opportunities to participate actively in sports and physical education;

h. Access to specific educational information to help to ensure the health and well-being of families, including information and advice on family planning.

Article 11

1. States Parties shall take all appropriate measures to eliminate discrimination against women in the field of employment in order to ensure, on a basis of equality of men and women, the same rights, in particular:

a. The right to work as an inalienable right of all human beings;

b. The right to the same employment opportunities, including the application of the same criteria for selection in matters of employment;

c. The right to free choice of profession and employment, the right to promotion, job security and all benefits and conditions of service and the right to receive vocational training and retraining, including apprenticeships, advanced vocational training and recurrent training;

d. The right to equal remuneration, including benefits, and to equal treatment in respect of work of equal value, as well as equality of treatment in the evaluation of the quality of work;

e. The right to social security, particularly in cases of retirement, unemployment, sickness, invalidity and old age and other incapacity to work, as well as the right to paid leave;

f. The right to protection of health and to safety in working conditions, including the safeguarding of the function of reproduction.

2. In order to prevent discrimination against women on the grounds of marriage or —maternity and to ensure their effective right to work, States Parties shall take appropriate measures:

a. To prohibit, subject to the imposition of sanctions, dismissal on the grounds of pregnancy or of maternity leave and discrimination in dismissals on the basis of marital status;

b. To introduce maternity leave with pay or with comparable social benefits without loss of former employment, seniority or social allowances;

c. To encourage the provision of the necessary supporting social services to enable parents to combine family obligations with work responsibilities and participation in public life, in particular through promoting the establishment and development of a network of child-care facilities;

d. To provide special protection to women during pregnancy in types of work proved to be harmful to them.

3. Protective legislation relating to matters covered in this article shall be reviewed periodically in the light of scientific and technological knowledge and shall be revised, repealed or extended as necessary.

Article 12

1. States Parties shall take all appropriate measures to eliminate discrimination against women in the field of health care in order to ensure, on a basis of equality of men and women, access to health care services, including those related to family planning.

2. Notwithstanding the provisions of paragraph I of this article, States Parties shall ensure to women appropriate services in connection with pregnancy, confinement and the post-natal period, granting free services where necessary, as well as adequate nutrition during pregnancy and lactation.

Article 13

States Parties shall take all appropriate measures to eliminate discrimination against women in other areas of economic and social life in order to ensure, on a basis of equality of men and women, the same rights, in particular:

a. The right to family benefits;

b. The right to bank loans, mortgages and other forms of financial credit;

c. The right to participate in recreational activities, sports and all aspects of cultural life.

Article 14

1. States Parties shall take into account the particular problems faced by rural women and the significant roles which rural women play in the economic survival of their families, including their work in the non-monetized sectors of the economy, and shall take all appropriate measures to ensure the application of the provisions of the present Convention to women in rural areas.

2. States Parties shall take all appropriate measures to eliminate discrimination against women in rural areas in order to ensure, on a basis of equality of men and women, that they participate in and benefit from rural development and, in particular, shall ensure to such women the right:

   a. To participate in the elaboration and implementation of development planning at all levels;

   b. To have access to adequate health care facilities, including information, counselling and services in family planning;

   c. To benefit directly from social security programmes;

   d. To obtain all types of training and education, formal and non-formal, including that relating to functional literacy, as well as, inter alia, the benefit of all community and extension services, in order to increase their technical proficiency;

   e. To organize self-help groups and co-operatives in order to obtain equal access to economic opportunities through employment or self employment;

   f. To participate in all community activities;

   g. To have access to agricultural credit and loans, marketing facilities, appropriate technology and equal treatment in land and agrarian reform as well as in land resettlement schemes;

   h. To enjoy adequate living conditions, particularly in relation to housing, sanitation, electricity and water supply, transport and communications.

PART IV

Article 15

1. States Parties shall accord to women equality with men before the law.

2. States Parties shall accord to women, in civil matters, a legal capacity identical to that of men and the same opportunities to exercise that capacity. In particular, they shall give women equal rights to conclude contracts and to administer property and shall treat them equally in all stages of procedure in courts and tribunals.

3. States Parties agree that all contracts and all other private instruments of any kind with a legal effect which is directed at restricting the legal capacity of women shall be deemed null and void.

4. States Parties shall accord to men and women the same rights with regard to the law relating to the movement of persons and the freedom to choose their residence and domicile.

Article 16

1. States Parties shall take all appropriate measures to eliminate discrimination against women in all matters relating to marriage and family relations and in particular shall ensure, on a basis of equality of men and women:

   a. The same right to enter into marriage;

   b. The same right freely to choose a spouse and to enter into marriage only with their free and full consent;

   c. The same rights and responsibilities during marriage and at its dissolution;

   d. The same rights and responsibilities as parents, irrespective of their marital status, in matters relating to their children; in all cases the interests of the children shall be paramount;

   e. The same rights to decide freely and responsibly on the number and spacing of their children and to have access to the information, education and means to enable them to exercise these rights;

   f. The same rights and responsibilities with regard to guardianship, wardship, trusteeship and adoption of children, or similar institutions where these concepts exist in national legislation; in all cases the interests of the children shall be paramount;

   g. The same personal rights as husband and wife, including the right to choose a family name, a profession and an occupation;

   h. The same rights for both spouses in respect of the ownership, acquisition, management, administration, enjoyment and disposition of property, whether free of charge or for a valuable consideration.

2. The betrothal and the marriage of a child shall have no legal effect, and all necessary action, including legislation, shall be taken to specify a minimum age for marriage and to make the registration of marriages in an official registry compulsory.

PART V

Article 17

1. For the purpose of considering the progress made in the implementation of the present Convention, there shall be established a Committee on the Elimination of Discrimination against Women (hereinafter referred to as the Committee) consisting, at the time of entry into force of the Convention, of eighteen and, after ratification of or accession to the Convention by the thirty-fifth State Party, of twenty-three experts of high moral standing and competence in the field covered by the Convention. The experts shall be elected by States Parties from among their nationals and shall serve in their personal capacity, consideration being given to equitable geographical distribution and to the representation of the different forms of civilization as well as the principal legal systems.

2. The members of the Committee shall be elected by secret ballot from a list of persons nominated by States Parties. Each State Party may nominate one person from among its own nationals.

3. The initial election shall be held six months after the date of the entry into force of the present Convention. At least three months before the date of each election the Secretary-General of the United Nations shall address a letter to the States Parties inviting them to submit their nominations within two months. The Secretary-General shall prepare a list in alphabetical order of all persons thus nominated, indicating the States Parties which have nominated them, and shall submit it to the States Parties.

4. Elections of the members of the Committee shall be held at a meeting of States Parties convened by the Secretary-General at United Nations Headquarters. At that meeting, for which two thirds of the States Parties shall constitute a quorum, the persons elected to the Committee shall be those nominees who obtain the largest number of votes and an absolute majority of the votes of the representatives of States Parties present and voting.

5. The members of the Committee shall be elected for a term of four years. However, the terms of nine of the members elected at the first election shall expire at the end of two years; immediately after the first election the names of these nine members shall be chosen by lot by the Chairman of the Committee.

6. The election of the five additional members of the Committee shall be held in accordance with the provisions of paragraphs 2, 3 and 4 of this article, following the thirty-fifth ratification or accession. The terms of two of the additional members elected on this occasion shall expire at the end of two years, the names of these two members having been chosen by lot by the Chairman of the Committee.

7. For the filling of casual vacancies, the State Party whose expert has ceased to function as a member of the Committee shall appoint another expert from among its nationals, subject to the approval of the Committee.

8. The members of the Committee shall, with the approval of the General Assembly, receive emoluments from United Nations resources on such terms and conditions as the Assembly may decide, having regard to the importance of the Committee's responsibilities.

9. The Secretary-General of the United Nations shall provide the necessary staff and facilities for the effective performance of the functions of the Committee under the present Convention.

Article 18

1. States Parties undertake to submit to the Secretary-General of the United Nations, for consideration by the Committee, a report on the legislative, judicial, administrative or other measures which they have adopted to give effect to the provisions of the present Convention and on the progress made in this respect:

   a. Within one year after the entry into force for the State concerned;

   b. Thereafter at least every four years and further whenever the Committee so requests.

2. Reports may indicate factors and difficulties affecting the degree of fulfilment of obligations under the present Convention.

Article 19

1. The Committee shall adopt its own rules of procedure.
2. The Committee shall elect its officers for a term of two years.

Article 20

1. The Committee shall normally meet for a period of not more than two weeks annually in order to consider the reports submitted in accordance with article 18 of the present Convention.

2. The meetings of the Committee shall normally be held at United Nations Headquarters or at any other convenient place as determined by the Committee. (amendment, status of ratification)

Article 21

1. The Committee shall, through the Economic and Social Council, report annually to the General Assembly of the United Nations on its activities and may make suggestions and general recommendations based on the examination of reports and information received from the States Parties. Such suggestions and general recommendations shall be included in the report of the Committee together with comments, if any, from States Parties.
2. The Secretary-General of the United Nations shall transmit the reports of the Committee to the Commission on the Status of Women for its information.

Article 22

The specialized agencies shall be entitled to be represented at the consideration of the implementation of such provisions of the present Convention as fall within the scope of their activities. The Committee may invite the specialized agencies to submit reports on the implementation of the Convention in areas falling within the scope of their activities.

PART VI

Article 23

Nothing in the present Convention shall affect any provisions that are more conducive to the achievement of equality between men and women which may be contained:

   a. In the legislation of a State Party; or
   b. In any other international convention, treaty or agreement in force for that State.

Article 24

States Parties undertake to adopt all necessary measures at the national level aimed at achieving the full realization of the rights recognized in the present Convention.

Article 25

1. The present Convention shall be open for signature by all States.

2. The Secretary-General of the United Nations is designated as the depositary of the present Convention.

3. The present Convention is subject to ratification. Instruments of ratification shall be deposited with the Secretary-General of the United Nations.

4. The present Convention shall be open to accession by all States. Accession shall be effected by the deposit of an instrument of accession with the Secretary-General of the United Nations.

Article 26

1. A request for the revision of the present Convention may be made at any time by any State Party by means of a notification in writing addressed to the Secretary-General of the United Nations.

2. The General Assembly of the United Nations shall decide upon the steps, if any, to be taken in respect of such a request.

Article 27

1. The present Convention shall enter into force on the thirtieth day after the date of deposit with the Secretary-General of the United Nations of the twentieth instrument of ratification or accession.

2. For each State ratifying the present Convention or acceding to it after the deposit of the twentieth instrument of ratification or accession, the Convention shall enter into force on the thirtieth day after the date of the deposit of its own instrument of ratification or accession.

Article 28

1. The Secretary-General of the United Nations shall receive and circulate to all States the text of reservations made by States at the time of ratification or accession.

2. A reservation incompatible with the object and purpose of the present Convention shall not be permitted.

3. Reservations may be withdrawn at any time by notification to this effect addressed to the Secretary-General of the United Nations, who shall then inform all States thereof. Such notification shall take effect on the date on which it is received.

Article 29

1. Any dispute between two or more States Parties concerning the interpretation or application of the present Convention which is not settled by negotiation shall, at the request of one of them, be submitted to arbitration. If within six months from the date of the request for arbitration the parties are unable to agree on the organization of the arbitration, any one of those parties may refer the dispute to the International Court of Justice by request in conformity with the Statute of the Court.

2. Each State Party may at the time of signature or ratification of the present Convention or accession thereto declare that it does not consider itself bound by paragraph I of this article. The other States Parties shall not be bound by that paragraph with respect to any State Party which has made such a reservation.

3. Any State Party which has made a reservation in accordance with paragraph 2 of this article may at any time withdraw that reservation by notification to the Secretary-General of the United Nations.

Article 30

The present Convention, the Arabic, Chinese, English, French, Russian and Spanish texts of which are equally authentic, shall be deposited with the Secretary-General of the United Nations.

IN WITNESS WHEREOF the undersigned, duly authorized, have signed the present Convention.

Part Four

---— ❧❧❧ —---

Freedom and Oppression

Freedom and Oppression

Freedom is an important and wide-ranging topic for philosophers. *Metaphysical Freedom* concerns the question of whether our actions are causally determined and whether we are free to act other than how we actually do behave. Social and political philosophers typically take it for granted that we are in some sense metaphysically free and focus on questions of *Social Freedom*, particularly, to what degree and in what ways do social constraints compromise our freedom and constitute Oppression? Thus it makes some sense to approach the question of freedom negatively, that is, by characterizing Oppression, or the denial of Freedom.

This section includes three readings on Oppression and one on Social Freedom. In the first reading the late Chicago political philosopher Iris Young explores five ways that social groups are oppressed. The next two articles explore poverty as a kind of Oppression. Indian born Nobel Prize winning economist and philosopher Amartya Sen discusses the conflict between property rights and the right not to be hungry, suggesting that in some cases our right to own property might conflict with others' right to life. The third reading is by the journalist and writer Jonathon Kozol, who describes the conditions under which poor children in New York schools struggle to achieve equal educational opportunities to their more affluent fellow citizens. The final article was written by the editor as the concluding chapter to her 2006 book, *Analyzing Oppression*. It argues that for any of us to achieve true freedom, we need to seek to end all forms of Oppression.

STUDY QUESTIONS:

1. What is Oppression? What are its five faces?

2. Is poverty a form of Oppression?

3. Is severe income inequality a form of Oppression?

4. Why does Cudd think that privileged persons will gain from the end of Oppression?

Five Faces of Oppression

Iris Marion Young

⊷⊶

Someone who does not see a pane of glass does not know that he does not see it. Someone who, being placed differently, does see it, does not know the other does not see it.

When our will finds expression outside ourselves in actions performed by others, we do not waste our time and our power of attention in examining whether they have consented to this. This is true for all of us. Our attention, given entirely to the success of the undertaking, is not claimed by them as long as they are docile. . . .

Rape is a terrible caricature of love from which consent is absent. After rape, oppression is the second horror of human existence. It is a terrible caricature of obedience.

—Simone Weil

I have proposed an enabling conception of justice. Justice should refer not only to distribution, but also to the institutional conditions necessary for the development and exercise of individual capacities and collective communication and cooperation. Under this conception of justice, injustice refers primarily to two forms of disabling constraints, oppression and domination. While these constraints include distributive patterns, they also involve matters which cannot easily be assimilated to the logic of distribution: decisionmaking procedures, division of labor, and culture.

Many people in the United States would not choose the term "oppression" to name injustice in our society. For contemporary emancipatory social movements, on the other hand—socialists, radical feminists, American Indian activists, Black activists, gay and lesbian activists—oppression is a central category of political discourse. Entering the political discourse in which oppression is a central category involves adopting a general mode of analyzing and evaluating social structures and practices which is incommensurate with the language of liberal individualism that dominates political discourse in the United States.

A major political project for those of us who identify with at least one of these movements must thus be to persuade people that the discourse of oppression makes sense of much of our social experience. We are ill prepared for this task, however, because we have no clear account of the meaning of oppression. While we find the term used often in the diverse philosophical and theoretical literature spawned by radical social movements in the United States, we find little direct discussion of the meaning of the concept as used by these movements.

In this chapter I offer some explication of the concept of oppression as I understand its use by new social movements in the United States since the 1960s. My starting point is reflection on the conditions of the groups said by these movements to be oppressed: among others women, Blacks, Chicanos, Puerto Ricans and other Spanish-speaking Americans, American Indians, Jews, lesbians, gay men, Arabs, Asians, old people, working class people, and the physically and mentally disabled. I aim to systematize the meaning of the concept of oppression as used by these diverse political movements, and to provide normative argument to clarify the wrongs the term names.

Obviously the above-named groups are not oppressed to the same extent or in the same ways. In the most general sense, all oppressed people suffer some inhibition of their ability to develop and exercise their capacities and express their needs, thoughts, and feelings. In that abstract sense all oppressed people face a common condition. Beyond that, in any more specific sense, it is not possible to define a single set of criteria that describe the condition of oppression of the above groups. Consequently, attempts by theorists and activists to discover a common description or the essential causes of the oppression of all these groups have frequently led to fruitless disputes about whose oppression is more fundamental or more grave. The contexts in which members of these groups use the term oppression to describe the injustices of their situation suggest that oppression names in fact a family of concepts and conditions, which I divide into five categories: exploitation, marginalization, powerlessness, cultural imperialism, and violence.

In this chapter I explicate each of these forms of oppression. Each may ential or cause distributive injustices, but all involve issues of justice beyond distribution. In accordance with ordinary political usage, I suggest that oppression is a condition of groups. Thus before explicating the meaning of oppression, we must examine the concept of a social group.

OPPRESSION AS A STRUCTURAL CONCEPT

One reason that many people would not use the term oppression to describe injustice in our society is that they do not understand the term in the same way as do new social movements. In its traditional usage, oppression means the exercise of tyranny by a ruling group. Thus many Americans would agree with radicals in applying the term oppression to the situation of Black South Africans under apartheid. Oppression also traditionally carries a strong connotation of conquest and colonial domination. The Hebrews were oppressed in Egypt, and many uses of the term oppression in the West invoke this paradigm.

Dominant political discourse may use the term oppression to describe societies other than our own, usually Communist or purportedly Communist societies. Within this anti-Communist rhetoric both tyrannical and colonialist implications of the term appear. For the anti-Communist, Communism denotes precisely the exercise of brutal tyranny over a whole people by a few rulers, and the will to conquer the world, bringing hitherto independent peoples under that tyranny. In dominant political discourse it is not legitimate to use the term oppression to describe our society, because oppression is the evil perpetrated by the Others.

New left social movements of the 1960s and 1970s, however, shifted the meaning of the concept of oppression. In its new usage, oppression designates the disadvantage and injustice some people suffer not because a tyrannical power coerces them, but because of the everyday practices of a well-intentioned liberal society. In this new left usage, the tyranny of a ruling group over another, as in South Africa, must certainly be called oppressive. But oppression also refers to systemic constraints on groups that are not necessarily the result of the intentions of a tyrant. Oppression in this sense is structural, rather than the result of a few people's choices or policies. Its causes are embedded in unquestioned norms, habits, and symbols, in the assumptions underlying institutional rules and the collective consequences of following those rules. It names, as Marilyn Frye puts it, "an enclosing structure of forces and barriers which tends to the immobilization and reduction of a group or category of people" (Fyre, 1983a, p. 11). In this extended structural sense oppression refers to the vast and deep injustices some groups suffer as a consequence of often unconscious assumptions and reactions of well-meaning people in ordinary interactions, media and cultural stereotypes, and structural features of bureaucratic hierarchies and market mechanisms—in short, the normal processes of everyday life. We cannot eliminate this structural oppression by getting rid of the rulers or making some new laws, because oppressions are systematically reproduced in major economic, political, and cultural institutions.

The systemic character of oppression implies that an oppressed group need not have a correlate oppressing group. While structural oppression involves relations among groups, these relations do not always fit the paradigm of conscious and intentional oppression of one group by another. Foucault (1977) suggests that to understand the meaning and operation of power in modern society we must look beyond the model of power as "sovereignty," a

dyadic relation of ruler and subject, and instead analyze the exercise of power as the effect of often liberal and "humane" practices of education, bureaucratic administration, production and distribution of consumer goods, medicine, and so on. The conscious actions of many individuals daily contribute to maintaining and reproducing oppression, but those people are usually simply doing their jobs or living their lives, and do not understand themselves as agents of oppression.

I do not mean to suggest that within a system of oppression individual persons do not intentionally harm others in oppressed groups. The raped woman, the beaten Black youth, the locked-out worker, the gay man harrassed on the street, are victims of intentional actions by identifiable agents. I also do not mean to deny that specific groups are beneficiaries of the oppression of other groups, and thus have an interest in their continued oppression. Indeed, for every oppressed group there is a group that is *privileged* in relation to that group.

The concept of oppression has been current among radicals since the 1960s partly in reaction to Marxist attempts to reduce the injustices of racism and sexism, for example, to the effects of class domination or bourgeois ideology. Racism, sexism, ageism, homophobia, some social movements asserted, are distinct forms of oppression with their own dynamics apart from the dynamics of class, even though they may interact with class oppression. From often heated discussions among socialists, feminists, and antiracism activists in the last ten years a consensus is emerging that many different groups must be said to be oppressed in our society, and that no single form of oppression can be assigned causal or moral primacy (see Gottlieb, 1987). The same discussion has also led to the recognition that group differences cut across individual lives in a multiplicity of ways that can entail privilege and oppression for the same person in different respects. Only a plural explication of the concept of oppression can adequately capture these insights.

Accordingly, I offer below an explication of five faces of oppression as a useful set of categories and distinctions which I believe is comprehensive, in the sense that it covers all the groups said by new left social movements to be oppressed and all the ways they are oppressed. I derive the five faces of oppression from reflection on the condition of these groups. Because different factors, or combinations of factors, constitute the oppression of different groups, making their oppression irreducible, I believe it is not possible to give one essential definition of oppression. The five categories articulated in this chapter, however, are adequate to describe the oppression of any group, as well as its similarities with and differences from the oppression of other groups. But first we must ask what a group is.

THE CONCEPT OF A SOCIAL GROUP

Oppression refers to structural phenomena that immobilize or diminish a group. But what is a group? Our ordinary discourse differentiates people according to social groups such as women and men, age groups, racial and ethnic groups, religious groups, and so on. Social groups of this sort are not simply collections of people, for they are more fundamentally intertwined with the identities of the people described as belonging to them. They are a specific kind of collectivity, with specific consequences for how people understand one another and themselves. Yet neither social theory nor philosophy has a clear and developed concept of the social group (see Turner et al., 1987).

A social group is a collective of persons differentiated from at least one other group by cultural forms, practices, or way of life. Members of a group have a specific affinity with one another because of their similar experience or way of life, which prompts them to associate with one another more than with those not identified with the group, or in a different way. Groups are an expression of social relations; a group exists only in relation to at least one other group. Group identification arises, that is, in the encounter and interaction between social collectivities that experience some differences in their way of life and forms of association, even if they also regard themselves as belonging to the same society.

As long as they associated solely among themselves, for example, an American Indian group thought of themselves only as "the people." The encounter with other American Indians created an awareness of difference; the others were named as a group, and the first group came to see themselves as a group. But social groups do not arise only from an encounter between different societies. Social processes also differentiate groups within a single society. The sexual division of labor, for example, has created social groups of women and men in all known societies. Members of each gender have a certain affinity with others in their group because of what they do or experience, and differentiate themselves from the other gender, even when members of each gender consider that they have much in common with members of the other, and consider that they belong to the same society.

Political philosophy typically has no place for a specific concept of the social group. When philosophers and political theorists discuss groups, they tend to conceive them either on the model of aggregates or on the model of associations, both of which are methodologically individualist concepts. To arrive at a specific concept of the social group it is thus useful to contrast social groups with both aggregates and associations.

An aggregate is any classification of persons according to some attribute. Persons can be aggregated according to any number of attributes—eye color, the make of car they drive, the street they live on. Some people interpret the groups that have emotional and social salience in our society as aggregates, as arbitrary classifications of persons according to such attributes as skin color, genitals, or age. George Sher, for example, treats social groups as aggregates, and uses the arbitrariness of aggregate classification as a reason not to give special attention to groups. "There are really as many groups as there are combinations of people and if we are going to ascribe claims to equal treatment to racial, sexual, and other groups with high visibility, it will be mere favoritism not to ascribe similar claims to these other groups as well" (Sher, 1987a, p. 256).

But "highly visible" social groups such as Blacks or women are different from aggregates, or mere "combinations of people" (see French, 1975; Friedman and May, 1985; May, 1987, chap. 1). A social group is defined not primarily by a set of shared attributes, but by a sense of identity. What defines Black Americans as a social group is not primarily their skin color; some persons whose skin color is fairly light, for example, identify themselves as Black. Though sometimes objective attributes are a necessary condition for classifying oneself or others as belonging to a certain social group, it is identification with a certain social status, the common history that social status produces, and self-identification that define the group as a group.

Social groups are not entities that exist apart from individuals, but neither are they merely arbitrary classifications of individuals according to attributes which are external to or accidental to their identities. Admitting the reality of social groups does not commit one to reifying collectivities, as some might argue. Group meanings partially constitute people's identities in terms of the cultural forms, social situation, and history

that group members know as theirs, because these meanings have been either forced upon them or forged by them or both (cf. Fiss, 1976). Groups are real not as substances, but as forms of social relations (cf. May, 1987, pp. 22–23).

Moral theorists and political philosophers tend to elide social groups more often with associations than with aggregates (e.g., French, 1975; May, 1987, chap. 1). By an association I mean a formally organized institution, such as a club, corporation, political party, church, college, or union. Unlike the aggregate model of groups, the association model recognizes that groups are defined by specific practices and forms of association. Nevertheless it shares a problem with the aggregate model. The aggregate model conceives the individual as prior to the collective, because it reduces the social group to a mere set of attributes attached to individuals. The association model also implicity conceives the individual as ontologically prior to the collective, as making up, or constituting, groups.

A contract model of social relations is appropriate for conceiving associations, but not groups. Individuals constitute associations, they come together as already formed persons and set them up, establishing rules, positions, and offices. The relationship of persons to associations is usually voluntary, and even when it is not, the person has nevertheless usually entered the association. The person is prior to the association also in that the person's identity and sense of self are usually regarded as prior to and relatively independent of association membership.

Groups, on the other hand, constitute individuals. A person's particular sense of history, affinity, and separateness, even the person's mode of reasoning, evaluating, and expressing feeling, are constituted partly by her or his group affinities. This does not mean that persons have no individual styles, or are unable to transcend or reject a group identity. Nor does it preclude persons from having many aspects that are independent of these group identities.

The social ontology underlying many contemporary theories of justice, I pointed out in the last chapter, is methodologically individualist or atomist. It presumes that the individual is ontologically prior to the social. This individualist social ontology usually goes together with a normative conception of the self as independent. The authentic self is autonomous, unified, free, and self-made, standing apart from history and affiliations, choosing its life plan entirely for itself.

One of the main contributions of poststructuralist philosophy has been to expose as illusory this metaphysic of a unified self-making subjectivity, which posits the subject as an autonomous origin or an underlying substance to which attributes of gender, nationality, family role, intellectual disposition, and so on might attach. Conceiving the subject in this fashion implies conceiving consciousness as outside of and prior to language and the context of social interaction, which the subject enters. Several currents of recent philosophy challenge this deeply held Cartesian assumption. Lacanian psychoanalysis, for example, and the social and philosophical theory influenced by it, conceive the self as an achievement of linguistic positioning that is always contextualized in concrete relations with other persons, with their mixed identities (Coward and Ellis, 1977). The self is a product of social processes, not their origin.

From a rather different perspective, Habermas indicates that a theory of communicative action also must challenge the "philosophy of consciousness" which locates intentional egos as the ontological origins of social relations. A theory of communicative action conceives individual identity not as an origin but as a product of linguistic and practical interaction (Habermas, 1987, pp. 3–40). As Stephen

Epstein describes it, identity is "a socialized sense of individuality, an internal organization of self-perception concerning one's relationship to social categories, that also incorporates views of the self perceived to be held by others. Identity is constituted relationally, through involvement with—and incorporation of—significant others and integration into communities" (Epstein, 1987, p. 29). Group categorization and norms are major constituents of individual identity (see Turner et al., 1987).

A person joins an association, and even if membership in it fundamentally affects one's life, one does not take that membership to define one's very identity, in the way, for example, being Navaho might. Group affinity, on the other hand, has the character of what Martin Heidegger (1962) calls "thrownness": one *finds oneself* as a member of a group, which one experiences as always already having been. For our identities are defined in relation to how others identify us, and they do so in terms of groups which are always already associated with specific attributes, stereotypes, and norms.

From the thrownness of group affinity it does not follow that one cannot leave groups and enter new ones. Many women become lesbian after first identifying as heterosexual. Anyone who lives long enough becomes old. These cases exemplify thrownness precisely because such changes in group affinity are experienced as transformations in one's identity. Nor does it follow fom the thrownness of group affinity that one cannot define the meaning of group identity for oneself; those who identify with a group can redefine the meaning and norms of group identity. Indeed, in Chapter 6 I will show how oppressed groups have sought to confront their oppression by engaging in just such redefinition. The present point is only that one first finds a group identity as given, and then takes it up in a certain way. While groups may come into being, they are never founded.

Groups, I have said, exist only in relation to other groups. A group may be identified by outsiders without those so identified having any specific consciousness of themselves as a group. Sometimes a group comes to exist only because one group excludes and labels a category of persons, and those labeled come to understand themselves as group members only slowly, on the basis of their shared oppression. In Vichy France, for example, Jews who had been so assimilated that they had no specifically Jewish identity were marked as Jews by others and given a specific social status by them. These people "discovered" themselves as Jews, and then formed a group identity and affinity with one another (see Sartre, 1948). A person's group identities may be for the most part only a background or horizon to his or her life, becoming salient only in specific interactive contexts.

Assuming an aggregate model of groups, some people think that social groups are invidious fictions, essentializing arbitrary attributes. From this point of view problems of prejudice, stereotyping, discrimination, and exclusion exist because some people mistakenly believe that group identification makes a difference to the capacities, temperament, or virtues of group members. This individualist conception of persons and their relation to one another tends to identify oppression with group identification. Oppression, on this view, is something that happens to people when they are classified in groups. Because others identify them as a group, they are excluded and despised. Eliminating oppression thus requires eliminating groups. People should be treated as individuals, not as members of groups, and allowed to form their lives freely without stereotypes or group norms.

This book takes issue with that position. While I agree that individuals should be free to pursue life plans in their own way, it is foolish to deny the reality of groups. Despite the modern myth of a decline of parochial attachments and ascribed identities, in modern society group differentiation remains endemic. As both markets and social administration increase the web of social interdependency on a world scale, and as more people encounter one another as strangers in cities and states, people retain and renew ethnic, locale, age, sex, and occupational group identifications, and form new ones in the processes of encounter (cf. Ross, 1980, p. 19; Rothschild, 1981, p. 130). Even when they belong to oppressed groups, people's group identifications are often important to them, and they often feel a special affinity for others in their group. I believe that group differentiation is both an inevitable and a desirable aspect of modern social processes. Social justice, I shall argue in later chapters, requires not the melting away of differences, but institutions that promote reproduction of and respect for group differences without oppression.

Though some groups have come to be formed out of oppression, and relations of privilege and oppression structure the interactions between many groups, group differentiation is not in itself oppressive. Not all groups are oppressed. In the United States Roman Catholics are a specific social group, with distinct practices and affinities with one another, but they are no longer an oppressed group. Whether a group is oppressed depends on whether it is subject to one or more of the five conditions I shall discuss below.

The view that groups are fictions does carry an important antideterminist or antiessentialist intuition. Oppression has often been perpetrated by a conceptualization of group difference in terms of unalterable essential natures that determine what group members deserve or are capable of, and that exclude groups so entirely from one another that they have no similarities or overlapping attributes. To assert that it is possible to have social group difference without oppression, it is necessary to conceptualize groups in a much more relational and fluid fashion.

Although social processes of affinity and differentiation produce groups, they do not give groups a substantive essence. There is no common nature that members of a group share. As aspects of a process, moreover, groups are fluid; they come into being and may fade away. Homosexual practices have existed in many societies and historical periods, for example. Gay men or lesbians have been identified as specific groups and so identified themselves, however, only in the twentieth century (see Ferguson, 1989, chap, 9; Altman, 1981).

Arising from social relations and processes, finally, group differences usually cut across one another. Especially in a large, complex, and highly differentiated society, social groups are not themselves homogeneous, but mirror in their own differentiations many of the other groups in the wider society. In American society today, for example, Blacks are not a simple, unified group with a common life. Like other racial and ethnic groups, they are differentiated by age, gender, class, sexuality, region, and nationality, any of which in a given context may become a salient group identity.

This view of group differentiation as multiple, cross-cutting, fluid, and shifting implies another critique of the model of the autonomous, unified self. In complex, highly differentiated societies like our own, all persons have multiple group identifications. The culture, perspective, and relations of privilege and oppression of these various groups, moreover, may not cohere. Thus individual persons, as constituted partly by their group affinities and relations, cannot be unified, themselves are heterogeneous and not necessarily coherent.

THE FACES OF OPPRESSION

Exploitation

The central function of Marx's theory of exploitation is to explain how class structure can exist in the absence of legally and normatively sanctioned class distinctions. In precapitalist societies domination is overt and accomplished through directly political means. In both slave society and feudal society the right to appropriate the product of the labor of others partly defines class privilege, and these societies legitimate class distinctions with ideologies of natural superiority and inferiority.

Capitalist society, on the other hand, removes traditional juridically enforced class distinctions and promotes a belief in the legal freedom of persons. Workers freely contract with employers and receive a wage; no formal mechanisms of law or custom force them to work for that employer or any employer. Thus the mystery of capitalism arises: when everyone is formally free, how can there be class domination? Why do class distinctions persist between the wealthy, who own the means of production, and the mass of people, who work for them? The theory of exploitation answers this question.

Profit, the basis of capitalist power and wealth, is a mystery if we assume that in the market goods exchange at their values. The labor theory of value dispels this mystery. Every commodity's value is functions of the labor time necessary for its production. Labor power is the one commodity which in the process of being consumed produces new value. Profit comes from the difference between the value of the labor performed and the value of the capacity to labor which the capitalist purchases. Profit is possible only because the owner of capital appropriates any realized surplus value.

In recent years Marxist scholars have engaged in considerable controversy about the viability of the labor theory of value this account of exploitation relies on (see Wolff, 1984, chap. 4). John Roemer (1982), for example, develops a theory of exploitation which claims to preserve the theoretical and practical purposes of Marx's theory, but without assuming a distinction between values and prices and without being restricted to a concept of abstract, homogeneous labor. My purpose here is not to engage in technical economic disputes, but to indicate the place of a concept of exploitation in a conception of oppression.

Marx's theory of exploitation lacks an explicitly normative meaning, even though the judgment that workers are exploited clearly has normative as well as descriptive power in that theory (Buchanan, 1982, chap. 3). C. B. Macpherson (1973, chap. 3) reconstructs this theory of exploitation in a more explicitly normative form. The injustice of capitalist society consists in the fact that some people exercise their capacities under the control, according to the purposes, and for the benefit of other people. Through private ownership of the means of production, and through markets that allocate labor and the ability to buy goods, capitalism systematically transfers the powers of some persons to others, thereby augmenting the power of the latter. In this process of the transfer of powers, according to Macpherson, the capitalist class acquires and maintains an ability to extract benefits from workers. Not only are powers transferred from workers to capitalists, but also the powers of workers diminish by more than the amount of transfer, because workers suffer material deprivation and a loss of control, and hence are deprived of important elements of self-respect. Justice, then, requires eliminating the institutional forms that enable and enforce this process of transference and replacing them with institutional forms that enable all to develop and use their capacities in a way that does not inhibit, but rather can enhance, similar development and use in others.

The central insight expressed in the concept of exploitation, then, is that this oppression occurs through a steady process of the transfer of the results of the labor of one social group to benefit another. The injustice of class division does not consist only in the distributive fact that some people have great wealth while most people have little (cf. Buchanan, 1982, pp. 44–49; Holmstrom, 1977). Exploitation enacts a structural relation between social groups. Social rules about what work is, who does what for whom, how work is compensated, and the social process by which the results of work are appropriated operate to enact relations of power and inequality. These relations are produced and reproduced through a systematic process in which the energies of the have-nots are continuously expended to maintain and augment the power, status, and wealth of the haves.

Many writers have cogently argued that the Marxist concept of exploitation is too narrow to encompass all forms of domination and oppression (Giddens, 1981, p. 242; Brittan and Maynard, 1984, p. 93; Murphy, 1985; Bowles and Gintis, 1986, pp. 20–24). In particular, the Marxist concept of class leaves important phenomena of sexual and racial oppression unexplained. Does this mean that sexual and racial oppression are nonexploitative, and that we should reserve wholly distinct categories for these oppressions? Or can the concept of exploitation be broadened to include other ways in which the labor and energy expenditure of one group benefits another, and reproduces a relation of domination between them?

Feminists have had little difficulty showing that women's oppression consists partly in a systematic and unreciprocated transfer of powers from women to men. Women's oppression consists not merely in an inequality of status, power, and wealth resulting fom men's excluding them from privileged activities. The freedom, power, status, and self-realization of men is possible precisely because women work for them. Gender exploitation has two aspects, transfer of the fruits of material labor to men and transfer of nurturing and sexual energies to men.

Christine Delphy (1984), for example, describes marriage as a class relation in which women's labor benefits men without comparable remuneration. She makes it clear that the exploitation consists not in the sort of work that women do in the home, for this might include various kinds of tasks, but in the fact that they perform tasks for someone on whom they are dependent. Thus, for example, in most systems of agricultural production in the world, men take to market the goods women have produced, and more often than not men receive the status and often the entire income from this labor.

With the concept of sex-affective production, Ann Ferguson (1979; 1984; 1989, chap. 4) identifies another form of the transference of women's energies to men. Women provide men and children with emotional care and provide men with sexual satisfaction, and as a group receive relatively little of either from men (cf. Brittan and Maynard, pp. 142–48). The gender socialization of women makes us tend to be more attentive to interactive dynamics than men, and makes women good at providing empathy and support for people's feelings and at smoothing over interactive tensions. Both men and women look to women as nurturers of their personal lives, and women frequently complain that when they look to men for emotional support they do not receive it (Easton, 1978). The norms of heterosexuality, moreover, are oriented around male pleasure, and consequently many women receive little satisfaction from their sexual interaction with men (Gottlieb, 1984).

Most feminist theories of gender exploitation have concentrated on the institutional structure of the patriarchal family. Recently, however, feminists have begun to explore relations of gender exploitation enacted in the contemporary workplace and through the state. Carol Brown argues that as men have removed themselves from responsibility for children, many women have become dependent on the state for subsistence as they continue to bear nearly total responsibility for childrearing (Brown, 1981;cf. Boris and Bardaglio, 1983; A. Ferguson, 1984). This creates a new system of the exploitation of women's domestic labor mediated by state institutions, which she calls public patriarchy.

In twentieth-century capitalist economies the workplaces that women have been entering in increasing numbers serve as another important site of gender exploitation. David Alexander (1987) argues that typically feminine jobs involve gender-based tasks requiring sexual labor, nurturing, caring for others' bodies, or smoothing over workplace tensions. In these ways women's energies are expended in jobs that enhance the status of, please, or comfort others, usually men; and these gender-based labors of waitresses, clerical workers, nurses, and other caretakers often go unnoticed and undercompensated.

To summarize, women are exploited in the Marxist sense to the degree that they are wage workers. Some have argued that women's domestic labor also represents a form of capitalist class exploitation insofar as it is labor covered by the wages a family receives. As a group, however, women undergo specific forms of gender exploitation in which their energies and power are expended, often unnoticed and unacknowledged, usually to benefit men by releasing them for more important and creative work, enhancing their status or the environment around them, or providing them with sexual or emotional service.

Race is a structure of oppression at least as basic as class or gender. Are there, then, racially specific forms of exploitation? There is no doubt that racialized groups in the United States, especially Blacks and Latinos, are oppressed through capitalist superexploitation resulting from a segmented labor market that tends to reserve skilled, high-paying, unionized jobs for whites. There is wide disagreement about whether such superexploitation benefits whites as a group or only benefits the capitalist class (see Reich, 1981), and I do not intend to enter into that dispute here.

However one answers the question about capitalist superexploitation of racialized groups, is it possible to conceptualize a form of exploitation that is racially specific on analogy with the gender-specific forms just discussed? I suggest that the category of *menial* labor might supply a means for such conceptualization. In its derivation "menial" designates the labor of servants. Wherever there is racism, there is the assumption, more or less enforced, that members of the oppressed racial groups are or ought to be servants of those, or some of those, in the privileged group. In most white racist societies this means that many white people have dark- or yellow-skinned domestic servants, and in the United States today there remains significant racial structuring of private household service. But in the United States today much service labor has gone public: anyone who goes to a good hotel or a good restaurant can have servants. Servants often attend the daily—and nightly—activities of business executives, government officials, and other high-status professionals. In our society there remains strong cultural pressure to fill servant jobs—bellhop, porter, chambermaid, busboy, and so on—with Black and Latino workers. These jobs entail a transfer of energies whereby the servers enhance the status of the served.

Menial labor usually refers not only to service, however, but also to any servile, unskilled, low-paying work lacking in autonomy, in which a person is subject to taking orders from many people. Menial work tends to be auxiliary work, instrumental to the work of others, where those others receive primary recognition for doing the job. Laborers on a construction site, for example, are at the beck and call of welders, electricians, carpenters, and other skilled workers, who receive recognition for the job done. In the United States explicit racial discrimination once reserved menial work for Blacks, Chicanos, American Indians, and Chinese, and menial work still tends to be linked to Black and Latino workers (Symanski, 1985). I offer this category of menial labor as a form of racially specific exploitation, as a provisional category in need of exploration.

The injustice of exploitation is most frequently understood on a distributive model. For example, though he does not offer an explicit definition of the concept, by "exploitation" Bruce Ackerman seems to mean a seriously unequal distribution of wealth, income, and other resources that is group based and structurally persistent (Ackerman, 1980, chap. 8). John Roemer's definition of exploitation is narrower and more rigorous: "An agent is exploited when the amount of labor embodied in *any* bundle of goods he could receive, in a feasible distribution of society's net product, is less than the labor he expended" (Roemer, 1982, p. 122). This definition too turns the conceptual focus from institutional relations and processes to distributive outcomes.

Jeffrey Reiman argues that such a distributive understanding of exploitation reduces the injustice of class processes to a function of the inequality of the productive assets classes own. This misses, according to Reiman, the relationship of force between capitalists and workers, the fact that the unequal exchange in question occurs within coercive structures that give workers few options (Reiman, 1987; cf. Buchanan, 1982, pp. 44–49; Holmstrom, 1977). The injustice of exploitation consists in social processes that bring about a transfer of energies from one group to another to produce unequal distributions, and in the way in which social institutions enable a few to accumulate while they constrain many more. The injustices of exploitation cannot be eliminated by redistribution of goods, for as long as institutionalized practices and structural relations remain unaltered, the process of transfer will re-create an unequal distribution of benefits. Bringing about justice where there is exploitation requires reorganization of institutions and practices of decisionmaking, alteration of the division of labor, and similar measures of institutional, structural, and cultural change.

Marginalization

Increasingly in the United States racial oppression occurs in the form of marginalization rather than exploitation. Marginals are people the system of labor cannot or will not use. Not only in Third World capitalist countries, but also in most Western capitalist societies, there is a growing underclass of people permanently confined to lives of social marginality, most of whom are racially marked—Blacks or Indians in Latin America, and Blacks, East Indians, Eastern Europeans, or North Africans in Europe.

Marginalization is by no means the fate only of racially marked groups, however. In the United States a shamefully large proportion of the population is marginal: old people, and increasingly people who are not very old but get laid off from their jobs and cannot find new work; young people, especially Black or Latino, who cannot find first or second jobs; many single mothers and their children; other people involuntarily unemployed; many mentally and physically disabled people; American Indians, especially those on reservations.

Marginalization is perhaps the most dangerous form of oppression. A whole category of people is expelled from useful participation in social life and thus potentially subjected to severe material deprivation and even extermination. The material deprivation marginalization often causes is certainly unjust, especially in a society where others have plenty. Contemporary advanced capitalist societies have in principle acknowledged the injustice of material deprivation caused by marginalization, and have taken some steps to address it by providing welfare payments and services. The continuance of this welfare state is by no means assured, and in most welfare state societies, especially the United States, welfare redistributions do not eliminate large-scale suffering and deprivation.

Material deprivation, which can be addressed by redistributive social policies, is not, however, the extent of the harm caused by marginalization. Two categories of injustice beyond distribution are associated with marginality in advanced capitalist societies. First, the provision of welfare itself produces new injustice by depriving those dependent on it of rights and freedoms that others have. Second, even when material deprivation is somewhat mitigated by the welfare state, marginalization is unjust because it blocks the opportunity to exercise capacities in socially defined and recognized ways. I shall explicate each of these in turn.

Liberalism has traditionally asserted the right of all rational autonomous agents to equal citizenship. Early bourgeois liberalism explicitly excluded from citizenship all those whose reason was questionable or not fully developed, and all those not independent (Pateman, 1988, chap. 3; cf. Bowles and Gintis, 1986, chap. 2). Thus poor people, women, the mad and the feebleminded, and children were explicitly excluded from citizenship, and many of these were housed in institutions modeled on the modern prison: poorhouses, insane asylums, schools.

Today the exclusion of dependent persons from equal citizenship rights is only barely hidden beneath the surface. Because they depend on bureaucratic institutions for support or services, the old, the poor, and the mentally or physically disabled are subject to patronizing, punitive, demeaning, and arbitrary treatment by the policies and people associated with welfare bureaucracies. Being a dependent in our society implies being legitimately subject to the often arbitrary and invasive authority of social service providers and other public and private administrators, who enforce rules with which the marginal must comply, and otherwise exercise power over the conditions of their lives. In meeting needs of the marginalized, often with the aid of social scientific disciplines, welfare agencies also construct the needs themselves. Medical and social service professionals know what is good for those they serve, and the marginals and dependents themselves do not have the right to claim to know what is good for them (Fraser, 1987a; K. Ferguson, 1984, chap. 4). Dependency in our society thus implies, as it has in all liberal societies, a sufficient warrant to suspend basic right to privacy, respect, and individual choice.

Although dependency produces conditions of injustice in our society, dependency in itself need not be oppressive. One cannot imagine a society in which some people would not need to be dependent on others at least some of the time: children, sick people, women recovering from childbirth, old people who have become frail, depressed or otherwise emotionally needy persons, have the moral right to depend on others for subsistence and support.

An important contribution of feminist moral theory has been to question the deeply held assumption that moral agency and full citizenship require that a person be autonomous and independent. Feminists have exposed this assumption as inappropriately individualistic and derived from a specifically male experience of social relations, which values competition and solitary achievement (see Gilligan, 1982; Friedman, 1985). Female experience of social relations, arising both from women's typical domestic care responsibilities and from the kinds of paid work that many women do, tends to recognize dependence as a basic human condition (cf. Hartsock, 1983, chap. 10). Whereas on the autonomy model a just society would as much as possible give people the opportunity to be independent, the feminist model envisions justice as according respect and participation in decisionmaking to those who are dependent as well as to those who are independent (Held, 1987b). Dependency should not be a reason to be deprived of choice and respect, and much of the oppression many marginals experience would be lessened if a less individualistic model of rights prevailed.

Marginalization does not cease to be oppressive when one has shelter and food. Many old people, for example, have sufficient means to live comfortably but remain oppressed in their marginal status. Even if marginals were provided a comfortable material life within institutions that respected their freedom and dignity, injustices of marginality would remain in the form of uselessness, boredom, and lack of self-respect. Most of our society's productive and recognized activities take place in contexts of organized social cooperation, and social structures and processes that close persons out of participation in such social cooperation are unjust. Thus while marginalization definitely entails serious issues of distributive justice, it also involves the deprivation of cultural, practical, and institutionalized conditions for exercising capacities in a context of recognition and interaction.

The fact of marginalization raises basic structural issues of justice, in particular concerning the appropriateness of a connection between participation in productive activities of social cooperation, on the one hand, and access to the means of consumption, on the other. As marginalization is increasing, with no sign of abatement, some social policy analysts have introduced the idea of a "social wage" as a guaranteed socially provided income not tied to the wage system. Restructuring of productive activity to address a right of participation, however, implies organizing some socially productive activity outside of the wage system (see Offe, 1985, pp. 95–100), through public works or self-employed collectives.

Powerlessness

As I have indicated, the Marxist idea of class is important because it helps reveal the structure of exploitation: that some people have their power and wealth because they profit from the labor of others. For this reason I reject the claim some make that a traditional class exploitation model fails to capture the structure of contemporary society. It remains the case that the labor of most people in the society augments the power of relatively few. Despite their differences from nonprofessional workers, most professional workers are still not members of the capitalist class. Professional labor either involves exploitative transfers to capitalists or supplies important conditions for such transfers. Professional workers are in an ambiguous class position, it is true, because, as I argue in Chapter 7, they also benefit from the exploitation of nonprofessional workers.

While it is false to claim that a division between capitalist and working classes no longer describes our society, it is also false to say that class relations have remained unaltered since the nineteenth century. An adequate conception of oppression cannot ignore the experience of social division reflected in the colloquial distinction between the "middle class" and the "working class," a division structured by the social division of labor between professionals and nonprofessionals. Professionals are privileged in relation to nonprofessionals, by virtue of their position in the division of labor and the status it carries. Nonprofessionals suffer a form of oppression in addition to exploitation, which I call powerlessness.

In the United States, as in other advanced capitalist countries, most workplaces are not organized democratically, direct participation in public policy decisions is rare, and policy implementation is for the most part hierarchical, imposing rules on bureaucrats and citizens. Thus most people in these societies do not regularly participate in making decisions that affect the conditions of their lives and actions, and in this sense most people lack significant power. At the same time, as I argued in Chapter 1, domination in modern society is enacted through the widely dispersed powers of many agents mediating the decisions of others. To that extent many people have some power in relation to others, even though they lack the power to decide policies or results. The powerless are those who lack authority or power even in this mediated sense, those over whom power is exercised without their exercising it; the powerless are situated so that they must take orders and rarely have the right to give them. Powerlessness also designates a position in the division of labor and the concomitant social position that allows persons little opportunity to develop and exercise skills. The powerless have little or no work autonomy, exercise little creativity or judgment in their work, have no technical expertise or authority, express themselves awkwardly, especially in public or bureaucratic settings, and do not command respect. Powerlessness names the oppressive situations Sennett and Cobb (1972) describe in their famous study of working-class men.

This powerless status is perhaps best described negatively: the powerless lack the authority, status, and sense of self that professionals tend to have. The status privilege of professionals has three aspects, the lack of which produces oppression for nonprofessionals.

First, acquiring and practicing a profession has an expansive, progressive character. Being professional usually requires a college education and the acquisition of a specialized knowledge that entails working with symbols and concepts. Professionals experience progress first in acquiring the expertise, and then in the course of professional advancement and rise in status. The life of the nonprofessional by comparison is powerless in the sense that it lacks this orientation toward the progressive development of capacities and avenues for recognition.

Second, while many professionals have supervisors and cannot directly influence many decisions or the actions of many people, most nevertheless have considerable day-to-day work autonomy. Professionals usually have some authority over others, moreover—either over workers they supervise, or over auxiliaries, or over clients. Nonprofessionals, on the other hand, lack autonomy, and in both their working and their consumer client lives often stand under the authority of professionals.

Though based on a division of labor between "mental" and "manual" work, the distinction between "middle class" and "working class" designates a division not only in working life, but also in nearly all aspects of social life. Professionals and nonprofessionals belong to different cultures in the United States. The two groups tend to live in segregated neighborhoods or even different towns, a process itself mediated by planners, zoning officials, and real estate people. The groups tend to have different tastes in food, decor, clothes, music, and

vacations, and often different health and educational needs. Members of each group socialize for the most part with others in the same status group. While there is some intergroup mobility between generations, for the most part the children of professionals become professionals and the children of nonprofessionals do not.

Thus, third, the privileges of the professional extend beyond the workplace to a whole way of life. I call this way of life "respectability." To treat people with respect is to be prepared to listen to what they have to say or to do what they request because they have some authority, expertise, or influence. The norms of respectability in our society are associated specifically with professional culture. Professional dress, speech, tastes, demeanor, all connote respectability. Generally professionals expect and receive respect from others. In restaurants, banks, hotels, real estate offices, and many other such public places, as well as in the media, professionals typically receive more respectful treatment than nonprofessionals. For this reason nonprofessionals seeking a loan or a job, or to buy a house or a car, will often try to look "professional" and "respectable" in those settings.

The privilege of this professional respectability appears starkly in the dynamics of racism and sexism. In daily interchange women and men of color must prove their respectability. At first they are often not treated by strangers with respectful distance or deference. Once people discover that this woman or that Puerto Rican man is a college teacher or a business executive, however, they often behave more respectfully toward her or him. Working-class white men, on the other hand, are often treated with respect until their working-class status is revealed. In Chapter 5 I will explore in more detail the cultural underpinnings of the ideal of respectability and its oppressive implications.

I have discussed several injustices associated with powerlessness: inhibition in the development of one's capacities, lack of decisionmaking power in one's working life, and exposure to disrespectful treatment because of the status one occupies. These injustices have distributional consequences, but are more fundamentally matters of the division of labor. The oppression of powerlessness brings into question the division of labor basic to all industrial societies: the social division between those who plan and those who execute. I examine this division in more detail in Chapter 7.

Cultural Imperialism

Exploitation, marginalization, and powerlessness all refer to relations of power and oppression that occur by virtue of the social division of labor—who works for whom, who does not work, and how the content of work defines one institutional position relative to others. These three categories refer to structural and institutional relations that delimit people's material lives, including but not restricted to the resources they have access to and the concrete opportunities they have or do not have to develop and exercise their capacities. These kinds of oppression are a matter of concrete power in relation to others—of who benefits from whom, and who is dispensable.

Recent theorists of movements of group liberation, notably feminist and Black liberation theorists, have also given prominence to a rather different form of oppression, which following Lugones and Spelman (1983) I shall call cultural imperialism. To experience cultural imperialism means to experience how the dominant meanings of a society render the particular perspective of one's own group invisible at the same time as they stereotype one's group and mark it out as the Other.

Cultural imperialism involves the universalization of a dominant group's experience and culture, and its establishment as the norm. Some groups have exclusive or primary access to what Nancy Fraser (1987b) calls the means of interpretation and communication in a society. As a consequence, the dominant cultural products of the society, that is, those most widely disseminated, express the experience, values, goals, and achievements of these groups. Often without noticing they do so, the dominant groups project their own experience as representative of humanity as such. Cultural products also express the dominant group's perspective on and interpretation of events and elements in the society, including other groups in the society, insofar as they attain cultural status at all.

An encounter with other groups, however, can challenge the dominant group's claim to universality. The dominant group reinforces its position by bringing the other groups under the measure of its dominant norms. Consequently, the difference of women from men, American Indians or Africans from Europeans, Jews from Christians, homosexuals from heterosexuals, workers from professionals, becomes reconstructed largely as deviance and inferiority. Since only the dominant group's cultural expressions receive wide dissemination, their cultural expressions become the normal, or the universal, and thereby the unremarkable. Given the normality of its own cultural expressions and identity, the dominant group constructs the differences which some groups exhibit as lack and negation. These groups become marked as Other.

The culturally dominated undergo a paradoxical oppression, in that they are both marked out by stereotypes and at the same time rendered invisible. As remarkable, deviant beings, the culturally imperialized are stamped with an essence. The stereotypes confine them to a nature which is often attached in some way to their bodies, and which thus cannot easily be denied. These stereotypes so permeate the society that they are not noticed as contestable. Just as everyone knows that the earth goes around the sun, so everyone knows that gay people are promiscuous, that Indians are alcoholics, and that women are good with children. White males, on the other hand, insofar as they escape group marking, can be individuals.

Those living under cultural imperialism find themselves defined from the outside, positioned, placed, by a network of dominant meanings they experience as arising from elsewhere, from those with whom they do not identify and who do not identify with them. Consequently, the dominant culture's stereotyped and inferiorized images of the group must be internalized by group members at least to the extent that they are forced to react to behavior of others influenced by those images. This creates for the culturally oppressed the experience that W.E.B. Du Bois called "double consciousness"—"this sense of always looking at one's self through the eyes of others, of measuring one's soul by the tape of a world that looks on in amused contempt and pity" (Du Bois, 1969 [1903], p. 45). Double consciousness arises when the oppressed subject refuses to coincide with these devalued, objectified, stereotyped visions of herself or himself. While the subject desires recognition as human, capable of activity, full of hope and possibility, she receives from the dominant culture only the judgment that she is different, marked, or inferior.

The group defined by the dominant culture as deviant, as a stereotyped Other, *is* culturally different from the dominant group, because the status of Otherness creates specific experiences not shared by the dominant group, and because culturally oppressed groups also are often socially segregated and occupy specific positions in the social division of labor. Members of such groups express their specific group experiences and interpretations of the world to one another, developing and perpetuating their own culture. Double consciousness, then,

occurs because one finds one's being defined by two cultures: a dominant and a subordinate culture. Because they can affirm and recognize one another as sharing similar experiences and perspectives on social life, people in culturally imperialized groups can often maintain a sense of positive subjectivity.

Cultural imperialism involves the paradox of experiencing oneself as invisible at the same time that one is marked out as different. The invisibility comes about when dominant groups fail to recognize the perspective embodied in their cultural expressions as a perspective. These dominant cultural expressions often simply have little place for the experience of other groups, at most only mentioning or referring to them in stereotyped or marginalized ways. This, then, is the injustice of cultural imperialism: that the oppressed group's own experience and interpretation of social life finds little expression that touches the dominant culture, while that same culture imposes on the oppressed group its experience and interpretation of social life.

In several of the following chapters I shall explore more fully the consequences of cultural imperialism for the theory and practice of social justice. Chapter 4 expands on the claim that cultural imperialism is enacted partly through the ability of a dominant group to assert its perspective and experience as universal or neutral. In the sphere of the polity, I argue, claim to universality operates politically to exclude those understood as different. In Chapter 5 I trace the operations of cultural imperialism in nineteenth-century scientific classifications of some bodies as deviant or degenerate. I explore how the devaluation of the bodies of some groups still conditions everyday interactions among groups, despite our relative success at expelling such bodily evaluation from discursive consciousness. In Chapter 6, finally, I discuss recent struggles

by the culturally oppressed to take over definition of themselves and assert a positive sense
of group difference. There I argue that justice
requires us to make a political space for such
difference.

Violence

Finally, many groups suffer the oppression of
systematic volence. Members of some groups
live with the knowledge that they must fear
random, unprovoked attacks on their persons or
property, which have no motive but to damage,
humiliate, or destroy the person. In American
society women, Blacks, Asians, Arabs, gay men,
and lesbians live under such threats of violence,
and in at least some regions Jews, Puerto Ricans,
Chicanos, and other Spanish-speaking Americans
must fear such violence as well. Physical violence
against these groups is shockingly frequent. Rape
Crisis Center networks estimate that more than
one-third of all American women experience an
attempted or successful sexual assault in their
lifetimes. Manning Marable (1984, pp. 238–41)
catalogues a large number of incidents of racist
violence and terror against blacks in the United
States between 1980 and 1982. He cites dozens
of incidents of the severe beating, killing, or rape
of Blacks by police officers on duty, in which the
police involved were acquitted of any wrongdoing. In 1981, moreover, there were at least five
hundred documented cases of random white
teenage violence against Blacks. Violence against
gay men and lesbians is not only common, but
has been increasing in the last five years. While
the frequency of physical attack on members
of these and other racially or sexually marked
groups is very disturbing, I also include in this
category less severe incidents of harrassment,
intimidation, or ridicule simply for the purpose
of degrading, humiliating, or stigmatizing group
members.

Given the frequency of such violence in our
society, why are theories of justice usually silent
about it? I think the reason is that theorists do
not typically take such incidents of violence
and harrassment as matters of social injustice.
No moral theorist would deny that such acts
are very wrong. But unless all immoralities
are injustices, they might wonder, why should
such acts be interpreted as symptoms of social
injustice? Acts of violence or petty harrassment
are committed by particular individuals, often
extremists, deviants, or the mentally unsound.
How then can they be said to involve the sorts
of institutional issues I have said are properly
the subject of justice?

What makes violence a face of oppression
is less the particular acts themselves, though
these are often utterly horrible, than the social
context surrounding them, which makes them
possible and even acceptable.

What makes violence a phenomenon of
social injustice, and not merely an individual
moral wrong, is its systemic character, its existence as a social practice.

Violence is systemic because it is directed
at members of a group simply because they are
members of that group. Any woman, for example, has a reason to fear rape. Regardless of what
a Black man has done to escape the oppressions of marginality or powerlessness, he lives
knowing he is subject to attack or harrassment.
The oppression of violence consists not only in
direct victimization, but in the daily knowledge
shared by all members of oppressed groups that
they are *liable* to violation, solely on account
of their group identity. Just living under such a
threat of attack on oneself or family or friends
deprives the oppressed of freedom and dignity,
and needlessly expends their energy.

Violence is a social practice. It is a social
given that everyone knows happens and will
happen again. It is always at the horizon of
social imagination, even for those who do not
perpetrate it. According to the prevailing social
logic, some circumstances make such violence
more "called for" than others. The idea of rape

will occur to many men who pick up a hitch-hiking woman; the idea of hounding or teasing a gay man on their dorm floor will occur to many straight male college students. Often several persons inflict the violence together, especially in all-male groupings. Sometimes violators set out looking for people to beat up, rape, or taunt. This rule-bound, social, and often premeditated character makes violence against groups a social practice.

Group violence approaches legitimacy, moreover, in the sense that it is tolerated. Often third parties find it unsurprising because it happens frequently and lies as a constant possibility at the horizon of the social imagination. Even when they are caught, those who perpetrate acts of group-directed violence or harrassment often receive light or no punishment. To that extent society renders their acts acceptable.

An important aspect of random, systemic violence is its irrationality. Xenophobic violence differs from the violence of states or ruling-class repression. Repressive violence has a rational, albeit evil, motive: rulers use it as a coercive tool to maintain their power. Many accounts of racist, sexist, or homophobic violence attempt to explain its motivation as a desire to maintain group privilege or domination. I do not doubt that fear of violence often functions to keep oppressed groups subordinate, but I do not think xenophobic violence is rationally motivated in the way that, for example, violence against strikers is.

On the contrary, the violation of rape, beating, killing, and harrassment of women, people of color, gays, and other marked groups is motivated by fear or hatred of those groups. Sometimes the motive may be a simple will to power, to victimize those marked as vulnerable by the very social fact that they are subject to violence. If so, this motive is secondary in the sense that it depends on a social practice of group violence. Violence-causing fear or hatred

of the other at least partly involves insecurities on the part of the violators; its irrationality suggests that unconscious processes are at work. In Chapter 5 I shall discuss the logic that makes some groups frightening or hateful by defining them as ugly and loathsome bodies. I offer a psychoanalytic account of the fear and hatred of some groups as bound up with fears of identity loss. I think such unconscious fears account at least partly for the oppression I have here called violence. It may also partly account for cultural imperialism.

Cultural imperialism, moreover, itself intersects with violence. The culturally imperialized may reject the dominant meanings and attempt to assert their own subjectivity, or the fact of their cultural difference may put the lie to the dominant culture's implicit claim to universality. The dissonance generated by such a challenge to the hegemonic cultural meanings can also be a source of irrational violence.

Violence is a form of injustice that a distributive understanding of justice seems ill equipped to capture. This may be why contemporary discussions of justice rarely mention it. I have argued that group-directed violence is institutionalized and systemic. To the degree that institutions and social practices encourage, tolerate, or enable the perpetration of violence against members of specific groups, those institutions and practices are unjust and should be reformed. Such reform may require the redistribution of resources or positions, but in large part can come only through a change in cultural images, stereotypes, and the mundane reproduction of relations of dominance and aversion in the gestures of everyday life. I discuss strategies for such change in Chapter 5.

APPLYING THE CRITERIA

Social theories that construct oppression as a unified phenomenon usually either leave out groups that even the theorists think are oppressed, or leave out important ways in which groups are oppressed. Black liberation theorists and feminist theorists have argued persuasively, for example, that Marxism's reduction of all oppressions to class oppression leaves out much about the specific oppression of Blacks and women. By pluralizing the category of oppression in the way explained in this chapter, social theory can avoid the exclusive and oversimplifying effects of such reductionism.

I have avoided pluralizing the category in the way some others have done, by constructing an account of separate systems of oppression for each oppressed group: racism, sexism, classism, heterosexism, ageism, and so on. There is a double problem with considering each group's oppression a unified and distinct structure or system. On the one hand, this way of conceiving oppression fails to accommodate the similarities and overlaps in the oppressions of different groups. On the other hand, it falsely represents the situation of all group members as the same.

I have arrived at the five faces of oppression— exploitation, marginalization, powerlessness, cultural imperialism, and violence—as the best way to avoid such exclusions and reductions. They function as criteria for determining whether individuals and groups are oppressed, rather than as a full theory of oppression. I believe that these criteria are objective. They provide a means of refuting some people's belief that their group is oppressed when it is not, as well as a means of persuading others that a group is oppressed when they doubt it. Each criterion can be operationalized; each can be applied through the assessment of observable behavior, status relationships, distributions, texts and other cultural artifacts. I have no illusions that such assessments can be value-neutral. But these criteria can nevertheless serve as means of evaluating claims that a group is oppressed, or

adjudicating disputes about whether or how a group is oppressed.

The presence of any of these five conditions is sufficient for calling a group oppressed. But different group oppressions exhibit different combinations of these forms, as do different individuals in the groups. Nearly all, if not all, groups said by contemporary social movements to be oppressed suffer cultural imperialism. The other oppressions they experience vary. Working-class people are exploited and powerless, for example, but if employed and white do not experience marginalization and violence. Gay men, on the other hand, are not qua gay exploited or powerless, but they experience severe cultural imperialism and violence. Similarly, Jews and Arabs as groups are victims of cultural imperialism and violence, though many members of these groups also suffer exploitation or powerlessness. Old people are oppressed by marginalization and cultural imperialism, and this is also true of physically and mentally disabled people. As a group women are subject to gender-based exploitation, powerlessness, cultural imperialism, and violence. Racism in the United States condemns many Blacks and Latinos to marginalization, and puts many more at risk, even though many members of these groups escape that condition; members of these groups often suffer all five forms of oppression.

Applying these five criteria to the situation of groups makes it possible to compare oppressions without reducing them to a common essence or claiming that one is more fundamental than another. One can compare the ways in which a particular form of oppression appears in different groups. For example, while the operations of cultural imperialism are often experienced in similar fashion by different groups, there are also important differences. One can compare the combinations of oppressions groups experience, or the intensity of those oppressions. Thus with these criteria one can plausibly claim that one group is more oppressed than another without reducing all oppressions to a single scale.

Why are particular groups oppressed in the way they are? Are there any causal connections among the five forms of oppression? Causal or explanatory questions such as these are beyond the scope of this discussion. While I think general social theory has a place, causal explanation must always be particular and historical. Thus an explanatory account of why a particular group is oppressed in the ways that it is must trace the history and current structure of particular social relations. Such concrete historical and structural explanations will often show causal connections among the different forms of oppression experienced by a group. The cultural imperialism in which white men make stereotypical assumptions about and refuse to recognize the values of Blacks or women, for example, contributes to the marginalizaion and powerlessness many Blacks and women suffer. But cultural imperialism does not always have these effects.

Succeeding chapters will explore the categories explicated here in different ways. Chapters 4, 5, and 6 explore the effects of cultural imperialism. Those chapters constitute an extended argument that modern political theory and practice wrongly universalize dominant group perspectives, and that attention to and affirmation of social group differences in the polity are the best corrective to such cultural imperialism. Chapters 7 and 8 also make use of the category of cultural imperialism, but focus more attention on social relations of exploitation and powerlessness.

REFERENCES

Ackerman, Bruce.1980. *Social Justice and the Liberal State.* New Haven: Yale University Press.

Alexander, David. 1987. "Gendered Job Traits and Women's Occupations." Ph.D. dissertation, Economics University of Massachusetts.

Altman, Dennis. 1982. *The Homosexualization of American Society.* Boston: Beacon.

Boris, Ellen and Peter Bardaglio.1983. "The Transformation of Patriarchy: The Historic Role of the State." In Irene Diamond. ed., *Families, Politics and Public Policy.* New York: Longman.

Bowles, Samuel and Herbert Gintis. 1986. "Crisis of Liberal Democratic Capitalism: The Case of the United States." *Politics and Society* 11:51–94.

Brittan, Arthur and Mary Maynard. 1984. *Sexism, Racism and Oppression.* Oxford: Blackwell.

Brown, Carol. 1981. "Mothers, Fathers and Children: From Private to Public Patriarchy." In Lydia Sargent, ed., *Women and Revolution.* Boston: South End.

Buchanan, Allen. 1982. *Marx and Justice.* Totowa, N.J.: Rowman and Allenheld.

Coward, Rosalind and John Ellis. 1977. *Language and Materialism.* London: Routledge and Kegan Paul.

Delphy, Christine. 1984. *Close to Home: A Materialist Analysis of Women's Oppression.* Amherst: University of Massachusetts Press.

Du Bois, W.E.B.1969 [1903]. *The Souls of Black Folk.* New York: New American Library.

Easton, Barbara. 1978. "Feminism and the Contemporary Family." *Socialist Review* 39(May/June): 11–36.

Epstein, Steven. 1987. "Gay Politics, Ethnic Identity: The Limits of Social Constructionism." *Socialist Review* 17(May-August): 9–54.

Ferguson, Ann. 1984. "On Conceiving Motherhood and Sexuality: A Feminist Materialist

Approach." In Joyce Trebilcot, ed., *Mothering: Essays in Feminist Theory*. Totowa, N.J.: Rowman and Allenheld.

—. 1989 *Blood at the Root*. London: Pandora.

Ferguson, Kathy. 1984. *The Feminist Case against Bureaucracy*. Philadelphia: Temple University Press.

Fiss, Owen. 1976. "Groups and the Equal Protection Clause." *Philosophy and Public Affairs* 5(Winter): 107–76.

Foucault, Michel. 1977. *Discipline and Punish*. New York: Pantheon.

Fraser, Nancy. 1987a. "Women, Welfare and the Politics of Need Interpretation." *Hypatia* 2(Winter): 103–22.

—. 1987b. "Social Movements vs. Disciplinary Bureaucracies: The Discourse of Social Needs." CHS Occasional Paper No. 8. Center for Humanistic Studies, University of Minnesota.

French, Peter. 1975. "Types of Collectivities and Blame." *The Personalist* 56(Spring): 160–69.

Friedman, Marilyn. 1985. "Care and Context in Moral Reasoning." In Carol Harding, ed., *Moral Dilemmas: Philosophical and Psychological Issues in the Development of Moral Reasoning*. Chicago: Precedent.

Friedman, Marilyn and Larry May. 1985. "Harming Women as a Group." *Social Theory and Practice* 11(Summer): 297–334.

Fyre, Marilyn. 1983. "Oppression." In *The Politics of Reality*. Trumansburg, N.Y.: Crossing.

Giddens, Anthony. 1981. *A Contemporary Critique of Historical Materialism*. Berkeley and Los Angeles: University of California Press.

Gilligan, Carol. 1982. *In a Different Voice*. Cambridge: Harvard University Press.

Gottlieb, Rhonda. 1984. "The Political Economy of Sexuality." *Review of Radical Political Economy* 16(Spring): 143–65.

Gottlieb, Roger. 1987. *History and Subjectivity*. Philadelphia: Temple University Press.

Habermas, Jürgen. 1987. *The Theory of Communicative Competence*. Vol. 2.: *Lifeworld and System*. Boston: Beacon.

Hartsock, Nancy. 1983. *Money, Sex and Power*. New York: Longman.

Heidegger, Martin. 1962. *Being and Time*. New York: Harper and Row.

Held, Virginia. 1987. "A Non-Contractual Society." In Marsha Hanen and Kai Nielsen, eds., *Science, Morality and Feminist Theory*. Calgary: University of Calgary Press.

Holmstrom, Nancy. 1977. "Exploitation." *Canadian Journal of Philosophy* 7(June): 353–69.

Lugones, Maria and Elizabeth Spelman. 1983. "Have We Got a Theory for You! Feminist Theory, Cultural Imperialism and the Demand for 'the Woman's Voice.'" *Women's Studies International Forum* 6:573–81.

Macpherson, C. B. 1973. *Democratic Theory: Essays in Retrieval*. Oxford: Oxford University Press.

Marable, Manning. 1984. *Race, Reform and Revellion: The Second Reconstruction in Black America, 1945–82*. Jackson: University Press of Mississippi.

May, Larry. 1987. *The Morality of Groups: Collective Responsibility, Group Based Harm, and Corporate Rights*. Notre Dame: Notre Dame University Press.

Murphy, Raymond. 1985. "Exploitation or Exclusion?" *Sociology* 19(May): 225–43.

Offe, Claus. 1985. *Disorganized Capitalism*. Cambridge: MIT Press.

Pateman, Carole. 1988. *The Sexual Contract*. Stanford: Stanford University Press.

Reich, Michael. 1981. *Racial Inequality*. Princeton: Princeton University Press.

Reiman, Jeffrey. 1987. "Exploitation, Force, and the Moral Assessment of Capitalism: Thoughts on Roemer and Cohen." *Philosophy and Public Affairs* 16(Winter): 3–41.

Roemer, John. 1982. *A General Theory of Exploitation and Class*. Cambridge: Harvard University Press.

Ross, Jeffrey. 1980. Introduction to Jeffrey Ross and Ann Baker Cottrell, eds., *The Mobilization of Collective Identity*. Lanham, Md.: University Press of America.

Rothschild, Joseph. 1981. *Ethnopolitics*. New York: Columbia University Press.

Sartre, Jean Paul. 1948. *Anti-Semite and Jew*. New York: Schocken.

Sennett, Richard and Jonathon Cobb. 1972. *The Hidden Injuries of Class*. New York: Vintage.

Sher, George. 1987."Groups and the Constitution." In Gertrude Ezorsky, ed., *Moral Rights in the Workplace*. Albany: State University of New York Press.

Symanski, Al. 1985. "The Structure of Race." *Review of Radical Political Economy* 17(Winter): 106–20.

Turner, John, Michael Hogg, Penelope Oakes, Stephen Rucher, and Margaret Wethrell. 1987. *Rediscovering the Social Group: A Self-Categorization Theory*. Oxford: Blackwell.

Wolff, Robert Paul. 1984. *Understanding Marx*. Princeton: Princeton University Press.

Property and Hunger

Amartya Sen

In an interesting letter to Anna George, the daughter of Henry George, Bernard Shaw wrote: "Your father found me a literary dilettante and militant rationalist in religion, and a barren rascal at that. By turning my mind to economics he made a man of me" (George, 1979, p. xiii). I am not able to determine what making a man of Bernard Shaw would exactly consist of, but it is clear that the kind of moral and social problems with which Shaw was deeply concerned could not be sensibly pursued without examining their economic aspects. For example, the claims of property rights, which some would defend and some (including Shaw) would dispute, are not just matters of basic moral belief that could not possibly be influenced one way or the other by any empirical arguments. They call for sensitive moral analysis responsive to empirical realities, including economic ones.

Moral claims based on intrinsically valuable rights are often used in political and social arguments. Rights related to ownership have been invoked for ages. But there are also other types of rights which have been seen as "inherent and inalienable,"[1] and the American Declaration of Independence refers to "certain unalienable rights," among which are "life, liberty and the pursuit of happiness." The Indian constitution talks even of "the right to an adequate means of livelihood."[2] The "right not to be hungry" has often been invoked in recent discussions on the obligation to help the famished.

RIGHTS: INSTRUMENTS, CONSTRAINTS, OR GOALS?

Rights can be taken to be morally important in three different ways. First, they can be considered to be valuable *instruments* to achieve other goals. This is the "instrumental view," and is well illustrated by the utilitarian approach to rights. Rights are, in that view, of no intrinsic importance. Violation of rights is not in itself a bad thing, nor fulfillment intrinsically good. But the acceptance of rights promotes, in this view, things that are ultimately important, to wit, utility. Jeremy Bentham rejected "natural rights" as "simple nonsense," and "natural and imprescriptible rights" as "rhetorical nonsense, nonsense upon stilts."[3] But he attached great importance to rights as instruments valuable to

From *Economics and Philosophy*, Volume 4, Number 1, 1988 by Amartya Sen. Reprinted with the permission of Cambridge University Press.

the promotion of a good society, and devoted much energy to the attempt to reform appropriately the actual system of rights.

The second view may be called the "constraint view," and it takes the form of seeing rights as *constraints* on what others can or cannot do. In this view rights *are* intrinsically important. However, they don't figure in moral accounting as goals to be generally promoted, but only as constraints that others must obey. As Robert Nozick has put it in a powerful exposition of this "constraint view": "Individuals have rights, and there are things no person or group may do to them (without violating their rights)" (Nozick, 1974, p. xi). Rights "set the constraints within which a social choice is to be made, by excluding certain alternatives, fixing others, and so on" (Nozick, 1974, p. 166).

The third approach is to see fulfillments of rights as goals to be pursued. This "goal view" differs from the instrumental view in regarding rights to be intrinsically important, and it differs from the constraint view in seeing the fulfillment of rights as goals to be generally promoted, rather than taking them as demanding only (and exactly) that we refrain from violating the rights of others. In the "constraint view" there is no duty to help anyone with his or her rights (merely not to hinder), and also in the "instrumental view" there is no duty, in fact, to help unless the right fulfillment will also promote some other goal such as utility. The "goal view" integrates the valuation of rights—their fulfillment and violation—in overall moral accounting, and yields a wider sphere of influence of rights in morality.

I have argued elsewhere that the goal view has advantages that the other two approaches do not share, in particular, the ability to accommodate integrated moral accounting including inter alia the intrinsic importance of a class of fundamental rights (Sen, 1982c; 1985b). I shall not repeat that argument here. But there is an interesting question of dual roles of rights in the sense that some rights may be *both* intrinsically important and instrumentally valuable. For example, the right to be free from hunger could—not implausibly—be regarded as being valuable in itself as well as serving as a good instrument to promote other goals such as security, longevity or utility. If so, both the goal view and the instrumental view would have to be simultaneously deployed to get a comprehensive assessment of such a right. This problem of comprehensiveness is a particularly important issue in the context of Henry George's discussion of rights, since he gave many rights significant dual roles.

The instrumental aspect is an inescapable feature of every right, since irrespective of whether a certain right is intrinsically valuable or not, its acceptance will certainly have other consequences as well, and these, too, have to be assessed along with the intrinsic value of rights (if any). A right that is regarded as quite valuable in itself may nevertheless be judged to be morally rejectable if its leads to disastrous consequences. This is a case of the rights playing a *negative* instrumental role. It is, of course, also possible that the instrumental argument will *bolster* the intrinsic claims to a right to be taken seriously. I shall presently argue that such is the case in George's analysis with the right of labor to its produce.

There are two general conclusions to draw, at this stage, from this very preliminary discussion. First, we must distinguish between (1) the intrinsic value of a right, and (2) the overall value of a right taking note inter alia of its intrinsic importance (if any). The acceptance of the intrinsic importance of any right is no guarantee that its overall moral valuation must be favorable.[4] Second, no moral assessment of a right can be independent of its likely consequences. The need for empirical assessment of the effects of accepting any right cannot be escaped. Empirical arguments are quite central to moral philosophy.[5]

PROPERTY AND DEPRIVATION

The right to hold, use and bequeath property that one has legitimately acquired is often taken to be inherently valuable. In fact, however, many of its defenses seem to be actually of the instrumental type, e.g., arguing that property rights make people more free to choose one kind of a life rather than another (see, for example, Friedman and Friedman, 1980). Even the traditional attempt at founding "natural property rights" on the principles of "natural liberty" (with or without John Locke's proviso) has some instrumental features.[6] But even if we do accept that property rights may have some intrinsic value, this does not in any way amount to an overall justification of property rights, since property rights may have consequences which themselves will require assessment. Indeed, the causation of hunger as well as its prevention may materially depend on how property rights are structured. If a set of property rights leads, say, to starvation, as it well might, then the moral approval of these rights would certainly be compromised severely. In general, the need for consequential analysis of property rights is inescapable whether or not such rights are seen as having any intrinsic value.

Consider Henry George's formula of giving "the product to the producer" (George, 1981, p. 451; 1979). This is, of course, an ambiguous rule, since the division of the credits for production to different causal influences (e.g., according to "marginal productivities" in neoclassical theory, or according to human efforts in classical labor theory) is inevitably somewhat arbitrary, and full of problems involving internal tensions (on this see Sen, 1978). But no matter how the ambiguities are resolved, it is clear that this rule would give no part of the socially produced output to one who is unemployed since he or she is producing nothing. Also, a person whose productive contribution happens to be tiny, according to *whichever* procedure of such accounting we use, can expect to get very little based on this so-called "natural law." Thus, hunger and starvation are compatible with this system of rights. George thought that this would not occur, since the economic reforms he proposed (including the abolition of land rights) would eliminate unemployment, and provision for the disabled would be made through the sympathetic support of others. These are empirical matters. If these empirical generalizations do not hold, then the outlined system of rights would yield a serious conflict. The property rights to one's product (however defined) might be of some intrinsic moral importance, but we clearly must also take note of the moral disvalue of human misery (such as suffering due to hunger and nutrition-related diseases). The latter could very plausibly by seen as having more moral force than the former. A positive intrinsic value of the right to one's product can go with an overall negative value, taking everything into account.

This type of problem arises most powerfully in assessing the ethical force of some of the standard theories of rights. For example, neither a straightforward moral theory asserting inalienable property rights, nor an elaborate theory of an entitlement system of the kind outlined by Robert Nozick, can escape having to face the possibility that when applied to an actual society, the rights in question may yield hunger, starvation, and even large-scale famine. I have tried to argue elsewhere—not in the context of disputing these moral theories but in trying to understand the causation of famines in the modern world—that famines are, in fact, best explained in terms of failures of entitlement systems.[7] The entitlements here refer, of course, to legal rights and to practical possibilities, rather than to moral status, but the laws and actual operation of private ownership economies have many features in common with the moral system of entitlements analyzed by Nozick and others.

The entitlement approach to famines need not, of course, be confined to private ownership economies, and entitlement failures of other systems can also be fruitfully studied to examine famines and hunger. In the specific context of private ownership economies, the entitlements are substantially analyzable in terms, respectively, of what may be called "endowments" and "exchange entitlements." A person's endowment refers to what he or she initially owns (including the person's own labor power), and the exchange entitlement mapping tells us what the person can obtain through exchanging what he or she owns, either by production (exchange with nature), or by trade (exchange with others), or a mixture of the two. A person has to starve if neither the endowments, nor what can be obtained through exchange, yields an adequate amount of food.

If starvation and hunger are seen in terms of failures of entitlements, then it becomes immediately clear that the total availability of food in a country is only one of several variables that are relevant. Many famines occur without any decline in the availability of food. For example, in the Great Bengal famine of 1943, the total food availability in Bengal was not particularly bad (considerably higher than two years earlier when there was no famine), and yet three million people died, in a famine mainly affecting the rural areas, through rather violent shifts in the relative purchasing powers of different groups, hitting the rural laborers the hardest (Sen, 1981, Chap. 6). The Ethiopian famine of 1973 took place in a year of average per capita food availability, but the cultivators and other occupation groups in the province of Wollo had lost their means of subsistence (through loss of crops

and a decline of economic activity, related to a local drought) and had no means of commanding food from elsewhere in the country (Sen, 1981, Chap. 7). Indeed, some food moved *out* of Wollo to more prosperous people in other parts of Ethiopia, repeating a pattern of contrary movement of food that was widely observed during the Irish famines of the 1840s (with food moving out of famine-stricken Ireland to prosperous England which had greater power in the battle for entitlements) (Sen, 1981, Chap. 10). The Bangladesh famine of 1974 took place in a year of *peak* food availability, but several occupation groups had lost their entitlement to food through loss of employment and other economic changes (including inflationary pressures causing prices to outrun wages) (Sen, 1981, Chap. 9; see also Alamgir, 1980; Ravallion, 1987). Other examples of famines without significant (or any) decline in food availability can be found, and there is nothing particularly surprising about this fact once it is recognized that the availability of food is only one influence among many on the entitlement of each occupation group. Even when a famine *is* associated with a decline of food availability, the entitlement changes have to be studied to understand the particular nature of the famine, e.g., why one occupation group is hit but not another (Sen, 1981, Chaps. 8 and 10). The causation of starvation can be sensibly sought in failures of entitlements of the respective groups.

There is, however, no great moral dilemma in this if property rights are treated as purely *instrumental.* If the goals of relief of hunger and poverty are sufficiently powerful, then it would be just right to violate whatever property rights come in the way, since—in this view—property rights have no intrinsic status. On the other hand, if property rights are taken to be morally inviolable irrespective of their consequences, then it will follow that these policies cannot be morally acceptable even though they might save thousands, or even millions, from dying. The inflexible moral "constraint" of respecting people's legitimately acquired entitlements would rule out such policies.[8]

In fact this type of problem presents a reductio ad absurdum of the moral validity of constraint-based entitlement systems. However, while the conclusions to be derived from that approach might well be "absurd," the situation postulated is not an imaginary one at all. It is based on studies of actual famines and the role of entitlement failures in the causation of mass starvation. If there is an embarrassment here, it belongs solidly to the consequence-independent way of seeing rights.

I should add that this dilemma does not arise from regarding property rights to be of intrinsic value, which can be criticized on other grounds, but not this one. Even if property rights *are* of intrinsic value, their violation may be justified on grounds of the favorable consequences of that violation. A right, as was mentioned earlier, may be intrinsically valuable and still be justly violated taking everything into account. The "absurdum" does not belong to attaching intrinsic value to property rights, but to regarding these rights as simply acceptable, regardless of their consequences. A moral system that values both property rights and other goals—such as avoiding famines and starvation, or fulfilling people's right not to be hungry—can, on the one hand, give property rights intrinsic importance, and on the other, recommend the violation of property rights when that leads to better overall consequences (*including* the disvalue of rights violation).[9]

The issue here is not the valuing of property rights, but their alleged inviolability. There is no dilemma here either for the purely instrumental view of property rights or for treating the fulfillment of property rights as one goal among many, but specifically for consequence-independent assertions of property rights and for

the corresponding constraint-based approaches to moral entitlement of ownership.

That property and hunger are closely related cannot possibly come as a great surprise. Hunger is primarily associated with not owning enough food[10] and thus property rights over food are immediately and directly involved. Fights over that property right can be a major part of the reality of a poor country, and any system of moral assessment has to take note of that phenomenon. The tendency to see hunger in purely technocratic terms of food output and availability may help to hide the crucial role of entitlements in the genesis of hunger, but a fuller economic analysis cannot overlook that crucial role. Since property rights over food are derived from property rights over other goods and resources (through production and trade), the entire system of rights of acquisition and transfer is implicated in the emergence and survival of hunger and starvation.

THE RIGHT NOT TO BE HUNGRY

Property rights have been championed for a long time. In contrast, the assertion of "the right not to be hungry" is a comparatively recent phenomenon. While this right is much invoked in political debates, there is a good deal of skepticism about treating this as truly a right in any substantial way. It is often asserted that this concept of "right not to be hungry" stands essentially for nothing at all ("simple nonsense," as Bentham called "natural rights" in general). That piece of sophisticated cynicism reveals not so much a penetrating insight into the practical affairs of the world, but a refusal to investigate what people mean when they assert the existence of rights that, for the bulk of humanity, are not in fact guaranteed by the existing institutional arrangements.

The right not to be hungry is not asserted as a recognition of an institutional right that already exists, as the right to property typically is. The assertion is primarily a moral claim as to what should be valued, and what institutional structure we should aim for, and try to guarantee if feasible. It can also be seen in terms of Ronald Dworkin's category of "background rights"—rights that provide a justification for political decisions by society in abstract" (Dworkin, 1977, p. 93). This interpretation serves as the basis for a reason to change the existing institutional structure and state policy.

It is broadly in this form that the right to "an adequate means of livelihood" is referred to in the Constitution of India: "The state shall, in particular, direct its policy towards securing . . . that the citizens, men and women equally, have the right to an adequate means of livelihood." This does not, of course, offer to each citizen a guaranteed right to an adequate livelihood, but the state is asked to take steps such that this right could become realizable for all.[11]

In fact, this right has often been invoked in political debates in India. The electoral politics of India does indeed give particular scope for such use of what are seen as background rights. It is, of course, not altogether clear whether the reference to this right in the Indian constitution has in fact materially influenced the political debates. The constitutional statement is often cited, but very likely this issue would have figured in any case in these debates, given the nature of the moral and political concern. But whatever the constitutional contribution, it is interesting to ask whether the implict acceptance of the value of the right to freedom from hunger makes any difference to actual policy.

It can be argued that the general acceptance of the right of freedom from acute hunger as a major goal has played quite a substantial role in preventing famines in India. The last real famine in India was in 1943, and while food availability per head in India has risen only

rather slowly (even now the food availability per head is no higher than in many sub-Saharan countries stricken by recurrent famines), the country has not experienced any famine since independence in 1947. The main cause of that success is a policy of public intervention. Whenever a famine has threatened (e.g., in Bihar in 1967–68, in Maharashtra in 1971–73, in West Bengal in 1978–79), a public policy of intervention and relief has offered minimum entitlements to the potential famine victims, and thus have the threatening famines been averted. It can be argued that the quickness of the response of the respective governments (both state and central) reflects a political necessity, given the Indian electoral system and the importance attached by the public to the prevention of starvation.[12] Political pressures from opposition groups and the news media have kept the respective governments on their toes, and the right to be free from acute hunger and starvation has been achieved largely because it has been seen as a valuable right. Thus the recognition of the intrinsic moral importance of this right, which has been widely invoked in public discussions, has served as a powerful political instrument as well.[13]

On the other hand, this process has been far from effective in tackling pervasive and persistent undernourishment in India. There has been no famine in post-independence India, but perhaps a third of India's rural population is perennially undernourished. So long as hunger remains non-acute and starvation deaths are avoided (even though morbidity and mortality rates are enhanced by undernourishment), the need for a policy response is neither much discussed by the news media, nor forcefully demanded even by opposition parties. The elimination of famines coexists with the survival of widespread "regular hunger." The right to "adequate means" of *nourishment* does not at all seem to arouse political concern in a way that the right to "adequate means" to *avoid starvation* does.

The contrast can be due to one of several different reasons. It could, of course, simply be that the ability to avoid undernourishment is not socially accepted as very important. This could be so, though what is socially accepted and what is not is also partly a matter of how clearly the questions are posed. It is, in fact, quite possible that the freedom in question would be regarded as a morally important right if the question were posed in a transparent way, but this does not happen because of the nature of Indian electoral politics and that of news coverage. The issue is certainly not "dramatic" in the way in which starvation deaths and threatening famines are. Continued low-key misery may be too familiar a phenomenon to make it worthwhile for political leaders to get some mileage out of it in practical politics. The news media may also find little profit in emphasizing a non-spectacular phenomenon—the quiet survival of disciplined, non-acute hunger.[14]

If this is indeed the case, then the implications for action of the goal of eliminating hunger, or guaranteeing to all the means for achieving this, may be quite complex. The political case for making the quiet hunger less quiet and more troublesome for governments in power is certainly relevant. Aggressive political journalism might prove to have an instrumental moral value if it were able to go beyond reporting the horrors of visible starvation and to portray the pervasive, non-acute hunger in a more dramatic and telling way. This is obviously not the place to discuss the instrumentalities of practical politics, but the endorsement of the moral right to be free from hunger—both acute and non-acute—would in fact raise pointed questions about the means which might be used to pursue such a goal.

MORAL ASSESSMENT AND SOCIAL RELATIONS

Henry George's advice to Bernard Shaw to study economics may well be supplemented by advising the economist to study politics and sociology, and the "moral scientist," to use an old-fashioned term, to study them all. When fulfillments of such rights as freedom from hunger are accepted as goals (among other possible goals), the moral assessment of actions and institutions will depend crucially on economic, social, and political analyses of how best to pursue these goals.

If there is one thing that emerges sharply from the discussion I have tried to present in this paper, it is the importance of factual analysis for moral assessment, including moral scrutiny of the acceptability and pursuit of specific rights. This is so even when the right in question is acknowledged to have intrinsic moral value, since valuing a right is not the same thing as accepting it. To affirm acceptability independently of consequences can be peculiarly untenable, as was discussed in analyzing entitlements and hunger. In assessing the claims of property rights, or the right not to be hungry, the examination cannot be confined to issues of basic valuation only, and much of the challenge of assessment lies in the empirical analysis of causes and effects. In the world in which we live—full of hunger as well as wealth—these empirical investigations can be both complex and quite extraordinarily important. The big moral questions are frequently also deeply economic, social, or political.

Shortened version of Henry George Lecture *at* Williams College, *April* 29, 1985.

NOTES

[1] The expression "inherent and unalienable" occurs in Thomas Jefferson's original draft of the Declaration of Independence.

2 This is presented as a "Directive Principle of State Policy." It does not have a direct operational role in the working of the Indian legal system, but it has considerable political force.

3 Ross Harrison (1983) provides an illuminating discussion of Bentham's treatment of rights, in *Bentham,* Chapter IV.

4 The reasoning here (and in earlier arguments) is based on the permissibility of pluralist moral structures, so that moral goodness is not necessarily seen as a simple monotonic function of one homogeneous primitive quantity (e.g., utility, as it is supposed to be in "monist" utilitarian accounting). I have tried to discuss the issue of pluralism, among other things, in my "Well-being, Agency and Freedom: The Dewey Lectures 1984" (Sen, 1985a).

5 On this see Sen, 1967; 1970, Chap. 5 and 6.

6 Allan Gibbard (1976) has argued convincingly that these attempts at justification of natural property rights are not successful.

7 Sen, 1981. The motivation for that work was to understand the nature and causation of poverty and famines and to draw lessons for practical policy (based on a number of case studies). The question of its moral relevance was not posed there.

8 Even Robert Nozick keeps open the possibility of justly violating rights to avoid "catastrophic moral horrors." However, once consequential rejection of rights is admitted in a system that started off with a simple assertion of consequence-independent rights, it is not at all clear where and how lines are to be drawn. See Sen, 1985c.

9 This statement has more of a "consequentialist" ring than is necessary for making the point at issue. A consequence-sensitive system (even when not fully consequentialist) can recommend the violation of property rights in the light of consequential assessment (despite the intrinsic value of those property rights). There is the further issue of "agent-relativity" in dealing with this question, and while that adds to the complexity of the picture, the possibility of justly violating intrinsically valuable rights is not altered by that. I have tried to discuss the relationships among consequentialism, consequence-sensitivity, agent-relativity and goal-rights in Sen (1982c, 1985a, 1985b) and in my response (Sen, 1983b) to some interesting and important critical points made by Donald Regan (1983).

10 This is, however, not the only causal link in the generation of hunger. There is the further problem of division of food *within* the family, which is not really a matter of ownership (since the food owned by the family is shared by all the members of it), but of intra-family distribution. In many of the poorer countries evidences of sex bias (against women) and of age bias (against children) are quite powerful, and this non-ownership issue is a matter of real practical importance. On this see Sen, 1984b, Chap. 15 and 16.

11 In fact, strictly speaking this is a right to have a state policy that genuinely tries to achieve the right to adequate means for all. Elsewhere (Sen, 1982b), I have tried to analyse the right to a *policy p(x)* to achieve x as a "metaright" to x. The constitutional Directive Principle, thus, asserts a metaright to adequate means.

12 In fact, the elimination of famine is one of the few major achievements of independent India. It is an achievement that deserves recognition, especially since famines have occurred in many other poor countries. A gigantic one took place even in China in 1958–61, in which excess mortality has been estimated to be "about 30 million" (Ashtom

et al., 1984), and this happened despite the fact that China's general record in improving nutritional standards and in reducing average morbidity and mortality rates is very impressive—far superior to India's. I have tried to discuss elsewhere the role of news media and opposition pressures in the prevention of famines in India (see Sen, 1982a, 1983a; see also Ram, 1986).

[13] It is, in fact, hard to find an example of a substantial famine that has occurred in any country with electoral politics and a free press. However, much importance need not necessarily be attached to this empirical observation, since such countries are also typically rather rich. India, because of its poverty as well as its relatively free press, is thus one of the few test cases. There are also interesting contrasts within Africa, on which see Drèze and Sen, forthcoming.

[14] This is discussed in Sen, 1982a; 1983a. The nature of property rights in the news media is a further issue that requires examination in this context. While state-owned newspapers (and radio or T.V. services) tend very often to be a "wash out" in asserting people's rights (especially vis-à-vis the state), privately owned newspapers have their own biases as well.

REFERENCES

Alamgir, M. 1980. *Famine in South Asia: Political Economy of Mass Starvation in Bangladesh.* Cambridge, Mass.: Oelgeschlager, Gunn, and Hain.

Ashton, B., Hill, K., Piazza, A., and Zeitz, R. 1984. "Famine in China, 1958–61." *Population and Development Review* 10:613.–45.

Drèze, Jean, and Sen, Amartya, editors. Forthcoming. *Hunger: Economics and Policy.* 4 vols. Oxford: Clarendon Press.

Dworkin, Ronald. 1977. *Taking Rights Seriously.* London: Duckworth.

Friedman, Milton, and Friedman, Rose. 1980. *Free to Choose.* London: Secker and Warburg.

George, Henry. 1979. *Poverty and Progress.* Centenary edition, with foreword by Agnes George de Mille. New York: Robert Schalkenbach Foundation.

—. 1981. *The Science of Political Economy.* New York: Robert Schalkenbach Foundation.

Gibbard, Allan. 1976. "Natural Property Rights." *Nous* 10:77–88.

Harrison, Ross. 1983. *Bentham.* London: Routledge.

Nozick, Robert. 1974. *Anarchy, State, and Utopia.* Oxford: Blackwell.

Ram, N. 1986. "An Independent Press and Anti-Hunger Strategies." WIDER Conference Paper. In *Hunger: Economics and Policy,* edited by J. Dreze and A. Sen. Oxford: Clarendon. Forthcoming.

Ravallion, Martin. 1987. *Markets and Famines.* Oxford: Clarendon Press.

Regan, Donald. 1983. "Against Evaluator Relativity: A Response to Sen." *Philosophy and Public Affairs* 12:93–112.

Sen, Amartya. 1967. "The Nature and Classes of Prescriptive Judgments." *Philosophical Quarterly* 17:46–62.

—. 1970. *Collective Choice and Social Welfare.* San Francisco: Holden Day. Reprint. Amsterdam: New Holland, 1979.

—. 1978. "On the Labour Theory of Value: Some Methodological Issues." *Cambridge Journal of Economics* 2:175–90.

—. 1981. *Poverty and Famines: An Essay on Entitlement and Deprivation.* Oxford: Clarendon Press; New York; Oxford University Press.

—. 1982a. "How is India Doing?" *New York Review of Books* 29, No. 20 (December

16):41–45. Reprinted in D. K. Basu and R. Sisson, eds., *Social and Economic Development in India* (Beverly Hills: Sage, 1986).

—. 1982b. "The Right Not to be Hungry." In *Contemporary Philosophy,* Vol. 2, edited by G. Fløistad, pp. 343–60. Boston: Martinus Nijhoff.

—. 1982c. "Rights and Agency." *Philosophy and Public Affairs* 11:3–39.

—. 1983a. "Development: Which Way Now?" *Economic Journal* 93:745–62. Reprinted in *Resources, Values and Development.*

—. 1983b. "Evaluator Relativity and Consequential Evaluation." *Philosophy and Public Affairs* 12:113–32.

—. 1984a. "Food Battles: Conflicts in the Access to Food." *Food and Nutrition,* FAP 10, Tenth Anniversary Issue. (FAD, United Nations, Rome).

—. 1984b. *Resources, Values, and Development.* Oxford: Blackwell and Cambridge: Harvard University Press.

—. 1985a. "Well-being, Agency, and Freedom: The Dewey Lectures 1984." *Journal of Philosophy* 82:185–203.

—. 1985b. "Rights as Goals." In *Equality and Discrimination: Essays in Freedom and Justice,* edited by S. Guest and A. Milne. Stuttgart: Franz Steiner.

—. 1985c. "The Moral Standing of the Market." In *Ethics and Economics,* edited by E. F. Paul et al. Oxford: Blackwell.

—. 1986. "Food, Economics, and Entitlements." *Lloyds Book Review,* No. 160, April.

The Savage Inequalities of Public Education in New York

Jonathon Kozol

"I n a country where there is no distinction of class," Lord Acton wrote of the United States 130 years ago, "a child is not born to the station of its parents, but with an indefinite claim to all the prizes that can be won by thought and labor. It is in conformity with the theory of equality . . . to give as near as possible to every youth an equal state in life." Americans, he said, "are unwilling that any should be deprived in childhood of the means of competition."

It is hard to read these words today without a sense of irony and sadness. Denial of "the means of competition" is perhaps the single most consistent outcome of the education offered to poor children in the schools of our large cities; and nowhere is this pattern of denial more explicit or more absolute than in the public schools of New York City.

Average expenditures per pupil in the city of New York in 1987 were some $5,500. In the highest spending suburbs of New York (Great Neck or Manhasset, for example, on Long Island) funding levels rose above $11,000, with the highest districts in the state at $15,000.

"Why . . . ," asks the city's Board of Education, "should our students receive less" than do "similar students" who live elsewhere? "The inequity is clear."

But the inequality to which these words refer goes even further than the school board may be eager to reveal. "It is perhaps the supreme irony," says the nonprofit Community Service Society of New York, that "the same Board of Education which perceives so clearly the inequities" of funding between separate towns and cities "is perpetuating similar inequities" right in New York. And, in comment on the Board of Education's final statement—"the inequity is clear"—the CSS observes, "New York City's poorest . . . districts could adopt that eloquent statement with few changes."

New York City's public schools are subdivided into 32 school districts. District 10 encompasses a large part of the Bronx but is, effectively, two separate districts. One of these districts, Riverdale, is in the northwest section of the Bronx. Home to many of the city's most sophisticated and well-educated families, its elementary schools have relatively few low-income students.

The other section, to the south and east, is poor and heavily nonwhite.

The contrast between public schools in each of these two neighborhoods is obvious to any visitor. At Public School 24 in Riverdale, the principal speaks enthusiastically of his teaching staff. At Public School 79, serving poorer children to the south, the principal says that he is forced to take the "tenth-best" teachers. "I thank God they're still breathing," he remarks of those from whom he must select his teachers.

Some years ago, District 10 received an allocation for computers. The local board decided to give each elementary school an equal number of computers, even though the schools in Riverdale had smaller classes and far fewer students. When it was pointed out that schools in Riverdale, as a result, had twice the number of computers in proportion to their student populations as the schools in the poor neighborhoods, the chairman of the local board replied, "What is fair is what is determined . . . to be fair."

The superintendent of District 10, Fred Goldberg, tells the *New York Times* that "every effort" is made "to distribute resources equitably." He speculates that some gap might exist because some of the poorer schools need to use funds earmarked for computers to buy basic supplies like pens and paper. Asked about the differences in teachers noted by the principals, he says there are no differences, then adds that next year he'll begin a program to improve the quality of teachers in the poorer schools. Questioned about differences in physical appearances between the richer and the poorer schools, he says, "I think it's demographics."

Sometimes a school principal, whatever his background or his politics, looks into the faces of the children in his school and offers a disarming statement that cuts through official ambiguity. "These are the kids most in need," says Edward Flanery, the principal of one of the low-income schools, "and they get the worst teachers." For children of diverse needs in his overcrowded rooms, he says, "you need an outstanding teacher. And what do you get? You get the worst."

In order to find Public School 261 in District 10, a visitor is told to look for a mortician's office. The funeral home, which faces Jerome Avenue in the North Bronx, is easy to identify by its green awning. The school is next door, in a former roller-skating rink. No sign identifies the building as a school. A metal awning frame without an awning supports a flagpole, but there is no flag.

In the street in front of the school there is an elevated public transit line. Heavy traffic fills the street. The existence of the school is virtually concealed within this crowded city block.

In a vestibule between the outer and inner glass doors of the school there is a sign with these words: "All children are capable of learning."

Beyond the inner doors a guard is seated. The lobby is long and narrow. The ceiling is low. There are no windows. All the teachers that I see at first are middle-aged white women. The principal, who is also a white woman, tells me that the school's "capacity" is 900 but that there are 1,300 children here. The size of classes for fifth and sixth grade children in New York, she says, is "capped" at 32, but she says that class size in the school goes "up to 34." (I later see classes, however, as large as 37.) Classes for younger children, she goes on, are "capped at 25," but a school can go above this limit if it puts an extra adult in the room. Lack of space, she says, prevents the school from operating a prekindergarten program.

I ask the principal where her children go to school. They are enrolled in private school, she says.

"Lunchtime is a challenge for us," she explains. "Limited space obliges us to do it in three shifts, 450 children at a time."

Textbooks are scarce and children have to share their social studies books. The principal says there is one full-time pupil counselor and another who is here two days a week; a ratio of 930 children to one counselor. The carpets are patched and sometimes taped together to conceal an open space. "I could use some new rugs," she observes.

To make up for the building's lack of windows and the crowded feeling that results, the staff puts plants and fish tanks in the corridors. Some of the plants are flourishing. Two boys, released from class, are in a corridor beside a tank, their noses pressed against the glass. A school of pinkish fish inside the tank are darting back and forth. Farther down the corridor a small Hispanic girl is watering the plants.

Two first grade classes share a single room without a window, divided only by a blackboard. Four kindergartens and a sixth grade class of Spanish-speaking children have been packed into a single room in which, again, there is no window. A second grade bilingual class of 37 children has its own room but again there is no window.

By eleven o'clock, the lunchroom is already packed with appetite and life. The kids line up to get their meals, then eat them in ten minutes. After that, with no place they can go to play, they sit and wait until it's time to line up and go back to class.

On the second floor I visit four classes taking place within another undivided space. The room has a low ceiling. File cabinets and movable blackboards give a small degree of isolation to each class. Again, there are no windows.

The library is a tiny, windowless and claustrophobic room. I count approximately 700 books. Seeing no reference books, I ask a teacher if encyclopedias and other reference books are kept in classrooms.

"We don't have encyclopedias in classrooms," she replies. "That is for the suburbs."

The school, I am told, has 26 computers for its 1,300 children. There is one small gym and children get one period, and sometimes two, each week. Recess, however, is not possible because there is no playground. "Head Start," the principal says, "scarcely exists in District 10. We have no space."

The school, I am told, is 90 percent black and Hispanic; the other 10 percent are Asian, white or Middle Eastern.

In a sixth grade social studies class the walls are bare of words or decorations. There seems to be no ventilation system, or, if one exists, it isn't working.

The class discusses the Nile River and the Fertile Crescent.

The teacher, in a droning voice: "How is it useful that these civilizations developed close to rivers?"

A child, in a good loud voice: "What kind of question is that?"

In my notes I find these words: "An uncomfortable feeling—being in a building with no windows. There are metal ducts across the room. Do they give air? I feel asphyxiated . . . ."

On the top floor of the school, a sixth grade of 30 children shares a room with 29 bilingual second graders. Because of the high class size there is an assistant with each teacher. This means that 59 children and four grown-ups—63 in all—must share a room that, in a suburban school, would hold no more than 20 children and one teacher. There are, at least, some outside windows in this room—it is the only room with windows in the school—and the room has a high ceiling. It is a relief to see some daylight.

I return to see the kindergarten classes on the ground floor and feel stifled once again by lack of air and the low ceiling. Nearly 120 children and adults are doing what they can to make the best of things: 80 children in four kindergarten classes, 30 children in the sixth grade class, and about eight grown-ups who are aides and teachers. The kindergarten children sitting on the worn rug, which is patched with tape, look up at me and turn their heads to follow me as I walk past them.

As I leave the school, a sixth grade teacher stops to talk. I ask her, "Is there air conditioning in warmer weather?"

Teachers, while inside the building, are reluctant to give answers to this kind of question. Outside, on the sidewalk, she is less constrained: "I had an awful room last year. In the winter it was 56 degrees. In the summer it was up to 90. It was sweltering."

I ask her, "Do the children ever comment on the building?"

"They don't say," she answers, "but they know."

I ask her if they see it as a racial message.

"All these children see TV," she says. "They know what suburban schools are like. Then they look around them at their school. This was a roller-rink, you know . . . . They don't comment on it but you see it in their eyes. They understand."

On the following morning I visit P.S. 79, another elementary school in the same district. "We work under difficult circumstances," says the principal, James Carter, who is black. "The school was built to hold one thousand students. We have 1,550. We are badly overcrowded. We need smaller Classes but, to do this, we would need more space. I can't add five teachers. I would have no place to put them."

Some experts, I observe, believe that class size isn't a real issue. He dismisses this abruptly. "It doesn't take a genius to discover that you learn more in a smaller class. I have to bus some 60 kindergarten children elsewhere, since I have no space for them. When they return next year, where do I put them?

"I can't set up a computer lab. I have no room. I had to put a class into the library. I have no librarian. There are two gymnasiums upstairs but they cannot be used for sports. We hold more classes there. It's unfair to measure us against the suburbs. They have 17 to 20 children in a class. Average class size in this school is 30.

"The school is 29 percent black, 70 percent Hispanic. Few of these kids get Head Start. There is no space in the district. Of 200 kindergarten children, 50 maybe get some kind of preschool."

I ask him how much difference preschool makes.

"Those who get it do appreciably better. I can't overestimate its impact but, as I have said, we have no space."

The school tracks children by ability, he says. "There are five to seven levels in each grade. The highest level is equivalent to 'gifted' but it's not a full-scale gifted program. We don't have the funds. We have no science room. The science teachers carry their equipment with them."

We sit and talk within the nurse's room. The window is broken. There are two holes in the ceiling. About a quarter of the ceiling has been patched and covered with a plastic garbage bag.

"Ideal class size for these kids would be 15 to 20. Will these children ever get what white kids in the suburbs take for granted? I don't think so. If you ask me why, I'd have to speak of race and social class. I don't think the powers that be in New York City understand, or want to understand, that if they do not give these children a sufficient education to lead healthy and productive lives, we will be their victims later on. We'll pay the price someday—in violence, in economic costs. I despair of making this appeal in any terms but these. You cannot issue an appeal to conscience in New York today. The fair-play argument won't be accepted. So you speak of violence and hope that it will scare the city into action."

While we talk, three children who look six or seven years old come to the door and ask to see the nurse, who isn't in the school today. One of the children, a Puerto Rican girl, looks haggard. "I have a pain in my tooth," she says. The principal says, "The nurse is out. Why don't you call your mother?" The child says, "My mother doesn't have a phone." The principal sighs. "Then go back to your class." When she leaves, the principal is angry. "It's amazing to me that these children ever make it with the obstacles they face. Many *do* care and they *do* try, but there's a feeling of despair. The parents of these children want the same things for their children that the parents in the suburbs want. Drugs are not the cause of this. They are the symptom. Nonetheless, they're used by people in the suburbs and rich people in Manhattan as another reason to keep children of poor people at a distance."

I ask him, "Will white children and black children ever go to school together in New York?"

"I don't see it," he replies. "I just don't think it's going to happen. It's a dream. I simply do not see white folks in Riverdale agreeing to cross-bus with kids like these. A few, maybe. Very few. I don't think I'll live to see it happen."

I ask him whether race is the decisive factor. Many experts, I observe, believe that wealth is more important in determining these inequalities.

"This," he says—and sweeps his hand around him at the room, the garbage bag, the ceiling—"would not happen to white children."

In a kindergarten class the children sit cross-legged on a carpet in a space between two walls of books. Their 26 faces are turned up to watch their teacher, an elderly black woman. A little boy who sits beside me is involved in trying to tie bows in his shoelaces. The children sing a song: "Lift Every Voice." On the wall are these handwritten words: "Beautiful, also, are the souls of my people."

In a very small room on the fourth floor, 52 people in two classes do their best to teach and learn. Both are first grade classes. One, I am informed, is "low ability." The other is bilingual.

"The room is barely large enough for one class," says the principal.

The room is 25 by 50 feet. There are 26 first graders and two adults on the left, 22 others and two adults on the right. On the wall there is the picture of a small white child, circled by a Valentine, and a Gainsborough painting of a child in a formal dress.

"We are handicapped by scarcity," one of the teachers says. "One fifth of these children may be at grade level by the year's end."

A boy who may be seven years old climbs on my lap without an invitation and removes my glasses. He studies my face and runs his fingers through my hair. "You have nice hair," he says. I ask him where he lives and he replies, "Times Square Hotel," which is a homeless shelter in Manhattan.

I ask him how he gets here.

"With my father. On the train," he says.

"How long does it take?"

"It takes an hour and a half."

I ask him when he leaves his home.

"My mother wakes me up at five o'clock."

"When do you leave?"

"Six-thirty."

I ask him how he gets back to Times Square.

"My father comes to get me after school."

From my notes: "He rides the train three hours every day in order to attend this segregated school. It would be a shorter ride to Riverdale. There are rapid shuttle-vans that make that trip in only 20 minutes. Why not let him go to school right in Manhattan, for that matter?"

At three o'clock the nurse arrives to do her recordkeeping. She tells me she is here three days a week. "The public hospital we use for an emergency is called North Central. It's not a hospital that I will use if I am given any choice. Clinics in the private hospitals are far more likely to be staffed by an experienced physician."

She hesitates a bit as I take out my pen, but then goes on: "I'll give you an example. A little girl I saw last week in school was trembling and shaking and could not control the motions of her arms. I was concerned and called her home. Her mother came right up to school and took her to North Central. The intern concluded that the child was upset by 'family matters'—nothing more—that there was nothing wrong with her. The mother was offended by the diagnosis. She did not appreciate his words or his assumptions. The truth is, there was nothing wrong at home. She brought the child back to school. I thought that she was ill. I told her mother, 'Go to Montefiore.' It's a private hospital, and well respected. She took my advice, thank God. It turned out that the child had a neurological disorder. She is now in treatment.

"This is the kind of thing our children face. Am I saying that the city underserves this population? You can draw your own conclusions."

Out on the street, it takes a full half hour to flag down a cab. Taxi drivers in New York are sometimes disconcertingly direct in what they say. When they are contemptuous of poor black people, their contempt is unadorned. When they're sympathetic and compassionate, their observations often go right to the heart of things. "Oh . . . they neglect these children," says the driver. "They leave them in the streets and slums to live and die." We stop at a light. Outside the window of the taxi, aimless men are standing in a semicircle while another man is working on his car. Old four-story buildings with their windows boarded, cracked or missing are on every side.

I ask the driver where he's from. He says Afghanistan. Turning in his seat, he gestures at the street and shrugs. "If you don't, as an American, begin to give these kids the kind of education that you give the kids of Donald Trump, you're asking for disaster."

Fashioning Freedom

Ann E. Cudd

When I walked out of prison that was my mission, to liberate the oppressed and the oppressor both. Some say that has now been achieved. But I know that this is not the case. The truth is that we are not yet free; we have merely achieved the freedom to be free, the right not to be oppressed. We have not taken the final step of our journey, but the first step on a longer and even more difficult road. For, to be free is not merely to cast off one's chains, but to live in a way that respects and enhances the freedom of others. The true test of our devotion to freedom is just beginning.

—*Nelson Mandela, Long Walk to Freedom*

OPPRESSION, JUSTICE, FREEDOM

Freedom, in addition to justice, requires overcoming oppression. This book has focused on the injustice of oppression, its causes, and our duty to overcome it. I argued that our psychological propensity to categorize, which together with our social nature, leads to stereotyping. Invidious discrimination based on these stereotypes sets the stage for oppression. Oppression is caused initially by direct material forces (violence,

economic deprivation) imposed from outside, and then reinforced by internalized, indirect, material and psychological forces. In chapter 7 I explored several ways that particular cases of oppression can be resisted and projected the hope that by strong resistance any one case of oppression will end. In this concluding chapter I turn from justice to the question of freedom to consider whether, even if we are able to resist the injustices of oppression, we may yet not be free. I shall argue, as suggested by the quote from Nelson Mandela, that freedom requires something more than an end to any particular case of oppression; full freedom requires that all cases of oppression end. This claim, whether true or not, raises crucial questions, however. What is the future of our species with respect to oppression? Are we headed for a state of freedom in which all cases, not just this case and that case, of oppression will be rare and short-lived? Or will we forever be plagued by some cases of long-standing oppression?

Some will argue that it is not possible to overcome oppression, given our psychological makeup, which is largely fixed in its predisposition to categorize and our strong propensity to form social groups. It seems that overcoming all oppression requires us to either change

From Analyzing Oppression by Ann E. Cudd. Reprinted by permission of Oxford University Press, Inc.

our psychological makeup (which I assume is impossible without ceasing to be us) or to prevent each other from forming close knit social groups. Even if we were able to overcome our sociality, it is not clear that we would want to. Everything of value in human life is bound up with its sociality; we cannot even imagine what life would be like as a solitary species like the bear or the coyote, for it would be language-less and so beyond our understanding. Our propensity to form close social bonds seems as fixed as our propensity to categorize. Thus, we must take the existence of social groups for granted in exploring how oppression is to be overcome, but we may be able to reinvent them or mold them to suit us. If social groups will exist, then perhaps we can change our stereotypes and discourage invidious discrimination. That would require the privileged to give up their privileges, and persons would have to resist the temptation to take advantage of others through the kind of group level processes that we seem to learn as children: bullying, teasing, peer pressure, and the like. What would motivate such changes?

The history of political philosophy offers us a parallel. In his classic *Federalist Paper* #10, James Madison wrote about the danger of factions, by which he meant groups that share a common interest that is opposed to the rights of others or the interest of the whole community (Hamilton, Madison, and Jay 1961, 77–83). He reasoned that either we could prevent such factions from forming, or we could try to find a way to prevent factions from succeeding in their "schemes of oppression." We cannot prevent factions from forming, Madison noted, without sacrificing freedom, since that would either require us to ensure that we all have the same interests (through some sort of brainwashing) or to prevent groups from forming to discuss their common interests. Thus, the only way we can maintain freedom yet avoid the oppressive forces of factions is to find a way to prevent them from succeeding in satisfying

their perfidious interests. Madison proposed that a representative democracy of the sort he had outlined in the proposed U.S. Constitution would be the solution because it would encourage discussion of general philosophies of government rather than particular policy interests if the people were to vote not on issues but on representatives. The record must be judged as mixed here. But in any event, we seek to solve a broader social problem. That is, we seek to project not only a government that will not oppress its citizens, but also a collage of unconnected but overlapping social groups that will not oppress each other. Like the people that Madison was trying to lead, the oppressed can reach freedom only by acting with good faith and good will toward others within a social system that does not reward them for doing otherwise, but instead rewards them when others are free, as well. Toward achieving this end, governments may well play a role, but it cannot be the only force for change without reinstituting oppression through the repression of our individual and social natures. We must, in effect, reward each other for our freedom.

In the last chapter I looked at a number of ways that particular cases of oppression can be resisted. Oppression can be resisted at all levels: by legal means backed up by coercive force, by groups who attempt to alleviate poverty and invest in the abilities of the poor, by individuals who refuse their unjust privileges, or oppressed individuals who refuse to help keep the others in their social groups to the norms that advantage the oppressors. In this chapter I take up the question of what a group is to do when the bonds of oppression are loosened. At that point we embark on the journey of which Mandela writes, the "longer and even more difficult road," on which we must learn "to live in a way that respects and enhances the freedom of others," for only by this route can true freedom be found. Our problem, however, is that we do not yet know what that route looks like or where, precisely, it is going. Our only guide is knowledge that it is our duty not to oppress others and to resist oppression where possible, and our enhanced ability to recognize oppression when it occurs.

The oppression of women, as has been noted by many, is the longest standing case of oppression. Women have become accustomed to being the subordinate sex, and to fashioning their lives within the unequal constraints that societies have imposed on them for at least most of human history. In doing so, women have in many ways forfeited their right to freedom. They rarely demand equality with men and often satisfy themselves with doing better than the next woman or the next subordinate of their society. This has been the individual's rational response to her oppression, after all: attempting to do as well as they can for themselves within the constraints they are offered, rather than futilely refusing to comply with sexist norms. Because women have done so well at accommodating themselves to oppression, in ways both rational and emotional, ending the oppression of women and overcoming sexual subordination is the biggest challenge to our hopes for freedom. For this reason, in what follows I will focus on how women can liberate themselves. Perhaps our struggle to liberate women, then, will unveil the path to freedom for all.

There are several reasons why women's path to freedom might be generalizable to that of other social groups. First, in order to free women, we must learn to change some of the most deep-seated norms of power and subordination. For, they are both long-standing and originate in natural inequalities or differences. Second, in order to change the status of women globally, we will have to learn how to see people as members of multiple social groups not of their choosing; those in power (men) will have to allow members of their social groups ("their" women) to claim other groupings as, at least temporarily, their most important or most threatened aspect of their identity, and those subordinated (women) will have to learn how to insist on it. For it is only if women and men see themselves as part of a gender hierarchy that cuts across race, class, ethnicity and other groupings, that we can address the oppression that gender entails. Gender oppression will not go away by ignoring or denying it, by insisting that there are no women or that women do not have common interests. Third, in the process of seeking their own liberation, women will have to forge friendships and alliances across social groups. In coming to see others as allies despite great differences, we will learn how to be sisters in affirming our common humanity. Well-intentioned men from different social groups may first join out of allegiance to their own race or ethnic grouping, but eventually they too will join this humanistic sorority that stretches across those groups. Then it will be a short step to seeing all of humanity as united in a struggle for universal freedom.

TWO SENSES OF FREEDOM

Many theorists of freedom, particularly since the influential paper by Isaiah Berlin (1969), "Two Concepts of Liberty," have recognized two senses of "freedom." Berlin named them "positive" and "negative," but others have more usefully distinguished between "internal" and "external" (Hirschmann 2003). Negative or external freedom means something like the absence of interference from outside the person, while positive or internal freedom means the capacity to seek and attain, provided that there is no external interference, one's own good. Positive freedom is often understood as autonomy, the ability to be a self-lawmaker, and this requires that one is not manipulated by the social structure under which one lives. One's desires are one's own and one's beliefs are rationally generated. Berlin ultimately rejects the idea of positive freedom because he thought that to posit a breach of positive freedom one would have to impose desires on individuals that they do not acknowledge. For governments to attempt to guarantee positive freedom, then, they would have to posit a good for their citizens and entice them to seek it, that is, in Rousseau's famous phrase, to force their citizens to be free. Berlin, as a liberal, argues that freedom requires merely imposing no impediments to individuals' given preferences. Positive freedom, Berlin concludes, insinuates a totalitarian menace.

In this book I have characterized oppression as being caused by social constraints, and I have asserted the liberal conviction that individuals are of primary moral importance. It may appear that my theory of oppression entails only or primarily a problem of negative or external freedom. But this inference would be too quick. I have also characterized psychological forces and harms of oppression that clearly work internally to the person, even while some of them, such as sterotyping, are externally imposed on the individual. Internal and external freedom cannot be easily distinguished; they are inevitably intertwined, just as the social forces of oppression work together to maintain an effective prison around the oppressed. The distinction that Berlin drew between negative and positive freedom is not neatly drawn, and his rejection of positive freedom involves two confusions. First, he failed to see that a persistent lack of negative freedom for a social group harms the individuals of that group psychologically, causing them to lack positive freedom, as chapters 3 through 6 have demonstrated. Second, even though the idea that a government might posit an individual's good for her raises the specter of totalitarianism, that fact does not vitiate the claim that an individual's freedom can be compromised by a lack of vision of viable alternative options.

A person can lack freedom without there being a clear way for the person to attain freedom in the future.

The first of these confusions suggests that the positive/negative distinction drawn by Berlin does not do the philosophical work we need it to do. Violations of negative freedom turn out to result in deeper harms that slide over into the kinds of harms that violations of positive freedom entail. Violence, for example, results in post-traumatic stress disorder, which robs victims of their ability to plan a coherent life. I shall adopt the terms "internal" and "external" freedom, to detach my theory from Berlin's distinction and to suggest a connection to my terms "indirect" and "direct" forces of oppression. As I shall use the terms, internal freedom requires that there be no indirect forces of oppression imposing on a person, and external freedom requires freedom from direct forces of oppression. These are necessary, not sufficient, conditions for freedom. Recall that the distinction between these two kinds of oppressive force turns on the contribution of the oppressed individual's internal mental processes of belief and desire formation. Indirect forces come about through the oppressed person's own psychological mechanisms. Direct forces of oppression begin a vicious cycle that may begin mainly depriving its victims of outer freedom, but as it continues to traumatize them and their fellow social group members, those forces cause their victims to relinquish their hopes and dreams for a better future, which in turn atrophies the ability to imagine a future of freedom. This description fits women's lack of freedom under patriarchy, or the global domination of men. Women have accepted their lesser status in much of the world and work within the constraints to achieve what they can without questioning or challenging the starting assumption that sex must impose a hierarchy of status.[1]

Since the two kinds of oppressive forces often work in concert and reinforce each other, internal and external freedom often fail together, though this is not necessarily the case. A person is not free so long as she is the victim of forces of oppression. As I have argued, indirect forces of oppression are in a sense self-imposed, even though ultimately caused by external forces. Resisting internal forces of oppression, as we have seen, requires restraining individuals (in the best case, individuals restraining themselves) from doing what they want, sometimes rationally, to do. The goal of achieving freedom thus imposes both social responsibility and individual responsibility. As I argued in chapter 7, those who are most privileged by oppression are surely the most responsible for resisting it. Yet, they are also often the least motivated, for they have the most to lose. The privileged have even more to lose than their undeserved privileges if oppression is inevitable and by releasing some from oppression they risk bringing it upon themselves. Motivation for ending oppression, then, may only come after the bonds of oppression are loosened by the oppressed themselves, working with the well-intentioned and insightful privileged who work actively to end oppression. For at this point the possibility of backlash against the oppressors is great, yet engaging in that backlash risks a continuing cycle. Thus, it behooves us all to seek a kind of freedom that is freedom for all if only as defense against catastrophe.

Berlin was correct to worry about the totalitarian menace; formulating someone else's desires or beliefs for them is to deny freedom, and even trying to assess others' true desires and beliefs is fraught with dangers. Yet there is, I believe, a greater danger in standing idly by while freedom is actively denied. This poses something of a dilemma, for it seems that because oppression is so intertwined with our existing social institutions, either we must seek

freedom or deny it, and if we seek it we must have a vision of what we seek, and this entails devising conditions under which persons will develop autonomous beliefs and desires. In framing those conditions, we risk totalitarianism. But perhaps that last claim is too extreme. If there is a way between these horns, then it is, I shall argue, through a gradual process of resistance to oppression combined with the will and intention not to oppress new or other social groups. In the next section I sketch out how this process could go.

BREAKING THE VICIOUS CYCLE OF OPPRESSION

Since oppression acts through social institutions, the starting point for us must be to begin by attacking the self-generating cycles that those institutions support. Oppression runs a typical sequence: it begins when members of one group violently attack individuals in another social group and proceeds as the dominant group wields economic force on the subordinates. The oppressed respond rationally by choosing within the constraints that they are offered by the oppressors, and they gradually accommodate their beliefs and desires to the oppressive conditions that they find through both rational and nonrational psychological processes. It is at this point in the process that all the most puzzling and tenacious features of oppression appear. Direct forces may become less visible as time wears on and generations adopt the coping mechanisms of their parents; the privileged come to believe that their superiority is natural; the oppressed come to believe in their own inferiority, and become dependent on the dominant social groups for material support and moral leadership. At this point, oppression cannot be successfully defeated by ending only the direct forces. Rather, we need to break the link between material deprivation and dependence of the oppressed social group on others. Achieving freedom then will require not only breaking the interlocking links of the chain but also setting the oppressed on a course toward independence.

By independence I do not mean disconnection from others, but rather the material and psychological preconditions for the ability to form one's own beliefs and desires without oppressive constraints. I have argued that the oppressed are cognitively and emotionally constrained in unjust ways to conform their beliefs and desires to benefit the dominant. These constraints impose emotive and cognitive forces of shame and low self-esteem, the cognitive process of false consciousness, and the cognitive/affective process of deformed desire, causing oppressed persons to believe ideologies that oppress them and to desire the situations, goods, and ways of life that keep them subordinate. By molding the oppressed to desire their position (as well as the privileged to believe they are entitled to theirs), they are made dependent on the desires of the dominant. This is the sense of dependence that we must object to. Dependence on others in the form of reliance on their charity, good will, cooperation, companionship, and good work to make one's own life better is not objectionable. Indeed, such dependence is a part of our sociality that makes human life uniquely wonderful.[2]

The first step toward freedom, then, is to end direct forces of oppression: violence, threats of violence, enslavement, and the blatantly unfair economic practices of invidious wage and hiring discrimination and enforced labor segregation. For women this would be a radical step. Ending violence would mean ending violence against women in the forms of domestic abuse, sexual assault, and sexual slavery. Curtailing direct economic forces would mean ending sex discrimination in hiring and wages, cracking down on sexual harassment, ending the segre-

gation of women into lower paid occupations and jobs, and providing equal opportunities for education and training regardless of sex. But we must recognize that even these enormous steps will not end oppressive dependence, and that there remains a social responsibility on the privileged to do more. The personalities, beliefs, desires of the oppressed and the privileged alike have been formed under conditions of oppression, after all. Changing those conditions will not immediately change the personalities. Future generations will be raised by parents and other adults who retain the personalities of oppressed, oppressor, and privileged. Consider how young women of today are still attracted to positions of sexual, political, and economic submission, despite the advances in economic opportunity that their mothers' and grandmothers' generations have made. Young men are often resentful of their loss of some privilege and even tend to see themselves as victimized by social efforts to end oppressive practices (Faludi 1999). Psychological progress comes slowly, not only in individuals, but also generationally. The psychology of freedom will not come to us in an instant; it is not an immediate result of the psychology of resistance.

The crucial next step toward freedom is to suggest alternative social practices that would be attractive to a wide variety of persons (not just the oppressed), and yet would help to break the cycle of dependency on the dominant groups. The privileged have to be recruited in the struggle for freedom so that they will not resent and resist change. Large and significant psychological changes will have to be directed also at the youngest members of society. In the United States, single mothers tend to be poor and poor single mothers are less able to equip their children and communities with skills for independence. Low income women tend to need child care in order to get more education, retain their jobs, or move to better ones (Lee

2004). At the same time, quality childcare is costly, which means that poor women cannot afford it. Yet good quality childcare is crucially important to children's health, well-being, and development of capacities for freedom from internal oppression. To fight the economic forces of poverty for women, by helping make women independent in the economy, and to develop a future of free citizens, broadly available subsidized child care should be socially provided.[3] This step helps to fashion a free society in a variety of ways. It addresses (though does not solve) the problems of women's and poor persons' oppression in our society. It helps develop the capacities for autonomy and independence from domination by the children who receive the good quality care. Furthermore, it is politically feasible even in a society that is not yet free. It appeals to large numbers of men and women across racial and class lines, since people everywhere want their children to be well cared for, and for the most part they want other people's children to be well cared for, too. Steps such as this one, which have multiple effects on resisting oppression and developing capacities to internal freedom approach freedom gradually, through small changes that are popularly and democratically adopted. They may not be inexpensive, and so the wealthy will have to be convinced that it is their duty to contribute more for the elimination of oppression. But they do not intrude upon individuals' decisions about how to use what wealth they retain. They make no effort to directly change preferences of any but the children, whose preferences will be formed by some social process or other, and clearly good child care is to be preferred to bad by all rational people of good will. Yet they offer the opportunity for women to take steps toward economic independence, defeating one of the forces of oppression.

These first two steps, while required by justice, will still not bring about a widespread psychology of freedom. There will still be those whose interests are best served by maintaining their position in the existing hierarchy: men who gain economically, sexually, or psychologically by asserting their dominance and claiming that it is natural for them to do so; women who gain economically or psychologically by selling their sexual subordination, given the current incentives. These people have to be provided incentives to forego those interests and develop new ones. These incentives could be carrots or sticks, but carrots are better for co-opting someone to a progressive cause, and sticks are unwarranted except as punishment for oppressive, not simply privilege-seeking, behavior. Men and women should be given incentives to enter into consensual relations that will enhance women's freedom as well as men's. For instance, small steps that would work through changing incentives to bring about the social provision of child care would include allowing tax credits to employers for providing child care at the work site or awarding block grants to communities for child care centers or for lengthening the school year and the school day to match the working day.[4] Larger steps to undermine economic oppression would include offering scholarship assistance for young women to enter male-dominated professions, tax credits for businesses to hire them or for women to start their own businesses. We must also work toward a vision of freedom at the same time that we undermine the forces of oppression, and social incentives for this vision-work could be offered. Awards might be made available for popular works of art and music that offer visions of a future without oppression. The legal definition of religion might be expanded so that groups who seek to articulate notions of freedom can garner the benefits provided to religions.[5]

Social change will be resisted not only by those who think they will lose their privileges but also by those who are rewarded by the current structures of incentives to continue in their path, even if they do not support its outcome. For example, many people who pursue research on pharmaceuticals are initially motivated to do so by their concern to cure illness. Those persons would presumably be most motivated by research that cures the most disease. Yet they find that the reward structures for drug development are not connected to the numbers of persons whose illnesses they can help to cure, but rather to the amount of wealth that ill persons have. Thomas Pogge (2003) proposes an ingenious solution to the problem of incentives for drug manufacturers to develop drugs for the diseases that primarily and disastrously afflict Third World countries. He proposes a transnational organization that would collect revenues from drug sales and use them to reward inventor firms in proportion to the impact that their inventions have on the global disease burden. The point of doing this is to realign the incentive structures away from just trying to cure the diseases that are relatively trivial in terms of numbers and effects but strike rich persons toward curing the diseases that are life-threatening for masses of persons. The interest of inventor firms and generic drug manufacturers would then come together, and drugs of great significance would be made in great quantities, reaping financial rewards for both types of firms. "Inventor firms would *want* their inventions to be widely copied, mass produced, and sold as cheaply as possible, as these would magnify the impact of these health inventions" (Pogge 2003, 23). This solution requires governmental intervention on behalf of ending oppression (in this case the severe human rights violation of poverty, as argued by Pogge), but the mechanism works through an incentive that makes both the agents of change and the oppressed better off.[6] This is an example of how incentives can be structured to bring together the interests of many in solving problems of oppression.

This third step goes beyond the direct social provision of resources to imagine how society might restructure incentives to bring about envisioned alternative social practices that enhance freedom. Such incentives work through individuals' free choices, rather than through the imposition of beliefs or preferences, and go beyond and improve upon the direct social provision of goods in three ways. First, offering incentives to behave in certain ways is more likely to change beliefs and desires than the previous step (direct social provision to the oppressed) in fashioning freedom. Second, as economists often argue with respect to markets for goods (or bads) subject to externalities (and hence free rider problems), giving incentives for socially beneficial behavior and then allowing individuals to choose the actions that are in their interest is the most efficient way to solve the problem of free riding. A standard example of this is the market for pollution, in which firms are allotted pollution rights that they can trade in the market. The alternative is to put an absolute prohibition on pollution above a certain threshold for each firm. The market solution, it has been argued, works better, by giving firms incentives to innovate where possible and not to cheat, since when they cannot innovate they can still run their business legally by buying the pollution credits from other firms (Varian 1994). The model relies on there being good information about the existing levels of pollution, and since firms have little incentive to provide this information, they have to be monitored by government agencies. The analogy between pollution and oppressive social norms has already been made. What I am arguing here is that there is also an analogy between market-based solutions to pollution problems and incentive-based solutions to changing oppressive social norms. By giving persons incentives to act in ways counter to oppressive social norms, they will choose to do so, and perhaps choose to do so in better ways than could have been devised from those farther removed from the problem. Third, socially structured incentives indirectly change beliefs and desires, in that they entice persons to do things that will enhance their independence. Just as there can be indirect forces of oppression, I am suggesting that there can be indirect forces of freedom enhancement. Joshua Cohen's discussion of the notion of a social ethos and its connection to social institutions supports my claim. By social ethos, a term he takes from G. A. Cohen, he means "socially widespread preferences and attitudes about the kinds of rewards it is acceptable to insist on, and, associated with those preferences and attitudes, a sense about the ways of life that are attractive, exciting, good, and worthy of pursuit" (Cohen 2001, 365). Cohen argues that it is at least plausible that the choice of social institutions causally affects the social ethos, so that, within a Rawlsian framework we can expect justice to require social institutions that instill an ethos conducive to freedom from oppression. If this substantive assumption holds, then people will be led by social institutions that they accept to develop the preferences and attitudes necessary for freedom—not by direct intervention in their lives but by the constitutive shaping of their personalities that must occur through one set of social institutions or another (Cohen 2001, 384).

One might object that such indirect forces are coercive because they manipulate people—indeed, they are specifically designed to manipulate people. But this is just where they differ from indirect forces of oppression. They are not coercive because they do not fit the definition of coercion I argued for in chapter 5: "An institution (economic system, legal system, or norm) is coercive if the institution unfairly

limits the choices of some group of persons relative to other groups in society." That is, these incentives do not, by hypothesis, *unfairly* limit choices. It is important to reiterate here a point made in the earlier discussion of coercion. I am using coercion in the moralized sense, that is, coercion is lack of choice relative to a set of choices that is deemed fair or moral by some background moral theory. That background moral theory has not been elaborated in this book, and I will not set out to do that now in the final pages of the work. I have in mind a liberal contractarian view of the sort developed by John Rawls in *A Theory of Justice,* or the more libertarian version of David Gauthier in *Morals by Agreement.* The claim that any particular incentive structure that is proposed to take this third step in fashioning freedom is noncoercive stands or falls on the claim that the social institution it seeks to counteract is oppressive. But that claim itself relies on the background moral theory that I am assuming in this book.

A liberal like Berlin might argue that these incentives amount to just the kind of preference re-education project that portends the slide to totalitarianism. But I think that this is not the case, and that a liberal can defend structuring social incentives through government intervention (as well as private incentive provision), or through international quasi-governing institutions. The key to the argument is to see that the government must structure incentives in favor of some set of conditions. It may structure incentives either to maintain the privileges of some social groups or to shift the benefits to others. What makes a totalitarian state evil is that it structures incentives for persons to be coerced into doing what they do not wish, absent that coercion, to do. If a set of incentives do not coerce, then they cannot be part of a totalitarian evil. It is not open to the libertarian to respond by arguing that any set of incentives is totalitarian, since there will be a social structure of incentives regardless. The only argument is over the source and the direction of the incentives.

TWO SERIOUS PROBLEMS FOR SOCIAL ENGINEERING

I have argued that engineering social incentives to change people's beliefs about and preferences for oppressive social norms is not coercive, and that this forestalls Berlin's totalitarian menace objection. There remain two serious problems with social engineering projects that must be addressed. I shall call the first of these problems the problem of unintended consequences and the second the communitarian menace.

The Problem of Unintended Consequences

One of the basic lessons of the history of macroeconomic policy is that social projects always have unintended consequences (some negative and some positive). There is little reason to doubt that providing incentives for persons to change social norms in the direction of enhancing freedom will sometimes go awry. Consider the record of the World Bank, which has as its main mission to fight poverty by helping people to help themselves.[7] Many well-intended programs have resulted in benign failures or worse. International nongovernmental organizations (NGOs) have had similar experiences (Walley 2004/5). National governments that have tried fiscal or monetary policies have sometimes brought about the reverse of their intended consequences. Sometimes the unintended consequences have been beneficial, such as the building of a railroad in Tanzania that was intended for what we can now see as an unrealistic at best goal, but has resulted in encouraging a thriving trading route.

The planners of TAZARA [Tanzania's national railway] were not expecting any such transformation when they initiated the project in the late 1960s. They imagined a grand national railway owned by the state that would be used for large-scale regional shipments of copper and other goods from Zambia—a project that would rival Egypt's recently completed, Soviet-funded Aswan Dam. Their primary goal was not to promote rural economic development or improve the lives of rural producers by connecting local markets. But that has been TAZARA's real impact. (Monson 2004/5)

What examples like these tell us is that large-scale social change is to some degree unpredictable and fraught with dangers of making things worse (or better). Yet, just as we cannot shy away from trying to make change in the face of the possibility of totalitarianism, so we cannot shy away from trying to find freedom in the face of failure. What we must do is try to characterize the ways that socially provided incentive structures can fail and try to foresee problems of the same kind from our proposals.

Three kinds of problems are generalizable. First, when incentives are offered and awarded on a competitive basis, then there are incentives for corruption and gaming the system. In many development projects in the Third World, for example, the local government is the intermediary between NGOs and the people in need. It is then easy for the local government officials to skim off a portion of the aid. Another way aid is siphoned off is by apparently legitimate local businesses that supply their services or goods at higher rates than would be required by the market. Corruption and gaming often go in concert, since opening the market to competitor firms should reduce the rents that the businesses can charge to zero. But if the government prohibits or places obstacles in the way of competitor firms, then the system can be successfully gamed. Second, there are incentives for shirking and cheating. This sort of problem arises when there are set rules with incentives for adhering to them and no objective and accurate way of determining compliance. For example, if there are set-asides for minority-owned businesses, but no effective oversight to determine which businesses are minority-owned, then persons from the dominant community can set up businesses that only appear to be minority-owned in order to capture the set-aside. To avoid such problems, incentives should be structured so that either there is little opportunity for cheating or little incentive for it. Third, there may be rent-seeking behavior that relies on an exogenously determined market failure that is ignored by the NGO (Young 2005; Ackerly 2005). For example, micro-credit organizations that make loans to women sometimes fail to benefit those women because the loans are not structured in a way that prevents their male relations from capturing that benefit. In Pakistan, the Grameen Bank often loans money to women who buy rickshaws that have to be operated by their husbands because of the background social norms about what labor women may or may not perform and whom they may work with. The social norm creates a market failure, in the sense that women do not have the freedom to enter the market. Husbands are able effectively to take ownership of the rickshaw and make their wives dependent on them and vulnerable to desertion, violence, and deprivation. Avoiding such problems is possible by making certain restrictions on the loans to prevent women from getting into a position to be exploited. This requires close attention to how social norms interact to create incentive structures.

What would be some of the potential unintended consequences of the incentive structures that might be proposed to enhance freedom? It seems unlikely that there can be any general answer to that question, beyond the concerns for creating incentives for corruption, cheating, shirking, or rent-seeking. But there is one more kind of bad unintended consequence that can occur with incentives for freedom enhancement. Resistance to oppression is likely to raise backlash on the part of the persons who are losing their privileges (Superson and Cudd 2002, 3-16). Loss of privilege is part and parcel of the end of oppression, though, so it is not possible to avoid the loss of privilege. Individuals must be convinced, then, that they are being compensated for their loss of privileges. In the final section of this chapter I shall complete the argument that the freedom of all is good for all. This argument, if it were generally understood and accepted, would be sufficient to rationally motivate. But because privilege is so difficult emotionally to forego, there need to be appeals at a more emotional and immediate level in order to motivate people even to consider that argument. In some ways the women's movement has been successful at this. Men who are fathers of daughters, or who have sisters or other loved ones who are women, can often be convinced that some loss of privilege to men generally is a worthwhile cost to bear for the benefits of seeing the women they love gain opportunities and succeed. It is commonplace (though sadly not exceptionless) among my female peers that their fathers told them that "they could be anything" when they grew up. And while this was not quite true (professional athletics was almost out of the question but for tennis players and golfers, and there has still never been a female U.S. president), many of these fathers thought that women should have equal opportunity to succeed and perhaps even fought for women's access to equal employment opportunities. Yet it is also the case that progress has been marked by backlash periods. Now, for example, in the United States there is a serious backlash against the Title IX requirements of equal funding for women's and men's educational opportunities when it comes to funding of athletics, despite the fact that this law has been responsible for a ninefold increase in the participation of women in college sports (Brady 2002). While many men see opportunities for their daughters as clearly a good, others (indeed, sometimes the very same men) resent the loss of men's nearly exclusive privilege to playing sports as endangered by having to share the resources for providing opportunities for women. The example nonetheless illustrates how incentives for oppressed individuals to break out of existing oppressive social norms can also appeal to members of privileged groups who have something to lose by that breach. Looking for these alliances, as well as appealing to the sense of justice and good will of the privileged helps to forestall backlash, but does not completely eradicate it.

The Communitarian Menace

My fundamental political and moral orientation in this book is liberal. That is, I take the individual to be primary morally and ontologically. Thus, I insist that social policies preserve liberal civil rights. Any social policy that is aimed at disrupting one form of oppression must not be unjust in this liberal framework. The communitarian menace is the looming problem that preference re-education might be so successful that it would result in a homogenization of society. Perhaps if the homogenization were complete, this would not be a serious problem, since it might result in social unity and cohesion that would be equally satisfying to each member. But the fact is that there will always be dissidents and persons who just do

not fit the social norms, yet who are themselves decent persons.[8] In a homogeneous community they will suffer from ostracization. This threatens the individual, then, in a way that is not oppression, but still a violation of the principle of liberalism. It prioritizes the community's needs and interests over that of the individual. If individuals are going to differ over deeply important matters like sexual preference, religious belief, aesthetic tastes, or philosophical views, or more low-brow matters such as tastes in sports, food, or how their homes should be decorated, then it is best for them if there are a variety of lifestyles from which they can choose. John Stuart Mill wrote eloquently about the value to individuals of living in a society with a variety of experiments in living (Mill 1978, ch. 3). If a society is so homogenous that it does not contain a variety of flourishing experiments in living, then it will not be hospitable for individuals.

Although I take the communitarian menace seriously in general, I do not believe that the incentive-based preference transformation program that I recommend is likely to lead to homogenization of preference or belief. While the incentives will cause individuals to change their behavior to accommodate those incentives, if the incentives act as they are supposed to and enhance freedom, then they are more likely to expand the variety of experiments in living rather than contract them. Still, this concern suggests that something needs to be done to forestall homogenization and its danger of intolerance for diversity. Namely, there must be a background understanding of the advantages of and social support for the value of diversity and tolerance.

Perhaps the greater concern with homogenization, however, comes from the worry that persons who have lived under conditions of oppression will lack the imagination for coming up with diverse lifestyles. Drucilla Cornell's (1998) work on freedom and liberalism helps to illuminate the ways in which society can encourage a variety of experiments in living by supporting the imaginary domain. For Cornell, the imaginary domain is the psychic space that allows a free play of sexual fantasy. She argues that this freedom to explore one's sexual life in imagination lies at the very foundation of self-respect. Although I agree that persons who are constructed under the current oppressions are unable fully to conceive the possibilities for liberation, if we expand the notion to encompass the whole realm of human expression, not only sex but also work, thought, feeling, art, and religion, the imaginary domain offers a glimpse of freedom for individuals. Under conditions of severe enough oppression, persons may be unable to conceive any alternative world at all. But when the bonds of oppression have been loosened to some degree, we can imagine life that is different from what we have known, institutions that are less oppressive.[9] We cannot simply design a future society and take the optimal steps to bring it about. We must be careful what we wish for, as our wishes may unwittingly be for further oppression. Yet, we must continue to wish and strive to make our visions reality. The imaginary domain is our capacity to imagine other ways of being, apart from the social norms that now constrain us.[10] The imaginary domain is the repository from which alternative conceptions of norms and social structures might arise. We are able to imagine them because each of us have different social group memberships, allowing most of us to experience at once privilege and oppression with respect to one or another of them, and giving us experiences of social groups with different ways of life. As I shall argue, the society that succeeds in supporting diversity and tolerance will reap the greatest benefits of freedom, while ensuring the lasting freedom of each individual.

THE SOCIAL UNION OF SOCIAL UNIONS: ENHANCING THE FREEDOM OF OTHERS

In examining how oppression happens and how it maintains itself through generations, I have assumed that each person seeks a short-term to medium-term maximum of preference satisfaction, and their interests in the short to medium term account in large part for their behavior. Yet, if freedom is to be possible, it will be necessary for at least some persons to look beyond their short- to medium-term interests and work toward a transformation of society that may be costly over that horizon. What would motivate persons to do this? I have tried to suggest ways that well-intentioned persons can argue, cajole, or bribe their fellows to join them in resisting oppression and seeking gradual enhancements of freedom. At the very least, though, a philosopher should offer a rational argument that would appeal to persons to work toward these ends. I conclude this book with an argument for the claim that the freedom of all is good for each. This claim may seem problematic in two ways. First, it appears to conflict with the argument I have developed throughout that a primary reason that persons, both privileged and oppressed, participate in oppressive social institutions is because it is in their interest to do so. The conflict in this case is merely apparent. One's long-term interest can conflict with one's short-to medium-term interest, with the latter motivating behavior. Indeed, that is one way of explaining the existence of akratic behavior. Second, it may appear problematic in that it is utopian to think that we can reach freedom. In the previous chapter and in the first parts of this chapter I have tried to describe how we might make social transformations that lead to freedom. At this point I am only trying to argue for the rationality for each of seeking freedom for all.

In *A Theory of Justice*, John Rawls provides the outlines of the argument. Rawls argues that humans tend to obey a basic generalization of psychology, which he calls the Aristotelian Principle. The principle states: "Other things equal, human beings enjoy the exercise of their realized capacities (their innate or trained abilities), and this enjoyment increases the more the capacity is realized, or the greater its complexity" (Rawls 1971, 426). This principle posits a basic motivational principle that seems to be born out by our everyday experiences. As we grow and mature we often seek out new challenges, and we take pleasure in developing our capacities to enjoy them. Our love of sport, art, craft-making, reading, decorating our homes, cooking food, entertaining our friends, and a thousand other occupations and enjoyments testify to the validity of the principle. The second premise of the argument is supplied by the fact, noted by philosophers from Aristotle to Marx to Rawls that humans are deeply social creatures. As Rawls explains it, "Humans have in fact shared final ends and they value their common institutions as good in themselves. We need one another as partners in ways of life that are engaged in for their own sake, and the successes and enjoyments of others are necessary for and complementary to our own good" (Rawls 1971, 522-523). Humans must join and cooperate with others to carry out projects large and small. Over time our projects deepen in complexity and nuance. The opportunities and ways of life that any individual may choose from are bequeathed by previous generations who themselves built upon those they inherited from and built in cooperation with others. In participating in these projects our achievements are made possible by the achievements of others. The social units that humans form

Rawls (following Humboldt) calls "social unions."

The Aristotelian Principle suggests then that individuals find pleasure in the achievements of their social unions, which also means that they find pleasure in the achievements of others in those groups. At its best, participating in social unions effects a transformation of individual psychology that avoids envy and expands our concern for others. Marcia Homiak writes that through shared activity, we

expand our conception of who we are, thereby making us more continuously active and providing us with more continuous pleasure. When, as members of shared activities, we begin to see ourselves as part of a larger enterprise, our perception of who we are and of what we can do expands to cover the activities of others who are fulfilling other parts of the overall task. (Homiak 1985, 104)

Furthermore, we come to see that by expanding our circle of concern to others who were once excluded we can increase our pleasure.[11]

This idea of finding pleasure in each other's achievements and coming to identify with them is an extremely attractive idea for a political philosopher. Rawls, for instance, argues that the well-ordered society is the "social union of social unions," that is, that the society that is structured by his two principles of justice exemplifies this admirable virtue of each taking pleasure in the achievements, the flourishing, of others. I take it that this is true of the society of free persons, which is not only free of current oppressions, but whose members seek to free all persons of oppression. For in such a society the individuals are able to seek their own good with good will toward others as well. They seek to encourage diversity and enhance the freedom of others. They take pleasure in and identify with the accomplishments of others. And further, they come to see their own freedom as connected to that of the others.

We can, I believe, take steps toward a free society because we are able to transform ourselves—make ourselves better—through good willed participation in social unions that are gradually transformed by increasing freedom. A concrete example of how enhancing women's freedom enhances the pleasure of others comes in the achievements of Mia Hamm. She was born in the United States in 1972, the very year that Title IX, which outlawed sex discrimination by federally funded educational institutions, became law. Mia Hamm retired in December 2004 as the most prolific scorer—male or female—in the history of international soccer. At the time of her retirement she was one of the most recognizable people on earth and is a shining example of what determination, hard work, ferocious competitiveness, and athletic talent can produce. But her achievement was an achievement of the social unions of soccer and of democratic society more generally. Mia Hamm's achievements were made possible by a history of soccer players who developed the sport through developing rules and practices of fair play and a game that could highlight and refine certain human abilities and skills, fans who made it popular, and in her case, a long history of women who fought for women's opportunities in sport. More importantly, through taking pleasure in the achievements of Mia Hamm we are able to see how the inclusion of a formerly excluded group (women) from a cherished activity (soccer) makes us all better off. Her achievements were made possible only by these social unions, as well as her natural talents and in turn they have brought the world much pleasure. We are better for having international women's soccer because Mia Hamm was able to showcase her talents, in it. Moreover, we take pride in the very progress of society that allowed Mia Hamm to shine. We can clearly see in this case, as we can see in thousands of other less spectacular cases that

we experience closer to home, the enhanced freedom of women has made the world better for all.

In enjoying the achievements of others, we experience freedom from what Marx called the alienation of man from man. We gain valuable information about alternative ways of life that others pursue with interest and devotion. This in turn develops our own capacities, our imaginary domains, which allow each of us the psychic space to enhance our freedom and take pleasure in it. In learning the value of diversity and tolerance, we become motivated to end oppression and privilege, both our own and others. This transformation is not easy; it requires moral character to resist the enticements of privilege or accommodation (Homiak 1991). But at least we can now see that it is rational to seek the freedom of others as well as ourselves. For, to be free is not merely to cast off one's chains, but to live in a way that respects and enhances the freedom of others.

NOTES

1 This is what is going on, I believe, when women criticize feminists for claiming that veiling or female circumcision is oppressive. These women ask feminists to concentrate on what they see as the real issues, such as poverty. But to accept veiling and circumcision is to accept the hierarchy of sex, and that is forfeiting freedom at a basic level.

2 The importance of connection to others has been described particularly well by contractarian thinkers. Rawls, as I will discuss shortly, writes that "In a fully just society persons seek their good in ways peculiar to themselves, and they rely upon their associates to do things they could not have done, as well as things they might have done but did not . . . . It is a feature of human sociability that we are

by ourselves but parts of what we might be" (Rawls 1971, 529). Yet contractarians are also quick to insist that shared activities must not be coerced. David Gauthier, writing about the passage of Rawls just cited, states: "if each participant is to find shared activity intrinsically valuable, then it must satisfy the standard of fairness" (Gauthier 1986, 338).

[3] An excellent presentation of the argument for and policy plans for providing child care in America, see Helburn and Bergmann (2002).

[4] Or even better, perhaps we could shorten the working day and lengthen the school day so that they match, but so that we have more leisure time with our children or other projects. Joan Williams (2000) writes persuasively that the current norms of the ideal worker are bad for both men and women, and that the full commodification of carework would lead to a far worse outcome for individuals and families than reshaping work life altogether. While I appreciate her concerns over the full commodification model, I worry that there will always be a wage-based motivation to be the hardest working worker in a capitalist economy, and hence that attempts to shorten the working day will be thwarted by the collective outcome of the struggles of each individual to have a competitive advantage over the next.

[5] Among the benefits provided to religions I would include not only the tax exemptions of the organizations themselves and tax deductions provided to individuals who contribute to them but also social benefits of respect or the benefits of attention by media to the leaders and so on. Generally, religions are regarded as having a special corner on morality. Yet surely those who articulate notions of freedom and seek to achieve them are acting morally and with vision, perhaps even in ways that religious persons label "spiritual."

[6] This is not to say that there are no losers here. Drug invention resources will be skewed toward curing more common diseases and away from less common diseases and problems that are described as lifestyle choice, such as those that Viagra or Cialis are meant to combat.

[7] Full mission statement available from the World Bank website, www.worldbank.org.

[8] John Rawls (1993) accounts for the existence of deep disagreements over social, moral, and religious matters by appeal to what he calls the facts of reason.

[9] We can do this because we belong to different social groups, some of which are privileged and some oppressed relative to others. Our multiple identities help us to escape the paradox of social construction, which Hirschmann describes as the puzzle of: "How can we ever figure out who 'we' are or what 'we want' if the language and concepts we must use are antagonistic to the enterprise we seek to carry out, that is, are themselves barriers to women's freedom?" (Hirschmann 2003, 99).

[10] Lugones (1990) nicely states the difficulty for theories of oppression that locate oppression in social structures and that want to recommend liberatory strategies.

[11] See also Homiak (1990, esp. 175–176).

REFERENCES

Ackerly, Brooke. 2005. "Comments on Young's The Gendered Cycle of Vulnerability in the Less Developed World". Presented at the Susan Moller Okin memorial conference, Stanford University, Feb. 4, 2005.

Berlin, Isaiah. 1969. "Two Concepts of Liberty". In *Four Essays on Liberty*. London: Oxford University Press.

Brady, Eric. 2002. *Major changes debated for Title IX.* Online. Available: http://www.usatoday.com/sports/college/2002?12?17?1a?title?ix?cover_x.htm

Cohen, Joshua. 2001. "Taking People as They Are". *Philosophy and Public Affairs* 30(4):363–386.

Cornell, Drucilla. 1998. *At the Heart of Freedom: Feminism, Sex, and Equality.* Princeton, N.J: Princeton University Press.

Faludi, Susan. 1999. *Stiffed: The Betrayal of the American Man.* New York: W. Morrow and Co.

Gauthier, David P. 1986. *Morals By Agreement.* New York: Oxford University Press.

Hamilton, Alexander, Madison, James, and Jay, John. 1961. *The Federalist Papers.* New York: New American Library.

Helburn, Suzanne W., and Bergmann, Barbara R. 2002. *America's Child Care Problem : The Way Out.* New York: Palgrave for St. Martin's Press.

Hirschmann, Nancy J. 2003. *The Subject of Liberty: Toward a Feminist Theory of Freedom.* Princeton: Princeton University Press.

Homiak, Marcia L. 1985. "The Pleasure of Virtue in Aristotle's Moral Theory". *Pacific Philosophical Quarterly* 66:93–110.

—. 1991. "On the Malleability of Character". In *Feminist Ethics*, edited by Claudia Card. Lawrence, Kan.: University Press of Kansas.

Lee, Sunhwa. November 2004. "Women's Work Supports, Job Retention, and Job Mobility: Child Care and Employer-Provided Health Insurance Help Women Stay on Jobs". *Research News Reporter.*

Lugones, Maria. October, 1990. "Structure/Antistructure and Agency under Oppression". *The Journal of Philosophy* 90:500–507.

Mill, John S. 1978. *On Liberty.* Indianapolis: Hackett.

Monson, Jamie. December 2004/Jan. 2005. "Freedom Railway: The Unexpected Successes of a Cold War Development Project". *Boston Review.*

Pogge, Thomas. 2003. *Severe Poverty as a Human Rights Violation.* http://www.law.utoronto.ca/documents/globalization/Pogge_Sept%2030th_04.pdf.

Rawls, John. 1971. *A Theory of Justice.* Cambridge, Mass.: Harvard University Press.

—. 1993. *Political Liberalism.* New York: Columbia University Press.

Superson, Anita M., and Cudd, Ann E., eds. 2002. *Theorizing Backlash : Philosophical Reflections on the Resistance to Feminism.* Lanham, Md.: Rowman & Littlefield.

Varian, Hal. 1994. A Solution to the Problem of Externalities when Agents are Well Informed. *American Economic Review* 84(5):1278–1293.

Walley, Christine J. December 2004/Jan. 2005. "Best Intentions: The Story of Tanzania's Peoples Park". *Boston Review.*

Williams, Joan. 2000. *Unbending Gender: Why Family and Work Conflict and What to do about It.* New York: Oxford University Press.

Young, Iris Marion. 2005. "The Gendered Cycle of Vulnerability in the Less Developed World". Presented at the Susan Moller Okin memorial conference, Stanford University, Feb. 4, 2005.